D0938791

e
ry

DATE DUE			

Oakland Community College
Orchard Ridge Library
27055 Orchard Lake Road
Farmington Hills, MI 48334

DEMCO

Food and Memories of Abruzzo,

Italy's Pastoral Land

FOOD AND MEMORIES OF ABRUZZO,

Italy's Pastoral Land

ANNA TERESA CALLEN

Hungry Minds
New York, NY • Cleveland, OH • Indianapolis, IN

To my Abruzzesi friends with whom I shared my growing pains: Virginia Falcone, Maria Improta, Anna de Blasis, Anna Maria Parere, and the unforgettable Paolo, Giorgio and Rosanna Calanca, Renato and Elvira Alfonsi, Giuliana Borgatti, Guido and Anna Scoponi, and the Rosica and Palmerio cousins.

But most of all this book is dedicated to Gianna, Franca, and Adriana, my most beloved cousins, and my nieces Marcella and Paola. They are the last remaining of my immediate family. Together with their children and my dear husband Harold, they make my life a joy to live.

HUNGRY MINDS, INC.
909 Third Avenue
New York, NY 10022

For general information on Hungry Minds' products and services please contact our Customer Care department; within the U.S. at 800-762-2974, outside the U.S. at 317-572-3993 or fax 317-572-4002.

Library of Congress Cataloging-in-Publication Data

Callen, Anna Teresa
    The pastoral land: food and memories of Abruzzo / Anna Teresa Callen.
        p. cm.
    Includes index.
    Includes index. ISBN: 0-02-520915-9 (alk. paper)
    1. Cookery, Italian. 2. Cookery—Italy—Abruzzo.
        3. Abruzzo (Italy)—Social life and customs. I. Title.
TX723.2.N65C35 1996   96-5553
641.5945'71—dc20   CIP

Manufactured in the United States of America

10 9 8 7 6 5 4 3 2

Book design by Nick Anderson

Contents

Acknowledgments

At the beginning of my career, it was Barbara Kafka who kept telling me, "You must write a cookbook on your region!" The idea lingered in my head, but I went about writing other books. I felt that Americans were not interested in the regional foods of Italy, let alone those of Abruzzo. Barbara insisted and, many years later, I complied.

This, however, could not have been accomplished without the encouragement of dear friends, pupils who attend my cooking school, colleagues, and some food writers, who discovered me and put me on the gastronomic map. They are:

The unforgettable late Ellie Volpe Greene and Peter Kump; and my very supportive friends, Florence Seligman, Midge Balterl, Andrea Di Noto, Roberto Talignani, Tom and Susan De Vito, and Anna Amendolara Nurse.

The late John Musilli, my boss at CBS, who produced and directed my first food show, and my colleagues there, Stephen Chodorof and Joanna Young, who were my invaluable collaborators during the period I worked for the prestigious CBS-Camera 3.

Florence Fabricant, Peggy Katalinich, Nancy Harmon Jenkins, and the unforgettable Bert Greene, who first wrote articles about me.

Arthur Schwartz keeps me and my books on the airwaves of his witty radio show, as does Bea Lewis on hers.

This acknowledgment cannot end without my expression of gratitude to the indefatigable and helpful staff at Balducci's, including Joe Reda, Roberto Tramontana, Alex Pogoceanu, Chef Vittorio Giacometti, Chef Dennis Natoli, Mario Spina, Gino Rosselli, Joseph Milazzo, Maurizio Madonna, Jose Ramos, Elias Melendez, Louis Arena, Vinny Schirippa, Frank Lo Verde, Doris Acosta, Jaque Zrimba, and Gerome Gay.

Introduction

Years ago, at the beginning of my culinary career, I wanted to write a cookbook on Abruzzo, my native region of Italy, a land of colorful festivals, brooding traditions, gargantuan banquets, and ancient superstitions, where the accidental spilling of oil is a sure sign of tragedy. I also wanted to share the experience of growing up in a family of good cooks where food was an expression of love and caring.

The food of this region reflects the environment: From the hilly heartland comes the cuisine of the farmers, wholesome and flavorful, with succulent poultry dishes, robust roasts, and a myriad of vegetables; from the mountains, that of the shepherds which makes our lamb famous even in Milan; and from the sea, that of the fishermen with their succulent *brodetti* (fish stews), and the *grigliate* (grilled fish), briny and fresh tasting, touched only by a few drops of good olive oil, lemon, and a pinch of fresh herbs.

This is simple cooking, for the most part, its flavors kept fresh and clean. Yet, the food of Abruzzo is also famous for elaborate and quite unique dishes. These are reserved for special occasions, to receive and please guests in the most special way. If nothing else, the Abruzzese people are famous for their hospitality. In fact, our motto is *Abruzzo, forte e gentile*, Abruzzo, strong and kind.

THE MYTH OF NORTHERN ITALY

Although editors were intrigued by my proposal, they felt that there was no real interest in the regional food of Italy. Americans had, in fact, progressed beyond spaghetti and meatballs to embrace something called "Northern Italian" cuisine, interpreted as the refined cooking of Italy (without the tomato sauce, garlic, and oregano). Yet there was no true understanding that the food of Italy is not Northern, Southern, Eastern, or Western but regional. Like the rest of Italy, the North is made up of many regions, each with its own traditional cuisine.

Americans, who are so health conscious, didn't notice at first that this type of food was also fattening. But, as a marketing tool devised by smart newcomer restaurateurs, who had seldom, if ever, used cream in Italy, it worked.

Things have changed. Frequent travel to Italy with trips to the countryside has taught Americans that there is more to Italian cuisine than the repetitious offerings on American menus—pesto sauce, tirami sù, saltimbocca, and caponata, to name a few. Americans are learning that Italian food is indeed made of ingredients and dishes that are intimately linked to the country's different regions.

A STEP BACK IN TIME

Although Americans have ventured beyond Rome and Venice, Abruzzo is still virtually undiscovered. Perhaps this is why it hasn't changed and has remained unique. For years, its mountains, the highest of the Apennines, rivaled only by the Alps, have been a difficult barrier to cross, keeping this land out of the mainstream.

Even now, with the new *autostrade* cutting through the mountains, Abruzzo remains somewhat isolated, leaving the quaint villages and towns of the interior unspoiled and its cuisine untouched by the culinary whims that sweep through other parts of the country. Only the coast, because of its beautiful sandy beaches and charming holiday resort towns, attracts outsiders.

Abruzzo is also famous for its *Scuola Alberghiera* school of hotel management, in Villa Santa Maria, whose origins go back to the Middle Ages. This school has produced some of the most famous chefs in the world. At one time there was neither an ocean liner nor a famous restaurant in New York, Paris, or London that didn't have an Abruzzese cook.

Many dishes from Abruzzo, such as *maccheroni alla chitarra* ("guitar" macaroni), *brodetto di pesce* (fish stew), and *porchetta* (roast pig), have, of course, traveled. But most of them are still the treasured secrets of families. They travel no further than the next generation. I, for one, started to cook from memory during my years of college and traveling. Grown up and away from home, I went back to the glorious days of my childhood when my grandmother and her maids prepared wonderful feasts for the family or guests. The dinners for special occasions were the most memorable, yet I still remember the everyday aromas permeating the house, and I still cook with these in mind.

How could I ever forget the perfume of the *ragù* for the *maccheroni alla chitarra*? Or the aroma pervading the house when *pollo alla canzanese* was being prepared?

BRINGING ABRUZZO TO AMERICA

I feel that the American public, which has already learned to appreciate Italian cuisine so well, will now be eager to learn even more about new specialties from little-known places such as Abruzzo.

Many of the recipes, tested and adapted during my years as a professional food writer and teacher, are personal and original. I also collected recipes from small towns and villages during my frequent trips to Abruzzo. These and others from enthusiastic friends with gastronomic reputations, and some from my favorite local restaurants are included, too.

Keeping in mind that people's attitudes about food and nutrition have changed, I adapted my recipes to modern methods of cooking. Fatty ingredients and salt are used at a minimum. But I kept the heart of Abruzzo food; that is, the use of fresh food, which is essential in obtaining a maximum of flavor and nutrition. In fact, nutrition was always important in my house. Everyday meals were balanced, seasonal, and aromatic with the fragrance that comes only from fresh ingredients.

AN INAUSPICIOUS BEGINNING

I must have been born with a selective palate. Milk was not my favorite food. At the age of three months, I was told, I began to refuse it. My mother, who didn't have any milk, dramatically declared that I knew it wasn't her breast that fed me. Maybe so, but either way it is a mystery how I survived my first months of life.

I showed the first glimmer of interest in food during a visit with an aunt. While everybody was enthralled by the beauty, the gurgles, and most of all the robustness of my twin brother

Mimmo, I, a feeble, almost mute baby, was left aside in the arms of a maid. Trays with all sorts of goodies were being passed around and one stopped in front of me. Perhaps it was the vivid color that made me stretch a hand toward a marzipan tomato. After I had grabbed it, three adults were unable to dislodge my little hand from my mouth—I finished the entire thing. My uncle Tommaso, the doctor, who was taking a *passeggiata*, walk, with his brother Agostino, the veterinarian, was immediately summoned. They both came and declared that since I had finally eaten something, this might be a turning point.

UNCLE TOMMASO

Although my uncle Tommaso died when I was seven or eight years old, he was one of the most important people in my life. I remember him with affection, even though he came as a harbinger of terror all throughout my infancy and childhood. For me, his visits meant medicines, purges, the needle, and worst of all—the enema. Yet, the moment he appeared, followed by the solicitous presence of my grandmother, my mother, father, and soon the entire family, a sense of calm spread over me. He exuded love, patience, and, most of all, well-being. I felt better, mother and grandmother felt better, and soon after, my room (or that of some other member of the family who was sick), would become the center of

a family gathering with *tarallucci e vino,* the eternal Italian panacea of pastry and wine offered all around.

To walk with Uncle Tommaso in the street was amazing. People used to stop to talk to him imparting looks of respect and admiration. It made me proud without even knowing the reason. Often during this *passeggiata*, we met farmers pulling their mules. Before anybody could prevent it, the farmers would kneel on the ground, grab his hand, and start kissing it.

I always heard stories about Uncle Tommaso getting up in the middle of the night to rush to somebody's bedside. He was a country doctor and tended one of the poorest districts. Many a time his wife, *Fides*, Faith, an appropriate name for the companion of such a man, related incidents of Uncle Tommaso's coming home without his coat, jacket, or pullover, left to one of his patient who, as he had put it, needed it more than he did.

Everybody said that I owed my life to him. I was born a twin, breathless and voiceless, to my brother "the heir," who thundered angry cries the moment I appeared. Discarded for dead in a corner, all attention turned to him and my poor mother who was in danger of bleeding to death. My compassionate grandmother kept glancing at me with great sorrow and suddenly noticed a movement in my lips. She alerted my uncle, who grabbed me by my feet and, since the entire scene was taking place in mother's bedroom

(those were the days previous to maternity wards), he started to use me like a menacing bell, slapping my backside and yelling until I finally joined the bedlam with a screeching aria. Uncle Tommaso and grandmother used to tell me this story with great relish, often fighting over the credit of my salvation.

After the episode of the marzipan tomato, my meals, according to family reports, consisted of small morsels of food prepared in a loving competition between my grandmother and assorted relatives who were determined to fatten me up. I must have enjoyed those meals, because I thrived.

BIRTH OF A PASSION

When I was about five, I discovered that the marvelous perfumes permeating the house at certain hours exuded from the kitchen. Mother, who was a good cook by osmosis but not passion, didn't like to have me around when she was cooking. I loved to be in the kitchen, but it was a struggle. Thank God for summers, when in later years our dispersed families returned to grandmother's house in Guardiagrele. It was in my grandmother's kitchen that I served my apprenticeship by watching and helping as often as she would let me.

I never really cooked, but growing up with good cooks and *buongustai*, connoisseurs, I did know what good food tasted like. Still, I had a long way to go before becoming a food lover. In fact, my uncle Raf was convinced that I would never be one because at fourteen I adamantly refused to eat gorgonzola cheese, which he loved. I could not stand its odor. My uncle considered it an exquisite aroma to be surpassed only by that of truffles and smoked salmon, which I also refused to taste.

I guess I was in the "Yuk!" period so common to teenagers. I actually sneered at my father's passion for smoked salmon, which he called "food for princes." Fortunately for me, and because it was expensive and considered an exotic delicacy, it was bought only "when a Pope died," an Italian expression meaning very seldom. Personally, I felt that marzipan was more appropriate for royalty. As a matter of fact, in our region marzipan is called *pasta reale,* royal paste.

Later in my life, I was sent to England to learn English. For my family, this was an essential part of our education. One day, I was invited to a high tea. On the beautifully set table, prominently displayed, were little canapés topped with smoked salmon. Too polite to refuse, I daintily bit into one. It made my gustatory papillae dance. I didn't eat the whole tray because, again, politeness took over. I concluded that my father, after all, knew what he was talking about. Consequently, it was easy to develop a taste for caviar, truffles, 1,000-year-old-eggs, and even gorgonzola.

From Dabbler to Pro

It was in England that I started cooking, mostly out of necessity. At the Italian Institute of Culture, where I worked, I met Giuliana, a colleague, who became a dear friend. We decided to share an apartment. It was natural to start cooking some of our meals to save money. We began with two dishes that we remembered from home: Giuliana's *bolognese* sauce, which is the one I still use today, and my father's *brodetto di pesce,* a fish stew similar to the French *bouillabaisse.* They became a resounding success with our young colleagues and the semi-deprived Italian students who congregated around the Institute.

Although Giuliana and I became good cooks and loved to entertain, many years passed before I changed my career and became a food professional. How did it happen? Well, I always say, jokingly, that I used to be an intellectual. I studied to become an archeologist. In England, I taught Italian in two English colleges. One day, I was invited to come to America as a lecturer on a ship. I had a visa for a month. How many Europeans get the opportunity to come to America as I did, *gratis et amore Dei,* for free and with the grace of God?

In the end, I decided to stay for "awhile." I got a job at the Italian Tourist Office in New York. In a couple of years, I said to myself, I would go back to England, which I loved. But I met Harold Callen, a playwright with a great sense of humor, an interesting, mischievous face, ill-fitting clothes, and a taste for Automat food. I fell in love, I married him, failed to make an *arbiter elegantiarum* (arbiter of elegance) out of him, but won over his palate with my homemade Italian food.

We lived in California for awhile, where Harold wrote television and stage plays. Upon our return to New York, I went to work as a researcher for an educational program called "Camera Three," which aired nationwide every Sunday morning on CBS. It was during this period that I read an article in *The New York Times* about Marco Polo bringing spaghetti to Italy. I was so incensed at this falsehood that I barged into my producer's office brandishing the offending article and telling him that we should do a show on the history of macaroni. This was 1976, before macaroni became "pasta."

The producer not only thought it was a good idea, he allowed me to write and narrate the show, called "Let Them Eat Pasta." In it, I showed many slides of art works related to cooking, including one of an Etruscan tomb which had a wall decorated with all the accouterments needed to make pasta, debunking the Marco Polo legend. (The Etruscans lived centuries before Marco Polo returned from China.) We received 5,000 complimentary letters.

For the next show, called "Nature's Masterpiece, the Egg," Kriss Forbes, the curator of Malcom Forbes's fabulous art collection, graciously lent me some of the Fabergé eggs from the collection. This elicited another avalanche of complimentary letters, including one from the Metropolitan Museum of Art in New York, suggesting that I do a show about famous paintings related to food.

I was all prepared to become the "Italian Julia Child," as I had been called by some newspapers, when CBS canceled our long-running, educational, non-sponsored show for a more lucrative one.

Among the people I admire, Craig Claiborne continues to be my hero. I admired his good taste, his witty and beautiful writing style, his honesty, and his knowledge and appreciation of Italian food. I felt he was a kindred spirit. I do not know how I had the courage at one time to write him a letter and dispute his answer to a query about tomato paste in the now defunct "Q&A" column. But write I did, and he published my letter entirely. Mimi Sheraton was another inspirational source, and I remain an admirer of her to this day. Julia Child, of course, is another story. She is the one who taught me and the whole country that cooking could be fun, and that it is all right to make mistakes.

Still, having accidentally turned an interest into a passion, I wasn't about to give up my new love. I opened a cooking school in New York. It was an instant success. Florence Fabricant of *The New York Times*, the unforgettable Bert Greene of the *Daily News*, and Peggy Katalinich, then an editor at *Newsday*, all gave me favorable reviews. Pupils came, and many have faithfully returned, session after session.

My first cookbook, *The Wonderful World of Pizzas, Quiches and Savory Pies*, was published in 1981. It was a thrill when Jean Hewitt gave me permission to reproduce one of her recipes in it. Because of her, many of my recipes were later published in *The New York Times* and *Family Circle*, where she held the position of editor.

I guess my life as a food person had to happen. As I said, love for good food runs in the family. In fact, a few years ago, I surprised my nephew Carlo, barely four, who was slivering truffles on his well buttered slice of bread with the expertise of a French chef. When I startled the child by asking what he was doing, he answered, "Zia, la merenda!" ("Auntie, my afternoon snack!") What a kid.

It is also true that kids will be kids. Upon my ritual returns to Italy from the States, Carlo would soon catch me alone and whisper in my ear the big secret: He knew where Mummy hid the Nutella, another passion we share when truffles are not available. Nutella, a spread made with hazelnuts and chocolate, is the Italian equivalent of peanut butter. Oh well, if once in a while Carlo wants to include me, his mature aunt in his gorging of semi-forbidden food, why should I refuse? After all, my life as a gourmand started with marzipan.

My family gave me a passion for food. The rituals that were practiced in my grandmother's kitchen are still with me. All this has remained part of my life and cooking for family and friends is a constant joy for me. To celebrate and make people happy are the reasons why I wrote this book.

Useful Culinary Tips

Above all, be organized. Have all the ingredients and utensils you need in front of you before you start cooking.

On pasta: Always cook your pasta in boiling salted water. You will need a couple of tablespoons of kosher salt for 1 pound of pasta. If you have a medical problem prohibiting the use of salt, the juice of a lemon, or a shot of vinegar are good substitutes. Add the salt only when the water boils.

Always cover your pot after putting the pasta in, but give a good stir to the pasta first. You want your pasta to come back to a boil quickly. If this doesn't happen your pasta will become "very friendly" at the bottom of the pot and you will have a blob.

Never put oil in the water—never. It makes the sauce slide off the pasta. If you use good pasta, and my method of cooking it, you will have excellent results. Also, do not overdrain your pasta, and wisely, keep some of its cooking water to loosen up the pasta when necessary.

Pastry bags: When using a pastry bag, wet the inside first. It will make what you put inside easy to pipe.

To make bread crumbs: Keep all the leftover bread in a tin; when you have enough, place the pieces of bread in an oven which has been preheated at 500°F. Immediately switch the oven off, and when the oven is cool remove the bread and process in a food processor. You will have wonderful bread crumbs. Keep the crumbs in a plastic container in the refrigerator.

Leftover salad: Do not throw it away; place it in a food processor, add a can or two of V8, process to a puree, and serve with diced cucumber. Gazpacho? Well, sort of.

Leftover vegetables make great soups. Place them in plastic containers; you can mix and match. When you have enough, combine the vegetables in a food processor and puree. Add broth according to how liquid you want your soup, heat, and serve with good crusty bread.

Parmesan rinds: Rinse and scrape the waxy part under the water, and add to broth, soups, ragùs.

Prosciutto: Buy and keep in the refrigerator or freezer the end pieces of prosciutto which cost half the price of the real one, and it is ideal for chopping.

Beef: If you must freeze steaks, marinate them first. For bigger pieces of meat, smear with olive oil, wrap, and freeze.

In umido: This term is used often in this book. It means to cook something, especially meat, with some liquid, hence "humidity."

Washing gritty vegetables: Leeks are the worst, and sometimes spinach, arugola, etc. Trim and cut these vegetables according to your recipe, place in a large bowl, add 1 tablespoon kosher salt and fill with water. Toss a few times and let stand 15 to 20 minutes. Gently remove the vegetable from the bowl and place in a colander. You will see how much sand is at the bottom of the bowl; discard the liquid and rinse your vegetables in abundant water a few times.

Mozzarella: Fresh mozzarella is wonderful to eat as in an antipasto, for instance. But it is not good for pizzas, lasagna, or in a stuffing. It exudes too much water. For these occasions buy a good mozzarella from the supermarket; I rely very much on the Polly-O brand.

Mushrooms: I always wash my mushrooms, but I do not soak them. Place the mushrooms in a bowl, add 1 tablespoon of kosher salt, fill the bowl with water, toss the mushrooms vigorously a few times, then lift the mushrooms to a colander. Check one by one if any grit is still clinging; if so, quickly rinse the mushroom under water. Place all the finished mushrooms in a colander lined with paper towels.

Do not soak dry mushrooms for more than 20 minutes. Lift the mushrooms from the water without disturbing the bottom. Filter the water through a paper towel and use it according to the recipe or freeze in ice cube trays to add to soups, stews, or sautés.

To skim the fat from a sauce or a soup: Let the preparation rest 10 to 20 minutes so that the fat rises to the surface. Better yet, place it in the freezer for 5 minutes. Gently place a paper towel over the fat and leave it a few seconds. The paper will absorb the fat. Remove the paper and discard; repeat if necessary.

About larding: Larding means to insert some sort of condiment (chopped garlic, prosciutto, lard, herbs, or a mixture of these things) after opening a hole with a small knife or a skewer into a piece of meat or fish.

Broth and stocks: I always make my own broth and I do not skim the broth unless I need a very clear soup. Skimming will remove part of the nutrient.

When you drain the broth, remove all the vegetables and herbs to a food mill and puree. You will have a delicious cream of vegetable soup. This puree can also be used as a base for risotto. And by all means, pick all the meat from the bones used in the broth and make a nice salad.

Store the clear broth in a container and freeze it for future use.

To make your own broth cubes: Freeze some of the broth in ice cube trays. Then remove the cubes to a bag and keep them in the freezer. These are extremely useful to add to food when you are sautéing or roasting instead of more oil or butter.

I use a large boullion cube quite often when I do not have enough meat for my broth. I find Knorr quite good and a godsend to enhance the flavor of soups and some sauces.

Diavoletto, or Italian hot red pepper, is practically the emblem of Abruzzo. Cook the *diavoletto* in your food without breaking it. The seeds are what makes the food hot. You can also use hot pepper flakes.

Wine: Do not get hung up when a recipe calls for red wine and you only have white. It is not exactly the same but, quite often whatever is open will do. Of course, if a recipe calls for a specific wine, you should oblige, because its flavor is important.

Dried tomatoes: Soak dried tomatoes 15 to 20 minutes before using them. Dried tomatoes are also sold soaked in olive oil. But they are expensive. I usually place the soaked and patted dry tomatoes in extra virgin olive oil myself and I add a little basil and sometimes a clove of garlic. You can use these as they are.

Olives: For cooking and in sauces, I prefer to use California olives in a can. They are sweet and their flavor is not too intrusive.

Mussels and clams: Soak them in cold water to which 1 tablespoon of flour has been added. This will make them spit out any sand residuals.

On frying: Use canola or vegetable oil, but always add $^1/_4$ cup olive oil; it adds flavor. You can reuse the oil 3 to 4 times, but when frying fish keep this oil just for fish. Put a piece of bread soaked in vinegar in your oil when using it again. This will purify the oil. Also, when the bread floats and starts to sizzle it means that the oil is ready.

PART I

LA CASA DI GUARDIAGRELE

The House in Guardiagrele

...oes back to the Middle Ages when the ...village, were being attacked by barbarians. ...hilltop encampment to guard their village ..., was the name they gave to this defensive ...lley, practically disappeared in later years, a town grew and prospered on the site of the garrisoned settlement.

THE HOUSE IN GUARDIAGRELE

The history of Guardiagrele goes back to the Middle Ages when the people of Grele, a small valley village, were being attacked by barbarians. The besieged inhabitants built a hilltop encampment to guard their village below. *Guardiagrele*, guard Grele, was the name they gave to this defensive outpost. But while Grele, in the valley, practically disappeared in later years, a town grew and prospered on the site of the garrisoned settlement.

Guardiagrele's stone houses are perilously perched on a high hill at the foot of the Maiella Mountains. Gabriele D'Annunzio, a celebrated native poet, loved Abruzzo and called Guardiagrele, *la nave di pietra*, stone ship. The ancient walls which surrounded the town are now gone, but the old tower still stands guard over the valley as a memento of past turmoil. Until I was nine, I lived in Guardiagrele with my grandmother, an uncle, and two young aunts, while my parents and twin brother, Mimmo, lived in Palermo. This separation, I was repeatedly told, was dictated by the fact that I was a delicate child in need of special attention and the natural air. Besides, my mother would be too burdened with two babies of the same age and no help from family or the good maids roaming grandmother's house. Whatever the reason, I was happy in this loving nucleus.

SPRING IN GUARDIAGRELE

Although I was born on a windy, snowy day at the beginning of March, my earliest recollections are of the gentle spring. I remember waking early in the morning, sensing the warmth outside, and thinking, "It must be spring." A chirping outside my balcony told me I was right. The swallows had come back to the one nest I managed to save, hidden by a jasmine vine. Their return was my little victory. You see, in late autumn, my grandmother ordered all the nests destroyed "so they won't come back." She didn't do it out of nastiness (my grandmother was "as good as a piece of bread" as the Italian expression goes), but because the birds did indeed make

a mess. After the first ones were back, however, and the nests began again, grandmother, defeated, could be heard scorning anyone *not* saving the crumbs for the former "enemy."

Although I felt like turning over and dozing a little longer, each morning I would get up. The aroma of freshly baked brioches permeated the house, and a musical clattering of kitchen utensils resounded through the floor. I sensed festivity in the air. Then, as now, I was not a breakfast person, but I could not resist that seductive calling.

My joy at spring's arrival in Guardiagrele was so strong that long after I moved away from Abruzzo, the desire to return always surfaced in the spring.

We celebrated many festive dinners in my grandmother's house during this

The family in Guardiagrele. From top left: Uncle Filippo; my mother; Aunt Cettina; my father; Aunt Ela; seated is nonnina *(grandmother) and, in the foreground, the twins—myself and Mimmo. We were seven years old.*

season. My family would return from Palermo for some of the occasions. First came Mimmo's and my birthday, on the fifth of March. The menu was planned with our favorite dishes and began with *Timballini di Maccheroni alla Nonnina* (page 186), grandmother's macaroni timbale, or a soup we all liked a lot, *Pastina Tic Tic* (page 65), so named because my grandmother, cutting the homemade noodles into tiny dots, made a tic-tic sound with her knife.

The second big dinner was in honor of my father on the nineteenth of March, which is also the feast of San Giuseppe (St. Joseph), his saint's name. On this date platters of *Zeppole*, special fritters (page 442), are traditionally prepared and served to well-wishers. My father always said that he had chosen his feast days very well. He was born the day after Christmas, *La festa di Santo Stefano,* is a national holiday.

Spring culminated in Easter week, with all its ceremonies and traditions. I particularly looked forward to Easter Sunday dinner, which featured most of my favorite dishes. But what we children considered the best part of the festivities was the traditional picnic on Easter Monday, another national holiday in Italy, when the entire country seemed to hit the road.

Armed with blankets, an immaculate tablecloth, and baskets of food, we embarked on a long walk—always a part of the event—heading for the mountains or the nearby woods of

Papà, young and handsome.

Colle Granaro. Here we delighted in picking bunches of violets and tiny wild strawberries. Later we ate the berries with a simple dusting of sugar and sprinkling of lemon juice. But this was only our foraged dessert.

The full repast consisted of delicious *panini* (the Italian equivalent of American sandwiches), an assortment of cheeses, a traditional *pizza rustica*, rice or Russian salads, and for dessert, the aforementioned strawberries, a *macedonia di frutta* (mixed fruit), and an array of traditional pastries. My father never went on a picnic without a few bottles of *lambrusco di Sorbara*, a sparkling wine which is ideal for these sorts of repasts. A stream had to be found in which to cool the wine, and that was the children's job.

At sunset, a car came to pick up some of us who were too tired to jour-

ney back on foot. I always ended up going home on foot—my father's feet that is—since he carried me on his shoulders.

SUMMER REUNIONS

As a child, I especially longed for the summer in Guardiagrele. That was the time of year our families, friends, and relatives living in different cities all over Italy returned "home." Guardiagrele was home for everybody. The town was, and is, a holiday resort, picturesquely set on top of a hill at the foot of the imposing Maiella Mountains. For us as children, this meant a continuous influx of new friends.

When I was nine, I went to live with my parents in Bari, a large city in the south where my father had been transferred. It was exciting; a big city, new friends, a large school! But as soon as school closed for the summer, to my great joy, I was sent back to Abruzzo.

The social exchanges there were intense and fun. The rituals began in the morning when everybody went to "take the air" at the *Villa Comunale,* the local park. The ladies wore large elegant hats, the men, dashing Panamas or the straw hat made famous by Maurice Chevalier, an actor popular with my parents' generation. We children wore jumpers and shorts, but we had to behave ourselves and not get dirty, which was difficult with our hide-and-seek games, bicycle races, and ball games.

It was at the *Villa* that the activities for each day were planned, from a simple, late afternoon walk outside the city walls to tea at some friend's house with *merenda* (snacks) for the children. Of course, when the grown-ups planned a picnic in Mount Granaro's woods or an all-day hike to one of our beautiful surrounding mountains, we were delighted.

But the quiet afternoons spent at home were just as memorable. After lunch, which was the main meal in Italy, everybody retired for a siesta. We children, unwillingly, followed the custom. I remember my room suffused with the sweet smell of jasmine blooming on the balcony. There, in the semi-darkness behind green wooden shutters, I used to try to read the book I had hidden in advance. In the distance, the *acciottolio,* noise of pots and pans being washed and put away by the maids, blended into the silence, providing a distant, familiar din. Then quiet, interrupted at times by a sudden burst of cicadas singing their joy to the sun. And, finally, sleep.

I would be awakened by the pungent smell of coffee wafting from the kitchen. I didn't drink coffee at that time, but this redolent tradition made such an impression on me that now, in the afternoon, I have to make myself a cup of espresso.

As the afternoon began, coffee for the grown-ups was served in the kitchen with no fuss. If a friend happened to drop in, everybody moved to the family room. We children were served a snack

My brother, my father, and I, when we lived in Bari.

consisting of *panini* (sandwiches), smeared with butter and jam or filled with prosciutto, or the favorite, bread and chocolate. If we were lucky, there would be grandmother's brioches or an assortment of cookies, which came with a cup of dense chocolate.

Later in the afternoon, if visitors came, the "good" living room was opened, and the service became more elaborate. It was tea for the ladies and *aperitivi* for the gentlemen. Colorful canapés, *pizzette* (little pizzas), and *rustici (*savory pastries) were offered.

When my uncle Raf built a new terrace, these afternoon ceremonies were performed there. The terrace was magnificent. It stretched from the top floor of the house to a border of little white columns on which you could lean and gaze at the perilous cliffside dropping into the immense valley below. The valley, a green and brown checkerboard punctuated by farmhouses, isolated little villages, and small, dark, spotty woods, looked like a quilt embroidered by clever hands.

The panorama was incredible, especially in the afternoon when the sun's rays had dimmed. To the south loomed the imposing Maiella Mountains, sloping down to the east and toward the Adriatic Sea. Their jagged edges were softened by a surreal blue-green color that enveloped the peaks like a cuddly mohair blanket.

On a clear day, the distant, shimmering line of the Adriatic could be seen melting into the horizon. To the north, rust-colored roofs descended toward the round elegant curve of the *Villa Comunale*. At night, the *Villa*, surrounded by slender lampposts when seen from afar resembled a crowned queen sitting on a throne.

Throughout the many summers I returned to my grandmother's house, the view never changed. Looking at the unending horizon in front of me I dreamed of faraway worlds. That terrace influenced my life, and now that I live in a distant world, I think of it with nostalgia. It is forever part of my past.

WINTER FEASTS

After fall, which was sometimes so glorious it seemed like the continuation of summer, there was winter and the first snow. So much of it! I remember walking between white, soft walls, above which even the grown-ups could not see.

Snow meant Christmas, and Christmas was a time of joy. The first celebration of the season was on the eighth of December, the feast of the Madonna's Conception. The first big dinner was given on this occasion. It was something of a rehearsal for the Christmas festivities to come. During this period, at least in those early years of my life, there was another tradition which was great fun. The *tombola*, or bingo, came out from its carton, and the entire family engaged in this vociferous game. Sometimes we children were even allowed to call the numbers.

During this period, the preparations in the kitchen accelerated dramatically. First cookies and candies were made, because they could be kept longer and had to be ready for visiting well-wishers. Then about two weeks before Christmas the turkeys or the capons were brought from the farm. A few days before Christmas the *baccalà* (salt cod) was soaked and, most important of all, the *capitone*, or conger eel—without which even today there is no Christmas in Italy—was ordered.

Everybody gravitated to the kitchen where the aroma of burning laurel mingled with that of mandarin peels, which were deliberately thrown in the fireplace to perfume the house. The fireplace was the focal point. I still have a letter from my friend, Lillino de Victoris Medori, a gastronome and food journalist, in which he reminds me of Christmas Eves celebrated long ago in our small towns at the edge of the *Maiella Madre,* as we Abruzzesi call "our mountain." The letter tells of the immense fireplaces of our youth in which the coal, like incandescent lava, heated the grill on which the "just sacrificed *capitoni* wriggled" (*i capitoni appena sacrificati*). On the stove, a pot for the pasta stood ready to boil; a skillet of oil waited for other fish, bubbling. On the side board, next to a humble crèche, the uncooked *Cavicionetti* (page 415) resembling "little adoring white sheep rested before the splash into the hot oil, which released the perfume of almonds, walnuts, raisins, and wine."

These dishes were part of the ritual nine entrées served at Christmas Eve dinner, a number commemorating the months of pregnancy of the Madonna. They consisted of an antipasto of stuffed mussels, fried *baccalà,* and fried vegetables, followed by spaghetti with clams, a *brodetto* or fish stew made with several kinds of white fishes like whiting, sole, bass, and a variety of mollusks. The feast consisted of all of this plus two kinds of vegetables, a salad, and a dessert of fresh and dried fruit.

Christmas dinner started with a grand antipasto consisting of all sorts of cold cuts. The first jars of the vegetables grandmother had pickled during the summer were opened. The traditional first course was a soup made of *cardone* (cardoon), cooked in a simmering capon broth until the tiniest meatballs ever, bounced gently on the surface. The meatballs were my mother's masterpiece; nobody could make such tiny balls so uniformly precise.

Next, my father magistrally carved a cold galantine of capon and set the marbled slices on a tray to be surrounded by homemade *giardiniera,* a mixture of pickled vegetables.

Lamb or veal was roasted in the oven and served with a crown of burnished potatoes. After the roast, there was *il piatto di mezzo* (literally, a middle dish), consisting of a vegetable *tortino,* similar to a *frittata*.

After the main part of the meal, a tray with all sorts of cheeses was served with homemade bread or focaccia. Baskets of fruit adorned with ribbons graced the table just before the big *Zuppa Inglese,* the so-called "English soup," made its monumental entrance. This dessert is a sponge cake whose layers are perfumed with several sprinklings of varied liqueurs and filled with rich custard and chocolate mousse. There was no whipping cream in our *Zuppa Inglese.* Its unadulterated taste was the perfect mingling of simple, traditional ingredients. My grandmother's was the best and her recipe is the one my cousins and I still make.

Following the *Zuppa Inglese,* coffee was served in the living room, and the first *panettone* of the season was cut and offered amidst protestations prompted by the fact that, an understatement for sure, we had eaten too much. But my uncle Filippo insisted that everybody had to have a bite. After all, it was tradition!

New Year's Eve was almost a repeat of Christmas Eve, with Papà's famous *brodetto di pesce,* fish stew, standing in for the *capitone.* For New Year's Day dinner, the soup was *tortellini* or *tagliolini* (thin noodles) served in a limpid, soothing broth meant to restore spirits exhausted by the previous night's revelries. I remember the rhythmic sound my mother made with her knife when cutting the *tagliolini* from the delicate sheets of homemade dough. Hers were the thinnest I have ever seen.

If we had had capon at Christmas, on New Year's Day there was a *Tacchino Mille Sapori,* turkey with "one thousand flavors," a hot galantine of turkey with a myriad of flavors. This was my father's creation, invented because we children always protested about the Christmas galantine which was cold, as all galantines are.

Other dishes of meat or fish were also served, such as a roast bass, veal, or pork. On this day, tradition was relaxed and the cooks could be more inventive; also they didn't want to repeat the Christmas dinner menu.

The day after Christmas, Santo Stefano, which is a national holiday in Italy, there was another special dinner. It was also my father's birthday, and he always requested *le laganelle spezzellate.* This is a typical Abruzzese specialty made with homemade pasta. The noodles, similar to *pappardelle,* are cut with a crinkled pastry wheel to make the noodles *spezzellate,* meaning with a jagged edge. *Carne alla Genovese* (page 329), a potted veal roast, provided a succulent sauce for the pasta as well as a luscious second course. Mushrooms, fresh from the woods if the snow had not frozen them, or dried porcini, accompanied the dish. For dessert Papà liked *panettone ripieno,* a *panettone* stuffed with a mixture of ricotta and *torrone,* nougat. This dessert gave my mother the opportunity to make good use of those cakes, which we received in abundance during the holidays.

The dinner always ended with a round of *digestivo,* digestives such as an Amaro or the ever-present Fernet Branca, which was indeed needed. But my father refused it every time saying, "I have eaten so well, why would I want to digest!" This familiar joke made everybody laugh.

For us children, though, the most exciting time was the morning of Epiphany, January 6, after *la Befana's* visit. *La Befana* is the benevolent witch who brings presents to children, the Santa Claus of Italy. Her presents were piled up near the fireplace because she too descended from the chimney. We woke early, even though we had been allowed to stay up late the night before to play *tombola.* The anticipation was simply too much.

The joyful expectation could be shattered by bitter disappointment,

Our maid, Annina

however, if the first thing we saw was a pile of coal. It meant we had been bad and didn't deserve better. But our loving maid, Annina, before desperation set in, quickly removed the coal and the black cloth that obscured the presents. Happiness was restored. The afternoon was generally filled with children's parties, and our relatives dropped in on the ones we were attending in order to exchange good wishes and more *panettone, torrone, caviciunetti,* and other delights.

Returning home on the cold winter's night, we sang happily, our voices shattering the silence. Annina at a certain point, would pick me up and wrap me in her shawl, so I would not catch a cold. Her shawl rests now on my bed here in New York, a warm reminder of my beloved nanny.

Unfortunately, Santa is creeping into our lives, and nowadays Italians are not only substituting him for our witch, but also replacing the crèche with the Christmas tree. My relatives in Abruzzo are continuing the old traditions—together with the new ones. *Così fan tutte.*

CHAPTER 1

ANTIPASTI

Appetizers

As children we loved it when guests came to dinner. We knew company meant a sumptuous *antipasto* (singular). Also, if there were other children, a table was set just for our little party. We were always forbidden to eat anything before a meal; therefore, the serving of *antipasto*, with all those delicious tidbits, was indeed reason to rejoice.

You should know that *antipasti* (plural) are not served at an everyday meal in Italy. They are dishes for special occasions, and are served before the first course. The average daily menu starts with a first course, which could be soup, pasta, or rice. It is followed by a second course of meat or fish, accompanied by vegetables and a salad. A plate of cheese and fruit is the usual finale. Cakes and sweets are also saved for special occasions, although as children, we always had brioches for breakfast and a treat like ice cream during the day.

Following are a mixture of traditional and personal recipes, all favorites at our table.

GRANDE ANTIPASTO ALL'ITALIANA

Grand Antipasto Italian Style (*Makes 12 servings or more*)

12 thin slices prosciutto
12 thin slices salami of your choice
12 thin slices ham, baked or boiled
12 thin slices mortadella
24 bocconcini mozzarella, about 3 pounds total
One 6-ounce jar marinated artichokes
Freshly ground pepper to taste

One 3³/₄-ounce can rolled anchovies, drained
4 hard-boiled large eggs, peeled and cut into thin rounds
¹/₂ pound mixed Italian cured black and green olives
Fresh curly parsley for garnish

1. Alternate the different meats, arranging them in a decorative fashion on a large round platter, leaving space in the center for the bocconcini and artichokes. If you wish, roll up the slices of ham and mortadella. This will save space on the platter.

2. Pat the mozzarella dry and place in a mixing bowl. Pour the oil from the jar of artichokes over the mozzarella. Add a grinding of pepper and toss. Place the dressed mozzarella in the center of the platter.

3. If the artichokes are large, cut them into halves or quarters. Set them around the mozzarella. Place the eggs around the edge of the platter. Top the eggs with the rolled anchovies. Scatter the olives over all and garnish with the parsley.

MOZZARELLA ALL'ERBETTE

Mozzarella with Herb Sauce (**Makes 4 to 6 servings**)

I LIKE TO PREPARE THIS SIMPLE ANTIPASTO during the summer when fresh herbs are abundant. The touch of anchovy and assertive sprinkling of capers add the right tanginess to the delicate mozzarella. Together with the now-famous *Caprese*, the mozzarella, tomato, and basil antipasto from Capri, this is one of my favorite dishes. Serve it at room temperature with a nice *pane casareccio*, home-style bread, and a good glass of *Prosecco*, a sparkling white wine from the Veneto area, in the north.

One 16-ounce fresh mozzarella cheese;
   or 1 pound bocconcini
¼ cup extra virgin olive oil
3 sprigs fresh Italian parsley
½ cup loosely packed fresh basil leaves
3 or 4 fresh mint leaves
5 or 6 fresh oregano leaves

Leaves from 1 sprig fresh thyme
1 tablespoon freshly grated parmesan cheese
2 or 3 anchovy fillets, drained
Freshly ground pepper to taste;
   or ¼ teaspoon hot chili pepper flakes
2 tablespoons small capers in brine,
   drained

1. Cut the mozzarella into 12 slices. If the mozzarella is a large one, cut the slices in half. Place in a serving dish, slightly overlapping the edges. Cut large bocconcini in half if using (do not cut small bocconcini) and place in the serving dish.

2. Place all the remaining ingredients except the capers in a food processor and puree.

3. Pour this sauce on the cheese and sprinkle with the capers. Refrigerate, covered, for at least 1 hour or overnight. Serve at room temperature.

CHEESE THE ABRUZZESE WAY

Mozzarella and scamorza are very much part of the Abruzzese diet. The charming town of Rivisondoli, a holiday and ski resort, is famous for its scamorze. These two fresh cheeses are made of cow's milk. They have a stringy, soft texture and a sweet flavor. The difference between the two is that scamorza is aged at least 12 days before being sold, and in the process it acquires a yellow bloom. They are both eaten as table cheeses and much used in the layering of baked dishes.

ANTIPASTO DI ROLLATINE DI SALAME E CARCIOFI

Salami and Artichoke Rolls (Makes 6 servings)

FOR THIS REAL QUICK TREAT, ALL YOU DO is spread a mixture of pureed marinated artichokes, combined with mayonnaise, and bread crumbs on slices of salami, roll them up, and spear with a toothpick.

One 6-ounce jar marinated artichokes
1 tablespoon mayonnaise
1/2 tablespoon very fine plain bread crumbs
12 thin slices salami of your choice
Lettuce leaves

1. Drain the artichokes and place them in a food processor or blender. Process while adding the mayonnaise and the bread crumbs until creamy.

2. Spread the artichoke mixture on the slices of salami and roll. Secure with toothpicks. Serve on lettuce leaves.

Variation: For another speedy antipasto, spread the slices of salami with olive paste, found in Italian food stores, instead of the artichoke mixture.

INSALATA DI RISO

Rice Salad (Makes 8 to 10 servings)

RICE SALAD, WHICH IS MUCH APPRECIATED in Italy, is practically unknown in this country. Yet a rice salad can be deliciously flavorful and delicate. It lends itself much better to salad dressings, like vinegar, lemon, or mayonnaise, which I think are awful on pasta. (Pasta should never be treated as a vegetable and I even resent when it is served on the side.)

Cold rice can be easily combined with a variety of ingredients: good

2 tablespoons extra virgin olive oil
Juice of 1/2 lemon
1/2 cup mayonnaise, optional
1 tablespoon minced fresh parsley
2 anchovy fillets, drained and mashed to a paste; or 1 teaspoon anchovy paste
3 cups cooked rice (about 1 1/2 cups raw)
2 tablespoons capers in brine, drained
1 cup shelled peas, blanched (see Note)
1/4 pound diced boiled ham
1/4 pound provolone cheese, diced
4 or 5 marinated artichokes, quartered
1/2 cup black California pitted olives
3 plum tomatoes, cubed
2 hard-boiled large eggs, peeled and sliced
Curly parsley for garnish

In a mixing bowl large enough to contain all the ingredients, combine the first 5 ingredients and mix well. Add the rice, mix, and add all the remaining ingredients except the eggs and curly parsley. Let it stand at room temperature for 20 to

canned tuna, ham, cheeses, vegetables, seafood, etc. I prefer to use an American rice, like Uncle Ben's, because the grains remain more separate. The Italian kind, which is excellent for risotto, tends to clump. The basic condiment should be a fruity extra virgin olive oil, a good, even if light mayonnaise, and lemon or vinegar.

This recipe is for a more complex salad since, in my house, it was often served as an antipasto for an important buffet or as a main dish in summer.

30 minutes. Then set in a serving dish and decorate with the eggs and the curly parsley. Serve at room temperature.

NOTE: TO BLANCH PEAS, ADD THEM TO PLENTY OF BOILING SALTED WATER, COOK UNTIL TENDER, ABOUT 5 MINUTES, AND DRAIN.

Variation: Replace the ham with good Italian canned tuna packed in olive oil. Use its oil to dress the rice. You can also remove the cheese but add more mayonnaise. This version was a favorite Friday supper.

AN UNSUITABLE SALAD

I will never understand why pasta salads, which in my opinion are an abomination, have become so popular in this country—they are now being exported to Italy! This is true! Twice during my last visit there I was served cold pasta, even by one friend who should have known better. Fortunately, the offending presence appeared only at the buffet table, which also offered many appealing choices.

ANTIPASTO DI CAVOLFIORE E RAVANELLI

Cauliflower and Radish Antipasto (Makes 6 servings)

HERE'S AN EASY APPETIZER—THE ABRUZZO version of a raw vegetable platter with dip—which I like to serve at the coffee table while my guests have drinks before dinner. The dressing is delicious and suited for all sorts of *crudités*.

1 medium-size cauliflower, separated into flowerets
1 bunch red radishes, well washed, trimmed at the bottom but short green leaves left on, if any

Lemon juice
1 cup mayonnaise
1 ¹/₂ tablespoons capers in brine, drained
2 cornichons or 1 small sour pickle, chopped
2 tablespoons minced fresh Italian parsley

1. Set the cauliflower flowerets and radishes around a serving plate or a basket, leaving a space in the middle. Sprinkle with lemon juice.

2. Combine the mayonnaise with all the remaining ingredients. Pour into a small bowl and set in the middle of the vegetables. Serve.

INSALATA RUSSA

Russian Salad (Makes 12 servings)

IN ITALY, THERE IS NO BUFFET TABLE AT which *insalata russa* does not appear. Sometimes it is enriched with seafood, including lobster, and colorfully embellished with hard-boiled eggs or roasted peppers. I can hardly resist buying some when I see it prominently displayed in the appetizing windows and cases of the chic *tavole calde* and *rosticcerie*, which are the take-out places of Italy.

In the States, however, this dish is not appreciated. The people at Balducci's, New York's great Italian specialty shop, told me that the dish didn't sell well, although they had made a great one. My assumption is that Americans get frightened by the mantle of mayonnaise covering the vegetables. For this reason I reduced the amount of mayonnaise by half in my recipe. I use a commercial, reduced-fat mayonnaise and it works well. I know that when I make *insalata russa* for my guests it vanishes. They all like it. Besides, it is one of the few salads you can prepare in advance, and this is such a bonus when cooking for a crowd.

1 bunch broccoli, washed, trimmed, cut into flowerets, and blanched
1 bunch cauliflower, washed, trimmed, cut into flowerets, and blanched
One 1-pound bag frozen mixed vegetables, cooked
2 large boiling potatoes, boiled until tender, peeled, and diced
2 sprigs fresh Italian parsley, minced

1 clove garlic, peeled and minced
1 sour pickle, chopped
¼ cup red wine vinegar
One 16-ounce jar marinated artichokes
Salt to taste, optional
2 cups mayonnaise
Juice of 1 lemon
1 red bell pepper, roasted until blackened on all sides, peeled, seeded, and cut into strips (see Step 1, page 117)

1. Reserve 3 or 4 flowerets of the broccoli and cauliflower for decoration. Chop the remaining flowerets into small pieces. Peel the stems of the broccoli and the cauliflower and cut into small dice.

2. Combine the mixed vegetables with the broccoli and cauliflower, turn the vegetables into a mixing bowl, and add the potatoes.

3. In a small bowl, combine the parsley, garlic, pickle, and vinegar. Add the oil from the artichoke jar, reserving the artichokes, and add the salt, if used, and 1 cup of the mayonnaise. Mix well. Add this sauce to the vegetables and toss.

EDIBLE ART

Insalate composite, literally composed salads as opposed to tossed, are made with many ingredients including vegetables, meat, fish, shellfish, and rice, but never with cold pasta—at least not at my table! Often greens are an afterthought in these salads, and used just for garnish. *Insalate composite* are a must in a buffet table where they are placed as a centerpiece for their colorful decorations of hard-boiled eggs, *cornichons* (tart pickles), capers, shrimp, or lobster. These, too, would make a nice main dish for a luncheon.

---

4. Turn this mixture onto a round or oval platter and flatten into a smooth surface. Cut the reserved artichokes into neat wedges and reserve.

5. Combine the remaining mayonnaise with the lemon juice and pour it evenly on the vegetables, smoothing the top with a spatula. Garnish the salad with the red peppers, reserved artichokes, and flowerets of the broccoli and cauliflower. Refrigerate until ready to serve.

Variation: It is also nice to set the salad on a bed of lettuce leaves.

   If some of the salad remains, use it to stuff tomatoes, cooked artichokes, or avocados.

IN NAME ONLY

There is some disagreement about who invented *insalata russa*. According to legend, an Italian chef working in Russia at the court of a czar came up with this delightful mixture of vegetables dressed with a luscious, lemony mayonnaise. The French say the same story but the chef . . . is French.

BRUSCHETTA

(Makes 12 servings or more)

IT IS AMAZING TO SEE HOW HUMBLE snacks like *bruschetta* and *crostini* have taken the United States by storm. Chefs have even found ways of embellishing them so that at times a few slices of *bruschetta* or a plate of *crostini* can become a meal.

   Bruschetta, as everybody now knows, are slices of toasted bread rubbed with fresh garlic and sprinkled with olive oil. They originated in

1 loaf Italian bread (long or round), cut into 1-inch slices
½ cup extra virgin olive oil

1 large clove garlic, peeled
Pinch of diavoletto (dried Italian hot red pepper), optional

1. Preheat the oven to 375°F.

2. Place the slices of bread on cookie sheets.

3. In a food processor, place all the remaining ingredients and blend thoroughly.

continues

Abruzzo and from there traveled to the bordering regions of Umbria and Lazio, and then to the rest of Italy. Very simple to prepare, *bruschetta*, in its simplest form (such as this recipe), is also a wonderful accompaniment to soups, stews, and other foods.

4. Brush the bread with the oil mixture and bake for about 10 minutes. Reduce the oven temperature to 250°F and let the bread toast until golden, about 10 more minutes. Turn the oven off. Leave in the oven until ready to serve. The longer it stays in the oven, the crispier it becomes. If necessary, reheat.

Variation: *Bruschetta* can also be topped with chopped fresh tomatoes dressed with a little olive oil and oregano or basil, or other vegetables like cooked onions or thinly sliced mushrooms. Cooked, shelled shellfish like mussels (see page 223) can also be used.

CANAPÉS ALLA RUSTICA

Rustic Canapés *(Makes 6 servings)*

MY GUESTS AND PUPILS LOVE THIS colorful *antipasto* of sliced tomato, zucchini, and mozzarella, and I make it often since zucchini are always on hand. It can be served at the dinner table or passed around with drinks.

1 or 2 cloves garlic, peeled and cut in half
Three ³/₄-inch slices bread cut from a large, round Italian crusty loaf, each slice cut in half; or 12 slices from a baguette
4 ripe plum tomatoes, cut into thin, round slices

1 or 2 medium-size zucchini, cut into very thin rounds
Freshly ground pepper to taste
¹/₂ teaspoon dried oregano
One 16-ounce mozzarella cheese, cut into thin slices
Extra virgin olive oil for drizzling

1. Preheat the oven to 375°F.

2. Rub the garlic over the slices of bread and place them on a cookie sheet. Cover each slice with overlapping slices of tomatoes and zucchini. Sprinkle with pepper and oregano. Place 1 slice of mozzarella on each canapé and then drizzle with olive oil.

3. Cover loosely with foil and bake 15 minutes. Remove the foil and bake until slightly brown at the top, about 5 more minutes. Serve hot.

ANTIPASTO DI FEGATINI ALL'ABRUZZESE

Chicken Livers Abruzzo Style (Makes 6 servings)

I HAVE CONVERTED MANY HATERS OF liver with this tasty antipasto. The livers are cut into bite-size pieces and then quickly sautéed with onions, *cornichon*s, and wine. At home it was always served hot with *bruschetta,* and I do the same.

3 tablespoons extra virgin olive oil
1 large onion, thinly sliced
1/4 cup dry white wine
3 cornichons or 1/2 sour pickle, chopped
1 pound chicken livers, trimmed, washed, dried, and cut into bite-size pieces
1/2 teaspoon sugar
Salt to taste, optional
Freshly ground pepper to taste
1 tablespoon minced fresh parsley

1. Place the oil and onion in a 10-inch skillet, cover, and cook, stirring often, over medium heat until the onion is soft, about 10 minutes. While cooking, add the wine a little at a time. Stir in the *cornichons* or pickle and cook 5 more minutes.

continues

2. Add the livers to the skillet. Raise the heat to high and cook the livers, stirring, for 5 minutes. Add the sugar, salt, if used, and pepper. Stir again and cook until the livers lose their pink color and are done, 5 to 10 minutes. Do not overcook. Sprinkle with the parsley and serve.

Variation 1: If some of the antipasto remained, my father, the inventive one, turned it into an elegant pâté by chopping the liver mixture very finely.

Variation 2: My mother didn't use *cornichon*s, as I suggest, but ¼ cup chopped *sottaceti* (a mixture of colorful pickled vegetables), which dotted the dish with colors. *Sottaceti* are the usual accompaniment to poached meats and fish in Italy. They can be found in Italian food stores under the name *giardiniera*.

SPIEDINI (ROSTICINI)

Grilled Skewered Meat (Makes 10 to 12 servings)

IN ABRUZZO *SPIEDINI*, THE COMMON word for brochettes or shish kebab, are also called *rosticini*, little roasts, because meat is cut into small pieces, then roasted quickly over charcoal. Lamb is the favorite, but other meats are also used.

Ideally *spiedini* should be cooked over charcoal. But they can also be broiled in a home oven with excellent results.

1 cup dry wine, white or red
2 bay leaves, broken in half
2 cloves garlic, peeled and sliced
2 or 3 sprigs fresh Italian parsley
1 sprig fresh rosemary, broken into
*   4 pieces; or 1 teaspoon dried*

1 tablespoon ketchup
Freshly ground pepper to taste
4 pounds lean boneless meat like lamb,
*   pork, beef, or chicken, cut into*
*   1½-inch cubes*
Salt to taste, optional

1. In a large nonreactive bowl, combine all the ingredients except the meat and salt, if used. Mix well, then add the meat. Toss again and let marinate in a cool place for 1 hour; refrigerate, covered, if longer. Stir the mixture once in a while.

2. Thread the cubes of meat onto skewers. Discard the marinade. Cook over medium heat on a charcoal grill or under a broiler, turning often, until done, 10 to 20 minutes, depending on the meat used. If using salt, lightly sprinkle the *rosticini* at this point. Serve hot.

Variation: Instead of meat, use scallops or shrimp, or a mixture of both. Eliminate the ketchup. You can wrap the shrimp or scallops in a bit of prosciutto or bacon.

ANTIPASTO DI GAMBERI E FAGIOLI

Shrimp and Bean Antipasto (Makes 6 servings)

THIS COUNTRY DISH, A MARINATED SALAD of shrimp and cranberry beans with diced vegetables, is found in many rustic *trattorie Abruzzesi*. I serve it as an antipasto, or as a main dish for lunch. The liquid in which the shrimp cook can be saved and used as the broth for a seafood risotto, or as poaching liquid for some other fish.

Assemble this dish 2 to 3 hours before serving it.

³/₄ pound fresh cranberry beans, or use any dried beans, soaked overnight
7 cups water
2 bay leaves
1¹/₂ medium-size onions, cut into quarters
Salt to taste, optional
1 carrot, peeled and cut into 4 pieces
1 rib celery, cut into 4 pieces
1 sprig fresh Italian parsley

¹/₄ cup red wine vinegar
1³/₄ pounds medium-size shrimp
Freshly ground pepper to taste
¹/₄ cup extra virgin olive oil
1 large tomato, peeled, seeded, and diced
1 clove garlic, peeled and minced
Juice of 1 lemon
2 tablespoons balsamic vinegar
1 tablespoon minced fresh Italian parsley

1. Place the beans in a 2-quart casserole and cover with 3 cups of the water. Add 1 bay leaf, half the onions, and the salt if used. Cover the casserole. Bring to a boil over high heat, then immediately reduce the heat to a minimum. Simmer the beans until tender, about 30 minutes for the fresh beans and about 1 hour for the dried. Drain and discard the bay leaf and the onions. Set aside.

2. In a medium-size pot, place the remaining onion and bay leaf, the carrot, celery, and parsley. Add 4 cups of water and the wine vinegar and bring to a boil over high heat.

continues

3. While the water is coming to a boil, peel and devein the shrimp. Add the shrimp shells to the pot and reduce the heat to medium. Season the broth with salt if used and pepper and simmer covered 20 minutes. Add the shrimp and cook, covered, just until they become red, about 5 minutes. Drain the shrimp and discard the bay leaf, onions, and shells. Dice the carrot and the celery.

4. In a mixing bowl, combine the remaining ingredients, add the cooked beans and shrimp, which can be diced if you prefer, and the diced carrot and celery. Toss the mixture, place it on a serving plate, and serve.

BACCALÀ TRICOLORE

Tricolored Baccalà **(Makes 8 servings or more)**

BACCALÀ, SALT COD, USED TO BE THE FOOD of the poor who could not afford fresh fish. Today it has become a delicacy and it is quite expensive.

This antipasto is still often served during the Christmas holidays. With strips of red and green grilled peppers surrounding the snowy white fish, the presentation is quite festive and colorful.

2 pounds salt cod fillet, soaked in cold water for 24 hours
1 medium-size onion, quartered
1 rib celery, cut into 4 pieces
6 sprigs fresh Italian parsley
2 or 3 anchovy fillets, drained
1 sour pickle; or 3 or 4 cornichons
1 large clove garlic, peeled
1 shallot or small red onion
2 tablespoons red wine vinegar
Extra virgin olive oil

1 small potato, boiled, peeled, and mashed
Lemon juice, if needed
1 red bell pepper, roasted over the gas flame (see Step 1, page 117) until blackened on all sides, peeled, seeded, and cut into strips
1 green bell pepper, roasted until blackened on all sides, peeled, seeded, and cut into strips
1 tablespoon capers in brine, drained
Curly parsley for decoration

1. Drain the fish and remove any skin and bones. Cut the fish into pieces. Place in a pot and add the onion, celery, and 2 sprigs of the parsley. Add water to cover, bring to a boil over high heat, then reduce the heat to low and simmer, covered, until the fish is soft and flakes easily, 10 to 15 minutes. Cool the fish in its water.

2. Drain the fish well and pat dry with paper towels, place it on a serving plate, and flake it.

3. In a food processor, finely chop the remaining 4 parsley sprigs, the anchovies, pickle, garlic, and shallot or onion. Add the vinegar and $\frac{1}{4}$ cup of the oil. Mix well.

Turn into a mixing bowl and add the mashed potato. It should be loose and spreadable. If the mixture is too thick add a little more oil or some lemon juice. Pour this sauce on the fish.

4. Place the peppers in a mixing bowl, add 2 tablespoons of oil, and mix. Arrange the peppers all around the fish. Sprinkle the capers over all and decorate with parsley sprigs.

COZZE ALLO ZAFFERANO

Mussels with Saffron *(Makes 8 servings)*

ABRUZZO, AND PERHAPS SARDINIA, ARE the only regions in Italy where saffron is cultivated, yet we Abruzzesi do not use it much. This recipe of sautéed mussels served on the half shell is one of the rare examples.

Do not be too generous with this wonderful and expensive spice. A little goes a long way; too much will make your food taste of medicine.

2 pounds mussels, scrubbed and debearded
2 shallots, each quartered; or 1 onion, quartered
2 sprigs fresh Italian parsley
1 sprig fresh thyme; or 1/2 teaspoon dried
2 bay leaves

3/4 cup dry white wine
1/4 cup water
Freshly ground pepper to taste
1/2 teaspoon saffron, preferably powdered
3 tablespoons extra virgin olive oil

1. Place all the ingredients in a large skillet. Cook over medium heat, shaking the skillet often, until the mussels open, 5 to 8 minutes. Remove the open mussels and discard half of the shell. Discard the mussels that have not opened. Place the remaining half with the mollusk on a serving plate. Keep warm.

2. With a slotted spoon, remove the solids from the skillet and discard. Strain the liquid through a paper towel into a small saucepan. Bring the liquid to a boil and if there is more than 3/4 cup, reduce it by boiling it. Pour the liquid over the mussels and serve. This dish can also be served chilled.

Variation: *Pepata di Cozze*—Peppered Mussels
This is a spicy dish from the resort town of Termoli, but found in many coastal towns of Abruzzo and neighboring Molise. It is a must during the feast of the patron saint, San Basso, which takes place at the beginning of August. During this celebration, and since the city is so geared to its beautiful coast, sea spectacles are the main attraction.

This dish is often served with *fett'onta*, crusty slices of bread drizzled with olive oil and grilled. (Unlike *bruschetta*, *fett'onta* contains no garlic.)

The preparation for the *pepata* is similar to the *Cozze allo Zafferano*. The *zafferano* is replaced by a touch of *diavoletto* and a good grinding of pepper.

REMEMBRANCES OF MUSSELS AND CLAMS

My family loved mussels and clams with a passion, most of all because we went to the sea and gathered them ourselves. My dearest Aunt Ela and Uncle Raffaele used to rent a villa in a picturesque holiday resort called San Vito, on the Adriatic coast. Their place was like a second home to me. Their daughters were and are the most beloved members of my family.

In that part of Abruzzo, the sandy beaches on the north give way to a series of coves with pebble beaches and beautiful rock formations. These rocks were at one time covered with clusters of plump mussels. You can still gather mussels there, but they are not as plentiful.

When I was a teenager, my cousins and I went to the rocks for our harvest and came home with buckets of mussels. It was a job to separate them from the beard, which attached them to the rock, and to scrub them clean. But we all did it, and as a group effort it was fun.

The preparations varied according to the mood of the cook or the most intriguing suggestions given by the would-be eaters, probably my father or Uncle Raf. They were always the ones with innovative tastes.

Some of the mussels were eaten raw, as an antipasto, simply dressed with drops of lemon. There was no pollution at that time, and nobody ever got sick.

Clams were gathered in a different way, and the best harvest was done in Pescara, the town where we had a house. My family spent the summer in this city when we were children, and later returned to live there. Bucket and fork in hand, we used to go to the beach early in the morning (always an adventure to me, not an early riser) and walk carefully and slowly into the clear waters of the sea. The point was to spot the bit of clam protruding from the sand and dig it out with the fork. Our clams, called *telline,* are small; therefore, you have to have sharp eyes and not ripple the water too much.

Ever ready for a gastronomic treat, we carried lemons so that we could eat the sweet *cannolicchi,* razor clams, on the spot. These clams were also imbedded in the sand and had to be extracted with the fork. They were quite abundant then. I remember squeezing one out of the shell directly in my mouth and dribbling a few drops of lemon onto my tongue . . . . I will never forget that pure marine flavor, it was like swallowing the sea.

In my opinion there is no better condiment for raw mollusks, including oysters, than the fresh juice of a lemon. I do not care for red cocktail sauces. If I want a real sauce I make one with a light mayonnaise, which I dilute with lemon juice and the liquor from the clams, or mussels, or a little clam broth.

Mussels and clams are, of course, delicious in sauces for pasta, and a great enhancer of flavor in many fish dishes, especially the *brodetti* or *zuppe di pesce* (fish stews).

ANTIPASTO ALLA GIULIESE

Fish Antipasto Giulianova Style (Makes 6 to 8 servings)

GIULIANOVA, IN ABRUZZO, IS A SUNNY little town on the littoral. It has a beautiful sandy beach with a backdrop of palm trees swaying in the breeze. The food is delicate and definitely marine, like this marinated salad of fish, shrimp, and squid.

5 cups Fish Broth (page 63)
1 pound shrimp, peeled and deveined, shells reserved
3/4 pound mixed whole or filleted white fish, such as scrod, cod, monkfish, bass, or flounder, cut into serving pieces
1 pound squid, cleaned
1 1/2 pounds mussels, scrubbed and debearded
1/2 cup extra virgin olive oil
Juice of 1 lemon
Salt to taste, optional

Freshly ground pepper to taste
One 6- to 7-ounce can imported Italian tuna packed in oil, drained
1 teaspoon anchovy paste
2 tablespoons capers in brine, drained
2 cornichons
2 cloves garlic, peeled
1 tablespoon red wine vinegar
4 or 5 sprigs fresh Italian parsley, chopped
Lettuce leaves, tomato slices, cured olives, etc., for garnish

1. Bring the court-bouillon to a boil over medium heat in a medium-size pot.

2. Tie the shells of the shrimp in a cheesecloth, and add to the broth. Add the white fish. Cook 5 minutes and then add the shrimp. Cook until the shrimp turn pink, about 5 minutes. Add the squid and cook just until tender-firm, 2 to 3 minutes (see Note). Cool the fish in the cooking liquid at room temperature.

3. Cut the squid into circles and halve or quarter the tentacles, depending on size. Flake the fish. Cut the shrimp into 3 or 4 pieces. Place in a large mixing bowl. Strain the court-bouillon and reserve for another use.

4. Place the mussels in a large skillet over medium heat. Cook, shaking the skillet, until they open, 5 to 8 minutes.

5. Discard the mussel shells, working over the skillet so you can collect all the juice. Strain the remaining mussel juice through a paper towel into the bowl.

6. In a food processor, place all the remaining ingredients except the parsley and the garnish. Process until smooth. Pour the sauce on the fish and toss gently. Refrigerate, covered, at least 1 hour.

continues

7. To serve, place the antipasto on a serving platter and sprinkle with the parsley. Decorate with the lettuce leaves, tomato slices, olives, etc., if desired.

NOTE: ITALIANS USUALLY COOK SQUID FOR A LONG TIME, ESPECIALLY WHEN USED IN A SAUCE OR STEW. FOR THIS SALAD, HOWEVER, AND SIMILAR DISHES, I FOLLOW THE CHINESE WAY OF COOKING THEM IN LIQUID FOR A FEW MINUTES, AND THEN REMOVING THEM AS SOON AS THE WATER GETS CLOUDY.

ASPARAGI PRIMAVERILI

Spring Asparagus *(Makes 6 servings)*

GLI ASPARAGI, ASPARAGUS, ARE THE TRUE harbingers of spring. I still remember the pleasure I felt as a child when the first asparagus arrived. They were so tender and flavorful, and so welcome. After all, we had waited an entire year to eat them. Now we can have asparagus practically year-round, a good thing for sure. But the sheer delight of seeing the *primizie*, the Italian name for early vegetables and fruits, is lost forever.

Because we wanted to taste their full fresh flavor, the first asparagus were always prepared in the simplest manner: briefly cooked, cooled, and then served with a drizzling of oil and lemon. It was like savoring spring itself.

36 spears asparagus, washed
3 tablespoons extra virgin olive oil, or more to taste
Juice of ¹/₂ lemon
6 radicchio leaves

1. Snap off the bottom part of the asparagus where it naturally breaks. (Reserve the tough ends for stock or soup.) Peel the stalks with a vegetable peeler, if you wish.

2. In a skillet large enough to hold the asparagus in one layer, bring 2 inches water to a boil over medium heat. Add the asparagus and cook until tender, 5 to 6 minutes. To test for doneness, pick up 1 asparagus spear with a pair of tongs; if the tip bends a little when lifted the asparagus is done. Drain and rinse in cold water. Dry with paper towels.

3. Combine the oil and lemon juice. Taste and add more oil if needed. Dress the asparagus with this mixture.

4. Place 1 radicchio leaf on each plate, arrange 6 asparagus on the leaves, and serve.

Variation: After dressing the asparagus, wrap 3 to 4 stalks with a slice of ham. Serve garnished with watercress.

FIORI DI ZUCCHINE

Deep-Fried Zucchini Flowers *(Makes 6 servings)*

I KNOW, FRIED FOOD IS NOT POPULAR these days. But zucchini flowers are rare and have a short season, so why not indulge once or twice in this delicious dish?

When deep frying, do not skimp on the oil. The more oil the better, because food swimming in oil absorbs less.

The oil used in frying can be strained and reused once or twice. When frying fish, however, reuse the oil only for fish.

It is a good idea to purify your oil, even if you are using it for the first time. A simple method consists of dropping a piece of bread soaked in vinegar into the hot oil. This will also tell you if the oil is ready, because the bread floats to the top of the oil heated to the proper temperature.

18 zucchini flowers
1 large egg
1 cup cornstarch
1 cup water, or more as needed
2 ice cubes
Oil for deep frying (see page xvi)
Salt to taste, optional

1. Remove the stems and the little spiked leaves surrounding the flowers. Gently rinse outside and inside the flowers. Drain.

2. In a mixing bowl, beat the egg, then add the cornstarch, water, and ice cubes. The batter should be thin; if not, add a little more water or a few more ice cubes.

3. In a 10-inch skillet, heat the oil to the smoking point. Dip each flower into the batter and gently place in the oil. Do not crowd the skillet. Cook, turning once, until golden, about 8 to 10 minutes in all. Drain on paper towels. Sprinkle with salt, if desired. Serve hot.

Variation: Place a small piece of mozzarella inside the flowers before dipping them into the batter.

WASHING MUSHROOMS

I know most cookbooks tell you to wipe the mushrooms with a cloth instead of washing them, the reason being that mushrooms absorb water. But nowadays I wash everything. The method I suggest is a quick wash, with kosher salt helping to extract the grit.

Place the fresh mushrooms in a large bowl. Add 1 tablespoon of kosher salt and lukewarm water to abundantly cover the mushrooms. Quickly toss the mushrooms around to wash them well. Place them in a colander, rinse with cold water, drain, and gently dry with paper towels.

FUNGHI ALLA FRANCESCA E LUIGI

Francesca and Luigi's Mushrooms **(Makes 6 servings)**

LUIGI AND FRANCESCA ARE THE CHILDREN of my cousin Adriana. At one time they were both at the university in Rome sharing an apartment. On one of my returns to Italy I stayed with them for a few days and they surprised me with this beautiful antipasto.

1 pound large portobello mushrooms, stems removed
Extra virgin olive oil
1 cup plain bread crumbs
2 tablespoons minced fresh Italian parsley

¼ teaspoon dried oregano
2 cloves garlic, minced
Salt to taste, optional
Freshly ground pepper to taste

1. Quickly wash and dry the mushrooms (see box, page 25). Cut each mushroom in half. Reserve the stems for another use.

2. Oil a cookie sheet large enough to fit the mushrooms in one layer.

3. In a mixing bowl, combine the remaining ingredients and sprinkle this mixture on the mushrooms. Bake until the mushrooms are soft, 20 to 25 minutes. Serve hot and pass the pepper mill.

FUNGHETTI MARINATI ALLO SCALOGNO

Marinated Mushrooms with Shallots **(Makes 6 servings)**

HERE'S A SIMPLE AND CONVENIENT antipasto that can be prepared in advance. At the table I like to serve the mushrooms on a leaf of radicchio, the whole sprinkled with minced parsley and a few drops of lemon juice. When people are balancing drinks and dishes at the coffee table, I use toothpicks.

¼ cup extra virgin olive oil
Juice of ½ lemon
1 shallot, cut in half
2 cloves garlic, peeled
2 cornichons; or 1 small sour pickle

1 tablespoon capers in brine, drained
1 pound medium-size white mushrooms, rinsed and dried (see box, page 25), caps only
¼ cup dry white wine

1. In a food processor or blender, place all the ingredients except the mushrooms and wine. Process until almost liquid.

2. Place the mushrooms in a large saucepan and add the wine. Cook over high heat for 5 minutes, then add the sauce. Bring to a boil, reduce the heat to low, and simmer until they are tender, about 5 minutes. Cover and refrigerate for about 2 hours.

MELANZANE IN SALSA PICCANTE

Eggplants in Savory Sauce **(Makes 6 to 8 servings)**

THIS DISH SHOULD BE PREPARED THE night before to give the eggplants time to absorb the flavor of the sauce, a bonus for the hostess or host who will have a dish ready in advance for a dinner party. It also makes a simple antipasto. To serve this as finger food with drinks, roll up the eggplant slices and secure with toothpicks.

6 small or 3 medium-size eggplants
Extra virgin olive oil
6 to 8 fresh oregano leaves, minced;
*   or ¹/₂ teaspoon dried*
2 cloves garlic, peeled

4 or 5 anchovy fillets, drained;
*   or 1¹/₂ teaspoons anchovy paste*
¹/₄ teaspoon hot red chili pepper flakes
4 or 5 sprigs fresh parsley
3 tablespoons balsamic vinegar
Fresh basil leaves for garnish

1. Preheat the oven to 375°F.

2. Cut the eggplants into ¹/₄-inch-thick rounds. Brush with olive oil and sprinkle with the oregano. Bake, turning once, until soft, 10 to 20 minutes.

3. Place the garlic, anchovies, hot red pepper, and parsley in a food processor or blender. Add 3 tablespoons of olive oil and the vinegar and puree.

4. Arrange the eggplant slices on a serving plate and pour the sauce over them. Refrigerate, covered, for 2 hours or longer.

5. Let the dish come to room temperature before serving. Decorate with the basil leaves.

CHAPTER 2

PANINI, PIZZE RUSTICHE E TORTINI

Sandwiches, Savory Pies, and Flans

*A*t the mention of these tantalizing specialties, I am transported back to my childhood before a special outing when an important picnic was being planned. I remember the feverish preparation of *panini* filled with varied ingredients, the precise slicing of some *pizza rustica* made the day before, and then the wrapping and storing of everything in colored picnic baskets. What fun it was.

I also remember returning home, exhausted by the day's activities, being greeted by the smells of a soup bubbling on the stove and the delicate aroma of a *tortino* baking in the oven. And then, into a cool bed for much needed rest. What a pleasant day it had been.

Panini are strictly for afternoon snacks and for taking along on picnics and travels. Coffee bars in Italy make tiny *panini* which Italians eat while drinking their aperitifs of Cinzano, Chinotto, or a powerful Negroni.

Pizze rustiche are pies filled with cheeses, meats, vegetables, and fish—in other words, not sweet. We would never call a pizza a pie. *Pizze rustiche* are also for snacks, but they are often served at teatime or with drinks before dinner, too, and make lovely lunch and

---

IL PANINO CLASSICO
The Classic "Panino"

The most classic *panino* is the one with prosciutto and mozzarella, but salami or mortadella make favorite *panini*, too. The bread is first smeared with butter, and a slice of cheese, often mozzarella, is added. There is seldom lettuce in it.

---

light supper entrées.

Tortini, similar to flans, are mostly made with vegetables and look like thick baked frittatas. They are reserved for suppers, buffet tables, or as an extra

course called *piatto di mezzo,* at an important dinner. Here, in America, I find them ideal dishes for lunch, and I serve them often, accompanied by a light salad and a fruit dessert.

PANINI DI MORTADELLA CON MASCARPONE E NOCCIOLE

Mortadella, Mascarpone, and Hazelnut Sandwiches (Makes 6 servings)

A LUSCIOUS CREAM OF NUTS AND CHEESE embellishes this *panino*. The nuts can vary according to what is available. I prefer hazelnuts or pistachios, but walnuts and almonds also work well with this recipe. The secret is to lightly toast whichever nuts you use.

Other cheeses, like ricotta, robbiola, brie, or good American cream cheese, are possible substitutions.

3/4 pound mascarpone cheese, at room temperature
1/2 cup hazelnuts, toasted (see Note) and chopped
2 tablespoons heavy cream or milk, if needed

6 standard-size hard-crusted rolls
12 thin slices mortadella, folded in half
6 lettuce leaves

1. Combine the cheese with the nuts. If the mixture seems too dry, add the heavy cream or milk. Mix well.

2. Split the rolls in half. Spread equal amounts of the mascarpone mixture on both halves of the rolls. Sandwich 2 slices of mortadella and 1 lettuce leaf in each roll and serve.

NOTE: TO TOAST HAZELNUTS, SPREAD THEM ON A COOKIE SHEET AND BAKE, STIRRING ONCE, IN A 350°F OVEN UNTIL GOLDEN, 5 TO 7 MINUTES.

PASTA PER FOCACCIA E PIZZA

Focaccia and Pizza Dough (Makes one 9 × 12-inch rectangular focaccia, or two 12-inch pizzas)

THERE IS NOT MUCH DIFFERENCE BETWEEN a pizza and a focaccia. They are made with the same dough and both are flat breads. They can be cooked completely unadorned with a sprinkling of salt and a drizzle of oil. Pizza, after the dough has risen once, is usually stretched very thin (the way I like it) and topped with some condiment. Focaccia should rise twice, and it is thicker than pizza. The focaccia takes very simple toppings, a drippling of olive oil, a sprinkling of kosher salt, rosemary, or sage, a few pieces of fresh tomatoes, anchovies, or sautéed onions. Its dough can be mixed with chopped olives with a combination of herbs.

1 package active dry yeast
1 cup lukewarm water (105 to 115°F)
1/2 teaspoon sugar

About 3 1/2 cups all-purpose or bread flour
1 1/2 teaspoons salt
3 tablespoons extra virgin olive oil

1. Proof the yeast: Combine the yeast, water, sugar, and 1 teaspoon of the flour. Mix and let stand 5 to 10 minutes. If a bubbly foam forms at the top, your yeast is alive and you can proceed with the recipe. If this doesn't happen, start with a fresh package of yeast.

2. In a food processor, combine 3 cups of the flour and the salt; add the oil and yeast mixture. Process until a ball forms on the blades. If this doesn't happen, add enough water to make the dough come together. On the other hand if the mixture is too wet, add more flour to obtain a smooth, pliable ball.

3. Turn the dough onto a floured board. Knead and slap the dough on the board for 10 to 15 minutes, adding more flour if the dough is sticky. The dough should be elastic, smooth, and pliable.

4. Gather the dough into a ball and place it in a lightly oiled bowl. Mark a cross on top of the dough with a knife. Cover the bowl with plastic wrap and a few kitchen towels, set it in a warm place, and let the dough rise until doubled in bulk, about 1 hour. After the first rising, the dough can be punched down, removed from the bowl, and used right away. Or it can be wrapped in plastic wrap and refrigerated or frozen. If frozen, thaw in the refrigerator overnight before using.

5. If the dough is to be used for a focaccia, let it rise a second time, until double in bulk.

Variation: For a crispier dough, use 1 cup whole wheat flour mixed with 2 cups of the all-purpose or bread flour.

PIZZA CLASSICA ALLA NAPOLETANA

Classic Neapolitan Pizza (*Makes two 8-inch pizzas or one 16-inch pizza*)

A NEAPOLITAN WILL TELL YOU THAT ONE can live with a piece of bread, a tomato, and a little olive oil. True! You will often see Italian children snack on a slab of thick bread smeared with olive oil and topped with a few slices of fresh, red tomatoes. It takes only one step and a little inventiveness to go from this simple repast to a succulent pizza. Like the Neapolitan snack, *pizza classica napoletana* is topped simply with fresh tomatoes, olive oil, and a touch of oregano or basil. There is no tomato sauce; the sauce is an embellishment used in pizzerias.

1 recipe Focaccia and Pizza Dough
  (page 30)
Extra virgin olive oil
2 cups sliced tomatoes

8 fresh oregano leaves, chopped;
  or ¹/₂ teaspoon dried
Salt to taste, optional

1. Preheat the oven to 400°F. Lightly oil the appropriate pans or pan.

2. Place the dough on the prepared pans or pan. With oiled fingers, stretch the dough to the size of the pan you are using and as thin as possible. Build a "wall," pushing the dough all around the pan to better contain the topping. Set aside.

3. In a mixing bowl, place the tomatoes and the oregano. Add 2 tablespoons of the oil, toss, and spread the mixture evenly on the dough. Sprinkle with a little salt, if using. Bake until the edge of the dough starts to brown, 15 to 20 minutes. Serve hot, cut into wedges.

Variation: To make pizza Margherita, slice or shred 8 ounces mozzarella cheese. I do not recommend fresh mozzarella because it is too watery. I use Polly-O

continues

whole-milk mozzarella. Toss the mozzarella with a little olive oil and a few fresh leaves of basil snipped by hand. Distribute this mixture evenly over Classic Neapolitan Pizza 5 minutes before the end of cooking. Decorate with additional fresh whole basil leaves before serving.

A SLICE OF PIZZA HISTORY

The pizza that made more conquests than the legions of Caesar is the *pizza Margherita*. According to legend, a smart Neapolitan *pizzaiolo*, pizza maker, a certain Mr. Esposito, invented this pizza in honor of the Italian queen, Margherita. The patriotic pizza he presented to the Queen sported the colors of the Italian flag: red (tomato), white (mozzarella cheese), and green (basil). So history was made.

PIZZA VEGETARIANA

Vegetarian Pizza

You do not need a recipe for this pizza, which is simply topped with vegetables and sometimes a bit of mozzarella. I change the vegetables according to the seasons. In the spring I use tender asparagus, in the summer, peppers or zucchini. In the fall, mushrooms are the prime element, and in the winter I turn to sun-dried tomatoes and whatever is available.

Whole wheat dough (see Variation, page 30) is a good base for this type of pizza. And for the meat eaters, just add a few cooked slices of sausage. In fact, what is called *pizza povera*, humble pizza, in Abruzzo is a pizza topped with inexpensive ingredients like sautéed broccoli di rape, which are cheap and abundant in Italy, and the addition of juicy, sweet sausages, also an inexpensive item.

FOCACCIA DELLA VIGILIA

Christmas Eve Focaccia   (Makes 8 or more servings)

THIS FOCACCIA, seasoned simply with anchovies, salt, pepper, and olive oil, is traditionally eaten at lunch on Christmas Eve to break the fast prescribed on this day by the Catholic religion. Of course for Americans eating something like a pizza for lunch is not much of a sacrifice, but do not forget that in Italy the main meal is at lunchtime.

Extra virgin olive oil
1 recipe Focaccia and Pizza Dough
   (page 30)

5 or 6 anchovy fillets, drained and
   cut into 1/4-inch pieces
Kosher salt to taste, optional
Freshly ground pepper to taste

1. Preheat the oven to 400°F. Lightly oil a 10 × 15-inch cookie sheet.

2. Place the dough on the prepared sheet. With oiled fingers, stretch the dough into a 3/4-inch-thick rectangle the size of the cookie sheet.

3. With your fingers, make "dimples" in the dough about 2 inches apart. Press the pieces of anchovy into them. Drizzle with olive oil and sprinkle with salt, if used, and pepper. Bake until the edges of the focaccia start to brown, 15 to 20 minutes. Cut into squares and serve.

PIZZA DEL LUNEDÌ DI PASQUA

Easter Monday Pizza   (Makes 30 to 40 squares)

EASTER MONDAY IS A TRADITIONAL DAY for picnics in Italy, as is the Fourth of July in the United States. This pizza was especially conceived just for such occasions and comes from the kitchen of my cousin, Gianna Amore.

As you will notice, this pizza is a little unusual. The crust, with no yeast, is similar to that of a tart. The lard makes it very tender. If lard is a no-no in your diet, use vegetable shortening.

DOUGH
3 cups all-purpose flour
1/2 teaspoon salt
6 tablespoons lard, chilled and cut into
   pieces, plus 2 tablespoons lard, softened
1 large egg, lightly beaten
About 1/2 cup white wine

FILLING
1 pound ricotta, drained
1/2 cup freshly grated parmesan cheese
1/2 cup freshly grated pecorino romano cheese
2 large eggs, beaten
1/2 pound Italian salamino (see Note),
   or any sweet salami, coarsely chopped
Freshly ground pepper to taste

1. Prepare the dough: In a food processor, combine the flour and salt. Add the chilled lard and process by turning the machine on and off until the mixture

continues

Because of the filling, this dish can be considered a *pizza rustica*. Italians call many breads—flat, topped, stuffed, and even rolled—pizza. In Abruzzo, cakes filled with custard or sweetened ricotta are often called *pizza dolce*. And, do not laugh, when we go to the movies, if the show is a bore, the usual reaction is "Mamma mia what a pizza."

resembles coarse meal. Add the egg and pulse 2 to 3 times. Gradually add the wine, processing until a ball forms on the blades.

2. Turn the dough onto a floured board and knead for 4 to 5 minutes. The dough should be soft. Gather the dough into a ball and wrap in plastic wrap. Refrigerate for 20 minutes.

3. Roll the dough into a rectangle. Brush with the softened lard. Fold in thirds, like a letter, and roll into a rectangle again. Repeat this operation (rolling, brushing, and folding) one more time. Fold the dough in thirds again and wrap in plastic wrap. Refrigerate for 20 minutes. Repeat the rolling and folding and refrigerating 3 more times.

4. Prepare the filling: In a mixing bowl, combine the ricotta, grated cheeses, and eggs. Beat until smooth and creamy. Add the remaining ingredients, stir, and set aside.

5. Preheat the oven to 350°F. With a little lard, brush a standard size 14 × 11-inch cookie sheet with sides. Set aside.

6. Divide the refrigerated dough into 2 equal parts. On a floured surface, roll out one part into a rectangle slightly larger than the prepared cookie sheet and fit it in. Pierce the dough in several places with a fork. Pour in the filling, leaving a clean rim all around, and smooth the top evenly.

7. On a floured surface, roll out the remaining dough into a rectangle large enough to cover the entire filling. Place this piece of dough on top, fold the edges of the bottom layer of dough over the top layer, and pinch all around to seal the pizza.

8. Bake until the top is golden, about 45 minutes. Cool on a rack. Cut into squares and serve at room temperature.

NOTE: *SALAMINO* IS A SMALL SALAMI THE SIZE OF AN ITALIAN SAUSAGE. ANY GOOD QUALITY SALAMI WILL DO, BUT A *SALAMINO ALLA CACCIATORA* IS THE BEST. IT IS FOUND IN ITALIAN SPECIALTY STORES AND IN SOME SUPERMARKETS.

BUDINO CALDO DI PANE E FORMAGGIO

Cheese and Bread Pudding *(Makes 6 servings)*

When I was growing up, the midday Sunday meal was a celebration. It always had an antipasto on the menu and some sort of pastry for dessert, bought at the local *caffè*.

After lunch we went for long walks. Sometimes we took along stuffed focaccia and fruit, just in case. Often we ended up in a *caffè* for a luscious ice cream.

In the evening, surprisingly, we'd be ready to eat again, and mother would make one of her specials. There was always an element of surprise in these dishes, and we would try to guess (with some trepidation) what she had put in this time. We knew she was recycling! Oh yes, mother was a great one for leftovers, and I think that I have taken after her. Here's one of my own specials, a savory bread pudding flavored with onion, pancetta, and fontina.

Plain bread crumbs
2 tablespoons extra virgin olive oil
1 medium-size onion, peeled and chopped
1 clove garlic, peeled and minced
1 thick slice pancetta, about 2 ounces, diced
3 cups cubed stale bread
1/2 cup dry white wine
1 cup shredded fontina cheese or a mixture of other cheeses
2 cups milk, heated
4 large eggs, beaten
Salt to taste, optional
Freshly ground pepper to taste
1/2 cup freshly grated parmesan or grana padano cheese

1. Preheat the oven to 350°F. Butter a 1 1/2-quart soufflé dish. Sprinkle the bottom and sides with bread crumbs.

2. In a 9-inch skillet, heat the oil over medium heat and add the onion, garlic, and pancetta. Cook, stirring often, until the pancetta is light brown, about 5 to 8 minutes. Set aside.

3. Place the bread in a mixing bowl, add the wine and toss until the bread has absorbed all the wine. Add the pancetta mixture and all the remaining ingredients, reserving 1 tablespoon of the grated cheese to sprinkle on top of the pudding. Toss well and transfer to the prepared dish. Smooth the top and sprinkle with the reserved grated cheese.

4. Bake until nicely brown, about 1 hour. If top browns too much, cover it loosely with aluminum foil. Serve hot.

Variation 1: My father's hand sometimes traveled to this dish and he would add, without my mother noticing, a shot of kirsch or Cognac to the mixture.

Variation 2: For a simpler version, line the bottom of a buttered baking dish with slices of bread. Top each individual slice with a slice of mozzarella, a piece of anchovy, a slice of tomato, and some basil. Cover each slice with same amount of bread. Beat 3 to 4 eggs with 1 tablespoon of grated parmesan cheese and pour over the bread. Bake until the top is golden brown, 15 to 20 minutes.

CROSTATA DI POLLO ALL'ALLORO

Chicken Pie with Bay Leaves   *(Makes 6 servings)*

ALLORO, LAUREL OR BAY LEAF, IS WHAT gives this pie such intense aromatic flavor. No using leftovers here; the chicken must be cooked with the bay leaf from scratch. I suggest chicken breast, because it cooks quickly, but I have also used the meat from turkey legs. Turkey needs a little more cooking time; also, its flavor is more pronounced and equally good.

1 1/2 tablespoons butter
1 tablespoon extra virgin olive oil
4 bay leaves, torn in half
1 whole chicken breast, skinned, boned, and diced

1/4 cup dry wine
1/4 pound boiled ham in 1 slice, diced
1/4 pound fontina cheese, shredded
1 recipe Simple Pie Dough (page 407)

1. In a 9-inch skillet, heat the butter and oil over medium heat and add 1 bay leaf. Cook a few seconds to let the flavor of the bay leaf explode, then remove the bay leaf. Add the chicken and remaining bay leaves and cook, stirring, until lightly brown, about 5 minutes. Add the wine and let evaporate. Turn the chicken into a mixing bowl; remove and discard the bay leaves. When the chicken has cooled, add the ham and fontina cheese. Mix well. Set aside.

2. Preheat the oven to 375°F. Butter a 9-inch pie plate from which you can serve.

3. Cut the dough in half. On a floured surface, roll out one part of the dough into a circle slightly larger than the prepared plate and fit it in. Pierce the bottom in several places with a fork. Add the chicken mixture and smooth the top.

4. On a floured surface, roll out the remaining dough into a circle large enough to cover the entire filling. Place this piece of dough on top, fold the bottom layer of dough over the top layer, and pinch all around to seal the pie while forming a decorative edge. Insert a pie funnel in the middle of the pie, or build one with aluminum foil to let the steam escape.

5. Bake until the top is golden brown, 30 to 40 minutes. Cool on a rack 10 minutes before slicing.

Variation: My mother used to make this pie with shrimp. Add 3/4 pound shrimp, peeled, deveined, and cooked exactly like the chicken. Add 1 cup of mushrooms sautéed in 1/2 tablespoon of butter and then simmered with 1/4 cup heavy cream. Instead of fontina cheese, add 1/4 cup freshly grated parmesan cheese and a grating of nutmeg.

PIZZA E FUIE

Pizza and Greens **(Makes 6 servings or more)**

THIS IS A PEASANT DISH MUCH BELOVED by the Abruzzesi. It consists of a *pizza gialla*, yellow cornmeal pizza, served as bread with sautéed greens, *fuie*, usually broccoli di rape, field chicory (wild dandelions), or escarole.

Although palates have become more sophisticated, this dish, which is a first course like pasta or a *minestra*, soup, is still served today at family dinners. The crumbling, crunchy crust and the soft inside make a perfect foil for the garlicky, slightly bitter broccoli and the piquant *diavoletto,* the little devil of a hot red pepper so popular in this region. I've given instructions for making this pizza by hand, which gives a more authentic, textured pizza.

For the full effect of a traditional Abruzzese meal, follow this dish with a platter of fried fish or sausages.

DOUGH

1 pound yellow cornmeal (polenta)
3/4 teaspoon salt
About 1 cup hot water

TOPPING

2 tablespoons extra virgin olive oil
3 cloves garlic, peeled and smashed
1 small diavoletto (dried Italian hot red pepper)
3 pounds strongly flavored leafy greens such as broccoli di rape, dandelion greens, and escarole, trimmed, cut into large pieces, and washed (see Tips, page xv)
1 teaspoon kosher salt

1. Preheat the oven to 375°F. Lightly oil a standard-size pizza pan (about 15 to 16 inches in diameter).

2. Place the flour in a large bowl, add the salt, and pour enough hot water to knead the dough into a soft ball. Pat the dough into a thick, round pizza 1 1/4 inches high and 14 inches in diameter.

3. Transfer the pizza to the prepared pan and bake until the top is golden and crusty, and the middle is still slightly soft, 45 to 50 minutes. Keep warm.

4. In a large skillet, heat the oil over medium heat. Add the garlic and hot pepper; cook a few minutes, stirring occasionally. Add the greens and salt. Toss, cover the pan, reduce the heat to low, and cook 5 minutes. Remove the lid and stir-fry the greens until they are done, about 10 minutes or longer. The greens tend to dry while cooking; if necessary add 3 to 4 tablespoons of water.

5. Serve on individual plates and pass the pizza around for everyone to tear off a piece by hand.

PIZZA RICCA DI GRANONE

Rich Corn Pizza   (Makes 8 or more servings)

THIS UNUSUAL "PIZZA" IS ALSO KNOWN BY the amusing name of *polenta maritata,* married polenta. In Abruzzo, every household has its own version of it. It was a favorite meal in my home for cold winter nights. With it, my mother always served soup, salad, and a light fruit dessert. My father's choice of wine was a Chianti Classico from Tuscany or a robust Montepulciano d'Abruzzo.

2 tablespoons extra virgin olive oil, plus additional for the pie plate
3/4 pound sweet Italian sausages
1 1/4 cups yellow cornmeal (polenta)
3 1/2 cups milk

Freshly grated parmesan or grana padano cheese
6 large eggs, separated
8 ounces mozzarella cheese, diced
1 1/2 cups Sugo Finto *(page 96)*
1 cup Salsa Balsamella *(page 92)*

1. Preheat the oven to 375°F. Lightly oil a 12-inch pie plate from which you can serve.

2. Place the sausages in a 10-inch skillet, pierce them in several places with a fork, cover with water, and cook over medium heat until the water has evaporated, about 10 minutes. Continue cooking the sausages by turning them in their own rendered fat until brown. Reserve 2 tablespoons of the fat. Remove the sausages to a plate and cool. Slice them into thin rounds. Set aside (see Note).

3. Place the cornmeal in a large heavy saucepan and gradually add the milk, stirring constantly to prevent lumping. Cook over medium heat, stirring, until the mixture starts to leave the sides of the pan, about 20 to 30 minutes. At this point the mixture will be quite dense. Remove from the heat and add the reserved 2 tablespoons of fat, 2 tablespoons of the olive oil, 5 tablespoons of the grated cheese and, one at a time, the egg yolks, beating after each addition.

4. Beat the egg whites until stiff, and fold into the cornmeal mixture.

5. Spoon one third of the cornmeal mixture into the prepared plate and smooth the top. Arrange half of the sliced sausages in one layer. Scatter half the mozzarella on top of the sausages.

6. Combine 1/2 cup of the *Sugo Finto* with the *Salsa Besciamella*. Pour some of this on the sausage-mozzarella layer. Cover with one-third more cornmeal mixture, spreading it in a layer, and top with the remaining sausages, mozzarella, and *Sugo-Finto-Salsa Balsamella*. Finish with another layer of the remaining cornmeal mixture and top with the remaining *Sugo Finto*. Sprinkle with additional grated cheese.

7. Bake about 45 minutes. Let the pizza cool slightly on a rack for 15 minutes before serving.

NOTE: THIS PIZZA REHEATS WELL. STEP 2 OF THIS RECIPE IS THE WAY I USUALLY COOK MY SAUSAGES, ESPECIALLY IF I WANT TO SERVE THEM AS A MAIN COURSE. THE BEST ACCOMPANIMENT? BROCCOLI DI RAPE SAUTÉED IN OIL AND GARLIC AND A LITTLE OF THE SAUSAGE FAT.

VILLA SANTA MARIA AND FARA SAN MARTINO

In this book, I talk often about Villa Santa Maria, a quaint village in the heart of Abruzzo. It is reached by a well-paved road that snakes through forbidding mountains. The final approach is breathtaking. Through a viaduct, which seems suspended in the air, you see the village, half clinging to a mountain and half spilling into a narrow valley guarded by snow-capped peaks. The village appears sliced in half by a jagged rim protruding from the mountainside. Staircases of perilous steps connect its ancient stone houses. The air is pure and cool; the silence interrupted only by the chirping of birds.

Its history began in A.D. 828, when it was founded by Benedictine monks. It was destroyed by the Saracens in the tenth century and then rebuilt by the Princes Caracciolo dynasty during the Middle Ages. The remains of their castle can still be admired there.

PATRON OF CHEFS

Prince Francesco Caracciolo, now a saint, is attributed with establishing Villa Santa Maria as *il paese dei cuochi*, the town of chefs. The Caracciolos were passionate about gastronomy and taught their young servants how to cook. They protected and promoted the best, sending them to other noble houses as far away as Naples and Rome to be employed as chefs. This was 400 hundred years ago, and the beginning of what was to become the town's Scuola Alberghiera (school of hotel management).

The chefs of Villa Santa Maria became renowned for passing down their profession from generation to generation. They served at the court of the czars, where the famous *insalata russa*, Russian salad, was invented, and at the White House, where Chef Luigi Turto prepared tasty dishes for Eisenhower, who could not have salt in his diet. Many famous restaurants of New York, London, and even Paris are often tended by a chef from Villa Santa Maria.

The chefs of Villa Santa Maria are also credited with a famous rescue mission. In 1944, the village was almost destroyed again, this time by the Germans, who mined the towns as they abandoned them. General Kesserling, in charge of the remaining Nazi troops in Italy, was instrumental in saving the village thanks to his Villese chefs, who pleaded with him to save Villa Santa Maria.

FARA SAN MARTINO

In a nearby narrow valley, there is another rustic village, Fara San Martino. The two most famous, modern, and important pasta factories of Italy, Del Verde and De Cecco, are located there. Verde is the river whose water is used to make the pasta. This is the reason why the pasta of Abruzzo is the best. Its water is considered the purest and the most pleasant tasting in all of Italy.

These two towns are beacons for the food professionals of Italy. One teaches, the other produces. They should both be visited often and remembered.

FIADONE VILLESE

Fiadone from Villa Santa Maria (Makes 8 servings)

IL FIADONE IS A *PIZZA RUSTICA* TRADITIONALLY prepared, nowadays, only for the Easter holidays. It's a humble pie whose simple ingredients—eggs, cheese, flour, and milk—reflect the pastoral aspect of this land.

This recipe was given to me by Antonio Stanziani, a renowned chef, and at one time the director of the famous cooking school of Villa Santa Maria. He pointed out that this is a local recipe, which in the old times was often served for dessert, especially during cold, snowy, winter nights. It's always a good excuse to have a couple of glasses of *vino cotto*. This is a wine made with cooked must which is reduced until it becomes dense. Must is the grape juice before fermentation.

DOUGH

3 large eggs
2 tablespoons baking powder
¼ cup extra virgin olive oil
1 tablespoon sugar
About 3½ cups all-purpose flour
⅓ cup milk, plus about 2 tablespoons
*   additional milk or water*

FILLING

Unsalted butter for the pan
5 large eggs
1 tablespoon baking powder
1 pound freshly grated pecorino romano
*   or sardo cheese, or a combination of*
*   pecorino and parmesan*
Freshly ground pepper to taste
½ teaspoon grated nutmeg

1. Prepare the dough: Beat the eggs in a large mixing bowl. Remove 2 tablespoons of the egg and reserve. Add the baking powder and oil. Beat, blending in the sugar, flour, and milk. If necessary add about 1 tablespoon additional milk or water. This can also be done in a food processor.

2. Turn the dough onto a floured surface and knead it until smooth, about 10 minutes. Gather the dough into a ball, cover with a bowl, and set aside.

3. Preheat the oven to 350°F. Butter and flour a 12-inch pie plate.

4. Prepare the filling: Beat the eggs in a large mixing bowl until frothy. Add all the remaining ingredients and mix well.

5. Divide the dough in half. On a floured surface, roll out one-half into a round slightly larger than the prepared plate and fit it in. Pierce the dough in several places with a fork. Pour the filling in. On a floured surface, roll out the remaining dough into a circle large enough to cover the entire filling. Place this piece of dough on top, fold the bottom layer of dough over the top layer, and pinch all around to seal the pie while forming a decorative edge. If you wish, you can make decorations like leaves or doves with the remaining dough, if any.

6. Add 1 tablespoon of water or milk, to the reserved beaten eggs and mix. With this egg wash, lightly paint the top of the pie. Pierce the top with a toothpick to let steam escape and bake until golden, about 1 hour. Cool on a rack before slicing and serve at room temperature.

My uncle Filippo, the "pater familias"

FIADONE AND FAMILY

While other pizzas of this kind were made often in my house, either for supper or for our Sunday outings, *il fiadone* was made only at Eastertime.

My uncle Filippo, the patriarch of the family, used to bring up a carafe of his good *vino cotto* from the cellar to serve with *il fiadone*. And he always reminded everybody that he had made the wine the year his daughter, Ela, was born. To her chagrin, he also invariably announced the precise date, making everybody aware of her age.

GATTÒ DI PATATE GIANNA AMORE

Potato Pie Gianna Amore **(Makes 6 to 8 servings)**

GATTÒ IS A CORRUPTION OF THE FRENCH word *gâteau.* (Without the accent on the "o" it means "cat" in Italian.)

The crustless, layered *gattò* is a classic Neapolitan preparation which my mother learned to make when we lived in Naples. She loved the dish and served it often for Sunday supper or as an elegant accompaniment to meats. It became a favorite with our extended family, each contingent adding his or her own touch. But my cousin,

4 to 5 baking potatoes, about 2¹/₂ pounds, unpeeled
6 tablespoons unsalted butter
²/₃ cup freshly grated parmesan cheese
1 cup milk
2 large eggs, lightly beaten
8 ounces smoked mozzarella cheese, diced
¹/₄ pound prosciutto, chopped
2 to 3 sprigs fresh parsley, minced
Salt to taste, optional
Freshly ground pepper to taste
Plain bread crumbs
4 ounces plain mozzarella cheese, thinly sliced

1. Boil the potatoes until soft. Drain and cool. Peel them, mash them in a ricer or a food mill, and turn into a mixing bowl. Add 5 tablespoons of the butter and the parmesan cheese, mix well, and add the milk, eggs, smoked mozzarella, prosciutto, parsley, and salt and pepper. Mix well.

continues

Gianna Amore, has made it even more personal. Her addition of smoked mozzarella was a stroke of genius and adds a subtle, unsuspected flavor to the dish. My mother, after tasting Gianna's version, started to make her *gattò alla Gianna*.

2. Preheat the oven to 375°F. Butter a 9- to 10-inch pie plate from which you can serve. Sprinkle it with bread crumbs.

3. Spoon half of the potato mixture into the prepared pie plate, smooth the top, and cover with the plain mozzarella slices in one layer. Spoon the remaining potato mixture on top, smooth, sprinkle with bread crumbs, and dot with the remaining butter.

4. Bake until the top is golden, 40 to 45 minutes. Cool 10 to 15 minutes and serve.

NOTE: THIS PIE REHEATS WELL.

Variation 1: My mother prepared several versions of this *gattò*. She would make it meatless (without the prosciutto) by adding a layer of fresh vegetables like broccoli, zucchini, baby artichokes, and peas sautéed in butter or oil. When she used peas, she would mix them with the potato and cook the pie in a deeper pan so that when the *gattò* was cut, the slices showed the vibrant green dots.

Everybody in the family tried to "improve" on my mother's savory potato *gattò*, and so did I. My version came about because, after a feast of corn, I was left with one ear only. I also had a solitary zucchini, so it too went into the pie. No need to tell you that you can use other vegetables if you wish.

Variation 2: *Pizza degli Avanzi*—**The Kitchen Sink Pie**
I named this pie "The Kitchen Sink Pie" for obvious reasons. The filling can be assembled with whatever you have in the refrigerator. While I call it a pie, this dish doesn't have a pastry crust. After buttering the pie plate, I sprinkle it with bread crumbs, fill it with whatever I have, and top it with a layer of mashed potatoes. You can put the mashed potatoes at the bottom, too.

TORTINO DI ZUCCHINE

Zucchini Flan **(Makes 6 servings)**

A *TORTINO* IS A BAKED *FRITTATA*, OR omelet. This is another dish that can be made from scratch or with leftovers. It's a good dish for lunch or a lighter supper. Leftover *tortino* can be cut into small squares and served cold with drinks.

3 tablespoons extra virgin olive oil
2 cups thinly sliced zucchini rounds
1 clove garlic, peeled and chopped
5 large eggs
2 sprigs fresh parsley, minced
1 tablespoon all-purpose flour

Salt to taste, optional
Freshly ground pepper to taste
8 ounces mozzarella cheese, shredded
1 tablespoon freshly grated parmesan
   or grana padano cheese

1. Preheat the oven to 375°F.

2. In a 10-inch ovenproof skillet, preferably cast iron, heat the oil over high heat and add the zucchini and the garlic. Cook, stirring, until the zucchini start to color, about 5 to 8 minutes.

3. In a mixing bowl, beat the eggs until frothy, add all the remaining ingredients, mix, and pour over the zucchini. Cook 4 to 5 minutes over medium to low heat to let the bottom set, then place the skillet in the oven.

4. Bake until the eggs are set and the top starts to brown, 15 to 20 minutes. Cut into wedges and serve.

Variation: Like a *frittata*, this preparation lends itself to many variations. You can use any kind of vegetable or a mixture of several, from spinach to artichokes, cauliflower, broccoli, and more.

UOVA

Eggs

hen I was a child, and a poor eater, I relished my one egg a day. It was fed to me religiously because my family believed in the high nutritional value of eggs. My uncle Filippo used to amuse me by making an account of all the eggs I had eaten since infancy, telling me how much money I owed for all the eggs. It seemed to me an astronomical sum.

Contrary to the Americans and the English, the Italians seldom eat eggs for breakfast. Eggs are mostly reserved for family suppers, and in the old days at least, given to children, mostly soft-boiled, as a snack in the afternoon. If the eggs were really fresh, we children ate them raw. My maid, Annina, used to take me to the chicken coop to gather the eggs which had just been "donated," as she put it, by the hens. She would pinch the bottom and top with a pin and I would suck the still warm nectar. It tasted of sun and earth and it was delicious. We knew nothing of salmonella!

I do remember the huge frittatas my grandmother used to make. Often they contained sausages, and I still see all the greedy eyes, especially mine, affixed to the spot where more sausages had accumulated. On Fridays, the frittatas were made with vegetables like broccoli, zucchini, chopped spinach, or endive, and even potatoes. My mother, on the other hand, used to break a bunch of eggs in a stew of simmering peppers and tomatoes, then cover the pan and cook the whole thing for a few minutes until the whites of the eggs had coagulated. We were all served one egg with a spoonful of its fragrant stew. While eating, the yolk, still running, would mingle with the vegetables and result

in a succulent mixture in which we greedily soaked our pieces of crusty bread.

There were so many ways in which eggs were prepared in my house. They were regarded as real food and not a spur-of-the-moment idea.

What a pity that lately, in Italy as well as the United States, eggs have been maligned, fallen victim to those food nutritionists whom Julia Child so charmingly calls "food terrorists." For cholesterol conscious people, they are the enemy.

I continue to love eggs with a passion, and since my husband and I do not have the high "C" problem, we indulge in them at least twice a week. There is nothing more soothing and rewarding on a night when you have had a big lunch to come home and cook a couple of eggs for yourself. Eggs are also my favorite lunch.

Eggs are still economical and a great source of highly digestible protein, vitamins, and minerals. The

white of the egg contains no fat, therefore it can be eaten without restriction. It is the yolk that contains 6 grams of fat which, unfortunately, is unsaturated and tends to raise the cholesterol level in the blood. Moderation is the key for those who have to be on the alert.

SHAKE, RATTLE, AND ROLL

When buying eggs at a supermarket, first of all, make sure they are not cracked. When nobody is looking (otherwise people think you are crazy), pick up an egg and shake it near to your ear. If it rattles, the egg is not fresh. My mother taught me this, but it is scientific because, as the egg ages, its natural gas escapes causing some evaporation. Put your egg back and select one in another carton. If the one egg you tried rattled, it is very likely the others will, too.

UOVA AL FORMAGGIO

Boiled Eggs with Cheese **(Makes 6 servings)**

BOILED EGGS ARE SO VERSATILE YOU could invent a recipe every day. Following are five of my favorite boiled egg dishes. They make great first courses and are ideal for lunch.

6 hard-boiled large eggs, peeled
2 tablespoons soft cheese such as mascarpone or stracchino, at room temperature
1 teaspoon extra virgin olive oil, if needed

Freshly ground pepper to taste
1 tablespoon minced fresh parsley
Lettuce leaves, preferably red, or radicchio
Dressing for My Everyday Salad (page 389)

1. Cut the eggs in half vertically. Remove the yolks to a bowl, add the cheese, and mash until smooth. If the mixture seems dry, mix in the oil. Add the pepper and parsley, mix again, and fill the white of the eggs with this mixture.

2. Place lettuce leaves on individual dishes, drizzle some salad dressing on the leaves, set 2 egg halves in the center of the dish, and serve.

Variations: Other cheeses like gorgonzola can be used, especially if mixed with mascarpone or cream cheese. And of course, caviar. Mix it with the yolks, add 1 tablespoon chopped scallion and 1 teaspoon minced parsley or a few drops of lemon juice. Fill the whites and serve on radicchio leaves for a more dramatic presentation.

UOVA TONNATE

"Tunnied" Eggs **(Makes 6 servings)**

A DELICIOUS LUNCH DISH WITH THE TANGY flavor of capers. For a truly Italian taste, use Italian tuna fish packed in olive oil.

6 hard-boiled large eggs, peeled
One 6-ounce can imported Italian tuna packed in olive oil
1 teaspoon anchovy paste

1 tablespoon light mayonnaise
1 tablespoon small capers in brine, drained
2 or 3 sprigs fresh minced parsley
Boston, red lettuce, or radicchio leaves

1. Cut the eggs in half vertically and remove the yolks to a mixing bowl.

2. Drain most of the oil from the tuna and add it to the egg yolks. Add the anchovy paste, mash, and add the mayonnaise; mix until smooth. This can be done

in a food processor but I like a little texture in the tuna. Mix in all the remaining ingredients except the lettuce. Fill the whites of the eggs.

3. Place some of the lettuce on individual dishes, set 2 egg halves on each dish, and serve.

NOTE: THESE EGGS CAN BE PREPARED IN ADVANCE AND CHILLED.

Variation 1: These eggs make a wonderful stuffing for avocados. I chop the egg whites coarsely and I either mix them with the yolks, or sprinkle them on the filled avocados.

Variation 2: Instead of tuna, use chopped cooked shrimp or crabmeat.

UOVA DELICATE

Delicate Eggs *(Makes 6 servings)*

THESE ARE "MELT IN THE MOUTH" EGGS. And this is exactly what I called this recipe when I made it on television during the filming of my show, *Nature's Masterpiece, the Egg*. It is a family recipe which is served mostly during the Easter holidays.

6 *hard-boiled large eggs, peeled*
3 *tablespoons* Salsa Balsamella
    (page 92) (see Note 2)
3 *tablespoons freshly grated parmesan or*
    grana padano cheese
$^1/_4$ *teaspoon grated nutmeg*

Salt to taste, optional
Freshly ground pepper to taste
All-purpose flour
1 large egg, beaten with 1 tablespoon milk
Plain bread crumbs
Oil for deep-frying (see page xvi)

1. Cut the eggs in half vertically. Remove the yolks to a bowl, mash them, and add the *Salsa Besciamella*, cheese, nutmeg, salt, if used, and pepper. Mix well. Stuff half of the eggs with this mixture and cover with the other half to reshape the egg. If some filling remains, set it aside.

2. Roll the eggs in flour, dip them in the beaten egg, and roll in bread crumbs. Refrigerate until the coating is set, about 20 minutes.

continues

3. Heat plenty of oil in a 10-inch frying pan or deep fryer. As soon as the oil reaches the smoking point, fry the eggs until golden. Serve hot.

NOTE 1: THE LEFTOVER FILLING, IF ANY, CAN BE ADDED TO SOUP OR USED AS STUFFING FOR CHERRY TOMATOES.

NOTE 2: ABOUT THE *SALSA BALSAMELLA*, YOU WILL SURELY MAKE AT LEAST 1 CUP. IT KEEPS IN THE REFRIGERATOR, COVERED, FOR 2 TO 3 DAYS. USE IT TO MAKE AU GRATIN PASTA, POTATOES, OR VEGETABLES.

UOVA AL CESTINO

Eggs in a Basket (Makes 6 servings)

HERE'S AN AMUSING AND DELIGHTFUL WAY to cook eggs. They are always greeted with pleasant surprise when brought to the table.

Extra virgin olive oil for the ramekins
Plain bread crumbs
4 cups Marinara Sauce *(page 97) or* Sugo Finto *(page 96)*

6 large eggs
Shredded gruyère or mozzarella cheese
Unsalted butter, optional

1. Preheat the oven to 375°F.

2. Lightly oil six 4- to 5-inch ramekins and sprinkle them with bread crumbs. Divide the *Marinara* or *Sugo Finto* equally (about ⅔ cup each) among the ramekins. Break 1 egg into each ramekin, set the ramekins on a cookie sheet, add the cheese on top of each, and bake until the cheese has melted and the whites are set, about 10 minutes. Dot with butter, if used. Serve hot.

UOVA IN BRODETTO

Eggs in Tomato Sauce **(Makes 6 servings)**

A FAVORITE SUPPER DISH, WHICH WE REL-
ished after a busy afternoon on the
town, this is homey and totally satisfying. It was served with thick slices of
crusty bread, salad, and a bowl of fresh
fruit.

2 tablespoons extra virgin olive oil
1 onion, coarsely chopped
2 sprigs fresh parsley
1 clove garlic, peeled and smashed
1 tablespoon wine vinegar

One 16-ounce can peeled tomatoes,
*   chopped (see Note)*
2 to 3 leaves fresh basil; or ¹/₂ teaspoon
*   dried*
6 large eggs

1. In a 10-inch skillet, heat the oil over medium heat. Add the onion, 1 sprig parsley, and the garlic. Cook, stirring, until the onion starts to soften, about 5 minutes.
Add the vinegar and let evaporate.

2. Add the tomatoes and their juices to the skillet. Bring to a boil over medium-
high heat and cook, stirring occasionally, until reduced a little, about 15 minutes.
Remove the garlic and parsley and discard.

3. Mince together the remaining parsley and the basil, add to the sauce, and stir.
Gently break the eggs into the sauce, cover, and simmer about 5 minutes for a soft-
consistency yolk and until the whites have solidified. Remove the skillet from the
heat and let rest 5 minutes longer. Serve hot.

NOTE: IN SUMMERTIME USE FRESH RIPE TOMATOES.

FRITTATA DI SPINACI

Spinach Frittata (*Makes 6 servings*)

THIS IS A BASIC VEGETABLE *FRITTATA*. Instead of spinach you can use other vegetables. Zucchini and artichokes are particularly good, as is broccoli and, a very Abruzzese one, potatoes and onions.

1 pound spinach, stems removed, washed and blanched (or use leftover cooked spinach)
2 tablespoons extra virgin olive oil
2 leeks or 1 onion, chopped

6 large eggs, beaten
Salt to taste, optional
Freshly ground pepper to taste
1 to 2 tablespoons freshly grated parmesan or grana padano cheese

1. Squeeze the spinach dry and finely chop.

2. In a 9-inch skillet, heat the oil over medium heat. Add the leeks or onion and cook, stirring, until soft, about 5 minutes.

3. In a mixing bowl, combine the eggs, spinach, and all the remaining ingredients. Pour the mixture into the skillet. Cook until the bottom has settled, about 5 to 8 minutes.

4. Holding a flat lid or a platter over the skillet turn the *frittata* onto its other side and then slide it back into the skillet. Cook 5 minutes longer. Serve immediately.

Variation: Instead of spinach, combine the eggs with small cherry tomatoes, peas, or a mixture of both. When we were children we called this fun frittata *"a palline,"* with little balls, or dots.

FRITTATA AL FORNO CON LA MOZZARELLA

Baked Frittata with Mozzarella (*Makes 6 servings*)

THE SIMPLEST AND MOST-LOVED *FRITTATA,* a version of this is prepared all over Italy. My recipe is a little more personal.

In Abruzzo my mother always made this *frittata* with the marvellous scamorze cheese from Rivisondoli, a mountain town famous for its dairy products. You can find scamorze in Italian specialty stores; I buy mine at my beloved Balducci's.

6 large eggs
Salt to taste, optional
Freshly ground pepper to taste
1 sprig fresh Italian parsley
6 fresh basil leaves

2 tablespoons extra virgin olive oil
8 ounces mozzarella or scamorza cheese,
  thinly sliced
1 plum tomato, cut into thin rounds

1. Preheat the oven to 350°F.

2. Beat the eggs until frothy, add the salt, if used, and the pepper.

3. Chop together the parsley and basil and add to the eggs.

4. Heat the oil in a 9-inch ovenproof skillet (I use a cast-iron one) over medium heat. Pour the eggs in and cook briefly until the bottom has settled, about 5 minutes. Remove from the heat and add the scamorza or mozzarella, arranging it in one layer, and dot with the slices of tomato.

5. Bake until the eggs are set and the cheese has melted, 20 to 25 minutes. Serve in the skillet, but wrap a colorful napkin on its handle.

LE FRITTATINE RIPIENE DI MAMMA

Mamma's Stuffed Little Frittatas (*Makes 6 servings*)

AN ELEGANT WAY OF SERVING EGGS, THESE little stuffed omelets are served in a light tomato sauce. They make a nice first course or a main course for lunch. My mother also served them as an antipasto for a special dinner.

8 large eggs
Extra virgin olive oil
4 ounces mozzarella cheese, chopped

4 ounces prosciutto, cut into thin strips
8 large eggs, beaten
2 cups Sugo Finto *(page 96)*

1. Beat the eggs. In a small skillet (I use a 5-inch one), heat 1 teaspoon oil over medium heat. Add ½ cup of the beaten egg and tilt the skillet to distribute the egg well. Cook until the bottom is set, 3 to 4 minutes, and turn on the other side. Remove the *frittatine* to a platter and continue making more until all the beaten eggs are finished.

2. Distribute the mozzarella and prosciutto among the *frittatine* and fold them in half.

3. In a large skillet, heat the sauce to the boiling point and add the *frittatine*. Reduce the heat to low, cover, and simmer until the mozzarella starts to ooze out, about 5 minutes. Serve immediately.

Variation: The stuffing can vary according to what's around, whether vegetables, cheeses, or meats, but the usual stuffing is mozzarella and prosciutto.

FRITTATA CON LE SALSICCE

Frittata with Sausages (Makes 6 servings)

I REMEMBER ONE EVENING AT GRAND-mother's house. We were all sitting around the table in the kitchen, in front of a huge fireplace, as we often did in winter, when a large *frittata* arrived at the table all neatly cut into wedges. But for some reason, one of the wedges contained more sausages then the others and all the forks point-ed to that one. So a coin was tossed and it went to my father who, politely, offered it to his friend Modesto della Porta, who was our guest. Modesto, a poet of some repute, later on described the scene in a funny poem which he wrote in Abruzzese dialect.

1 sweet Italian sausage, about ¹/₂ pound, cooked

2 tablespoons extra virgin olive oil

1 leek, trimmed, washed and sliced in thin circles

6 large eggs

1 tablespoon minced fresh parsley

Freshly ground pepper to taste

1. Cut the sausage in thin rounds.

2. In a 10-inch skillet, heat the oil and add the leek, cooking over low heat until soft.

3. Beat the eggs, add the parsley, pepper, and sausage.

4. Pour the mixture into the skillet, raise the heat to medium, and stir a little, trying to distribute the slices of the sausage evenly. Cook 5 to 8 minutes, or until the bottom is set. Holding a flat lid or a platter over the skillet, turn the *frittata* onto its other side and then slide it back into the skillet, cook 5 minutes longer. Serve immediately.

A MATTER OF TASTE

In the old days, eggs were available every day in an Italian household. Chickens where raised in courtyards or backyards in affluent and poor houses alike. Odd as it may seem, raw eggs were considered a nutritional boost, and children were given one every afternoon, still warm from the chicken! As I related in this chapter's introduction, the egg was pierced at the top and bot-tom with a pin and we sucked with gusto. Nowadays, not knowing where the egg came from, it is better to cook the eggs properly to avoid the risk of salmonella.

PALLOTTE CACIO E OVA

Cheese and Egg Balls (Makes 6 servings)

I COULD NOT CLOSE THIS CHAPTER ON EGGS without including this typical Abruzzese recipe. In my home, this dish was often the main course for a Friday meal, when meat was not served. The first course was a spicy dish of Spaghetti *Aglio, Olio e Peperoncino* (see page 95) or some other simple pasta. The *pallotte* were served with a green vegetable. It made a complete, pleasant meal.

I had forgotten this recipe and I could not find one in my files, but Chef Antonio Stanziani of the Villa Santa Maria cooking school came to my rescue with his recipe.

Chef Stanziani, for the sake of authenticity, recommends using pecorino cheese, which should be *"semifresco,"* not too aged and sweet. This is not easy to find here. But he also suggests using well-drained ricotta, and for a more delicate taste, parmesan.

These balls are deep-fried first. Use as much oil as possible because they will absorb less when they can swim in the oil. I use canola oil, to which I add ¹/₂ cup olive oil. To make sure that your oil is ready, drop in a small piece of bread soaked in vinegar. It should bounce to the surface and start frying immediately. Remove the bread and eat it—it is delicious.

¹/₂ pound freshly grated parmesan cheese
¹/₂ cup grated pecorino romano cheese
1¹/₂ cups bread crumbs
1 tablespoon minced fresh parsley
2 cloves garlic, peeled and minced
6 large eggs, beaten
Oil for deep-frying (see page xvi)
1 recipe Marinara Sauce (page 97)

1. In a mixing bowl combine the cheeses, bread crumbs, parsley, and garlic. Add the eggs and mix well. If the mixture is too loose, add some more bread crumbs to bind the ingredients together.

2. Wet your hands and form medium-size balls, 2 or 3 per person. Chill 20 minutes.

3. In a deep skillet or pan, heat the oil and when ready gently drop in the balls. Do not crowd the pan. Fry until brown. Remove to a paper towel to drain.

4. In a clean skillet, warm up the sauce, add the balls, and simmer 15 minutes, turning the balls once or twice. Serve hot.

NOTE: MY FAVORITE ACCOMPANIMENTS FOR THIS DISH, APART FROM A GREEN VEGETABLE, ARE RICE, POLENTA, AND A GOOD POTATO PUREE.

PART II

LA CASA DI ORTONA

The House in Ortona

I would be packed off to Abruzzo to spend

, who had practically raised me, and her

charming town of Ortona a Mare which,

top of a hill overlooking the undulating

lar trees, with their trembling leaves,

seemed to stand guard over the little harbor. It was quite active at sunset

THE HOUSE IN ORTONA

When school closed for the summer, I would be packed off to Abruzzo to spend a few months with my aunt Cettina, who had practically raised me, and her husband, Mario. They lived in the charming town of Ortona a Mare which, as so many Italian towns do, sat on top of a hill overlooking the undulating coastline of the Adriatic. The poplar trees, with their trembling leaves, seemed to stand guard over the little harbor. It was quite active at sunset when fishing boats would return with their daily catch. On both sides of the harbor, the solemn olive trees, with their silvery leaves and contorted trunks, gave a sense of mystery to the hills sloping toward the sea.

There was a window in my aunt's place, perhaps symbolic since it was located in the kitchen, which looked over the *piazza*. Her apartment was on the top floor of a high building, and this window was a good observation point for the unfolding of the town's life.

Life in Ortona was pure summer for me. At about ten o'clock in the morning, we would descend through a winding, terraced path to the beach

below. The walk took half an hour and my aunt considered it good exercise. The beach was a small half moon wedge reclaimed from the harbor on one side and the rocky coast on the other. It was where social encounters took place, from umbrella to umbrella,

Me with my two beloved aunts, Zia Cettina on the left, and Zia Ela in the middle.

all through the morning. The water of the sea was clean then, and shallow for quite a distance, making the place ideal for children.

At lunchtime, everybody went back to town, not on foot, but with an amusing funicular in which we were usually packed like sardines. We children loved it. Unfortunately this beach does not exist anymore; the port ate it up. Now the people of Ortona have to go a little distance to swim—to the "Molo dei Saraceni," the landing of the Saracens, another beach where we also went on occasion for picnics and to spend the day. This beach is so named because at one time it was a favorite spot for the Saracens to land and start their frequent invasions.

In the late afternoon, after the obligatory siesta, off we went, all dressed up, for the *passeggiata*. This is the ritual stroll which still takes place in small towns all over Italy. In Ortona, the stroll started from the *piazza*, it went up and down the *corso*, the main street, and continued on to the *panoramica*, panoramic, which ended dramatically at a little park dominated by the picturesque ruins of a medieval castle. This was the street which afforded a commanding view of the sea, and from which one could observe the coming to life of the *faro*, the lighthouse on the promontory of Punta Penne, guiding the boats returning to port. It was also the place to linger with friends and perhaps make plans for meeting again after dinner.

It was on this *panoramica* that I was glanced at, for the first time, by a boy. I looked mature for my age. It made my heart flutter and it scared me. I wasn't ready to grow up, not yet anyway. So nothing happened.

It was because of the terrace in grandmother's house in Guardiagrele and this panoramic street in Ortona, that I started to have dreams of distant places. I knew that the horizon was not the limit. The fascination of the beyond lured me.

Back then I was always dreaming and observing, leaning on the ledge of the kitchen window. Meanwhile, just behind me, the dramatic art of cooking was being acted out by my aunt and her maid, Maria.

Maria, the daughter of my grandmother's maid, Annina, had grown up with me and we loved each other like sisters. Maria had a special way with the fishermen selling their catch. They would always give her the best and the freshest, not of course, without the usual teasing bargaining. She used to take me to the fish market and sometimes we went down to the pier to buy fish. I loved these expeditions, and was very fond of Maria, a sweet and loving creature. When she died in childbirth, she was very young, just a few years older then me, and it was a great tragedy.

My aunt Cettina was a marvelous cook. She loved elegant dinners and liked to experiment. She was the one who, contrary to my mother, let me linger in the kitchen. She loved to make special dishes for me. I was also, quite often, her appreciative guinea pig.

She had a way with pasta, recreating with a touch of inventiveness, some of her mother's dishes. Sometimes, just the presentation was different. Her *timballi*, timbales, for instance, were cooked in smaller molds to make them look more elegant and not in the monumental traditional molds.

My aunt Cettina also died young, she was only forty-two. She was my second mother in a way. I loved her dearly and still miss her. But the memories of our life together remain vivid and joyful.

CHAPTER 4

BRODI, ZUPPE
E MINESTRE

Broths and Soups

*T*he custom in Italy dictates *brodo* on Saturday. Most Italians still work half a day on Saturday. When they come home around noon for the middle of the day dinner, the effusive fragrance of a good broth greets them. In my home it was eagerly expected.

Since the cuisine of Italy is regional, the ingredients for the soup, of which the broth is the base, would change from region to region, and according to the seasons, from robust to light. Often leftover soups would be reserved for the evening meal, and in the winter they also appeared when a light supper was being served.

In general, when we say *brodo*, we mean soup. But a soup whose base is clear broth will contain only *pastina* (small pasta), elegant *tortellini*, *tagliolini* (homemade thin noodles), dumplings, and similar, more delicate ingredients.

In Italian, there are many words for different kinds of soup. We have *zuppa*, which usually contains vegetables and seldom pasta or rice. There's also *minestra*, which has two or three ingredients and a thicker consistency, like a *pasta e fagioli* (pasta and beans); *minestrone*, meaning "big *minestra*" because it usually contains many ingredients; and *minestrina*, in which some semolina or little pasta is cooked in the clear broth.

STOCK OR BROTH?

Often the word broth is used interchangeably with stock. They are not the same thing and they are not made the same way. To make broth, which is homier, meat, bones, vegetables, and liquid are placed together in a pot and cooked on the stove at a bare simmer for several hours. To make classic stock, the meat and vegetables are first roasted in the oven and then placed in a pot with the liquid and simmered like broth.

Italians seldom make stocks. Stocks are usually reserved for elaborate dishes *alla francese*, French style, or for restaurant cooking. Italians make broth.

BROTH BASICS

For homemade soup, there is nothing better than homemade broth, and it is so easy to prepare. Broth freezes well, so you can always have a supply for soups, *risotti*, braised dishes, and more.

Italian broth is usually a mix of chicken, veal, and bones. I always buy my chicken whole, and unless I am roasting it, I cut the chicken into pieces and freeze the neck, giblets (without the liver), back, and wing tips until I collect enough to make a broth. When I have a good amount of these parts, I ask my butcher to give me a couple of veal bones. The veal bones add flavor and gelatin to the broth. I also like to put in a couple of turkey legs or thighs, which I then use for a salad, and, of course, the customary "*odori di cucina*"—celery, carrot, onion, and parsley.

Nothing gets wasted in my broth. After straining the liquid with a fine-mesh sieve, I separate the meat and bones from the vegetables. I pick off all the meat attached to the bones and make a salad with it. As for the vegetables, I puree them in a food mill to make a delicate *crema di verdure*, cream of vegetable soup. This vegetable cream can also be used as a thickener for sauces and as a base for risotto. It also freezes well.

I seldom skim the broth so as not to eliminate the many nutrients rising to the surface, but if you want a clear broth, you have to skim.

It is advisable to make the broth in advance, straining and then refrigerating it. This way the fat, which congeals at the top, can be easily removed from the surface. Broth will keep for three to four days in the refrigerator. Freeze some of the defatted broth in an ice cube tray, then bag the cubes. They are a godsend when sautéing or braising and can be used if one doesn't want to add more oil or butter.

BRODO DI POLLO

Chicken Broth **(Makes 8 cups broth or more)**

*One 3-pound chicken or other fowl, or
    the equivalent in backs, bones, necks,
    wings, giblets (no liver, which will
    make the broth bitter), and other
    scraps
2 veal bones
2 to 3 ribs celery, cut into 2 pieces
1 large carrot, peeled and cut into 4 pieces*

*1 medium-size onion, peeled, studded
    with 2 cloves, and with a cross cut at
    the root end of the onion
3 sprigs fresh parsley
1 bunch of the green "beard" or fronds
    of a fennel; or 1 bunch fresh dill
10 peppercorns
1 bay leaf
Salt to taste, optional*

1. Place all the ingredients in a stockpot. Add enough cold water to cover the solids by 2 inches. Bring to a boil over high heat, reduce the heat to low, and simmer, half covered, for about 3 hours.

2. If using a whole chicken, remove it after 1 hour. Cool the chicken, remove the skin, and pull off all the meat from the bones. Discard the skin but return the bones to the pot. Reserve the chicken meat for another use. Continue simmering the broth for 2 more hours. When done, strain the broth.

NOTE: REMEMBER TO PUREE THE VEGETABLES FROM THE BROTH IN A FOOD MILL AND USE THE PUREE AS A BASE FOR A *RISOTTO*, OR AS A SAUCE THICKENER. THE PUREE WILL MAKE AN EXCELLENT CREAM OF VEGETABLE SOUP. A TOUCH OF SOY OR WORCESTERSHIRE SAUCE GIVES AN EXOTIC AND DELICIOUS FLAVOR TO THIS SOUP.

Variation 1: Brodo di Manzo, **Beef Broth**
Substitute the 3 pounds of chicken and bones with 3 pounds beef and bones, preferably the chine or shoulder. Proceed as per chicken broth.

Variation 2: Brodo di Vitello, **Veal Broth**
Substitute the chicken with 3 pounds of veal, preferably the chine or shoulder, plus a few bones. Proceed as per chicken broth.

BRODO DI CAPPONE

Capon Broth   **(Makes about 8 cups broth)**

Capon broth is made in exactly the same way as the chicken broth (page 61), replacing the chicken with a capon. Therefore just follow the previous recipe.

However, since this is the land of oversize birds (I had never seen a turkey weighing 14 pounds before coming to America), and American capons are much bigger than Italian ones, this is what I do. First of all, try to find a capon that doesn't weigh more than 6 or 7 pounds, and plan to make a galantine (page 292) with the boned capon. For the capon broth, use all the bones, the gizzards, any scraps of meat, add 1 veal bone, and proceed as for a regular broth. After preparing a galantine, and when the broth has simmered for a couple of hours, I strain it and poach the galantine in this broth, enriching it to a full delicious flavor.

Incidentally, boiled capon is delicious, and you can always turn it into a tasty salad or dress it with a savory tuna fish and mayonnaise sauce. Another sauce that goes well with boiled capon or any other boiled meat, is *Salsa per Bollito di Mamma*, Mother's Sauce for Boiled Meat (page 94).

BRODO DI PESCE

Fish Broth   (Makes 6 cups poaching liquid)

The base for a brodo di pesce (fish broth) can be made either with a combination of water and lemon juice or water and vinegar plus the usual *odori di cucina*, onion, carrot, celery, parsley, and garlic. This mixture is better known in this country as court bouillon. Fish is poached in this liquid, and the resulting broth should be reserved for other uses.

A regular fish broth is augmented by fish heads and bones, or fish trimmings. This broth is used for fish soups, fish *risotti*, or as a base for some *brodetti*, or *zuppe di pesce*, fish stews.

1 rib celery, cut into 4 pieces

1 medium-size carrot, peeled and cut into 4 pieces

1 medium-size onion, quartered

2 sprigs fresh parsley

2 bay leaves

1 clove garlic, peeled and smashed

1/4 cup wine vinegar; or juice of 1 lemon

5 1/2 cups cold water

10 peppercorns, crushed

Place all the ingredients in a stockpot. Bring to a boil over high heat, reduce the heat to low, and simmer, uncovered, 30 minutes. Strain, discard the solids, and cool.

NOTE: WHEN POACHING, ALWAYS ADD THE FISH TO A COLD LIQUID. IF NOT, THE FISH WILL CURL OR CONTRACT AND WILL LOOK UNAPPETIZING.

Variation 1: To make 6 to 8 cups of more robust fish broth, add 3 pounds fish bones, heads, with gills removed, and other trimmings. Add 7 cups cold water and 1 1/2 cups dry white wine instead of vinegar or lemon. Add a bunch of fresh thyme for extra flavor. Shrimp or lobster shells can be added, too.

Variation 2: For lobster broth, when poaching lobsters, reserve the poaching water. Add the shells, heads, and feet, if any, and the usual *odori di cucina*, celery, onion, carrot, parsley, and garlic. Also add a 1-inch-long piece of fresh gingerroot, unpeeled and coarsely chopped.

BRODO DI FUNGHI

Mushroom Broth **(Makes about 8 cups broth)**

I DID NOT FIND THIS RECIPE AMONG MY mother's notes; I had to reconstruct it from memory. Always the thrifty one, Mother made this broth from less-than-perfect mushrooms which were broken and stems that were too big or too tough. She also added a good handful of dried porcini for a truly bosky aroma. To further enhance its flavor, she also dropped into it a Knorr bouillon cube which, especially during the lean years of the war, she considered an extra bonus.

The broth was used mostly for soups and *risotti*, but also to intensify the taste of fish and meat dishes.

Nowadays, I like to use my Chicken Broth (page 61) as a base. But I would not hesitate to use the ubiquitous Knorr cube. As a matter of fact, I always have some around. They are a godsend!

¹/₄ cup dried porcini mushrooms
3 cups mushroom pieces and stems, cut up
1 clove garlic, peeled and smashed
1 bunch scallions, greens included, cut into 4 pieces
1 medium-size carrot, peeled and sliced
1 rib celery, cut into 8 pieces
2 sprigs fresh parsley

2 bay leaves
1 sprig fresh thyme, or ¹/₄ teaspoon dried
2 cloves
¹/₄ teaspoon Seven Herbs (see headnote, pages 297–98)
5 or 6 peppercorns
1 tablespoon tomato paste
8 cups chicken broth, preferably homemade (page 61)

1. Soak the dried porcini mushrooms in 1 cup of lukewarm water for about 15 to 20 minutes. Gently, so as not to upset the sediment resting at the bottom, lift the porcini mushrooms out of the water and set aside. Strain the water through a paper towel or coffee filter. Set aside.

2. In a 4-quart stockpot, place all the remaining ingredients, including the soaked mushrooms and strained soaking liquid. Bring to a boil over high heat, reduce the heat to low, and simmer until the mushrooms are soft and the soup is well flavored, about 35 minutes. Strain the broth and use as desired. If you wish, after removing and discarding the bay leaf, you can puree the solids through a food mill. The puree can be used as a thickener or a base for a sauce. Both freeze well.

PASTINA TIC TIC IN BRODO

Small Homemade Pasta in Broth (Makes 6 to 8 servings)

I CAN STILL HEAR THE "TIC TIC" SOUND OF my grandmother's knife cutting the long strands of homemade narrow noodles into tiny dots of *pastina*, very small pasta. On my birthday, I always requested this dish, which is a most simple one, but utterly delicious since the *pastina* is always cooked in a superlative broth made with chicken or capon. Nothing is added to it but a little parmesan cheese. Fortunately, my twin brother Mimmo liked it too.

My cousin Dina Lullo, also from Guardiagrele, remembered this passion of mine, and every time I returned for a visit to my birthplace, she would invite me for dinner and always have the *pastina tic tic*, as my grandmother made it. After all she had learned it from her.

1 recipe Basic Homemade Pasta (page 140) made with 3 eggs

2 1/2 quarts chicken broth, preferably homemade (page 61)
Freshly grated parmesan cheese, optional

1. Knead the dough: Cut the dough in 3 parts. Keep the unused portions under a bowl. Flatten one piece of the dough with your hands. Position the rollers of a pasta machine at their maximum opening. Insert the piece of dough between the rollers, turn the handle, and roll the dough through. Sprinkle the dough with flour, fold the dough in thirds, like a letter, and roll again. Do this 2 to 3 times until the dough is smooth and not sticky.

2. Stretch the dough: Move the rollers one notch tighter and roll the dough without folding. Continue stretching through the consecutively tighter notches, flouring the dough as necessary. Do not go to the last two notches. The sheet of dough should be a little thick. Place the sheet of dough over kitchen towels. Repeat the operation with the remaining dough. Dry the sheets of dough for 10 minutes. If left for longer the dough will dry out and become difficult to cut.

3. Cut the noodles: Feed the sheets of dough, one at a time, through the narrow cutters of the pasta machine. Set the noodles loosely and lengthwise over kitchen towels.

4. Cut the noodles into *pastina*: Place one bundle of noodles, lengthwise, on a cutting board and cut into tiny pieces. They should resemble little square dots. Spread the *pastina* over kitchen towels to dry. Continue cutting likewise until you finish all the noodles.

5. Bring the broth to a boil over high heat in a large saucepan and plunge the *pastina* into it. Stir, bringing the broth back to a boil, and cook until the *pastina* is done, about 3 to 5 minutes. Serve in soup bowls with a sprinkling of parmesan cheese, if desired.

TAGLIOLINI IN BRODO

Thin Noodles in Broth (Makes 6 to 8 servings)

DOCTOR MONTEFREDINE, AN ABRUZZESE gastronome with a flare for poetry, used to say, "*I tagliolini in brodo*, thin like hair, light like a feather, perfumed like a flower."

My mother's *tagliolini* were famous. The above mentioned *dottore* would have approved. They were exactly as he described them. I can still see my mother rolling up the perfectly rounded *sfoglia*, the stretched dough (no pasta machine for her), and then rolling the *sfoglia* and cutting across it with swift motions into the thinnest noodles imaginable. When one *sfoglia* was finished, she would gingerly pick up the noodles and lay them gently on a linen-covered tray, ready to be cooked in boiling broth.

Keep in mind that you can knead and stretch the dough with a pasta machine, but you have to cut the *tagliolini* by hand.

1 recipe Basic Homemade Pasta (page 140), made with 3 eggs, stretched as thin as possible

7 to 8 cups defatted chicken broth, preferably homemade (page 61)
Freshly grated parmesan cheese, optional (see Note)

1. Make the dough according to the recipe. Stretch the dough as thinly as possible. As soon as you finish one sheet, sprinkle it lightly with flour, roll it up, and, with a sharp knife, cut into very thin strands. Unravel the strands and set on trays lined with kitchen towels. Repeat until you finish all the dough.

2. Bring the broth to a boil in a large saucepan over high heat. Add the *tagliolini* and stir gently. Let the broth come up to a boil and cook until the *tagliolini* are done, 2 to 3 minutes. Ladle the soup into individual soup bowls, or serve in a tureen. Pass the cheese, if used, separately.

NOTE: IF I HAVE A VERY GOOD BROTH, I PREFER MY *TAGLIOLINI* WITHOUT CHEESE, BUT I ALWAYS PUT A BOWL OF FRESHLY GRATED PARMESAN ON THE TABLE.

Variation 1: The soup can be garnished with ¾ cup chicken livers cut into small pieces and sautéed in 1 tablespoon of olive oil with a little chopped onion and 2 or 3 diced tomatoes.

Variation 2: It's also nice to serve strands of both plain and green *tagliolini*. Leave half the dough plain and color the other half green with spinach (page 142).

MORE ABOUT TAGLIOLINI

Nice Cortelli Lucrezi, the author of a delightful book *Le Ricette della Nonna: L'Arte di Mangiar Bene in Abruzzo (Grandmother's Recipes: The Art of Eating Well in Abruzzo)*, points out that our *tagliolini* are related to those from Piedmont in northwest Italy. King Victor Emmanuel II, the father of the country, used to eat them with great gusto, sporting a large napkin knotted behind his ears to protect his uniform and medals.

SCREPPELLE 'MBUSSE

Crepes in Broth **(Makes 6 to 8 servings)**

IF YOU EVER PICK UP A BOOK ON THE CUI-
sine of Abruzzo and come across this
recipe, you'll surely find passages rhap-
sodizing this unique and delicious
soup. With rolled crepes floating in a
limpid broth, it is indeed one of the
most delicate soups and an exquisite
beginning to an elegant dinner. It is
often served at festive occasions, like
important banquets and weddings.

For these *scrippelle*, a capon broth
(page 62) is usually *de rigeur*.

4 large eggs
6 tablespoons all-purpose flour
Freshly grated parmesan cheese
1 tablespoon minced fresh Italian
  parsley
¹/₄ teaspoon grated nutmeg

¹/₄ teaspoon salt, optional
¹/₄ cup milk
¹/₂ cup water
1 tablespoon butter
10 to 12 cups chicken or capon broth,
  preferably homemade (page 61 or 62)

1. In a food processor, place the eggs, flour, 2 tablespoons of the parmesan, the parsley, nutmeg, and salt. Process until smooth and then add the milk and water. Stop the machine when thoroughly blended. Refrigerate, covered with plastic wrap, for 30 minutes.

2. Lightly butter a crepe pan or a small skillet. (I use a 5-inch skillet because I like my crepes small.) Wipe the skillet with a paper towel to remove excess butter and heat over medium heat. Pour ¹/₄ cup of the crepe batter at a time into the skillet. Tilt and rotate the skillet to distribute the batter evenly. Cook until the edges start to turn gold, about 2 to 3 seconds, and turn the crepe over. Cook a few seconds longer and turn the crepe onto a platter. Set aside while continuing to make the rest of the crepes. At some point you may need to lightly butter your pan again. The crepes can be prepared in advance and refrigerated overnight.

3. When ready to serve, sprinkle each crepe with parmesan cheese, roll, and place 2 or 3 in individual soup bowls. Pour boiling broth on them and serve with a bowl of parmesan cheese.

NOTE: FOR A MORE AUTHENTIC FLAVOR, USE PECORINO ROMANO CHEESE INSTEAD OF PARMESAN.

CRAZY FOR CREPES

Abruzzesi have a predilection for crepes. They appeared in our region around 1798, during the French occupation, and have remained part of our cuisine ever since. Crepes, called *screppelle* or *scrippelle,* turn up in scrumptious *timballi* (timbales), as wrappers (instead of pasta) in cannelloni, and folded around dessert mousses and soufflés.

ZUPPA DELLA BUONA SALUTE

Soup of Good Health *(Makes 6 servings)*

MY MOTHER CONSIDERED THIS SOUP A restorative health booster, since it is light and nourishing. She made it often, especially when someone was "under the weather."

2 bunches endive or escarole, about 1 1/2 pounds total, trimmed and washed
2 tablespoons extra virgin olive oil
2 cloves garlic, peeled and minced
1 medium-size carrot, peeled and shredded
One 16-ounce can tomato puree
2 or 3 leaves of fresh basil or oregano, or 1/2 teaspoon dried

2 cups chicken or beef broth, preferably homemade (page 61)
30 mozzarella ciliegine cheeses (see Note); or 8 ounces fresh mozzarella, cut into 30 small cubes
Freshly grated parmesan cheese

1. Blanch the greens for a few minutes in boiling water. Drain them, reserving 2 cups of the cooking water. When the greens are cool enough to handle, chop them coarsely.

2. Heat the oil in a large skillet over medium heat, add the garlic and shredded carrot, and cook, briefly stirring, until the vegetables are soft, 5 to 8 minutes. Stir in the tomato puree. Fill the empty tomato puree can halfway with water, swish it around to loosen any remaining tomato puree, and add to the skillet. Add the herb, bring to a boil over medium heat, and simmer, uncovered, for 10 minutes. Add the chopped greens and cook, stirring, for 5 minutes and then add the broth. Stir again and cook until the greens are tender, about 10 minutes. If necessary, and if you like a thinner soup, add more of the reserved cooking water.

3. Ladle the soup into individual soup bowls and float 5 mozzarella ciliegine or mozzarella cubes in each bowl. Serve with parmesan cheese.

NOTE: CILIEGINE ARE SMALL, FRESH MOZZARELLAS MADE BY POLLY-O AND SOLD IN PLASTIC CONTAINERS AT THE SUPERMARKET.

ITALIAN PENICILLIN

My favorite *in brodo* when I was a child was with *pastina*, and it had to be *acini di pepe*, peppercorn pasta, because these pastina bits are as tiny as peppercorns. As a matter of fact, one of the pleasures of being in bed with a cold or a fever, was the expectation of a bowl of pastina served in a good chicken soup.

ZUPPA REALE DEL DOTTORE SERAFINI

Dr. Serafini's Royal Soup *(Makes 6 to 8 servings)*

DR. NINO SERAFINI, A DEAR FRIEND FOR many years, is a true *buongustàio*, or gourmand. He is also very lucky to have a wife, Anna, who is not only a native of Bologna (the best eating city in Italy), but an excellent and enthusiastic cook, who likes to indulge him. Nino, who loves to dabble in the kitchen himself, always cooks at least one dish when friends come to dinner.

The following recipe for Royal Soup, which features tiny custard squares floating in the broth, is the most elegant and suave of soups.

Unsalted butter for the pan
All-purpose flour for the pan
Butter for the pan
Flour
Freshly grated parmesan cheese
4 large eggs
6 large egg yolks
4 cups milk
One 8-ounce fresh mozzarella cheese,
(2 to 3 days old), shredded
Zest of 1 lemon, finely chopped
1/2 teaspoon ground cinnamon
12 cups chicken or capon broth, preferably
homemade (page 61 or 62), heated

1. Preheat the oven to 350°F. Butter and flour a 10 × 14-inch baking pan.

2. In a mixing bowl, place 1/4 cup of the parmesan cheese and add all the remaining ingredients except the broth. Mix well, then pour the mixture into the prepared pan. Set the pan in a larger one with high sides. Place both in the oven. Pour hot water into the larger pan to come halfway up the sides of the smaller pan.

3. Bake until the mixture is set, about 30 minutes. Carefully remove from the oven and cool the smaller pan on a rack. Unmold the custard and cut into 1-inch squares. This can be prepared in advance up to this point and refrigerated, well-covered with foil, overnight.

4. Divide the squares among individual soup bowls. Add enough broth to each to let the squares float and serve with additional parmesan cheese.

PASTA E FAGIOLI CON LE VONGOLE E COZZE

Pasta and Beans with Clams and Mussels **(Makes 6 to 8 servings)**

THE FIRST TIME I ATE THIS UNUSUAL COMbination was at the Restaurant Lo Squalo Blu in Termoli, a pretty town on the Adriatic where we have the "summit of the cousins" (see the box on the next page). At that time, I didn't think of asking for the recipe from the generous Bobo, the chef and one of the owners. But the memory of this fabulous dish lingered. I couldn't forget it. The ingredients were clear: fresh, red-speckled beans in a luscious broth combined with plump mussels and tiny *tellines*, the small Adriatic clams. I have recreated this *minestra* several times with good American clams. It works well.

BEANS

2 cups fresh or dried cranberry beans
1 clove garlic, peeled
1 bay leaf
Salt to taste, optional

SAUCE

1 small onion, finely chopped
1 rib celery, finely chopped
1 sprig fresh parsley, minced
A few flakes of hot red pepper, optional
¹/₄ cup extra virgin olive oil

MOLLUSKS

24 small clams, scrubbed
24 mussels, scrubbed and debearded
3 tablespoons extra virgin olive oil
2 cloves garlic, peeled and minced

PASTA

¹/₂ pound Basic Homemade Pasta
    (page 140) made with 2 eggs, cut into
    ¹/₂-inch-wide noodles
Freshly ground pepper to taste

1. Shell the fresh beans and rinse. If using dried beans, sort the beans to remove any stones or possible impurities and wash them. Plunge the dried beans into plenty of boiling water. Cook for 10 minutes and then rinse under cold water. Place the fresh or dried beans in a 4-quart pot, preferably terra-cotta, and add the garlic and bay leaf. Bring to a boil over medium heat and cook at a simmer until the beans are tender. If fresh beans are used, cook them 20 to 25 minutes, about 1 hour for dried. Add salt toward the end.

2. While the beans are cooking, place all the ingredients for the sauce in a 9-inch skillet. Cook, stirring, uncovered, until the vegetables are soft, about 5 minutes. When the beans are half done, add this sauce to the beans. Reserve the skillet.

3. In a large skillet, place the clams and mussels. Cook, uncovered, over medium heat, shaking the skillet often, until they open, 5 to 8 minutes. Immediately remove the open ones to a bowl. Discard the shells.

4. Reserve any juice from the mollusks and strain it using a paper towel or a coffee filter. Add this strained liquid to the cooked beans. Set the clams and mussels aside.

5. In the reserved skillet where the sauce cooked, heat the 3 tablespoons oil over medium heat. Add the minced garlic and cook for about 3 minutes. Remove from the heat, add the clams and mussels, and cook for a few seconds, stirring. Set aside.

6. Cook the noodles in boiling, salted water until tender, 3 to 4 minutes. Drain, reserving 2 cups of the cooking water.

7. Add the reserved pasta water to the cooked beans. Bring the beans to a boil over medium heat and add the drained pasta. Bring to a boil again and add the reserved clams and mussels mixture. Cook just enough to heat through. This *minestra* should be rather soupy; if necessary, add more hot water. Serve in soup bowls with a good grinding of pepper.

A FAMILY GET-TOGETHER

When my husband and I return to Abruzzo in the summer, our families from the region and from Campania in the south have a reunion at a restaurant on the Adriatic. We call it "the summit of the cousins." And what a reunion it is! Often friends join in. Sometimes we are more than thirty people. An entire side of the restaurant is reserved for us with one large table for the kids.

We, the Abruzzesi, try to arrive first, because I like to chat with Bobo, the owner of the restaurant, before he gets too busy with our group. Bobo has made the place famous for fish, and some of his specialties are really inspired.

Bobo is a fanatic about his fish. On the cover of his book, *La Cucina di Bobo*, he is humorously and elegantly photographed in a blue suit, shirt, and tie, walking out of the green waters of the Adriatic carrying a basket full of just-caught fish.

CICORIA SEDUTA

Sitting Chicory *(Makes 6 servings)*

An odd name isn't it? The funny thing, though, is that it does makes sense. The greens in this dish, after being made into a flan and sliced, are served "sitting" at the bottom of soup bowls before the broth is added.

The kind of chicory one should use is the *cicoria di campo*, field chicory or dandelion greens, but regular chicory will do, too.

The recipe comes from the restaurant Vecchia Trattoria da Tonino, a family-owned restaurant in Campobasso. Maria Lombardi, the "mamma" and also the cook, calls this dish a flan in broth.

Unsalted butter for the pan
1 pound dandelions greens,
   trimmed and washed
6 1/2 cups broth of your choice, preferably
   homemade (pages 61 to 64)
6 large eggs
Salt to taste, optional

Freshly ground pepper to taste
1/2 pound freshly grated parmesan cheese
1/2 pound caciocavallo cheese, grated
   (see Note 2)
About 1 1/4 cups vegetable oil for frying
3 slices of crusty bread, cut into small cubes

1. Preheat the oven to 375°F. Butter a 9-inch soufflé dish.

2. Blanch the greens in plenty of boiling, salted water and cook until wilted, about 5 minutes, and drain. Rinse in cold water, drain again, and squeeze to extract as much water as possible.

3. Chop the greens finely and place them in a 2-quart saucepan with 1/2 half cup of the broth. Cook over medium heat for about 5 minutes, turn into a mixing bowl, and cool. If too much liquid accumulates, drain it.

4. Beat the eggs until frothy, add the salt, if used, the pepper, 2 tablespoons of the parmesan, and 2 tablespoons of the caciocavallo. Mix well and add the greens to this mixture.

5. Pour the mixture into the prepared soufflé dish. Sprinkle some of the cheeses on top and bake until the top is slightly crusty, about 25 to 30 minutes. Cool completely.

6. Cut the flan into 6 wedges, distribute it among individual soup bowls, and let it come to room temperature.

7. Bring the broth to a boil over high heat.

8. In a 9-inch skillet, heat the oil over medium heat and quickly fry the bread cubes until golden on all sides, about 5 minutes. Drain on paper towels.

9. Distribute the bread cubes among the soup bowls. Ladle the broth into the bowls, sprinkle some of the parmesan and caciocavallo over the top, and serve. Serve with additional cheese on the side.

NOTE 1: THE FLAN CAN BE REFRIGERATED, COVERED, FOR UP TO ONE DAY.

NOTE 2: CACIOCAVALLO IS AN ITALIAN CHEESE SIMILAR TO PROVOLONE. LIKE PROVOLONE IT CAN BE EITHER MILD OR PIQUANT.

Variation: Escarole or endive can be used instead. I don't recommend spinach because of its pronounced flavor.

My mother (far left, standing) with her nieces and cousins

IL CARDONE

Cardoon Soup *(Makes 6 servings or more)*

IN ABRUZZO, THIS *MINESTRA* IS SIMPLY called *il cardone.* It is another of this region's great soups and it is eaten as the first course of the traditional Christmas dinner. Piedmont is another region where cardoons are cultivated and eaten. I do not know why this vegetable, with a delicate taste of artichokes, is not very popular in other parts of Italy—and practically unknown in the United States. Since I am fortunate enough to live near Balducci's, the quintessential Italian specialty store, where cardoons are always available during the winter season, I serve them often as a vegetable.

The first three steps of this recipe can be done one day in advance. In any case, the cardoons must be prepared the day before, because after they are cut, they must be soaked overnight in water acidulated by the juice of a lemon to remove the slight bitterness of the stalks.

CARDOONS

Juice of 1 lemon

Water

1 bunch cardoons (about 4 pounds)

1 tablespoon kosher salt

2 tablespoons all-purpose flour

10 cups chicken or capon broth, preferably homemade (page 61 or 62)

Cooked meatballs (recipe follows)

4 large eggs

3 tablespoons freshly grated parmesan cheese

MEATBALLS

1/2 pound ground beef

1 teaspoon minced fresh parsley

1/4 teaspoon dried sage

1 tablespoon freshly grated parmesan

1 large egg, beaten

Salt to taste, optional

Freshly ground pepper to taste

1 tablespoon extra virgin olive oil

1 tablespoon unsalted butter

1/4 cup dry Marsala or sherry wine

GIBLETS

Giblets from the chicken or capon used to make the broth

1 tablespoon butter

1 tablespoon extra virgin olive oil

1/2 tablespoon unsalted butter

1/4 cup dry wine, white or red

1/2 cup broth of your choice, preferably homemade (pages 61 to 64)

Salt to taste, optional

Freshly ground pepper to taste

THE DAY BEFORE:

1. Prepare the cardoons: Squeeze the lemon juice into a large bowl and fill the bowl with water. Work with one rib at a time. Using a paring knife, and as you would do with celery, remove the stringy portions and filaments, and peel the white skin from the inside of the rib. Dice the rib and drop into the prepared bowl of acidulated water. Refrigerate overnight and continue the cardoon preparation the next day.

2. Prepare the meatballs: Mix all the ingredients together except the oil, butter, and wine. Form tiny meatballs the size of chick peas. Refrigerate 20 minutes. Heat the oil and butter in a 9-inch skillet over medium heat. Add the meatballs and cook, stirring until brown, about 10 minutes. Add a little of the wine, let evaporate, cool, and refrigerate.

3. Prepare the giblets: Cut the gizzard, heart, and liver into pieces. Heat the oil and butter in a small skillet over medium heat. Add the giblets and cook, stirring, until brown, about 5 to 8 minutes. Add the wine and let evaporate. Add a little broth and the seasoning. Cover the skillet, reduce the heat to a minimum, and cook until the giblets are cooked through, about 10 minutes. When cool enough to handle, dice the pieces and refrigerate.

THE NEXT DAY:

4. Continue working on the cardoons by bringing water to a boil in a large pot. Add the kosher salt and flour. Stir and bring to a boil again. Add the cardoons, bring the pot back to a boil, and cook 10 minutes. Drain.

5. In the same pot where the cardoons cooked, place the broth, bring to a boil, and add the drained cardoons. Bring back to a boil, reduce the heat to low, and cook until the vegetable is tender, about 10 to 15 minutes. Add the meatballs and giblets. Continue cooking at a gentle boil.

6. Beat the eggs and parmesan cheese together and stir into the boiling soup. Remove from the heat and serve. Serve with additional parmesan cheese on the side.

LE VIRTÙ

The Virtues (Makes 6 to 12 servings—see Note 1, below)

THE ESSENTIAL ABRUZZESE MINESTRONE is called *Le Virtù*. It is a specialty of the city of Teramo, and it is traditionally prepared on the first of May. An offer of this dish to friends signals good things to come.

The derivation of this poetic name is attributed to a charming folk legend. It tells the story of seven beautiful and virtuous young ladies, each one of them adding something to this complex soup—an aromatic herb, a condiment, a vegetable, and so on. Others say that it symbolizes the virtues of the Abruzzese woman who utilizes any remaining food.

The elaborate preparation of this soup, prompted the urbane Waverley Root, author of *The Food of Italy*, to give this wry, amusing explanation of its name: "only a woman of great virtues," he wrote, "would be willing to launch herself into a preparation of a dish which requires at least six separate cooking operations. . . ."

But do not get discouraged by his musing. True, it takes time to prepare this dish, but it is worth it. Also, keep in mind that, because of the sheer assortment of ingredients used, it will yield a generous lot. The soup reheats beautifully (the flavors increase with time) and it freezes well. Although I

¹/₂ pound pork rind (see Note 2, page 79)
2 pig trotters (see Note 2, below)
1 pig's ear (see Note 2, below)
1 ham or prosciutto bone, cut into 2 pieces (see Note 1, page 79)
¹/₂ pound flanken with bone; or one 1-pound beef shank
1 large onion, peeled and with a cross cut at its root end
2 whole cloves
1 rib celery, cut into 2 pieces
2 to 3 sprigs fresh Italian parsley
Salt to taste, optional
2 cups mixed dried legumes, beans, lentils, and chick peas, picked over for stones and seeds and washed
2 bay leaves
1 medium-size onion, sliced
¹/₄ pound prosciutto in 1 slice, diced
3 tablespoons extra virgin olive oil
1 clove garlic, peeled and chopped

4 or 5 scallions, green parts included, chopped
2 or 3 sprigs fresh parsley, minced
1 bulb fennel, chopped
2 medium-size carrots, peeled and diced
4 large ripe tomatoes, cubed; or 2 cups peeled canned tomatoes, with their juice
1 cup fresh shelled fava beans or lima beans
2 cups fresh shelled peas
4 or 5 leaves fresh mint
4 or 5 leaves fresh marjoram
Leaves from 1 bunch fresh thyme
Freshly ground pepper to taste
¹/₂ teaspoon grated nutmeg
8 cups chopped mixture of cabbage, endive, and spinach, blanched (see Note 3, below)
1 pound remnants of dried pasta or noodles, broken into short pieces
Freshly grated parmesan or pecorino cheese

1. Place the pork rind, pig trotters and ear, ham or prosciutto bone, and the flanken or beef shank in a large pot. Stud the onion with the cloves and add it along with the celery and sprigs of parsley to the pot. Add 16 cups water and bring to a boil over high heat. Reduce the heat to medium-low and cook, covered, until the meats are tender, about 2 hours. Taste the broth and add the salt if needed.

2. Strain the broth and return it to the pot. Discard the vegetables. When cool enough to handle, strip the meats from the bones, shred all the meats, and return them to the pot with the broth. These first 2 steps can be done in advance.

have simplified this recipe, and omitted many ingredients, each bowl still makes a full meal.

This soup is also called *cucina*, kitchen. The funny part is that I comprehended the true meaning of this name when I came to America and learned the expression "everything but the kitchen sink." In fact, anything can go into this soup but the kitchen sink! A meal in itself, as I said, but what a meal!

One word of advice: To make your work easier and before you start cooking, have your ingredients ready in the order in which you will be using them. And the same goes for the utensils. Better yet, do steps 1 and 2 the day before. Chill the broth because this will give you the opportunity to defat it.

3. While the meats cook, place the dried beans in a 4-quart pot and cover with water. Bring to a boil over high heat and cook 10 minutes. Drain and rinse under cold water. Return the dried beans to the pot, add the bay leaves, sliced onion, diced prosciutto, and 5 cups of water. Bring to a boil over high heat, reduce to low, and cook, covered, for about 45 minutes or until legumes are almost done; drain and set aside. This step, too, can be done in advance.

4. When ready to finish the soup, remove the bay leaves from the beans and discard. Add the bean mixture to the meat in the main pot.

5. In a 10-inch skillet, heat the oil over medium heat, add the garlic, scallions, minced parsley, fennel, and carrots and cook, stirring, until the vegetables are somewhat tender, about 10 minutes. If using canned tomatoes, drain the tomatoes, and reserve their juice. Add the tomatoes to the skillet. Reduce the heat to low and simmer to let the flavors mingle, 10 to 15 minutes. Add some of the reserved tomato juice from the tomatoes if the sauce tends to dry out. Add any remaining tomato juice to the main pot. Add the fava beans and the peas to the tomato mixture, stir, and cook, until tender, about 5 minutes. Turn all this into the main pot. Add all the herbs, a good grinding of pepper, and the nutmeg. Bring to a boil over high heat, then lower the heat and simmer 20 minutes. Add the blanched greens and cook 5 minutes longer.

6. Partially cook the pasta in boiling, salted water. Drain, reserving the water. Add the pasta to the mixture in the pot. Add as much of the reserved pasta water as you like according to the desired consistency of the soup. Keep in mind, though, that this soup is traditionally rather dense. Bring the soup to a boil and cook until the pasta is done. Serve with the parmesan cheese separately.

NOTE 1: I GIVE A WIDE RANGE FOR THE NUMBER OF SERVINGS. IT IS UP TO YOU IF YOU WANT TO SERVE LARGE OR SMALL PORTIONS. AND ALWAYS MAKE SURE YOU HAVE LEFTOVERS!

NOTE 2: PIGS' TROTTERS AND EARS ARE USUALLY AVAILABLE AT BUTCHER STORES.

NOTE 3: TO BLANCH THE MIXED CABBAGE, ENDIVE, AND SPINACH, ADD THEM TO PLENTY OF BOILING SALTED WATER AND COOK FOR ABOUT 5 MINUTES, THEN DRAIN.

NOTE 4: FOR A MORE ELEGANT TOUCH, USE FRESH TORTELLINI INSTEAD OF THE DRIED PASTA.

PASTA E FAGIOLI CON LE COTICHE ALL'ABRUZZESE

Pasta and Beans with Pork Rind Abruzzo Style **(Makes 6 to 8 servings)**

THIS IS THE QUINTESSENTIAL *PASTA E fagioli.* Plebeian food no doubt, but with a delicious taste. This *minestra* also appears on elegant tables, however, to the delight of the gourmands.

Around L'Aquila, the capital of Abruzzo, it is traditionally eaten on the 17th of January, the day of the feast of Saint Anthony, the Abbot's feast. It was, and still is today, cooked in a terra-cotta pot called *la fagioliera* and served in rustic *tegamini,* little pots.

BEANS

1 pound dried cannellini or borlotti (kidney or cranberry) beans, picked over for stones and seeds and washed

1 prosciutto or ham bone, (see Note 1, below)

1 rib celery, leaves included

2 cloves garlic, peeled and smashed

2 sprigs fresh parsley

2 bay leaves

1/2 pound fresh pork rind, or 1/4 pound prosciutto skin, washed, trimmed of excess fat, and cut into thin strips (see Note 2, below)

SAUCE

1 thick slice prosciutto with fat, cut into 4 pieces

1 medium-size onion, quartered

1 medium-size carrot, peeled and cut into 4 pieces

1 rib celery, cut into 4 pieces

1 sprig fresh parsley

2 tablespoons extra virgin olive oil

One 16-ounce can pureed tomatoes

1 teaspoon tomato paste

Freshly ground pepper to taste

1/2 hot red pepper, optional

PASTA

1 cup short pasta, such as tubetti *or* lumachine

1. Prepare the dried beans and plunge them into boiling water. Cook 10 minutes, then rinse under running water. Place them in a large pot, preferably a terra-cotta one, and cover with water. Bring to a boil over high heat and cook 10 minutes. Drain and rinse under cold water. This will remove the indigestible "patina" on the skin of the beans. Set the beans aside.

2. Place the prosciutto bone, not the ham bone, in a pot into which it fits snuggly. Cover with cold water, and bring to a boil over high heat, cook 10 minutes, and discard the water. This will eliminate the excess salt in the bone. This step is not necessary if using a ham bone.

3. Return the dried beans to the pot, add the bone you are using, the celery, garlic, parsley, and bay leaves. Add 2 1/2 quarts of cold water. Bring to a boil.

4. Add the pork or prosciutto rind to the beans. Reduce the heat to medium-low, cover the pot, and simmer until the beans are tender, about 2 hours.

5. Prepare the sauce: Place the prosciutto and vegetables, including the parsley, in a food processor and chop finely.

6. In a 10-inch skillet, heat the oil over medium heat and add the chopped vegetable mixture. Cook, stirring, until soft, about 5 to 8 minutes. Add the canned tomatoes and tomato paste, stir, add pepper and the hot pepper, if used. Cook the sauce over medium-low heat at a simmer, stirring often, 10 to 15 minutes.

7. With a slotted spoon, remove the celery, garlic, and parsley that was cooked with the beans. Place these in a food processor and add 1 cup of the beans. Puree and set aside.

8. Remove the bone from the beans and cool. Remove the bay leaves and discard. Scrape all the meat from the bone, and chop if the pieces are big. Return the meat to the pot together with the bean puree. Add the sauce, bring the soup back to a boil, reduce the heat to low, and simmer 10 to 15 minutes longer.

9. Meanwhile, cook the pasta in plenty of boiling, salted water for about 5 minutes. Drain, reserving 2 cups of the cooking water. Add the pasta to the beans and some of the reserved water according to how soupy you want your *minestra*. Bring the soup back to a boil and cook until the pasta is done, 5 to 8 minutes. Let the soup rest 5 minutes before serving.

NOTE 1: AFTER COOKING, THE PROSCIUTTO BONE (NOT THE HAM, WHICH AT THIS POINT HAS RELEASED ALL ITS FLAVOR) CAN BE WASHED, DRIED, AND FROZEN FOR ANOTHER *MINESTRA*.

NOTE 2: PORK RIND, WHICH IS ESSENTIAL IN THIS DISH, IS NOT EASY TO FIND, BUT CAN BE ORDERED FROM A BUTCHER. I SUGGEST USING THE SKIN OF PROSCIUTTO BUT IN REDUCED QUANTITY BECAUSE IT IS SALTY. IF YOU BUY YOUR PROSCIUTTO IN A GOOD ITALIAN DELICATESSEN, ASK FOR A PIECE OF THE SKIN AND THE BONE, ANOTHER ESSENTIAL ELEMENT.

ZUPPA DI FUNGHI

Mushroom Soup (Makes 6 to 8 servings)

PESCARA, THE TOWN WHERE MY PARENTS lived when father retired and where I spent many happy summer holidays, is situated on the Adriatic Sea. Nowadays, it is a modern bustling city. Very little remains of the charming small holiday resort of the past since it was almost completely destroyed by the war.

But one of Pescara's most famous features, apart from its wonderful sandy beaches, is still there. It is the *Pineta Dannunziana*, a pine wood, which is dedicated to Gabriele D'Annunzio, a much admired Italian poet and a native son. He wrote a stupendous poem called "*La Pioggia nel Pineto,*" or "The Rain in the Pine Woods," which is very lyrical and describes in almost musical terms the sound of the rain on the trees. It made, of course, the *pineta* of Pescara famous. I remember the

³/₄ cup dried porcini mushrooms
¹/₄ cup extra virgin olive oil
2 slices bacon, chopped
1 medium-size onion, chopped
2 medium-size potatoes, peeled and diced
2 medium-size carrots, peeled and diced
1 leek, white and pale green leaves only (trimmed of the tough green leaves), washed and thinly sliced

8 cups chicken or beef broth, preferably homemade (page 61)
¹/₂ pound fresh mushrooms, trimmed and coarsely chopped
Freshly ground pepper to taste
Salt to taste, optional
1 cup heavy cream, optional
¹/₄ cup minced fresh parsley
Freshly grated parmesan cheese

1. Soak the dried porcini in 1½ cups of lukewarm water for 20 minutes.

2. In a 5-quart pot, place 2 tablespoons of the oil and the bacon, and heat over medium heat. Add the onion and cook, stirring, until the onion is soft and translucent, 5 to 8 minutes. Add the potatoes, carrots, and leek. Cook, stirring, until wilted, 5 to 8 minutes, and add the broth. Bring to a boil over high heat and then reduce the heat to low to maintain a simmer.

3. Gently lift the porcini out of the water. Strain the water through a paper towel or coffee filter and add to the pot. Chop the porcini coarsely and add these too. Again bring the pot to a boil and then reduce to a simmer.

many picnics we had there, both as a child and a grown-up, and of course a few romantic *passeggiate*, strolls, at sunset!

On a more prosaic and rather funny note, I have to talk about dear Carolina, our washerwoman (these were the days before the washing machine), who lived near the *pineta*. When she came to pick up the laundry or bring it back, she would always have a basket of wild mushrooms which she had gathered the night before in the woods. To Mother's look of uncertain gratitude (could some of them be poisonous?) she would mischievously reply "Signora, don't worry,. I gave them to 'him' last night." "Him," of course, was her husband.

My mother, and father, too—he loved to get into the act—prepared the mushrooms in many ways. The large ones were grilled; the medium-size stuffed; the smaller, quartered and sautéed or made into a soup like the following one.

I always add a certain amount of dried porcini mushrooms when cooking fresh ones. This way, I recreate that certain woodsy flavor that was so characteristic of Carolina's wild mushrooms.

4. In a 9-inch skillet, heat the remaining oil over high heat. Add the fresh mushrooms and cook, stirring often, over high heat until they release their water, 10 to 15 minutes. Add the seasoning and continue cooking for 5 to 6 minutes. Add these mushrooms to the pot and simmer 30 minutes longer.

5. If using the cream, and you should, add it during the last 5 minutes of cooking. Add parsley, stir, and serve with the grated parmesan cheese on the side.

La "Ciavidella" di Federico

Egg and Tomato Soup *(Makes 6 servings)*

FEDERICO SPERA IS A COUSIN BY MAR-
riage. A dark, serious man, he looks a
little dangerous until you see him
walking the wards of Lanciano's hospital, where he is head of the pediatrics
department. All the children, at least
those who can, will jump out of their
beds to run to him. Soon the *professore*,
as he is called at the hospital, will be
cavorting on the floor under the
amused surveillance of his entourage,
which often includes one or two nuns.

Federico, actually has a great sense
of humor and jokes about being called
"uncivilized" by his colleagues because,
in these days of population control, he
has produced six offspring with my
cousin Adriana. The kids are all wonderful and although some, with professions of their own, have abandoned
the nest, they return often and always
at traditional festivities.

Federico is a great lover of music
and a connoisseur of good food and
wine. During my frequent returns to
Abruzzo, I always spend a few days in
Lanciano with the Speras. They compete with their friends in preparing the
most delicious dinners for me and my
husband. I always return home with a
bevy of new recipes. And this is one
from the last time I was there.

3 tablespoons extra virgin olive oil
3 medium-size onions, peeled and chopped
1 sweet dried pepper (available in Italian
*   specialty stores), chopped (see Note)*
6 or 7 ripe medium-size tomatoes,
*   chopped coarsely*
4 cups cold water
Salt to taste, optional
Freshly ground pepper to taste
6 slices Bruschetta (page 15)
6 large eggs

1. In a large saucepan, heat the oil over medium heat. Add the onions and dried
pepper. Cook, stirring, until the onions are soft and translucent, about 10 to 15
minutes. Cover the pan, reduce the heat to a minimum, and continue cooking,
stirring occasionally, until the onions are very soft and slightly colored, about 20
to 30 minutes. Add a little water if the mixture looks dry. Add the tomatoes, and
cook, stirring once in awhile, for 10 minutes, then add the water, salt, if used, and
the pepper. Cover the pan, bring to a boil, reduce the heat to medium-low, and
cook 10 minutes longer.

2. Place a slice of Bruschetta into six individual soup bowls.

3. Prepare the eggs: Break 3 eggs into the simmering soup without letting them
touch. Cover and simmer until the whites of the eggs are set, about 5 minutes. The
yolks should remain soft. With 2 large spoons, and being careful not to break the
egg, scoop out 1 egg at a time with some of the vegetable mixture and place it in
one of the prepared bowls. Cook and remove the remaining 3 eggs in the same
way. Spoon all the remaining soup around the eggs and serve.

NOTE: I PREDICT THAT SWEET DRIED PEPPERS, WHEN DISCOVERED BY AMERICANS, WILL
BECOME AS POPULAR AS DRIED TOMATOES. IN THIS COUNTRY, WHEN FRESH, THEY GO BY THE
NAME OF ITALIAN FRYING PEPPERS, OR CUBANELLE. THE PEPPERS ARE SWEET AND RED-
COLORED. THEY ARE SUN-DRIED, AND CAN BE FOUND IN ITALIAN, SPANISH, AND KOREAN
GREENGROCER STORES. THEY ADD A DELICATE SWEET FLAVOR TO MANY DISHES, ESPECIALLY
STEWS, SOUPS, FISH, AND POTTED MEATS.

CREMA DI CARCIOFI

Cream of Artichoke Soup **(Makes 6 to 8 servings)**

WHEN I THINK OF ROME, WHERE ARTI-chokes reign supreme, I see people at the renowned market of Campo dei Fiori, carrying away their bunches of long-stemmed artichokes as if they were roses. The stems are very tender and are also used in a sauce for pasta, *Pasta con Gamberi e Carciofi* (page 133).

This soup is rich yet delicate, with a very seductive flavor. It should be served in small portions. For many recipes, when I cannot find fresh baby artichokes, I use frozen ones. This is one vegetable which, in addition to peas, I do not mind to buying frozen. Do not use canned artichokes, however; they are packed in brine and will give a funny flavor to the soup.

10 to 12 fresh baby artichokes; or two 12-ounce packages frozen artichokes, defrosted and drained
1 tablespoon extra virgin olive oil
1 tablespoon unsalted butter
3 shallots, peeled and chopped
1 medium-size carrot, peeled and chopped
1 sprig fresh mint

1 sprig fresh parsley
6 cups chicken broth, preferably homemade (page 61)
1 cup heavy cream
1/4 teaspoon grated nutmeg
Salt to taste, optional
3/4 cup shredded Swiss cheese
Additional sprigs fresh mint or parsley for garnish

1. Do not use scissors or a knife on the outer leaves of the artichokes. Remove the tough leaves by bending the top of each leaf outward with your fingers and snapping it off. When you reach the tender core, trim 1 inch from the tops with a sharp knife. Peel the stems, if any, and cut the artichokes lengthwise into 4 or 6 wedges. Plunge them into a large bowl of acidulated water (water with the juice of 1/2 lemon) to prevent discoloration. If using frozen artichokes, cut them into halves.

2. In a 10-inch skillet or sauté pan, heat the oil and butter over medium heat. Add the shallots, carrot, mint, and parsley and cook, stirring, until the vegetables are somewhat soft, about 10 minutes. Add the artichokes and cook, stirring, about 5 minutes. Add the broth and bring to a boil, then reduce the heat to medium-low and simmer until the artichokes are tender, about 25 to 35 minutes.

3. Puree the artichoke mixture in a food mill to remove any stringy parts. Return the puree to the pan and add the cream, nutmeg, and salt, if used. Stir and serve in individual soup bowls with a sprinkling of Swiss cheese. Decorate with the herb sprigs.

PASTA CON LA CHICUCCIA (ZUCCA)

Pasta and Pumpkin (Makes 6 to 8 servings)

As a young teenager, I was a finicky eater and thought of myself as having a rather sophisticated palate. This plebeian dish, a recipe typical of the Abruzzese *cucina povera*, cooking with humble ingredients, was not one of my favorites. But now I love it. It is a flavorful dish and just right for a fall day.

1 small yellow or "Turkish head" pumpkin, about 2 pounds
3 tablespoons extra virgin olive oil
1 tablespoon prosciutto fat or bacon, chopped
1 large onion, sliced
One 16-ounce can peeled tomatoes, with their juice
4 or 5 leaves fresh basil, or 1 teaspoon dried

Salt to taste, optional
Freshly ground pepper to taste
2 cups chicken or beef broth, preferably homemade (page 61)
3/4 pound small pasta, such as shells, tubetti, wheels, or bow ties
1 tablespoon minced fresh parsley
Freshly grated pecorino romano cheese

1. Preheat the oven to 350°F.

2. Cut the pumpkin in half and remove the seeds and filaments. Place the halves on a cookie sheet, cut side down, add 1 cup of water, and bake until partially tender, 20 to 30 minutes. This will make the pumpkin softer and easier to cut. Cool, peel, and cut into small cubes.

3. In a 10-inch saucepan, heat the oil over medium heat, add the prosciutto fat or bacon, and cook 2 to 3 minutes. Add the onion and cook, stirring, until soft and translucent, about 10 minutes. Add the pumpkin and cook, stirring, 5 minutes, then add the tomatoes. Cook 10 minutes and stir in the basil and seasonings. Add 1½ cups of broth. Cook, covered, until the pumpkin is soft, about 30 minutes. If the mixture tends to get dry, add more broth.

4. Cook the pasta in plenty of boiling, salted water according to the package directions, but keep quite al dente. Drain and add to the pumpkin mixture. Add a little more broth if the soup seems too dry—this is up to you, but the soup should be dense. Cook until the pasta is done. Turn into a tureen and sprinkle with the parsley. Serve with a bowl of pecorino romano separately.

A SAVORY PASTIME

Don't discard the seeds of a pumpkin or other hard-shell squash! They can be washed and then dried in a slow 200°F oven for 45 minutes to 1 hour. If you wish, sprinkle them with a little salt before baking. Remove the shell before eating. In Sicily they are much appreciated and sold from pushcarts with the amusing name of *spassatiempo,* pastime.

ZUPPA DI FAVE E PECORINO

Fava Bean and Pecorino Cheese Soup **(Makes 6 servings or more)**

MY FATHER LOVED THIS RUSTIC SOUP. IN the summer, fresh fava beans were used, and we children loved to remove them from their wooly pods. Of course some ended up in our mouths. In winter the beans were dried and they had to be soaked overnight.

2 pounds fresh fava beans, shelled;
*   or 1 pound dried, soaked overnight*
1 head escarole, trimmed, washed,
*   and cut up*
2 or 3 shallots, peeled and coarsely chopped
2 cloves garlic, peeled
1 sprig fresh thyme

1 fresh hot red pepper, optional
2 tablespoons extra virgin olive oil
2 cloves garlic, chopped
2 sprigs fresh Italian parsley, minced
³/₄ cup freshly grated pecorino romano or
*   sardo cheese, shredded*

1. In a large saucepan, place the fava beans, escarole, shallots, the 2 whole cloves garlic, thyme, and hot pepper, if used. Add enough water to come up 2 inches above the solids. Bring to a boil, reduce the heat to low, and simmer 30 minutes if using fresh favas, 1 hour for dried ones.

2. Puree the mixture in a food processor and return it to the pan.

3. In a small skillet, heat the oil over medium heat. Add the chopped garlic and cook until it starts to fry, about 2 minutes, then add the parsley. Pour this into the soup. Ladle into soup bowls and sprinkle each bowl with some of the cheese.

SAGNATIELL' E LENTICCHIE

Noodles and Lentil Soup (Makes 6 servings)

WOULD YOU BE SURPRISED IF I TOLD YOU that when I was growing up in Italy I didn't like pasta? I was a finicky eater with a penchant for the unusual. Store-bought pasta, which my family ate almost every day, didn't appeal to me, unless it was part of a soup. My pasta had to be homemade and dressed with a special sauce. But life is full of unexpected events. Many years later, I ended up writing a TV documentary for CBS on the history of pasta and a book, *Anna Teresa Callen's Menus for Pasta*, which goes to prove that tastes change.

As a youngster, I really preferred soups, from the delicate to the robust. And I loved them with a passion. I still feel that way, although nowadays I could eat pasta even for breakfast, since I learned to love it.

The following soup recipe is another simple and humble fare, with all the flavors of a country kitchen. The lentils are combined with the *sagnatiell'*, large noodles cut 2 inches in length and 1 inch wide. The noodles, too, are rustic fare, made simply with flour, egg whites, and a little water. The soup is finished with a typical *Abruzzese* condiment called *adacciata*, which is a pesto of garlic, prosciutto, and herbs.

1 1/2 cups lentils, picked over for stones
    and seeds and washed
1 medium-size potato, unpeeled, scrubbed
2 bay leaves
3 tablespoons extra virgin olive oil
1 medium-size onion, finely chopped
One 32-ounce can peeled tomatoes,
    with their juice
1 small hot red pepper, optional

Salt to taste, optional
1 recipe L 'Sagne (page 155),
    made with 4 egg whites

ADACCIATA
2 cloves garlic, peeled
2 sprigs fresh parsley
6 leaves fresh basil
1 slice prosciutto with a little fat

1. Place the lentils in a large pot, add the potato, bay leaves, and water to come up 2 inches above the solids. Bring to a boil, reduce the heat, and simmer until the potato is done, about 35 to 40 minutes.

2. Remove the potato from the lentils and peel it. Puree it and return it to the pot.

3. In a 9-inch skillet, heat the oil over medium heat. Add the onion and cook, stirring, until the onion is soft and translucent, about 5 to 8 minutes. Drain the tomatoes and add the juice to the pot with the lentils. Add the tomatoes to the skillet. Break up the tomatoes with a wooden spoon while stirring. Add the hot pepper and salt, if used, and cook the sauce, stirring often, over medium heat, about 10 minutes. Add this to the lentils and continue cooking at a simmer about 10 minutes.

4. Meanwhile, cook the pasta in a large pot of boiling, salted water for 4 to 5 minutes. Drain, reserving 1 cup of the cooking liquid. Add the pasta to the lentils and cook a few more minutes to mingle the flavors.

5. Chop all the ingredients for the *adacciata* and stir into the lentil mixture. If you like your soup thinner, add some of the reserved pasta water. Cook a few minutes longer to let the flavors mingle and serve.

continues

Variation: *Pasta e Ceci*, Pasta and Chick Peas, is made similarly to noodle and lentil soup. The chick peas must be soaked overnight. Next day, cover with water, add 2 bay leaves, and simmer about 40 minutes. You may either add or omit the *adacciata*.

NOTE: BEFORE ADDING THE PASTA, YOU CAN REMOVE 1 CUP OF THE COOKED CHICK PEAS AND PUREE IT. ADD THE PUREE BACK INTO THE SOUP. THIS WILL GIVE THE SOUP A CREAMY TEXTURE.

FIT FOR A POET

It is interesting to know that *Pasta e Ceci* was the favorite dish of the Roman poet Horace. In one of his *Satires*, he writes about his longing to return home, after a hard day's work and eat a steamy "bowl of pasta and chick peas."

Dried beans and chick peas are much loved in Abruzzo; in fact we have many *minestre* (soups) similar to this one, called *all'Abruzzese*. They are made with all sorts of dried beans, but *ceci*, chick peas, are the preferred. My grandmother always made special *tacconi*, homemade noodles, to go with them.

MINESTRA DI FARRO

Emmer Soup **(Makes 6 to 8 servings)**

FARRO IS A MOUNTAIN GRAIN OF THE Gramineae family. Cultivated since antiquity, this grain has been found in the most ancient Egyptian tombs, in the remains of pile dwelling villages, and among the ruins of burned Troy. The Romans, after toasting it, milled it and used it for food. Together with salt they offered it to the gods during ceremonial sacrifices.

BROTH

1 medium-size onion, peeled, with a cross cut at its root end
2 whole cloves
1 ham bone, split in 2 pieces (see Note)
1 medium-size carrot, peeled and cut into to 4 pieces
1 rib celery, trimmed and cut into to 4 pieces
2 bay leaves
2 sprigs fresh parsley

Green part from the end of 1 or 2 leeks
Green feathery part of a fennel
10 peppercorns, crushed
Salt to taste, optional

FARRO

1 1/2 cups farro (available in health food stores and Balducci's), picked over for impurities and washed

Farro almost became extinct, but now it is being revived, thanks to chefs' reclaiming gastronomic castoffs and nutritionists' hailing its healthy values.

The mountain people of Abruzzo have continued its cultivation. In their villages, this *minestra* is quite popular. Local restaurants, which have never discarded the old traditions, serve it often.

My uncle Filippo always told us children of its ancient history, so when we ate it, we felt like ancient Romans. I have been bringing my supply of farro back from Abruzzo. My relatives and friends make sure I do not leave without it.

1. Prepare the broth: Stud the onion with the two cloves. Place it in a stockpot and add all the remaining ingredients. Add enough water to come up 2 inches above the solids, cover, and bring to a boil. Reduce the heat to low and let simmer about 2 hours. This can be done in advance. The broth keeps in the refrigerator for up to 3 days.

2. Prepare the farro: Place the cleaned farro in a 4-quart terra-cotta pot, preferably, or an enamel one. Add enough water to cover the grain by 2 inches. Cover the pot and bring to a boil. Reduce the heat to low and let it simmer until the water is absorbed, about 30 to 45 minutes.

3. Reheat the broth and start adding it to the farro, 2 to 3 ladles at a time, and continue adding and simmering until the farro is cooked, about 30 minutes or longer. The finished *minestra* should be rather dense.

NOTE: | USUALLY STRIP THE BONE OF ANY PIECES OF MEAT AND ADD IT TO THE *MINESTRA* AT THE END.

Variation 1: In the province of Teramo, the farro is cooked with water only. It is then dressed with pieces of salted herring that have been lightly cooked in olive oil. A true dish from the *cucina povera,* and as usual with these humble preparations, quite tasty.

Variation 2: Another characteristic Abruzzese soup is *La Zuppa di Cicerchie,* Chicerchie Soup. A cross between a fava bean and a chick pea, *cicerchia* is an ancient legume, which, like fava, had almost vanished in Italy. It was made into soup for the Roman legionnaires, who were fed *pane,* bread, and *cicerchie* before their long marches. *Cicercula* was its Latin name, and for the Abruzzese, who have always cultivated it, this legume is still called by its Roman name.

Its sturdy plant grows better in rocky terrain and requires little care. *Cicerchie* appear in many Abruzzese *minestroni,* often together with other beans. In this country one can find *cicerchie* in some Italian or health food stores.

The characteristics of this soup are the presence of *adacciata* (page 87) and *diavulillo,* a common feature in Abruzzese cooking.

It is important to soak the *cicerchie* for 24 hours to soften the woodsy texture of this legume.

CHAPTER 5

SALSE, SUGHI

E RAGÙ

Sauces

At the end of August, my family would leave the Adriatic shores to spend the last

days of summer at my grandmother's house in Guardiagrele. We passed the time

on joyous picnics in nearby woods or climbing surrounding mountains. This was

also the time for the *bottiglie*, or bottles.

PRESERVING AT HOME

In Italy, *fare le bottiglie*, literally, "to make the bottles," means only one thing:

putting up tomato sauce and tomato paste for winter.

We children viewed the frenzied activities going on in the household during those days with great excitement. The aroma of tomato sauce perfumed with basil mingled with that of burned sugar, spilling from the cauldrons of jams my mother loved to make. And then there were the vegetables. Many, like baby artichokes, tender zucchini, and string beans, had already been preserved earlier in the summer, and were sitting on shelves in the pantry. But still to come were the late-ripening vegetables, the peppers, eggplants, and pumpkins.

Distant cousins were summoned to help. Children, too, were given assignments, and we loved it and felt important. My father had his hands on everything, and uncle Filippo serenely organized the traffic. In the middle of the afternoon there was always a sumptuous *merenda*, snack, and later on when the men would come to pick up the women, it became a party.

The evening ended with a lovely *passeggiata fuori le mura*, a walk outside the city walls, and a stop at a *caffè*. A *bibita*, soft drink, or espresso for the ladies; ice cream for the children; and a *digestivo*, digestive, which most of the time meant a cognac or a grappa, for the men.

Those were the golden days, before the war forced us to make many of these provisions out of necessity.

Now when I go back to Italy, I sometimes catch the scent of *le bottiglie*, or preserves, being made. Often it is not an illusion; peasants and the working class still follow tradition. They set up their worktables outside the door, and everybody stops to watch and comment.

Fortunately, we have excellent canned tomatoes in America. My pupils always ask me which brand of tomato they should buy. And I always make them laugh when I tell them, "Whatever's on sale at the supermarket." But if you see among them canned tomatoes from San Marzano, Italy, stock up! They are the best in the world.

BEYOND TOMATO SAUCE

"What would Italy do without the tomato?" you might ask. True, true, Italians have undoubtedly been credited (and deservedly) with glorifying the tomato. But our sauces come in more colors than red, even for pasta.

One of the reasons Italian food is so easy to prepare and so naturally flavored is because it doesn't always require making a separate sauce. In most cases, the sauce is an integral part of a dish. The sauce is usually enriched with wine, which evaporates during the cooking process. Sometimes cream is added, but that is a modern influence and prevails mostly in the northwest of Italy.

SALSA, SUGO, OR RAGÙ?

The basic sauces in Italian cuisine are *salsa*, *sugo*, and *ragù*. They all mean sauce. When a sauce is served separately, it is usually called *salsa*, like *salsa verde*, or green sauce, which usually accompanies fish or boiled meat. *Sugo*, instead, is the sauce that dresses a dish or is incorporated into something else, mostly pasta. This is why *ragù*, a corruption of the French word *ragoût*, made with a variety of meats, also goes by the name of *sugo*. The meat is either chopped, as in *sugo* or *ragù alla bolognese*, or kept in large pieces as in *ragù all'Italiana* or *ragù alla napoletana*. A *ragù* is the quintessential sauce for pasta. Nowadays, some chefs call a fancy vegetable stew a *ragù*, but in my opinion that is a fanciful misnomer.

For me, the aroma of a *ragù* wafting in the air announces Sunday dinner. In Abruzzo at one time, the Sunday *ragù* was a test of culinary merit. Luigi Braccili, a noted Abruzzese writer, wrote that its perfume indicated "status, economic condition, and even culture." Of course, this is a thing of the past. Still, although I do not expect a *ragù* every Sunday, I still get worried when I am invited to *dinner* on that day and smell nothing.

In Abruzzo, the favorite Italian sauces for pasta are the so-called *ragù della festa*, festive sauces, rich with meat. But the simple *sugo finto,* "fake" sauce—made with the basic aromatic vegetables onion, carrot, and celery along with parsley, tomato, and herbs—is the one that dresses everyday pasta.

One of the most popular pasta sauces of the *cucina povera,* which is now becoming quite fashionable, is *aglio, olio e peperoncino* (garlic, oil, and hot red pepper). As I said before, *cucina povera,* literally "poor cooking," does not mean the cuisine of the poor but cooking with simple, inexpensive ingredients like oil, vegetables, legumes, and herbs.

Not so long ago it was important to establish which sauce went with which kind of pasta. But things have changed. For instance, when I was growing up, nobody dressed homemade pasta or commercial short pasta with a fish sauce. Only spaghetti or linguine were dressed so. Today it goes according to the individual taste, and I approve.

If the amount of sauce I suggest for dressing a pound of pasta does not seem enough, remember that Italians abhor pasta drowned in sauce. The sauce should complement the pasta not obliterate it.

SALSA BALSAMELLA

Béchamel Sauce **(Makes 1 cup)**

ALSO CALLED *BESCIAMELLA* IN ITALIAN, this is a basic sauce used for many preparations.

1 tablespoon unsalted butter
1 heaping tablespoon all-purpose flour
1 cup cold milk

Pinch of salt
Freshly ground white pepper to taste
1/4 teaspoon grated nutmeg

1. In a 1-quart heavy saucepan, preferably an enameled one, melt the butter over medium heat. Add the flour and cook, stirring, for a few minutes until the mixture forms a paste.

2. Remove the pan from the heat and slowly add the milk, whisking constantly until the mixture is smooth. Return the pan to the heat and cook the sauce, whisking constantly, until it thickens and begins to "puff," about 10 to 12 minutes. Let the sauce puff once or twice and remove from the heat. Season with salt, pepper, and nutmeg.

NOTE: IF A RECIPE CALLS FOR A THICKER *BALSAMELLA*, ADD 1/2 TABLESPOON MORE FLOUR AT THE BEGINNING. FOR A LOOSER ONE, ADD A LITTLE MORE MILK AT THE END ACCORDING TO HOW LIQUID YOU WANT THE BÉCHAMEL.

SALSA VERDE

Green Sauce **(Makes about 2 cups)**

WHEN WE SAW MOTHER MAKING THIS green sauce, we didn't even ask which dish it was for. We loved the sauce so much it didn't matter. Indeed, this sauce, a must for a *Bollito Misto* (page 316), is so versatile that it can be used for many other preparations. It accompanies grilled and poached fish beautifully. It dresses seafood salads perfectly. It doubles as a sparkling dip for vegetables, cold lobster, and shrimp, and makes a delicate topping for raw or cooked oysters, clams, and mussels on the half shell. As for practical matters, it is a cinch to make and it keeps for a week in the refrigerator, but must be covered with oil.

For a flavor bonus in soups and stews, add 1 teaspoon of this sauce per person just before serving.

2 cloves garlic, peeled
¹/₄ cup plain bread crumbs
1 hard-boiled large egg, peeled and quartered
3 anchovy fillets, drained; or 1¹/₂ teaspoons anchovy paste
1¹/₂ cups fresh parsley leaves

2 tender ribs celery, with as many leaves as possible, cut into pieces
1 tablespoon wine vinegar
Juice of 1 lemon
³/₄ cup extra virgin olive oil
2 tablespoons small capers in brine, drained

In a food processor, place all the ingredients except the oil and capers. Start the machine and slowly pour in the oil. Process until the mixture is pureed. Turn into a mixing bowl and stir in the capers.

NOTE: IF THE MIXTURE IS TOO THICK, ADD A LITTLE MORE LEMON JUICE, VINEGAR, OR EVEN BROTH.

SALSA PER BOLLITO DI MAMMA

Mother's Boiled Meat Sauce **(Makes about 4 cups)**

MOTHER ALWAYS SERVED THIS FLAVORFUL pepper and tomato sauce when the *Bollito Misto* (page 316) was an affair *in famiglia*. When guests were present, Mother prepared *Salsa Verde* (page 93). She considered it more elegant.

I like this sauce for its homey look and garden-fresh taste. An added bonus: Try warming up the leftover *Bollito Misto* in this sauce. It's excellent.

3 tablespoons extra virgin olive oil
1 clove garlic, peeled
1 sprig fresh parsley
1 bunch fresh rosemary
4 bell peppers, cored and cut into strips
1 1/2 pounds ripe plum tomatoes; or one 28-ounce can peeled tomatoes, with their juice, drained

3 or 4 fresh basil leaves, or 1/2 teaspoon dried
1 diavoletto (dried Italian hot red pepper), optional
1 tablespoon minced fresh parsley

In a 10-inch skillet, heat the oil over medium heat. Add the garlic, parsley sprig, and rosemary and cook, stirring, until the garlic starts to color, about 3 to 4 minutes. Remove the parsley and rosemary and discard. Add the bell peppers, and cook, stirring often, about 10 minutes. Add all the remaining ingredients except the minced parsley and continue cooking until the peppers are soft, about 10 minutes. Sprinkle with the minced parsley and serve.

PESTO ALLA GENOVESE

Pesto Sauce Genoa Style **(Dresses 1 pound of pasta)**

PESTO IS A LIGURIAN SPECIALTY BUT, LIKE *cotolette alla Milanese*, Milan-style cutlets, or a Sicilian *caponata*, it is eaten all over Italy. Many of these enticing specialties do not have frontiers, and a good thing, too. We Abruzzesi love pesto and enjoy it often.

I have friends who make great amounts of pesto when fresh basil is available and freeze it for years to come. There's no need to do this. First

PESTO BASE (SEE NOTE)
5 cups (about 5 bunches) basil leaves including tender stems
1 sprig fresh parsley
1/3 cup extra virgin olive oil

PESTO FINISH
3 cloves garlic, peeled
1/4 cup pignoli (pine nuts)
1/2 cup freshly grated parmesan cheese
2 tablespoons butter

1. Prepare the pesto base: In a food processor, place all the ingredients and puree.

2. Finish the pesto: In a food processor, place the pesto base and all the remaining ingredients. Puree.

of all, basil is available all year round. Besides, if you freeze the finished recipe for pesto, after a while the sauce will loose its pungency. Stick to making a pesto base and add the rest of the ingredients when you are ready to eat your pesto.

NOTE: THE BASE KEEPS WELL FOR A LONG TIME, WEEKS AND WEEKS IN THE REFRIGERATOR, IF WELL COVERED WITH OIL. USE IT BY THE TEASPOON FOR RECIPES CALLING FOR FRESH BASIL. IT CAN ALSO BE FROZEN.

Variation: During one of my recent visits to Abruzzo, my niece Francesca made a delicious dish of pappardelle, homemade broad noodles, dressed with a surprising sauce made with arugula instead of basil. It has a more pungent flavor then pesto and it is delightfully refreshing. I have also tried it with fusilli and it works beautifully.

To dress 1 pound of pasta you will need 1 bunch arugula, about 2 cups loosely packed leaves. Proceed as for pesto, but eliminate the pignoli.

AGLIO, OLIO E PEPERONCINO ALL'ABRUZZESE

Garlic, Oil, and Hot Red Pepper Abruzzo Style *(Dresses 1 pound of spaghetti or linguine)*

ALSO CALLED THE *SUGO DEI CINQUE MINUTI*, or five-minute sauce, because it takes no time to prepare, this is the sauce Italians make when they get together for an impromptu *spaghettata*. This means to go to somebody's home, usually after an evening at the theater or the movies, to cook and eat some spaghetti.

Use a large skillet to make the sauce, so you can toss the pasta directly in the sauce. Do not overdrain the pasta. Remember that the Neapolitans, masters of pasta cooking, say, "*lo spaghetto con la goccia*" (spaghetti with the "drop"), or a little bit of water clinging to drained spaghetti.

Before starting the sauce, have your linguine or spaghetti cooking and almost done.

¹/₄ cup extra virgin olive oil
3 large cloves garlic, peeled and smashed
1 small diavoletto *(dried Italian hot red pepper)*

2 tablespoons minced fresh parsley
Freshly ground pepper to taste

In a large skillet, heat the oil over medium heat. Add the garlic and hot pepper and cook, stirring, until the garlic starts to color, about 3 to 5 minutes. Stir in the parsley, remove the skillet from the heat, and add your chosen pasta. Toss and serve immediately.

SUGO FINTO

"Fake" Sauce (Dresses 1 pound of pasta)

THIS IS A SIMPLE AND FLAVORFUL TOMATO sauce which tastes as if it were made with meat; hence, the "fake" in its name. Sometimes my mother cheated by adding a little chopped prosciutto with the vegetables or a knob of butter at the end. It was good!

This and Marinara Sauce (page 97) are the sauces Italians use most often to dress their daily pasta.

1 medium-size onion, cut into 6 pieces
1 medium-size carrot, cut into 4 pieces
1 rib celery, cut into 4 pieces
1 sprig fresh Italian parsley
3 tablespoons extra virgin olive oil
2 fresh sage leaves, chopped,
*   or ¼ teaspoon dried*
1 teaspoon tomato paste

4 pounds ripe tomatoes; or one 32-ounce
*   can peeled tomatoes, both strained*
*   through a food mill*
5 or more fresh basil leaves,
*   or ½ teaspoon dried*
Salt to taste, optional
Freshly ground pepper to taste

1. In a food processor, chop the vegetables and the parsley. Set aside.

2. In a 3-quart saucepan, heat 2 tablespoons of the oil over medium heat. Add the chopped vegetables and the sage and cook, stirring, until the vegetables are wilted, about 10 minutes. Add the tomato paste and cook, stirring, for a few minutes, then add the tomatoes and cover the pan.

3. Bring the sauce to a boil, then reduce the heat to low, add half the basil, and simmer 30 minutes. Add the seasoning and remaining basil. Remove from the heat and stir in the remaining oil.

NOTE 1: NEVER PUREE YOUR TOMATOES IN A FOOD PROCESSOR. IT WILL CRUSH THE SEEDS AND MAKE THE SAUCE BITTER.

NOTE 2: THIS SAUCE FREEZES WELL.

Variation: For *Sugo coi Finocchi* (Sauce with Fennel), add 1 large fennel bulb, trimmed, cut into very thin slices and blanched, to the "sugo." Cook at a simmer for 10 minutes. Reserve some of the fronds from the fennel for decoration.

SUGO ALLA MARINARA

Marinara Sauce *(Dresses 1 pound of pasta)*

ALTHOUGH THE WORD *MARINARA* COMES from the Latin *mare*, sea, it does not mean that the sauce contains fish. Rather, marinara sauce is often used as a base for fish dishes. According to legend, Italian fishermen used to take this simple sauce, which doesn't spoil easily, on their fishing expeditions to dress their spaghetti and also cook some fish in it. It is the base for the classic *Brodetto di Pesce* (page 227), the Italian equivalent of *bouillabaisse*.

One 8-ounce can tomato puree
1 teaspoon tomato paste
2 tablespoons extra virgin olive oil
2 cloves garlic, peeled and smashed

2 sprigs fresh Italian parsley
4 to 5 leaves fresh basil or oregano, or ¹/₂ teaspoon dried

1. Place all the ingredients in a 3-quart saucepan. Cover the pan and bring to a boil, then reduce the heat to low, and simmer, covered, about 20 minutes. Stir once in a while. If the sauce seems too watery, remove the lid and cook a little longer.

2. Remove the garlic and the parsley, or strain through a food mill.

NOTE: THIS SAUCE FREEZES WELL.

Variation: For *Sughetto al Filetto di Pomodoro e Basilico* (Tomato and Basil Sauce), make this quick and simple, rustic sauce with a tangy, luscious flavor of summer, with fresh, ripe tomatoes, peeled, seeded, and cut in strips, hence the *filetti*. Cherry tomatoes are a worthy alternative since they seem to taste good all year round. Proceed as for Marinara, but add ¹/₂ cup basil leaves chopped with 1 clove garlic at the the very end.

SUGHETTO DI SALVATORE

Salvatore's Little Sauce *(Dresses 1 pound of pasta)*

SALVATORE, A NEPHEW BY ADOPTION (HE is the cousin of my nieces), devised this unusual sauce when he was a student away from home. It is quick and simple, but utterly delicious over spaghetti or linguine. This is a summer sauce though, and it must be made with fresh, ripe tomatoes.

5 or 6 medium-size ripe tomatoes, coarsely chopped
2 cloves garlic, peeled and chopped
5 or 6 basil leaves, chopped

1 heaping tablespoon capers in brine, drained
2 tablespoons plain bread crumbs
3 tablespoons extra virgin olive oil

1. Preheat the oven to 375°F

2. Combine all the ingredients in a baking pan. Bake until the sauce has reduced a little, 20 to 25 minutes. Serve on spaghetti or linguine.

SUGO BIANCO DI MARE

White Fish Sauce **(Dresses 1 pound of pasta)**

BECAUSE OF THE EXTENSIVE COASTLINE IN Abruzzo, we have many fish specialties. Marine, or seafood, cuisine is quite simple; it requires a short cooking time to retain the freshest flavors and perfumes of the sea. This sauce is a good example, as even the tomato is omitted as not to mar the true saline flavor of the seafood.

1 dozen small clams, scrubbed
1 pound mussels, scrubbed and debearded
1 pound squid, cleaned
4 tablespoons extra virgin olive oil
1 small onion, finely sliced
1 clove garlic, peeled and chopped
$^1/_2$ cup minced fresh parsley
$^3/_4$ pound small shrimp, peeled, deveined, and cut in half lengthwise

1. Place the clams and mussels in a large skillet over medium heat. Cook, shaking the skillet often. As soon as the mollusks start to open, remove them to a bowl. Discard the shells, making sure that all the juices from the mollusks are collected at the bottom of the bowl together with the clams and mollusks. Discard any unopened shells. Set the bowl aside. Wipe the skillet clean. Reserve.

2. Cut the squid into small pieces and place in a food processor. Lift the mussels and clams from the bowl, reserving the liquid, and add to the squid. Process briefly. You want a chunky mixture.

3. Heat 3 tablespoons of the oil in the reserved skillet over low heat. Add the onion, garlic, and half the parsley. Cook, stirring, until the onion is soft and translucent, about 5 to 8 minutes. Stir in the shrimp, add the chopped seafood mixture, and cook, stirring, for 5 minutes. Strain the juice from the clams and mussels into the skillet, and cook until the sauce has somewhat reduced, about 10 minutes. Add the remaining parsley and the remaining oil, stir, and remove from the heat.

NOTE: THE MUSSELS AND CLAMS CAN BE ADDED TO THE SAUCE WHOLE.

Variation: For a fish-vegetable sauce, you can add 1 cup shelled peas; 1 cup asparagus, cut into $^1/_2$-inch pieces; or 1 cup baby artichokes, trimmed and cut into thin wedges.

Cook the vegetables in boiling water until tender (the artichokes need the most cooking), then add to the sauce and cook until heated through.

SUGO DI VITELLO AI FUNGHI

Veal and Mushroom Sauce *(Makes 2 cups)*

THIS UNCOMPLICATED AND FLAVORFUL sauce is ideal for homemade pasta or polenta. It's also good on short tubular pasta like penne or rigatoni.

3 tablespoons butter
1 tablespoon extra virgin olive oil
1 large onion, cut in half
1 medium-size carrot, peeled and
    cut into 4 pieces
1 rib celery, cut into 4 pieces
$1/2$ pound shoulder or rump of veal in one
    piece, and preferably with bones
$1/4$ cup dry white wine

$1/2$ cup dried porcini mushrooms, soaked
    in $3/4$ cup lukewarm water
1 teaspoon tomato paste
One 32-ounce can peeled tomatoes,
    with their juice
$1/4$ pound chicken livers, trimmed and
    cut into small pieces
Salt to taste, optional
Freshly ground pepper to taste

1. In a heavy 4-quart pot, heat 2 tablespoons of the butter and the oil over medium heat. Add the onion, carrot, and celery and cook, stirring, until the vegetables are tender, about 10 minutes. Add the veal and brown it on all sides. Add the wine and let evaporate.

2. Gently remove the porcini mushrooms from the water. Reserve the water. Add the mushrooms to the veal. Strain the mushroom water through a paper towel or a coffee filter and add to the veal. Reduce the heat to medium-low and cook at a simmer, covered, 10 to 15 minutes. Add the tomato paste and tomatoes. Stir, breaking up the tomatoes with a wooden spoon. Bring to a boil, reduce the heat to low, and simmer until the veal is quite tender, 45 minutes to 1 hour. Stir often.

3. Remove the veal and reserve for another use. Strain the sauce through a food mill. Do not use a food processor; it crushes the seeds of the tomatoes and makes the sauce bitter. Return the sauce to the saucepan.

4. In a small skillet, melt the remaining butter over medium heat. Add the chicken livers and cook, stirring, until the livers lose their pinkness, about 5 to 10 minutes. Add the seasoning and pour the livers into the sauce during the last 5 minutes of cooking.

Variation: The meat of the reserved veal can be chopped and added to the sauce.

RAGÙ D'AGNELLO E PEPERONI ALL'ABRUZZESE

Lamb and Pepper Sauce Abruzzo Style (*Dresses 1 pound of pasta*)

ABRUZZO LAMB IS THE BEST AND THE most flavorful as the flocks are nourished by the fragrant herbs carpeting the slopes of our mountain. The shepherds roast the lamb in wood-fired stoves and prepare it in succulent casseroles cooked in open-air fires.

Lean lamb is required for this *ragù*, flavored with bell peppers.

1/4 cup extra virgin olive oil
2 cloves garlic, peeled
2 bay leaves
3/4 pound boneless lean lamb, chopped
1/4 cup dry wine, white or red
One 32-ounce can tomato puree

2 or 3 basil leaves, or 1/2 teaspoon dried
Salt to taste, optional
Freshly ground pepper to taste
3 bell peppers of different colors, roasted, peeled, seeded, and cut into strips

1. In a heavy 4-quart pot, heat the oil over medium heat. Add the garlic and bay leaves and cook until the garlic starts to brown, about 2 to 3 minutes. Add the lamb and cook, stirring, until browned. Add the wine and let evaporate. Add the tomato puree and fill the empty can halfway with water, swish it around to loosen any remaining tomato puree, and add to the sauce. Stir and add the basil, season with salt, if used, and pepper. Cover the pot and cook over low heat at a simmer 45 minutes to 1 hour. Stir often. Add the pepper strips during the last 5 minutes.

2. Remove the bay leaves before using.

Variation: For a more elegant sauce, you can puree the peppers before adding them.

Ragù all'Abruzzese con la Papera Muta

Abruzzo Style Sauce with Mute Duck **(Dresses 1 pound of pasta or more)**

GEOGRAPHICALLY, ABRUZZO IS LOCATED in central Italy. It is often referred to as the last region of the north or the first region in the south. But when it comes to *ragù*, and we have many kinds, Abruzzo definitely belongs to the south, where the *ragù*, any *ragù*, is king.

This is perhaps the most complex of the local meat sauces. It contains beef, pork, duck, and lamb. To be authentic, the duck should be of the kind we call *papera muta,* literally "mute duck," and the lamb should be *castrato,* the meat from a castrated lamb. In the United States, I use a good Long Island duck and I do not ask questions about the lamb. In any case, I find the *castrato* flavor a little strong.

Only the sauce is used for the pasta; the meat and the onion, cut into pieces, are eaten separately. Still, my mother sometimes poured this *ragù,* meat and all, over a bowl of polenta and I assure you, it was heaven!

Homemade pasta, stuffed pasta, timbales, short pasta like rigatoni or shells, and fusilli are the best for this sauce.

One 4- to 5-pound duck
1/4 cup extra virgin olive oil
2 medium-size onions, each cut with
  a cross at their root end
1 pound beef chuck, cubed
1 pound boneless shoulder of pork, cubed
1 pound boneless shoulder of lamb, cubed
1/2 cup dry white wine

Salt to taste, optional
2 teaspoons tomato paste
Two 32-ounce cans peeled tomatoes,
  strained through a food mill
1 small diavoletto *(dried Italian hot red*
  pepper), optional
6 or more basil leaves

1. Remove the skin and all visible fat from the duck. Remove the breast and reserve it for another use. Cut the remaining duck into small pieces. Leave the legs whole. The bones give a good flavor to the sauce.

2. In a large, heavy pan, heat the oil over medium heat. Add the onions and all the meats and cook, stirring, until the meats are brown. Add the wine and let evaporate. Add all the remaining ingredients, except the basil leaves, which are added at the end. Cover the pan, reduce the heat to low, and cook at a simmer about 2 1/2 hours.

NOTE: LEFTOVER SAUCE, IF ANY, CAN BE USED TO REHEAT THE MEAT TO BE EATEN AS A *SECONDO* WITH SOME VEGETABLES. THE SAUCE ALSO FREEZES WELL.

RAGÙ DI AGNELLO RIPIENO

Stuffed Lamb Sauce *(Dresses 1 pound of pasta or more)*

THIS RECIPE, IN WHICH A STUFFED LAMB shoulder cooks in the sauce, lending an incomparable flavor, definitely belongs to the menus *della festa*, festive menus. It's a colorful spring dish that tastes absolutely delicious when prepared with a young lamb. The meat used to make the sauce is usually served as a second course with an accompaniment of sautéed baby artichokes or tender peas.

One 4-pound shoulder of lamb, boned
Salt to taste, optional
Freshly ground pepper to taste
$1/2$ cup plain bread crumbs
1 clove garlic, peeled and minced
1 sprig fresh parsley, minced
$1/4$ pound pancetta, cut into strips
2 hard-boiled large eggs, peeled and cut into 6 wedges
$1/4$ cup grated pecorino romano or sardo cheese

$1/4$ cup extra virgin olive oil
$1/4$ cup dry white wine
1 medium-size onion, quartered
1 small carrot, peeled and quartered
1 rib celery, cut into 4 pieces
1 sprig fresh parsley
1 clove garlic, peeled
2 bay leaves
1 heaping teaspoon tomato paste
Two 28-ounce cans peeled tomatoes, with their juice

1. Cut open the boned lamb and try to flatten it with a meat pounder as much as possible so that it resembles a rectangle. The butcher can do this for you. Sprinkle the meat with salt, if used, and the pepper.

2. Combine the bread crumbs with the minced garlic and parsley and spread this mixture over the meat. Distribute the pancetta strips evenly. Place the egg wedges lengthwise in one line in the middle of the meat. Sprinkle the pecorino cheese all over, roll up the meat starting with the long end, and tie with strings.

3. In a large, oval, heavy pot, heat the oil over medium heat. Add the meat and brown it on all sides. Add the wine and let it evaporate. Add the onion, carrot, celery, parsley, garlic clove, and bay leaves and cook 10 more minutes, then add the tomato paste and peeled tomatoes. Cook, covered, at a simmer over low heat for about $2^1/_2$ hours. Turn the meat once in a while and scrape the bottom of the pan.

4. Remove the meat and keep warm. Discard the bay leaves and strain the sauce through a food mill. Rewarm the sauce before using.

NOTE: THIS AMOUNT OF MEAT WILL SERVE 4 TO 6 PEOPLE. IF YOU HAVE ANY SAUCE LEFT, USE IT TO REWARM THE MEAT OR FREEZE IT.

Variation: The same *ragù* can be made with a shoulder of pork.

RAGÙ ALLA BOLOGNESE

Bolognese Sauce **(Dresses 1 pound of pasta)**

THE MOST ITALIAN OF ALL SAUCES, *bolognese* is done from Bologna to Napoli, from Milano to Palermo. It is the essential sauce for dressing fresh homemade noodles, the type the people from Bologna call tagliatelle and those from Rome call fettuccine.

There's no need to tell you that if you put five Italians together to discuss *bolognese* sauce, each one has a different version. Well, we are such individualists! This is my recipe.

1 slice prosciutto, 1/4-inch thick, cubed
1 sprig fresh parsley
1 medium-size onion, quartered
1 rib celery, cut into 4 pieces
1 medium-size carrot, peeled and cut into 4 pieces
2 tablespoons extra virgin olive oil
2 tablespoons unsalted butter
1 pound mixed boneless beef, veal, and pork, chopped together

2 fresh sage leaves, or 1/4 teaspoon dried
Salt to taste, optional
Freshly ground pepper to taste
1/4 cup dry wine, preferably red
2 cups chicken broth, preferably homemade (page 61)
3 tablespoons tomato paste
1/4 cup heavy cream, optional

1. In a food processor, combine the prosciutto, parsley, onion, celery, and carrot. Process until the mixture is finely chopped.

2. In a 4-quart saucepan, heat the oil and butter over medium heat. Add the prosciutto-vegetable mixture and cook, stirring, until lightly browned, about 8 to 10 minutes. Stir in the meat and sage and cook, stirring frequently, until brown. Season with salt, if used, and the pepper. Add the wine and let evaporate.

3. Blend the broth into the tomato paste and stir into the meat. Cover and simmer over low heat, stirring occasionally, about 1 hour. Add the cream, if used, stir, and remove from the heat.

NOTE: THIS SAUCE CAN ALSO BE USED FOR SHORT PASTA LIKE RIGATONI, PENNE, FUSILLI, CONCHIGLIE, ETC.

RAGÙ ALL'ITALIANA

Meat Sauce for Pasta (Dresses 1 pound of pasta or more)

IN MY HOME THIS WAS THE FAVORITE sauce for *maccheroni alla chitarra*, "guitar" macaroni (page 144). In Abruzzo, many people add a piece of lamb to the *ragù*, especially in spring when the lamb is young and its flavor is quite delicate. The meats are kept in one piece and then sliced at the table. A green vegetable such as string beans, zucchini, or broccoli, accompanies the dish.

My mother served the *ragù* meats only at family dinners. For company, she didn't think it was right to have the meats after the *maccheroni* because then the two dishes would have the same flavor. But I do serve it as a main course, and nobody has ever complained.

However, if you want to keep the *ragù* meat for another use, make sure you also have some of the sauce to reheat it with.

¹/₄ cup extra virgin olive oil
2 medium-size onions, each with a cross cut at the bottom
1 rib celery, cut into 2 pieces
1 medium-size carrot, peeled and cut into 2 pieces
1 sprig fresh parsley
1 pound beef chuck or rump
1 pound pork shoulder, preferably with bone
1 pound veal shoulder, preferably with bone
1 pound sweet Italian sausages
Salt to taste, optional
Freshly ground pepper to taste
1 cup dry red wine
¹/₄ cup tomato paste
6 pounds fresh, ripe tomatoes, cut into pieces and strained through a food mill; or two 32-ounce cans tomato puree
2 or 3 fresh basil leaves, or ¹/₄ teaspoon dried

1. In a large, heavy 5-quart pot, heat the oil over medium heat. Add the onions, celery, carrot, and parsley.

2. Cook briefly, stirring, and add the meats. Pierce the sausages in several places with a pointed knife. This will prevent the sausages from cracking. Add them to the pot and cook until all the meats are well browned. Turn the meats often and scrape the browned bits at the bottom of the pot. Season with salt, if used, and pepper.

3. Add the wine and let evaporate. Add the tomato paste, tomatoes, and basil. If using canned tomato puree, fill the empty can halfway with water, swish it around to loosen any remaining tomato puree, and add to the pot.

4. Stir well, cover, reduce the heat to very low, and cook, stirring often, at a simmer until the meats are very tender, about 3 hours.

NOTE: ANY LEFTOVER SAUCE CAN BE FROZEN. THE AMOUNT OF MEAT IN THIS *RAGÙ* WILL SERVE 6 PEOPLE.

RAGÙ DI CARNE ALLO SPUMANTE

Meat Ragù with Sparkling Wine (Dresses 1 pound of pasta)

SPUMANTE, A SPARKLING WINE WITH A touch of sweetness, is not an ordinary table wine. Often it is misunderstood and drunk with the wrong food. Italians drink spumante as an aperitif with antipasti like mozzarella, prosciutto (especially when served with melon or figs), and other cured meats. But most of all, it is a wine that goes splendidly with desserts. We have excellent sparkling wines similar to Champagne, like the great Proseccos from the Veneto area, which we drink with food.

Still, spumante is a very good cooking wine in certain dishes. This succulent sauce is perfect. In fact, keep the remaining spumante for this dish. It does not matter if the spumante gets a little flat.

3 tablespoons extra virgin olive oil
4 ounces pancetta, diced
1 large carrot, peeled and cut into 2 pieces
1 rib celery, cut into 2 pieces
2 whole cloves
1 large onion, peeled and cut with a cross at its root end
1 1/2 pounds ground beef
2 bay leaves
1/2 bottle spumante
2 cups chicken or beef broth, preferably homemade (page 61)
Salt to taste, optional
Freshly ground pepper to taste

1. In a heavy 4-quart saucepan, heat the oil over medium heat. Add the pancetta and cook until the pancetta starts to color, about 4 to 5 minutes, then add the carrot and celery.

2. Stick the 2 cloves into the onion and add to the pan. Cook, stirring, for a few minutes, then add the beef and cook until brown. Add the bay leaves, stir, and start adding the spumante, a little at a time. Continue cooking and stirring until the wine evaporates. Add the broth, cover the pan, and bring to a boil. Reduce the heat to low and cook at a simmer, stirring often, about 1 hour. Add the seasoning while cooking.

3. With a slotted spoon, remove the carrot, celery, and onion. Puree the mixture in a food processor. Remove the bay leaves and discard. Return the puree to the pan and rewarm the sauce before using.

PASTA

About Pasta

Although much has been written about pasta, when I lecture around the country, I find that people are still confused by one thing: the difference between fresh homemade pasta, fresh pasta, and dry pasta.

COMMERCIAL PASTA

In Italy time-honored homemade pasta is made with all-purpose flour and eggs and is prepared at home. Dry pasta is made with semolina, or durum wheat (no eggs), and is generally prepared in factories and sold dry in packages.

It is the latter pasta, the dry one, that Italians eat almost every day. It is nutritious, light, and not fattening if dressed with simple sauces.

Because I am an Italian food person, people say to me, with a hint of envy, "Of course, you make your own pasta." They expect me to whip up spaghetti, penne, fusilli, rigatoni, etc. in my kitchen! In fact, these pastas are only good when made in a pasta factory where powerful machines can properly knead the semolina, which is a hardy flour, with water.

I know that there are electric pasta machines, which, after the ingredients are put in, start to spit out all sorts of pasta in a matter of seconds. I have tried with the result being a pasty, mushy, gooey mess. If you, dear reader, have one of those machines, give it away to a friend you do not like! Buy yourself a simple hand-cranked pasta machine. It is the only one you will need. The best, in my opinion, is the Imperia, sold in kitchenware stores. It makes only flat dough, but that is the only dough one should make with a machine.

In Italy the classic homemade pasta dough is prepared with all-purpose flour only (no whole wheat, buckwheat, or other kinds of flour) and eggs. This is the type of pasta used for all sorts of flat noodles, including tagliatelle, fettuccine, lasagne, and *tagliolini;* and for stuffed pasta such like cannelloni, ravioli, tortellini, and agnolotti, to name a few.

In some regions of Italy, other types of flour may be used to make local pasta specialties. Good examples are the buckwheat *pizzoccheri* from Valtellina in Lombardy, the *orecchiette* and *cavatelli* from Apulia, made partially with semolina, and whole wheat *bigoli* from the Veneto area. These are the preparations of the *cucina povera,* humble cooking, which is the thrifty cuisine of the peasants and the working class. The ingredients are humble, but the dishes are substantial and flavorful, and they are often dressed with unusual sauces. These preparations are wonderful to eat when you're in the mood for soul food of some kind, or if you are in the towns or regions where they are traditional.

The so-called "fresh" pasta sold in supermarkets and specialty food stores has nothing to do with homemade pasta, since it is made with semolina and sometimes, eggs. It is a convenience food. I buy it occasionally, in sheets, to make cannelloni or ravioli, which are time-consuming. But by no means does it resemble homemade pasta, which is light and delicate. Semolina flour produces a hardy pasta that looks good in a display case for days. This is why it has become so popular in this country. Pasta made with all-purpose flour dries quickly and becomes brittle. It is not suitable for display. In my opinion, one is better off buying packaged dry egg noodles, imported from Italy, than this so called "fresh pasta."

What Color Is Your Pasta?

Another pet peeve of mine: I do not like all the absurd flavors and colors added to pasta dough. A pasta that tastes of garlic or whatever, may conflict with its sauce. The sauce should be the one element giving flavor to the pasta and not the other way around.

About coloring pasta: We Italians use only pureed spinach for green pasta, pureed red beets for red pasta, and the squid ink of the squid for black pasta. Sometimes, when I'm feeling whimsical and perhaps at *Carnevale* (Mardi Gras), I make *Tagliatelle Arlecchino* (see box, page 142). One batch of tagliatelle is made with a touch of unsweetened cocoa powder to add another color to the bowl of red, green, and yellow (plain) noodles.

Saffron noodles are another peeve of mine. What a waste of a good spice! If you use too much, it tastes medicinal; too little and it doesn't give any color to the pasta. You want a yellow pasta? Do as the Piedmontes do; make your dough with only egg yolks instead of whole eggs and forget the cholesterol.

In a word, simpler is better; it's hard to beat the tried-and-true combinations of generations of Italian cooks—simplicity and moderation are the rules to follow.

Today dietitians recommend pasta as a substitute for many proteins found in meat. Pasta is rich in nutritive properties essential to the human body and is prominent in the health diets of Weight Watchers, Pritikin, and the Heart Association of America.

COOKING PASTA

As long as I live, I will remember the commotion that went on in the kitchen of my ancestral homes when the pasta was ready to be dropped into the pot of boiling water. It was a kind of frenzied ceremony which was repeated almost every day. The children were told to keep out of the way, if not out of the kitchen. My grandmother, or who ever was in charge, checked to make sure that everything was in place—the salt for the boiling water, the long fork for stirring, the cold water for dumping into the pot at the moment the pasta was ready to stop its cooking, the colander for draining, and the serving bowl for serving.

As soon the pasta was sauced and ready, everyone relaxed and became serene and happy again in anticipation of the good food to come.

I, too, in my minuscule Manhattan kitchen, where organization is an absolute must, become a little frenzied and always need the help of my husband to hold the colander in place when I drain the pasta.

And these are rules for cooking pasta properly. Hopefully, they will make cooking pasta less frantic:

- Use a large 4- to 6-quart capacity pot, not a stockpot, which is too heavy and will take too long for the water to reboil after the pasta is in.
- Fill the pot with cold water, cover the pot, and bring it to a boil over high heat. Add the salt only after the water boils, not before, otherwise your water and the pasta will taste metallic. I seldom give the quantity of salt in my recipes, leaving it up to you. However, I always use 2 to 3 tablespoons of kosher salt, which is purer than table salt and melts quickly, for 1 to 1^1/$_2$ pounds of pasta. If this seems like too much to you, remember that pasta is bland and needs the salt to give it flavor; the sauce will not do it. Besides, most of the salt remains in the water. Still, if you have a medical problem and cannot have salt, use a shot of vinegar, about ^{1}/$_4$ cup, or the juice of 1 lemon to boost the flavor.
- Drop the pasta into the pot, stir, and cover the pot, because you want the water to come back to a boil as quickly as possible. If you do not cover the pot, your pasta will sit at the bottom of the pot and become friendly with each other (they will stick together) and you will have a blob. After the water comes back to a boil, you can remove the lid. But remember, pasta must boil at all times, not simmer.
- Do not add oil to the water. It will make the sauce slide off the pasta,

---

GRATING CHEESES FOR PASTA

- Parmigiano reggiano, or parmesan, is produced only in the provinces of Parma, Mantova, and Bologna, and it is made only from April to November with whole milk from cows fed with fresh grass.
- Grana padano is similar to parmesan but it is produced all year round in the area north of the Po River. It is made with skim milk from cows that are fed hay. I use this more often than parmesan.
- Pecorino, or romano, as it is better known here, is made with whole sheep's milk. It is aged for grating, but also sold fresh for eating. There are many types of pecorino, apart from the better known romano. They are the Abruzzese, Sardinian, and Sicilian.
- These cheeses are not interchangeabe. Pecorino, although it is an excellent cheese, is sharp and salty at the same time. To suggest the use of either parmesan or romano, as often indicated in cookbooks or touted on television food shows, is often wrong. On a few dishes, either cheese can be used, but to sprinkle pecorino over a dish of *tagliatelle alla bolognese* is to ruin it.
- Keep in mind the taste of these cheeses and use them accordingly. Pecorino, in particular, should be reserved for strong-flavored dishes containing pancetta, prosciutto, or quite a bit of onion or garlic. When in doubt, use parmesan or grana; you will not go wrong.

when you want the sauce to stick instead. I suspect that this terrible habit started because people didn't know that pasta had to "swim" in lots of boiling water while cooking, and used small pots with too little water. Also, at one time, the pasta was often overly starchy because it was made with the wrong flour, and therefore became sticky. Nowadays, even the pastas made in the United States are excellent.

- Taste your pasta for doneness. Although you will often find instructions on the package for how long you should cook it, cooking times are just a guide. Only tasting guarantees perfectly cooked pasta, which should be "al dente," meaning a little resistant to the tooth. Nowadays though, this al dente business has gone too far and often we are eating raw pasta, raw vegetables, and raw fish.

- When the pasta is ready, dump a glass of cold water into the pot to stop the boiling. Drain the pasta, but not too much. The Neapolitans, masters of pasta cooking, advise: *lo spaghetto con la goccia*, the spaghetti with the drop, meaning not too dry. Some Neapolitans insist on removing the spaghetti with a fork without draining it at all. I use a colander but I do not shake it too much because, as I said, the pasta should remain a little wet.

- Always reserve 1 cup of the cooking water. You can add it to the pasta if the sauce, especially a creamy one with cheese, has made the pasta clump together. A bit of pasta cooking water will inhibit the need for more butter, cream, or oil to loosen up the mixture.

- Never put cheese on pasta dressed with fish sauces, especially if the sauce contains oil, garlic, and tomato. One exception: If the fish sauce is cream-based, you can use parmesan or grana padano, which are delicate in flavor.

- Serve your pasta as soon as it is ready, unless the recipe calls for a period of rest.

- As for the quantity of pasta to cook, one pound of dry pasta will usually feed six people, if served Italian style, as a first course. But if you wish to serve the pasta as a main course, add $1/2$ pound more pasta for the same number of servings.

- Another thing to consider is the type of sauce you are using. A chunky sauce, for instance, or one that contains other ingredients, like vegetables, fish, or meat, will increase the volume of your dish.

Pasta Secca (Dried Pasta)

Spaghetti con gli Asparagi

Spaghetti with Asparagus (Makes 6 servings)

In my home this dish was made with the wild asparagus that we used to gather during our outings in the countryside. They were so tender, nothing needed to be discarded, and since they were also very thin, they could almost be twirled with the spaghetti.

If you can find pencil-thin asparagus, just remove the bottom end of the spears at the point where it breaks naturally. For regular asparagus follow the recipe.

2 tablespoons unsalted butter
1 tablespoon extra virgin olive oil
18 spears asparagus, trimmed, peeled, blanched (see Note), and cut into 1-inch pieces
Zest of 1 lemon, very finely chopped
3/4 cup heavy cream
1 pound spaghetti
2 tablespoons lemon juice
Freshly grated parmesan cheese

1. In a large skillet, heat the butter and oil over medium heat. Add the asparagus and cook, stirring, about 5 minutes. Add the lemon zest and heavy cream, bring to a boil, reduce the heat to low, and simmer until the asparagus are done, about 5 minutes.

2. Meanwhile, cook the spaghetti in boiling salted water according to the package directions. Drain, reserving 1 cup of the cooking water. Add the spaghetti to the skillet with the asparagus, and cook for a few seconds, tossing the mixture to let the flavors mingle. Add the lemon juice. If the mixture seems a little dry, add some of the reserved water. Serve with the parmesan cheese.

NOTE: To blanch asparagus, add it to plenty of boiling, salted water (as for pasta) and cook until slightly tender, about 5 minutes.

What Do Fifty Million Italians Have in Common?

Mario Soldati, the famous Italian writer and movie director, said more or less that the unification of Italy didn't happen with Garibaldi. "The Italians," he said, "are united once a day, at around midday, when the pasta all over Italy is plunged into a boiling pot."

SPAGHETTI RUSTICI

Rustic-Style Spaghetti **(Makes 6 servings)**

THIS RECIPE IS A TYPICAL PEASANT DISH with the assertive scent of autumn.

Before dried tomatoes became the rage in this country, one would encounter them only in certain rural areas of Italy. Drying tomatoes were as much a sign of fall as bottling tomatoes. Bunches of them, still attached to the vine, festooned the fronts of humble whitewashed houses, adding color to the landscape.

I remember these *pomodorini*, or little tomatoes, also hung on the walls of our most sunny terraces, until the first frost crusted them with sparkling droplets. Then they were taken inside to simply decorate one corner of the kitchen.

They were not, by any means, considered gourmet food. They were essential for adding flavor to a tomato sauce and were used sparingly. This peasant dish is a good example of how dried tomatoes are traditionally used in Italy.

³/₄ cup sun-dried tomatoes soaked in oil, drained (see box)
2 medium-size red onions, chopped
1 clove garlic, peeled
¹/₄ cup extra virgin olive oil
¹/₄ cup dry red wine
1 teaspoon tomato paste
About ¹/₂ cup, or more, chicken broth, preferably homemade (page 61), or use bouillon
A few flakes diavoletto (dried Italian hot red pepper), optional
1 pound spaghetti or linguine
2 sprigs fresh parsley, finely minced

1. In a 9-inch skillet, combine the tomatoes, onions, garlic, and 2 tablespoons of the oil. Cover and cook over low heat, stirring often, about 20 minutes.

2. Stir the wine into the tomato paste and add to the skillet. Cook briefly and add ¹/₂ cup of broth. Cook over medium-low heat at a simmer, covered, until the tomatoes and onions are tender, about 20 to 30 minutes. If the tomatoes are not tender enough, add more broth. Pour this sauce into a food processor and process until finely chopped. Return it to the skillet. Add the *diavoletto*, if used.

3. Cook the pasta in boiling, salted water according to the package directions. Drain, reserving 1 cup of the cooking water.

4. Reheat the sauce. Remove from the heat and add to it the remaining 2 tablespoons of oil, pour on the pasta, and toss. If the pasta seems a little dry, add some of the reserved water. Add the minced parsley and serve.

DRIED TOMATOES IN OIL

Dried tomatoes are now easily available in this country. There is no need to buy those in olive oil, which are quite expensive. I do the olive oil bit myself. Just soak the dried tomatoes in lukewarm water for 30 minutes, drain, and dry them. Place the tomatoes in jars and pour in good extra virgin olive oil to cover. If you wish you can add either a sprig of rosemary or 5 to 6 leaves of basil. They keep for long time if stored in a cool, dark place or in the refrigerator.

SPAGHETTI AI CAPPERI

Spaghetti with Capers *(Makes 6 servings)*

THIS QUICK, UNCOOKED SAUCE FOR AN impromptu *spaghettata*, a speedy dish of spaghetti, was one of my father's favorites. He would prepare it in the middle of the night when, with my mother and a few friends, they would come home from an opera or a movie. We children, attracted by the aroma, would appear instantly.

In this recipe, the dried tomatoes and the capers add an intriguing, tangy taste to the sauce, and the nuts give a crunchy texture and exotic touch. But what outshines them all here is the pure herbivorous aroma of the basil.

1 ½ pounds spaghetti
2 pounds ripe tomatoes, diced; or 1 pint
   cherry tomatoes, halved
1 cup sun-dried tomatoes in oil, drained
   (see box, page 111), coarsely chopped
1 ½ tablespoons capers in brine, drained

2 cloves garlic, peeled and finely minced
¼ cup extra virgin olive oil
1 cup loosely packed fresh basil leaves,
   snipped by hand
½ cup pine nuts or chopped walnuts

1. Cook the spaghetti in boiling, salted water according to the package directions.

2. While the pasta cooks, combine all the remaining ingredients in a pasta serving bowl. Mix well. When the pasta is ready, drain it, but not too much, and add to the pasta bowl, toss, and serve.

Mamma e Papà

BUCATINI CON RICOTTA SALATA

Bucatini with Salted Ricotta (*Makes 6 servings*)

THE *RICOTTA SALATA*, AVAILABLE IN ITALIAN specialty stores and some supermarkets, is not all that salted. The ricotta is aged, therefore it becomes dry and can even be grated. It is a specialty of the South, but it is sold all over Italy. It is also eaten as a table cheese.

In this recipe the ricotta adds a bite to this savory pasta dish, flavored simply with pancetta, tomatoes, wine, and aromatic vegetables.

1 slice, pancetta, about 2 ounces
1 medium-size onion, peeled and quartered
1 medium-size carrot, peeled and cut into 4 pieces
1 rib celery, trimmed and cut into 4 pieces
1 tablespoon extra virgin olive oil
$\frac{1}{2}$ cup dry white wine
1 teaspoon tomato paste

One 16-ounce can peeled tomatoes, with their juice
2 to 4 fresh basil leaves, or $\frac{1}{4}$ teaspoon dried
Freshly ground pepper to taste
$1\frac{1}{2}$ pounds bucatini or linguine
4 ounces ricotta salata
1 small clove garlic, peeled and minced
1 tablespoon fresh parsley, minced

1. In a food processor, place the pancetta, onion, carrot, and celery. Process until very finely chopped.

2. In a 10-inch skillet, heat the oil over medium heat. Add the vegetable mixture. Cook, stirring, about 5 minutes. Gradually add the wine a little at a time and the tomato paste. Mix well and then add the peeled tomatoes and basil.

3. Stir and cook, breaking up the tomatoes with a wooden spoon. Cover and cook over medium-low heat at a simmer about 30 minutes, stirring once in a while. Add the seasoning.

4. Cook the pasta in boiling, salted water according to the package directions.

5. While the pasta cooks, crumble the ricotta in a pasta serving bowl and combine it with the garlic and parsley.

6. Drain the pasta, reserving 1 cup of the cooking water. Add $\frac{1}{2}$ cup of this water to the prepared pasta bowl, mix, and add the pasta. Pour the sauce over the pasta, toss, and serve.

SPAGHETTI ALLA CARBONARA

Coal Man's Spaghetti *(Makes 6 servings)*

AN ITALIAN CLASSIC. WHO DOESN'T LOVE this spaghetti? In the days before cholesterol became a dreaded household word, we used to eat it quite often. It was another favorite dish for a *spaghettata* (quick meal of spaghetti). The sauce is actually a specialty of the Roman cuisine, but where do you think the *carbonari* come from? Abruzzo, of course.

The cream, by the way, is a modern addition. You can leave it out if you wish. But what the heck, it is so good, and as the Romans said, "*semel in anno licet insanire.*" It means "once in a year it is all right to go mad." So once in a while go mad and enjoy the spaghetti *alla carbonara*.

1 ½ pounds spaghetti
3 large eggs
½ cup freshly grated parmesan cheese, plus additional for serving (see Note 2)
1 tablespoon extra virgin olive oil
3 ounces pancetta in 1 or 2 slices, coarsely chopped
½ cup heavy cream, optional
Freshly ground black pepper to taste

1. Cook the spaghetti in boiling, salted water according to the package directions.

2. In a pasta serving bowl, beat together the eggs and ½ cup of the parmesan cheese. Set aside.

3. In a small skillet, heat the oil over medium heat. Add the pancetta and cook, stirring, until crisp, about 5 to 8 minutes. Set aside.

4. Drain the spaghetti, reserving 1 cup of the cooking water. Pour the spaghetti into the serving bowl and toss quickly with the egg sauce. Add the pancetta and the cream, if used, and a good grinding of pepper. If the mixture seems too dry, add some of the reserved water. Serve with the additional parmesan cheese separately.

NOTE 1: MIX THE PASTA WITH THE EGG SAUCE AS SOON AS YOU DRAIN IT. THE HOT PASTA WILL COOK THE EGG, ELIMINATING ANY DANGER OF SALMONELLA.

NOTE 2: SOME PEOPLE PREFER TO USE PECORINO ROMANO CHEESE. IT IS INDEED MORE AUTHENTIC AND IT GIVES A MORE PUNGENT TASTE TO THE DISH.

SPAGHETTI DEL POLLAIOLO

Chicken Man's Spaghetti *(Makes 6 servings)*

As a child I remember that chickens were considered special. We didn't eat them as often as we do today. In my grandmother's house, they were raised in a coop in a distant backyard and every night the maids would go and feed them. I liked to go too, when I didn't have anything better to do. We would gather the eggs generously released by the hens, and discuss which one was the next chicken destined for the pot. A bit cruel nowadays, when I think of it, but then it was a matter of daily life.

A slaughter of chickens always happened when guests came for dinner or for other special occasions, like birthdays, saint's name days, and similar festivities. Often there was an abundance of *frattaglie* (gizzards, hearts, and livers), which were saved to make other delicious dishes or sauces. This is one sauce which my aunt Cettina liked to prepare.

The livers were not actually used in this dish. They were reserved for the *Antipasto di Fegatini all'Abruzzese* (page 17).

Keep in mind that a mixture of hearts and giblets are often sold in supermarkets.

1 large red onion, quartered
1 rib celery, cut into 4 pieces
1 small carrot, peeled and cut into 4 pieces
1 sprig fresh parsley
1 clove garlic, peeled
1/4 cup extra virgin olive oil
1 pound frattaglie, or chicken giblets and hearts, trimmed and cut in half (see Note)
Salt to taste, optional
Freshly ground black pepper to taste
1 cup dry wine, preferably red
2 tablespoons tomato paste
About 3 cups chicken or beef broth, preferably homemade (page 61)
1 pound spaghetti
Freshly grated parmesan or grana padano cheese

1. Coarsely chop all the vegetables, the parsley, and the garlic in a food processor.

2. In a heavy 2-quart pot, heat the oil over medium heat. Add the chopped vegetables, and cook, stirring, over medium heat until wilted, about 5 to 8 minutes.

3. Add the giblets and hearts and continue cooking until the meat is brown. Add the seasoning and the wine and let the wine evaporate. Stir in the tomato paste and add 2 cups of the broth. Stir, cover, and bring to a boil over high heat, then reduce the heat to low and simmer until the gizzards are tender, about 45 minutes. Add more broth if the sauce becomes too dry.

4. Pour the sauce into a food processor and process until finely chopped. Return the sauce to the pot and add a little more broth. At the end, this sauce should be a little thin. When the pasta is almost ready, reheat the sauce before serving.

5. Cook the spaghetti in boiling, salted water according to the package directions. Drain, reserving 1 cup of the cooking water, and dress with the sauce. If the pasta mixture seems too dry, add some of the reserved water. Serve with a bowl of parmesan or grana padano cheese separately.

Variation: I often add a handful of dried porcini mushrooms soaked for 15 minutes and drained, which I chop and cook, stirring, with the vegetables. Or I add 1 cup of frozen peas at the very end. They both bring extra richness and color to the dish.

Hiking on the Majella, one of the highest mountains of Abruzzo, in 1946

SPAGHETTI ALLA PECORARA

Shepherd's or Herdsman's Spaghetti **(Makes 6 servings)**

BEING ABRUZZO THE "PASTORAL LAND," there are many dishes named after the fabled shepherds who, with their white flocks and gentle fluffy dogs, are so much a part of the landscape. But, alas, they are no longer wearing the colorful costumes that made them so recognizable as they descended from their mountains to sell wool and buy their supplies. Those costumes are now reserved for special occasions like parades, festivals, and shows. In fact you can still see the *Zampognari Abruzzesi,* Abruzzo's bagpipers, who are shepherds, at Christmas time in the Piazza Navona in Rome. They play the *"Novena,"* a special prayer recited for nine days. The *Zampognari Abruzzesi* wear sheepskin coats and their characteristic sandals laced over white socks ending below the short, slightly bouffant pants. But I doubt if these shepherds still have a flock to tend. I suspect they sit on the local board of tourism. Anyway, they still make quite a scene, and are very colorful.

This is a dish of pastoral origins because of the cheese, which the shepherds make with sheep's milk.

3 bell peppers of different colors
2 slices smoked bacon
2 cloves garlic, peeled
1/2 teaspoon dried rosemary
2 tablespoons extra virgin olive oil
1 teaspoon tomato paste
One 16-ounce can peeled tomatoes, with their juice
2 or more fresh basil leaves
1 pound spaghetti
One 8-ounce smoked mozzarella cheese, diced
Freshly grated pecorino Abruzzese or romano cheese
1 tablespoon minced fresh parsley

1. Roast the peppers directly in the flames of a gas burner until the skin is charred on all sides, or roast them on a foil-lined cookie sheet under a broiler until the skin is charred. Place the roasted peppers in a brown paper bag and close the bag tightly, or if oven-roasted, simply wrap them in the foil. This will make the peeling of the peppers easier. When cool, peel the peppers with your fingers or a small knife. (Do not surrender to the temptation to wash the pepper skins off under the faucet; you will also wash away the smoky flavor of the roasted peppers.)

2. In a food processor, place the peppers, bacon, garlic cloves, and rosemary. Puree.

3. In a large skillet, heat the oil over medium heat. Add the pepper mixture. Cook, stirring, for 5 minutes, then add the tomato paste, peeled tomatoes, and basil. Stir, bring to a boil, then reduce the heat to low and simmer until the sauce reduces slightly, 5 to 8 more minutes.

4. Meanwhile, cook the spaghetti in boiling, salted water according to the package directions, and drain, reserving 1 cup of the cooking water. Turn the drained spaghetti into the skillet, toss, and cook until all the flavors mingle, about 5 minutes. If the mixture seems too dry, add some of the reserved cooking water. Add the mozzarella and parsley, toss, and serve with the grated pecorino cheese separately.

NOTE: ADD THE MOZZARELLA ONLY AT THE VERY END. IT SHOULD MELT WHILE YOU ARE EATING THE PASTA.

Capellini alla Zia Cettina

Aunt Cettina's Capellini (Makes 6 servings)

CAPELLINI, OR ANGEL HAIR PASTA, WAS always served in broth in my home, especially when someone was sick. It made a soothing and delightful soup.

Nowadays, there seems to be a passion for angel hair pasta. Every Italian restaurant I go to seems to have an offering of it, but I have not yet seen it served in broth. For this reason, I tried capellini in this family recipe, which my aunt Cettina used to make with *tagliolini,* homemade noodles. It worked quite well.

Keep in mind that fine pasta should not be drained too much. If too dry, it tends to clump together. As I suggest, always keep some of the cooking water which you can add to the pasta if it sticks or clumps.

¹⁄₄ cup extra virgin olive oil
1 large clove garlic, peeled and smashed
3 to 4 baby aritichokes, washed, trimmed (see Step 1, page 83) and cut into wedges
About ¹⁄₂ cup water
6 spears asparagus, washed, trimmed, and cut into ¹⁄₂-inch pieces
1 cup frozen peas, defrosted
1 tablespoon unsalted butter
¹⁄₄ pound chopped meat, veal, turkey, or chicken

¹⁄₄ cup dry white wine
1 cup peeled and seeded fresh tomatoes; or same amount canned peeled tomatoes with their juice
Salt to taste, optional
Freshly ground pepper to taste
12 mussels, scrubbed and debearded
12 clams, any kind, scrubbed
6 medium-size shrimp, cooked, peeled, and diced
1 pound capellini or angel hair pasta
1 tablespoon minced fresh parsley

1. In a large skillet, place 3 tablespoons of the oil, the garlic, and artichokes. Add ¹⁄₂ cup water, cover the skillet, and cook over medium heat until the artichokes are almost tender, about 10 minutes. Add the asparagus and, if the juices have reduced too much, add a little more water. Continue cooking 5 minutes longer, until the asparagus is tender, then add the peas and cook just to heat through. Set aside.

2. In a 9-inch saucepan, heat the butter and the remaining oil over medium heat. Add the meat and cook, stirring, until brown, about 10 minutes. Add the wine, and let evaporate. Add the tomatoes and seasoning. Cover and bring to a boil, then reduce the heat to low and simmer for 20 to 25 minutes. Pour this sauce into the skillet with the vegetables. Set aside.

3. In a large skillet, place the mussels and the clams. Cook, shaking the skillet, until they open, 5 to 8 minutes. Remove the mollusks to a bowl as soon as they start to open. Filter any juice remaining in the skillet through paper towels and add to the vegetable-meat sauce. Discard the shells and add the clams, mussels, and the diced shrimp to the sauce. Reheat over low heat just before the pasta is ready.

4. Cook the pasta according to the package directions, drain quickly, reserving 1 cup of the cooking water. Add the pasta to the skillet, or turn it into a pasta serving bowl, add the sauce, and toss. Sprinkle with the parsley and serve.

SPAGHETTI CON LE COZZE

Spaghetti with Mussels *(Makes 6 servings)*

EVERY TIME I MAKE THIS DISH IT IS LIKE filling my kitchen with memories and the scent of the Adriatic. This was such a favorite in my home. We had it often, especially when relatives arrived unannounced, since it was so easy to prepare. In this country, most mussels come from cultivated marine reserves; therefore they are quite clean and safe to eat. But it is still advisable to scrub them before using.

$1^1/_2$ pounds mussels, scrubbed and debearded
$^1/_4$ cup water
1 tablespoon flour or cornmeal
$^1/_4$ cup extra virgin olive oil
2 sprigs fresh parsley

2 cloves garlic, peeled and smashed
1 teaspoon tomato paste
One 16-ounce can tomato puree
2 tablespoons minced fresh parsley
1 pound linguine or spaghetti

1. Place the mussels in a bowl, cover with water, add the flour, and toss. Let stand for 15 to 20 minutes This will make the mussels spit out any residual sand.

2. Rinse the mussels, place them in a large skillet, add the $^1/_4$ cup water, and set over medium heat. Cook, shaking the skillet, until they open, 5 to 8 minutes. As soon as they start to open remove the opened ones to a bowl. Discard the mussels which have not opened.

3. Working over the bowl to collect all the juices, remove the mussels from the shells, discard the shells, and place the mussels in a clean bowl. Strain the juices accumulated in the first bowl through a paper towel and set aside.

4. In a 2-quart saucepan, heat the oil over medium heat. Add the sprigs of parsley and garlic cloves. As soon as the garlic starts to sizzle, add the mussels, and cook, stirring, about 5 minutes.

5. Combine the tomato paste with the mussel liquid and add to the mussels. Stir in the tomatoes from the can. Stir well, cover, and bring to a boil, and immediately reduce the heat to very low. Simmer 15 minutes. Add the minced parsley and remove from the heat.

6. Cook the pasta in boiling, salted water according to the package directions. Drain the pasta and turn it into a pasta serving bowl. Dress with the sauce and serve.

Variation: *Spaghetti alle Vongole* is prepared the same way. I cook the mussels only 5 minutes and omit the tomato.

SPAGHETTI CON LE FAVE E COZZE

Spaghetti with Fava Beans and Mussels (Makes 6 servings)

A HOMEY DISH, SIMPLE AND FLAVORFUL. Having the mussels so readily available, the Abruzzesi use them in many ways. Mixing them with legumes is a specialty from the coastal towns around Vasto.

In my home this simple and flavorful dish was prepared with fresh fava beans in summer, and with the dried favas in the winter.

If you use the dried legume, soak it overnight.

1 pound mussels, scrubbed and debearded
1 tablespoon flour
3 pounds fresh fava beans; or 1 1/2 cups dried, soaked overnight in enough water to cover
3 tablespoons extra virgin olive oil
4 ounces pancetta, in one slice, cut into thin strips

1 medium-size onion, sliced
2 cloves garlic, peeled and smashed
1 small diavoletto (dried Italian hot red pepper), optional
2 sprigs fresh parsley
1 pound spaghetti
1 tablespoon minced fresh parsley

1. Place the mussels in a bowl, cover with water, add the flour, and toss. Let stand for 15 to 20 minutes. This will make the mussels spit out any residual sand.

2. Shell the fresh fava beans and set aside. If you are using the dried kind, drain, remove and discard the outer skin, if any, from the fava beans, and set aside.

3. In a heavy 4-quart pot, heat 1 tablespoon of the oil over medium heat, add the pancetta, and cook, stirring, until slightly brown, about 5 minutes. Add the onion and cook, stirring, until the onion is soft and translucent, 5 minutes longer. Add the fava beans and, cook for a few minutes, stirring, then add 1 1/2 cups of hot water if using fresh favas, or 3 cups for the dried favas. Bring to a boil, then reduce the heat to low, simmer and cook until the favas are tender, 15 to 20 minutes for the fresh, and 40 to 45 minutes for the dried.

4. In a large skillet, heat the remaining oil over medium heat, add the garlic, hot pepper, if used, and the parsley sprigs and cook for about 3 minutes. Drain, rinse, and add the mussels to the skillet with 1/2 cup of water. Cover and cook, shaking the skillet, until they open, about 5 minutes or longer. As soon as they start to open remove the opened ones to a bowl. Discard the mussels which have not opened. Discard the shells. Set the mussels aside. Strain the broth remaining in the skillet through a paper towel. Discard the solids. Add the liquid to the fava beans, and if the favas are done, add the mussels too. Set aside but keep warm.

5. Cook the spaghetti in boiling, salted water according to the package directions. Drain, reserving 1 cup of the cooking water. Combine the spaghetti with the fava beans and the mussels. If the mixture seems dry, add some of the reserved water. Toss and serve with a sprinkling of minced parsley.

SPAGHETTI AI FRUTTI DI MARE

Spaghetti with Seafood (Makes 6 servings)

THIS WAS A DISH THAT WAS EATEN AT least once a week in my home. While our young friends would consider Friday, the day when Catholics are forbidden to eat meat, a day of punishment, in my house it was almost a feast. We knew that Papà was making one of his favorite specialties, the *spaghetti ai frutti di mare*, spaghetti with "the fruits of the sea." It was so well liked in the family that when relatives came to dinner, they would often request this dish.

My father always put one or two whitings in the sauce. These delicately flavored fish were abundant in the Adriatic Sea. It is difficult to find good whitings here, but a monkfish is a good substitute.

$^1/_4$ pound medium-size shrimp
1 sprig fresh parsley
1 small diavoletto *(dried Italian hot red pepper), optional*
2 cloves garlic, peeled
12 small clams, scrubbed and washed
18 mussels, scrubbed and debearded
1 bay leaf
$^1/_4$ *cup water*
6 tablespoons extra virgin olive oil
$^1/_2$ *pound squid, cleaned and cut into circles*
$^3/_4$ *cup dry white wine*

1 teaspoon tomato paste
One 28-ounce can peeled tomatoes, with their juice
2 small whiting, about $^1/_2$ *pound total, gutted with head on if possible; or 1 monkfish tail, about* $^1/_2$ *pound*
1 pound spaghetti or linguine
$^1/_4$ *pound scallops, cut into 4 pieces if large*
Salt to taste, optional
Freshly ground pepper to taste
2 tablespoons minced fresh parsley

1. Peel the shrimp but do not discard the shells. Tie the shells in a cheesecloth together with the parsley sprig, hot pepper, if used, and 1 clove of garlic. Set aside. Devein the shrimp and cut in half lengthwise. Set aside.

2. In a large skillet, place the clams and mussels, add the bay leaf and water. Cover and set on the heat. Steam, shaking the skillet once or twice, until they open, about 5 minutes or longer. Remove the lid and take out all the clams and mussels that have opened. Set these in a bowl to cool. Discard the unopened ones. Strain the liquid accumulated in the skillet through a coffee filter or paper towel and reserve. Working over a bowl to collect all the juices, remove the clams and mussels from their shells. Discard the shells but keep 18 half-shells to garnish the pasta.

3. In a large skillet, heat 3 tablespoons of the oil over medium heat. Chop the remaining garlic clove and add. Cook, about 2 to 3 seconds, then add the bundle with the shell mixture. Cook, turning the bundle 2 or 3 times, until the flavor is released, about 3 to 5 minutes. Add the squid. Cook, stirring, 2 to 3 minutes, then add the wine. Let it reduce by half.

continues

4. Add the tomato paste and the can of peeled tomatoes. Break up the tomatoes with a wooden spoon. Cover the skillet, and bring to a boil over medium heat, then reduce the heat and cook over very low heat until the squid is tender, about 40 minutes. Stir often; if the sauce looks a little dry add some or all of the liquid collected from the clams and mussels. Push the bundle with the shells to one side of the skillet and place the whiting or monkfish in the middle of the skillet. Cover and continue cooking until the fish is done, 8 minutes for the whiting, 15 for the monkfish. Remove the fish to a plate, and when cool, discard the skin and bones and flake the fish. Set aside.

5. Remove the skillet from the heat but keep warm. Remove the bundle with the shells, squeeze out as much juice as possible into the skillet, and discard the bundle.

6. Cook the pasta in boiling, salted water according to the package directions.

7. When the pasta is almost ready, return the skillet to the heat, add the remaining juices from the clams and mussels, if any, and add the scallops and shrimp. Cook until the shrimp become red and the scallops opaque, about 8 to 10 minutes. Return the flaked fish to the skillet. Season with salt, if used, and the pepper. Add the remaining 3 tablespoons of the oil, stir, and remove from the heat.

8. Drain the pasta and turn it into the skillet if large enough, or use a pasta serving bowl. Toss the pasta with the fish sauce. Sprinkle with the minced parsley, toss again, and serve. Garnish the bowl, or the individual plates, with the reserved shells.

A WORD ABOUT SQUID

A crucial ingredient in Spaghetti with Seafood, squid should be cooked very little when poached or pan-fried. But when used in a sauce or *brodetto*, fish stew, the cooking time should be from 45 minutes to an hour. What happens is this: After about 3 to 5 minutes of cooking, the squid toughens. To make it tender again, you must cook it until it gets soft again. In this recipe and similar ones, you want as much flavor as possible from the little beast, therefore cook it longer.

LINGUINE AL SUGO DI RAZZA

Linguine with Ray Sauce (*Makes 4 to 6 servings*)

I'M SO GLAD THAT THE DELICATE RAY, OR skate, is becoming more popular in this country. In Italy it has always been much appreciated. In my home, this dish was a Friday special.

The ray was so fresh and slithery. I was always fascinated by the dexterity of our maid, Annina, in removing its head and the skin, leaving the beautiful wings intact. When small rays were used, they were just gutted because, according to expert fish cookers, the heads give a good flavor to a sauce, as do the bones.

In this country, most of the time, ray is cleaned and skinned, and only the wings, with bones removed are sold. But for this recipe try to get a ray with the bones. It will give much more flavor to the sauce.

*One 2-pound (approximately) ray fish,
   gutted, head removed, and skinned*
¼ cup extra virgin olive oil
2 cloves garlic, peeled and chopped
1 sprig fresh rosemary, or ½ teaspoon dried

2 tablespoons minced fresh parsley
*One 28-ounce can peeled tomatoes,
   drained*
1 pound linguine

1. Cut the ray into 5 or 6 pieces and set aside.

2. In a 10-inch skillet, heat the oil over medium heat and add the garlic, rosemary, and pieces of fish. Cook the fish, turning the pieces around at least once, about 5 minutes. Remove the rosemary and add half the parsley and the tomatoes. Bring to a boil over medium heat, then reduce the heat to low and cook at a simmer until the fish is cooked and the sauce has gained its flavor, about 10 minutes.

3. Meanwhile, cook the linguine in boiling, salted water according to the package directions.

4. Remove the fish from the sauce, let cool, and flake it, discarding the bones. Return the flaked fish to the sauce, and heat through. Add the remaining parsley.

5. Drain the linguine and dress with the sauce.

BUCATINI AL SUGO DI SEPPIA

Bucatini with Squid Sauce **(Makes 6 servings)**

ONE SUMMER, MY DEAR FRIEND LELLA Delfino Spiga arrived for our appointment at the restaurant Da Michele in Pescara, breathless and waving a piece of paper on which a recipe was hurriedly written. I was having a grand dinner with a group I had brought to Abruzzo from the French Culinary Institute of New York. Lella and I hadn't seen each other in a year and since she had organized the dinner, I invited her to stay. We had a great time, and later on her husband and daughter also joined us. Since they all spoke English, my group enjoyed the added thrill of being entertained by local people.

The recipe, Lella told me, was given to her by a local fisherman, and I must put it in the book. They had cooked the dish on the fisherman's boat during a fishing expedition she had participated in. Here it is. It is a savory dish with the briny taste of the sea, blended with the tenacious aroma of fresh garlic and the sweetness of dried peppers.

6 medium-size squid with tentacles, cleaned
6 small sprigs fresh parsley
6 small cloves garlic, peeled
3 dried sweet peppers (see box)
3 tablespoons extra virgin olive oil
1 large clove garlic, chopped
2 cups tomato puree
³/₄ cup water
Salt to taste, optional
Freshly ground pepper to taste
1 small diavoletto (dried Italian hot red pepper), optional
1 pound bucatini or linguine
1 tablespoon minced fresh parsley

1. Stuff each squid with its tentacles, 1 sprig of parsley, and 1 clove of garlic. Secure with strings or a toothpick. Set aside.

2. Remove the stems and seeds from the dried sweet peppers and grind them very finely in a food processor. Set aside.

3. In a heavy sauté pan, into which the squid can be placed in one layer, place the oil, and add the chopped garlic. Before the oil gets too hot, add the dried sweet peppers. Cook, stirring, over low heat for 1 minute, being careful not to burn the peppers. Add the squid and sauté for 5 to 8 minutes, turning them often. Add the tomato puree, water, seasoning, and hot pepper, if used. Cover the pan and bring to a boil over medium heat, then reduce the heat to low and simmer until the squid are tender, about 45 minutes. If the sauce reduces too much, add a little more water.

4. Cook the pasta in boiling, salted water, according to the package directions. Drain and turn into a pasta serving bowl.

5. Remove the squid to a plate, untie them, and remove the string or toothpick. Dress the pasta with the sauce, sprinkle with the minced parsley, and toss. Serve, placing 1 squid on each plate.

NOTE: THE DRIED PEPPERS ARE AVAILABLE IN ITALIAN SPECIALTY STORES AND PRODUCE STORES. TWO TABLESPOONS OF SWEET PAPRIKA ARE A GOOD SUBSTITUTE.

SPAGHETTI AL CARTOCCIO

Spaghetti in a Pouch *(Makes 6 servings)*

THIS DISH IS A NEW ADDITION TO THE gastronomy of Abruzzo. I certainly never ate it when I was growing up. Now, however, many restaurants on the coast will present you, with great flourish, this funny looking package which, when opened, assaults you with the most marvelous marine scent.

It is an amusing dish for a dinner party. It never fails to make an impression when brought to the table, especially if you manage to crimp the foil in the shape of a boat or a fish.

3 medium-size half-ripe tomatoes
10 clams
10 mussels, debearded
1 tablespoon flour
1/4 cup extra virgin olive oil
2 cloves garlic, peeled and smashed
1 small diavoletto *(dried Italian hot red pepper), optional*
8 medium-size fresh shrimp, peeled, deveined, and diced, shells reserved

About 3/4 cup cold water
1 1/2 pounds squid, cleaned and cut into thin circles
1/2 cup dry white wine
1/2 pound red snapper, preferably whole, clean and ready to cook
4 or 5 fresh basil leaves
8 large scallops, quartered
1 pound spaghetti
1 tablespoon minced fresh parsley

1. Preheat the oven to 450°F.

2. Plunge the tomatoes in boiling water for 1 minute. Drain and let cool. Peel the tomatoes, discard the seeds, and dice. Set aside.

3. Set the clams and mussels in a bowl, cover with cold water, and add the flour. Toss and let stand for 15 to 20 minutes.

continues

4. In a 10-inch skillet, heat 3 tablespoons of the oil over medium heat. Add the garlic and the hot pepper, if used, and cook until the garlic starts to sizzle, about 2 minutes. Add the reserved shells from the shrimp. Cook, stirring, for 5 minutes, then add the water. Bring to a boil over high heat, reduce the heat to low, cover, and cook at a simmer for 5 minutes. Strain this sauce in a colander and return it to the skillet. Bring to a boil, add the squid, and cook about 5 minutes. Add the wine. Cover and cook the squid over low heat until tender, about 30 minutes. If the liquid reduces too much, add some water to let the squid cook *in umido,* with humidity.

5. Add the red snapper and cook, turning once or twice, until it starts to flake when touched with a fork, 8 to 10 minutes; cook about 5 minutes longer if the fish is on the bone. Remove the fish to a plate, cool, bone it if whole, and flake it. Return the fish to the skillet, add the tomatoes and basil, and cook 5 minutes. Add the diced shrimp and the scallops and cook about 5 minutes.

6. Drain the clams and the mussels, rinse them, and add them to the skillet, cover, and cook, shaking the skillet, until the mollusks open, 5 to 8 minutes. As soon as the clams and mussels start to open, remove the skillet from the heat. Discard the unopened ones. Add the remaining olive oil.

7. Preheat the oven to 450°F.

8. While preparing the sauce, cook the spaghetti in boiling, salted water for about 8 minutes. The pasta should not be stiff. Drain, but not too much. Combine the spaghetti with the fish sauce. Without removing the shells of the mussels and clams, add them along with the parsley.

9. On a cookie sheet, place a large sheet of heavy-duty aluminum foil. Pour the spaghetti lengthwise in the middle of the foil. Fold the foil to enclose the spaghetti and crimp to seal. Bake 15 minutes. The pasta will not overcook. Place the pouch on a serving platter. Open the pouch at the table and serve.

MACCHERONI ESTIVI CON LA SALSA CRUDA

Summer Pasta with Uncooked Tomato Sauce (Makes 6 servings)

IT IS ESSENTIAL TO USE THE BEST, FRESH, ripest tomatoes in this sauce. Therefore, try this dish only in summer when vine-ripened tomatoes are available. If you follow these rules, you will eat an unforgettable dish, redolent of all the summer perfumes.

This is, of course, a pasta that can be eaten at room temperature—not cold. I detest cold pasta, but given its popularity in this country, I cannot avoid proposing some recipes for it in this book. But please do not even think of putting this pasta in the refrigerator. Also, If you really want to eat cold pasta, eat it at room temperature only and avoid adding grated cheese, which will make your pasta gooey. The mozzarella is all right, but add it just before serving.

4 to 5 tablespoons extra virgin olive
2 cloves garlic, peeled and smashed
1 tablespoon tomato paste
5 or 6 ripe tomatoes, coarsely chopped
½ cup loosely packed fresh basil leaves, snipped
A few flakes of hot red pepper flakes, optional
1 cup canned, pitted black California olives, cut into circles
1 pound fusilli, penne, or rigatoni
One 8-ounce mozzarella di bufalo, diced

1. In a pasta serving bowl, place all the ingredients except the pasta and mozzarella. Toss and let it stand at room temperature for 30 minutes or longer.

2. Cook the pasta according to the package directions. Drain and add to the pasta bowl. Toss well, sprinkle with the mozzarella, and serve.

MACCHERONI AL GRATIN

Aunt Ela's Macaroni Gratin **(Makes 4 to 6 servings)**

MY BELOVED AUNT ELA, THE MOTHER OF my three cousins, Gianna, Franca, and Adriana, used to say that she had four daughters, and I was the first one since I was the oldest of the girls of the house.

I spent many summers with my Aunt Ela and her husband Raffaele, called Raf. From the very beginning, I had a crush on Uncle Raf. Not only had he come with a shiny car, the first in the family, but he had a passion for picnics, loved to hike mountains, and go on rides to the many scenic villages of the surrounding area. He would not hesitate to pack his fiancée, us children, and a chaperone (which was *de rigueur* at that time), who would fit into the not-very-big Balilla Fiat and go.

When we went on these outings with Uncle Raf, most of the time we brought food for a picnic. Sometimes, though we would stop at a rustic *osteria*, country inn, to eat *porchetta*. This is a young pig, roasted in a wood-burning oven, and is a specialty of Abruzzo.

But before leaving the house on a family outing, Aunt Ela would prepare her famous *maccheroni al gratin*, a pasta dressed with *salsa balsamella* (béchamel sauce), mozzarella, and parmesan cheese. It would be baked on our return. Hot, light, and a little crunchy at the top, it was delicious and just right after a day in the wilderness.

Unsalted butter
1 pound penne or rigatoni
¹/₄ cup heavy cream
Freshly grated pepper to taste

1 cup Salsa Balsamella (page 92)
One 8-ounce mozzarella, diced
¹/₂ cup freshly grated parmesan cheese

1. Preheat the oven to 375°F. Butter a gratin dish from which you can serve, and where the pasta can be spread evenly and not more than 2 inches high. Set aside.

2. Cook the pasta in boiling, salted water according to the package directions. Drain well, turn into a mixing bowl, and add all the remaining ingredients except the parmesan cheese. Toss well and add half of the parmesan cheese and 1 tablespoon of butter. Toss again and turn the mixture into the prepared pan. Smooth the pasta evenly on the top, sprinkle with the remaining parmesan, and dot with ¹/₂ tablespoon butter. Bake until top starts to brown, 40 to 45 minutes.

NOTE: YOU CAN FINISH THIS UNDER THE BROILER (5 TO 10 MINUTES WILL DO) TO GIVE THE DISH A MORE CRUSTY LOOK.

Aunt Ela

PASTA CON CAVOLFIORE BIANCO O NERO

Pasta with White or Purple Cauliflower *(Makes 6 servings)*

TWICE A YEAR, IN THE SPRING AND THE fall, the newly established green markets of America sport lovely cauliflower in its many colors: candid white, mellow green, and dramatic purple. They are so esthetically beautiful to me that, when I have a dinner party, I use them to compose an edible centerpiece for the table or a still life for the living room.

A versatile vegetable, the cauliflower can be used for many dishes, from antipasti to salad. Choose the freshest you can get, and, if you prefer the white kind, make sure they are unblemished and have green and squeaky leaves at the base of the head. The following dish, with a tomato-cauliflower sauce, was prepared in my house in the fall and the spring.

1 medium-size head cauliflower, white or purple
1 medium-size onion, quartered
1 medium-size carrot, peeled and cut into 4 pieces
1 clove garlic, peeled
3 tablespoons extra virgin olive of oil
One 28-ounce can peeled tomatoes, with their juice
5 fresh basil leaves, or 1 teaspoon dried
5 fresh oregano leaves, or ¼ teaspoon dried
Leaves from 1 small sprig fresh rosemary, or ½ teaspoon dried
Salt to taste, optional
Freshly ground pepper to taste
1 small diavoletto (dried Italian hot red pepper), optional
3 tablespoons kosher salt
1 pound macaroni (penne, fusilli, rigatoni, or small shells)

1. Wash and trim the cauliflower and separate it into flowerets. Cut the tender stems into bite-size pieces. Set aside. Reserve the larger stems to peel and slice into a salad.

2. In a food processor, chop the onion, carrot, and garlic.

3. In a 3-quart pot, heat the oil over medium heat. Add the chopped vegetables and cook, stirring, until wilted, about 5 to 8 minutes. Add the tomatoes, herbs, seasoning, and *diavoletto,* if used. Bring to a boil over medium heat, reduce the heat to low, and simmer 20 to 25 minutes.

4. Bring a 4-quart pot of water to a boil over high heat and plunge the cauliflower in. Boil until partially cooked, about 8 minutes, then remove the cauliflower with a slotted spoon. Do not discard the cooking water. Add the cauliflower to the pan with the tomato sauce and continue cooking until the cauliflower is tender but not mushy, about 10 minutes.

5. Bring the cauliflower cooking water back to a boil. Add the kosher salt and as soon as the water comes back to a boil, add the pasta. Cook according to the package directions until al dente. Drain the pasta and dress with the cauliflower-tomato sauce.

NOTE: IF YOU WISH, YOU CAN SERVE THIS PASTA WITH GRATED PECORINO ROMANO CHEESE.

PASTA AFFUMICATA

Smoked Pasta *(Makes 6 servings)*

THIS RECIPE IS AN INVENTION OF MINE. You must have a good smoked mozzarella, preferably fresh, because the flavor of the pasta sauce depends on it. It is a satisfying and filling little dish, practically a meal in itself, which I round out with just a good, juicy pear. Sometimes, I am even tempted to slice the pear into the pasta. Well, you can try!

You must know that cheese and pears are a favorite Italian dessert. We have a proverb, a little nasty perhaps, reflecting this fondness. "*Al cafon non far saper quant'è buon formaggio e per.*" ("Don't let the peasant know how good his cheese and pear are together.") It means that if the *cafon*, peasant, learns to eat these good things himself, he will not bring them to the market anymore.

1 pound penne, rigatoni, fusilli,
or small shells
2 cups ricotta

4 ounces fresh mozzarella, diced
4 ounces fresh smoked mozzarella, diced

1. Cook the pasta in boiling, salted water according to the package directions.

2. Place the ricotta in a heated shallow pasta serving bowl.

3. Drain the pasta, reserving 1 cup of the cooking water. Stir $^1/_4$ cup of the cooking water into the ricotta. Add the pasta and toss. If the mixture seems too dry add a little more of the reserved water. Sprinkle the pasta with the two mozzarellas. Toss once and serve.

NOTE: THE MOZZARELLAS SHOULD MELT ON THE HOT PASTA WHILE EATING.

FUSILLI PINOLATI

Fusilli with Pine Nuts *(Makes 6 servings)*

HERE'S AN UNUSUAL SAUCE OF RICOTTA cheese, spinach, roasted red pepper, and pine nuts, which my cousin Franca prepared for me on a recent visit to Italy. It pleased me so much, not only because it was a delicious dish, but because it proved, once again, that in the family there are still good inventive cooks, as in the time of our grand-mothers.

1 pound whole-milk ricotta
½ cup pinoli, pine nuts
1 red bell pepper, roasted until blackened
*   on all sides, peeled, seeded*
*   (see Step 1, page 117), and diced*
1 tablespoon extra virgin olive oil
1 clove garlic, peeled and minced

1 pound fresh spinach, trimmed and
*   washed, the leaves cut in half*
1 pound fusilli or small shells
2 tablespoons unsalted butter
Freshly grated grana padano or
*   parmesan cheese*
Freshly ground pepper to taste

1. Preheat the oven to 200°F.

2. In a pasta serving bowl, combine the ricotta, pine nuts, and bell pepper. Set aside.

3. In a large skillet, heat the oil over medium heat. Add the garlic and cook until it sizzles, then add the spinach, toss, and cook until the spinach has wilted. Turn the mixture into the pasta serving bowl, mix well, cover with aluminum foil, and set the bowl in the oven. Leave the door ajar.

4. Cook the pasta in boiling, salted water according to the package directions. Drain, reserving 1 cup of the cooking water.

5. Remove the bowl from the oven and add the pasta to the spinach-ricotta mix-ture. Add ½ cup of the reserved water and toss well. If the mixture seems dry, add more water. Add the butter, mix again, and serve with the grated cheese and a touch of pepper separately.

PENNETTE RIGATE AL SUGO DI GAMBERI

Grooved Penne with Shrimp Sauce *(Makes 6 servings)*

IN ABRUZZO THIS SAUCE IS MADE WITH *panocchie* or *cannocchie,* a flat, pinkish crustacean, 8 inches long and about 2 inches wide, which is found only in the Adriatic Sea and Japan. The name in English is squil or mantis shrimp. It is the sweetest crustacean you can eat.

Because the *pannocchie* are cut into small pieces, the sauce, which is ubiquitous in many *trattorie* along our shores, is served over spaghetti or linguine. Since I use small shrimp, which I peel, devein, and cut lengthwise, I prefer small, grooved penne.

To give the sauce a more fragrant marine flavor, I add a handful of clams.

1 1/2 pounds small fresh shrimp
1/4 cup extra virgin olive oil
1 bay leaf
1 sprig fresh parsley
2 cloves garlic, peeled and chopped
1 diavoletto *(dried Italian hot red pepper), optional*

1 teaspoon tomato paste
One 16-ounce can peeled tomatoes, with their juice
24 clams, any size, scrubbed
1 clove garlic, peeled and smashed
1 pound grooved penne rigate
1 tablespoon minced fresh parsley

1. Soak the shrimp in salted water for 10 minutes to refresh them, then rinse (see Note). Peel the shrimp, reserving the shells. Devein the shrimp, cut in half lengthwise, and set aside.

2. In a 9-inch skillet, heat the oil over medium heat. Add the bay leaf and the parsley sprig and cook, stirring until the flavor of the herbs comes through. Add the chopped garlic, the hot pepper, if used, and the shrimp shells. Cook, stirring, about 5 mintues. Add the tomato paste and the peeled tomatoes. Cover the skillet and simmer over low heat for 15 minutes.

3. Place the clams in a large skillet and add 1/2 cup water and the clove of garlic. Cover, set over medium heat, and cook, shaking the skillet, until the clams open, 5 to 8 minutes. As soon as the clams start to open, remove the open ones to a bowl. Discard the unopened ones. Reserve any liquid remaining in the skillet. Working over a bowl to collect any liquid, remove the clams from the shells. Strain the clam liquid through a paper towel and add to the cooking sauce. Set the clams aside.

4. Strain the tomato sauce in a colander, pushing the solids to extract all the juices. Discard the solids and return the sauce to the skillet. If the sauce seems too watery, reduce a little, otherwise add the shrimp and cook until they turn red, 5 to 8 minutes. Add the clams and cook just to heat throughout.

5. Cook the pasta in boiling, salted water according to the package directions. Drain. Turn into a pasta serving bowl and dress with the shrimp sauce. Sprinkle with the minced parsley and serve.

NOTE 1: IF YOU WISH, AND ESPECIALLY IF THE CLAMS ARE SMALL, YOU CAN LEAVE THEM IN THEIR SHELLS. BUT MAKE SURE, WHEN YOU SERVE THE PASTA, TO PLACE SOME LITTLE BOWLS STRATEGICALLY ON THE TABLE WHERE THE GUESTS CAN DISCARD THE SHELLS.

NOTE 2: MY FRIEND, MARK BITTMAN, THE AUTHOR OF A WONDERFUL AND INSTRUCTIVE BOOK, *FISH* (MACMILLAN), TAUGHT ME ALWAYS TO "BRINE" SHRIMP. THIS MEANS TO KEEP THE SHRIMP IN A BATH OF SALTED WATER FOR 15 TO 20 MINUTES. IT WILL REVITALIZE THE SHRIMP SINCE THEY ARE VERY SELDOM SOLD FRESH. THEY ARE FLASH FROZEN ON THE FISHING BOAT AND DEFROSTED AT THE FISH MARKET.

PASTA CON GAMBERI E CARCIOFI

Pasta with Shrimp and Artichokes   **(Makes 6 servings)**

I REMEMBER THE DISMAY MY MOTHER FELT when she found a choke in an artichoke. She would sigh and say, "What a pity the artichoke season is finished, we have to wait for next year!" This would happen at the beginning of every summer, and we were all sad for this announcement since we all loved artichokes.

In this country we have artichokes all the time—huge, tough, and full of choke. Because of my mother, I avoid them totally. I use baby artichokes. Living in New York, I can find them quite easily, but not so in other parts of the country. Frozen artichokes are quite acceptable in these recipes; they are certainly much better than those woody monster globes into which one has to dig for the choke as if it were a

Extra virgin olive oil
3/4 pound medium-size shrimp, peeled and deveined, shells reserved
4 cloves garlic, peeled
4 sprigs fresh parsley
1/2 cup dry white wine
2 teaspoons tomato paste
1 1/2 cups water
8 baby artichokes, preferably with stems
1 pound short pasta, such as penne, fusilli, rigatoni, or bow ties
2 tablespoons minced fresh parsley

1. In a 2-quart saucepan, heat 1 tablespoon of the oil. Add the shrimp shells and cook, stirring, about 5 minutes. Smash 1 clove of garlic and add it to the skillet together with 1 sprig of parsley. Cook, stirring, until the parsley has wilted, about 3 minutes. Add the wine and tomato paste. Cook, stirring, for 5 minutes. Add the water, cover, and bring to a boil, then reduce the heat to low and cook at a simmer for 30 minutes.

2. Prepare the artichokes: Remove the tough leaves from the artichokes, trim the tops, and peel the stems. Cut the artichokes in 4 or 6 wedges, according to their size. Keep the finished artichoke pieces in a bowl of acidulated water to prevent discoloration.

3. Chop together 1 garlic of clove and 1 sprig of parsley.

continues

hidden treasure. In fact I think that, among the frozen vegetables, artichokes and peas, especially peas, are often better than the fresh.

4. In a 10-inch skillet, heat 2 more tablespoons of the oil over medium heat. Add the garlic-parsley mixture and cook, stirring, for about 3 seconds. Add the artichokes and $1/2$ cup of the acidulated water. Cover and let the artichokes cook over low heat for 10 minutes. Remove the cover and, if there is still some water, let it evaporate, then stir-fry the artichokes until tender, about 5 minutes longer.

5. Strain the shell broth in a colander, pushing on the solids to extract as much juice as possible. Discard the solids. Set the broth aside but keep warm.

6. Wipe the saucepan in which the shells were cooked and add 2 more tablespoons of the oil. Heat over medium heat. Add the remaining 2 cloves of garlic and sprigs of parsley and cook, stirring, until they start to sizzle, about 3 minutes. Add the shrimp and cook, stirring, until the shrimp turn red, about 5 to 8 minutes. Add the artichokes and the shrimp broth. If you have too much liquid, slightly reduce over high heat for a few minutes. The sauce should be thin. Remove from the heat. Just before the pasta is ready, reheat this sauce.

7. Cook the pasta in boiling, salted water according to the package directions. Drain and dress with the shrimp sauce. Sprinkle with the minced parsley and serve.

PASTA MARE E GIARDINO

Sea and Garden Pasta *(Makes 6 servings)*

IN THESE DAYS WHEN MEDITERRANEAN food is heralded so much, I cannot help remembering the enthusiasm with which my family embraced the fresh, and, at times, unusual vegetables our maid Annina would bring back from the green market. She used to go to the green market at five in the morning to get the best and the freshest produce, and later on, when the farmers were ready to go home, for the bargains. Squishy tomatoes were her best bargain and biggest pride because, being really ripe, they would make the sweetest sauce. The overripe fruits would make delicious jams and pies, all for a fraction of the price the farmers had been asking in the early hours. She would have loved the delicate snap peas—unknown in Italy then—that I added to this family recipe. Like my family, I love vegetables.

We used to call this dish *Mare e Giardino* because it contains the fruits of the garden and those of the sea.

6 tablespoons extra virgin olive oil
2 cloves garlic, peeled and smashed
2 sprigs fresh parsley
2 shallots, chopped
1 basket, about 1 pint, ripe cherry tomatoes, cut in half
2 or 3 leaves fresh basil, or 1/4 teaspoon dried
1/2 pound sugar snap peas
2 cloves garlic, peeled and chopped
1/2 pound small shrimp, peeled, deveined, and diced
1/2 pound scallops, quartered if large
1/2 cup shucked clams, chopped
3/4 cup bottled clam juice
4 scallions, trimmed, washed, and coarsely chopped
1 pound fusilli
2 tablespoons minced fresh parsley

1. In a 10-inch skillet, heat 3 tablespoons of the oil over medium heat. Add the smashed garlic and the sprigs of parsley and cook until the garlic starts to sizzle and their flavor explodes, about 2 to 3 minutes, then remove the garlic and the parsley and discard. Add the shallots to the skillet and cook, stirring, until soft and translucent, about 5 minutes. Add the tomatoes and basil and cook about 5 minutes. Add the sugar snap peas and cook, stirring, about 5 minutes, then turn the whole into a bowl. Set aside.

2. Wipe the skillet clean and add the remaining oil. Heat the oil over medium heat, add the chopped garlic, and cook until the garlic starts to sizzle, about 2 to 3 minutes. Add the shrimp and cook about 8 to 10 minutes. Add the scallops and cook, stirring, until they turn opaque, about 5 to 8 minutes, then add the clams, stir, and cook until heated through, a few seconds. With a slotted spoon, remove the whole to the bowl with the vegetables. Add the clam broth to the skillet, bring to a boil, and add the scallions. Cook a few minutes and set aside but keep warm.

3. Cook the pasta in boiling, salted water according to the package directions. Drain.

4. Add the pasta to the serving bowl and toss. Serve sprinkled with the chopped parsley.

Pasta all'Amatriciana (Matriciana)

Pasta in the Style of Amatrice (Makes 4 to 6 servings)

A WELL-KNOWN RECIPE, THIS ONE, A classic, is fortunately still being served in good Italian restaurants in the United States. I say fortunately, because, with the mania of being new and innovative, some of these excellent, traditional dishes are being discarded.

How many people know that *Pasta all'Amatriciana* or *Matriciana* originated in Abruzzo? The town of Amatrice borders on the region of Lazio, of which Rome is the capital, and Abruzzo. Nowadays, though, because this town is part of the Lazio jurisdiction, its most famous recipe is often referred to as being part of the Roman cuisine. So be it.

2 tablespoons extra virgin olive oil
1 medium-size onion, chopped
¼ pound pancetta or prosciutto, in 1 slice, diced
¼ cup dry white wine
1 teaspoon tomato paste
1 pound fresh, ripe tomatoes, peeled, seeded, and chopped; or one 16-ounce can peeled tomatoes, with their juice

Freshly ground pepper to taste
A few flakes diavoletto *(dried Italian hot red pepper)*
1 pound penne or ziti
Freshly grated pecorino romano cheese or a combination of pecorino and parmesan

1. In a 10-inch skillet, heat the oil over medium heat. Add the onion and cook, stirring, until it is soft and translucent, about 5 to 8 minutes. Add the pancetta, or prosciutto, and cook briefly, stirring, until it releases its flavor, about 5 to 8 minutes. Add the wine and let evaporate. Stir in the tomato paste, tomatoes, pepper, and *diavoletto*, if used. Bring to a boil over medium heat, reduce the heat to low, and simmer about 15 to 20 minutes.

2. Meanwhile, cook the pasta in boiling, salted water according to the package directions. Drain and dress with the sauce. Serve with the grated cheese separately.

PENNE AL COCCIO

Penne in an Earthenware Pan (Makes 4 to 6 servings)

THIS DELICIOUS DISH OF PASTA, WHOSE sauce is cooked in a *coccio*, or earthenware pan, is a recipe invented in a huff when two friends of mine from Italy, were visiting New York. We had spent the day sightseeing and eaten at the delightful Union Square Cafe restaurant. In the evening, we were not really hungry, perhaps just a bite would be fine.

The inspiration came from a bag of dried porcini mushrooms—a permanent fixture in my house—and a box of frozen peas. I was particularly happy when I noticed the peas, which I thought would give a touch of color to the drabness of the mushrooms. And I was right. When I presented the dish in the earthenware pan, it looked lovely and appetizing, rustic yet elegant at the same time.

The truffle paste I added to the sauce at the end was a stroke of luck. I had a bit of it left from an extravagant past dinner. On other occasions I have not used the paste, since there was none in the house, but I assure you, it does go very well with this dish. So when you make it, splurge a little. It is worth it.

To make my earthenware pan more presentable, I tie a colorful napkin to the handle before bringing it to the table.

2 tablespoons unsalted butter
1 tablespoon extra virgin olive oil
1/4 pound prosciutto or ham, chopped
3/4 cup dried porcini mushrooms, soaked in 3/4 cup lukewarm water
1 1/2 cups frozen peas, thawed
1 cup heavy cream
1 tablespoon truffle paste, optional (see Note)
1 pound penne
Freshly grated parmesan cheese

1. Heat the butter and oil in a large, heatproof earthenware pan or skillet over medium heat. Add the prosciutto, or ham, and cook, stirring, until it releases its flavor, about 5 minutes.

2. Gently lift the mushrooms from the water. Reserve the water. Chop the mushrooms coarsely and add to the pan. Strain the water from the mushrooms through a paper towel and add a little to the pan. Cook the mushrooms until they are tender, for about 10 minutes. Add more of the mushroom water, a little at a time, while cooking. Before all the water evaporates, add the peas and cook until heated through. Add the cream, bring to a boil over medium heat, and stir in the truffle paste, if used. Set aside, but keep warm.

3. Cook the pasta in boiling, salted water according to the package directions. Drain and pour the penne into the pan with the sauce. Toss well and serve with a bowl of freshly grated parmesan cheese.

NOTE: TRUFFLE PASTE IS SOLD IN ITALIAN SPECIALTY STORES, ALONG WITH TRUFFLE OIL. A COUPLE OF SPOONS OF TRUFFLE OIL, ADDED AT THE END, IS A GOOD SUBSTITUTE.

IL COCCIO

In Italy, many things are cooked in a *coccio*, a special earthenware pan. My grandmother and mother swore by them; they felt that in order to retain the true flavor of food, *il coccio* was a must. Unfortunately, I possess only one *coccio*, but in it go my beans, lentils, chick peas, chicken stews, and much more.

RIGATONI ALLA MAIELLA CON SALSA ALLO ZAFFERANO

Rigatoni Maiella Style with Saffron Sauce **(Makes 4 to 6 servings)**

THIS RECIPE, ADAPTED BY ME, IS A creation of Dr. Bruno Adriano Piselli, the dietitian of the Del Verde Pasta Factory (see box). This dish, with its little *ragù* of native lamb and local saffron, has a true Abruzzese flavor.

2 tablespoons extra virgin olive oil
1 clove garlic, peeled and chopped
1 medium-size onion, chopped
1/2 pound minced lamb
1/2 cup dry white wine
1 teaspoon saffron, preferably in powder
1 cup broth of your choice, preferably homemade (pages 61 to 64)

1 leaf fresh sage, or 1/4 teaspoon dried (see Note)
1 diavoletto (dried Italian hot red pepper), optional
Salt to taste, optional
1 pound rigatoni
2 large eggs, beaten
Freshly grated pecorino romano cheese

1. Heat the oil in a 10-inch skillet over medium heat. Add the garlic and stir briefly. Add the onion and cook, stirring, over medium heat until soft and translucent, about 5 minutes. Add the meat and cook, stirring, until brown, about 10 to 15 minutes. Add the wine and let evaporate.

2. Dissolve the saffron in the broth and add to the meat. Add the sage, hot pepper, and salt, if used. Cover and simmer over low heat, stirring often, 25 to 30 minutes.

3. Cook the pasta in boiling, salted water according to the package directions. Drain the pasta and return it to the pot. Add the beaten eggs, toss, and add the sauce. Cook over low heat, stirring, until the mixture is well-bound together, about 5 minutes. Serve with the pecorino romano cheese.

NOTE: DR. PISELLI SERVED THE DISH WITH A GRACEFUL GARNISH OF ADDITIONAL FRESH SAGE LEAVES.

PASTA MADE AT HOME

Homemade Pasta: Noodles, Stuffed Pasta, Gnocchi, and Crepes

There is nothing more rewarding than a good dish of homemade pasta. The look of surprise on the faces of my guests or pupils when they taste a strand of homemade tagliatelle for the first time makes up for all the work I might have done.

No doubt this pasta is delicious, but it isn't the kind one should eat every day. Apart from containing eggs, homemade pasta usually calls for a rich sauce. But this rule is changing. We are now dressing homemade noodles with fish sauces and even filling ravioli and lasagna with fish. In the past this was unheard of. As for gnocchi, I like them simply coated with a tomato sauce. These light sauces make eating homemade pasta possible more frequently.

Whatever sauce you prefer, do not deprive yourself of such delicious treats entirely. Do as the Italians do, reserve homemade pastas for special occasions—Sundays, birthdays, the arrival of guests, etc.

Some people balk at the idea of making pasta. But it is not difficult and it isn't all that time-consuming. Once you have "taken the hand at it," as we Italians say, it will become easy. You do not need much equipment either: a simple hand-cranked pasta machine, a wooden board for kneading the dough, a tablecloth on which to lay your sheets of pasta, and cookie sheets covered with kitchen towels on which to dry your finished product.

Of course, if you want to make stuffed pastas, like ravioli, tortellini, cannelloni, and crepes, then, yes, these are time-consuming. But even then there are many steps you can do in advance. Again, reserve these for the "grand occasion."

PASTA FATTA IN CASA

Basic Homemade Pasta (Serves 4 to 6 people)

IT IS DIFFICULT TO CALCULATE HOW MUCH flour is needed to make homemade pasta. I give you an approximate amount of flour, so do not mix the whole amount all at once with the eggs. The amount you need depends on the size of the eggs.

The best way to gauge your portions is by the eggs. If you are planning to serve the pasta as a main dish or you are feeding people with an earthy appetite, you should figure 1 large egg per person. When serving pasta as a first course with a main dish to follow, 4 large eggs will feed 6 people adequately. My basic recipe calls for 4 eggs since in this book pasta is usually served as a first course. Also, most recipes for stuffed pasta call for a batch of dough made with 4 eggs.

As a matter of fact, my grandmother gave me an invaluable lesson when I was a child. Inviting me into the kitchen one day she said, "Let's make 4

FOUR-EGG DOUGH
4 cups all-purpose flour, approximately
4 large eggs

THREE-EGG DOUGH
3 cups all-purpose flour, approximately
3 large eggs

TWO-EGG DOUGH
2 cups all-purpose flour, approximately
2 large eggs

MIXING DOUGH BY HAND:

1. Place the flour in a mound in the middle of a floured work surface. Make a well in the center and break the eggs into it. Beat the eggs with a fork until mixed, about 5 minutes.

2. Using a fork, gradually blend as much flour into the eggs as they can absorb, and as needed to gather the dough into a ball. You will not need all the flour. Knead until smooth and elastic, adding more flour if the dough gets sticky. The dough should be firm to the touch but not hard.

3. Place the dough under an inverted bowl and let it rest about 20 minutes.

MIXING DOUGH IN A FOOD PROCESSOR:

1. Place the eggs in a food processor. Turn the machine on and process until the eggs are mixed, for a few seconds. Add 1 cup of flour and process, adding more flour until a ball forms on the blades. Too much flour will turn the dough into dry

eggs of pasta." She proceeded by pouring flour on a *spianatoia,* the wooden board which is placed on the marble table for such a chore. She gathered the flour into a "mountain" and then formed a "well" in the middle. When she started to break the 4 eggs into the well, I noticed that she had not measured the flour, and I said so. Her answer was, "Oh, I have no idea how much flour I need. You must use only the amount of flour the eggs want to drink." Very sound advice, which I have never forgotten. Yes indeed, it all depends on the size of the eggs. And if you notice how small the large eggs have become nowadays, you will understand how important it is to add the flour gingerly.

Remember, pasta should not be made on a cold surface. Use wood or your counter if it is not made of marble.

pellets. If this happens, turn the mixture onto a floured work surface and gather it into a ball with your hands. You may need a little water. If the dough should come out too soft, knead it, adding more flour.

2. Place the dough under an inverted bowl and let it rest about 20 minutes.

NOTE: IF NECESSARY, THE DOUGH CAN BE PREPARED THE DAY BEFORE AND REFRIGERATED, WELL WRAPPED IN PLASTIC WRAP OR FOIL. LET IT COME TO ROOM TEMPERATURE BEFORE USING. THE DOUGH CAN ALSO BE FROZEN. DEFROST AT THE BOTTOM OF THE REFRIGERATOR THE NIGHT BEFORE.

KNEADING DOUGH BY HAND:

1. Knead the dough on a floured work surface until smooth and elastic, about 10 to 15 minutes, adding a little more flour if the dough seems sticky.

2. Place the dough under an inverted bowl and let it rest for about 20 minutes.

KNEADING, STRETCHING, AND CUTTING THE DOUGH WITH A PASTA MACHINE:

1. Divide the dough into 6 parts. Feed the dough, one piece at a time, through the larger opening of the pasta machine rollers, which is usually marked as #1. Fold the sheet of dough into 3 parts, like a letter, lightly flour it, and repeat 3 to 4 times until the dough is smooth and not sticky. Turn the rollers to the next setting and stretch the dough through them, one time only, without folding. Continue doing so, again turning the rollers to the next setting until you reach the desired thinness. Sprinkle the sheet with flour when necessary.

2. Place the finished sheets on kitchen towels to dry. Do not use paper. Repeat stretching and rolling until you finish all the dough. It is advisable to keep the sheets of dough covered with kitchen towels. This will prevent the pasta from becoming dry, brittle, and difficult to cut.

3. To cut the pasta, feed the sheets of dough, one at a time, through the cutting blades of the desired width. Place the noodles on kitchen towels to dry until ready to cook.

NOTE: IF NECESSARY, THE DOUGH CAN BE PREPARED THE DAY BEFORE AND REFRIGERATED, WELL WRAPPED IN PLASTIC WRAP.

ABOUT COLORED AND FLAVORED HOMEMADE PASTA

Italians, at one time, used to color the pasta dough with spinach for the green, red beets for the red, and squid ink for the black. Nowadays people use all sorts of things because pasta in several colors looks pretty. For we Italians, substance and taste is more important then looks. I do not think that, among the colors, carrots give a good hue to pasta and the same goes for artichokes, olives, and other absurdities.

And let's not talk of adding saffron! What a waste of a good spice—too much of it and the pasta tastes medicinal, and too little does nothing. You want a yellow pasta? Make it with egg yolks only, like the people of Turin do, and forget the cholesterol. Tomato paste is acceptable as a coloring but the flavor seeps through.

I do not approve at all of flavored pastas, and putting garlic in the mixture is absolutely idiotic. The flavor in the pasta should come from the sauce, and not the other way around.

And now that I have expressed my opinion, here is what I do.

TO MAKE 1 BATCH PASTA MADE WITH 4 EGGS:

Variation 1: For green pasta made with 4 eggs, add $1/4$ cup cooked, well-squeezed, finely chopped spinach to the eggs, mix and process as with regular pasta.

NOTE: IF YOU ARE USING A FOOD PROCESSOR, START PROCESSING THE SPINACH BEFORE ADDING THE EGGS AND THE FLOUR. PROCEED AS ABOVE.

Variation 2: For red pasta made with 4 eggs, boil 1 trimmed, medium-size red beet until soft. Peel and puree the beet and add it to the eggs. Proceed as above.

Variation 3: For black pasta made with 4 eggs, add squid ink to the eggs.

NOTE: I WOULD NOT BOTHER EXTRACTING THE INK SACK FROM THE SQUID. FIRST OF ALL, MOST OF THE TIME THEY ARE SOLD CLEAN—WITH THE INTERIORS REMOVED, INCLUDING THE INK. BESIDES, FISH STORES SELL LITTLE POUCHES OF FRESH OR FROZEN INK. EACH POUCH IS 0.05 OUNCE.

IF YOU WISH TO USE THE INK FROM A SQUID, FREEZE THE SQUID FOR 20 MINUTES. THIS WILL PREVENT THE INK SACK, WHICH IS VERY FRAGILE, FROM BREAKING AND MAKES THE EXTRACTION EASIER. COMBINE 2 POUCHES OF SQUID INK, OR 2 TO 3 INK SACKS FROM FRESH SQUID, WITH THE EGGS. PROCEED AS DIRECTED FOR GREEN PASTA.

Variation 4: For chocolate pasta made with 4 eggs, mix $1^1/_2$ tablespoons unsweetened cocoa powder with 2 of the eggs. Proceed as above.

NOTE: THIS IS A WHIMSICAL RECIPE, BUT NOT A DESSERT.

I make the above pasta for *Carnevale,* or Mardi Gras, as it is called here. In fact, I call the dish *Tagliatelle Arlecchino.* It consists of a bowl of noodles made with batches of dough in different colors, yellow, green, red, and brown. I dress them with a lot of butter and grated parmesan or grana padano cheese. You can use cream, if you like, but do not dress this pasta with a sauce that masks the colors. You need a white, transparent sauce to make the colors come out.

PASTA DI FARINA INTEGRALE

Whole Wheat Pasta (*Makes 4 to 6 servings*)

FOR WHOLE WHEAT PASTA MADE WITH 4 eggs, use 2 cups of whole wheat flour and about 1½ cups all-purpose flour. Add 1 tablespoon extra virgin olive oil to the eggs. This type of pasta is used mostly for *pappardelle* (page 152).

2 cups whole wheat flour
1½ cups all-purpose flour, plus additional
   for kneading

4 large eggs
1 tablespoon extra virgin olive oil

BY HAND:

1. Combine the whole wheat flour and 1 cup of the all-purpose flour on a floured work surface and make a well in the center. Break the eggs in it, add the oil, and beat briefly with a fork.

2. Blend in the flour, a little at a time, letting the eggs absorb only the amount of flour necessary to gather the dough into a ball. Knead until smooth and elastic, adding more flour if the dough feels sticky. The dough should be firm to the touch but not hard.

3. Place the dough under an inverted bowl and let it rest for 10 to 15 minutes.

BY FOOD PROCESSOR:

1. Place the eggs and the oil in a food processor. Process a few seconds and start adding the flour, stopping as soon as a ball forms on the blades. Too much flour will make the dough break into pellets. If this happens, turn the mixture on a floured work surface and gather it into a ball with your hands. You may need some water. If the dough should come out too soft, knead it on the work surface, adding more flour. In either case, knead the dough until smooth and elastic, about 10 minutes.

2. Place the dough under an inverted bowl and let it rest about 20 minutes.

NOTE: IF NECESSARY, THE DOUGH CAN BE PREPARED THE DAY BEFORE AND REFRIGERATED, WELL WRAPPED IN PLASTIC WRAP. LET IT COME TO ROOM TEMPERATURE BEFORE USING.

THE DOUGH CAN BE FROZEN. DEFROST AT THE BOTTOM OF THE REFRIGERATOR THE NIGHT BEFORE.

continues

TO CUT DOUGH:

1. Divide the dough into 6 parts.

2. Feed the dough, one piece at a time through the larger opening of the pasta machine rollers, which is usually marked #1. Fold the sheet of dough into 3 parts, like a letter, lightly flour it, and repeat 3 to 4 times until the dough is smooth and not sticky. Turn the rollers to the next setting and stretch the dough through them, one time only, without folding. Continue doing so, again turning the rollers to the next setting until you reach the desired thinness. Sprinkle the sheet with flour when necessary.

3. Place the finished sheets of dough on kitchen towels to dry. Do not use paper towels. Repeat stretching and rolling until you finish all the dough. It is advisable to keep the sheets of dough covered with kitchen towels. This will prevent the pasta from becoming dry and brittle, and difficult to cut.

4. Cut the sheets of dough one at a time through the chosen cutter of the pasta machine. *Pappardelle*, which are larger noodles, are cut by hand. Set noodles on kitchen towels to dry.

NOTE: THESE NOODLES CAN BE COVERED WITH A KITCHEN TOWEL AND KEPT IN A COOL PLACE FOR A WEEK OR STORED IN THE REFRIGERATOR. THEY CAN ALSO BE FROZEN.

MACCHERONI ALLA CHITARRA

"Guitar" Macaroni (Makes 6 servings)

As I said before, if one mentions the food of Abruzzo, the first thing that comes to mind is, of course, *la chitarra*. A guitar? The musical instrument? Well, yes and no. Here we are talking of the one that is used to make the famous *Maccheroni alla Chitarra*. Yes, the macaroni are made on a guitar, but not the type used to serenade a

1½ cups all-purpose flour, approximately
2 cups bread flour

4 large eggs

BY HAND:

On a floured work surface (not marble), combine both flours in a mound. Dig a well in the center of the mound and break the eggs into it. Beat the eggs with a fork and gradually incorporate the flour into the eggs. You may not need all of the flour depending on how much the eggs will absorb. As soon as you feel that you have a consistent bundle, start kneading, using the palms of your hands. Knead for

sweetheart, although you can also play a tune on it!

When we were children, Grandmother would run after us with a rolling pin when we were caught playing with one of her guitars. Let me explain. This guitar—and the picture on the cover—is indeed an instrument, consisting of a rectangular frame made of beechwood and strung with wires set a few millimeters apart from each other. The distance between the wires varies. You choose your guitar according to how wide you want your noodles. A household in Abruzzo might have three or four guitars with varying widths.

A sheet of homemade pasta is placed on the wires of the guitar and a rolling pin is rolled in a back and forth motion over the pasta, cutting it into noodles.

Guitars used for cutting macaroni are ancient instruments and are illustrated in thirteenth-century manuscripts. Today, however, modern cooks—even in Abruzzo—rely on the less time-consuming hand-cranked pasta machine.

As I explained in the segment "About Pasta" (page 106), homemade pasta in Italy is generally made with all-purpose flour and eggs. There are exceptions and this is one. In Abruzzo, the pasta for these noodles is made with a mixture of durum wheat (or semolina) flour and all-purpose flour. In this country it is difficult to find finely milled durum wheat flour. Therefore I use bread flour, which works well for this preparation.

at least 15 minutes sprinkling the dough with a little more flour when it feels sticky. Form into a ball, place under an inverted bowl, and let the dough rest 15 minutes.

BY FOOD PROCESSOR:

Place the eggs in a food processor. Process a few seconds and start adding both flours. Stop as soon as a ball forms on the blades. Remove to a floured work surface and knead 5 minutes. Form into a ball, place under an inverted bowl, and let the dough rest 15 minutes.

TO ROLL AND CUT DOUGH WITH A PASTA MACHINE:

1. Cut the dough into 4 parts. Keep unused portions under a bowl. Flatten the dough with your hands. Position the rollers of the machine at their maximum opening, which is usually marked #1. Insert the piece of dough between the two rollers, turn the handle, and roll the dough through. Sprinkle the dough with flour, fold the dough into thirds, like a letter, and roll again. Do this 2 to 3 times until smooth and not sticky.

2. Move the rollers one notch and roll the dough without folding. Continue rolling the dough through consecutively tighter notches sprinkling the sheets of dough lightly with flour when it feels sticky.

3. Place the sheets of dough over kitchen towels to dry for 10 minutes. If left for longer, the dough will become dry and brittle, and difficult to cut.

4. To cut: Feed the sheets of dough through the narrow cutters of the pasta machine. Set the noodles on kitchen towels. At this point the noodles can be dried and kept up to a week in a cool place, covered with kitchen towels.

5. To serve: Bring a 5-quart pot of water to a boil. Add 3 tablespoons of kosher salt, wait for the water to come back to a boil over high heat, and add the pasta. Stir and cover the pot to let the water come back to a boil over high heat. Remove the lid, stir again, and continue boiling the pasta. When the pasta is done, it should float at the top. Remove from the heat and add a cup of cold water to stop the cooking. Drain the pasta and dress with the desired sauce.

MACCHERONI ALLA CHITARRA CON SUGO DI FUNGHI

Guitar Macaroni with Mushroom Sauce **(Makes 6 servings)**

In this recipe, the *MACCHERONI* are finished with an assertive mushroom sauce, redolent with porcini and a pinch of garlic.

3/4 cup dried porcini mushrooms, soaked in 1 cup lukewarm water for 20 minutes
4 tablespoons extra virgin olive oil
2 cloves garlic, peeled
1 leek, trimmed and thoroughly washed (leeks are very gritty), white and light green parts cut into thin slices
1/2 pound fresh mushrooms, trimmed and coarsely chopped

Salt to taste, optional
Freshly ground pepper to taste
4 or 5 sprigs fresh parsley, minced
1 recipe Maccheroni alla Chitarra *(page 144)*
Freshly grated parmesan or grana padano cheese

1. Gently, so as not to upset the sediment resting at the bottom, lift the porcini mushrooms out of the water, chop, and set aside. Strain the water through a paper towel or coffee filter. Set aside.

2. In a medium-size skillet, heat 3 tablespoons of the oil over medium heat. Add the garlic and the leek and cook, stirring briefly, then add the drained mushrooms. Stir in half of the reserved liquid and let evaporate. Add the fresh mushrooms, salt, if used, and the pepper. Stir and add half the parsley. Cook over medium heat until the mushrooms are tender, about 15 minutes. Continue, adding the remaining mushroom water while cooking and stirring often. Add the remaining oil toward the end. Stir and keep warm.

3. Cook the pasta in a large pot of boiling, salted water, stirring often, until done, 2 to 4 minutes. Taste the pasta for doneness as soon as the water returns to a boil. Drain, reserving 1 cup of the cooking water. Dress the pasta with the mushroom sauce and add a generous grinding of pepper. Toss gently but well. If the mixture seems too dry, add some of the reserved cooking water. Sprinkle the remaining parsley over the pasta and serve with the grated cheese separately.

TAGLIATELLE CON ARAGOSTA
E ZUCCHINE

Tagliatelle Noodles with Lobster and Zucchini (*Makes 6 servings*)

I COULD EAT LOBSTER EVERY DAY, AND I am so happy that in this country it is so widely available and not too expensive. This recipe, in fact, came about during a summer in East Hampton where my husband, Harold, and I vacation. Besides lobster, there was also an abundance of zucchini. Remembering a similar pasta that my mother used to make with crabmeat, I tried this version and it worked beautifully.

It is important to use fresh herbs in this recipe.

SAUCE

One 1½-pound lobster
¼ cup wine vinegar
3 tablespoons extra virgin olive oil
3 cloves garlic, peeled and smashed
4 or 5 sprigs fresh parsley
2 sprigs fresh thyme
2 bay leaves
1 sprig fresh rosemary
1 tablespoon tomato paste
2 tablespoons cognac
½ cup dry white wine
1 cup heavy cream

ZUCCHINI AND TAGLIATELLE NOODLES

1 tablespoon extra virgin olive oil
2 tablespoons unsalted butter
1 large onion, chopped
1 large carrot, peeled and chopped
2 medium-size zucchini, cut into matchstick strips
1 recipe Basic Homemade Pasta (page 140), made with 4 eggs, stretched thinly, and cut into ⅜-inch-wide tagliatelle
Freshly grated parmesan cheese

1. Prepare the lobster: Bring a large pot of water to a boil; add the lobster and the vinegar. Cook until bright red, about 5 minutes. Remove the lobster and cool, reserving the water. When the lobster is cool enough to handle, remove the meat from the shell, working over a bowl to collect its juices. Reserve these juices. Reserve the shells and the head of the lobster, as well. Dice the meat. Set aside.

2. Prepare the sauce: In a large skillet, heat the oil over medium heat, add the garlic and all the herbs, and cook, stirring, until slightly softened, about 3 to 4 minutes. Add the reserved lobster shells and head, broken in half, and stir in the tomato paste. Cook 2 to 3 minutes, stirring, and then add the cognac. Let evaporate, add the wine, and cook until reduced by half, about 5 minutes. Pour in enough of the reserved lobster cooking water to cover the solids in the skillet. Bring to a boil over high heat, reduce the heat to low, and simmer until the flavors have been released, 20 to 30 minutes. If the liquid evaporates too much and the mixture seems dry, add a little more of the lobster water.

continues

3. Strain the sauce through a colander, pressing on the solids to extract as much juice as possible. Discard the solids. If you have more than $1^1/_4$ cups sauce, continue to simmer until it reduces to 1 cup. Return the strained sauce to the skillet and add any reserved juices from shelling the lobster and the heavy cream. Bring to a boil over high heat, add the lobster meat, reduce the heat to low, and simmer 3 minutes. Remove from the heat but keep warm.

4. Prepare the zucchini: In a clean medium-size skillet, heat the oil and butter over medium heat. Add the onion and carrot and cook, stirring often, until the vegetables are softened, about 10 minutes. Add the zucchini and cook until tender, about 8 minutes. Combine with the lobster sauce.

5. Cook the pasta in a large pot of boiling, salted water, stirring often, until done, 2 to 4 minutes. Taste the pasta for doneness as soon as the water returns to a boil. Drain. Reheat the sauce if necessary and dress the pasta with it. Serve with a bowl of parmesan cheese on the side.

TAGLIATELLE ALLA BOLOGNESE

Tagliatelle with Bolognese Sauce **(Makes 4 to 6 servings)**

WHAT WOULD AN ITALIAN COOKBOOK, from any region, be without this ultra-Italian dish!

The amusing story of the sauce for these tagliatelle is that I taught it to my mother, or I should say I improved on my mother's version. But the truth of the matter is that I learned it from my friend Giuliana Trevisan. The two of us shared a "flat" in England, during a period we called the British Campaign. We were improving our English. One night, while counting our money, we realized that we could either go to a restaurant or to the theater, but not both. Those were the days when you could buy a ticket at the last minute. Well, rummaging in several pocket-books, we scrounged enough money for a Whimpy, the British hamburger, and then went to the see a show.

Afterward, we discussed the fact that we were actually spending too much money eating out all the time. It would be a good idea to start cooking at home. But our experience being limited, we began with what we remembered most from our homes. I came up with the *Brodetto di Pesce di Papà* (page 227), my father's inimitable fish stew, and Giuliana with her mother's Bolognese sauce. To our great surprise, both turned out to be delicious.

1 recipe Basic Homemade Pasta (page 140), made with 4 eggs
3 cups Bolognese Sauce (page 103)
$1/_2$ cup heavy cream
Freshly grated parmesan cheese

1. Cut the pasta into tagliatelle according to the recipe on page 147. Set on cookie sheets lined with kitchen towels.

2. Reheat the sauce over low heat, add the cream, and simmer 5 minutes.

3. Cook the pasta in a large pot of boiling, salted water, stirring often, until done, 2 to 4 minutes. Taste the pasta for doneness as soon as the water returns to a boil. Drain and dress with the sauce. Serve with a bowl of parmesan cheese.

FETTUCCINE NERE AL SUGO DI GRANCHIO

Black Fettuccine with Crab Sauce *(Makes 6 servings)*

AT FIRST SIGHT, THE REACTION TO THESE fettuccine is one of alarm. Who ever saw such a funereal sight in the kitchen? One of the polite reactions I get from my guests is: "Oh! This would appeal to Hitchcock!" When my mother made this dish, invariably someone would make the sign against the evil eye. Abruzzesi are superstitious. Gabriele D'Annunzio, our main poet and writer, wrote one of his most famous dramas based on the spilling of oil, which is a sure sign of bad luck. But do not fear, the only bad luck here is if you over-cook the pasta and ruin the dish.

Any fish sauce, like the *Sugo Bianco di Mare*, White Fish Sauce (page 98), is excellent with this pasta. When I serve the black fettuccine, sometimes I add a teaspoon of red caviar to each dish. And I always add a good handful of minced fresh parsley to color the pasta with a brilliant green hue.

The following sauce is one of my favorites. A bit rich, but worth the indulgence once in a while. Try it.

DOUGH
1 recipe black Basic Homemade Pasta (page 140), stretched thin and cut into 1/4- to 3/8-inch-wide fettuccine

SAUCE
2 cups heavy cream
4 ripe plum tomatoes, peeled, seeded, and diced
1 pound fresh crabmeat, flaked
1 abundant tablespoon minced fresh parsley
Freshly grated parmesan or grana padano cheese (see Note)
1 heaping tablespoon minced fresh parsley

1. Cut the fettuccine according to the recipe on page 140. Set on cookie sheets lined with kitchen towels.

2. Place the cream into a medium saucepan and bring to a boil over medium-high heat. Reduce the heat to low and simmer until slightly reduced, 5 to 6 minutes. Add the tomatoes and cook at a simmer, 5 minutes longer. Add the crabmeat and 2 tablespoons of the grated cheese and cook just to heat through. Set aside, but keep warm.

3. Cook the fettuccine in a large pot of boiling, salted water, stirring often, until done, 2 to 4 minutes. Taste the pasta for doneness as soon as the water returns to a boil. Drain, reserving 1 cup of the cooking water. Dress the fettuccine with the crabmeat sauce. If the mixture seems too dry, add some of the reserved water. Sprinkle the pasta with the minced parsley and serve with a bowl of the grated cheese.

NOTE: BECAUSE OF ITS CREAM BASE, THIS RECIPE IS AN EXCEPTION TO THE USUAL "NO NO" OF CHEESE ON FISH SAUCES.

Variation: If you prefer, you can make this fettuccine in two tones, coloring half a batch black, and half green.

TAGLIATELLE AL LIMONE

Tagliatelle in Lemon Sauce (Makes 6 servings)

HERE'S A DELIGHTFUL, SIMPLE SAUCE WITH the clean fragrance of fresh lemons. Choose lemons with unblemished, plump skins.

1 recipe Basic Homemade Pasta (page 140), made with 4 eggs, stretched thin and cut into tagliatelle

Zest of 1 large lemon, or 2 medium-size ones, very finely chopped

3 tablespoons unsalted butter

2 cups heavy cream, lightly heated until bubbles appear around the edge

Freshly grated parmesan cheese

1. Stretch the dough according to the pasta recipe and cut into tagliatelle according to the recipe on page 147. Spread them on kitchen towels.

2. In a pasta serving bowl, place the lemon and butter. Keep in a warm place.

3. Cook the tagliatelle in plenty of boiling, salted water stirring often until done, about 2 to 4 minutes. Taste the pasta for doneness as soon as the water returns to a boil. Drain, reserving 1 cup of the cooking water. Turn the tagliatelle into the pasta bowl, toss, and add the cream. Toss gently but thoroughly and if the mixture seems a little dry add some of the reserved water. Serve with a bowl of parmesan cheese.

PAPPARDELLE CON LA LEPRE

Pappardelle with Hare Sauce **(Makes 6 to 8 servings)**

AT THE END OF AUGUST, OUR FAMILIES— mine and the aunts'—would return to my grandmother's house in Guardiagrele. We would remain there part of the fall, or until we children were due back at school. Other family friends and relatives would also return for a fall holiday from Rome, Milan, or Naples. It was a grand reunion.

We kids couldn't wait to get together and start over from where we had left off the year before. The most important thing was to plan our mountain excursions. We were passionate climbers, grown-ups and children alike.

This was also the beginning of the hunting season. Some of the uncles and older cousins were hunters. We all loved game. Having grown up with a twin brother, I was, needless to say, a tomboy, and often went along. I actually loved the dogs more than the shooting.

Since the hare was the best catch of the month, we ate it often, cooked into delicious *salmí* (a kind of stew, page 360) for which the center of Italy is famous. At times the hare would be made into a succulent ragout and served over homemade *pappardelle* (broad noodles). In my household, this recipe was also made with rabbit, duck, or wild duck.

MARINADE

One 4-pound hare, approximately, cut into 8 to 10 pieces
2 large onions, quartered
1 medium-size carrot, peeled and cut into thick slices
1 large rib celery, leaves included, cut into chunks
2 sprigs fresh parsley
2 cloves garlic, peeled and smashed
2 bay leaves
7 whole cloves
1/2 bottle full-bodied red wine, such as Chianti or a Montepulciano

Flour for dredging
2 tablespoons extra virgin olive oil
3 tablespoons unsalted butter
1 thick slice prosciutto, about 1/4 pound, diced
1/2 cup Marsala wine
1 tablespoon tomato paste
About 1 cup chicken broth, preferably homemade (page 61), or low-sodium canned broth
1/2 cup dried porcini mushrooms, soaked in 3/4 cup lukewarm water for 15 to 20 minutes
1 recipe Basic Homemade Pasta (page 140) made with 4 eggs, stretched thin and cut into 1-inch-wide pappardelle
Freshly grated parmesan or grana padano cheese

THE DAY BEFORE:

1. Prepare the marinade one day ahead: Place the hare in a nonreactive bowl and add the onions, carrot, celery, parsley, garlic, bay leaves, and cloves. Stir well and pour in the wine. Refrigerate, covered, overnight. Turn the hare pieces a few times to distribute the flavors.

THE NEXT DAY:

2. Remove the hare from the marinade and dry the pieces with paper towels. Dredge the pieces in the flour, shaking off any excess.

3. Remove all the remaining ingredients from the marinade. Chop finely. Set the marinade aside.

4. In a large skillet, heat the oil and 1 tablespoon butter over medium heat. Add the chopped vegetable mixture and cook, stirring, until softened, about 5 to 8 minutes. Add the prosciutto and the hare. Cook until the meat is brown. Add the Marsala wine and let evaporate.

5. Dilute the tomato paste in $^1/_2$ cup of the wine from the marinade, add this mixture to the skillet, and cook 5 minutes. Add the remaining wine from the marinade and $^3/_4$ cup of the broth.

6. Gently, so as not to upset the sediment resting at the bottom, lift the porcini mushrooms out of the water, and set aside. Strain the water through a paper towel or coffee filter and add it to the skillet. Chop the mushrooms coarsely and set aside. Cover the skillet and continue cooking the hare over medium-low heat at a simmer, stirring often and adding more broth as needed if mixture dries out, until the hare is tender, about 2 hours. Add the chopped mushrooms during the last 10 minutes of cooking.

7. In a large pot of boiling, salted water, cook the pappardelle until al dente, 4 to 5 minutes.

8. Drain the pappardelle, and place them in a shallow serving bowl. Add the remaining 2 tablespoons of butter, spoon some of the sauce from the hare over the pasta, and toss. Spoon the remaining sauce and hare over the pasta. Serve with grated cheese on the side.

NOTE: IF THE LIVER OF THE HARE IS AVAILABLE, CHOP IT AND ADD WITH THE MUSHROOMS. IT CAN BE MARINATED IN THE MARSALA TOGETHER WITH THE HARE.

Pappardelle con l'Anatra

Pappardelle with Duck   (Makes 4 to 6 servings)

This dish of *PAPPARDELLE* is more interesting when its dough is made with whole wheat flour. The richness of the duck is somewhat softened by the rustic, nutty flavor of the whole wheat dough. This is an intensely flavored dish. My father, mother permitting, loved to accompany this dish with copious libations of Montepulciano d'Abruzzo.

Ducks in Abruzzo were rather lean, therefore they were often simply cut into pieces and braised or sautéed. In this country though, ducks are generally fat, so when I cook a duck this way, I remove the skin and all the clumps of fat before I cut it up.

One 3-pound duck, with its liver (see Note)
1 rib celery, preferably with leaves attached, washed, trimmed, and cut into 4 pieces
1 medium-size carrot, peeled and cut into 4 pieces
1 large onion, quartered
2 sprigs fresh parsley
2 ounces prosciutto
3 tablespoons extra virgin olive oil
1 teaspoon fresh thyme leaves, or ½ teaspoon dried
½ cup dry wine, white or red
¾ cup chicken broth, preferably home-made (page 61), or low-sodium canned, or bouillon

1 teaspoon tomato paste
One 32-ounce can peeled tomatoes, with their juice
Salt to taste, optional
Freshly ground pepper to taste
1 recipe Basic Homemade Pasta (page 140), made with 4 eggs, stretched thin and cut into 1-inch-wide pappardelle; or 1 recipe Whole Wheat Pasta (page 143), made with 4 eggs; or use same amount of regular homemade dough stretched thin and cut into 1-inch-wide pappardelle
Freshly grated parmesan or grana padano cheese

1. Remove the skin and all visible fat from the duck and discard it.

2. Cut the duck into 6 or 8 pieces. Coarsely chop the liver and set both aside.

3. In a food processor, chop together the celery, carrot, onion, parsley, and prosciutto.

4. In a large skillet, heat the oil over medium-high heat, add the vegetable mixture and thyme, and cook, stirring, until softened, about 5 to 8 minutes. Add the duck, but not the liver, and cook until brown. Add the wine and let evaporate. Add the broth and cook until the mixture has thickened, about 20 minutes. Stir in the tomato paste.

5. Drain the tomatoes, reserving the liquid. Add the tomatoes to the skillet, breaking them into pieces with a wooden spoon. Cover the skillet and simmer over low heat until thickened, about 1 hour. Check once in a while to make sure that the

sauce is not reducing too much. If liquid is needed, add some of the reserved juice from the tomatoes. Uncover the skillet during the last 10 to 15 minutes. Add the reserved liver during the last 10 minutes of cooking.

6. With a slotted spoon remove the duck pieces from the skillet and cool. Remove the meat from the bones and chop coarsely. Discard bones. Add the meat to the sauce and reheat it.

7. Cook the pasta in a large pot of boiling, salted water, stirring often, until done, 3 to 5 minutes. Taste the pasta for doneness as soon as the water returns to a boil. Drain and turn them into a shallow bowl.

8. Dress with the duck sauce and serve with a bowl of grated cheese on the side.

NOTE: IF THE DUCK COMES WITHOUT THE LIVER, USE 2 CHICKEN LIVERS.

L'SAGNE

Abruzzo Broad Noodles **(Makes 1 pound of dough)**

IT'S IMPOSSIBLE TO TRANSLATE THIS NAME. It is an Abruzzese dialect word similar to the Italian *le sagne* which means a type of noodle. It is a kind of rustic, very simple homemade pasta made with flour, water, and a pinch of salt. My mother used to add some egg whites when she had them; otherwise the dough is made without eggs. In Abruzzese dialect, these kinds of pastas are also called *sagnatiell'*, or *laganelle.*

L' sagne are quite often combined with legumes, especially beans, chick peas, lentils, and *cicerchie* (see the variation, *La Zuppa di Cicerchie,* page 89), and some vegetables. They are rustic dishes belonging to the *cucina povera,* of which I spoke before.

2 cups all-purpose flour, plus more for kneading

¹/₂ teaspoon salt
³/₄ cup water, approximately

BY HAND:

On a wooden board place the flour in a mound. Form a well in the center and add the salt. Add the water a little at a time, while mixing in the flour and water with a fork. Using both hands, knead the dough into a ball, adding more flour as necessary, to obtain a smooth pliable dough. Set the dough under an inverted bowl and let it rest 15 minutes.

BY FOOD PROCESSOR:

1. Place the flour and the salt in a food processor. With the machine running, slowly start adding the water. Stop as soon as a ball forms on the blades. Remove the dough from the machine and knead until smooth and pliable, about 10 minutes. Set the dough under an inverted bowl and let it rest 15 minutes.

continues

2. Stretch the dough with a rolling pin to the required thickness or use a pasta machine. See instructions for stretching dough in Basic Homemade Pasta (page 140).

3. Cut the dough into $3/4$-inch-wide noodles. Cut the noodles into 2- to 3-inch-long pieces.

L'SAGNE ABBOTTA PEZZENTE
Poor Man's Stuffer

This is a poor man's dish, made with readily available ingredients, hence the name. Everybody in Abruzzo will brag about his or her sagne, although nowadays they are rarely eaten (since palates have become more sophisticated) and have become part of memory food. In my home, they were made on winter evenings when my father felt nostalgic about his abandoned "paese."

When I was a child, and if the family had eaten the midday meal out, perhaps on a Sunday, we would go home and the maids would mischievously announce that they were going to make *l'sagne* that evening, and that meant an invitation to partake. After declining for lack of appetite, the family would nevertheless end up congregating in the kitchen to "taste" . . . you guessed it, *l'sagne.*

TACCOZZELLE ALLA RICOTTA VERDE

Noodles with Green Ricotta Sauce (*Makes 4 servings*)

TACCOZZELLE, TACCONI, AT TIMES CALLED "ancient people noodles," were an everyday *minestra,* a soup, or first course on the table of the peasants. The dough is that of *L'Sagne* made with just flour and water. At one time, the flour was whole wheat, which made it even cheaper than the more refined white flour. The condiment was also quite simple—made with garlic, onion, tomatoes, a pinch of *diavoletto* (the ever-present little hot pepper), and a piece of *pancetta,* bacon, *guanciale,* or *muso,* cheek, snout, or any other humble piece of pork. It filled the stomach with lots of intriguing flavors.

In my house, this was a dish the servants made for themselves when the family ate out. Eating out was nearly always a midday affair, since this is when the Italians have their main meal of the day.

On these occasions the evening supper was a *spuntino,* which I used to love because it consisted of delicious tidbits. Having eaten such a large midday meal, this simple assortment was enough. But as soon as the perfume of the *taccozzelle* started to permeate the house, as I have written before, we all ended up in the kitchen eager to "taste" the humble meal.

DOUGH
1 recipe L'Sagne *(page 155)*

SAUCE
1 pound spinach, washed, trimmed, cooked, and drained
1 pound ricotta cheese
Freshly grated pecorino romano cheese
1/4 teaspoon grated nutmeg
1 tablespoon unsalted butter
1 carrot, peeled, boiled, and diced

1. Prepare the dough according to the recipe. Stretch the dough in not-too-thin sheets. Stop stretching before reaching the last two notches of the pasta machine. Lightly flour 3 or 4 stretched sheets at a time, pile them right on top of each other, and cut into squares that measure 1 × 1-inch. Set on cookie sheets lined with kitchen towels.

2. Prepare the sauce: Place the spinach in a food processor and process until finely chopped. Add the ricotta, 1/4 cup of the grated cheese, and the nutmeg. Process until the mixture is creamy and smooth. Turn into a pasta serving bowl and keep in a warm place, like the corner of the stove.

3. In a small skillet, heat the butter over medium-high heat and add the carrots and cook, stirring often, about 5 minutes. Set aside and cover, but keep warm.

4. Cook the taccozzelle in a large pot of boiling, salted water, about 3 minutes. Taste for doneness as soon as the water returns to a boil. Drain the pasta, reserving 1 cup of the cooking water. Add half of this water to the bowl with the ricotta mixture. Add the taccozzelle and gently toss. If the mixture seems too dry add some more of the reserved water. Top with the diced carrot and serve with additional grated pecorino cheese.

NOTE 1: WHEN I MAKE THIS SAUCE FOR RAVIOLI, I USE PARMESAN OR GRANA PADANO INSTEAD OF THE PECORINO ROMANO WHICH IS TOO SHARP.

NOTE 2: TO WARM THE SAUCE, KEEP THE PASTA BOWL ON TOP OF THE POT OF HOT WATER IN WHICH THE PASTA WILL BE COOKED. AN ALTERNATIVE IS TO PUT THE BOWL IN A 300°F OVEN FOR 10 TO 15 MINUTES.

STUFFED HOMEMADE PASTA

According to Italian folklore, *ravioli,* one of the most well-known stuffed pastas, were invented by the thrifty Ligurians, who could not bare to throw away food. So they filled pasta with their leftovers. Thank God for that! Now from north to south, all Italy can enjoy these delicious morsels.

In Florence and other parts of Italy, the *ravioli* are also called *tortelli.* After the *lasagne,* which Cicero loved *cum caseo,* with cheese, tortelli are the earliest known stuffed pasta in history. Other stuffed pastas include *tortellini* or *cappelletti,* which look like little peaked caps and are the glory of Bologna. Then there are *tortelloni,* a larger variety of *tortellini.* Others include *agnolotti,* which are half-moon shaped, and of course *cannelloni.*

In the States, *cannelloni* are often confused with *manicotti.* The homemade *cannelloni* are rectangular pieces of dough that are filled, rolled, sauced, and baked. Quite often in Abruzzo, the *cannelloni* are made with crepes. *Manicotti,* on the other hand, are usually made with commercial dried pasta and sold in a preformed tubular shape. Their fillings can be the same as those used for *ravioli.*

The following recipes will specify the number of eggs needed to make the dough, the ingredients for the varied fillings, and instructions for how to cut and shape them. Keep in mind though, that the ingredients for the recipes are for full, Italian-style portions, not restaurant portions, where sometimes they dare serve only three ravioli per person. *Che orrore!*

RIPIENO PER RAVIOLI O CANNELLONI ALLA ANNA TERESA

Stuffing for Ravioli or Cannelloni alla Anna Teresa

(Makes enough filling for about 130 2-inch square ravioli or 40 3 × 5-inch cannelloni)

THIS STUFFING IS THE ONE I NORMALLY USE for my regular ravioli and cannelloni.

It is difficult to establish the precise amount of ravioli or cannelloni one can make from a given recipe. The quantity of the dough depends on the size of the eggs, how thin you make your pasta, and how big you make each one. Therefore, the amounts below are approximate.

1 pound fresh spinach; or one 10-ounce package frozen spinach
1 teaspoon unsalted butter
1/4 pound gruyère cheese, cut into chunks
1 Italian salamino, or 1 dry sausage, cut in pieces (see Note)
15 ounces ricotta
Salt to taste
Freshly ground black pepper to taste
1 large egg
1 teaspoon nutmeg
3 tablespoons grated parmesan or grana padano cheese

1. Wash and trim the fresh spinach. Defrost the package if you are using frozen spinach.

2. In a skillet, heat the butter over high heat and add the spinach. Cook, stirring, until the excess water has been absorbed. Cool the spinach and squeeze all the remaining moisture from it. Set aside.

3. In a food processor, place the gruyère and *salamino* or sausage and chop until fine. Add the spinach and chop to combine. Add all the remaining ingredients and process until well blended. This recipe can be prepared up to 2 days in advance and stored in the refrigerator in a tightly covered container.

NOTE: THE *SALAMINO*, ALSO CALLED *CACCIATORINO*, AND THE DRY SAUSAGE ARE AVAILABLE IN ITALIAN SPECIALTY STORES. IF ALL ELSE FAILS, BUY FRESH SAUSAGE AND STORE IT UNCOVERED IN THE REFRIGERATOR. IT WILL BE DRY ENOUGH TO USE IN 5 OR 6 DAYS.

RAVIOLI DI RICOTTA ALLA ANNA TERESA

Ravioli with Ricotta Anna Teresa **(Makes 8 servings)**

CLASSIC RAVIOLI ARE SIMPLY MADE WITH a basic filling of ricotta, spinach, and parmesan cheese. From here, one can improvise, using imagination, inventiveness, and, as the Ligurians do, leftovers! Create your own original ravioli.

I sometimes add some chopped *salamino,* small salami, or dry sausage. Our homemade ravioli often included my favorite cheese, gruyère, too.

The proportions of this recipe are for a full dish of ravioli, Italian style. That is, 12 to 14 ravioli per person. We loved these ravioli and we did like to gorge on them. If you have a small appetite, reduce the ingredients.

FILLING

1 recipe Stuffing for Ravioli alla Anna Teresa (page 159)

SAUCE

1 recipe Ragù all'Italiana (page 104)

PASTA

1 recipe Basic Homemade Pasta (page 140), made with 4 eggs, stretched thin

1. Prepare the filling according to the recipe. Add ¹/₂ cup of the *ragù* and process to mix. Set aside.

2. Prepare the ravioli: Divide the dough into 2 parts and each part into 4 wedges. Roll one wedge at a time into thin sheets. I use the last notch on my pasta machine because I like my stuffed pasta very thin. Set the stretched pasta on kitchen towels (do not use paper towels) and cover with kitchen towels to prevent them from drying too much.

3. Cut the ravioli: If using a ravioli tray (see Note), place one sheet of dough over the tray and press the dough gently into its depressions. Place a small amount of filling (no more than a teaspoonful) into each depression. Dip a finger in a glass of water and run it along the lines where the ravioli will be cut. Cover the filled tray with another sheet of dough of equal size, pressing down along the dampened edges to make the two sheets stick. Use a rolling pin to go over the tray. This will seal and cut the ravioli. Turn the tray over and gently separate the ravioli. Set on cookie sheets lined with kitchen towels. Quickly gather all the scraps of dough and form into a ball. Roll the ball out to make additional ravioli before it gets too dry and cannot be rolled out. Repeat until all the remaining sheets of dough and filling have been used. Reserve any leftover filling to add to the sauce or use as a dip.

4. If using a ravioli cutter, place 1 teaspoon of filling at regular intervals in rows on a sheet of dough. Dip a finger in a glass of water and dampen the dough around the sides and along the lines where the pasta will be cut. Cover with a sheet of dough of equal size, press along the dampened lines to make the pasta adhere, and cut with a ravioli cutter or jagged-edged cookie cutter.

5. Cook the ravioli: Gently reheat the sauce. Cook the ravioli in a large pot of boiling, salted water, stirring once or twice, until done, 3 to 5 minutes. Taste a raviolo for doneness as soon as the water returns to a boil. Reheat the sauce. Drain the ravioli and dress with the sauce. Let the ravioli rest in the sauce for 5 to 8 minutes. Serve with a bowl of grated parmesan cheese.

NOTE: RAVIOLI TRAYS AND CUTTERS ARE AVAILABLE IN KITCHEN EQUIPMENT SHOPS. WHEN I EAT RAVIOLI MADE BY SOMEONE OTHER THAN ME, I OFTEN FIND THE EDGES UNDERCOOKED AND HARD. TO AVOID THIS, AFTER CUTTING THE RAVIOLI, PRESS WITH YOUR FINGERS ALL AROUND EACH RAVIOLO. THIS WILL MAKE THE EDGES THINNER, SO THAT EACH RAVIOLO WILL COOK EVENLY. THIS IS NOT NECESSARY WHEN USING A RAVIOLI TRAY.

FOR A LIGHTER SAUCE, DRESS THE RAVIOLI WITH *SUGO FINTO* (PAGE 96).

RAVIOLI ALLA BOSCAIOLA

Ravioli of the Woodsmen (Makes 6 to 8 servings)

IN ITALIAN *ALLA BOSCAIOLA* SIGNIFIES something from the *bosco*, or wood.

The featured recurrent ingredient in a dish *alla boscaiola* is the mushroom. These ravioli are filled with a mixture of mushrooms and ricotta cheese.

I have a tip for you: When cooking mushrooms, even the common white kind, do as I do—add a handful of dried porcini to the pan and you will have that delightful, bosky flavor that is found only in wild mushrooms.

This recipe makes approximately 110 2-inch-square, standard-size ravioli, providing that you make the dough as thin as I do. Leftover filling can be added to the sauce at the last minute.

FILLING

1 tablespoon unsalted butter
1 tablespoon extra virgin olive oil
1 leek, trimmed, washed, and coarsely chopped
2 sprigs fresh parsley, minced
2 cups sliced fresh white mushrooms
1/2 cup dried porcini mushrooms, soaked in 3/4 cup lukewarm water for 15 to 20 minutes
2 large eggs
1/4 cup freshly grated parmesan cheese
Freshly ground pepper to taste
1/2 teaspoon grated nutmeg
1 1/2 cups ricotta, drained

DOUGH

1 recipe Basic Homemade Pasta (page 140), made with 4 eggs, stretched as thin as possible

SAUCE

1 tablespoon unsalted butter
1 tablespoon extra virgin olive oil
1/2 pound ground beef
2 anchovy fillets, drained and chopped
1 tablespoon all-purpose flour
1/2 cup beef broth, preferably homemade (page 61), or bouillon
Freshly ground pepper to taste
2 cups tomato puree
2 or 3 fresh basil leaves, chopped
Freshly grated parmesan cheese

1. Prepare the filling: Heat the butter and oil in a medium-size skillet. Add the leek and half the parsley. Cook over low heat, stirring often, until the leek is softened, about 5 minutes. Add the fresh white mushrooms, raise the heat to high, and continue cooking.

2. Gently, so as not to upset the sediment resting at the bottom, lift the porcini mushrooms out of the water, and add to the skillet. Strain the water through a paper towel or coffee filter and add, a little at a time, to the skillet. Cook until the mushrooms are softened and the water has been completely absorbed, 10 to 15 minutes. Cool.

3. Turn the mushrooms into a food processor and puree until smooth. Add the eggs, parmesan cheese, pepper, nutmeg, and ricotta. Process until mixed well and set aside.

4. Prepare the ravioli: Cut dough into wedges. Using a pasta machine, roll one wedge at a time into a very thin sheet. Use the last notch if your machine allows it (some machines will break the dough when stretched too thin). Let the dough dry for 5 minutes.

5. Follow the procedure for cutting the ravioli given in step 3 of *Ravioli di Ricotta alla Anna Teresa* (page 160).

6. Keep the ravioli on cookie sheets lined with kitchen towels (not paper towels) until ready to cook.

7. Prepare the sauce: Heat the butter and oil in a medium-size skillet, add the beef and cook over medium-high heat until brown, about 10 minutes. Add the anchovy fillets and mix.

8. Combine the flour with the broth and add to the meat. Add a good grinding of pepper, the tomato puree, and the basil. Cover and bring to a boil over high heat. Immediately reduce the heat to low and simmer gently for about 1 hour.

9. Cook the ravioli in a large pot of boiling, salted water, stirring often, until done, 3 to 5 minutes. Taste a raviolo for doneness as soon as the water returns to a boil. Drain in a large colander.

10. Reheat the sauce if necessary. Pour half the sauce into a shallow pasta bowl, add the ravioli, toss gently, add the remaining sauce, and let it rest 5 minutes. Serve with a bowl of grated parmesan cheese on the side.

RAVIOLI DI MARE

Sea Ravioli (*Makes 6 to 8 servings*)

At one time, homemade pasta was seldom dressed with fish sauces because they were considered too assertive. Dry pasta was the preferred kind. But food evolves, and people with imagination like to experiment. I had these ravioli in a modest trattoria on the Adriatic Sea. The fragrant filling was wrapped in the most delicate homemade pasta, the whole thing melting in the mouth in a harmony of flavors.

FILLING

2 tablespoons extra virgin olive oil
1 clove garlic, peeled
1 to 2 sprigs fresh parsley
3/4 pound lobster, crab, or shrimp,
  or a mixture of the three
3/4 pound bay scallops
1/4 cup dry white wine
2 egg whites, lightly beaten

DOUGH

1 recipe Basic Homemade Pasta (page
  140), made with 3 eggs, stretched as
  thin as possible

SAUCE

4 tablespoons extra virgin olive oil
1 small onion, chopped
1 clove garlic, minced
1/2 cup dry white wine (same as used in
  the filling)
3/4 pound small shrimp, peeled and
  deveined, shells reserved
1/2 tablespoon all-purpose flour
1 1/2 tablespoons tomato paste
About 1 1/2 cups or more fish or
  chicken broth, preferably homemade
  (page 63 or 61)
1/4 cup heavy cream, optional

1. Prepare the filling: Heat the oil in a medium-size skillet. Add the garlic and parsley and cook for 1 minute over medium-high heat. Add the shellfish and the scallops and cook until the scallops turn opaque, 2 to 3 minutes. Add the wine and cook until it evaporates, then remove from the heat. Cool and turn the mixture into a food processor; add the egg whites. Process until finely chopped. Set aside.

2. Prepare the ravioli according to the recipe for *Ravioli di Ricotta alla Anna Teresa* (page 160), using the above mixture as the filling. Keep the ravioli on cookie sheets lined with kitchen towels (not paper towels) until ready to cook.

3. Prepare the sauce: Heat 2 tablespoons of the oil in a medium-size skillet. Add the onion and garlic and cook over low heat, stirring often, until the onion is very soft, about 8 minutes. Add a little wine to prevent the onion from coloring. Add the shrimp and cook 2 minutes. Add half of the wine and let evaporate. Cook about 5 minutes, or until the shrimp turn red. Remove to a mixing bowl and set aside. Wipe the skillet clean. Add the remaining 2 tablespoons of oil to the skillet. Add the reserved shrimp shells and cook, stirring, 2 to 3 minutes, or until the shells are red.

4. Combine the flour and tomato paste in a small bowl. Mix well. Stir in the remaining wine and mix until smooth. Add this mixture to the skillet. Cook over medium-low heat for 5 minutes, or until the flavors are released. Add 1 cup of the broth, increase the heat to high, and bring to a boil. Cook over high heat, stirring often, until slightly reduced, about 5 more minutes. Turn the mixture into a colander and press down to extract as much liquid as possible. Discard the solids and return the liquid to the skillet. If you have any leftover filling from the *ravioli*, add it to the sauce. Dice the shrimp and add to the sauce. If the sauce seems too thick, add a little more broth or the cream, if used. Remove the sauce from the heat and cover to keep warm. Set aside.

5. Cook the ravioli in two batches in a large pot of boiling, salted water. Drop half of the ravioli in and cook, stirring once or twice, until done, 3 to 5 minutes. Taste a raviolo for doneness as soon as the water returns to a boil. Remove the ravioli with a slotted spoon to a colander. Bring the water back to a boil over high heat and cook the remaining ravioli. Reheat the sauce, if necessary. Pour half of the sauce into a shallow pasta bowl, add all of the ravioli, and gently toss. Add the remaining sauce and serve.

RAVIOLI MARE E TERRA

Ravioli Sea and Land (Makes 6 to 8 servings)

THE DISHES THAT COMBINE THE FRUITS OF the sea and good things from the earth are called *mare e terra*, sea and land. They are usually made with fish and some vegetables; meat is seldom added. In the past, Italians never mixed fish and meat in the same dish, but we are now changing as we learn to adapt to the customs of other cuisines.

My mother and father called these dishes *mare e orto*, the *orto* being the kitchen garden. Often the fish was combined with vegetables and greens from our *orto*.

SAUCE AND FILLING

1 pound medium shrimp

2 tablespoons extra virgin olive oil

1 small carrot, peeled and cut into pieces

1 small onion, quartered

1/2 tender rib celery, cut into pieces

1 jigger (about 2 tablespoons) grappa or vodka

1 1/2 cups water

1/2 pound red snapper fillet, cut into 4 pieces

2 tablespoons unsalted butter

1 large egg

DOUGH

1 recipe Basic Homemade Pasta (page 140), made with 3 eggs

TOPPING

5 baby artichokes, preferably with stems

2 tablespoons extra virgin olive oil

2 cloves garlic, peeled

2 sprigs fresh parsley

3 to 4 ripe plum tomatoes, peeled, seeded, and diced

FINISH

2 cloves garlic, peeled

2 sprigs fresh parsley

1 tender rib celery

1. Prepare the sauce and the filling: Shell and devein the shrimp. Reserve the shells; set shells and shrimp aside.

2. In a medium-size skillet heat the oil over medium-high heat. Add the carrot, onion, and celery. Cook, stirring often, until softened, about 10 minutes. Add the reserved shells of the shrimp and cook until they turn red, about 5 minutes. Add the grappa or vodka and let evaporate. Pour in the water, increase the heat to high, and bring to a boil. Reduce the heat to medium-high and simmer until slightly reduced, about 10 minutes.

3. Strain the sauce through a colander, pressing on the solids to extract as much juice as possible. Return the sauce to the skillet, bring to a boil over high heat, and add the red snapper. Reduce the heat to medium-low and cook about 5 to 8 minutes, then add the shrimp. Cook until the fish flakes when touched with a fork, about 10 minutes longer.

4. Set a colander in a large bowl. Transfer the contents of the skillet to the colander and drain over the bowl, letting the fish cool while the sauce drips. Wipe out the skillet, pour the liquid from the bowl under the colander back into the skillet. Add the butter. Set the sauce aside.

5. Place the fish and shrimp in a food processor and add the egg. Process until finely chopped. Set aside.

6. Prepare the ravioli according to the recipe for *Ravioli di Ricotta alla Anna Teresa* (page 160) using the above fish and shrimp mixture as the filling. If some of the filling remains, it can be added to the sauce. Keep the ravioli on cookie sheets lined with kitchen towels (not paper towels) until ready to cook.

7. Prepare the topping: Remove all the tough leaves from the artichokes and trim the tops. If the artichokes have stems, peel and dice them. Cut the whole artichokes into thin wedges. Keep the artichokes and stems in a bowl of acidulated water (water with the juice of $1/2$ lemon) while working to prevent discoloration.

8. In another skillet heat the olive oil, add 1 clove garlic and 1 sprig of parsley. Cook briefly over medium-high heat for 2 to 3 minutes. Drain the artichokes, reserving half of the acidulated water. Add the artichokes to the skillet and cook, stirring often, until they start to soften, about 5 minutes. Pour in enough of the reserved water to cover the artichokes. Reduce the heat to low and cook the artichokes, covered, over low heat until they are tender, 5 to 8 minutes. Remove the garlic clove and parsley sprig and discard both. Add the tomatoes and cook until slightly reduced. Continue cooking 5 to 6 minutes. Cover to keep warm.

9. Prepare the finished dish: Chop together the remaining garlic, parsley, and celery. Add to the shrimp sauce and simmer for 2 to 3 minutes. Cover to keep warm.

10. Cook the ravioli in a large pot of boiling, salted water, about 5 minutes. Taste a raviolo for doneness as soon as the water returns to a boil. Drain and reserve 1 cup of the cooking water. Add $1/2$ cup of the cooking water to the shrimp sauce. Toss. Dress the ravioli with the sauce. Add a a little more of the cooking water if the mixture looks dry. Serve the ravioli topped with the stewed artichokes and tomatoes.

TORTELLI AL TACCHINO AFFUMICATO

Smoked Turkey Tortelli *(Makes 6 servings)*

AT HOME, AFTER A FEAST OF TURKEY, THE leftover meat was often used as stuffing for ravioli. To make it more flavorful, my mother used to combine the meat. Chopped leftover turkey with ricotta and smoked mozzarella make an excellent stuffing for ravioli. It was an unusual flavor but the ravioli were excellent.

It was in remembering this recipe that I came to invent the following one, thanks to my friend and colleague, Bobby Leavitt. She is famous for her delicious smoked turkey. I am the lucky one who often goes home with the carcass! On one occasion, I was able to pick out enough meat to try my mother's recipe using this smoked turkey rather than smoked mozzarella. I changed the format into *mezzelune tortelli* (half-moon shaped *tortelli* that are larger than ravioli) because I wanted to enclose more filling. It worked well. Not only did the tortelli look wonderful, the smoky flavor was even more pronounced than when using the smoked cheese.

Lacking Bobby's turkey, one can use smoked turkey from the delicatessen or revert to my mother's smoked mozzarella. By the way, I will never give this recipe to Bobby—she might want to keep the carcass for herself next time!

FILLING

1 cup smoked turkey, very finely chopped
1 cup ricotta, drained
1 egg, lightly beaten
2 tablespoons freshly grated parmesan or grana padano cheese
1/2 teaspoon grated nutmeg
Freshly ground white pepper to taste
1 tablespoon minced fresh parsley

PASTA

1 recipe Basic Homemade Pasta (page 140), made with 4 eggs

SAUCE #1

1 1/4 cups heavy cream
1 cup chicken broth, preferably homemade (page 61)
Freshly grated parmesan or grana padano cheese

SAUCE #2

1 tablespoon butter
1 heaping tablespoon all-purpose flour
2 cups chicken broth, preferably homemade (page 61)
1/4 teaspoon grated nutmeg
1/2 teaspoon white pepper
Salt to taste, optional

1. Combine the turkey, ricotta, egg, cheese, nutmeg, pepper, and parsley in a bowl. Mix well and set aside.

2. Cut the dough into 6 wedges. Use a pasta machine to roll the dough out as thin as possible, one wedge at a time. (See instructions on page 141). Reuse any scraps of dough by kneading them again into one of the remaining wedges of dough. Repeat until all the dough is finished. Lay the sheets of dough out one at a time on a large work surface. Keep the remaining dough covered with kitchen towels. Place 1 teaspoon of the filling at equal intervals in a line along one side of the sheet of dough. Dip a finger into a glass of water and run it around the filling where the tortelli will be cut. Fold the sheet over to cover the filling. Press around each filling with your fingers, and cut with a 2 1/2-inch tortellini cutter or a crinkle-edged round cookie cutter. Press with your fingers around the filling again to seal the tortelli well.

3. Keep the tortelli on cookie sheets lined with kitchen towels (not paper towels) until ready to cook. The tortelli can be prepared 1 day in advance to this point and refrigerated.

The tortelli are served with a simple cream sauce that should be unobtrusive and does not overpower the delicate smokiness of the turkey. In the following recipe I suggest two sauces which complement this dish well.

4. If using sauce #1, prepare the sauce while the tortelli are cooking. Combine the cream and broth in a small saucepan together. Bring to a boil over high heat, and remove from the heat immediately.

5. If using sauce #2, prepare it before cooking the tortelli. Heat the butter in a 1-quart saucepan, add the flour and cook for 1 minute, stirring constantly. Remove from the heat and start adding the broth, a little at a time, stirring the whole to a smooth liquidy sauce. Cook over medium heat stirring constantly until it starts to boil. Add remaining ingredients. Set aside but keep warm.

6. Cook the tortelli in a large pot of boiling, salted water, stirring once or twice until done, 5 to 8 minutes. Taste a tortello for doneness as soon as the water returns to a boil. Drain, reserving 1 cup of the cooking water.

7. Dress the drained tortelli with either sauce, toss, and sprinkle with the grated cheese. If the mixture seems too dry, add a little of the reserved cooking water. Serve with additional cheese on the side.

NOTE: ANY LEFTOVER FILLING CAN BE ADDED TO THE EITHER SAUCE.

CLASSIC TORTELLINI

(Makes 6 to 8 servings)

THIS IS A BASIC RECIPE, MADE WITH A chicken, mortadella, and nutmeg filling. These tortellini can be sauced like other pastas. Served in broth they become an elegant *minestra* called *Tortellini in Brodo*, a classic of Italian cuisine.

FILLING
1 tablespoon unsalted butter
1 tablespoon extra virgin olive oil
1/2 skinless, boneless chicken breast,
*   cut into cubes*
Salt to taste, optional
Freshly ground pepper to taste
1/2 teaspoon grated nutmeg

About 1 ounce mortadella cheese,
*   cut into large pieces*
1 small egg

DOUGH
1 recipe Basic Homemade Pasta (page
*   140), made with 2 eggs, stretched as*
*   thin as possible*

1. In a small skillet, heat the butter and the oil over medium heat. Add the chicken and cook, stirring, until brown, about 8 to 10 minutes. Season with salt and

continues

pepper. Place the chicken in a food processor and add the remaining ingredients for the filling. Process until very finely chopped. Set aside.

2. Using a 2-inch tortellini cutter or cookie cutter of the same dimension, cut the dough into rounds. Put a small amount of the filling, the size of a chick pea, in the center of each round. Dip a finger in water and run it around the perimeter of the round. Fold the round into a half-moon and press to seal. Pick up the half-moon and pinch the two pointed ends together forming a little peaked cap. Set the tortellini on cookie sheets lined with kitchen towels. Be sure to gather all the scraps of dough before they get too dried and reroll to make additional tortellini. Repeat until all the dough and filling have been used. Cook as directed.

NOTE 1: TORTELLINI CUTTERS ARE AVAILABLE IN KITCHEN EQUIPMENT STORES.

NOTE 2: TORTELLINI CAN BE PREPARED IN ADVANCE AND KEPT IN A COOL PLACE FOR A FEW HOURS. IF LONGER, REFRIGERATE. THEY CAN ALSO BE FROZEN.

Variation: My aunt Cettina, a patient cook who loved to fuss in the kitchen, made her tortellini into perfect little doughnut-shaped rounds to the astonishment of everybody. For very round tortellini like my aunt's, place the filling not in the center of the round, but near the border, then roll into a little tube. Pinch the ends together.

TORTELLINI BY ANY OTHER NAME

Tortellini are also called *cappelletti*, Italian for "little hats," and *agnolotti* when not pinched together and left in half-moon shapes.

TORTELLINI TRICOLORE AL FORNO

Baked Tricolored Tortellini (Makes 6 servings)

HERE IS A PASTA DISH WHICH IS LIGHT IN calories, yet elegant and satisfying. I use green pasta for the *tortellini* which renders the dish unique. Because it can be prepared in advance, it is ideal for entertaining.

1 recipe Basic Homemade Pasta, spinach dough variation (page 140), made with 3 eggs
Unsalted butter for greasing the dish and to dot the top before baking
2 tablespoons dried bread crumbs
8 to 9 plum tomatoes, peeled, seeded, and chopped
1 cup peas, blanched

½ teaspoon grated nutmeg
3 to 4 fresh basil leaves, or ½ teaspoon dried
Freshly ground pepper
½ cup ricotta
8 ounces mozzarella cheese, preferably bufalo, diced
About 1 cup freshly grated grana padano cheese to taste

1. Make the tortellini according to the recipe for Classic Tortellini (page 169), but using green pasta.

2. Preheat the oven to 375°F. Butter a 2-quart soufflé dish and sprinkle with bread crumbs. Set aside.

3. In a mixing bowl, combine the tomatoes, peas, nutmeg, and basil. Toss well to mix.

4. Cook the tortellini in a large pot of boiling, salted water, stirring often, until done, 5 to 8 minutes. Taste the pasta for doneness as soon as the water returns to a boil. Drain the tortellini, reserving ½ cup of the cooking water. Turn the tortellini into the mixing bowl that contains the vegetables, sprinkle with pepper, and toss.

5. Place the ricotta in a small bowl and add enough of the reserved water to make it the consistency of a light, creamy sauce. Add this to the tortellini and toss again. Add the mozzarella cheese and toss again.

6. Spoon one-third of the tortellini mixture into the prepared dish and sprinkle with 2 or 3 tablespoons of the grana padano cheese. Add another third of the tortellini and sprinkle again with the cheese. Add the remaining tortellini and sprinkle with grana padano. If you wish, dot the top with a small amount of butter. Bake until the top is golden, about 30 to 35 minutes.

CAPPELLETTI PASTICCIATI

Cappelletti in a Nice Mess *(Makes 6 servings)*

MY FATHER ALWAYS SAID THAT HE HAD chosen his birthday well. He was born on the 26th of December, the day after Christmas. This is a holiday in Italy, and my father always celebrated accordingly. The following recipe was one of his favorite dishes.

We used to call this *tortellini*, or *cappelletti pasticciati*, which is an acceptable culinary term that in Italian gastronomy means *with many things put together*. In other words, a nice mess! The filling is rich and unusual, one of my aunt Cettina's brilliant inspirations on which my father, he said, improved. True, the addition of the stracchino cheese in the filling was his idea.

For my father's birthday, the main ingredient for the filling was always made with capon meat. Since this bird was traditionally served during Christmas holidays, there always seemed to be several cooked capons around to use as leftovers. A turkey breast is equally good and my father would have not complained.

FILLING

2 tablespoons unsalted butter
1 tablespoon extra virgin olive oil
1 small pork chop, about $^1/_2$ pound
1 half capon breast, approximately 1
    pound, or same amount turkey breast,
    cut into 2 pieces
2 fresh sage leaves, or $^1/_2$ teaspoon dried
1 teaspoon fresh rosemary leaves,
    or $^1/_2$ teaspoon dried
$^1/_4$ cup Marsala wine or sherry
3 ounces stracchino cheese, cubed
    (available in Italian food stores)
2 tablespoons freshly grated parmesan
    cheese
2 large eggs
$^1/_2$ teaspoon grated nutmeg
1 large strip lemon peel, bitter white pith
    removed, cut into 2 pieces
Salt to taste, optional
Freshly ground black pepper to taste

DOUGH

1 recipe Basic Homemade Pasta (page
    140), regular or green, made with
    4 eggs

SAUCE

3 to 4 cups Ragù all'Italiana *(page 104)*
Freshly grated parmesan or grana
    padano cheese

1. In a large skillet, heat the butter and the oil, add the pork chop, and cook over medium heat until lightly browned, about 5 minutes on each side. Add the capon breast, sage, and rosemary. Cook until lightly browned, about 5 minutes on each side. Add the wine and let evaporate. Transfer the pork chop and the capon breast to a plate or platter and cool.

2. When the meats are cool enough to handle, remove the bone from the chop. Cube both meats. Transfer to a food processor and add the stracchino cheese, parmesan cheese, eggs, nutmeg, lemon peel, salt, and pepper, and process until very finely chopped.

3. Prepare the cappelletti using the recipe for Classic Tortellini (page 169) and the above filling.

4. Gently warm the sauce over low heat. Cook the cappelleti in a large pot of boiling, salted water for 5 to 8 minutes. Taste for doneness as soon as the water returns to a boil. Drain and dress with the sauce. Serve with the grated cheese on the side.

NOTE: IF YOU HAVE SOME LEFTOVER FILLING, IT CAN BE ADDED TO THE SAUCE OR RESERVED FOR ANOTHER USE. IT IS DELICIOUS SPREAD ON CRACKERS.

CAPPELLETTI ALL'ORTOLANA

Cappelletti a la Backyard (Makes 6 servings)

THE NAME OF THIS RECIPE, OF COURSE, comes from *orto*, the kitchen garden or backyard where the chickens were kept.

I like to use green dough for this *cappelletti*. The brown sauce matches the cool elegant color of the green pasta beautifully.

DOUGH
1 recipe Basic Homemade Pasta (page 140), green dough, made with 3 eggs

SAUCE
1 sweet Italian sausage, about 10 ounces
2 tablespoons unsalted butter
1 tablespoon extra virgin olive oil
1 medium-size onion, finely chopped
1 clove garlic, peeled and finely chopped
2 bay leaves
1 pound assorted chicken gizzards, hearts, giblets, and livers, coarsely chopped

Salt to taste, optional
Freshly ground pepper
1/2 cup dry wine, white or red
1 teaspoon tomato paste
1 cup chicken broth, preferably homemade (page 61), or bouillon
One 16-ounce can strained tomato sauce
1 1/2 cups broccoli flowerets, blanched; or frozen peas, defrosted
Freshly grated parmesan or grana padano cheese

1. Prepare the cappelletti as directed for Classic Tortellini (page 169).

2. Pierce the sausage in several places and place in a small skillet. Cover it with water, bring to a boil over high heat, and cook, turning often, until all the water has been absorbed. Remove from the skillet and cool.

3. In a large skillet, heat the butter and oil, add the onion and garlic and cook over medium heat, stirring, until soft and translucent, 8 to 10 minutes. Add the bay leaves and the chicken gizzards, hearts, and livers. Cook, stirring often, until lightly browned, 5 to 8 minutes. Add the salt, if used, the pepper, and the wine. Let evaporate. Stir in the tomato paste and broth. Simmer about 5 minutes. Add the tomato sauce. Cover the skillet and bring to a boil over high heat. Reduce the heat to low and simmer, stirring often, until the meat is tender, about 45 minutes.

continues

4. Remove and discard the skin of the sausage, crumble the meat, and add it to the sauce. Continue cooking at a simmer until the flavors are combined, about 10 minutes longer. If the sauce is too thick, add a little more broth. Add the broccoli or peas and cook until heated through, about 2 minutes. Set the sauce aside and keep warm.

5. Cook the cappelletti in a large pot of boiling, salted water for 5 to 8 minutes. Drain and dress with the sauce. Serve with the grated cheese on the side.

CANNELLONI ALLA ANNA TERESA

(Makes 6 to 8 servings)

MY SIGNATURE RECIPE. THESE *CANNELLONI* were a great success when I made them on television, during my special show, "Let Them Eat Pasta." The show was produced by CBS and aired nationwide. It was later repeated on PBS. During the show, I discussed the history of pasta, introducing a lot of historical background, starting with the Etruscans—and debunking the Marco Polo legend. This happened in the late sixties, at the beginning of the pasta invasion. I think that I was the first one to use the word *pasta*. We called it macaroni, remember? In fact, my friend and colleague, Nancy Verde Barr, wrote a lovely book with this title.

These cannelloni are also famous in my family because it was the first time my husband, who hates spinach, unknowingly ate and liked it. The spinach was part of the stuffing. We

1 recipe Basic Homemade Pasta (page 140), made with 4 eggs, stretched as thin as possible
2 tablespoons kosher salt
2 cups Stuffing for Ravioli or Cannelloni Anna Teresa (page 159)

Unsalted butter for pan
4 cups Ragù all'Italiana (page 104)
Freshly grated parmesan or grana padano cheese

1. Divide the dough into 4 wedges. Roll one wedge at a time into thin sheets. I use the last notch on my pasta machine.

2. Set the stretched dough on a cutting board and using a crinkled-edged cookie wheel, cut the sheets into rectangles that measure 5 by 6 inches. Set the rectangles on kitchen towels until ready to use.

3. Wet a large kitchen towel, preferably cotton or linen, wring out the water, and spread the towel on the counter or flat work surface.

4. Fill a shallow 2-quart pot with water. Bring to a boil over high heat, add the kosher salt, wait for the water to come back to a boil. Add 4 pieces of the pasta. As soon as the pasta rises to the surface, remove each piece with a slotted spoon to the bowl of cold water to cool.

had just been married and were visiting Italy together for the first time. A dear friend of my mother, Signora Maria Contegno, invited us to dinner and made these cannelloni, which I had eaten many times because my mother made them as well.

The stuffing is the original, which I also use to fill ravioli.

The recipe can be made in stages. Keep in mind that many steps for this recipe, like the stuffing and the sauce, can be prepared in advance. The finished dish can be made a day before, refrigerated overnight, and baked just before ready to serve.

The quantity of dough suggested will make approximately 40 *cannelloni*.

5. Spread the pieces of wet pasta on the prepared towel to drain. Continue cooking and draining the pasta until all the rectangles are cooked.

6. Butter one or two oven-to-table baking dishes large enough for the cannelloni to fit snugly in one flat layer.

7. Starting from the top end of the rectangle, spread 2 tablespoons of the stuffing along the edge, then roll to enclose the filling. Set the cannelloni close together in the prepared buttered dish.

8. Repeat until you finish cooking and filling all the pasta.

9. Preheat the oven to 375°F.

10. Reheat the sauce, dress the cannelloni with it, reserving the meat for another use or to serve as a second course. Sprinkle with plenty of grated cheese. Bake 45 minutes. Serve with additional cheese on the side.

SCREPPELLE DI PESCE

Crepes Stuffed with Fish (*Makes about 18 5-inch crepes*)

I HAVE ALREADY TALKED ABOUT MY FRIEND Bobo, who at one time was at the helm of the fabulous restaurant Lo Squalo Blue (the Blue Shark) on the Adriatic coast. I love and admire his cuisine because he so cleverly combines traditional food with novel inspiration. The following recipe, which I have adapted, is a good example of his expertise.

CREPES

4 large eggs
1/2 cup all-purpose flour
1 tablespoon minced fresh parsley
1/4 teaspoon salt
1/4 cup milk
1/2 cup water
1 tablespoon unsalted butter

FILLING

1 teaspoon kosher salt
3/4 pound firm white-flesh fish like cod, monk, sea bass, or red snapper
3/4 pound ricotta, drained
1 egg, beaten

1/4 teaspoon grated nutmeg
Freshly ground pepper to taste
2 tablespoons freshly grated parmesan cheese
1 cup Salsa Balsamella (page 92)

SAUCE

1/2 pound medium-size shrimp
1/4 cup extra virgin olive oil
1 clove garlic, peeled and minced
1 jigger (1 1/2 ounces) brandy or cognac
One 16-ounce can peeled tomatoes, drained
1 sprig fresh parsley, minced

1. Prepare the crepes: Place the eggs in a food processor and process briefly to mix. With the motor running, slowly add the flour, parsley, salt, milk, and water. Process until the batter is well mixed. Pour into a bowl. The batter should be the consistency of light cream. If not, add some water or milk to thin.

2. Melt 1/2 teaspoon of the butter in a crepe pan, or a small skillet (I use a 5-inch skillet, because I like my crepes small). Wipe the skillet with a paper towel to remove any excess butter and heat over medium heat. Using a ladle or a cup, pour the crepe batter 1/4 cup at a time into the skillet. Tilt and rotate the skillet to distribute the mixture evenly. Cook until the edges start to turn gold, 2 to 3 seconds, and turn the crepe on the other side.

3. Set aside while continuing to make the rest of the crepes. At some point you may need to lightly butter your pan again. The crepes can be prepared in advance and refrigerated overnight.

4. Prepare the filling: Fill a 2-quart pot with water and bring to a boil over high heat. Add the salt and the fish. Reduce the heat to medium-high and simmer the fish for 10 minutes. Remove from the water, reserving 1 cup of the cooking water. Drain the fish and set aside.

5. In a mixing bowl, combine the ricotta, egg, nutmeg, pepper, cheese, and *Salsa Balsamella*. Flake the fish and add to the ricotta mixture. Set aside.

6. Prepare the sauce: Peel and devein the shrimp. Reserve the shells. Cut the shrimp in half lengthwise. Place in a bowl of cold water to which 1 teaspoon of kosher salt has been added. Set aside for 10 minutes, then rinse and drain the shrimp.

7. In a medium-size skillet heat 2 tablespoons of the oil, add the shrimp shells and cook over medium heat until they turn red, about 5 minutes. Add the cup of reserved cooking water from the fish. Increase the heat to high and and boil until slightly reduced, about 10 minutes. Drain the mixture in a colander and reserve the liquid. Discard the shells.

8. Wipe the skillet clean and add the remaining oil. Set over medium heat and add the shrimp and garlic. Cook until the garlic starts to color, about 3 to 5 minutes, then add the brandy. Cook until the brandy has evaporated and add the tomatoes. Stir, breaking the tomatoes with a wooden spoon. Bring to a boil over high heat and cook over medium high heat until the liquid has reduced by half, 10 to 15 minutes. Add some of the reserved liquid from the shells of the shrimp and cook until thickened, about 5 minutes longer. The sauce should not be too thick.

9. In one or two skillets into which the crepes can be snugly set in one layer, pour half of the sauce.

10. Fill each crepe with 2 tablespoons of the fish mixture. Roll into cylinders and set them in the prepared skillet. Top them with the remaining sauce. Heat over medium-low heat until the crepes are hot, 5 to 10 minutes. Spoon the sauce over the crepes every once in a while and gently shake the pan occasionally to prevent sticking. Serve hot, sprinkled with the minced parsley.

CRESPELLE DI FARINA DI CECI CON FUNGHI

Chick Pea Flour Crepes with Mushrooms **(Makes 18 crepes)**

A TYPICAL EXAMPLE OF ABRUZZESE ingenuity is using peasant fare like chick pea flour for an elegant, sophisticated, and quite unusual dish.

Before you start, soak the dried porcini so you can use the water in which they soaked for the crepes.

¹/₂ cup dried porcini mushrooms, soaked in 1 cup of lukewarm water for 20 minutes

CREPES

2 large eggs
2 cups chick pea flour
1 tablespoon finely minced fresh parsley
Salt to taste, optional
Freshly ground pepper to taste
The water from the soaked porcini mushrooms
1 tablespoon unsalted butter

FILLING

³/₄ pound fresh mushrooms
2 tablespoons butter, plus more for finishing the dish
1 tablespoon extra virgin olive oil
³/₄ cup heavy cream
Butter for pan

SAUCE

2 tablespoons extra virgin olive oil
5 to 6 plum tomatoes, diced
¹/₄ cup heavy cream
2 to 3 basil fresh leaves
1 sprig fresh parsley

1. Gently, so as not to upset the sediment resting at the bottom, lift the porcini mushrooms out of the water and set aside. Strain the water through a paper towel or coffee filter. Set aside.

2. Prepare the crepes: Place the eggs in a food processor and process briefly to mix. Add the flour, parsley, salt, and pepper. Pulse to combine the mixture. Slowly and with the machine running, start to add the water from the dried mushrooms. The batter should be liquidy, and you may not need more water. Pour the batter into a bowl.

3. Lightly butter a crepe pan or small skillet (I use a 5-inch skillet). Wipe the skillet with a paper towel to remove any excess butter, and heat over medium heat. Using a ladle or a cup, pour about ¹/₄ cup of the crepe batter into the skillet. Tilt and rotate the skillet to distribute the mixture evenly. Cook until the edges start

to turn gold, 2 to 3 seconds. Turn the crepe to the other side and cook a few seconds longer. Turn the crepe out onto a platter. Set aside while continuing to make the rest of the crepes. At some point you may need to lightly butter the pan again. The crepes can be prepared in advance and refrigerated.

4. Prepare the filling: Coarsely chop the fresh mushrooms and the drained porcini.

5. In a medium-size skillet, heat 2 tablespoons of the butter and the oil, add all the mushrooms, and cook over medium-high heat, stirring occasionally, until all the water put out by the mushrooms has been absorbed. Add the cream. Bring to a boil over high heat, reduce the heat to low, and cook until the cream is slightly thickened, about 5 minutes.

6. Preheat the oven to 250°F. Butter a baking dish large enough to hold the filled and rolled crepes in one layer.

7. Spoon about 2 tablespoons of the mushroom mixture into each crepe, roll them into cylinders, and set them in the prepared pan. Dot with butter and keep the crepes warm in the oven while preparing the sauce.

8. Prepare the sauce: In a medium-size skillet, heat the oil over medium-high heat. Add the tomatoes and cook, 5 to 8 minutes. Add the cream and cook until it is quite hot and slightly reduced, 5 to 8 minutes.

9. Chop the basil and parsley together and add to the sauce; mix.

10. Serve 2 to 3 crepes per person, topped with a spoonful of the sauce.

GNOCCHI DI PATATE

Potato Gnocchi **(Makes 6 servings)**

WE ALL LOVED GNOCCHI IN MY HOME, and when we were children, we liked to gather around Grandmother to watch her and to help. We were all given a ball of the dough and taught how to make the cigar-shaped strips from which the gnocchi were cut and shaped. The shaping, ah the shaping! That is another story. Not easy, but with a little patience, one learns. And we did.

However, when I came to America I found that making gnocchi was not so easy. In fact, in my previous book, *Menus for Pasta*, I confessed to my friend Bruno Creglia that I was having problems. He was the owner of the restaurant Giordano, now defunct (as it often happens to good establishments in New York). They made superb gnocchi. Bruno sent me a recipe with a funny letter inviting me to take gnocchi lessons from his chef. His secret was the addition of 1 egg. In my house, eggs had been a no-no because, according to my grandmother, they made the gnocchi chewy (which, by the way is how I really like them—but do not tell anybody!).

One thing is important. Never use new potatoes. Italian books will often specify old potatoes, but it is not easy to guess the age of the potatoes we buy.

2 pounds boiling or baking potatoes
1 egg

½ teaspoon salt
2 cups or more all-purpose flour

1. Wash the potatoes but do not peel them. Place the potatoes in a large pot, cover with cold water, and bring them to a boil over high heat. Cook until tender. The cooking time depends on the size and type of potatoes. Test for doneness by piercing one or two potatoes with a fork. If the fork enters easily, the potatoes are done. Drain and cool the potatoes, peel, and rice with a potato ricer or a food mill—never use a food processor. Transfer the riced potatoes to a large mixing bowl. Add the egg and salt, mix well, and turn out onto a floured work surface. Add 1½ cups of the flour and start kneading the dough, adding more flour as necessary to prevent sticking. Stop the kneading as soon as the dough holds together into a soft, smooth dough. This dough should not be handled too much and it does not need to rest before cutting and shaping.

2. Break off a small amount of dough the size of an egg and shape it into a thin, round strip resembling a cigar. Do this on the floured work surface, then cut into 1-inch pieces. Holding a fork and resting the point on the work surface, gently press and roll down each piece on the tines of the fork. You can also roll the little pieces of dough on a cheese grater. This will make each piece of dough ridged and curled up into the shape of a shell. Set the gnocchi separately on cookie sheets lined with kitchen towels. Do not use paper towels, as they absorb the moisture and might stick to the gnocchi. Keep in a cool place until ready to cook, but no longer than 40 to 45 minutes. If necessary to keep longer, cover with kitchen towels.

3. To cook the gnocchi, bring a large pot of water to a boil and add salt. As soon as the water comes back to a boil, add the gnocchi and cook until they float to the surface. Let boil 2 to 3 minutes, taste for doneness, then drain. The gnocchi are done when tender but not mushy.

The best, in my opinion, are boiling or baking potatoes. But lately I tried the Yukon Gold potatoes with excellent results. And my advice is to use an egg. Believe me, your gnocchi will come out quite tender enough to satisfy the most rigid purist.

NOTE: FRESH GNOCCHI, FROZEN IN BUNCHES AND BAGGED WHEN HARD, KEEP WELL FOR 2 MONTHS OR MORE.

THE BEST SAUCES FOR GNOCCHI ARE SIMPLE ONES, MY FAVORITE IS THE *SUGO FINTO* (PAGE 96), A BASIC TOMATO SAUCE, OR SIMPLY BUTTER AND PARMESAN WITH A HINT OF SAGE. BUT THERE ARE MANY WAYS TO DRESS GNOCCHI, JUST REMEMBER THAT GNOCCHI SHOULD "SIT" IN THEIR SAUCE FOR 10 MINUTES BEFORE SERVING.

Variation: To make *Gnocchi di Patate Tricolore*, divide the dough into 3 parts. Add to one part $1/4$ cup puree of cooked red beets, and to the second part, $1/4$ cup puree of cooked spinach. Proceed as for above recipe using a little more flour for the colored dough. To keep the color of the gnocchi visible, I dress them with a simple and translucent sauce made with butter and a little cream, to which I add 8 ounces of mozzarella. Add the mozzarella just before serving and, of course, pass the parmesan.

GNOCCHI DI SEMOLINA ALL'ABRUZZESE

Semolina Gnocchi Abruzzo Style **(Makes 6 servings)**

POTATO GNOCCHI ARE INDIGENOUS TO ALL parts of Italy, but there are other kinds that are typical of certain regions and favor gnocchi made with other ingredients. Notable examples are the *gnocchi di semolina alla Romana* from Rome, the famous *cavatelli* from Apulia, or those made with ricotta from Emilia-Romagna, and so forth.

The gnocchi in this recipe are similar to those made in Rome. The Abruzzo region is adjacent to the Lazio region, of which Rome is the capital. The two regions often borrow recipes from each other.

These gnocchi are easy to make. They can be prepared in advance and baked just before serving.

1 quart milk
1³/₄ cups semolina
About 1 cup unsalted butter, at room temperature
3 tablespoons freshly grated parmesan cheese, plus more for sprinkling

1 egg, lightly beaten
¹/₂ cup finely chopped prosciutto
¹/₂ teaspoon grated nutmeg
Salt to taste, optional
1 tablespoon finely minced fresh parsley

1. Pour the milk into a large saucepan and bring it to a boil over high heat. Add the semolina to the milk in a steady stream, stirring constantly with a wire whisk. Reduce the heat to medium and cook until the mixture starts to pull away from the sides of the pan, 10 to 15 minutes. Remove from the heat and add half the butter, 3 tablespoons of the cheese, the egg, and the prosciutto. Season with the nutmeg and salt. Mix well.

2. Slightly wet a marble slab or a Formica countertop. Turn the semolina mixture over onto it. Let cool. Butter a 10-inch round ovenproof dish from which you can serve.

3. Wet your hands and pat the mixture to a ¹/₂-inch flat thickness. Cut the semolina into 1¹/₂-inch rounds (this can be done with a tortellini or a small cookie cutter) and arrange one layer of gnocchi on the bottom of the buttered dish. Sprinkle with parmesan and dot with a little of the remaining butter. Continue stacking the rounds of gnocchi, starting the second layer about ³/₄ inch from the border of the first layer. Make 2 to 3 or more layers in consecutively smaller stacks. The completed dish will have a cupola effect. Sprinkle each layer with cheese and dot with butter.

4. The dish can be prepared in advance up to this point. Refrigerate if kept overnight.

5. Preheat the oven to 375°F. Bake the stacked gnocchi until the top is nicely colored, 25 to 30 minutes. Sprinkle with the parsley and serve.

Variation: *Cupola di Polenta o Gnocchi Gialli*
In Fontavignone the gnocchi are made with polenta cooked in milk and cut and layered like the semolina gnocchi. Fontina cheese is also used between layers.

CAVATELLI CON L'ARUGULA

(Makes 4 to 6 servings)

THIS IS A MUCH-LOVED DISH THAT MOTHER made every time arugula was in season and abundant. She had brought back the recipe from Apulia, where we lived for a while, and made it part of her repertoire.

I make my own cavatelli since this is how the recipe started, but you can use store-bought cavatelli.

DOUGH
About 2¹/₂ cups all-purpose flour
1¹/₂ cups semolina
¹/₄ teaspoon salt
About 1 cup lukewarm water

SAUCE
5 tablespoons extra virgin olive oil
2 cloves whole garlic, peeled

One 16-ounce can peeled tomatoes,
or 1 pound fresh, ripe tomatoes
4 to 5 fresh basil leaves, or ¹/₂ teaspoon
dried
Salt to taste, optional
Freshly ground pepper to taste
3 bunches arugula, washed, trimmed,
and cut into 2-inch pieces
Freshly grated pecorino romano cheese
for serving

1. Prepare the dough: Combine the flour, semolina, and salt in a food processor. With the motor running, add enough water to knead the dough. Stop processing as soon as a ball forms on the blades.

2. Transfer the dough to a floured work surface and knead the dough, adding more flour if necessary, until smooth and elastic, about 10 minutes. Set the dough under an inverted bowl and let it rest 20 minutes.

3. When ready to make the *cavatelli*, break off pieces of dough about the size of an egg and roll into cigar-shaped cylinders. Cut each cylinder into ³/₄-inch pieces and, pressing each piece of dough down against the work surface with the thumb, form a little shell-like dumpling. Set on cookie sheets lined with kitchen towels.

4. Prepare the sauce: Heat the oil in a large skillet over medium heat. Add the garlic and cook until it starts to color, about 2 minutes. Let it sizzle for 1 minute and add the tomatoes, basil, salt, if used, and the pepper. Cover the skillet and simmer until the sauce is thick and slightly pulpy, 15 to 20 minutes.

5. In a large pot of boiling, salted water add the arugula. Cook over high heat until slightly wilted, about 30 seconds. Add the *cavatelli* and cook until the dumplings are done, about 5 to 8 minutes longer. Drain and dress with the sauce. Serve with a bowl of grated cheese on the side.

GNOCCHI NUDI

Naked Gnocchi **(Makes 24 gnocchi, serves 6 as a first course)**

THESE ARE THE MOST DELICATE GNOCCHI ever. Made with a spinach and ricotta mixture, they are dressed just with butter and parmesan cheese. They are called "naked" because they resemble the exposed filling often used to make ravioli.

My brother and I loved these gnocchi, but convincing our mother to prepare them was another story. It had to be a very special occasion because the gnocchi are a little tricky to make. If the right amount of flour is not used, they might melt into the boiling water and become a "polenta." (Italians call everything mushy and unappetizing a "polenta." We also call a boring person a "polenta," we are famous for insulting people with gastronomic names!) However, once when my gnocchi became a polenta, I simply drained the whole mess in a fine mesh colander, placed it in a buttered pie dish, baked it, and brazenly called it a flan. It was delicious!

1 pound fresh spinach, trimmed, washed, cooked, and squeezed dry
15 ounces ricotta, drained
3 large eggs, lightly beaten
About 1 cup freshly grated parmesan or grana padano cheese
1/2 teaspoon grated nutmeg
1/4 teaspoon salt
1/4 teaspoon freshly ground pepper
About 2 cups all-purpose flour
2 to 3 tablespoons unsalted butter plus more for dish
1 tablespoon kosher salt

1. Chop the spinach very finely by hand. Do not use a machine which will produce too much liquid. Squeeze the chopped spinach to remove excess moisture. Place the spinach in a large mixing bowl. Add the ricotta, eggs, $1/3$ cup of the cheese, nutmeg, salt, and pepper. Mix well. Start adding small amounts of the flour, 4 to 5 tablespoons at a time. The mixture should be soft, but not wet. If necessary, add a little more flour, in small amounts, as needed. (The amount of flour needed will depend on the dampness of the spinach.)

2. Preheat the oven to 375°F. Generously butter an ovenproof serving dish into which the gnocchi can be set in one layer. Set aside.

3. Sprinkle a work surface with flour. Form little croquette-shaped dumplings, about 2 inches long, and roll them in the flour. Set aside until all are finished. Do not handle too much.

4. Bring water to boil in a shallow, medium-size pan and add the kosher salt. When the water comes back to a boil, drop in 3 to 4 gnocchi at a time. Boil until they float to the top. Cook until firm, 3 to 4 minutes. Remove with a slotted spoon, drain in a colander, and transfer to the buttered baking dish. Continue until you finish all the gnocchi. Sprinkle the gnocchi generously with grated cheese and dot with butter. Place in the oven and bake until golden, about 15 minutes.

TIMBALLI

Timballi and Lasagne

Timballi and *lasagne* are the "glories" of the Italian cuisine. Lasagne need no explanation, everybody knows this dish.

But *timballi*, timbales in English, are less well-known and need, perhaps, to be explained.

There are many types of timbales. Most of them are made of dry pasta layered with an assortment of ingredients including cheeses, meats, fish, vegetables, etc. Some are made of semolina or polenta and there are unusual ones made with crepes. Their appearance, especially when they are made for a banquet, can be monumental, as the one made famous in the film *Big Night*. The preparation can be lengthy, but many steps can be performed in advance. Even the timbale itself can be finished in advance and be ready for the oven when you need it. Some freeze well, and some reheat beautifully.

It is inconceivable to think of a festive Abruzzese dinner without some sort of *timballo*. And let's not confuse this gastronomic masterpiece with baked macaroni. A *timballo*, even when made with macaroni, is a work of art; it ennobles the table. In his novel *The Leopard*, the great Italian writer, Giuseppe Tomasi di Lampedusa, dedicates an interesting page to the description of the really monumental *timballo* that the chef to the fictional Duke of Salaparuta had prepared for one of his great dinners. And talking of films, Luchino Visconti made a great movie from the novel. The dinner scene is a memorable one. Rent the movie; it is great.

The quintessential Abruzzese *timballo,* though, is made with "very fine, almost transparent" crepes, according to Luigi Braccili, a noted Abruzzese writer. In his book, *Abruzzo in Cucina*, he so describes a *timballo di scrippelle* (crepe timbale) and its customary serving place in a wedding menu. "The fourth course place," he says, "after the antipasti, the broth, which opens the stomach, and the chicken galantine." And I won't tell you the continuation of this banquet!

There are however, many *timballi* and *lasagne* in Abruzzo. There are *timballi in bianco,* in white, meaning without tomato sauce, and others layered with meat, fish, or just vegetables. A timbale is sometimes called *pasticcio* or *sformato*. Those versions, especially the *sformato,* are often made with potatoes or other vegetables, and layered with sausages and cheeses.

For festive occasions in my home, both in the past and now, the *Timballo di Maccheroni alla Nonnina*, (my grandmother's masterpiece) was our favorite. She didn't make her *timballo* in one large form, as is the custom, but in individual round baking dishes, 4 to 5 inches in diameter. When unmolded, these *timballini*, little timbales, enclosing their delicious flavor in a harmonious melody of tastes, were irresistible and elegant. The recipe follows.

Some Abruzzese *lasagne* are quite unique, like *Lasagna in Brodo* (page 193), a specialty of the city of Lanciano, or the *Timballo di Patelle* (page 195), which is layered with peas, mushrooms, little meatballs, and small pork cutlets, among other things. In this section you will also find *i rotoli*, or pasta rolls. These are usually stuffed with vegetable puree or finely chopped meat and fish. Contrary to lasagna, which is also made with commercial pasta, the *rotoli* are made with homemade pasta.

TIMBALLINI DI MACCHERONI ALLA NONNINA

Grandmother's Macaroni Timbales (Serves 8)

THIS IS A SPECIAL RECIPE THAT MY grandmother always made for me on my birthday. The word *timballo* comes from the Arabic and refers to dishes cooked in round vessels that resemble a drum, or *timpano*. This recipe can also be made in one 10-inch cake pan. But as my grandmother did, I use eight individual 1-cup capacity ramekins.

MEATBALLS
1/2 pound mixture ground veal, beef, and pork
1 teaspoon minced fresh parsley
1 teaspoon chopped fresh sage, or 1/4 teaspoon dried
Salt to taste, optional
Freshly ground pepper to taste
1 tablespoon unsalted butter
1 teaspoon extra virgin olive oil
2 tablespoons Marsala wine

TIMBALLO (TIMBALE)
Unsalted butter for pan and for topping
2 to 3 tablespoons dried bread crumbs plus more for the topping
One 16-ounce can tomato puree
4 cups Ragù alla Bolognese *(page 103)*
1 1/2 pounds tubular pasta, preferably penne
2 eggs, lightly beaten
1 to 1 1/2 cups freshly grated parmesan or grana padano cheese
1 pound mozzarella, shredded
5 thin slices prosciutto, shredded
1 cup sliced, cooked mushrooms, optional
3 hard-boiled eggs, sliced 1/4 inch thick

1. To prepare the meatballs: Combine the ground meat, parsley, sage, salt, and pepper in a large bowl. Use wet hands to shape into tiny meatballs about the size of a hazelnut.

2. Heat the butter and oil in a large skillet. Add the meatballs and cook over medium-high heat, stirring often, until browned, 5 to 8 minutes. Add the Marsala and let evaporate. Drain on paper towels. The meatballs can be made a day in advance.

3. To make the timbales: Preheat the oven to 375°F. Butter eight individual 1-cup ramekins or a deep, 10-inch round cake pan. Dust with bread crumbs. Set aside.

4. In a large saucepan, combine the tomato puree and ragù. Bring to a boil over high heat, reduce the heat to medium-high, and cook, stirring often, until slightly reduced, about 15 minutes.

5. Cook the pasta according to the package instructions but leave it quite al dente. Drain well and return the pasta to the pot in which it cooked. Add the beaten eggs and mix well. Stir in 3 to 4 ladlesful of the ragù mixture and $^1/_2$ cup grated parmesan cheese. Mix well.

6. Place a thin layer of the pasta in the bottom of each ramekin. Sprinkle on 1 teaspoon of the grated parmesan, 1 tablespoon of the mozzarella, and some of the prosciutto and mushrooms. Cover with a few slices of egg. Spoon 2 to 3 tablespoons of the ragù and repeat until all the ingredients are used. Finish the *timballini* with a layer of pasta, a few spoonsful of sauce, and a sprinkling of grated cheese. Dust the top with bread crumbs, dot with butter, and bake 40 to 45 minutes until the tops are slightly crusty. Cool for 10 minutes. Loosen the sides of the ramekins with a knife and unmold. Sprinkle with additional grated cheese and serve.

TIMBALLO DI SCRIPPELLE

Crepes Timbale (Serves 8)

THIS TIMBALLO IS A SPECIALTY OF THE Teramano, the province of which Teramo is the capital. Teramo is famous for its sophisticated cuisine.

SCRIPPELLE (CREPES)
10 eggs
2 cups all-purpose flour plus 2 tablespoons
1/2 teaspoon grated nutmeg
1/2 cup water
Unsalted butter for cooking the crepes

TIMBALLO (TIMBALE)
5 to 6 baby artichokes, trimmed of tough leaves, quartered, and kept in a bowl of acidulated water

2 1/2 tablespoons unsalted butter
1 tablespoon extra virgin olive oil
1 1/2 cups frozen peas, thawed
4 cups Ragù alla Bolognese (page 103), heated
4 hard-boiled eggs, sliced 1/4 inch thick
1 pound mozzarella cheese, coarsely chopped
About 1 cup grated parmesan cheese
1 large egg
2 tablespoons heavy cream

1. Prepare the *scrippelle:* Beat the eggs in a large bowl and stir in the flour. Add the nutmeg and enough water to make a smooth batter.

2. Lightly grease an 8-inch crepe pan or nonstick skillet. Heat over medium-high heat. Pour about 1/2 cup of the batter into the pan and twirl to evenly coat the bottom. Cook a few seconds, or until the edges start to brown. Turn over and cook the other side a few seconds longer, or until browned around the edges. Transfer to a platter and continue until all the batter is used. The crepes can be made a day in advance.

3. Prepare the *timballo*: Drain the artichokes and reserve 1/4 cup of the acidulated water. In a medium-size skillet, heat 2 tablespoons of the butter and the oil. Add the artichokes and the reserved water. Cover and cook over medium-low heat until the artichokes are tender, about 10 minutes. Add the peas, stir, and cook to heat through, 2 to 3 minutes.

4. Preheat the oven to 375°F. Butter a 10-inch round baking dish from which you can serve. Line the bottom and sides of the baking dish with crepes and let the crepes overlap. Add 2 to 3 ladlesful of the ragù and a layer of the artichoke mixture. Cover with 1 sliced egg, 2 to 3 tablespoons of the mozzarella, and 2 tablespoons of the parmesan cheese. Cover with a layer of crepes. Repeat the layering until all of the crepes are used. Fold the overlapping crepes over to enclose the *timballo*.

5. In a small bowl, beat the egg with 2 tablespoons of parmesan cheese and the cream. Pour over the *timballo* and sprinkle with more parmesan cheese. Dot with the remaining $1/2$ tablespoon of butter and bake for 1 hour and 30 minutes, or until the top is golden brown. Cool before slicing.

Variation: *Timballo di Scrippelle con Ragaglie di Pollo*
The crepes are layered with the same ragù used for *Spaghetti del Pallaiolo* (page 115).

TIMBALLO DI MACCHERONI PRIMAVERA

Macaroni Timbale Primavera **(Makes 6 to 8 servings)**

THIS IS A SIMPLE *TIMBALLO* FLAVORED WITH a sauce made of broccoli and mushrooms.

*Unsalted butter for the pan and
  for the topping
$1/4$ cup dried bread crumbs
2 tablespoons dried porcini mushrooms,
  soaked in lukewarm water for
  20 minutes
3 tablespoons extra virgin olive oil
1 clove garlic, peeled and smashed
$1/2$ pound fresh mushrooms, sliced
1 bunch broccoli, cut into flowerets,
  stems peeled and diced*

*3 to 4 ripe tomatoes, peeled, seeded,
  and diced
$1/2$ cup Pesto Sauce (page 94)
1 pound dried pasta, preferably penne
  or ziti
2 eggs, lightly beaten
$1/2$ pound mozzarella, thinly sliced
$1/2$ cup grated parmesan or grana padano
  cheese*

1. Preheat the oven to 375°F. Butter a 9- to 10-inch springform pan and dust with the bread crumbs.

2. Gently, so as not to upset the sediment resting at the bottom, lift the porcini mushrooms out of the water and set aside. Strain the water through a paper towel or coffee filter. Reserve the liquid and coarsely chop the porcini.

3. In a large skillet, heat the oil. Add the garlic, chopped porcini, and fresh mushrooms. Cook over medium-high heat, stirring often, until the water exuded by the mushrooms has been absorbed. Add the broccoli and cook, stirring, 2 to 3 minutes,

continues

then add the tomatoes, reduce the heat to medium-low, and cook until thickened, 8 to 10 minutes. Add the pesto and heat through, 2 to 3 minutes. Discard the garlic. Remove several of the broccoli flowerets for garnish.

4. Cook the pasta according to the package instructions, slightly undercooking. Drain and return the pasta to the pot it cooked in and add the eggs. Mix well. Add the mushroom-and-vegetable mixture and 1 tablespoon of the parmesan cheese. Mix well. If the mixture looks too dry, add a small amount of the mushroom soaking liquid.

5. Spread a third of the pasta mixture over the bottom of the prepared pan. Add half the mozzarella and a tablespoon of the parmesan cheese. Repeat with another layer of pasta, the remaining mozzarella cheese, and 1 more tablespoon of the parmesan cheese. Finish with a layer of the pasta mixture and sprinkle over the remaining parmesan. Dot with butter and bake for 30 to 40 minutes, or until the top is golden. Cool 10 minutes before slicing. Garnish with the reserved broccoli flowerets and serve.

SOUFFLÉ DI CAPELLI D'ANGELO

Angel Hair Pasta Soufflé **(Makes 6 servings)**

THIS FAMILY RECIPE CREATED A SENSATION when I made it for a demonstration class I was giving at the Culinary Institute of America. The big-toqued chef-professors sitting at the back of the auditorium felt that I didn't have enough sauce for the soufflé. I explained that we Italians don't drown our pasta in sauce. When they tasted the soufflé, they were delighted with the results and admitted that I was right about the amount of sauce. The sauce can be doubled, if more is desired, but please serve it on the side.

SAUCE

2 tablespoons unsalted butter
1 tablespoon extra virgin olive oil
1 large onion, chopped
1/2 pound ground veal
1/4 cup dry white wine
1 tablespoon tomato paste
1 1/2 cups homemade chicken broth or bouillon
1/2 cup heavy cream

SOUFFLÉ

Unsalted butter for the pan and for the topping
2 to 3 tablespoons dried bread crumbs
3/4 pound angel hair pasta
3 eggs, separated, plus one additional egg white
1 cup ricotta, drained
3 thin slices prosciutto, trimmed and minced
1/4 pound mozzarella, sliced
1/2 pound smoked mozzarella, sliced
Freshly grated parmesan or grana padano cheese to taste

1. Prepare the sauce: Heat the butter and the oil in a large skillet. Add the onion and cook over medium-high heat, stirring often, until soft and translucent, 3 to 5 minutes. Add the veal and increase the heat to high. Cook, stirring, until the veal is lightly browned. Add the wine and let evaporate.

2. In a small bowl, combine the tomato paste and broth. Add to the meat mixture, reduce the heat to medium, and cook, uncovered, until thickened, about 20 minutes. Add the cream, remove from the heat, and cool.

3. Prepare the soufflé: Preheat the oven to 375°F. Butter a 2-quart soufflé dish or a 10-inch springform pan and sprinkle with the bread crumbs.

4. Cook the pasta according to the package instructions, but keep it slightly under-cooked. Drain well.

5. In a large bowl, combine the egg yolks, ricotta, and prosciutto. Add the pasta and toss well. Add a fourth of the meat sauce and stir to blend.

6. Beat the egg whites until stiff and gently fold into the pasta mixture.

7. Layer one third of the pasta over the bottom of the prepared pan. Sprinkle over a third of the mozzarella cheeses, 2 to 3 tablespoons of the grated cheese, and 3 to 4 tablespoons of the sauce. Continue layering, finishing with the pasta. Top with the remaining sauce and grated parmesan cheese. Dot with butter and bake for 30 to 40 minutes, or until the top is browned. Cool 10 minutes before serving. Unmold the soufflé if cooked in a springform pan but do not turn it upside down.

NOTE: FOR AN ELEGANT PRESENTATION, MAKE THE SOUFFLÉ IN INDIVIDUAL 4-INCH SOUFFLÉ DISHES OR RAMEKINS. THIS RECIPE MAKES 8 TO 10 OF THESE SMALL SOUFFLÉS. DOUBLE THE AMOUNT OF THE SAUCE FOR SMALL SOUFFLÉS. YOU WILL WANT TO SERVE THEM WITH SOME SAUCE ON THE BOTTOM OR ON THE SIDE.

ROTOLO DI SPINACI E RICOTTA

Spinach and Ricotta Roll (*Makes 6 to 8 servings*)

THE FILLING IN THIS PREPARATION IS NOT enclosed in a classic sheet of pasta dough, rather in a kind of crepe. The dish is unusual but elegant and delicate.

DOUGH

4 eggs
1/4 cup all-purpose flour
2 tablespoons grated parmesan or grana padano cheese
1/2 teaspoon grated nutmeg
About 1 cup milk
Unsalted butter for the pan

FILLING

1 cup ricotta, drained
1/4 cup grated parmesan or grana padano cheese

1/4 teaspoon grated nutmeg
1/4 teaspoon freshly ground pepper
1 1/2 cups cooked spinach, squeezed dry
6 thin slices prosciutto cotto *or ham*
1/4 pound mozzarella, shredded

FINISH

Unsalted butter for the pan
2 cups Salsa Balsamella (*page 92*)
3 tablespoons grated parmesan or grana padano cheese

1. Preheat the oven to 400°F. Place two 16 × 11-inch cookie sheets in the oven.

2. Prepare the dough: Place the eggs in a food processor and process briefly to blend. With the motor running, gradually add the flour, cheese, and nutmeg. The batter will be thick. Add the milk, a little at a time, stopping as soon as the batter has the consistency of heavy cream.

3. Remove the heated sheets from the oven and brush with butter. Do not let the sheets cool. Divide the batter in half and pour each half onto a hot cookie sheet. Swirl to evenly coat the bottoms. Bake until the batter is set, about 10 minutes. Turn out onto clean kitchen towels and cool.

4. Prepare the filling: Place the ricotta, parmesan cheese, nutmeg, pepper, spinach, and *prosciutto cotto* in a food processor. Process until finely chopped. Remove to a mixing bowl and stir in half the mozzarella.

5. Pour half the prepared filling over each of the cooled sheets of dough. Spread evenly, then roll into a cylinder to enclose the filling. Wrap tightly in aluminum foil. Proceed with the second roll. Refrigerate 30 minutes or longer.

6. To finish the dish, preheat the oven to 375°F. Butter a medium-size baking dish from which you can serve. Cut the rolls into ³/₄-inch-thick slices and place them in the prepared dish, overlapping slightly. Pour the *Salsa Balsamella* over the slices and sprinkle with the grated cheese. Bake for 25 to 30 minutes, or until the top is bubbly and lightly browned.

NOTE: THE *ROTOLO* CAN BE FINISHED WITH *SUGO FINTO* (PAGE 96) INSTEAD OF *SALSA BALSAMELLA* IF DESIRED.

LASAGNA IN BRODO ALLA LANCIANESE

Lasagna in Broth, Lanciano Style **(Makes 8 servings or more)**

LANCIANO IS AN ANCIENT TOWN WHOSE story I will tell later. It is my last link to Abruzzo. It is the place to which I return at least once a year from America. My dear cousins, Adriana and Federico Spera and their children, live there. It is a second home for my husband and me.

This lasagna is the specialty of the town. As I have written before, Italian food is regional. Most well-known dishes have left the periphery of their own region and can be found almost everywhere in Italy. There are still many dishes which have remained local, however. I often say that Italians are *campanilisti*. It means that we are attached to our campanile, or local bell tower—and often, so is the food. This recipe is a good example.

Few people outside Lanciano know of this exquisite lasagna. Even there, it

BROTH

One 3-pound chicken or hen; or fowl or turkey legs, or same amount turkey meat, preferably the legs
3 sprigs fresh parsley
1 medium-size carrot, peeled and halved
2 ribs celery, trimmed and halved
1 large onion, with a cross cut at the bottom, studded with 2 cloves
2 strips lemon peel
¹/₄ teaspoon cinnamon

MEATBALLS

See recipe under Timballini di Maccheroni alla Nonnina, *page 186*

LASAGNA

1 recipe Basic Homemade Pasta (page 140), made with 4 eggs
1 tablespoon unsalted butter plus more for the pan
About 1 cup freshly grated parmesan or grana padano cheese
4 to 5 hard-boiled eggs, peeled and sliced into ¹/₄-inch slices
1¹/₂ pounds mozzarella cheese, coarsely chopped

1. Prepare the broth: Combine the fowl, parsley, carrot, celery, and onion in a large stockpot. Add water to come 2 inches above the solids. Bring to a boil over high heat, reduce the heat to low, and simmer 2 to 2¹/₂ hours. When done, strain the broth and reserve the chicken meat and vegetables for another use. This can be done a day in advance. When ready to make the lasagna, degrease the broth and place in a large saucepan. Add the lemon peel and cinnamon. Bring to a boil over

continues

has remained part of home cooking and is not found in restaurants. It is a deliciously surprising and elegant dish, done mostly for special occasions. The results are worth the extra effort.

Incidentally, the lasagna strips are not cooked in advance of assembling the dish, as is the case in many other lasagna dishes.

high heat. Reduce the heat to medium and simmer for 5 minutes, then remove the strips of lemon and discard. Set the broth aside until ready to assemble the dish.

2. Prepare the meatballs according to the recipe on pages 186–87. Set aside.

3. Prepare the lasagna: Cut the dough into wedges and roll each wedge through the cylinder of a pasta machine, notch by notch, as thinly as possible. I go to the last notch. Each strip of dough should be 18 to 19 inches long or long enough to fit the pan you are planning to use, letting the strips overlap. If not, cut accordingly. Also remember that the strips can be patched together. Set the strips on kitchen towels to dry.

4. Preheat the oven to 400°F. Butter a 14 × 10-inch lasagna pan from which you can serve.

5. Reserve 2 to 3 strips of lasagna for the top. Line the bottom and sides of the pan with one layer of lasagna strips, letting them overlap. Sprinkle 2 to 3 tablespoons of the grated cheese, a third of the egg slices, a third of the mozzarella, and a third of the meatballs. Add $1/_2$ cup of the broth and repeat the layering until all the ingredients are used. Fold over the overlapping dough and top with the reserved strips of dough. Sprinkle the top with $1/_4$ cup of the broth and some of the grated cheese. Dot with the butter. Cover with aluminum foil and bake about 30 minutes. Remove the foil and continue baking until the top is golden brown, about 30 minutes. Cool 15 minutes before cutting.

TIMBALLO DI PATELLE

(Makes 6 to 8 servings)

In certain parts of Abruzzo the strips of dough used for lasagna or cannelloni are called *patelle*.

MEATBALLS

1 medium-size onion, quartered

1 medium-size carrot, peeled and cut into pieces

1 sprig fresh parsley

6 tablespoons extra virgin olive oil plus more for the pan

1/2 pound ground pork meat

1/4 cup dry white wine

1 tablespoon grated pecorino romano cheese

1 egg, lightly beaten

Freshly ground pepper to taste

FILLING

1/2 pound pork cutlets (about 5), pounded to 1/4 inch thick

1 medium-size onion, quartered

1 rib celery, trimmed and cut into pieces

1/4 cup dried porcini mushrooms, soaked in 3/4 cup lukewarm water for 15 to 20 minutes

1/2 pound fresh mushrooms, cleaned, trimmed, and thinly sliced

2 1/2 cups frozen peas, thawed

PATELLE

1 recipe Basic Homemade Pasta (page 140), made with 4 eggs, stretched as thin as possible, each 18 to 19 inches long

2 1/2 cups Ragù all'Italiana (page 104, see Note)

Freshly grated pecorino romano cheese

3 hard-boiled large eggs, peeled and sliced about 1/4 inch thick

One 3/4-pound mozzarella, coarsely chopped

1. Prepare the meatballs: Place the onion, carrot, and parsley in a food processor and process until chopped.

2. In a medium-size skillet, heat 2 tablespoons of the oil. Add the chopped vegetables and cook over medium heat until soft, stirring often, about 10 minutes. Add the ground pork and continue cooking until brown, about 5 minutes. Pour in the wine and let evaporate. Remove to a mixing bowl. Wipe out the skillet and set aside. Add the grated cheese, egg, and pepper to the onion and meat mixture. Make small meatballs about the size of a hazelnut. Set aside.

3. Prepare the filling: Add 2 tablespoons of the oil to the wiped-out skillet and heat. Cook the cutlets over medium-high heat until brown, about 5 minutes per side. Remove the cutlets to a dish and, when cool, cut into 2 or 3 pieces. Set the cutlets aside and reserve the skillet.

continues

4. In a food processor combine the onion and celery. Process until chopped.

5. In the reserved skillet heat 2 more tablespoons of the oil. Add the onion and celery and cook over medium heat, stirring often, until the vegetables are softened, about 10 minutes.

6. Gently, so as not to disturb the sediment resting at the bottom, remove the porcini mushrooms from the soaking liquid. Strain the water through a sieve lined with a paper towel or coffee filter, and reserve. Coarsely chop the mushrooms and add to the skillet together with the sliced mushrooms. Cook until all the water that the mushrooms give off has been absorbed. Add the peas and the strained porcini soaking liquid. Cook for 5 minutes, or until the peas have absorbed the flavors in the skillet.

7. Preheat the oven to 375°F. Lightly oil a 10 × 14-inch lasagna pan.

8. Prepare the timbale: Set a bowl of cold water near the pan into which the stretched strips of dough will be cooked. Spread one or two dampened towels on the counter. Add 2 or 3 strips at a time to a large pot of boiling, salted water. As soon as the water comes back to a boil and the strips start to float, about 2 to 3 minutes, transfer each to the bowl of cold water with a slotted spoon. Cool, then set the strips on the dampened towels to drain. Continue until all the strips are cooked.

9. Line the bottom and the sides of the prepared pan with some of the strips and let the ends overlap. The strips can be patched together if necessary. Cover the bottom with a ladleful or so of the ragù. Sprinkle over 2 or 3 tablespoons of the grated cheese, 1 of the eggs, a third of the mozzarella, and a third of the meatballs. Top with a third of the mushroom-and-pea mixture. Lay a third of the pork pieces over. Add another ladleful or two of sauce and repeat layering the cheese, egg, and meatballs until all the ingredients are used, finishing with a layer of noodles. Fold in the overlapping strips of dough. Pour over the remaining sauce and sprinkle with grated cheese. Bake for 45 to 50 minutes, or until the top is lightly browned. Cool 15 minutes before cutting.

NOTE: I SOMETIMES USE THE *SUGO FINTO* (PAGE 96) IN PLACE OF THE RAGÙ. BUT IT ISN'T THE SAME AND ONE CAN ALWAYS SERVE THE MEAT OF THE RAGÙ AS A SECOND COURSE OR RESERVE IT FOR ANOTHER USE.

LO SCRIGNO DELLE TRE MARIE

Three Marys' Jewel Box *(Makes 8 timballini)*

HERE IS ANOTHER FABULOUS RECIPE FROM the restaurant Tre Marie in L'Aquila. These are small timbales or *timballini* that are enclosed in a delicate crepe.

The recipe is appropriately named. When the elegant little timbale comes to the table and is cut with a fork, "the jewels" roll out.

It is a rich dish, and it should be reserved for special occasions.

I prefer to use baby artichokes which do not have a choke or tough, stringy leaves as do the larger varieties.

CREPES
3 large eggs
6 tablespoons all-purpose flour
$1/4$ teaspoon salt, optional
3 tablespoons milk
$1/4$ cup cold water
Unsalted butter for the crepe pan

FILLING
8 baby artichokes
3 tablespoons extra virgin olive oil
1 clove garlic, peeled and smashed

2 tablespoons unsalted butter
$3/4$ pound chicken breast, skin removed and flesh diced
2 tablespoon Malvasia wine, or Marsala
1 thick slice (about 3 ounces) prosciutto, diced
$1/2$ teaspoon grated nutmeg
$3/4$ cup heavy cream
$1/2$ cup freshly grated parmesan or grana padano cheese
1 pound mozzarella, diced
Butter for ramekins

1. Prepare the crepes: Place the eggs in a food processor and process briefly to mix. With the motor running, add the flour and process until blended. Add the salt, milk, and water and process until all the batter is well mixed. The batter should be rather thin. If not, add more water or milk. Pour into a bowl.

2. Lightly butter an 8-inch crepe pan or skillet. Wipe the skillet with a paper towel to remove excess butter and heat over medium heat. Using a ladle or a cup, pour $1/4$ cup of the batter at a time into the skillet. Quickly tilt and rotate the skillet to distribute the batter mixture evenly. Cook until the edges start to turn gold, 2 to 3 seconds. Turn the crepe on the other side. Cook 2 to 3 seconds longer and turn the crepe out onto a platter.

3. Set aside while continuing to make the rest of the crepes. At some point you may need to lightly butter the pan again. The crepes can be prepared in advance and refrigerated overnight.

4. Prepare the filling: Remove the tough leaves from the artichokes. Peel the stems, if any, and cut into dice. Cut the artichokes into thin wedges. Keep the cut-up artichokes and stems in a bowl of acidulated water (water with the juice of $1/2$ lemon) to prevent discoloration while working. When ready to cook them, drain well, reserving $1/2$ cup of the water.

continues

5. In a large pan, heat 2 tablespoons of the oil, add the garlic and artichokes. Cook over medium-high heat, stirring until the artichokes start to soften, about 5 minutes. Add the reserved acidulated water, cover, and cook until the artichokes are tender, about 10 minutes longer. Stir often. If by the end you have too much liquid, remove the lid, reduce, and remove the artichokes to a bowl. Set aside.

6. Wipe out the pan in which the artichokes cooked. Use it to heat 2 tablespoons butter and 1 tablespoon of the oil. Add the diced chicken and cook, stirring, until browned, 5 to 8 minutes. Add the wine and let evaporate. Add the cooked artichokes, prosciutto, nutmeg, cream, and parmesan cheese. Mix well. Cool, then mix in the mozzarella and toss again.

7. Preheat the oven to 375°F.

8. Prepare the timbales: Butter eight 5-inch ramekins and line each one with a crepe. Fill the ramekins with the artichoke-and-prosciutto mixture, pressing down to tightly pack. Fold the overlapping crepe over the filling. Bake until the top is browned, about 15 minutes. Unmold on individual plates and serve.

NOTE: PAOLO SCIPONI, THE OWNER OF THE RESTAURANT, SUGGESTS SERVING THE TIMBALES WITH A *GRATTUGIATA*, OR SHAVING, OF BLACK TRUFFLES. THIS WAY, HE ADDS, THE *SCRIGNO* WILL BE MORE PRECIOUS. I AGREE.

RISO

Rice

*R*ice is one of the most ancient foods in the world. According to historians, the
Chinese were cultivating this precious aliment since the year 2800 B.C. A thousand years later, rice appeared in India. Alexander the Great introduced it to the
Greeks, and the Arabs to Sicily during their domination of the island in the ninth
and tenth centuries. Today, Italy is the major producer of rice in Europe.

It is wrong, however, to assume that rice is a prerogative of northern Italy.
Every region of the country consumes it and has its own way of cooking it and its
own specialties. In fact, two of the most famous rice dishes of Italy come from the
South. Naples has its *sartù di riso,* which is an elaborate rice timbale. From

Palermo come the delicious *arancini di riso,* rice balls stuffed with a delicate *ragù.*

Modern Romans often eat *suppli al telefono* while standing in one of the many coffee bars of the Eternal City, sipping an aperitif. This preparation is similar to *arancini,* but with the addition of mozzarella. The *al telefono* stands for telephone because when one bites into a *suppli,* the hot mozzarella pulls into threads like the wires of a telephone.

And now let's talk about risotto, which has become almost as popular in this country as pasta. Risotto is indeed a specialty of northern Italy. Nowadays though, it is made and eaten from Milano to Palermo.

In my family we have always eaten risotto because at a certain point we lived in Padua, near Venice. My mother, who was never too fond of rice, preferred *risotti.* Most Abruzzese serve rice cooked in broth as a *minestra* or baked in a timbale, but classic *risotti* are now very popular. In my home province, *risotti* are made with an Abruzzese touch, using local and traditional ingredients.

To cook rice in a broth is simple, but to make a timbale is a little more involved and often calls for the rice to be cooked first as a risotto.

Therefore it is important to know the unique technique for making risotto. After gently sautéing a base, mostly consisting of butter and onion, the rice is added and liquid, usually broth or water, is stirred in, a little at a time, until the rice is cooked al dente.

A word of warning: You have to learn to judge when to add the liquid. Keep in mind that if you let your rice get too dry before adding more liquid, your risotto will come out gummy. On the other hand, too much liquid at once will make your risotto boiled. But do not be put off; a couple of trials will show you how to master the art, and you will make a perfect risotto. As the Venetians and the Milanese say, the risotto at the end should be *all'onda,* with a wave, meaning with a touch of moisture.

RISO VERDE

Green Rice (**Makes 6 to 8 servings**)

IN ABRUZZO, RICE IS USUALLY SERVED IN a *minestra* and seldom shines on its own. When I was a child, *risotti* were fancy dishes made on special occasions. My father, the adventurous cook with an exquisite palate, loved to make risotto . . . or something similar. This is a recipe he invented. It has a pervasive garlic flavor and it is not quite a risotto.

My father used to add a contrasting color to this otherwise beautiful green

2 tablespoons extra virgin olive oil
4 or 5 cloves garlic, peeled and coarsely chopped
2 pounds fresh spinach, trimmed, washed, and coarsely chopped
2 sprigs fresh parsley, chopped

2 cups converted rice (see Note)
About 4 cups chicken broth, preferably homemade (page 61), hot
2 tablespoons currants
1/2 cup pine nuts
4 anchovy fillets, drained and chopped

1. In a 4-quart heavy saucepan, heat the oil over medium heat. Add the garlic and cook until it starts to sizzle, about 2 minutes. Stir in the spinach and parsley and cook 5 minutes over high heat to let the greens absorb the flavor of the oil and garlic.

rice in the form of diced tomatoes, carrot shavings, or diced boiled red beet. When he felt patriotic, he would make one risotto green, one white (plain), and one red. These are of course the colors of the Italian flag.

2. Stir in the rice, cook a few minutes, stirring, and add 2 cups of broth. Cover, reduce the heat to low, and cook about 10 minutes. Check the liquid in the pan; you may or may not have to add more broth. This depends on the moisture released by the spinach. The mixture should look a little soupy.

3. Add the currants and pine nuts. Continue cooking until the rice is al dente, about 8 or more minutes. Stir in the anchovies. Let the rice rest for 5 minutes before serving.

NOTE: SINCE THE RICE AT THE BEGINNING IS COOKED IN A LARGE AMOUNT OF BROTH AND NOT "IN *RISTRETTO*," MEANING IN REDUCED AMOUNT, AS IN A REGULAR RISOTTO, I USE CONVERTED RICE. THIS ABSORBS LESS LIQUID AND DOESN'T OVERCOOK IN THE BOILING AS THE ARBORIO (ITALIAN RICE) WOULD, IF ONE IS NOT CAREFUL.

RISOTTO ANNA TERESA

(Makes 6 servings)

THIS RISOTTO IS A CREATION OF THE CHEF-owner of Il Mulino restaurant in New York, Fernando Masci. A fellow Abruzzese, Fernando named this risotto, which I liked very much, after me.

The risotto, which I've adapted somewhat, contains quite a bit of shellfish. The crabmeat is optional only because of the cost. If you can afford it, by all means use it. The saffron, oregano, garlic, and an abundance of parsley add a real Abruzzese touch to this dish.

50 mussels, scrubbed and debearded
24 small cockles or clams, scrubbed
1/4 cup (1/2 stick) unsalted butter
2 or 3 shallots, chopped
2 cups Arborio rice
1/2 cup dry white wine
About 7 cups fish or chicken broth, preferably homemade (page 63 or 61), hot
1/2 teaspoon saffron
Salt to taste, optional

Freshly ground pepper to taste
3 tablespoons extra virgin olive oil
6 cloves garlic, peeled and smashed
12 medium-size shrimp, peeled and deveined
1 1/2 pounds bay scallops
1/2 teaspoon fresh oregano, or 1/4 teaspoon dried
1/4 pound cooked crabmeat, optional
3 sprigs fresh parsley, minced

1. Place the mussels in a large skillet and cook over high heat, shaking the skillet, until they open, 5 to 8 minutes. As soon as the mussels start to open remove the open ones to a bowl. Cool and discard the shells. Perform this operation over a bowl to collect all the juice.

continues

2. Add the clams to the same skillet, cover and cook, shaking the skillet, until they open, about 5 to 8 minutes. Clams may take longer to open. Remove the open ones to another bowl and let them cool. Strain the juice from the skillet, if any, through a paper towel. Remove the clams from the shells, add to the mussels, and discard the shells. Combine the juices accumulated at the bottom of the bowl with the juices from the skillet and set aside.

3. In a 4-quart heavy saucepan, melt 2 tablespoons of the butter over medium heat. Add the shallots and cook, stirring, until wilted, about 5 minutes. Add the rice and cook, stirring, for a few minutes, until it absorbs the flavor of the butter and shallots.

4. Add the wine; let evaporate but continue stirring. Start adding the broth, 1 cup at a time, while stirring constantly. Wait until each addition is almost completely absorbed before adding more broth. Add the reserved juices from the mussels and clams, a little at a time, and continue stirring and adding the cup of broth until the rice is done. Keep in mind that the rice will take about 20 minutes to cook. Stir in the saffron, salt, if used, and pepper.

5. While the rice is cooking, in a large skillet, heat the oil over medium heat. Add the garlic and cook until it starts to sizzle, about 2 minutes. Add the shrimp and cook until they start to turn red, about 5 minutes. Add the scallops and oregano and cook until the scallops become opaque, about 5 minutes. Add the mussels, clams, and crabmeat, if used, stir, cook until heated through, and remove from the heat. Discard the garlic.

6. Add the fish mixture to the risotto. Stir to combine. Remove from the heat and add the remaining 2 tablespoons butter, stir, and serve the risotto sprinkled with the parsley.

RISOTTO CON FUNGHI

Risotto with Mushrooms *(Makes 6 servings)*

AT THE ARRIVAL OF AUTUMN, AN INTOXI-cating aroma pervades the Italian markets and food shops. And if you enter an Italian restaurant at this time of the year, you are assaulted by the perfume of fresh porcini mushrooms. It is their season and one is bound to feast on them. Unfortunately, when they arrive in this country, that special aroma seems lost. And the price!

What to do? Invest in a large bag of dried porcini mushrooms. Yes I know, they do cost "one eye of the head" as we Italians say, meaning an arm and a leg. But one handful of these goes long way when combined with regular, inexpensive fresh white mushrooms. Believe me, this trick works. The dried porcini will give your risotto that touch of boskiness needed for it to be authentically Italian.

3 tablespoons unsalted butter
1 tablespoon extra virgin olive oil
1 large onion, sliced
12 ounces fresh mushrooms, trimmed and coarsely chopped (see Note)
¹/₂ cup dried porcini mushrooms, soaked in lukewarm water for 20 minutes, drained, chopped, with soaking water strained and reserved

2 cups Arborio rice
¹/₂ cup dry white wine, optional
About 6 cups chicken broth, preferably homemade (page 61), hot
Salt to taste, optional
Freshly ground black pepper to taste
Freshly grated parmesan cheese

1. In a 4-quart heavy saucepan heat 2 tablespoons of the butter and the oil over medium heat. Add the onion and cook over low heat until soft and translucent, about 5 minutes. Add all the mushrooms and cook, stirring often, until they give up their moisture and it evaporates, about 10 minutes.

2. Add the rice and cook, stirring, until well-flavored, about 2 to 3 minutes. Stir in the wine, if used. Let evaporate. Add the reserved mushroom water. Cook, stirring, a few minutes, then start adding the broth, 1 cup at a time, stirring constantly. Wait until each addition is almost completely absorbed before adding the next. Add another cup of broth and continue stirring and adding broth until the rice is al dente, about 20 minutes.

3. Remove the pan from the heat and stir in the remaining tablespoon butter. Serve with the parmesan.

NOTE: I DO NOT RECOMMEND USING ONLY DRIED PORCINI FOR THIS RISOTTO. THEIR FLAVOR IS TOO STRONG AND WILL BE OVERPOWERING.

Variation: This is a basic risotto. Instead of mushrooms, use either broccoli, asparagus, string beans, or any other vegetables you like. Cauliflower makes a surprising flavor. My twin brother, Mimmo, hated cauliflower. But one day I had the idea of making a risotto with it. To the amusement of my mother and father, and after expressing his enthusiasm, my brother asked for a second helping. When we told him what he was eating, good-natured as he was, he said that he would always eat my risotto, no questions asked.

RISOTTO VECCHIA ROMA

Vecchia Roma's Risotto **(Makes 6 servings)**

THE FOOD AT THE RESTAURANT VECCHIA Roma is always delicious, well prepared, and beautifully served. This shrimp risotto is one of my favorites among their many specialties. I adapted the recipe from rather whimsical, if enthusiastic, instructions I extracted from Armando, one of the waiters. What is the chef's little secret? The addition of cream at the end.

2 tablespoons unsalted butter
2 tablespoons extra virgin olive oil
1 large onion, chopped
1 1/2 cups Arborio rice
2 tablespoons brandy

1 tablespoon tomato paste
About 6 cups chicken broth, preferably homemade (page 61), hot
1/2 pound shrimp, peeled and deveined
1/2 cup heavy cream

1. In a 4-quart heavy saucepan, heat 1 tablespoon of the butter and 1 tablespoon of oil over medium heat. Add the onion and cook, stirring, over low heat until the onion is soft and translucent, about 5 minutes. Add the rice, stir, and cook until well-flavored, 2 to 3 minutes Add the brandy and let evaporate.

2. Blend the tomato paste into 1/2 cup of the broth, stir into the rice, and cook briefly. Continue cooking the rice, adding the broth 1 cup at a time, until the rice is al dente, about 20 minutes. Wait until each addition is almost completely absorbed before adding the next.

3. While the rice is cooking, cut 3 shrimp lengthwise. You should have 6 shrimp halves; set these aside. Dice the remaining shrimp.

4. Heat 1 tablespoon of butter and 1 of oil in a 9-inch skillet. Add the shrimp halves and cook, stirring, a few seconds, then add the diced shrimp and continue to cook, stirring, until they turn red. Do not overcook. Sort out the 6 shrimp halves and set aside but keep warm.

5. Add the diced shrimp to the rice, stir, and add the cream. Cook just to heat through. Use the shrimp halves to decorate the risotto.

RISOTTO COLLE VONGOLE E FUNGHI MARE E TERRA

Risotto with Clams and Mushrooms (Makes 6 servings)

THE COMBINATION OF INGREDIENTS IN this risotto is quite common in Abruzzo and reflects its three distinctive cuisines, that of the sea, the land, and the mountains.

As I said before, these dishes are often called *mare e terra*, an Italian version of surf and turf.

2 dozen cherrystone clams
Liquid from the clams
Bottled clam broth
3 cups water or Fish Broth (page 63)
5 tablespoons extra virgin olive oil
1 medium-size onion, thinly sliced
2 cloves garlic, peeled, 1 clove minced
2 cups coarsely chopped fresh mushrooms

1/4 cup dried porcini mushrooms soaked in 3/4 cup lukewarm water for 15 to 20 minutes, drained, and chopped
2 cups Arborio rice
1/2 teaspoon powdered saffron, or 1 teaspoon threads
2 teaspoons minced fresh parsley
1 tablespoon unsalted butter

1. Open the clams over a bowl to collect the juices. Chop the clams and reserve. Pour the liquid from the clams into a measuring cup. Add the bottled clam broth to measure 2 cups. Pour into a large pot and add the water or fish broth. Bring to a boil and keep at a low simmer.

2. Heat 3 tablespoons of the oil in a 4-quart heavy saucepan over medium heat. Add the onion and minced garlic and cook, stirring, until the onion is soft and translucent, about 5 minutes.

continues

3. Add all the mushrooms, reserving the water of the porcini, and cook, stirring often, until they give up all their moisture. Add the rice and cook, stirring, until the rice is well coated with the juices in the pan. Strain the water from the porcini through a paper towel and add. Let evaporate.

4. Start adding the simmering liquid, 1 cup at a time, while stirring constantly. Cook until the liquid is almost absorbed before adding another 1 cup. Continue cooking the rice, stirring and scraping the bottom of the pan while adding more liquid, until the rice is almost done, about 18 minutes. Add the saffron, stir to mix, and cook until rice is al dente, about 20 minutes total.

5. While the rice is cooking, in a 9-inch skillet, heat 2 tablespoons of the oil over medium heat. Add the remaining garlic clove and cook until it starts to sizzle, about 2 minutes. Add the chopped clams and cook just to heat through.

6. Remove the garlic clove from the mixture in the skillet and add the clams to the rice. Add the parsley, stir, and remove the pan from the heat. Stir in the butter and serve.

RISOTTO ALL'AGNELLO E FINOCCHIETTO

Risotto with Lamb and Fennel **(Makes 6 servings)**

THIS RISOTTO CAME ABOUT WHEN MY husband, Harold, saw two slices of roast lamb on the counter and said, "Oh no, not again!" Sound familiar? Well it is, especially in my home, because I am absolutely unable to throw away any food.

I knew I had to disguise it into some other food. So I went to work and the result was . . . "Darling, you never made this risotto before. It is delicious. I hope you are including it in your book!" I didn't even do the customary *mantecazione,* which is the stirring of a tablespoon of butter into the risotto after it is finished. I wanted to keep it as lean as possible, and I felt that the assertive flavor of the fennel would be enough.

2 tablespoons extra virgin olive oil
1 large onion, thinly sliced
½ cup red wine
About 6 cups broth of your choice, preferably homemade (pages 61 to 64), hot
2 cups Arborio rice
1 cup strained tomato, fresh or canned
Freshly ground black pepper to taste
1 cup cooked and diced lamb, trimmed of all fat
2 or 3 bunches of the "green beard" or fronds of a fennel, snipped
2 sprigs fresh parsley, minced
1 tablespoon unsalted butter, optional
Freshly grated parmesan cheese

1. In a 4-quart heavy saucepan, heat the oil over medium heat. Add the onion and cook over low heat adding a little of the wine. Let evaporate and add a little of the broth. Continue cooking until the onion is quite soft.

2. Stir in the rice and cook a few seconds. Add the remaining wine and cook, stirring, until the wine evaporates. Add half of the tomato and continue cooking and stirring over medium heat until the tomato is absorbed. Add the pepper and remaining tomato, and continue as before.

3. Start adding the remaining broth to the rice, 1 cup at a time, stirring constantly. Wait until each addition is almost absorbed before adding the next. Continue cooking and stirring while adding more broth, about 10 minutes. Add the meat and continue as before, adding broth and stirring until the rice is al dente, about 20 minutes.

4. Add the fennel, parsley, and butter, if used, stir, and serve with parmesan.

NOTE: IF YOU CANNOT FIND FENNEL FRONDS, USE DILL.

Variation: I make this risotto with other cooked meats, such as chicken, veal, and pork, too.

RISOTTO DI NATALE

Christmas Risotto **(Makes 6 servings)**

THIS RISOTTO IS A SPECIALTY OF THE region of Molise, which until 1963 was part of Abruzzo. It is a unique, rich rice dish. It is not cooked like a classic risotto—it does not require much stirring. For this reason it is easier to make. The unusual addition of walnuts gives a special flavor to the preparation. A good homemade broth is essential. In Molise a capon broth is used. Capon is the traditional bird for the holidays in both regions.

2 tablespoons extra virgin olive oil
1 large onion, chopped
½ pound sweet Italian sausages,
 cut into thin rounds
½ cup shelled walnuts, coarsely chopped

About 6 cups chicken broth or capon broth,
 preferably homemade (page 61 or 62)
2 cups Arborio rice
1 tablespoon unsalted butter
Freshly grated parmesan or grana
 padano cheese

1. In a 9-inch skillet, heat the oil over medium heat. Add the onion and cook, stirring, over low heat until soft and translucent, about 5 minutes. Do not brown. Add the sausages and cook, stirring, until brown. Add the walnuts and cook, stirring, for a few minutes. Set aside.

2. In a 4-quart heavy saucepan, bring 4 cups of the broth to a boil. Add the rice, stir, bring to a boil again, and cook over low heat, uncovered, for 15 minutes. Add the sausage mixture and continue cooking and stirring occasionally until the rice is al dente, about 5 minutes or longer. Add more broth when necessary. At the end, the risotto should be slightly wet. Remove the pan from the heat, add the butter and 2 to 3 tablespoons of the grated cheese. Stir well and serve with additional cheese on the side.

CHAPTER 8

POLENTA

$\mathcal{P}$olenta was not one of my favorite foods. During the war, our family went to live in Padua, which is practically the capital of the *polentoni*, polenta eaters! Bread was rationed, and polenta, a good filler whose flour was more available, became our daily sustenance. My mother used to make it more palatable for me by serving it with a lot of sauce, or layering it with a combination of ingredients like sausages, mushrooms, and mozzarella, and it was delicious.

After the war I rarely ate polenta. Then my pupils suddenly began to ask for polenta recipes. *Oy vay*, I said with my Italian accent. Now here I am writing a chapter on polenta, resurrecting all of my mother's concoctions and adding a few of my own. These I like—and you will too!

POLENTA IN ABRUZZO

In Abruzzo polenta never became a staple as it did in the north of Italy. However, there are many classic Abruzzese polenta recipes that are ancient and tied to religious tradition. *Fracchiata*, a kind of porridge, for instance, was considered a Lenten dish and served with a humble dressing of oil, garlic, anchovies, and hot pepper. Before the arrival of corn, *fracchiata* was made with chick pea flour, bean flour, or *cicerchie* flour, the cereal which has become almost extinct.

Nowadays, in many towns of the region, polenta has become a specialty: In Fontavignone the polenta is cooked in milk; in Pereto, a succulent snail sauce is its condiment. Pettorano sul Gizio, a picturesque town in the mountains where the women still wear their characteristic costumes topped by a starched white headdress, stages a New Year's Eve polenta festival, *Sagra della Polenta*. In reality, during these festivities, the polenta is just a bed on which to serve braces and braces of delicious local sausages.

The Abruzzesi like their polenta with a condiment—a modest one like a little oil, sautéed onions, a few salted sardines braised in oil, will do. But the favorite is undoubtly a good pork *ragù*. In the costal towns, the polenta is dressed with a savory *ragù* of clams and tomatoes. Recipes for these sauces are included.

POLENTA MIA

My Polenta *(Makes 6 to 8 servings)*

As I said before, I never cared too much for polenta. During the war and living in the north of Italy, polenta was "the bread" and I had had too much of it.

But then I remembered how my mother used to embellish her polenta. Most of the time, instead of water as was customary, she cooked the polenta in chicken broth or dissolved a reliable bouillon cube or two in the water. She also dressed it with a sauce or layered it with cheese, sausages, or vegetables. In fact there are several recipes in the Italian cuisine for *polenta maritata* ("married polenta") or *polenta pasticciata*, in which the polenta is layered or dressed with several condiments.

2 cups polenta flour (cornmeal)
7 cups chicken broth, preferably homemade
    (page 61), or water

Salt to taste, optional

Place the polenta in a 4-quart heavy pot, preferably a copper one. Start adding the broth or water a little at a time, while stirring to prevent lumps. Place over medium heat and cook, stirring constantly, for about 35 minutes. Add the salt. The polenta is done when it starts to pull away from the sides of the pan. Add more broth while cooking if the polenta is too dense. The final consistency of the polenta, soft or hard, is to your taste. I prefer mine a little soft.

NOTE: YOU CAN BUY INSTANT POLENTA, WHICH COOKS IN 5 MINUTES AND IS NOT BAD.

Variation: Polenta, cut in slices, can be reheated on a grill. Pour the hot cooked polenta into a meatloaf pan, chill, unmold, and cut into slices. In the Venetian area grilled polenta is very much in fashion.

POLENTA E CECI

Polenta and Chick Peas **(Makes 6 servings)**

THIS RECIPE IS A CLASSIC EXAMPLE OF THE cuisine belonging to the diminishing *civiltà contadina*, peasant civilization. Peasants would eat this polenta for breakfast, before a hard day's work in the field, and the leftovers, cut into slices and baked, made the evening meal.

Nowadays these dishes have become the passion of food researchers and are served at gastronomic conventions with reverence. This cooking is also much appreciated by vegetarians because, for once, and contrary to the Abruzzese taste, this dish doesn't contain any meat. It is indeed a simple, almost Spartan recipe, with an unadulterated earthy flavor.

1 pound dried chick peas, soaked overnight and drained
2 bay leaves
1 clove garlic, unpeeled
Kosher salt to taste

5 tablespoons extra virgin olive oil
3 cloves garlic, peeled and chopped
1 sprig fresh parsley, minced
1 recipe My Polenta (page 210), freshly made and hot

1. Place the chick peas in a large pot and add water to cover by 2 inches. Add the bay leaves and the unpeeled garlic. Add the salt and bring to a boil over high heat. Simmer over low heat until the chick peas are done, 45 minutes to 1 hour.

2. Drain, reserving some of the cooking water. Discard the bay leaves and garlic. Return the chick peas to the pot. Keep warm.

3. In a small skillet heat the oil over medium heat. Add the chopped garlic and the parsley and cook a few seconds until the garlic starts to sizzle.

4. Pour this sauce into the chick peas. Stir well. Add a bit of the reserved cooking water to loosen the chick peas and pour on the polenta. Serve immediately.

POLENTA PASTICCIATA AI FUNGHI

Baked Polenta with Mushrooms **(Makes 6 to 8 servings)**

THE ENGLISH TRANSLATION OF *PASTICCIO*, from which *pasticciata* comes from, is "mess." The meaning is the same in Italian, but gastronomically speaking, this kind of mess is always a delicious, baked dish of some sort. This polenta is a good example.

In certain parts of Italy a pasta timbale is also called a *pasticcio di maccheroni*.

2 tablespoons unsalted butter, plus more for the pan
1/2 cup dried porcini mushrooms, soaked in 3/4 cup lukewarm water for 15 to 20 minutes
1/2 pound fresh mushrooms, trimmed, preferably a mixture of different kinds
3 tablespoons extra virgin olive oil
1 large onion, chopped
2 cloves garlic, peeled and chopped
2 sprigs fresh parsley, minced
Salt to taste, optional
Freshly ground pepper to taste
1 recipe My Polenta (page 210), freshly made and hot

1. Preheat the oven to 375°F. Butter a 14 × 12-inch lasagna dish from which you can serve.

2. Drain the porcini mushrooms. Strain its water and reserve for another use. Clean the fresh mushrooms and chop both coarsely.

3. In a 12-inch skillet, heat the oil over medium heat. Add the onion and cook until translucent, about 5 minutes. Add the garlic and cook until the onion is soft, about 10 minutes. Add all the mushrooms and cook until the water exuded by the mushrooms has evaporated, about 10 minutes. Add the parsley, salt, if used, and the pepper. Remove from the heat.

4. Pour half the polenta into the prepared dish. Dot with half the butter, top with the mushroom ragout, and cover with the remaining polenta. Dot with the remaining butter and bake until top is slightly brown, 30 to 40 minutes. Serve hot.

POLENTA CON RAGÙ DI VONGOLE

Polenta with Clam Ragout *(Makes 1 1/2 cups sauce)*

FOR THIS RAGOUT, YOU WILL NEED 1 POUND of shelled clams. I recommend using canned ones. Some fish markets also sell containers of frozen clams, which are less expensive. I sometimes combine some fresh mussels with these clams. It is better to use water than broth for this polenta, to keep the marine flavor pure.

1/4 cup extra virgin olive oil
2 cloves garlic, peeled and chopped
4 sprigs fresh parsley
One 28-ounce can peeled tomatoes, with the juice

Two 6 1/2-ounce cans clams, drained
1 recipe My Polenta (page 210) made with water, hot

1. In a 10-inch skillet, heat the oil over medium heat. Add the garlic and 2 parsley sprigs, cook briefly, letting the flavor of the parsley explode into the oil, then remove the parsley. Add the tomatoes, breaking them up with a wooden spoon while stirring. Cook, covered, 20 to 25 minutes. Stir once in a while.

2. When ready to serve, add the clams. Mince the remaining parsley and add to the ragout. Cook 2 to 3 minutes just to heat the clams through.

3. Turn the polenta into a bowl and top with the clam ragout.

LA PASTUCCIA

(Makes 6 to 8 servings)

HERE'S AN ANCIENT DISH WHOSE NAME, loosely translated means "little paste." At one time it was the specialty of Teramo and its province. It was resuscitated in Pescara, together with *fracchiata*, during a convention of the Accademia Italiana della Cucina, a gastronomic society dedicated to the research and documentation of traditional regional dishes.

1/2 pound sweet Italian sausages
1 recipe My Polenta (page 210) made with water, hot
2 large egg yolks
1/4 cup raisins, soaked in lukewarm water

1 tablespoon extra virgin olive oil
1/4 pound pancetta, diced
1/4 pound pork cheeks, diced, optional (see Note)

1. Place the sausages in a small skillet, pierce them in several places, cover with water, and cook, uncovered, until all the water has evaporated. Brown the sausages in their own fat. Remove the sausages and reserve the fat in the skillet. When the sausages are cool, cut into 1/4-inch slices. Set aside.

continues

2. Add 2 tablespoons of the fat from the sausages to the hot polenta; mix. Add the egg yolks and sliced sausage. Drain the raisins and add to the polenta. Mix again.

3. Preheat the oven to 375°F.

4. In a 10-inch cast-iron skillet, heat the oil over medium heat. Cook the pancetta and pork cheeks, if used, stirring, until slightly brown, about 5 to 8 minutes. Remove half of it and set aside.

5. Spread the remaining pancetta mixture evenly in the skillet. Add the polenta, and flatten and smooth the top. Sprinkle with the remaining pancetta and bake until the top is brown and crusty, 30 to 40 minutes.

NOTE 1: THE TOP OF THE *PASTUCCIA*, BEFORE BAKING IT, IS CUSTOMARILY SPREAD WITH LARD. THIS IS A SUCCULENT, RICH WINTER DISH. FOR OBVIOUS REASONS I HAVE ELIMINATED THE LARD, AND IT IS UP TO YOU TO TRY THE REAL THING.

NOTE 2: PORK CHEEKS CAN BE ORDERED FROM AN ITALIAN BUTCHER OR ITALIAN SPECIALTY STORE.

POLENTA ROGNOSA O DEI CARBONARI

"Mangy" Polenta or Polenta in the Style of the Coal Men (Makes 6 to 8 servings)

THE ABRUZZESE WRITER LUIGI BRACCILI amusingly describes the making of this well-known polenta and the ancient utensils that are used. One important ingredient, he says, is *olio di gomito,* elbow grease and, while working, a good glass of red wine.

In a convivial gathering, the polenta is served in a flat wooden tray with raised edges. Each guest must mark the "borders" of his or her portion

1 1/2 cups polenta flour (cornmeal)
About 6 cups water
1/2 cup freshly grated pecorino romano
  cheese

2 tablespoons extra virgin olive oil
1/4 pound pancetta, diced
3 pounds sweet Italian sausages, cooked
  (see Step 1, page 213)

1. Make the polenta following the directions for My Polenta (page 210), but using only 1 1/2 cups polenta and 6 cups water. This polenta should be a little hard. Add the cheese and stir well.

2. In a 9-inch skillet heat the oil over medium heat. Add the pancetta and cook, stirring, until crisp, about 4 to 5 minutes.

before starting to eat. Sometimes, fork fights ensue, but they are all in fun.

This is made in Pettorano sul Gizio during their polenta festival.

3. Crumble the sausages and add to the pancetta. Cook just to heat through.

4. Turn the polenta onto a wooden board. Pour the pancetta-sausage sauce on top of the polenta. Serve immediately.

POLENTA AL RAGÙ DI MAIALE

Polenta with Pork Ragout **(Makes 6 servings)**

THIS DISH MAKES AN APPETIZING AND filling meal. The polenta is topped with succulent pork chops and crumbled sausages. A bit rustic in appearance, but oh, so delicious!

1 medium-size onion, quartered
1 clove garlic, peeled
1 large rib celery, cut into 4 pieces
1 large carrot, cut into 4 pieces
1 tablespoon extra virgin olive oil
2 ounces pancetta, diced
1 1/2 pounds pork chops, each cut into 3 pieces
1/2 cup dry red wine

1 teaspoon tomato paste
One 32-ounce can peeled tomatoes,
with the juice
1/2 pound sausages, cooked and crumbled
1 small diavoletto *(dried Italian hot*
red pepper), optional
1 recipe My Polenta (page 210),
freshly made and hot

1. In a food processor place the onion, garlic, celery, and carrot. Process until finely chopped.

2. In a 2-quart heavy saucepan, heat the oil over medium heat. Add the pancetta and cook until crisp, about 5 minutes. Add the pork chops and cook until brown on both sides. Add the wine, let evaporate, then add the tomato paste and tomatoes. Break up the tomatoes with a wooden spoon while stirring. Cover the pan, bring to a boil, and simmer, stirring occasionally, over very low heat for 1 hour. Add the sausages and the *diavoletto* during the last 15 minutes. If you wish, remove the bones from the chops before pouring the ragout on the polenta.

Variation 1: Mushrooms, fresh or dried, are often added to this sauce. Cook the mushrooms in oil separately until almost done, about 10 minutes, and add them to the sauce in Step 2 during the last 5 minutes.

Variation 2: No need to say that this sauce is also delicious on pasta.

CROSTINI DI POLENTA
Polenta Crostini

Delicious *crostini* can also be made with polenta. You do not need a recipe, but following are a few suggestions to spur your imagination.

The important thing to remember is to make the polenta a little hard, which is simple. Just cook it a little longer. Spoon the polenta into a loaf pan, and refrigerate it overnight.

The next day, unmold the polenta and cut it into slices. (You can recut the squares into triangles.) Top the pieces with your favorite ingredients. Bake the *crostini* in a preheated 375°F oven for 5 to 10 minutes, depending on the topping you are using.

The polenta slices can also be deep-fried or simply grilled and eaten as bread.

My favorite *crostini* toppings are:

- Mozzarella with a bit of parmesan or a drop of tomato paste and a basil leaf
- Fontina or gruyère cheese are also excellent toppings, as is gorgonzola
- Smoked mozzarella
- Mushroom or clam ragout
- A round slice or two of sausage, ham, or prosciutto, with or without a bit of mozzarella cheese
- Fried zucchini or eggplant
- Polenta marries well with nuts, especially walnuts.

PART III

LA CASA DI PESCARA

The House in Pescara

...t an apartment in Pescara just one block from ...ed, safe from mines. We had three bedrooms, ...with its own balcony. Another large balcony ...of the other rooms. I can still see my parents ...ntertaining their friends "al fresco." It was pleasant in the summer, when the sea breeze cooled the heat of the day.

After the war, my parents bought an apartment in Pescara just one block from the beach which finally had reopened, safe from mines.

We had three bedrooms, a living room and a large kitchen with its own balcony. Another large balcony faced the street and fronted almost all of the other rooms. I can still see my parents sitting there in the late afternoon, entertaining their friends "al fresco." It was pleasant in the summer, when the sea breeze cooled the heat of the day.

Sadly, buying this apartment cost us the house in Guardiagrele. With the older generation gone, we and Aunt Ela had been owners of the house. It was becoming more and more evident that the house was a luxury that could barely be afforded. We had to sell it.

It took me many years before I could walk again along Via dei Cavalieri, the street where the house stood. I would go to Guardiagrele often, to the cemetery, and to visit the relatives we still had there, but I would never pass that house. I did so many years later when I took my husband, Harold, for the first time to Guardiagrele. I could not avoid showing him the house of which I had spoken so often.

It was a beautiful day, and I felt calm and prepared, so after calling the new owners, whom I knew, we went for a visit. The house had been divided into four units, but the main core, the part in which we had lived in the most, had not changed much. The garden with my secret corners, where I used to hide and read forbidden books like *Madame Bovary,* seemed so small. The pine we had planted when my cousin Gianna was born was no longer there. It had been cut down by a cannon, shot during the war. Looking at that spot, I remembered a story I had heard many times about a hole near where the tree had been. The hole was where our silver had been buried before we were forced to abandon the house during the war. When the family returned, no one had bothered to look there, thinking that everything was gone. But Annina, our ever-wise maid who had done the digging, remembered that she had made a very deep hole, and this seemed shallow to her. With her innate Abruzzese stubbornness, and a little hope, she started to dig again, and lo and behold, our treasure was still there. She had done a really good job. The family silver was one of the few things saved from the war. So many things were lost forever.

One place I was afraid to see again was the terrace. How many happy days we had spent there with all the dear people who were no longer with us. How many dreams I dreamed on that terrace; how many games I played with my brother and cousins. Maybe because of Harold's presence I felt protected. Yes the ghosts came, I did cry, but it was a release. I could look at that familiar landscape of mountains and fields and feel grateful for many things.

My life in Pescara had many episodes of leaving and returning. When I went to the university in Rome, studying literature and specializing in archeology, I lived with a very dignified widow who had a daughter a little older than me. Although I loved living in Rome, I was happy to go back to Pescara for my vacations.

One year, while still at the university, I was offered a job at the Museum of Ostia Antica, near Rome. This was the ancient port of the Romans and is now an archeological site, similar to Pompei. The sea has now receded from its port and Ostia Antica lies inland. Modern Ostia, with its beautiful beach, has become the Coney Island of Rome, albeit a little more elegant.

I accepted the job in Ostia Antica because I wanted to become an archeologist. My job there was fascinating. But my destiny was not to be a "grave digger," as my brother called me— I was always excavating tombs. One summer I went to England to learn to speak English better. And my life took a turn. I never went back to Ostia Antica. I never became an archeologist; I left London and came to America, for good. And that is another story.

PESCE

Fish

ABOUT FISH

When I was a child and living in Guardiagrele, we would make expeditions to

nearby coastal cities like Pescara, Ortona, and Francavilla just to eat fish. When

we lived in Pescara on the coast, we had a continuous train of friends and relatives

coming to visit, wanting to go to one of our famous fish restaurants, unless my

father was making his famous *Brodetto di Pesce* (page 227). On these occasions I

would rush with him to the port, wait for the fishing boats to come in, and buy

some of the catch of the day. On our return home, what a feast he made.

A Love-Hate Relationship

Italians' natural love of fish, however, is somewhat complicated by the dietary restrictions of Catholicism. Italy, being blessed by an extensive coastline should be very keen on fish. Not so, at least not until recently. But I am afraid this was more a relic of religious restrictions which made the Italians "think" that they didn't like fish. Fish was the food of penance, the food of the *mangiare di magro,* lean (meatless) eating, the food of Friday, when Catholics are forbidden meat. Meat, although expensive, was infinitely more desirable for being off limits and less abundant.

Yet since antiquity, the Romans have used the flourishing fish market, *forum piscarium,* as a meeting place, and fish has played an important part in the gastronomy of Italy. The value of buying and eating fish has been amply recorded in the writing of famous people. Juvenal, a Roman poet and satirist, in his *IV Satire*—which sarcastically describes the Romans' vices—recounts the Emperor Domitian calling the crown council to decide the recipe for a turbot. The consul Asinio Celere, at the time of Caligula, bought a mullet for eight thousands sestertiums, a great deal of money at the time. Apicius, the greatest gourmand of antiquity, rhapsodizes about the quality of "blue" fish, mackerel, sardines, and anchovies.

Let's not forget that bluefish, and the anchovy in particular, are at the base of many famous sauces. Among them is the Worcestershire, a direct descendent of the famous *garum,* which the ancient Romans doused on practically every food they ate.

The Little Fishes of Abruzzo

Before the recent depletion of our seas, there were so many little, inexpensive fishes like the *pannocchie* (crawfish), *merluzzi* (whiting), and of course, sardines, anchovies, and a very small fish called *a riso,* as in rice, because of its very small size. They were inexpensive and the Italians loved them. True, these kinds of fishes were considered common, belonging to the *cucina povera,* and not elegant enough to serve to guests. Still, people would go out of their way to eat them in some little *trattoria* along the coast. Large fish were also abundant then, but they were always reserved for the wealthy populations. They were dispatched in shipments to the big inland cities like Rome, Milan, Florence, and Bologna.

Fish cooking in Abruzzo is part of its three cuisines: that of the sea, the heartland, and the mountains. The recipes are quite abundant, and I have put together, a sampling of the most famous and typical local specialties from my side of the Adriatic.

About Buying Whole and Filleted Fish, Storing, and Cooking Fish

For someone who grew up with the dictum "Look at your fish in the eye," I am lost in front of headless, cut-up, or filleted fish. In Italy, you look first at the eyes to see if the fish is fresh. When buying whole fish, the eyes should be clear and bright and not cloudy or opaque. The gills should be bright red. Look at the skin. It should be shining and not covered with mucus, unless you are buying eels, which usually have a certain viscosity. The scales should be tight against the skin. The flesh should look firm.

If you are not too squeamish, put your nose on the chosen fish. It should smell fresh and of the sea and not too fishy. In this country, the fish is always behind a barrier of glass, buried in pristine ice. The ice does keep the fish fresh, but it also dulls the taste. However, as the saying goes, *Paese che vai, usanze che trovi;* in other words: When in Rome, do as the Romans do. I had to learn to buy the fish as it comes.

Always buy from a reliable store where the fish is indeed kept on ice. If you can, choose your fish unboned and with the head. Remember that if you buy whole fish, with the bones and

head, your fishmonger will prepare it as you wish. Keep in mind, also, that the fish cooked on the bone is always more flavorful. Observe, as I said above, the brightness of the eye and the gleaming red color of the gills.

When buying fillets, make sure they look plump and moist with a pearly shine.

BUYING OTHER SEAFOOD

For shellfish, like mussels and clams, the shells should be tightly closed. As for shrimp, they should definitely not smell of ammonia. As you probably know, all the shrimp fished in this country arrive at the stores frozen. But the freezing operation is done with care, and usually the shrimp are quite good.

Never buy lobsters that are not swimming in water. When picked up, the tails should flap vigorously. That is also a sign that the lobster has not lost much meat, since it doesn't feed living in captivity.

Squid, which American people are warming to, needs a little explaining. It took some time for the Americans to overcome their reluctance for this delectable cephalopod. But they did and found that its meat, briny and sweet at the same time, can be deliciously enticing. The texture is what surprises people most, the unexpected chewiness, which nevertheless melts in the mouth.

To achieve a perfect texture, it is important to cook squid properly. The Chinese and Japanese way calls for cooking squid a few minutes over high heat, and I use this method for frying or poaching squid for a salad. By way of contrast, the Italian method for cooking squid takes almost one hour for most preparations, but it is done over very low heat.

In Italy we have three kinds of squid. The *seppia* has a short, oval body and a chalky bone inside (useful to canaries; you will see this bone in practically every cage in Italy). The *calamaro,* with an elongated, vigorous body, has an inside bone that looks like a piece of cellophane. This is the squid which is most common in the United States. Then there is the *totano,* with an arrowlike, muscular body, much appreciated in Italy where it is used mostly for stuffing.

Another mollusk, sold mostly in Greek markets and whose meat is deliciously succulent, is the *polpo,* or octopus. The octopus, if not quite small, needs to be treated with a good beating to soften the meat before cooking it. It is also a good idea to scrub it for quite a while to remove its viscosity. Fortunately, mollusks and all other fish in this country are sold clean and ready to cook. However, when necessary, instructions for cleaning fish will be given in the recipes that follow.

Buy the fish the day you plan to use it. Keep it in its wrapping and store it immediately in the refrigerator, preferably in a bowl of ice.

The recipes in this book will tell you how, and how long, to cook the fish. But keep in mind that overcooked fish isn't worth eating. So follow the instructions. Still, remember that it is important to cook the fish properly to avoid the possible peril of parasites. Perfectly cooked fish should flake easily, look opaque with no hint of pearliness, be moist, and of course, flavorful.

READ UP ON FISH

Several good books on fish have been published lately. Four in particular come to mind, the scholarly *The Official Fulton Fish Market Cookbook*, by Bruce Beck (Dutton), and the panoramic *Fish, The Complete Guide To Buying and Cooking*, by Mark Bittman (Macmillan). Both books are informative, instructive, and beautifully written. Ruth Spear's book, *Cooking Fish and Shellfish* (Doubleday), published in 1980, is a cavalcade on the fish cuisines of several countries of the world, and her choice of recipes is superb. *Fish and Shellfish*, by James Peterson (Morrow), is another good source. I highly recommend these books.

ABOUT MUSSELS AND CLAMS

My family loved mussels and clams with a passion, most of all because we would go to the sea and gather them ourselves. My dearest aunt, Ela, and uncle, Raffaele, used to rent a villa in a picturesque holiday resort called San Vito, on the Adriatic coast. Their place was like a second home to me. Their daughters were and are my most beloved relatives. In that part of Abruzzo, the sandy beaches in the north give way to a series of coves with pebble beaches and beautiful rock formations. These rocks, at one time, were encrusted with clumps and clumps of plump mussels. You can still gather mussels there, but they are not as plentiful anymore.

When I was a teenager, with my cousins in tow, we would go to the rocks for our harvest and come home with buckets of mussels. It was a job to separate them from the beard with which they attach themselves to the rock and scrub them clean. But we all did it, and as a choral labor it was fun. The preparations varied according to the mood of the cook—or the most intriguing suggestions given by the would-be eaters, probably my father or Uncle Raf. They were always the ones with innovative tastes.

Some of the mussels were eaten raw, as an antipasto, and simply dressed with drops of lemon. There was no pollution at that time, and nobody ever got sick.

In this country we have excellent mussels, they are farm raised and therefore quite clean. Sometimes they even come beardless, but it is a good idea to check them one by one and remove the beard if any. I also soak the mussels 10 to 20 minutes in cold water into which I sprinkle a tablespoon of flour. This supposedly makes them spit out any sand from their valves.

Clams were gathered in a different way, and the best harvest was in Pescara. My family spent summers in this city when we were children, and later returned to live there. Bucket and fork in hand, we would go to the beach early in the morning (always an adventure to me, a non-early riser) and walk carefully and slowly into the clear waters of the sea. The point was to spot the bit of clam protruding from the sand and dig it out with the fork.

Our clams, called *telline,* are small, therefore one has to have sharp eyes

and not ripple the water too much. We also carried a lemon with us so that we could immediately eat the sweet *cannolicchi,* razor clams, which were also imbedded in the sand and had to be extracted with the fork. They were quite abundant then. I remember squeezing one out of the shell directly in my mouth, a few drops of lemon on the tongue. I will never forget that pure marine flavor, it was like swallowing the sea.

Our preference was to eat part of our harvest raw, and simply sprinkled with lemon. In my opinion, there is no better condiment for raw mollusks, including oysters, than the fresh juice of a lemon. I do not care for these so-called red cocktail sauces. If I want a real sauce I make one with a light mayonnaise, which I dilute with lemon juice and the liquid from the clams or mussels, or a little clam broth.

Mussels and clams are of course delicious in sauces for pasta, and a great enhancer of flavor in many fish dishes, especially the *brodetti* or *zuppe di pesce,* fish stews.

BRODETTINO DI COZZE E ROSPO ALL'AGLIO E OLIO

Little Stew of Mussels and Monkfish with Garlic and Oil (*Makes 8 servings*)

Yᴏᴜ ᴍᴜsᴛ ʜᴀᴠᴇ ᴀ ʙᴀsᴋᴇᴛ ᴏғ *ʙʀᴜsᴄʜᴇᴛᴛᴀ* (page 15) or chunky pieces of Italian crusty bread to sop up the tangy sauce of this dish and fully appreciate its aromatic essence. It's simple, and quick, and most of all not even expensive. So enjoy it.

2 pounds mussels, scrubbed and debearded	*1 sprig fresh rosemary*
1 tablespoon all-purpose flour	*1 bay leaf*
¹/₄ cup extra virgin olive oil	*1 sprig fresh thyme*
4 cloves garlic, 1 peeled and smashed, and 3 peeled and coarsely chopped	*2 pounds skinless monkfish fillet, cut into 2-inch cubes*
1 sprig fresh parsley	*³/₄ cup dry white wine*
1 small diavoletto *(dried Italian hot red pepper), optional*	*1 tablespoon minced fresh parsley*

1. In a bowl place the mussels, add the flour, and cover with water. Let stand 15 to 20 minutes. This will make the mussels spit out residuals of sand. When ready to cook, scrub and rinse the mussels well and debeard them. Set aside.

2. In a large skillet, heat the oil over medium heat. Add the smashed garlic clove, the parsley sprig, and *diavoletto,* if used. Let their flavor explode, so to speak, then remove the garlic and parsley. Stir in the rosemary, the chopped garlic, bay leaf, and thyme, stir and add the monkfish. Cook over high heat, turning the fish often, until slightly colored, about 10 minutes. Add the wine, cover the skillet, and cook over low heat at a simmer until the fish is almost done, about 10 to 15 minutes. Remove the lid. If you have too much liquid, boil to reduce a little. At the end this dish should be a little soupy. Add the mussels and cook, covered, until all the mussels have opened, about 5 minutes. Sprinkle with the minced parsley and serve in pasta bowls.

COZZE ALLA POLACCA

Mussels Polish Style *(Makes 6 servings)*

WHY IS THIS EXOTIC NAME IN AN Abruzzese cookbook? Well, it is another elaboration of an evening special. At home this dish was made with hot dogs, but once I experimented with kielbasa sausage, and I liked it better. It was natural to call this dish *alla Polacca* since the kielbasa is Polish.

3 dozen mussels
1 tablespoon all-purpose flour
1 pound kielbasa sausage
2 tablespoons extra virgin olive oil
3 cloves garlic, peeled and chopped

$^1/_4$ cup dry wine, white or red
4 medium-size ripe tomatoes, peeled, seeded, and cubed
4 to 5 basil leaves, or $^1/_4$ teaspoon dried
3 sprigs fresh parsley, minced

1. In a bowl place the mussels, add the flour, and cover with water. Let stand 15 to 20 minutes. This will make the mussels spit out residuals of sand. When ready to cook, scrub and rinse the mussels well, and debeard them.

2. Cut the sausage in half lengthwise and then in $1^1/_2$-inch slices.

3. In a large skillet, heat the oil, add the sausage, and sauté a few minutes. Add the garlic, cook very briefly, and add the wine. Let evaporate, then add the tomatoes. Cook over low heat for 10 minutes, stirring often. Add the mussels, basil, and half the parsley. Cover and cook until the mussels have opened. Shake and stir the pan once or twice. Sprinkle with the remaining parsley and serve in soup bowls.

BRODETTO DI PESCE IN BIANCO E VERDE

Green and White Fish Stew *(Makes 8 servings or more)*

THIS IS ONE OF THE MANY ITALIAN *brodetti* (fish stews) without tomato. The greens from the leek and the scallions give a wonderful flavor to the stew and add a pleasing consistency and color to the sauce. When you buy the fish, ask your fishmonger for some lobster heads or extra shrimp shells. You can add these to the broth.

BROTH

1 tablespoon extra virgin olive oil
The shells from the shrimp (see below)
1 clove garlic, peeled and smashed
Green parts from the leeks and the scallions (see below)

2 sprigs fresh parsley
$^1/_2$ cup dry white wine
$1^1/_2$ cups water

FISH

3 tablespoons extra virgin olive oil	*1 pound skinless scrod or cod fillets, or*
5 cloves garlic, peeled and sliced	*other white fish, cut into large cubes*
1 diavoletto *(dried Italian hot red pepper)*	*2 pounds skinless monkfish fillet,*
1 leek, washed and trimmed, green parts	*cut into 2-inch slices*
reserved for the broth, white part	*4 sprigs fresh parsley*
chopped	*1 cup loosely packed fresh basil leaves*
1 bunch of scallions, washed and	*³/₄ pound medium-size shrimp, peeled*
trimmed, green parts reserved for	*and deveined*
the broth, white parts chopped	*³/₄ pound bay scallops*
Reserved broth	*32 mussels, scrubbed and debearded*
1 pound squid, cleaned and bodies cut	
into circles, tentacles cut in half	

1. Before starting, remove the green parts from the leeks and the scallions. Shell and devein the shrimp. You will need the greens and the shells to make the broth.

2. Prepare the broth: In a 4-quart saucepan, place 1 tablespoon of oil, the shrimp shells, and other shells if available, the garlic, the reserved green parts of the leek and scallions and the parsley. Sauté for a few minutes and add the wine, cook 5 minutes, and add the water. Bring to a boil and simmer 15 minutes. Strain this broth, pushing the solids down to extract all the liquid. Discard the solids and reserve the broth.

3. Prepare the fish: In a 12-inch skillet, large enough to contain all the fish in one layer, heat the oil, add 3 cloves garlic and the hot pepper, cook a few minutes, and add the leeks and scallions. Cook, stirring, for 5 minutes and add the reserved broth, heat, and add the squid. Cook 5 to 8 minutes, then add the scrod, cod, or other white fish, and the monkfish. Cook 10 minutes.

4. In a food processor, place the parsley and basil. Process and add to the skillet. Add the remaining shellfish. Cook until the shrimp turn red and the mussels have opened, about 8 to 10 minutes. Serve hot.

NOTE: CLAM BROTH IS A GOOD SUBSTITUTION FOR THE BROTH.

LEFTOVER *BRODDETTO* CAN BE USED AS A PASTA SAUCE. REHEAT IT IN A DOUBLE BOILER OR MICROWAVE.

BRODETTINO MARE E TERRA

Little Fish Stew with Vegetables "Sea and Earth" **(Makes 6 servings)**

WHEN MY FATHER ANNOUNCED "THIS evening, *brodettino*," we would all be happy. This is the Abruzzese version of surf and turf (here meaning seafood and vegetables). It was good in summer and in winter—indeed, a dish for all seasons. It was served with delicious croutons that my mother baked instead of frying, making the dish healthier and simpler. I explain the technique below.

CROUTONS
2 tablespoons extra virgin olive oil
1 clove garlic, peeled and smashed
1 bunch fresh rosemary, or 1/2 teaspoon dried
1 1/2 cups Italian bread cut into 1-inch cubes
Freshly ground pepper to taste

BRODETTINO
18 small clams
1 tablespoon all-purpose flour
3 tablespoons extra virgin olive oil

2 cloves garlic, peeled and chopped
1 sprig fresh rosemary, or 1/2 teaspoon dried
1 medium carrot, peeled and diced
2 bell peppers, 1 red and 1 green, seeded and cut into thin strips
2 small zucchini, cut into small cubes
One 16-ounce can peeled or strained tomatoes, with their juice
1 pound medium-size shrimp, peeled, deveined, and cut into 2 or 3 pieces
1 1/2 pounds bay scallops
1 cup frozen peas, thawed

1. In a small skillet, heat the oil over high heat. Add the garlic and rosemary and cook until flavor is released, about 2 to 3 minutes. Discard the garlic and rosemary and add the bread. Toss with a slotted spoon, sprinkle with a little pepper, and set aside.

2. Prepare the *brodettino:* Place the clams in a bowl, add the flour, and cover with water. Let stand 15 to 20 minutes. This will make the clams spit out any sand. When ready to cook, rinse the clams and set aside.

3. Fifteen minutes before serving, preheat the oven to 375°F and place the croutons on a cookie sheet. Bake until golden, about 10 minutes, switch off the oven, and keep the croutons warm in it.

4. In a large skillet, heat the oil over medium-high heat. Add the garlic and rosemary and cook about 2 to 3 minutes. Add the carrot and peppers and cook, stirring, until softened, 5 to 8 minutes, then add the zucchini and cook about 5 minutes. Add the tomatoes, cover, and cook at a simmer over low heat, about 10 minutes. Add the shrimp and cook until they start to turn red. Add the scallops, clams, and peas. Cook until the scallops turn opaque, about 5 minutes. Serve the *brodettino* in pasta bowls. Pass the croutons separately.

BRODETTO DI PESCE ALLA PAPÀ

My Father's Fish Stew **(Makes 6 to 8 servings)**

MY FATHER, GIUSEPPE VITA-COLONNA, was famous among his friends and relatives for his culinary expertise, but most of all for his *brodetto di pesce*, the Italian *bouillabaisse*. To be completely honest, my brother and I felt uncomfortable with this father who cooked and bragged about it. At that time in Italy, gentlemen didn't cook. But when my girlfriends and cousins began to get married, they would spent hours on the telephone consulting with my father about his *brodetto* and other dishes. Only then did it dawn on us that perhaps we had an unusual father, so we started to flaunt his originality.

Papà was generous with his recipe advice, but when he gave the recipe, it was never given with the same directions twice. He explained: For a *brodetto*, much depended on the type of fish available at the time, if the tomatoes where fresh or canned, and whether the oregano came from the mountains or a garden! "This time," he would say, "perhaps using basil instead of oregano would be a better idea, or an extra clove of garlic, a pinch of pepper, a touch of leek." These were his last-minute suggestions. Whatever the variation, the reports were always enthusiastic.

SAUCE

¹/₄ cup extra virgin olive oil

2 cloves garlic, peeled and smashed

One 32-ounce can peeled tomatoes, with their juice; or 2 pounds very ripe fresh tomatoes, peeled, seeded, and chopped

1 tablespoon tomato paste

2 sprigs fresh parsley

2 or 3 fresh basil leaves, or ¹/₂ teaspoon dried

1 small diavoletto *(dried Italian hot red pepper), optional*

2 or 3 strips fresh green or red bell pepper, optional

1 small leek, white part only, cut into thin rounds, optional

Salt to taste, optional

FISH

1 pound squid, cleaned, bodies cut into circles, tentacles cut in half

3 pounds assorted lean white fish, such as scrod, cod, monkfish, whiting, bass, red snapper, etc., large pieces cut in half (see Note)

¹/₂ pound small shrimp, peeled and deveined

¹/₂ pound bay scallops

25 mussels (or a mixture of mussels and clams), scrubbed and debearded

1 tablespoon minced fresh parsley

1 recipe Bruschetta *(page 15)*

1. Prepare the sauce: In a large skillet into which the fish can go in one layer, place all the ingredients for the sauce. Bring to a boil over medium heat, then simmer over low heat for 10 minutes.

2. Prepare the fish: Add the squid to the sauce and cook 5 minutes. Add the white fish and simmer until the fish is opaque throughout, 20 to 25 minutes.

3. Add the shrimp and cook until the they turn red. Add the scallops and mussels, or the mixture of mussels and clams, and cook until they open and the scallops are opaque, about 5 minutes. Sprinkle with the minced parsley and serve. Pass the *bruschetta* separately.

NOTE: IF YOU ARE USING FILLETS OF SOLE OR FLOUNDER, ROLL THEM UP.

PESCE BOLLITO

Poached Fish **(Makes 6 to 8 servings)**

I HAVE ALWAYS LOVED POACHED FISH. It can be served with a simple emulsion of oil and lemon. In my home in Abruzzo, the fish often came with a luscious warm sauce or a homemade mayonnaise. My mother didn't particularly like mayonnaise, but the rest of the family did, so I learned quite early how to make it by hand.

My mother preferred her fabulous *Salsa Verde* (page 93). Try it and decide.

1 rib celery, cut into 4 pieces
1 medium carrot, peeled and cut into 4 pieces
1 large onion, cut into 6 wedges
2 sprigs fresh parsley
2 bay leaves
1/4 cup wine vinegar
1 heaping teaspoon kosher salt
10 cracked peppercorns
One 6- to 7-pound whole fish with head on, such as sea bass or red snapper, cleaned

1. Place all the ingredients but the fish in a fish poacher or oval casserole into which the fish can be placed lengthwise. Add enough water to come 2 inches above the solids. Bring to a boil over high heat and cook, covered, over medium heat 15 to 20 minutes.

2. Place the fish rack or another rack into the poacher; it should rest just over the top of the water. Add the fish. Cover and cook 20 to 30 minutes depending on the size of the fish. To check the fish, pierce it with a small knife near the bone; the flesh should appear opaque. Cool slightly in the poacher. Peel the skin from the top of the fish. Gently, using a spatula, lift the entire (skinless) top fillet and place on the serving platter, skinned side down. Discard the bones and the head. Pick out all visible bones. Place the bottom fillet on top of the first fillet, recomposing the fish. Set the cooking liquid aside.

3. Serve the fish with a sauce of your choice. Reserve the poaching liquid for a fish risotto. Discard the vegetables.

NOTE: A NICE WAY TO SERVE THIS FISH IS SURROUNDED BY SPRIGS OF FRESH PARSLEY AND CHERRY TOMATOES. SERVE THE SAUCE ON THE SIDE.

CODA DI ROSPO ALLA GIANNA AMORE

Monkfish Gianna Amore **(Makes 6 servings)**

I DO NOT KNOW IF THE MONKFISH FROM the Adriatic is more flavorful than the one we get here, but the way this fish tastes when my cousin Gianna cooks it is incredible. As for a meat *ragù*, the fish is first sautéed, then the wine is added and cooked down, and then the tomatoes are added. The whole simmers for 35 minutes and the fish comes out tender and delicious. It is a superb dish and of infinite simplicity.

3 tablespoons extra virgin olive oil
2 cloves garlic, peeled and smashed
3 sprigs fresh parsley
Pinch of diavoletto *(dried Italian hot red pepper), optional*

One 3-pound skinless monkfish fillet, ready to cook
$^1/_4$ cup dry white wine
$^1/_2$ cup strained tomatoes, fresh or canned
Kosher salt, optional
4 or 5 fresh basil leaves

1. In a skillet into which the fish can fit snugly, heat the oil over medium heat, add the garlic, 2 sprigs parsley, and the hot pepper, if used. Add the fish and cook 5 to 6 minutes, then turn. Cook 5 minutes longer. Add the wine and let evaporate. Add the tomatoes and salt, if used. Cover the skillet, reduce the heat to medium-low, and cook until the fish is opaque throughout, about 35 minutes. If toward the end you have too much liquid, remove the lid and reduce the sauce.

2. Chop together the remaining sprig of parsley and the basil. Sprinkle this mixture on the fish and serve.

CODA DI ROSPO IN UMIDO

Potted Monkfish (**Makes 6 servings**)

MONKFISH, ALSO CALLED BY THE AMUSING name of *rana pescatrice*, fishing frog, is a very versatile fish and can be cooked in many ways. It is a must in *brodetto*, or *zuppa di pesce*. In this recipe, the fish is potted as if it were a meat.

¹/₄ cup extra virgin olive oil
2 whole cloves
1 smallish onion, peeled and cut with a cross at its root end (see Note)
16 pearl onions, peeled and cut with a cross at the root end of each
1 bay leaf
2 cloves garlic, peeled and chopped
1 tablespoon all-purpose flour
1 cup dry red wine
1 teaspoon tomato paste

1 red bell pepper, barbecued, or roasted directly over a gas flame, peeled, seeded, and pureed
1 cup fish broth (page 63), or bottled clam juice
Kosher salt, optional
Freshly ground pepper to taste
2 ¹/₂ to 3-pound skinless monkfish fillet, skinned and cut into 1 ¹/₂-inch cubes
1 tablespoon minced fresh parsley

1. In a heavy-bottomed oval casserole, into which the fish can fit snugly, heat 3 tablespoons of the oil over medium heat. Stick the cloves into the onion and add to the pot together with the pearl onions, bay leaf, and garlic. Cook, stirring, about 4 to 5 minutes, then add the flour. Cook, stirring, a few more minutes. Add the wine and cook, scraping the bottom of the pan, for 2 to 3 minutes. Add the tomato paste, bell pepper puree, and broth. Season with salt, if used, and pepper. Cover, bring to a boil, and simmer over low heat for 10 minutes.

2. Add the cubed fish and simmer until the fish is opaque throughout, 5 to 6 minutes. Remove the onion with the cloves and discard. (Or chop the onion and add it to the fish.) Add the remaining 1 tablespoon of olive oil, stir, sprinkle with the parsley, and serve.

NOTE: THE REASON A CROSS IS CUT AT THE ROOT END OF AN ONION IS TO PREVENT THE ONION FROM COLLAPSING. THIS WAY THE ONION RETAINS ITS SHAPE WHICH IS IMPORTANT FOR PRESENTATION.

Variation: Skate is also delicious cooked this way. It can also be added to the monkfish and, for a more complex dish, add a handful of peeled shrimp. Serve the stew with *Bruschetta* (page 15).

Spigola all'Acqua Cotta e Alloro

Sea Bass in "Cooked Water" and Bay Leaves (Makes 6 servings)

It means exactly what it says in the title, cooked water! Okay, let me explain. There are many recipes in Italy in which the main ingredient is water, not broth. Thus the name. But other ingredients are added: sometimes wine, always herbs, and, usually at the end, a little bit of butter or oil.

These "cooked water" dishes are very tasty because fresh ingredients are the rule. The flavor of the food should be as natural as possible, standing on its own, and not marred by heavy condiments. Make sure then, when you make this recipe, that your fish is really fresh.

1 rib celery, cut into 4 pieces
1 large onion, quartered
1 medium-size carrot, peeled and cut into 4 pieces
3 sprigs fresh parsley
1 teaspoon kosher salt, optional
Freshly ground pepper to taste
2 cups water

One 4-pound sea bass, cleaned but head on (see Note)
1 clove garlic, peeled
½ cup dry white wine
3 bay leaves
3 tablespoons extra virgin olive oil
2 tablespoons unsalted butter, optional

1. In a 2-quart pot, place the celery, onion, carrot, 1 sprig parsley, the salt, if used, and pepper. Add the water and bring to a boil over medium heat. Cook, uncovered, 20 minutes.

2. Preheat the oven to 375°F.

3. Place the fish in an oval baking dish from which you can serve. Fill the opening near the head of the fish with the remaining parsley and the garlic. Add the wine to the dish.

4. Strain the broth and pour on the fish. Discard the vegetables. Add the bay leaves and the oil. Bake until the flesh near the bone is opaque, or until the eye of the fish has popped out, about 15 to 20 minutes.

5. Discard the bay leaves. Swirl in the butter, if used. Peel the skin from the top of the fish. Gently, using a spatula, lift the entire (skinless) top fillet and place on the serving platter, skinned side down. Discard the bones and the head. Pick out all visible bones. Place the bottom fillet on top of the first fillet, recomposing the fish. Cut the fish into serving portions. Serve the fish with some of the broth.

NOTE: Any whole fish can be cooked this way, including a salmon.

Variation: Fillets (about 3 pounds for 6 servings) can also be used, but they should be at least 1 inch thick.

Spigola alle Erbe e Zafferano

Red Snapper with Herbs and Saffron *(Makes 6 servings)*

A SPECIALTY FROM THE COASTAL STRETCH around the charming town of Ortona a Mare. It is an ideal dish for lunch or a summer night because the fish is served cold.

I am not very fond of fresh coriander (cilantro). Only my friend Rosa Ross, the Chinese cookbook author and teacher, can make me eat it because she uses it sparingly. Coriander has an overpowering flavor, therefore must be used prudently. The Abruzzesi use it mostly with sausages, but I think that it goes well with this fish recipe.

The herbs used should be fresh. The olive paste for the sauce is available at Italian grocery stores and some supermarkets.

FISH

One 4-pound red snapper cleaned, but with head on
3 to 4 tablespoons extra virgin olive oil
2 or 3 cloves garlic, peeled and slivered
5 or 6 peppercorns, cracked
1 bunch green "beard" or fronds of a fennel; or 1 small bunch of fresh dill
1 sprig fresh coriander (cilantro)
1 sprig fresh thyme
2 bay leaves
1/2 teaspoon powdered saffron
1/2 cup dry white wine
Juice of 1/2 lemon
Lettuce leaves
10 cherry tomatoes, cut in half
2 or 3 large eggs, hard-boiled and peeled, cut into wedges
Lemon wedges
1 small bunch fresh curly parsley

SAUCE

3/4 cup light mayonnaise
1 tablespoon minced fresh parsley
1 tablespoon olivata (olive paste, see head note)

1. Prepare the fish: Place the fish in an oval casserole, pour 3 tablespoons of oil on it, and scatter the garlic, peppercorns, and all the herbs over the fish.

2. Combine the saffron with the wine and pour on the fish. Add the lemon juice. Cover with an oiled piece of wax paper and the lid. Cook over medium-low heat until the flesh near the bone is opaque, the flesh is flaky when touched with a fork, and the eye of the fish pops out, about 20 to 25 minutes. Cool the fish completely.

3. Place the lettuce leaves on an oval serving platter. Peel the skin from the top of the fish. Gently, using a spatula, lift the entire (skinless) top fillet and place on the serving platter, skinned side down. Discard the bones and the head. Pick out all visible bones. Place the bottom fillet on top of the first fillet, recomposing the fish. Set the cooking liquid aside. Garnish the fish with the cherry tomatoes, egg wedges, and lemon wedges. Place the bunch of curly parsley where the head was. Set aside.

4. Prepare the sauce: Strain the reserved liquid from the fish pushing the solids to extract all the juices. Combine this with the mayonnaise, minced parsley, and olive paste. Spoon some sauce on the fish. Serve the remaining sauce separately.

PESCE ALLE OLIVE E CAPPERI

Fish with Olives and Capers **(Makes 6 servings)**

ANY FISH CAN BE USED IN THIS TANGY-tasting recipe and it can be whole, filleted, or cut in slices. The puckery tang of the capers gives an assertive flavor to this dish. If fresh tomatoes are not available, use canned peeled tomatoes, instead of canned puree, to obtain a lighter sauce. For this reason I also prefer sweet California olives to the Italian salted or sun-dried. In my opinion, they make the sauce too harsh.

SAUCE

3 tablespoons extra virgin olive oil
1 1/2 cups pureed fresh tomatoes, or
    use canned peeled tomatoes
1 sprig fresh parsley, minced
2 or 3 fresh basil leaves, chopped, or
    1/4 teaspoon dried
1 clove garlic, peeled and chopped
1 small diavoletto *(dried Italian hot red*
    pepper), optional

FISH

All-purpose flour
Kosher salt, optional
Freshly ground pepper to taste
3 pounds fish fillets or steaks;
    or 5 to 6 pounds whole fish
2 tablespoons extra virgin olive oil
2 tablespoons unsalted butter
1/4 cup dry white wine
20 sweet California olives, pitted and
    cut into circles
2 tablespoons capers, drained

1. Prepare the sauce: Place all the ingredients in a 2-quart saucepan. Cover and bring to a boil over high heat. Uncover the pan and reduce the heat to a low simmer. Cook for 10 minutes. Remove the hot pepper, if used.

2. Prepare the fish: Combine flour, salt, if used, and pepper in a large bowl. Dredge the fish in this mixture, and shake to remove excess flour.

3. In a large skillet, the size in which the fish can fit snugly, heat the oil and the butter over medium heat. Cook the fish about 3 to 4 few minutes on each side. Add the wine and let evaporate. Add the cooked sauce and cook 5 to 10 minutes. Add the olives and capers and cook 5 minutes longer. The flesh of whole fish or fish steaks should be opaque near the bone. Fish fillets should be opaque throughout. Serve immediately.

MERLUZZO AL FORNO CON BROCCOLI E COZZE

Baked Cod with Broccoli and Mussels *(Makes 6 servings)*

My MOTHER LOVED BROCCOLI, THE ITALIAN type called broccoli di rape, and made many dishes with it. Because they are a little bitter (pleasantly so for me), when making this preparation for guests or my pupils, I often use the American broccoli. Try it both ways and see which one you like best.

Merluzzo is abundant in the sea surrounding Italy, and especially in the Adriatic. It is very much appreciated by the Italians. The *merluzzo* is a small fish called whiting in this country, and belongs to the cod family. It is difficult to find, therefore I suggest using cod fillets or steaks. Tile fish, halibut, and scrod are also excellent choices for this recipe.

Extra virgin olive oil for pan
Six 6-ounce cod fillets or steaks
1 pound broccoli di rape, trimmed at the bottom, each stalk cut in half; or same amount American broccoli cut into flowerets, with long stems cut in half, and blanched (see Note)
40 mussels (about 3 pounds), scrubbed and debearded
2 cloves garlic, peeled and chopped
4 sprigs fresh parsley, minced
3/4 cup dry white wine
Freshly ground pepper to taste
Kosher salt, optional

1. Preheat the oven to 400°F.

2. Lightly oil an oval baking pan into which the fish can fit in one layer. Add the fish. Place the broccoli and mussels all around. Scatter the garlic and half the parsley all over. Pour the wine in and sprinkle with pepper and salt, if used.

3. Cover the pan tightly with aluminum foil. Bake 15 minutes, then remove the foil and bake until the fish is opaque throughout, 10 minutes longer or more. The time depends on the thickness of the fish steaks. However, the fish is done if it flakes easily when touched with a fork.

NOTE: TO BLANCH BROCCOLI, ADD IT TO PLENTY OF BOILING, SALTED WATER AND COOK A FEW MINUTES.

Variation: Instead of broccoli, I often use mushrooms which I sauté with 1 clove garlic in oil over high heat, until the water from the mushrooms is released and evaporates. I like to serve the dish with rice or polenta to soak up the sauce.

FILETTI DI SOGLIOLE ALLE PERLE

Fillets of Sole with Pearls **(Makes 6 servings)**

THIS DISH, DEVISED BY ME, WAS ISPIRED by the "pearls," or our tiny clams from the Adriatic. But when I saw the little bay scallops here in New York, I knew I had found my real pearls.

2 tablespoons unsalted butter plus more
for the pan
12 small sole fillets, about 4 ounces each
3/4 pound bay scallops
Juice of 1/2 lemon

1/4 cup plain bread crumbs
2 or 3 sprigs fresh parsley, minced
Freshly ground pepper to taste
1/4 cup dry white wine

1. Preheat the oven to 375°F.

2. Lightly butter a shallow ovenproof dish from which you can serve and in which 6 fillets of sole can be laid flat. Place 6 fillets, skin side down, in one layer in the dish. Scatter the bay scallops over the fish, sprinkle with half of the lemon juice, bread crumbs, half of the parsley, and the pepper. Dot with a little butter. Cover these fillets with the remaining ones. Pour the wine around the fish, dot with the remaining butter, and bake until the fish is opaque throughout and starts to flake when touched with a fork, 20 to 25 minutes. Baste a few times while cooking, and add the remaining lemon juice.

3. Serve hot, sprinkled with the remaining parsley.

ORATA AL FORNO CON POMODORI SECCHI

Baked Porgy with Sun-Dried Tomatoes (Makes 6 servings)

THIS IS A RATHER COMMON FISH IN THE Adriatic and can be found in this country quite easily. However, a red snapper or bass will also do very well in this recipe.

In Italy, these fish are not too big and can be served one per person. Here, I have seen larger ones that can feed two to three people. Since the cooking method is the same for large or small alike, shop accordingly to your needs.

The dried tomatoes give a truly Mediterranean flavor to this recipe.

5 tablespoons extra virgin olive oil
Six 10- to 12-ounce porgies, cleaned,
    preferably with the heads on
6 cloves garlic, peeled and smashed
6 sprigs fresh parsley
3/4 cup dry white wine

Kosher salt, optional
Freshly ground pepper to taste
Juice of 1 lemon
1/2 cup sun-dried tomatoes in oil,
    drained and chopped
1 tablespoon minced fresh parsley

1. Pour the oil into a shallow baking dish from which you can serve, and into which the fish fits snugly. Add the fish and turn several times to coat both sides with the oil. Place 1 garlic clove and 1 sprig of parsley in the head or cavity of each fish. Pour on the wine and sprinkle with salt, if used, and pepper. Refrigerate, covered, 30 minutes or longer.

2. Preheat the oven to 400°F.

3. Place the fish in the oven and bake 15 to 20 minutes. Reduce the heat to 375°F. Add the lemon juice and tomatoes and continue cooking 10 more minutes. Baste the fish with its juices a few times. The fish is done when the flesh near the bone is opaque and it flakes easily if touched with a fork. Serve 1 fish with sauce per person.

NOTE: IF YOU COOK YOUR FISH WITH THE HEAD, THE FISH IS DONE WHEN THE EYE POPS OUT.

PESCE UBRIACO

Drunken Fish *(Makes 6 servings)*

THIS IS A WONDERFUL RECIPE FOR ANY FISH, but it works better with fatty fish: salmon, sturgeon, swordfish, tuna, bluefish. We called it "drunken fish" for obvious reasons.

1/4 cup extra virgin olive oil
Juice of 1/2 lemon
1 teaspoon dried rosemary leaves
3 tablespoons minced fresh parsley
1/4 teaspoon dried thyme leaves
1 cup dry white wine
2 cloves garlic, peeled and slivered

Salt to taste, optional
Freshly ground pepper to taste
6 steaks or fillets of salmon, sturgeon, swordfish, tuna, or bluefish, about 3 pounds
Lemon wedges

1. In a large shallow baking dish, into which the fish fits in one layer, combine 4 tablespoons of the oil, the lemon juice, rosemary, the 1 tablespoon parsley, the thyme, the wine, garlic, salt, if used, and pepper. Toss the fish in it, turning several times to coat both sides well. Marinate, covered, in the refrigerator for about 1 hour or longer.

2. Preheat the oven to 375°F.

3. Bake until the fish is opaque and the sauce has reduced by half, 35 to 40 minutes.

4. Serve the fish hot, sprinkled with the remaining parsley and surrounded by the lemon wedges.

PESCE ARROSTO ALLO ZENZERO

Roasted Fish with Ginger (*Makes 6 servings*)

ZENZERO, OR GINGER, WAS POPULAR during the Middle Ages and Renaissance. Later on, it fell out of use and almost vanished from the Italian cuisine. Probably the only region which continued to cook with it through the ages was Tuscany. Nowadays, due to the Asian cooking influence, which has also reached Italy, ginger has reappeared. In Abruzzo, where spices have always been used more than in any other region, it has been accepted gladly by chefs and home cooks.

A recipe similar to this, was prepared at a fish barbecue I attended at *Il Cavalluccio* (The Little Horse), my cousin Adriana's villa on the Adriatic. I had lost the recipe, but I remembered the flavor. There, the fish was barbecued over charcoal. I have decided to bake it, for convenience, and it works beautifully.

MARINADE

3 tablespoons extra virgin olive oil
2 tablespoons balsamic vinegar
Juice of 1/2 lemon
1 teaspoon grainy mustard
2 scallions, including green part, chopped
2 cloves garlic, peeled and sliced
3 or 4 slivers peeled fresh ginger

FISH

Extra virgin olive oil for pan
3 pounds thick fish fillets or steaks, such as salmon, bluefish, tuna, or swordfish steaks
1/2 cup dry white wine

1. Combine all the ingredients for the marinade in a bowl and set aside.

2. Lightly oil a baking dish into which the fish can fit in one layer. Add the fish, skin side down for fillets. Spoon the marinade on the fish. Marinate, covered, in the refrigerator for 30 minutes.

3. Preheat the oven to 400°F.

4. Pour the wine around the fish. Bake until the fish is opaque throughout and starts to flake when touched with a fork, 30 to 35 minutes.

PESCE ALLA PIZZAIOLA

Fish Pizzaiola **(Makes 6 servings)**

ALLA PIZZAIOLA MEANS COOKING WITH tomatoes that are cut into pieces, or in strips, as you would for a pizza. Fish fillets, and such meats as veal and turkey cutlets, and breast of chicken, can also be cooked *alla pizzaiola. It is an easy method and an ideal way to prepare a quick supper.*

All-purpose flour for dredging
2 ¹/₂ to 3 pounds white fish fillets, such as halibut, monkfish, red snapper, sea bass, or sole, larger fillets cut into portion size
3 tablespoons extra virgin olive oil
3 cloves garlic, peeled and smashed
1 small diavoletto *(dried Italian hot red pepper)*
1 sprig fresh parsley
1 sprig fresh rosemary, or 1 teaspoon dried
¹/₄ cup dry white wine

Salt to taste, optional
Freshly ground pepper to taste
¹/₂ cup chopped fresh tomatoes, or same amount canned peeled tomatoes, chopped and drained
¹/₂ cup fish broth (page 63), or water
16 cured olives, pitted and cut in half
24 mussels, about 1 ¹/₂ pounds, scrubbed and debearded, or same amount clams, or a mixture of both
1 tablespoon minced fresh parsley

1. Spread the flour on a large plate. Dredge the pieces of fish in the flour and set aside.

2. In a skillet large enough into which the fish can fit in one layer, heat the oil over medium heat. Add the garlic, hot pepper, parsley, and rosemary. As soon as the garlic starts to sizzle, add the fish. Cook a few minutes over medium-high heat, turning the fish once.

3. Add the wine, the salt, if used, and pepper. Cook over high heat until the wine reduces by half, about 5 minutes. Spread the tomatoes over the fish and add the fish broth, or water. Cook 10 minutes and add the olives. Place the mussels or clams all around the pan. Cover and cook until the shells open.

4. Serve sprinkled with the minced parsley.

RAZZA AI CAPPERI

Skate with Capers **(Makes 6 servings)**

SKATE IS A DELICATE FISH WHICH, A FEW years ago, could be found only on menus of restaurants catering to an Italian or French clientele. The popularization of this delectable fish is really due to ambitious new chefs who had encountered the fish in Europe and were not afraid to experiment.

In Italy we have always appreciated this fish and cooked it in many ways. The following is a family recipe, simple and quick to make, and thoroughly delectable.

My mother did not soak the fish in milk. Our skate is not too big and does not need to be tenderized. But since the skate in this country is sold a little aged, as it should be, I find that a little milk bath restores the freshness to the fish. This is a fish, by the way, that will improve if kept one day in the refrigerator before cooking it.

In this country, skate (of which only the wings are sold) comes to the market cleaned and often skinned, making the cooking process a cinch.

6 boneless, skinned, skate wings, weighing approximately 3 pounds total
3/4 cup milk
Kosher salt to taste, optional
Freshly ground pepper to taste
All-purpose flour
1/4 cup extra virgin olive oil
2 cloves garlic, peeled and smashed
Juice of 1 lemon
2 to 3 tablespoons capers in brine, drained
2 tablespoons minced fresh parsley

1. Place the fish in a large shallow baking dish, pour the milk on, sprinkle with salt, if used, and the pepper. Refrigerate, covered, for about 30 minutes or longer. Turn once.

2. Drain the fish and dredge in the flour, shaking off the excess.

3. In a skillet large enough for the fish to fit in one layer (or use two skillets, dividing the ingredients among them), heat the oil over medium heat. Add the garlic. As soon as the garlic starts to sizzle, add the fish. Cook until the fish browns on the bottom, 3 to 5 minutes, turn on the other side, and cook until golden brown, a few more minutes. Do not overcook. Add the lemon, sprinkle the wings with the capers, reduce the heat to low, and cook until the fish is opaque through, about 2 to 3 minutes longer. Sprinkle with the parsley and serve.

TORTIERA DI RAZZA E FUNGHI

Skate and Mushrooms Casserole **(Makes 6 servings)**

My mother used to make several *tortière*, or casseroles, with fish. This one is a particularly inspired way to bring out the delicacy of the skate. Another one she made with fresh sardines or anchovies, was also good. The recipe, *Alici o Sardine in Tortiera*, is on page 250.

4 boneless, skinned skate wings, weighing about 2 1/2 pounds total
3 tablespoons extra virgin olive oil
Salt to taste, optional
Freshly ground pepper to taste
2 cloves garlic, peeled
1 sprig fresh parsley

3/4 pound fresh mushrooms, trimmed and thinly sliced
1/4 cup dried porcini mushrooms, soaked in 1/2 cup lukewarm water for 15 to 20 minutes
1/4 cup plain dried bread crumbs
1 teaspoon freshly grated parmesan cheese
1 tablespoon minced fresh parsley

1. In a large sauté pan, cook the skate in boiling, salted water for a few minutes (as if blanching). Drain.

2. Preheat the oven to 350°F. Lightly oil a shallow baking dish from which you can serve, and into which the skate can be placed in one layer. Place the fish in the baking dish. Season with some pepper.

3. In a 10-inch skillet, heat 2 tablespoons of the oil over high heat. Add 1 clove garlic and the sprig of parsley. Cook a few minutes, then add the fresh mushrooms.

4. Gently, so as not to upset the sediment resting at the bottom, lift the porcini mushrooms out of the water and set aside. Strain the water through a paper towel or coffee filter. Set aside. Chop the mushrooms coarsely and add to the skillet. Stir and cook until the water released by the fresh mushrooms has evaporated. When done, remove the garlic and the sprig of parsley and discard. Spoon the mushrooms over the skate.

5. Chop the remaining garlic very finely and combine it with the bread crumbs, parmesan cheese, and minced parsley. Moisten this mixture with 2 or 3 tablespoons of the reserved water from the mushrooms and spread this mixture on the fish. Sprinkle with the remaining water from the mushrooms and drizzle 1 tablespoon of oil over all.

continues

6. Bake until the fish is opaque through, about 20 to 25 minutes. Serve hot.

NOTE: THE SKATE IS EVEN BETTER IF COOKED IN FISH BROTH, IF YOU HAVE IT HANDY.

Variation: For a change, use baby artichokes instead of the mushrooms. Slice the artichokes very thinly and cook them exactly as directed for the mushrooms.

TROTE ALLA MUGNAIA

Miller's Wife's Trout *(Makes 6 servings)*

ALLA MUGNAIA IS A COMMON WAY OF cooking fish in Italy. Sole, flounder, mullet, and, of course, trout are the preferred kind. Butter is used with a little oil, and the technique is quick and simple.

Trout are abundant in the Sangro River in Abruzzo and much appreciated. I buy my trout in America at the green market. They are farm raised and quite good, but they do not compare with the trout from the Sangro. If you can find wild trout, go for it.

Six ³/₄-pound trout, cleaned and gutted, but preferably with heads on
All-purpose flour, spread on a large plate
¹/₄ cup unsalted butter
1 tablespoon extra virgin olive oil
2 lemons
2 sprigs fresh parsley, minced

1. Dredge the trout in the flour. Shake off the excess.

2. In a large skillet into which the fish can fit snugly, heat 2 tablespoons of the butter and the oil over medium heat. Sauté the fish on both sides until nicely golden and the flesh near the bone is opaque, about 5 minutes per side. Remove the fish to a serving platter and keep warm. Discard the cooking fat and wipe the skillet clean.

3. Return the skillet to the heat and melt 2 tablespoons of butter in it over medium heat. Add the juice of 1 lemon and the minced parsley. Pour on the fish. Cut the remaining lemon into wedges and place around the fish. Serve immediately.

TROTE RIPIENE ALL'ABRUZZESE

Stuffed Trout Abruzzo Style (Makes 6 servings)

THIS SAVORY STUFFING COMBINES AMIABLY with the sweet pinkness of the delicate trout flesh.

I have made this recipe with a large salmon trout and it is delicious too.

2 tablespoons freshly grated parmesan cheese
1/4 cup plain bread crumbs
2 anchovy fillets, drained and chopped
1 clove garlic, peeled and minced
1 tablespoon minced fresh parsley
1 tablespoon extra virgin olive oil
Six small 1/2- to 3/4-pound trout, scaled,
*   gutted, cleaned, and boned for stuffing*

2 bay leaves
Salt to taste, optional
Freshly ground pepper to taste
3/4 cup dry white wine
1 tablespoon unsalted butter
Lemon wedges

1. In a bowl, combine the first 5 ingredients and mix well. Add the oil and mix well.

2. Preheat the oven to 350°F. Lightly oil a shallow baking dish into which the trout can fit snugly.

3. Open each trout flat on a work surface. Spoon an equal amount of the bread crumb mixture onto the inside of each trout. Close to re-form the fish and set in the prepared pan. Add the bay leaves, season with salt, if used, and pepper, and add the wine. Dot with the butter.

4. Place the pan in the oven and bake, basting occasionally, until the fish is opaque through, 20 to 25 minutes. Serve with the lemon wedges.

SGOMBRI AI FERRI

Grilled Mackerel **(Makes 6 servings)**

ITALIANS LOVE GRILLED FISH, OR FISH *ai ferri*, which means "on the irons."

All fish can be grilled and they all taste good that way. The preparation is easy—simply marinate the fish in herbs, lemon or vinegar, and wine. My favorite is basic and simple, oil and lemon and some herbs. When your fish is really fresh you do not need anything else.

Mackerel is not much appreciated in this country. This is a pity because the fish, when fresh—and it must be fresh—is delicious with a meaty texture and a very distinctive flavor. Bluefish, coming from Montauk Point in season, is also superb. Tuna and swordfish are good substitutions. Salmon can also be grilled in this simple way.

Six 8-ounce mackerel, cleaned, with heads on
6 bay leaves
6 cloves garlic, peeled
7 sprigs fresh parsley
3 to 4 tablespoons extra virgin olive oil
Juice of 1 lemon
Freshly ground pepper to taste
1/4 teaspoon dried oregano
Lemon wedges

1. In the body opening of each mackerel, place 1 bay leaf, and in the head stuff 1 garlic of clove and 1 sprig of parsley. Reserve the remaining sprig.

2. On a large platter, combine the oil, lemon juice, and a good grinding of pepper. Roll the fish in it. Refrigerate, covered, for 20 minutes or longer.

3. Preheat the broiler or prepare a charcoal fire. Lightly oil a grill or broiler rack.

4. Place all the fish on the rack. Sprinkle with the oregano and grill or broil, turning once, until the flesh near the bone is opaque, about 8 minutes on one side and 5 on the other. Using the remaining sprig of parsley as a brush, brush the fish with the lemon marinade while it cooks. Turn often; the fish is done when the eye pops out. Serve with lemon wedges.

NOTE: IDEALLY THE MACKEREL SHOULD BE COOKED OVER CHARCOAL. THIS IS A GREAT SUMMER RECIPE.

SALMONE A LETTO

Salmon in Bed (Makes 6 servings)

THIS RECIPE IS IDEAL FOR LARGE FILLETS, especially coho salmon, which is usually sold in half fillets. The salmon is cooked on a bed of lemon slices, hence the name.

Extra virgin olive oil for pan
1 large lemon, thinly sliced
3 pounds fresh salmon, preferably one
*   3-pound fillet*

2 bay leaves
2 tablespoons unsalted butter
1 tablespoon minced fresh parsley
Lemon wedges

1. Preheat the oven to 350°F. Lightly oil a shallow baking dish from which you can serve and in which the salmon can fit snugly.

2. Place the lemon slices in a layer in the prepared dish. Lay the salmon on top and add the bay leaves. Dot with the butter.

3. Bake until the fish is opaque throughout, 25 to 30 minutes depending on the thickness of the fillet. Baste often with the juices in the dish. Serve sprinkled with the minced parsley and surrounded by lemon wedges.

SALMONE IMPACCHETTATO

Salmon in a Packet (Makes 6 servings)

YEARS AGO, FRESH SALMON WAS QUITE rare in Italy. Now you can find it in every fish market and it is excellent. My mother used to prepare this recipe with *sgombri*, mackerels, which abound in the Adriatic Sea, but are not always available here. I have been making it with salmon with excellent results.

The leeks add a special, delicate taste to the salmon and it is more delicate than onions.

2 leeks, white and light green parts only,
*   cut into matchstick strips and blanched*
*   (see Note)*
Unsalted butter
6 salmon steaks (about 3 pounds total)

6 tablespoons dry white wine
Juice of ¹/₂ lemon
6 thin slices of lemon
Freshly ground pepper to taste

1. Trim the leeks, remove the green parts and discard, or reserve for another use. Cut the leeks in very thin julienne and place in a bowl of lukewarm water. Add a little kosher salt and let stand 10 minutes. This will remove the sand from the leaves. When ready, rinse the leeks under fresh water and blanch them for a few minutes, drain, and set aside. This step can be done in advance.

continues

2. Preheat the oven to 350°F.

3. Cut 6 pieces of aluminum foil, each large enough to enclose a salmon steak in a packet. Butter the foil sheets. Place 1 salmon steak on each foil. Distribute the leeks evenly among the tops of the steaks. Pour 1 tablespoon of wine over each steak. Sprinkle all with 1 teaspoon of the lemon juice, and top with the lemon slices. Grind some pepper on the steaks and dot each with $^1/_2$ teaspoon butter. Crimp the foil to enclose the steaks tightly.

4. Place them on a cookie sheet and bake until the fish is opaque throughout, about 25 minutes. Serve in their packets.

NOTE: TO BLANCH LEEKS, ADD THEM TO PLENTY OF BOILING, SALTED WATER AND COOK FOR A FEW MINUTES. (BLANCHING MEANS TO COOK VERY BRIEFLY, 1 TO 2 MINUTES IN BOILING WATER.)

Variation: Tuna steaks can be cooked the same way.

SALMONE ALLE ZUCCHINE

Salmon with Zucchini **(Makes 6 servings)**

As I SAID BEFORE, FRESH SALMON WAS NOT something I ate when I was growing up in Abruzzo. It wasn't really available. My father would buy smoked salmon for special occasions, and I didn't even wanted to taste it. I found the smell not very appealing and my poor Papà would get so annoyed at me for my lack of sophistication and taste, but I learned and now I love it.

On one of my frequent visits to Abruzzo, my friend and famous chef Nicola Ranieri invited us for dinner in his restaurant and served us salmon. I remember being a little disappointed by his choice. I wanted something

All-purpose flour, spread on a large plate
Salt to taste, optional
Freshly ground pepper to taste
Six $^3/_4$-inch-thick salmon steaks
2 large eggs, beaten, in a large shallow bowl

2 cups canola oil
4 zucchini, about $^3/_4$ pound total, cut into very thin rounds
$^1/_4$ cup extra virgin olive oil
Lemon wedges, optional

1. Season the flour with salt and pepper. Dredge the salmon steaks in the flour. Shake off the excess and dip the steaks in the beaten eggs. Refrigerate, covered, for 10 minutes or longer. Reserve the flour

2. In a large skillet, heat the canola oil to the smoking point over high heat. Dredge the zucchini in flour and fry them, in batches if necessary, until golden, about 5 minutes. Drain on paper towels. Keep warm.

3. Remove the oil from the skillet and reserve. (This oil can be reused for frying two more times.)

more *nostrano,* ours, from our sea, the Adriatic, and not an exotic fish from Norwegian waters. But since we were his guests, I didn't protest. And a good thing, too, because the dish was excellent. Here is the recipe.

4. Return the skillet to the heat, add the olive oil, and heat over medium heat. Add the salmon steaks. Do not crowd the steaks; they can be cooked in batches if necessary. Cook until the flesh near the bone is opaque, about 5 minutes on each side. Turn the steaks once or twice.

5. Set the steaks on a serving plate and pile the fried zucchini on top. Serve hot with the lemon wedges, if used.

NOTE: DO NOT USE TOO LITTLE OIL WHEN FRYING. WHEN THE FOOD SWIMS IN OIL, IT ABSORBS LESS OF IT.

PESCE SPADA AL DOLCINO

Sweet and Sour Swordfish **(Makes 6 servings)**

IN THE PAST, BALSAMIC VINEGAR WAS TOO expensive and quite rare to find outside Modena, where it is made.

For this reason, the Abruzzese version of *agro dolce,* a sweet and sour preparation, was always made with regular wine vinegar and sugar.

Today balsamic vinegar is readily available. It is wonderful for enhancing flavors. I often use it instead of regular vinegar, as in this recipe. Salmon and tuna can also be cooked this way.

6 swordfish steaks, about 6 ounces each
Salt to taste, optional
Freshly ground pepper to taste
All-purpose flour, spread on a large plate
3 tablespoons extra virgin olive oil
1/2 cup dry white wine
1/4 cup Marsala wine
1/4 cup balsamic vinegar
2 or 3 tablespoons capers in brine, drained
1 tablespoon minced fresh parsley

1. Lightly sprinkle the fish with salt, if used, and the pepper. Dredge the fish steaks in the flour. Shake off the excess. Set aside.

2. In a large skillet, heat the oil and quickly sauté the fish until lightly browned on both sides. This can be done in batches. Remove the fish to a platter and keep warm.

3. Pour off the oil in the skillet and add both wines. Cook over medium heat, scraping up the browned bits on the bottom and sides of the skillet. Add the balsamic vinegar, stir, and return the fish to the skillet. Cook until the fish is opaque throughout, about 8 to 10 minutes, adding the capers toward the end. Sprinkle the parsley over the fish and serve.

PESCE SPADA CON LA SALSA DI LIMONE E ZAFFERANO

Swordfish with Lemon and Saffron Sauce *(Makes 6 servings)*

THE BEST SAFFRON IN ITALY COMES FROM L'Aquila, the capital of Abruzzo, yet we Abruzzesi do not use it extravagantly. Traditionally, it is reserved for *Risotto alla Milanese*. Lately though, it seems that saffron has been rediscovered and it appears more often in our cuisine. This recipe is a good example.

1 small onion, finely chopped
4 scallions, white and green parts
  chopped separately
1/2 cup dry white wine
1 cup fish broth, preferably homemade
  (page 63); or bottled clam juice
1/4 teaspoon powdered saffron,
  or 1/2 teaspoon threads
Six 6-ounce swordfish steaks

Juice of 1 lemon
1/4 cup extra virgin olive oil
2 cloves garlic, peeled and minced
1 sprig fresh rosemary
Salt to taste, optional
Freshly ground pepper to taste
2 tablespoons unsalted butter
1 1/2 teaspoons all-purpose flour

1. In a 1-quart pan, place the onion, the white part of the scallions, the wine, half the broth, and the saffron. Bring to a boil, reduce the heat to medium-low, and simmer for 10 minutes. Strain, discarding the solids, and reserve.

2. Place the fish on a large platter, sprinkle with half of the lemon juice, 2 tablespoons of the oil, and the garlic. Turn the fish so that it is coated on both sides with the marinade. Set aside.

3. In a large skillet, or use two smaller ones, into which the fish can fit in one layer, heat the remaining oil over medium heat. Add the rosemary. Lift the fish from the marinade, reserving the marinade. Place the fish in the skillet and sauté until lightly browned on both sides, about 3 to 4 minutes per side. Add the marinade and cook, shaking the pan every once in a while and turning the fish once or twice, until the fish is opaque throughout, about 10 to 15 minutes. Season with salt, if used, and pepper. Remove the fish to a serving platter. Keep warm. Discard the rosemary.

4. Melt the butter in the same skillet over medium heat. Add the flour and stir, scraping the browned bits at the bottom and sides of the pan. Little by little, add the reserved broth, and cook, stirring constantly, until it starts to simmer. Add the remaining lemon juice. Cook a few seconds more.

5. Pour the sauce on the fish, sprinkle with the green parts of the scallions, and serve.

Variation: After removing the fish from the marinade, you can grill it, if you wish, and serve it with the same saffron-lemon sauce.

ALICI O SARDINE IN PADELLA

Anchovies or Sardines in a Skillet **(Makes 4 to 6 servings)**

WHEN I SEE FRESH ANCHOVIES AND SAR-dines at the fish market, I snatch them up immediately. It is a little of a bother to clean them, but if you always shop at the same place, your fishmonger might clean the fish for you. Whether or not you have help cleaning these little fish, do not deprive yourself, because fresh anchovies and sardines are delicious.

We Italians always like to cook our fish with the head on, and my mother did just so. She removed only the innards and gently scaled the fish. Because the anchovies are so small, some cooks do not even bother removing the innards. Especially when deep-frying them, everything tastes delicious.

You do not need to bone the fish. The bone is tender and can be eaten. Besides, it is good for you because it provides calcium. But you can remove the heads; it makes the cleaning easier.

Anchovies and sardines can be pan-fried, grilled, deep-fried with just a dusting of flour, or baked.

2¹/₂ pounds fresh anchovies or sardines
¹/₄ cup extra virgin olive oil
Salt to taste, optional
Freshly ground pepper to taste
2 tablespoons minced fresh parsley
1 clove garlic, peeled and minced
¹/₂ teaspoon dried oregano, more if fresh, chopped (measure after chopping)
1 tablespoon capers in brine, drained
¹/₂ cup dry white wine
6 medium-size ripe tomatoes, chopped

1. Gently scale the fish, if necessary. Pull off the heads. The innards will come out with the head. If not, remove them with your fingers. Wash the fish and pat dry.

2. Place the fish in a 9- to 10-inch skillet. Do not worry if they overlap a little. Add the oil, sprinkle with salt, pepper, 1 tablespoon of the parsley, the garlic, oregano, and capers. Set on medium heat and as soon as the fish start to sizzle, add the wine. Let evaporate over medium-high heat and add the tomatoes. Gently stir and shake the pan. Cook until the fish is done throughout, 5 to 10 minutes. Add the remaining minced parsley and serve.

ALICI O SARDINE IN TORTIERA

Potted Anchovies or Sardines **(Makes 6 or more servings)**

HERE'S ANOTHER OF MY MOTHER'S favorites. This time the anchovies, or sardines, are layered with potatoes and baked.

3 tablespoons extra virgin olive oil, plus additional for the baking dish
2 baking potatoes, peeled and cut into very thin slices
Salt to taste, optional
Freshly ground pepper to taste

2 tablespoons minced fresh parsley
2 pounds fresh anchovies or sardines, gutted and heads removed (see Step 1 previous recipe)
3 ripe tomatoes, cubed, optional
4 to 5 tablespoons plain bread crumbs

1. Preheat the oven to 375°F. Lightly oil a 10-inch shallow baking dish from which you can serve.

2. Place the potatoes in a mixing bowl and add 2 tablespoons of the oil, a little salt and pepper, and half the parsley. Toss well.

3. Place one-third of the potatoes in a layer in the prepared dish, add half the fish, and drizzle ½ tablespoon of the oil over them. Add half the tomatoes. Repeat the layering using one-third potatoes, the remaining tomatoes, and another layer of potatoes, all of the tomatoes, all of the fish, and ending with a layer of all of the remaining potatoes. Sprinkle with the remaining parsley. Season with a little more salt and pepper. Sprinkle the top with the bread crumbs and drizzle with a little oil.

4. Bake until the top is golden and the potatoes are soft when pierced with a fork, about 1 hour.

SCAMPI ALLA GRIGLIA

Grilled Shrimp (Makes 6 servings)

WHAT'S BETTER THAN A SUCCULENT BRACE of grilled shrimp, especially when they are cooked over subdued charcoal? You can also cook these shrimp under the broiler. Either way, the important thing is for them to marinate long enough to absorb the aromatic flavors.

My father, who was the family fish specialist, always cooked the shrimp in the shells. He first slit the shells from the top to the tails, making it easier to peel when cooked, and to remove the vein, although he always said to ignore the vein because, as he put it, "after all, it is . . . organic." He then marinated the shrimp for at least 30 minutes.

2 pounds medium or large shrimp
1 teaspoon kosher salt
2 sprigs fresh parsley
1/4 cup extra virgin olive oil
1 clove garlic, peeled and pressed through a garlic press
1/2 teaspoon minced sage or oregano, fresh or dried
Juice of 1 lemon
Freshly ground pepper to taste

1. Place the shrimp in a bowl of cold water, add the kosher salt, and refrigerate for 15 minutes to make a marinade.

2. Reserve 1 sprig fresh parsley and combine the other one with the remaining ingredients to make a marinade.

3. When ready to cook, drain the shrimp, peel and devein them, if desired, or slit the backstop of the shells with a knife or scissors. Place the shrimp on a platter, add the marinade, toss, and refrigerate for 30 minutes or longer.

4. Preheat the broiler or prepare a charcoal fire. Lightly oil a grill or broiler rack.

5. Grill or broil the shrimp, turning once or twice. Brush them, while cooking, with the marinade, using the remaining parsley sprig as a brush. Do not overcook. As soon as they turn red, the shrimp are done.

Variation: This is a basic method of marinating and grilling fish. You may or not use the garlic or as you wish, and you can change the herbs to suit the fish or shell-fish. For instance, with fatty fish, it is better to use rosemary or thyme.

Another delicious recipe we used to make, especially in the summer, was *spiedini.* After marinating the shrimp, they were put on skewers and grilled.

SCAMPI CON ASPARAGI ALLE DUE SALSE

Scampi and Asparagus with Two Sauces (Makes 6 servings)

WHEN MY AUNT CETTINA GOT MARRIED, she went to live in the port town of Ortona a Mare. As soon as school ended, I was sent to spend the summer with her. Like so many towns in Abruzzo, this one is located on top of a hill overlooking the Adriatic Sea. The ritual of the *passeggiata,* walk, which is performed in the late afternoon in every small town in Italy, takes place on the Lungomare, the panoramic street which ends dramatically at a little park dominated by the picturesque ruins of a medieval castle. This is the best point from which to admire the panorama of the undulated coastline below, the rugged aspect of the hills made gentle by silvery olive trees and solemn cypresses.

Being a port, Ortona had a lively fish market where the shrimp, fresh and still dripping with sea water, were bought for this dish. Aunt Cettina was an excellent cook, and, unlike my mother, she loved to be in the kitchen. She served this dish for one of her *cene fredde,* cold suppers, which are so fashionable in Italy during the summer.

This refreshing, cool entrée, which was accompanied by a salad of cucumber and tomatoes, made the entire meal a feast of contrasting colors. When the asparagus season ended, she substituted them with zucchini strips

24 spears asparagus, trimmed and washed
36 large shrimp
Kosher salt to taste, optional
Green parts from 3 leeks, trimmed
Green parts from a bunch of scallions, trimmed
2 green lettuce leaves
5 springs fresh parsley, tender part of the stems included
3 medium-size carrots, peeled and cut into 4 pieces
10 peppercorns
2 bay leaves
Salt to taste, optional
1/2 cup mayonnaise
Juice of 1 lemon
2 tablespoons extra virgin olive oil
1 small clove garlic, peeled and squeezed through a garlic press

1. Trim off 2 to 3 inches from the bottom ends of the asparagus and reserve. If asparagus are thick, peel them and discard the peels. Set aside the asparagus spears.

2. Place the shrimp in a bowl of cold water, add 1 teaspoon of kosher salt, and refrigerate for about 15 minutes. When ready to cook, drain, peel, and devein the shrimp. Set the shrimp aside. Tie the shells in a piece of cheesecloth and set aside.

3. In a stockpot, place the reserved bottom ends of the asparagus, the green parts of the leeks, scallions, lettuce, and parsley. Add the carrots, peppercorns, and bay leaves. Add enough water to cover the solids by 2 inches. Cover the pot, bring to a boil, and cook over medium heat for 20 to 30 minutes. Add the bundle with the shells, some salt, if used, and cook 15 minutes longer.

4. With a slotted spoon, remove the carrots from the pot. Puree in a food processor and set aside. Discard the bay leaves. Remove all the green parts from the pot and puree in a food mill. If you want to use a food processor, you may, but then you have to strain the puree to remove the stringy parts. Strain the broth, squeezing the juices out of the bundle with the shrimp shells. Discard the bundle. Strain the broth, taste the broth for flavor, and, if necessary, add a little salt. Set aside.

5. Blanch the asparagus spears in boiling, salted water. The asparagus are done if the tops bend slightly when picked up with tongs, about 5 minutes. Drain. Plunge in cold water, drain again, and wrap in paper towels. Refrigerate.

or green beans, producing the same striking effect.

6. Prepare the sauce: Add half of the mayonnaise and 2 tablespoons of the lemon juice to the carrot puree, and mix well. If the sauce is too dense, add a bit of the broth. Set aside. Do the same with the green puree. Taste for flavor, and, if necessary, add some lemon. Cover both sauces and refrigerate until ready to use.

7. Bring the reserved broth to a boil and add the shrimp. Cook until the shrimp turn red, about 5 minutes. Remove the shrimp with a slotted spoon. Reserve this wonderful broth for a fish risotto or a fish soup.

8. Combine the remaining lemon juice with the oil and the garlic. Mix well. Dress the shrimp with this mixture. Refrigerate.

9. When ready to serve, let the shrimp come to room temperature for about 10 to 15 minutes. Place 4 asparagus spears in the middle of each individual plate. Spoon the yellow sauce on one side of the plate, and the green on the other side. Place 3 shrimp on each side of the asparagus on top of the sauces, tails facing the edge of the plate.

NOTE: THIS IS A GOOD DISH FOR A BUFFET. SERVE IT AS SUGGESTED, BUT ON A LARGE SERVING PLATTER. SET THE REMAINING SAUCES IN TWO SEPARATE BOWLS.

SCAMPI ALLA GRAPPA

Shrimp with Grappa **(Makes 6 servings)**

HERE'S A DIFFERENT WAY OF COOKING shrimp scampi. The harshness of the grappa, which is a fiery liqueur much favored by the Italians as an after-dinner drink, is smoothed out by the delicate cream. Rice is a good accompaniment to this dish.

1 ½ pounds (about 30) medium-size shrimp	1 tablespoon unsalted butter
1 teaspoon kosher salt	2 shallots, finely chopped
Juice of 1 lemon	¼ cup heavy cream
Freshly ground pepper to taste	1 ¼ cups shelled peas
2 tablespoons extra virgin olive oil	2 slices prosciutto, finely shredded
½ cup grappa	2 sprigs fresh parsley, minced

1. Place the shrimp in a bowl, cover with cold water, and add the kosher salt. Let stand 15 minutes. Discard the water, rinse the shrimp, peel, and devein. Reserve the shells. Return the shrimp to the bowl, add the lemon juice, and sprinkle with pepper. Set aside.

2. In a 9-inch skillet, heat 1 tablespoon of the oil over medium heat. Add the shells. Cook, stirring, until the shells turn red, about 5 minutes. Slowly (it may flare up) add ¼ cup of the grappa. Reduce the heat to low and cook until the grappa evaporates, about 5 minutes. Add ¼ cup water, cover, and cook until the liquid reduces to a minimum, about 5 minutes longer. Strain into a bowl, squeezing out as much of the juices as possible. Discard the shells but reserve the juices.

3. Wipe the skillet and add to it the remaining oil and the butter. Heat over medium heat. Add the shrimp. and cook, stirring, until they turn red, about 1 minute, and add the shallots. Cook until wilted, about 5 minutes, and slowly add the remaining grappa, the cream, and the juice from the shells. Cook over high heat for 1 more minute. Transfer the shrimp to a plate and keep warm.

4. Add the peas to the skillet and cook until done. If you have too much sauce, remove the peas to the plate with shrimp and simmer the sauce over medium heat until reduced by half. Return the shrimp and the peas, if you have removed them, to the skillet, add the prosciutto, bring to a rolling boil, and add the parsley. Serve immediately.

SCAMPI ALLA DAVIDE

Davide's Scampi (*Makes 6 servings*)

DAVIDE SPERA IS ONE OF MY COUSIN Adriana's sons and an absolute *sagoma*. This is a slang word meaning "a character." And that he is, an amusing one. He is also a teacher and very serious and passionate about his profession. He likes good food and sometimes even cooks. This recipe, he told me, came from an expedition he made on a fishing boat. The just-caught shrimp were cooked by the fishermen while Davide took notes.

1 ¹/₂ pounds medium-size shrimp
1 teaspoon kosher salt
3 tablespoons extra virgin olive oil
1 tablespoon capers in brine, drained
1 clove garlic, peeled and smashed
Juice of ¹/₂ lemon

¹/₄ cup tomato puree, fresh or canned
¹/₄ cup fish broth or water, if necessary
7 or 8 fresh basil leaves, or ¹/₂ teaspoon dried
1 sprig fresh parsley

1. Place the shrimp in a bowl, cover with cold water, and add the kosher salt. Let stand 15 minutes. Discard the water, rinse the shrimp, peel, and devein.

2. In a 9-inch skillet, place the oil, capers, garlic, and lemon juice. Cook over medium heat for 2 to 3 minutes. Add the tomato puree and half of the basil. Cook 10 minutes over low heat. Add the fish broth and bring to a boil. Add the shrimp and cook, stirring, until they turn red, about 5 minutes.

3. Chop the parsley and the remaining basil together, add, and serve.

SCAMPI ALLA BUONGUSTAIA

Shrimp of the Connoisseur (*Makes 6 servings*)

HERE IS ANOTHER SIMPLE SHRIMP DISH, perhaps my favorite. The sauce is so delicious that it calls for something to soak it up. If you have some leftovers, which I doubt, chop the shrimp and dress some linguine with it.

My mother served this dish with *pan dorato*. These are slices of bread dipped in beaten eggs and deep-fried. They were delicious, but nowadays I prefer a simple *bruschetta*.

1 ¹/₂ pounds shrimp
1 teaspoon kosher salt
3 tablespoons of all-purpose flour
¹/₄ teaspoon powdered sage
A good grinding of pepper to taste

¹/₄ cup extra virgin olive oil
Juice of 1 lemon
³/₄ cup Marsala or sherry wine
1 tablespoon tomato paste
1 tablespoon minced fresh parsley

1. Place the shrimp in a bowl of cold water, add the salt, and refrigerate 15 minutes. When ready to cook, rinse the shrimp, peel, and devein them.

continues

2. Combine the flour with the sage and pepper. Dredge the shrimp in this mixture, shaking to remove excess flour.

3. In a skillet large enough to contain all the shrimp in one layer, heat the oil over medium heat and add the shrimp. Cook, turning once or twice, until they turn red, about 5 minutes. Add half of the lemon juice while cooking. Remove the shrimp to a platter and keep warm.

4. Add the wine to the skillet and cook over medium-high heat, scraping the bottom and sides, for 5 minutes. Stir in the tomato paste. Cover and cook at a simmer over low heat, stirring often, for 5 to 8 minutes. Return the shrimp to the skillet, add the remaining lemon juice, stir, and cook just to warm through. Sprinkle the parsley on top and serve.

GAMBERETTI "ALLA ME"

Shrimp My Style **(Makes 6 servings)**

HERE'S A WHIMSICAL RECIPE. IT CAME about because I poached too many for a luncheon antipasto. In the evening, to vary the menu—rather than eat the same thing again—I did the leftover shrimp in a gratin. Since the dish was quite good, and the family started to request it, I called it *"alla me."* After all, it had been my idea.

1 tablespoon unsalted butter, plus additional for buttering the dish
1 1/2 pounds cooked small shrimp
1 tablespoon all-purpose flour
1/2 cup milk

1/2 cup heavy cream
1 tablespoon minced fresh parsley
Freshly ground white pepper to taste
2 tablespoons sherry
2 tablespoons freshly grated parmesan cheese

1. Preheat the oven to 375°F.

2. Butter a baking dish from which you can serve and large enough to contain all the shrimp in one layer. Add the shrimp and set aside.

3. In a 1-quart saucepan, melt 1 tablespoon of the butter over medium heat, add the flour, and cook, stirring, for 2 to 3 minutes. Remove from the heat.

4. Combine the milk and cream. Using a whisk, stir this liquid, a little at a time, into the butter-and-flour mixture. Stir until thoroughly liquefied and smooth.

Cook, whisking constantly, over medium-low heat until the mixture starts to bubble. Add the parsley, pepper, sherry, and parmesan cheese. Pour this sauce on the shrimp.

5. Bake the shrimp in the center of the oven for 5 to 10 minutes. Set the pan under the broiler and broil until the top is slightly brown, about 5 minutes. Serve immediately.

FRITTELLE DI SCAMPI

Scampi Cakes **(Makes 6 to 8 cakes)**

THE ITALIAN VERSION OF CRAB CAKES?
Not quite, but similar. It is a good way
to use cooked shrimp.

3 large eggs
2 tablespoons soda water
About ¹/₄ cup all-purpose flour
1 jigger (¹/₄ cup) grappa or brandy
Kosher salt to taste
Freshly ground pepper to taste

1 tablespoon minced fresh parsley
4 cups cooked shrimp, diced
1¹/₂ cups canola, or other vegetable oil,
    for deep-frying
Lemon wedges

1. In a mixing bowl beat the eggs and add the soda water. Slowly mix in the flour and add the grappa or brandy. Mix well and add the salt, pepper, parsley, and shrimp, and mix again. If the mixture seems too thin, sprinkle with a little more flour and mix.

2. In a 9-inch deep fryer or sauté pan, heat the oil to the smoking point and start adding the shrimp mixture by the spoonful to form cakes 4 to 5 inches in diameter. Cook, turning the cakes 2 or 3 times, until golden on both sides, about 3 to 4 minutes per side. Drain on paper towels; serve hot surrounded by lemon wedges.

SPIEDINI DI CAPESANTE E GAMBERETTI

Scallops and Shrimp on the Spit (*Makes 6 servings*)

THERE IS AN AMERICAN ADDITION TO THIS very Italian dish—smoked bacon—pleasingly contrasting with the sweetness of the shrimp. My father used prosciutto or very lean pancetta, which is Italian bacon, but I feel that the smokiness of the American bacon is what makes this dish deliciously unusual.

I suggest serving this dish with a mixed salad. Italians serve the salad on the side or on a separate dish. We do not particularly like to put hot food on a cool salad as it is done today in fashionable restaurants.

3 tablespoons extra virgin olive oil, plus
  a little more for grill
24 jumbo shrimp, peeled and deveined
24 sea scallops
Juice of ½ lemon

5 or 6 fresh sage leaves, finely chopped,
  or ½ teaspoon dried
Freshly ground pepper to taste
24 thin slices bacon, each slice cut in half

1. Preheat the broiler or prepare a charcoal fire. Lightly oil a grill or broiler rack.

2. Place the shrimp and the scallops in a bowl and add the olive oil, sprinkle with the lemon juice, sage, and pepper. Toss. Wrap each shrimp and scallop in one piece of bacon and thread them, alternating the fish, on skewers.

3. Cook over medium heat on a charcoal grill or under a broiler, turning often, for 4 to 5 minutes. Do not overcook. Serve with a mixed salad.

CAPESANTE COI FUNGHI E CARCIOFI

Scallops with Mushrooms and Artichokes (*Makes 6 servings*)

PERHAPS IT IS BECAUSE THE SEA AND THE land are so close together that we in Abruzzo love to add vegetables to our fish and meat. Many farms in this region reside on top of hills overlooking the sea. No wonder, then, that cooks are inspired to combine the products of the sea with those from the land.

This dish is another example of what we call *mare e terra*, sea and land.

Extra virgin olive oil
2 cloves garlic, peeled and smashed
1 sprig fresh oregano, or ¼ teaspoon dried
1 sprig fresh parsley
3 cups fresh mushrooms, trimmed and
  quartered

8 baby artichokes, trimmed and quartered lengthwise; or one 10-ounce
  package frozen, defrosted
1¼ pounds bay scallops
1 tablespoon minced fresh parsley

1. In a large skillet, heat 2 tablespoons of the oil over medium heat. Add the garlic, oregano, and parsley, and cook briefly. Add the mushrooms and cook, stirring, until the mushrooms have released their water, about 10 minutes. Let the water evaporate, add the fresh artichokes, and cook until they are tender, about

10 minutes. You may need to add a little water while cooking the fresh artichokes. If using frozen artichokes, add them toward the end, just to heat through. Remove the vegetables to a bowl and keep warm. Discard the garlic and the sprigs of oregano and parsley.

2. Wipe the skillet where the vegetables cooked. Add 1 tablespoon of the oil and heat over medium heat. Sauté the scallops and cook, stirring, until they are opaque throughout, about 5 minutes.

3. Return the vegetables to the skillet, stir well to warm up, sprinkle with the minced parsley, and serve.

Variation: This dish can be made with string beans, cooked in advance.

Aragosta con Carciofi

Lobster with Artichokes **(Makes 6 servings)**

THIS IS A SUPERB RECIPE FROM THE GREAT chef Valentino Mercattilii of the San Domenico restaurant in Imola, Italy, owned by Gianluigi Morini. Valentino, a native Abruzzese, opened another San Domenico in New York together with the enterprising Tony May and Gianluigi Morini. After a few years, however, the two homesick Italians, went back to their restaurant in Italy.

The San Domenico in New York is still thriving and serving wonderful food, including some of Valentino's signature dishes.

Although I have somewhat adapted this recipe to make it more accessible to home cooks, I still serve it in the grand style of the San Domenico.

Six $^3/_4$- to 1-pound lobsters
6 tablespoons unsalted butter, cut into
  tablespoon-size pieces
1 or 2 strips prosciutto fat, optional
2 medium-size carrots, peeled and cut
  into thin rounds
1 large onion, thinly sliced
16 fresh artichoke bottoms

Juice of $^1/_2$ lemon
3 sprigs fresh flat-leaf parsley
About $^1/_4$ cup water or more
1 tablespoon fresh tarragon leaves,
  or $^1/_4$ teaspoon dried
Salt to taste, optional
Freshly ground white pepper to taste
1 bunch curly parsley for decoration

1. Cook the lobsters by plunging two at a time into a large pot of boiling, salted water. Remove and cool.

2. In a large saucepan, melt 2 tablespoons of the butter over medium heat and add the prosciutto fat, if used, and cook about 2 minutes, then remove and discard it. Add the carrots and onion and cook 5 to 8 minutes. Add the artichoke bottoms, lemon juice, and sprigs of parsley. Stir and cook 2 to 3 minutes, then add the water and continue cooking until the artichokes are tender, about 10 minutes.

continues

Drain the vegetables, reserving the liquid, and discard the sprigs of parsley. Reserve the pan.

3. Remove the head of the lobster first and set aside. Snip the tail off the body, remove the meat in it, and set it aside. Discard the tail shell. With scissors or poultry shears, cut the underbelly open lengthwise. Shell the lobsters, being careful to keep the carcasses as intact as possible.

4. Reserve the carcasses and the heads. Remove the meat from the claws. Cut all the meat into small cubes, add the meat from the tails, and set aside.

5. Separate the artichoke bottoms from the rest of the vegetables and dice them. Set aside.

6. Return the liquid from the vegetables to the pan and cook over medium heat until reduced by half, about 5 minutes. Add the remaining butter and cook, whisking, over very low heat. Do not let the sauce boil. Return all the vegetables and the lobster to the pan and add the tarragon. Add the salt and a good grinding of pepper. Cook a few minutes to heat through.

7. To serve: Place the carcasses of the lobsters into individual pasta bowls. Fill each one with some of the lobster mixture. Decorate with the head of the lobster and sprigs of curly parsley. Serve immediately.

NOTE: I ALWAYS ALLOW MY GUESTS TO PICK OUT THE GOOD STUFF FROM THE HEAD OF THE LOBSTER IN THEIR DISH. I JUST PASS A FEW PAPER NAPKINS.

CALAMARI FRITTI

Fried Calamari (*Makes 4 to 6 servings*)

FRIED CALAMARI, ONCE A LITTLE-KNOWN Italian specialty, has taken America by storm. Today it's a staple appetizer in many restaurants, and not only the Italian ones. Everybody likes the crunchiness of these delectable morsels, dipped (or not) in some kind of sauce. They are indeed delicious and addictive, in the sense that they stimulate one's appetite, and it becomes difficult to stop eating them.

My mother used to fry squid with just a dusting of flour to which a good grinding of pepper and a little salt had been added. We never ate them as an antipasto. First of all, Italians do not eat appetizers at every meal. Second, the fish was a cheap one, seldom served to guests, and therefore it was a family dish. Soup or pasta came first and then the fried squid, served with puckery wedges of lemon and a mixed salad. Considering that my father had just gotten the catch of the day from his favorite fisherman, the squid was an absolute delight.

With this recipe though, I am going away from my heritage because the best fried squid I have ever eaten were not made at home. They are those made by Michael Romano, the inventive chef of the Union Square Cafe in New York. And here is the recipe.

4 cups light or vegetable oil
1¾ cups all-purpose flour
1¾ cups graham cracker crumbs
1 teaspoon kosher salt, optional

2 pounds squid with tentacles, cleaned, bodies cut into circles; tentacles halved or quartered, depending on size
Lemon wedges

1. Heat the oil in a deep-fryer skillet or a sauté pan to 360°F. If you do not have a thermometer, drop a piece of bread soaked in vinegar in the oil. It should float to the surface immediately and get lightly brown. The vinegar will also purify the oil.

2. In a large bowl, combine the flour, graham cracker crumbs, and salt.

3. Toss approximately one-third of the squid at a time into the flour mixture. Toss to coat the squid well. Shake the squid in a colander to remove excess coating.

4. Drop the squid into the hot oil and turn once or twice using a slotted spoon. Do not crowd the pan. Fry until golden brown, about 5 minutes. Drain on paper towels, and keep warm until you finish frying all the squid. Serve hot with wedges of lemon.

HOW I GOT THE RECIPE

Michael asked if he could come to my cooking school one night. I was delighted and when I told my pupils that the following week we were going to have Michael Romano as a guest they flipped. But they made a request: Would Michael make his famous fried squid for us? Since he had practically fished for an invitation, I was bold enough to make the request. He accepted with enthusiasm and came prepared with a bag of the famous coating and a bowl of his fabulous dipping sauce. It was a feast. We not only enjoyed his squid, but also his charming company.

TOTANI RIPIENI

Stuffed Squid *(Makes 6 servings)*

IN MY HOUSE, SQUID WAS STUFFED MANY ways and eaten hot or cold, like miniature galantines. The following recipe is a family one, which my mother made often.

3 cloves garlic, peeled and chopped
¹/₂ cup pitted cured black olives
1 tablespoon capers in brine, drained
2 sprigs fresh parsley
5 tablespoons extra virgin olive oil
6 large squid with tentacles, cleaned

2 to 3 tablespoons plain fresh bread
*   crumbs per squid, according to size*
1 teaspoon anchovy paste
Salt to taste, optional
Freshly ground pepper to taste
³/₄ cup dry white wine
1 tablespoon minced fresh parsley

1. In a food processor, finely chop the garlic, olives, capers, and parsley sprigs. Remove the mixture and set aside. Do not wash the processor, set aside.

2. In a 9-inch skillet, heat 2 tablespoons of the oil over high heat. Add the tentacles of the squid and cook, stirring, for 4 to 5 minutes. Remove to the food processor and chop fine. Add the chopped garlic mixture and tentacles to the skillet and cook, stirring, for 2 to 3 minutes over medium heat. Add the bread crumbs, and cook, stirring, 2 to 3 minutes until the flavors have combined.

3. Turn the squid mixture into a bowl, add the anchovy paste, salt, if used, and pepper, and mix well. Cool, then stuff the squids loosely with this mixture. Secure the openings with toothpicks.

4. In a heavy sauté pan into which the squid can be placed in one layer, heat the remaining oil over medium heat. Add the stuffed squid and cook, turning often, until slightly brown, about 10 minutes. Add the wine, cover the pan, and simmer over low heat until the squid is tender, about 1 hour. Check for evaporation; if the sauce reduces too much, add a little water. Serve sprinkled with the minced parsley.

Variation 1: In summertime, my mother used to serve this dish cold, the squid cut into neat rounds surrounding a lovely mixed salad.

Variation 2: Cooked fish, especially shrimp, mixed with the crumb mixture, makes a good stuffing.

MOSCARDINI AI FUNGHI SECCHI E BIETOLE

Little Squid with Dried Mushrooms and Swiss Chard **(Makes 6 servings)**

MOSCARDINI IS A NAME GIVEN TO SMALL squid in Abruzzo. This is a succulent dish, but you must use dried porcini to obtain the full flavor of the preparation. They are expensive, but you do not need many.

Try to choose the smallest squid you can.

1/2 cup dried porcini mushrooms
1 large onion, quartered
1 medium-size carrot, peeled and cut into 4 pieces
1 rib celery, trimmed and cut into 4 pieces
1 clove garlic, peeled
2 sprigs fresh parsley
3 tablespoons extra virgin olive oil

2 1/4 pounds squid including tentacles, cleaned, washed, and cut into 1/4-inch circles
1/4 cup dry white wine
Salt to taste, optional
Freshly ground pepper to taste
1 pound Swiss chard, trimmed and washed
1/2 cup chicken broth, preferably homemade (page 61), or low-sodium canned

1. Soak the dried porcini mushrooms in 1 cup of lukewarm water for 15 to 20 minutes. Gently, so as not to upset the sediment resting at the bottom, lift the porcini mushrooms out of the water and set aside. Strain the water through a paper towel or coffee filter. Set aside.

2. In a food processor, very finely chop the onion, carrot, celery, garlic, and parsley.

3. In a 10-inch skillet, heat the oil over medium heat. Add the vegetable mixture and cook, stirring, until the vegetables are soft, about 5 to 8 minutes. Add the squid and cook, stirring, until it starts to color, about 5 to 8 minutes. Add the wine and let evaporate.

4. Add the mushrooms to the squid and cook, stirring, for 5 minutes. Add the mushroom soaking water to the pan. Add the salt, if used, and pepper. Cover the pan and reduce the heat to a minimum.

5. Cook the Swiss chard in boiling water until wilted, about 3 minutes. Drain, reserving 1 cup of the water. Rinse the chard under cold water. Squeeze the leaves dry and chop the leaves and ribs coarsely.

continues

6. Add the chopped chard to the squid. Cook, stirring, for 2 to 3 minutes, then add the broth. Stir well and continue cooking, covered, until the squid are soft, about 45 minutes to 1 hour. If the liquid reduces too much, add some of the water from the Swiss chard.

SEPPIE CON I CARCIOFI

Squid with Artichokes **(Makes 6 servings)**

ARTICHOKES, MUCH LOVED IN MY HOUSE, are a perfect foil for squid and shell-fish. The addition of anchovies makes this dish different.

1 lemon
8 baby artichokes
3 tablespoons extra virgin olive oil
3 cloves garlic, peeled
3 sprigs fresh parsley
3 pounds squid, cleaned and cut into
 1/4-inch circles

1/4 cup dry white wine
Salt to taste, optional
Freshly ground pepper to taste
About 1 cup chicken broth, preferably
 homemade (page 61), or low-sodium
 canned
2 anchovy fillets, drained

1. With a carrot peeler, remove the zest from the lemon and set aside.

2. Remove the tougher leaves from the artichokes and trim the tops. Cut the artichokes into thin wedges and add them to a bowl of acidulated water (water into which the juice of half a lemon is squeezed). This will keep the artichokes from turning black.

3. In a 10-inch skillet, heat the oil over high heat. Add 1 garlic clove and 1 parsley sprig. Cook until the garlic starts to sizzle, about 1 to 2 minutes. Add the squid and cook, stirring, for 5 minutes. Add the wine and let evaporate. Add the salt, if used, pepper, and broth. Cover, reduce the heat to a minimum, and simmer about 45 minutes. Make sure that the broth does not evaporate completely. If this happens add a little more broth or water.

4. Drain the artichokes, reserving 1/2 cup of the lemon water. Add the artichokes to the skillet and, if the skillet looks dry, a little of the lemon water. Cook until the artichokes are tender, about 10 to 15 minutes.

5. In a food processor, finely chop the remaining garlic and parsley, anchovies, and lemon zest. Add this mixture to the squid, stir, and serve.

Variation: 1 cup of frozen, defrosted peas can be added to the artichokes during the last 5 minutes.

POLPI IN PURGATORIO

Octopus in Purgatory *(Makes 6 servings)*

THIS IS AN ANCIENT RECIPE FROM THE coastal town of Vasto. The octopus are cooked in a sauce flavored with garlic and a touch of the ubiquitous dried hot red pepper of Abruzzo, the *diavoletto*. Add a small hot pepper, otherwise the octopus will be in Inferno and not in Purgatory anymore.

3 tablespoons extra virgin olive oil
2 cloves garlic, peeled and smashed
2 sprigs fresh parsley
1 small diavoletto *(dried Italian hot red pepper)*
2 pounds octopus, cleaned (see box) and cut into bite-size pieces

½ cup dry white wine
2 cups cubed tomatoes, fresh or canned
Salt to taste, optional
Freshly ground pepper to taste
1 tablespoon minced fresh parsley

1. In a 2-quart heavy-bottomed pan, preferably a terra-cotta one, heat the oil over medium heat. Add the garlic, parsley sprigs, and hot pepper and cook until the garlic starts to sizzle, about 1 to 2 minutes.

2. Add the octopus and cook, stirring, for 5 minutes. Add the wine and let evaporate. Add the tomatoes, cover, and simmer over low heat until the octopus are tender, about 1 hour. Add the salt, if used, and pepper, while cooking. Serve with a sprinkling of minced parsley.

NOTE: IN VASTO THIS DISH IS SERVED WITH AN ACCOMPANIMENT OF LENTILS.

CLEANING OCTOPUS

One of the things that makes people a little squeamish about octopus is the idea of cleaning them. No fear—in most markets octopus is sold already cleaned.

If not, just turn the head inside out "like a sock," says Mark Bittman, author of *Fish,* and remove the inside. Cut away the "mouth," which is the hard piece resembling an eye, and wash the octopus well.

FRITTURA DELLA VIGILIA

Christmas Eve Fried Vegetables and Fish (Makes 8 servings or more)

THIS RECIPE IS A GRAND DISH SERVED AT special occasions and is the equivalent of the famous *fritto misto all'Italiana*, which also contains meats, like brains and sweetbreads. Since on Christmas Eve Catholics are not supposed to eat meat, this *fritto* is composed of fish and vegetables exclusively. Considering that the rest of the dinner is all fish-based, often only vegetables are used. In my house *baccalà* (dried salt cod) was always included.

The Christmas Eve dinner or *cenone*, big supper, is very important in Italy. At one time, it was a day of fasting so to speak: No breakfast (which the Italians seldom eat anyway) was eaten, but at lunch, a slice of pizza studded with anchovies was served. Many people still observe this tradition. Keep in mind that *baccalà* must be soaked for 3 or 4 days to remove the salt. Its water must be changed once a day. Some Italian specialty stores sell *baccalà* already soaked.

1 small head cauliflower, divided into flowerets

1 bunch broccoli, about 1½ pounds, divided in flowerets

2 medium-size zucchini, cut lengthwise into sticks

2 or 3 ribs celery, cut into 2½-inch-long sticks

1 pound baccalà (salt cod), drained and cubed (see instructions in head note)

½ pound squid, cleaned, and bodies cut into ¼-inch circles

½ pound small shrimp, peeled and deveined

3 large eggs, separated

3 tablespoons all-purpose flour

About ¼ cup water

Kosher salt to taste, optional

Freshly ground pepper to taste

Canola oil for frying

Lemon wedges

1. Cook each vegetable separately in boiling water until tender but still crisp. Rinse in cold water. Drain and pat dry. Pat dry all the fish.

2. In a bowl, beat the egg yolks, add the flour, and enough water to make a soft batter. Add salt and pepper. Whip the whites of the eggs until stiff and fold into the batter.

3. In a deep-fryer or large sauté pan, heat the oil to the smoking point, 350°F. As a test, drop a piece of bread soaked in vinegar into the oil. If the bread floats to the surface, the oil is ready.

4. Working in batches, dip the vegetables into the batter and then drop them into the oil. Do not crowd the pot. Fry until golden, about 5 minutes, and then drain on paper towels. Keep warm until all the vegetables are done. Do the same with the salt cod and the fish.

5. Serve surrounded by lemon wedges.

NOTE: KEEP THE FRIED FOOD IN A WARM OVEN UNTIL ALL THE PIECES ARE READY.

CAPITONE ALLO SPIEDO

Conger Eel on a Spit **(Makes 6 servings)**

IN ABRUZZO AND OTHER PARTS OF ITALY, Christmas Eve dinner (*cenone*) and the eating of *il capitone* (conger eel) are sacred traditions. The most famous eels come from the so-called Comacchio Valleys (which in reality are not valleys but bodies of water), in the region of Emilia-Romagna. The eel fishermen in the picturesque village of Comacchio (often called little Venice because of its many canals and bridges) take advantage of the migratory habits of the eels. Leaving the sea to swim up its river streams, the eels end up in special traps. Released in the "valleys," they are then fattened to be sold on Christmas Eve in fish markets all over Italy.

The best way to cook *capitone* is to roast it on a spit over a wood-burning fire. The *capitone* can also be cooked on a grill with a rotisserie attachment or on skewers and turned by hand. The natural fat bastes the fish, making the skin crunchy and delicious.

2 1/2 to 3 pounds conger eel, scrubbed clean and cut into 6 pieces
1/4 cup vinegar plus 2 tablespoons
1/2 cup dry white wine
3 tablespoons extra virgin olive oil

Salt to taste, optional
Freshly ground pepper to taste
7 bay leaves
1 large sprig fresh parsley

1. Place the pieces of eel in a bowl, add the vinegar, and cover with cold water. Turn the eel in the liquid and let stand 10 minutes. Rinse well and set aside.

2. In a mixing bowl, combine all the remaining ingredients except the parsley. Place the eel in this mixture and turn the pieces so that each one is well coated, being careful not to break the bay leaves. Refrigerate, covered, for 1 hour or longer.

3. Prepare a charcoal fire and, if possible, set up the rotisserie attachment.

4. When ready to cook, on the spit or metal skewers, alternately thread 1 bay leaf and 1 piece of eel, repeat in this order until all pieces of eel and all bay leaves are used. Reserve the marinade. Cook the eel, turning often, if there is no rotisserie attachment to the spit. Baste with its own reserved marinade, using the sprig of parsley as a brush. Cook about 15 to 20 minutes. Cooking time varies according to the thickness of the eel.

NOTE: IT IS A GOOD IDEA TO PUT A PIECE OF BREAD AT EACH END OF THE SPIT; THIS WILL KEEP THE PIECES OF EEL IN PLACE.

A Christmas Fish Market

In an official ceremony at 2 A.M. on the twenty-fourth of December, the mayor of Rome opens the wholesale Via Ostiense fish market to the general public. This special ceremony is called *il cottio,* meaning the quoting of prices, and it's a big event. The fishmongers cook fish in many ways, and it is fun to attend and sample the food.

I have gone to *il cottio* many times during my student days in Rome. We used to spend the night dancing in a nightclub waiting for the opening of the market. Then we would sample the many offerings, knowing that we had to wait until the evening for our next meal since Christmas Eve is a day of fasting in Italy.

A Slippery Tradition

I will never forget a funny scene in my grandmother's house when we were all startled from our festive Christmas preparations by screams coming from the bathroom. One of my young aunts, finding the bathtub full of "snakes," had become hysterical. The eels, which were bought live, were happily swimming unaware of their destiny.

There is also an unforgettable scene in the movie, *Marriage Italian Style,* with Sophia Loren and Marcello Mastroianni running after a semi-chopped eel hiding under the furniture. But I do not want to go into details because I know that you tender-hearted Americans will cringe. Fortunately in this country, the conger eel swims in a tank in the fish shop and is given to you in a package ready to use.

CHAPTER 10

POLLAME E CONIGLIO

Poultry and Rabbit

ABOUT POULTRY AND RABBIT

Since the dawn of civilization, men have eaten meat. As soon as they learned to light a fire, they began to appreciate the sapid taste of meat, roasted or cooked on a boiling stone. The classification of men in prehistoric time begins with the hunter, then the shepherd, and finally the farmer. These are all professions which are related to meat.

Adam and Eve, though, must have been vegetarians, because it is difficult to imagine the slaughtering of animals in the garden of Eden. But after they consumed the most disastrous snack in history . . . well, what did they have to lose?

Pagan gods, in their pandemic battles, often ended up devouring each other, or their children and relatives, for fear of being dethroned. And how do you think Minerva-Athena broke out of Zeus's head? He had eaten his pregnant mother, but the kid refused to die and the rest is . . . mythology.

Meat was the *pièce de résistance* in biblical and Homeric banquets. The animal was often killed in front of the guests to ensure freshness.

Tenderizing was not important. Those ancestors must have had good teeth!

Homer, who wrote so lyrically of "blond loaves and smoking meats," never mentions chicken in those ancient times. They were consumed mostly in times of famine. It was only during the golden age of Pericles that poultry became a delicacy.

Abruzzo gastronomy has a wide range of recipes for poultry and meat, as you will see in this chapter and the next. I have assembled here the most traditional, the new, and many which often are the result of my experimentation and that of members of my family and friends.

About Buying, Storing, and Cooking Meat

Personally, when I need a specifc piece of meat for a recipe, I rely on my butchers at Balducci's and the Ottomanelli of Bleecker Street. Those men, most of whom are Italian, understand what I am talking about; they know what they are selling and can advise you accordingly. How many times Robert or Louis at Balducci's changed my mind, suggesting something other than the meat I had originally wanted. And they were right—the dish came out much better because of their suggestions. Here are a few pieces of advice that come from my experience.

When you buy meat, any kind, including chicken, look for clean, pinkish colors and no suspicious bruises or brown spots. If the meat is packaged, make sure the cellophane is not broken, and avoid a chicken with too much liquid concentrated at the bottom of its bag.

If you do not know exactly which is the best method to cook the meat you are planning to buy, ask your butcher. He can also tell you how the chicken, or the rabbit, or the chops should be cut. Most of the time, he will do the cutting for you.

Keep your meat and poultry in the refrigerator until ready to cook. If your recipe suggests that you have the meat at room temperature, follow the instruction. Most of the time this type of recipe calls for a marinade. In any case, do not let the meat stand unrefrigerated for more than one hour, especially if you are working in a warm kitchen.

If you can help it, do not freeze fresh meat. If you must do so, chill it in the refrigerator for 1 hour before putting it in the freezer, and make sure it is well wrapped to prevent frost spots.

Chicken should not be stored in the refrigerator for more then one night, the fresher the better. Remember, it has had time to tenderize because it does not arrive at the market the moment it is killed and, even worse, it might have been frozen. If, for convenience, you need to have poultry in the freezer, buy them already frozen, especially turkey, which will never freeze well in a home freezer.

There are many methods of cooking meat. Following are some suggestions:

Roasting is a method suitable to many kinds of meats and poultry. There are several ways to roast, like on the spit, the primordial technique, which is best for tender cuts of meat, like fillets, loins, and of course poultry. The meats are often marinated and, since the roasting occurs on an open fire, care must be taken for splattering and burning. Often basting is required.

In the oven, the meat is put in a pan with some condiments. Often a rack is used to hold the meat. This too needs constant basting.

Cooking in a pot is suitable for almost any meat. In fact, we Italians have a glorious chapter in our gastronomy with the unappealing name of *arrosti morti*, literally meaning "dead roasts." They are pot roasts, which, for

Americans, conjures visions of cheap meat, smothered with onions and cooked to death. Not our pot roasts. Some are cooked with expensive wines and ingredients, and turn out to be the most succulent preparations.

Stufato or *stufatino* and *spezzatino* are stews, and they belong in this category. Pieces of meat are sautéed in fat and doused with wine. An addition of broth or pureed tomato completes the sauce. The sauce is quite abundant in *stufato* or *stufatino,* just as in an American stew, but scarce in a *spezzatino.* Often vegetables are added to both. Polenta or potato puree are the preferred accompaniments. Rice is excellent too, but remember the Italians eat pasta and rice as a first course, seldom as an accompaniment for meat or fish, and never as a bed. But when in Rome, or should I say the United States. . . .

In braising, the meat is first browned in fat, then cooked slowly, and covered in a small amount of liquid which can be wine, water, broth, or tomato.

Sautéing is the quickest method of cooking tender or thin cuts of meat, like chicken breasts, *scaloppine,* or cutlets, in hot oil or butter. At times, wine is added.

Since I do not like to throw away food, I freeze leftover cooked meats, and I use plastic containers with well-fitting lids. Most cooked meat freezes well. When needed, defrost it overnight on the bottom shelf of the refrigerator.

Also remember that leftover meat can be chopped and turned into a wonderful ragout for pasta. Just add a good can or two of tomato sauce, and do not forget the delicious salads you can make with the remains of roasted or potted meats and chickens. There are some suggestions and recipes for these in this book. You will love the recipe for *Pollo Tonnato,* chicken with tuna fish sauce (page 280). This sauce is a godsend, and can be used not only on meats, but also fish and vegetables.

As I said before, no matter what you do with your meat, a good butcher, is the best ingredient.

Gastronomist Anthelme Brillat-Savarin wrote, "Poultry is for the cook what canvas is to the painter." I could not agree more. The versatility of poultry is exciting, stirs the imagination, and most of the time the preparation and cooking are easy and quick.

I wish rabbit were more acceptable in this country. Its tender, delicate, and flavorful meat can be prepared in many ways from a simple stew to an elegant galantine. It is also a meat which is light, nourishing, and contains no cholesterol, therefore quite healthy.

POLLO ALLA DIAVOLA

Grilled Chicken "Diavola" (Makes 6 servings)

AT ONE TIME WE ITALIANS ATE *POLLO ALLA diavola* only when we went on outings in the countryside. A rustic inn or a trattoria was considered the ideal place, and still is. In my own town of Pescara, which is on the Adriatic Sea, we would go, of all places, to a motel on the outskirts of the town. Their unassuming restaurant, set under a canopy of vine leaves with a barbecue in a corner, did indeed make an excellent *pollo alla diavola*. You see, for the best way to obtain that unique smoky flavor, the birds should be cooked over an open fire outdoors.

In the house, one can use a broiler. One little tip: Keep the door of your broiler open, so that some air can go in.

This dish is becoming popular with Americans. It is an ideal dish for summer when everybody is happy to deal with smoke and fire.

One word of caution: Always wash you chicken before you touch it. Rinse the chicken under cold, running water. Place it in a large bowl and cover with cold water. Add 2 tablespoons kosher salt to the water. Soak for about 20 minutes. And of course, wash everything the raw chicken has touched with hot water, soap, and vinegar.

Three 2½- to 3-pound broiler chickens
Extra virgin olive oil
Salt to taste, optional
Freshly ground pepper to taste
4 to 5 sprigs fresh parsley
2 lemons

1. Split each chicken on its back from neck to tail. Turn the chickens and press hard with your hand over the breasts to flatten the bones. Cover with a piece of waxed paper and pound with a mallet or a heavy frying pan to make the chickens as flat as possible.

2. Lightly coat both sides of the chickens with oil, sprinkle with the salt and a good amount of pepper. Scatter the parsley over, squeeze and add the juice of 1 lemon. Let stand at room temperature for 1 hour. If longer, refrigerate.

3. Prepare a barbecue or preheat the broiler. Set the grill or broiling rack 4 to 6 inches from the source of heat and cook chickens, turning often and brushing with the lemon marinade, until browned and done through, about 25 minutes per side.

4. Cut the remaining lemon in wedges and serve it with the chicken.

NOTE: FOR A LESS PEPPERY TASTE, INSTEAD OF PEPPER USE A MIXTURE OF CHOPPED HERBS LIKE OREGANO, SAGE, AND THYME. MY MOTHER CALLED THIS VERSION *ALLA CHERUBINO*, FOR ITS "ANGELIC" DRESSING.

POLLO ARROSTO ALLA PAPÀ

Father's Roasted Chicken *(Makes 4 to 6 servings)*

THIS IS MY FATHER'S RECIPE TO WHICH some of my own ideas have been added.

When mother or father announced *pollo arrosto questa sera*, roasted chicken tonight, we never knew how it would come to the table. Roasted chicken, especially if it is a free-range one, can be simplicity itself. What you need is a little oil, salt, pepper, a clove of garlic, a sprig of rosemary, and tender loving care. But, as usual with chicken, one can improvise. And did father improvise! Fortunately, he had exquisite taste, so we didn't worry.

At times he would put a crown of potatoes around the chicken, or a scattering of *odori di cucina*, onion, celery, carrots, and parsley, all chopped together and set underneath, around, or inside the chicken. And, when nobody was looking, an extra glass of wine went into the pan.

1 lemon
One large chicken, about 3 pounds, washed and dried
1 teaspoon Seven Herbs (see head note, pages 297–98)
1/2 teaspoon allspice
Freshly ground pepper
3 sprigs fresh parsley
1 rib celery, preferably with leaves attached, cut into 4 pieces
2 bay leaves
2 large cloves garlic, peeled
2 slices bacon or 2 strips prosciutto fat
1 sprig fresh rosemary
1/2 cup water
1/4 cup Marsala wine or sherry

1. Preheat the oven to 400°F.

2. Cut the lemon in half. Squeeze half of the lemon into the cavity of the chicken and place the shell of the lemon inside it. Sprinkle the cavity of the bird with the Seven Herbs mixture, allspice, and pepper, and insert the sprigs of parsley, celery pieces, bay leaves, and garlic. Drape the breast of the chicken with the bacon or prosciutto and truss the chicken. Place it in a roasting pan fitted with a rack, add the rosemary, and pour the water into the bottom of the pan. Bake for 20 minutes, then reduce the heat to 375°F and cook 1 hour longer or more. Baste the chicken with the wine and its own juice. Squeeze the remaining lemon over the chicken 10 minutes before taking it out of the oven. To make sure the chicken is done, pierce the meatier part of a thigh with a skewer. If the juices come out clear, the chicken is done. Let it rest 10 minutes before cutting. Discard what is inside the chicken before serving.

Variation: For a simpler version, omit the allspice, celery, bay leaves, and bacon or prosciutto.

NOTE: THIS CHICKEN IS COOKED WITHOUT SALT; THE LEMON AND THE BACON OR PROSCIUTTO ARE ENOUGH TO FLAVOR THE BIRD.

POLLETTI RIPIENI

Stuffed Cornish Hens *(Makes 3 to 6 servings)*

THIS IS AN ELEGANT PREPARATION WITH the aromatic perfume of mushrooms. The stuffing is made with a savory mix and some fresh ricotta, which makes it a special delicacy.

3 Cornish game hens, about 1 pound each, giblets reserved and chopped
Salt to taste, optional
Freshly ground pepper to taste
3 tablespoons unsalted butter
3 tablespoons extra virgin olive oil
2 medium-size onions, finely chopped
$^1/_2$ cup Marsala wine or sherry
$^1/_2$ cup dried porcini mushrooms, soaked in 1 cup of lukewarm water for 20 minutes

1 cup fresh mushrooms, trimmed and coarsely chopped
1 cup ricotta, drained
$^1/_4$ cup chopped prosciutto
1 large egg, lightly beaten
$^3/_4$ cup dried bread crumbs
2 tablespoons minced fresh parsley
1 sprig fresh rosemary

1. Wash and pat the hens dry. Sprinkle them inside and out with salt, if used, and pepper. Set aside.

2. In a large skillet, heat 2 tablespoons of the butter and 2 tablespoons of the oil. Add the giblets and the onion. Cook over medium-high heat, stirring, until browned, about 10 minutes. Add half of the Marsala and let evaporate.

3. Gently, so as not to disturb the sediment resting at the bottom, lift the porcini mushrooms from the bowl of water, and strain the soaking liquid through a paper towel or coffee filter. Add about $^1/_4$ cup of the liquid to the skillet, and reserve the rest. Chop the porcini coarsely and add to the skillet together with the fresh mushrooms. Cover and cook until all of the liquid has been absorbed, about 20 minutes. If the mixture appears too watery, remove the lid, increase the heat to high, and boil until reduced. Transfer to a bowl and cool.

4. In a large mixing bowl combine the ricotta, prosciutto, egg, bread crumbs, and parsley. Add the giblets and mushrooms and mix well. If the mixture seems too loose, add more bread crumbs. Be careful though; the mixture should not be too dry. Stuff the chickens with the ricotta mixture and truss them.

5. Preheat the oven to 400°F. Lightly oil a large roasting pan with the remaining oil. Place the chickens in the pan, breast side down, and dot with the remaining butter. Break the rosemary into pieces and scatter over the birds. Bake 10 minutes,

then turn the hens breast side up and reduce the temperature to 375°F. Pour the remaining water from the porcini into the bottom of the pan and sprinkle with some of the Marsala.

6. Baste the hens often with any accumulated pan juices and more Marsala. Continue baking until the joints move easily when twisted, about 45 minutes to 1 hour. Cool 10 minutes before cutting in half. To deglaze the pan, pour off the fat and place over high heat on top of the stove. Add some more Marsala or water to the pan. Bring to a boil, boil on top of the stove while scraping the brown particles at the bottom and sides of the pan with a wooden spoon. Boil until the liquid has slightly reduced and thickened. Pour over the hens just before serving.

POLLO ALLA CANZANESE

Chicken Canzano Style (Makes 8 servings)

CANZANO IS A SMALL TOWN IN THE province of Teramo where some of the most unique food of Abruzzo originates. At times the food is quite elegant, at others rustic and homey. It is nevertheless a sophisticated cuisine that is often prepared with ordinary ingredients and, given the thrifty nature of the Abruzzesi, from a need not to waste. This delicious chicken stew is a typical example.

I still remember our maid Annina, coming back from the chicken coop, which was in the back of my grandmother's large house, with a basket of eggs. She would announce to my grandmother that the red, or white, or gray chicken was not making eggs anymore. While the two of them mourned, the rest of the household

2 small chickens, about 3 pounds each, cut into 6 to 8 serving pieces
1 tablespoon kosher salt
2 sage leaves, or 1/2 teaspoon dried
4 bay leaves
3 cloves garlic, peeled and sliced
12 whole cloves
2 sprigs fresh rosemary, or 1 teaspoon dried

24 black peppercorns, crushed
1 small diavoletto (dried Italian hot red pepper)
Two 1/4-inch-thick slices prosciutto, diced
3/4 cup dry red wine
Water, if necessary
1 tablespoon minced fresh parsley

1. Place the chicken pieces in a large bowl and sprinkle with the kosher salt. Add enough cold water to cover and let stand 20 to 30 minutes.

2. Rinse the chicken and place in a skillet into which the pieces can fit in one flat layer. Add the sage, bay leaves, garlic, cloves, rosemary, peppercorns, red pepper, prosciutto, and wine.

3. Cover and cook over medium heat, stirring once or twice, until the chicken is almost tender, 30 to 35 minutes. Remove the lid from the skillet and cook until the sauce is reduced and the chicken starts to color. If necessary, add more wine or a little water. Sprinkle with parsley and serve.

continues

exulted, knowing the stew pot would soon be busy. We all knew that the little unconsidered beast would end up in this delicious stew.

Since this dish was always made with an old chicken, it needed a little advance preparation. To tenderize it, the chicken, was cut into serving pieces and left to soak in cold water and kosher salt for 1 hour. The first time my husband saw me prepare this chicken, and I told him it was from Nonnina's, he replied with amusement that he didn't know that my grandmother was Jewish. He explained that his mother, who was Jewish, did the same thing.

Here in America, I had eliminated this preliminary step since chickens are usually tender. But my friend Jack Ubaldi, the noted butcher and teacher, author of the *Meat Cookbook* (Macmillan), hearing of a nasty infection of salmonella I had contracted cutting a chicken, said to me: "Give it a bath, give it a bath before you touch any chicken." So now I always soak my birds in water and kosher salt, not so much as to tenderize them but to clean them. It is very important, and 20 minutes is enough. The rest of the preparation is simple. All the ingredients are put together at the same time, and it requires little stirring during the cooking.

Do not be put off by the rather large amount of herbs and spices.

Although we Italians rarely cook with more than one or two herbs, or more than one spice at a time, this dish is an exception. And when you eat it, you will see that the condiments are not overwhelming. People seldom guess the ingredients. The cloves, actually the secret of this dish, are barely detectable. And the aroma fills the house! If one follows the recipe closely, one will achieve a surprising blend of exquisite flavors. However, if the quantity of the chicken is increased, do not double the condiments; just add a little more of each herb and spice.

One of my favorite features of this dish is that it reheats particularly well.

POLLO DEGLI ZAMPOGNARI

Bagpipers' Chicken *(Makes 8 servings)*

WHEN YOU ARE A CHILD, EVERYTHING seems an adventure. At the beginning of November, we children used to wait with great expectation for the coming of the *zampognari*, or bagpipers. These players are shepherds who come down the Maiella Mountains to announce the coming of the Christmas season by playing the *novena* from house to house. They roam the countryside, pushing their way as far as Rome, where they always make a scene at their arrival in Piazza Navona, the end of their journey. Like their Scottish counterparts, the *zampognari* are dressed in colorful costumes, sheepskin vests, and short fitted pants secured at the knee, where they meet the intricate geometry of the lacing of the *chioche*, characteristic footwear resembling those worn by the ancient Romans.

My grandmother received them in our courtyard, and after they finished playing, our maids Annina and Maria would arrive with huge trays holding coffee and Nonnina's famous brioches.

The magical day always ended with a special family dinner. In fact, Annina, the house expert on these matters, was immediately dispatched to select and prepare a couple of *polli* (chickens) for a robust and zesty dish we called *Pollo degli Zampognari*, in honor of these men.

1 medium-size chicken, 3 to 4 pounds
1/4 cup dried porcini mushrooms, soaked in
  3/4 cup lukewarm water for 20 minutes
2 tablespoons extra virgin olive oil
2 cloves garlic, peeled and minced
1 sprig fresh rosemary, or 1/2 teaspoon dried
1 tablespoon tomato paste
1/2 cup dry wine
1 red bell pepper, diced

1 green bell pepper, diced
1 yellow bell pepper, diced
4 to 5 ripe tomatoes, diced;
  or one 16-ounce can peeled tomatoes
Salt to taste, optional
Freshly ground pepper to taste
2 to 3 fresh basil leaves
1 sprig fresh parsley

1. Remove the legs and the breast from the chicken. Reserve the backbone, neck, and giblets, if any, for another use. Cut the chicken into 8 serving pieces by separating the chicken legs into 4 pieces and the breast in half and each half in two.

2. Gently, so as not to disturb the sediment resting at the bottom, lift the porcini mushrooms from the water and strain the soaking liquid through a paper towel or coffee filter and set aside. Coarsely chop the mushrooms.

3. In a large skillet, heat the oil and add the garlic, rosemary, and mushrooms. Cook over medium-high heat a few minutes to release the flavor of the ingredients. Remove this mixture with a slotted spoon to a bowl and discard the rosemary. Add the chicken pieces to the skillet and cook, turning often, until lightly browned, 5 to 8 minutes. Add the tomato paste and the wine. Increase the heat to high and cook until evaporated. Add the water from the mushrooms, reduce the heat to medium-low, and cook, stirring often, until thickened, about 10 minutes.

4. Return the garlic-mushroom mixture to the skillet. Add the peppers, stir, and cook until the peppers start to soften, about 5 minutes. Add the tomatoes and season with salt, if used, and pepper. Cover and cook until the chicken pulls away from the bones, about 30 minutes.

5. Chop the basil and parsley together and add during the last 5 minutes of cooking.

NOTE: THIS DISH WAS OFTEN SERVED WITH POLENTA.

POLLO ALLA CACCIATORA

Chicken Hunter Style (Makes 4 to 6 servings)

THIS RECIPE IS A CLASSIC, SO TO SPEAK. Like the Bolognese sauce, another classic, opinions differ about the execution of the dish.

It is also quite basic so one can add and remove ingredients according to one's taste.

My *cacciatora* is a simple recipe, favored by my grandmother and mother. They, too, tried variations. Often they would add some mushrooms—perhaps to honor woodland hunters (because the "hunter" of the recipe title usually dwells in the woods)—or fresh tomatoes, peppers, or even olives.

Chicken is an invitation to experiment, and I do not mind it at all.

One 3-pound chicken, cut into 8 small pieces
¼ cup extra virgin olive oil
2 cloves garlic, peeled and smashed
1 small onion, quartered
1 small carrot, peeled and cut into 4 pieces
1 rib celery, trimmed and cut into 4 pieces
1 sprig fresh parsley
1 tablespoon prosciutto fat, optional

1 small diavoletto *(dried Italian hot red pepper)*
1 bay leaf
2 teaspoons tomato paste
¾ cup dry wine, white or red
Salt to taste, optional
Freshly ground pepper to taste
1 tablespoon minced fresh parsley

1. Wash and pat the chicken dry.

2. In a large skillet, heat the oil. Add the garlic and cook over medium-high heat until it starts to sizzle, about 2 to 3 minutes. Add the chicken and cook, turning often, until browned, 10 to 15 minutes.

3. In a food processor, place the onion, carrot, celery, parsley, and prosciutto fat, if used. Process until finely chopped. In Italian, this is called a *battuto*.

4. Add the *battuto* to the skillet. Cook over medium-high heat, stirring and turning the pieces of chicken often. Add the *diavoletto*, if used, the bay leaf, and tomato paste. Stir and add the wine. Let evaporate. Cook, stirring and turning the pieces of chicken often, until the chicken is done, 30 to 40 minutes. Add salt, if used, and the pepper. Remove the bay leaf and the hot pepper before serving. Serve hot, sprinkled with the minced parsley.

Variation 1: Cook veal chops the same way. You can add some mushrooms to them. Rabbit is also delicious cooked *alla cacciatora,* but add 2 cups peeled tomatoes after the wine evaporates.

Variation 2: *Pollo dell'Autunno,* Fall Chicken, is made the same way as the above recipe, but use ¾ cup dried tomatoes instead of fresh ones, and eliminate the peppers. It becomes a succulent hymn to autumn.

Variation 3: *Pollo alla Franceschiello* ("little Francesco"), salaciously named after a king of Naples, who was a little short. This contains 2 tablespoons of chopped sour pickles and 20 small black olives. No mushrooms, tomatoes, or peppers.

POLLO ALLA SALOMÈ

Chicken Salomè **(Makes 8 servings)**

RETURNING TO ITALY ONE YEAR, WE brought our cat Salomè with us. She was an excellent traveler who didn't mind the leash but hated the carrier.

During our stay in Italy, my husband was called to England regarding a play of his, which was being performed there. So we left Salomè with my parents, and off we went.

Unfortunately, our cat was rather finicky. Cat food was somewhat rare in Italy then, and we had instructed my father to give her fresh kidneys and some canned mackerel or tuna. When we returned, my father exclaimed, "What kind of a cat is this? She doesn't even eat spaghetti! But fortunately she likes one of your mother's chicken dishes, and, of course, kidneys."

The next day we went to buy a nice chicken and beef kidneys, but we were surprised at the bill. The butcher explained, "Signora, kidneys in Italy are a delicacy, and are expensive. But what can you do if the stupid American cat doesn't eat spaghetti!"

From then on, we stuck to mother's chicken, which was cheap, and started to call the dish *alla Salomè*.

2 small chickens, 2 to 3 pounds each, cut into 6 to 8 serving pieces
1 large onion, or 2 medium-size, chopped
½ cup wine vinegar
10 whole cloves
1 teaspoon grainy mustard
2 teaspoons tomato paste
1 tablespoon minced fresh parsley

1. Wash the chicken pieces and place them in a large skillet, or two, skin side down in one flat layer. Sprinkle the onion on top, add the vinegar, and scatter the cloves all over. Cover and cook over medium-low heat, until lightly browned, about 20 minutes.

2. In a small bowl, combine the mustard and tomato paste. Stir until well blended.

3. Remove the cover from the skillet and try to skim off as much fat as possible. Add the mustard and tomato mixture and stir well. Cook, covered, until the chicken begins to pull away from the bone, about 25 to 30 mintues. Remove the cloves, sprinkle with the parsley, and serve.

POLLO TONNATO

Chicken with Tuna Sauce (Makes 6 servings)

LEFTOVER CHICKEN AGAIN? WELL, MAYBE, but with this recipe it will taste deliciously differently. This tonnato sauce also works on leftover meats and fish, providing they were not originally prepared with a tomato or another prominently flavored sauce.

One 7-ounce can imported Italian tuna fish, packed in oil, undrained
2 anchovy fillets, drained and chopped; or 1 teaspoon anchovy paste
1/2 cup mayonnaise
Juice of 1/2 lemon, or more

2 sprigs fresh parsley
3 cups cooked chicken, boned, skinned, and chunked
2 tablespoons capers in brine, drained
2 hard-boiled eggs, peeled and sliced
Lettuce for garnish

1. In a food processor, combine the tuna fish and its oil, the anchovies, mayonnaise, lemon juice, and parsley. Process to a smooth cream.

2. Place the chicken on a serving platter, pour the tuna sauce over it. Sprinkle with capers and decorate with the eggs and lettuce.

NOTE: THE FLAVOR OF THIS DISH INCREASES IF IT IS PREPARED AT LEAST 2 HOURS BEFORE SERVING.

GAMBE DI POLLO ALLO ZENZERO, ZAFFERANO E GRAPPA

Chicken Legs with Ginger, Saffron, and Grappa **(Makes 6 servings)**

THE HISTORY OF ABRUZZO INCLUDES MANY invaders, and their subtle influences remain today. Certain herbs and spices, which are not generally found in Italian cooking, are extensively cultivated in Abruzzo. *Dragoncello* (tarragon) and *zafferano* (saffron) are two examples. This recipe for chicken legs came about from remembering how my father enjoyed experimenting with unusual condiments. I am adding ginger, which my father used sometimes, and instead of Worcestershire sauce, which he liked, I sometimes add soy sauce, a totally unknown ingredient to him. Had Chinese cuisine arrived in Italy a little sooner, my father would have loved it, experimented with its flavors, and perhaps enjoyed this recipe, which I call *Un Po' Cinese*—a little Chinese.

6 whole chicken legs with thighs, each cut in half
3 shallots, coarsely chopped
1 sprig fresh parsley, chopped
1 sprig fresh tarragon or rosemary, chopped
3 thin slices fresh ginger, cut into julienne
½ teaspoon of saffron, preferably in powder form
¼ cup grappa
Juice of ½ lemon
¼ cup water
Freshly ground black pepper to taste
3 to 4 tablespoons soy or Worcestershire sauce
1 tablespoon minced fresh parsley

1. Preheat the oven to 375°F.

2. Place the chicken legs into a large baking pan. Sprinkle with the shallots, herbs, and ginger. In a small bowl, combine the saffron with the grappa, lemon juice, and water. Mix well and add to the pan. Sprinkle with pepper. Place the pan in the oven and cook until the legs are done, about 1 hour. Baste often, adding the soy or Worcestershire sauce toward the end.

3. Serve sprinkled with minced parsley.

GAMBE DI POLLO IMPANATE CON PATATE

Breaded Chicken Legs with Potatoes   **(Makes 4 servings)**

THIS IS MY MOTHER'S UNUSUAL DISH MADE with skinless chicken legs and thighs.

I am sure that my mother started to skin the chicken when some Italian "food terrorist" (we have a few of those too) got to her. In fact, she announced this preparation as if it were the discovery of America, and was very proud of herself for being so modern.

I returned to Italy often, but this was one of the last dishes she cooked for me. My dear father had died and she was going to live with my brother, where she avoided the kitchen like hell. I could not blame her, considering my sister-in-law's attitude. She is a good cook, I admit, but one who is suspicious of anything she doesn't know. After much reservation, she once gave me the honor of trying my Spanish paella. (When I am in Italy, I cook exotic food!) Lo and behold, she liked it so much that I had to make it for her every time I returned to Abruzzo, although according to my brother, she had mastered the art herself.

With this recipe, you will have a juicy and flavorful dish to which the pecorino romano imparts a special delicate tang. You can use a whole chicken instead of the chicken legs. Simply cut it up in serving pieces and skin each part, of course.

¹/₄ cup balsamic vinegar
Extra virgin olive oil
2 cloves garlic, peeled and quartered
3 to 4 sprigs fresh parsley, snipped into little brunches
4 whole chicken legs with thighs attached, skin removed

1 cup dried bread crumbs
2 tablespoons grated pecorino romano cheese
2 small potatoes, peeled and cut into wedges
Salt to taste, optional
Freshly ground pepper to taste

1. In a small bowl, combine the vinegar, 2 tablespoons of the oil, garlic, and parsley.

2. Place the chicken in a nonreactive, dish and pour the vinegar mixture over. Turn the chicken once to coat and refrigerate for 1 hour, turning the chicken from time to time in its marinade.

3. When ready to cook, preheat the oven to 400°F. Lightly oil a baking dish large enough to contain the chicken and the potatoes.

4. In a large bowl, combine the bread crumbs and cheese.

5. Remove the chicken legs, drain, and pat dry with paper towels. Set aside. Strain the marinade, reserving both the solids and the liquid. Chop the solids very finely and combine with the bread-crumb mixture. Dredge the chicken in this mixture to coat and place in the oiled dish.

6. Pour the reserved marinade over the potatoes, add the salt, if used, and the pepper. Toss. Drain the potatoes, but reserve the marinade, and set the potatoes all around the chicken. Bake 10 minutes, then reduce the heat to 375°F. Continue baking until the potatoes are tender and the chicken is done, about 1 hour and 15 minutes. Every once in a while baste the potatoes and chicken with the marinade.

PETTI DI POLLO FRANCA

Breast of Chicken Franca **(Makes 6 servings)**

THE ORIGINALITY OF THIS SIMPLE RECIPE is in the fact that the breasts are cubed and cooked in a colorful mixture of carrots and zucchini. It is my cousin Franca Falcone's invention, and a good one.

2 whole chicken breasts, about 1½ pounds total
1 tablespoon extra virgin olive oil
1 tablespoon unsalted butter
1 medium-size carrot, peeled and diced
1 medium-size onion, finely chopped

2 medium-size or 3 small zucchini, cut into small cubes
Salt to taste, optional
Freshly ground pepper to taste
¼ cup dry white wine

1. Skin and bone the breasts, trim away any visible fat, and cut into 1-inch cubes.

2. In a large skillet, heat the oil and the butter. Add the carrot and cook over medium-high heat, stirring, until slightly softened, about 5 minutes. Add the onion and cook until soft and translucent, about 3 minutes. Add the zucchini and cook until tender, about 5 minutes longer. Add the chicken and cook, stirring often, until browned, about 5 minutes. Season with salt and pepper. Add the wine and cook until evaporated. Serve hot.

ROLLATINE DI POLLO ALLA LUCULLO

Rolled Chicken Lucullus (Makes 6 servings)

LUCULLUS, A ROMAN GENERAL WHO DIED around the year 57 B.C., was famous for his high standard of living. The word "Lucullan" was coined by the Romans for his lavish and extravagant banquets.

My father must have been an admirer of this lifestyle, because he was always telling stories about the Lucullan banquets he had attended when he was a bachelor. My mother regarded this boasting with amusement. But one day, after getting hold of some rare ingredients—pâté of *foie gras* and a truffle, probably a donation from one of my father's grateful employees—she included them in her *rollatine*, which normally she stuffed modestly, with chicken livers and cockscombs. My father liked the dish immensely and declared it worthy of Lucullus. So the name remained.

Foie gras was usually available in those days, if one wanted to spend the money, but truffles were another story, most of the time being too expensive or out of season. Mother often used her delicious cured olives instead, which were delicate and not salty. In the filling, they looked . . . like truffle. I find that sweet California olives work well as a substitute, and you can call it . . . mock truffles. Of course, if you can find some cockscombs, add them to the stuffing.

16 large boneless, skinless chicken breast halves, pounded thinly
$^1/_4$ cup plus 2 tablespoons Marsala wine
$^1/_4$ pound chicken livers, trimmed, washed, and picked over
1 sprig fresh parsley
2 fresh sage leaves, or $^1/_4$ teaspoon dried
1 large egg
$^1/_4$ pound pâté of foie gras, fresh or canned
1 small black truffle, minced
Salt to taste, optional
Freshly ground pepper to taste
2 tablespoons unsalted butter
1 tablespoon extra virgin olive oil

1. Remove 4 cutlets, the smallest of the bunch, cut these in pieces, and place in a food processor. Add 2 tablespoons of the Marsala, the chicken livers, parsley, sage, and egg. Process until very finely chopped. Add the *foie gras* and process until well mixed. Remove to a bowl and stir in the truffle, mixing with a fork. Season with salt, if used, and pepper.

2. Spread the liver mixture over the remaining cutlets, roll them up and tie with kitchen string.

3. In a large skillet, or using two, heat the butter and oil. Add the *rollatine* and cook over medium heat, gently turning often, until brown on all sides, about 10 minutes. (Do not overcrowd the skillet. Do in two batches if necessary to ensure proper browning.) Add half the remaining Marsala wine, cover, and cook over low heat for 10 more minutes. Remove the cover and let the wine evaporate. The total cooking time is about 30 minutes or so. When done, remove the *rollatine* to a serving plate and keep warm. Deglaze the pan with the remaining Marsala, scraping the skillet with a wooden spoon to dislodge all the brown particles clinging to the bottom and sides of the pan. Remove the strings from the *rollatine*, pour the sauce over, and serve hot.

NOTE: ALTHOUGH SOME WERE FOUND IN OUR REGION, BLACK TRUFFLES WERE EASILY TRANSPORTED TO ABRUZZO FROM NEARBY UMBRIA. BLACK TRUFFLES ARE THE PREFERRED TRUFFLE FOR COOKING, WHILE THE WHITE ARE BETTER RAW AND SIMPLY SHAVED OVER FOOD.

POLLO AL VERDE

Chicken in Green (Makes 6 servings)

THE COOLNESS OF THE GREEN *PESTO*, AND its colorful decoration of summer vegetables make this dish an ideal course for a lunch or dinner *al fresco*.

CHICKEN

3 whole chicken breasts, skinned, boned, and halved
1 leek, white part only, trimmed, washed, and sliced into thin rounds
2 fresh bay leaves
Kosher salt to taste, optional
Freshly ground pepper to taste
Juice of $1/_2$ lemon

SAUCE

1 cup loosely packed parsley leaves
$1/_2$ cup loosely packed basil leaves
1 clove garlic, peeled
2 or 3 cornichons; or use 1 sour pickle
1 rib celery, thinly sliced
$1/_4$ cup extra virgin olive oil

1 tablespoon balsamic vinegar
Juice of $1/_2$ lemon

GARNISH

2 red bell peppers, roasted until blackened on all sides, peeled, seeded, cored, and cut into strips (see Step 1, page 117)
2 yellow bell peppers, roasted until blackened on all sides, peeled, seeded, cored, and cut into strips (see Step 1, page 117)
1 tablespoon extra virgin olive oil
2 plum tomatoes, sliced in wedges lengthwise; or use 10 to 12 cherry tomatoes, halved
2 tablespoons capers in brine, drained

1. Prepare the chicken: Fill the bottom of a steamer with water. Place the chicken breasts on the rack, scatter the leeks on top, and add the bay leaves, salt, pepper, and lemon juice. Cover and steam until the chicken is opaque and the leeks are tender, about 30 minutes. Remove from the heat and cool in the steamer, uncovered. Reserve the cooking liquid.

2. Prepare the sauce: Combine the parsley, basil, garlic, *cornichons,* celery, oil, vinegar, and lemon juice in a food processor. Add the steamed leeks from the chicken and process until very finely pureed. If the sauce seems too dense, add a little of the reserved cooking liquid from the chicken.

3. To serve: Place the chicken on a large serving platter. Discard the bay leaves and pour the sauce over the chicken.

4. Garnish: Combine the peppers and oil. Set all around the chicken. Garnish with the tomatoes. Scatter the capers all over.

TEGAMINI DI POLLO AL PROSCIUTTO

Chicken Ramekins with Prosciutto **(Makes 6 servings)**

THIS IS ANOTHER DISH WHICH CAN BE prepared in advance. The flavor is delicious and the texture complex and succulent. The delicacy of ricotta and mozzarella is mingled with the savory taste of the prosciutto.

3 or 4 whole chicken breasts, boned, skinned, and cubed
3/4 cup dry Marsala wine
Extra virgin olive oil
1 cup plain bread crumbs
1 medium-size onion, chopped
2 sprigs fresh parsley
3/4 pound prosciutto in 1 slice, cubed

One 8-ounce mozzarella, cubed
1/2 cup ricotta, drained
1/2 cup freshly grated parmesan or grana padano cheese
2 large eggs
1/2 teaspoon nutmeg
Freshly ground pepper to taste
6 large radicchio leaves

1. Place the chicken in a shallow bowl and add the Marsala. Marinate the chicken 20 minutes at room temperature or overnight, refrigerated.

2. Preheat the oven to 375°F. Lightly oil six 1-cup ramekins. Sprinkle the interior with the bread crumbs.

3. In a medium-size skillet, place 1 tablespoon of the oil. Add the onion and sauté over medium-high heat, stirring often, until soft and translucent, 3 to 5 minutes. Set aside.

4. Drain the chicken and reserve the marinade. Place the chicken cubes into a food processor. Add the cooked onion, parsley, prosciutto, and mozzarella. Process until finely chopped. Add the ricotta, grated cheese, eggs, nutmeg, and pepper. Process to combine well. Fill the prepared ramekins with the chicken mixture. Pour about 1 tablespoon of the reserved Marsala marinade into each ramekin. Discard any remaining Marsala.

5. Bake until the mixture is firm and the top has browned, 40 to 45 minutes. Remove from the oven and cool for 10 minutes.

6. Place the radicchio leaves on individual plates. Unmold each ramekin onto the leaf and serve.

GALANTINA SEMPLICE MAMMA LELLA

Simple Galantine Mamma Lella (Makes 8 servings or more)

THIS IS MY MOTHER'S NAMESAKE master-piece, although all my life I heard my father protest, in annoyance, albeit *sottovoce*, that it was his innovation. And I am afraid it is true.

In our family, a classic galantine, usually made either with capon or turkey, was prepared only at Christmas or for some very special occasion, maybe because it was time-consuming. To make it properly, it often took two to three days. The galantine was poached, kept under a weight over-night, and then served cold, in aspic. And this was the reason my brother Mimmo and I never enjoyed it. We didn't like this masterpiece, mostly because it was eaten cold. My mother made a less complicated galantine with chicken, but it also was served cold. One time, my father decided to roast this simple galantine and serve it hot. Well, it was a revolutionary idea and an instant success, not only with us but the entire family. After that, we began making this marvelous idea of my father's often, especially when relatives or friends came to dinner. Although, as I said above, it was Papà's idea, and despite his protests, this special dish, in the history of my family, has remained the *Galantina Zia Lella*— Aunt Lella's Galantine—among the nephews and nieces, and *della signora*

1 large roasting chicken, about 5 pounds
3/4 cup dry Marsala wine
Salt to taste, optional
Freshly ground pepper to taste
1/4 cup plain dried bread crumbs
1 tablespoon minced fresh parsley
2 fresh sage leaves, chopped,
    or 1/2 teaspoon dried, crumbled
6 to 8 slices mortadella or ham, about
    5 ounces
8 pitted sweet olives, such as Apulian or
    Californian, coarsely chopped (see Note)
6 to 8 slices salami, about 2 1/2 ounces
    (Genoa, soppressata, or capocolla)
4 to 5 large eggs, hard-boiled and peeled
2 tablespoons unsalted butter plus more
    for the pan
Curly parsley for decoration

THE DAY BEFORE:

1. Prepare the chicken: To bone the chicken, use a sharp knife to detach the tips of the wings. To facilitate boning the leg, chop off about 1 inch at of the end of each drumstick. Slit the chicken along the length of the backbone without cutting through the bone. Using a boning knife, and working close to the carcass, scrape away the meat and the skin from one side, being careful not to pierce the skin. Do the same on the other side, opening the chicken like a book away from the carcass. Remove the carcass, carefully detaching it from the joints of the legs and wings. To remove the bones from the remaining pieces of the wings, insert the knife along each bone and dislodge the meat all around and pull the bone out. Leave the empty "sleeve" inside the chicken.

2. To bone the legs, dislocate the bones from the sockets and cut through the connective nerves. Bone the thigh on each side of the chicken, scraping as close to the bone as possible. When you reach the drumsticks, cut the meat by inserting the knife along the bone and scraping down in a circular motion until the bone is exposed enough for you to pull it out. Repeat with the other leg. Leave the empty legs inside the chicken. Reserve all the bones for a broth.

3. Rinse the chicken and pat dry, place it in a large bowl, and add the Marsala. Cover and refrigerate overnight, turning the chicken a few times.

continues

Lella, for friends. And poor Papà, he had to bask in the reflected glory all his life.

This galantine is not complicated. Of course the chicken has to be boned, but if you have a regular butcher, he will do it for you.

In our family, my father made it simpler. Instead of the so-called "glove boning," in which the chicken is boned from the inside and it remains whole, Papà used a simpler technique, which is described here.

Do not be afraid to try this dish. It is quite easy, and you will be quite pleased with your accomplishment. The finished galantine makes a stunning presentation.

THE GALANTINE:

4. Drain the chicken, reserving the Marsala. Spread the chicken out flat, skin side down, on a work surface. Sprinkle lightly with salt and pepper.

5. Preheat the oven to 350°F. Butter a 13 × 9-inch baking pan.

6. Cut 8 pieces of kitchen string, each about 16 inches long, and slide the strings under the chicken, spacing them evenly.

7. In a small bowl, combine the bread crumbs, parsley, and sage. Cover the inside of the boned chicken with half the mortadella slices, sprinkle with half the bread-crumb mixture, scatter the olives over, and cover with half the salami slices. Arrange the eggs, end to end, in a row down the center of the chicken. Cover with a layer of the remaining salami, sprinkle with the remaining bread-crumb mixture, and cover with the remaining mortadella. Gently fold the chicken from one side over the center. Repeat with the other side. Let one side overlap, pulling the skin and flesh taut at the seam to enclose the filling well.

8. Secure with toothpicks. (Sew the opening closed with needle and thread if desired.) Tie the strings tightly around the chicken, then remove the toothpicks. Tuck in both ends and tie the chicken with more string, like you would a package, to enclose the ends firmly. The final shape of the galantine should be that of a large roll, oval and about 12 inches long.

9. Place the galantine, seam side down, in the prepared pan. Add $1/2$ cup of the reserved Marsala to the bottom of the pan. Sprinkle with a little salt and pepper. Dot generously with the butter, cover the pan with foil, and place in the oven. Roast 50 minutes, basting often with the remaining Marsala and the pan juices. Remove the cover, baste again, and continue cooking, uncovered, 15 minutes longer or until golden brown, basting twice more. Cool 30 minutes before cutting with a serrated knife. The galantine needs all this cooling time, otherwise it will not cut evenly and the stuffing may crumble. If you wish, after cutting, it can be warmed up in the pan in which it cooked. With two spatulas, lift the entire galantine on both ends without dislodging the slices, and place into the pan in which it cooked. Add a touch of Marsala or broth and warm up, basting often.

10. To show the galantine's interior design, serve it on a round or oval dish with the slices slightly overlapping. Place a bouquet of parsley in the center.

Variation: If you wish, you can serve this galantine cold. In this case, make it and cook it the day before. Cool it completely, wrap tightly in aluminum foil, and refrigerate overnight. Next day, cut the galantine into thin slices and serve it as suggested above. Let it come to room temperature.

NOTE: IF YOU WANT TO SPLURGE AND IT IS THE SEASON, USE A SMALL TRUFFLE INSTEAD OF THE OLIVES.

STUFATINO DEL POVER'UOMO

Poor Man's Stew **(Makes 6 servings)**

DURING THE HOLIDAYS, THE KITCHEN OF my house in Pescara became a theater of many activities. Intense. Since the preparations always occurred a day or two before the actual event, the meals for the nights leading up to the big feasts were called "make do food." There was very little time to cook a proper dinner. When "make-do" menus were announced, we children didn't mind it at all. We knew that there would be all sorts of odds and ends. These often included not only the heads of lambs and rabbits, but a wonderful stew, and most of all the *ragaglie di pollo,* made with poultry gizzards, hearts, liver, and even blood. I know many modern families are unaccustomed to such things, but they were easy to prepare, economical, nutritious, deliciously cooked, and tasted so good.

We called these improvisations *del pover'uomo* because of their inexpensive ingredients.

1 pound Italian sweet sausages
2 cups fresh mushrooms, quartered
1¹/₂ pounds chicken gizzards and hearts, trimmed, washed, and picked over
2 tablespoons extra virgin olive oil
1 medium-size onion, coarsely chopped
1 medium-size carrot, peeled and coarsely chopped
1 rib celery, coarsely chopped
1 sprig minced fresh parsley
1 bay leaf
¹/₂ teaspoon ground cloves
1 tablespoon tomato paste
¹/₂ cup dry wine, white or red
One 8-ounce can tomato puree, or ¹/₂ cup fresh
2 medium-size potatoes, peeled and cubed
³/₄ cup sun-dried tomatoes, soaked for ¹/₂ hour in lukewarm water
¹/₂ pound chicken livers

1. Place the sausages in a large skillet, pierce them in several places, cover them with water, and bring to a boil over high heat. Reduce the heat to medium and cook until the water has evaporated. Once the water has evaporated, reduce the heat to low and cook, turning often, until well browned. When cool, cut them into 1-inch pieces. Set aside. Pour off the fat from the skillet and add the mushrooms. Cook until the water exuded by the mushrooms has been absorbed, 10 to 15 minutes.

2. Cut the gizzards into 3 or 4 pieces and halve the hearts; set aside.

3. In a large skillet, heat the oil and add the onion, carrot, celery, and parsley. Cook over medium-high heat, stirring often, until tender, 5 to 8 minutes. Stir in the gizzards, giblets, hearts, bay leaf, and cloves.

continues

4. Combine the tomato paste and wine in a small bowl and add to the skillet, cook 5 minutes, stirring, then add the tomato puree and $1/2$ cup water. Cover, reduce the heat to medium, and cook until slightly reduced, about 10 minutes. Add the potatoes and cook until they are tender, about 20 minutes. Drain the dried tomatoes, coarsely chop, and add to the skillet. Cook 15 minutes longer. Add the liver and cook until no longer pink, about 5 minutes. Add the sausages and mushrooms and cook to warm through, 2 to 3 minutes. Serve hot.

NOTE: I LIKE TO SERVE THIS STEW WITH RICE.

Variation: *Cibreo all'Abruzzese*

A simple variation of the above tasty stew is called *cibreo*. It was a favorite of Caterina dé Medici. It is said that she took an Abruzzese cook to France with her and he probably made this dish for the lady.

No sausages or mushrooms in a *cibreo*—they have to be omitted. *Cibreo* is also the base for the famous *Finanziera*, which often finishes a *Bolognese* sauce or other fancy dishes.

CAPPONE CON LA SALSA GHIOTTA

Capon with Glutton Sauce (Makes 8 servings)

WHILE SOMEWHAT LESS APPRECIATED IN this country, a capon in Italy has always been considered a delicacy and quite special. When guests are presented a capon at the dinner table, they know that they are being treated quite honorably.

In my home, capons were eaten during the winter, mostly at Christmas and sometimes for New Year's. Carnival, or Mardi Gras, were other occasions which usually called for capon.

I still remember the butcher's arrival at my grandmother's house to do the caponizing, which meant the castration of male chickens 4 to 5 months old. Caponizing was invented in ancient Greece, according to Richard Olney in his Time-Life book *The Good Cook—Poultry*. "The practice," he reports, "became widespread in classical Rome . . . . With a simple surgical procedure Roman poultry breeders . . . produced a bird that grew twice the size of a chicken while retaining all the tenderness of a young bird." Leave it to those Romans—anything to enhance their Lucullan dinners.

As capons go, this is a relatively simple recipe, yet the sauce is a gossamer mixture of delicate flavors.

CAPON

Extra virgin olive oil
1 capon, 9 to 10 pounds
Salt to taste, optional
Freshly ground pepper to taste
¼ pound prosciutto in 1 thick slice, cut into thin strips
2 sprigs fresh parsley
2 medium-size onions, coarsely chopped
1 medium-size carrot, peeled and coarsely chopped
2 tablespoons unsalted butter
½ cup dry white wine

SAUCE

1 cup heavy cream
Juice of ½ lemon
2 large egg yolks
¼ cup goose liver pâté or paste

1. Preheat the oven to 375°F. Lightly oil a roasting pan large enough to hold the capon.

2. Prepare the capon: Sprinkle the capon inside and out with salt, if used, and pepper. Insert half the prosciutto and the sprigs of parsley in the cavity of the bird. Truss the capon.

3. Spread the onions, carrots, and remaining prosciutto over the bottom of the prepared pan. Drizzle with a little oil and stir to coat. Arrange the capon on top of the vegetables, dot with the butter, and roast 30 minutes. Reduce the heat to 350°F and continue roasting, basting often with the pan juices and the wine, until the juices run clear when a meaty part of the bird is pierced with a skewer, about 2½ hours.

4. Prepare the sauce: Combine the cream, lemon juice, egg yolks, and pâté in a food processor. Process to blend well, and pour into a saucepan. Do not wash the processor.

5. Remove the capon to a platter and cover with aluminum foil to keep warm. With a slotted spoon, remove all the vegetables and the strips of prosciutto at the bottom of the pan and transfer to the food processor. Degrease the juices at the bottom of the pan and add them to the processor. Puree and add this to the sauce in the saucepan. Cook over low heat, stirring often, until heated through. Do not boil the sauce or it will curdle.

6. Carve the capon into serving pieces. Pour some of the sauce over the capon and serve the remainder in a sauce boat on the side.

GALANTINA DI CAPPONE NATALIZIO

Christmas Capon Galantine **(Makes 8 servings or more)**

NOT A SIMPLE DISH, THIS ONE, BUT absolutely exceptional. It requires time and patience. Although it takes three days, when you have finished the preparation and the poaching of the galantine, all that remains is to slice it and then bake it for 1 hour before serving.

One word of advice: Before you attempt this recipe, read the instructions carefully so that you have everything ready when you start working.

By the way, a turkey galantine is done exactly the same way.

CAPON

1 capon, 9 to 10 pounds
½ pound cooked tongue, diced
Marsala wine

BROTH

The bones of the capon
2 veal bones
1 medium-size onion, with a cross
*   cut at its root end*
2 whole cloves
1 medium-size carrot, peeled
1 rib celery
2 sprigs fresh parsley
2 bay leaves
10 whole black peppercorns
Kosher salt to taste

GALANTINE

Salt to taste, optional
Freshly ground pepper to taste
3 pounds veal, pork, and beef,
*   ground together*
½ teaspoon grated nutmeg
2 to 3 tablespoons pinoli nuts
½ pound prosciutto in 1 very thick slice,
*   diced*
¼ pound fatback, diced, optional
½ cup pitted sweet olives, preferably
*   Apulian or Californian, sliced*
4 to 5 small or medium-size hard-boiled
*   eggs, shelled*
Unsalted butter for the pan

TWO DAYS BEFORE:

1. Bone the capon according to Steps 1 and 2 for *Galantina Semplice Mamma Lella* on page 287. Place the boned capon in a large bowl.

2. Gently remove the breast meat from the boned capon and cut it into ½-inch-wide strips. Add the strips of breast and the tongue to the bowl with the boned capon. Add enough Marsala to cover. Add all the pieces of meat you can recover from the carcass.

3. Prepare the broth: Place the capon bones in a large stockpot. Add the veal bones, the onion with the cloves stuck in it, carrot, celery, parsley, bay leaves, peppercorns, and salt. Cover with enough water to come 4 inches above the solids. Bring to a boil, reduce the heat to medium-low and simmer for 1½ hours. Strain the broth, reserve the solids for another use, taste for flavor, and season with salt if necessary. If the broth is not flavorful, the galantine will come out insipid. Refrigerate the broth overnight.

4. Prepare the galantine: Place a large piece of cheesecloth on a large work surface. Drain the capon and lay the boned capon flat on the cloth, skin side down. Sprinkle very lightly with salt, if used, and pepper.

5. Remove and drain the breast strips and all the pieces of meat from the Marsala, but leave the diced tongue in the bowl. Add to the bowl the ground chopped meat, pepper to taste, the nutmeg, *pinoli,* prosciutto, fatback, if used, and the olives. Mix well with your hands.

6. Have a needle and thread ready to sew the galantine. Place half the ground meat mixture, which is called a *farcia,* lengthwise down the middle of the capon. Arrange the breast strips of meat on top of it and place the hard-boiled eggs in one line down the center on top of the *farcia.* Cover with the remaining *farcia.* Bring the two sides of the capon up to enclose the *farcia* completely. Sew the skin in place, letting some of the thread hang over on both ends. (This will make the removal of the thread easier.) Sew any other openings or tears which have occurred during the boning, always leaving a little of the thread hanging out. Tightly wrap the galantine with the cheesecloth and secure with string to give it a nice cylindrical shape. Place it in an oval heavy-bottomed pan large enough to hold the galantine comfortably. Set aside.

7. Poach the galantine: Skim the fat from the surface of the broth. Reserve 1 cup of the broth. If the broth has gelled, spoon on top of the galantine; if liquid, pour over enough of the chilled broth to cover the galantine completely. If you should be short of broth, add some water if necessary in order to completely submerge the galantine. Cover the pan, bring to a boil over high heat, and immediately reduce the heat to low. Cook about 2 hours at a constant, gentle simmer. When done, remove the lid and let the galantine completely cool in its own broth. (At this point, the galantine is not yet completely cooked.) Remove it to a platter and reserve the broth. Cut away the strings around the galantine and carefully remove the cheesecloth. Rinse the cloth in cold water and tightly rewrap it around the galantine. Place the galantine in a pan and set a weight (like a tray with a large book, for example) on top. Chill overnight in the refrigerator.

CHRISTMAS DAY:

8. Finish the galantine: Butter an ovenproof dish large enough to contain the galantine and from which you can serve.

continues

9. Unwrap the galantine. Gently pull out any threads used to sew up the galantine. With a sharp knife, thinly slice the galantine, taking care not to destroy its shape. Using two large spatulas, lift the entire galantine from both ends and transfer to the prepared pan. Dot the galantine with butter. Pour $3/_4$ cup of the reserved capon broth into the pan. Cover loosely with aluminum foil and place in a cold oven. Heat the oven to 350°F and bake about 1 hour to complete the cooking. Baste often with the Marsala, remaining broth, and its own juices. Remove the foil during the last 10 minutes of cooking to brown and crisp the top. Serve hot.

NOTE 1: A CLASSIC GALANTINE, WHICH THIS IS, SHOULD BE SERVED COLD. THE SLICES ARE SET FLAT ON A SERVING PLATTER AND COOL BROTH, TO WHICH A LITTLE MARSALA HAS BEEN ADDED, IS POURED OVER THE TOP. THEN THE GALANTINE IS CHILLED UNTIL THE BROTH GELS; THIS IS CALLED AN ASPIC. THIS WAY THE GALANTINE LOOKS BEAUTIFUL, AND IS, I ASSURE YOU, DELICIOUS. IF YOU INDEED WISH TO SERVE IT COLD, POACH THE GALANTINE 1 HOUR LONGER AND COOL IT COMPLETELY IN ITS OWN BROTH BEFORE SLICING IT AND POURING THE BROTH ON TOP OF THE SLICES FOR THE ASPIC.

YOU CAN ALSO SERVE THE GALANTINE DECORATED WITH OR SURROUNDED BY THE GELLED BROTH CUT INTO CUBES OR TRIANGLES.

NOTE 2: I RESERVE THE MEAT ATTACHED TO THE BONES, IF ANY, FOR A SALAD. STRAIN THE VEGETABLES AND USE THE PUREE FOR A SOUP OR TO THICKEN A SAUCE.

TACCHINO DEL GIORNO DOPO

Next Day Turkey **(Makes 4 servings)**

HAVEN'T WE ALL FOUND OURSELVES WITH too much leftover turkey at one time or another? I know you can make a hash, but this is how my mother solved the problem. Actually, we hoped to have leftovers from the splendid roast of the day before, because we liked this dish so much. I hope you will like it too.

2 tablespoons extra virgin olive oil
1 large potato, quartered and coarsely chopped
1 medium-size onion, quartered and coarsely chopped
4 cups cooked turkey, chopped
1/4 cup dry wine, white or red

1 teaspoon tomato paste
Salt to taste, optional
Freshly ground pepper to taste
1 cup shredded mozzarella cheese
1 sprig fresh parsley
5 to 6 basil leaves, chopped
2 ripe, firm tomatoes, sliced

1. In a large skillet, heat the oil. Add the potato and onion. Cook, stirring often, until the potatoes are softened, 10 to 15 minutes. You may need to add a little water or broth if the mixture starts to stick. Add the turkey and cook briefly, stirring.

2. Combine the wine and tomato paste and add to the skillet. Add the salt, if used, and the pepper. Cover and simmer 10 minutes.

3. Place the mozzarella cheese in a bowl. Chop together the parsley and basil and mix with the mozzarella cheese. Sprinkle this mixture on the turkey. Place the tomato slices all around the skillet in a decorative fashion, cover, and cook, without stirring, over low heat for 5 minutes.

4. Tie a colorful napkin on the handle of the skillet and serve.

ROTOLO DI TACCHINO ALLA GIANNA

Turkey Roll Gianna **(Makes 8 servings)**

Turkey is considered such an American bird that people are surprised when they find out that many delectable and important dishes in Italy are prepared with turkey. This one is the invention of my cousin Gianna Amore, who is a fabulous cook. It is a great dish for a party because it can be prepared in advance and it can be served cold. The presentation is very pretty.

Extra virgin olive oil
4 eggs, well beaten
2 tablespoons unsalted butter
1 pound trimmed and washed spinach
4 1/2 pounds breast of turkey, boned
Salt to taste, optional
Freshly ground pepper to taste

4 slices mortadella
2 tablespoons freshly grated parmesan cheese
1 sprig fresh rosemary, or 1/2 teaspoon dried
1/4 cup white wine
1 cup chicken broth, approximately, preferably homemade (page 61)

1. Heat 1 tablespoon of the oil in a 7- or 8- inch skillet. Add half the beaten eggs. Make a flat, thin omelet, turning it once. Set aside. Repeat with the remaining eggs; set aside. Wipe the skillet clean.

2. In the same skillet where the eggs cooked, heat 1 tablespoon of the butter. Add the spinach and cook, stirring once or twice until the water put out by the spinach has been absorbed, 5 to 8 minutes. Set aside.

3. Spread the turkey breast, skin side down, on a large work surface. Remove the fillets and set them aside. Flatten the breast somewhat to give it an even shape. Sprinkle with salt and pepper and place one omelet on top of the breast. Cover with the slices of mortadella. Spread the spinach over the mortadella and sprinkle with the parmesan cheese. Top with the remaining omelet. Place the reserved fillets lengthwise down the center. Fold in the two sides of the breast to enclose the filling. Secure with kitchen string, giving the meat the form of a big roll.

4. In a pan where the roll can fit snugly, heat the remaining butter and the remaining 2 tablespoons of oil. Add the rosemary and turkey roll. Cook over medium-high heat, turning often, until brown on all sides. Add the wine and let evaporate. Add half of the broth and cover. Reduce the heat to medium-low and cook about 1 1/2 hours. Turn the meat occasionally. If liquid evaporates, add more broth as needed. To test for doneness, insert a skewer into the thickest part. If the juices run clear, the turkey is done. Cool 15 to 20 minutes before slicing it.

ANATRA ALLE SETTE ERBE

Seven Herbs Duckling *(Makes 4 servings)*

IN OUR HOUSE, A MIXTURE OF HERBS, called *le sette erbe* (the seven herbs), was a staple used to flavor many things. If I remember it well, this combination of herbs was said to have been started by an old aunt who gave packets or jars of it as presents to family members and friends, a tradition that continues today. When we were children, and later on as teenagers, Grandmother would always ask that we bring back as many herbs as we could from our hiking expeditions in the mountains. We continued doing it as grown-ups. The bunches of fresh herbs were hung in the sun and when they were completely dry, they were crumbled and placed in jars to be kept in the cool pantry. I remember the kitchen air beautifully perfumed by the herbs at those times.

I still make the Seven Herbs mixture, but at this point my hiking takes me to the Union Square green market in Manhattan. And thank God for that, because I find all the herbs I need there. Because I am in New York, I dry them in my kitchen. The kitchen is small and hot, and the herbs dry quite quickly. Once jarred, I keep them in a cool clothes closet. The lingering perfume is delicious and even keeps the possible bugs away!

DUCK

1 duckling, 4 to 5 pounds
Salt to taste, optional
Freshly ground pepper to taste
1/2 lemon
2 bay leaves
2 to 3 slivers fresh ginger
1 small onion, quartered
1 medium-size apple, peeled, halved, and cored
1 tablespoon Seven Herbs (see head note, next page)
2 sprigs fresh parsley, minced
10 juniper berries, crushed
1/4 cup wine vinegar
1/2 cup Marsala wine

SAUCE

1 tablespoon unsalted butter
1 tablespoon extra virgin olive oil
2 large onions, chopped
1 teaspoon sugar
2 tablespoons wine vinegar
2 tablespoons Marsala wine
3/4 cup chicken broth, preferably homemade (page 61)
Salt to taste, optional
Freshly ground pepper to taste
Onion and apple from inside the duck

1. Prepare the duck: Remove the neck, gizzard, heart, and liver, if any, and set aside.

2. Bring to a boil a pot of water large enough to cover the duck when placed in it. Add the duck and return to a boil. Boil 5 to 7 minutes. This will exude some of the fat from the duck. Drain, discard the water, and dry the duck completely. This can be done the day before. If so, keep refrigerated loosely covered with waxed paper.

3. Preheat the oven to 400°F.

4. Season the duck, inside and out, with salt, if used, and pepper. Squeeze the lemon juice inside the duck and insert the squeezed lemon shell into the cavity of the duck, along with the bay leaves, ginger, onion, and apple. Truss the duck. Combine the Seven Herbs with the parsley, juniper berries, and a good grinding of pepper. Place the duck, breast side down, on a rack in a roasting pan.

continues

The seven herbs are sage, thyme, marjoram, rosemary, basil, oregano, and a pinch of mint. The mixture enhances almost any roast or sauce. Try it.

I adapted the following roast duck recipe from an old family recipe years ago, when I did a job for the Long Island Duck Council, and it was published in a couple of newspapers.

I kept the duck whole, while at home my mother used to cut the duck into pieces, and I add an apple, to make it more New York–style.

Mother served her duck with this sauce, a typical Abruzzese country sauce, which, incidentally, goes well with other roasts too.

Everybody likes a crisp skin on a roasted duck and so do I. To achieve this, I start with a Chinese method that my friend Marcella Hazan told me about which she uses. Simply plunge the duck into boiling water for 5 minutes and then dry it completely before cooking it. Marcella actually uses a hair dryer!

5. Chop the neck of the duck into 3 to 4 pieces and cut the gizzard in half. Scatter the neck, gizzard, and heart over the bottom of the pan. Reserve the liver. Roast for 30 minutes without opening the oven. Turn the duck over and roast 30 minutes longer.

6. Remove the pan from the oven and pierce the duck in several places with a skewer to allow the fat to ooze out. Pour off all the fat at the bottom of the pan. Pour the vinegar and the Marsala wine over the duck. Add $3/_4$ cup of water to the bottom of the pan. Return the pan to the oven and roast 30 minutes longer, basting the duck once or twice with the pan juices. Add the liver during the last 5 minutes. To test for doneness, pierce the thickest part of the thigh with a skewer. The duck is done when its juices run clear when pierced in a meaty place.

7. Remove from the oven. Remove the stuffing from inside the duck and set the apple and onion aside. Discard the rest of the stuffing. Cut the duck in half. Return the duck to the hot oven with the heat off, or place under a preheated broiler for a few minutes. This will crisp the skin. Discard the neck. Coarsely chop the gizzard, heart, and liver; set aside. Using a food processor, chop the onion and apple and set aside.

8. Prepare the sauce: Heat the butter and oil in a large saucepan. Add the onions and cook, stirring often, until softened, 5 to 8 minutes. Add the sugar, stir, and add the vinegar. Cook briefly and add the Marsala and broth. Add the onion-apple puree and the chopped giblets. Heat the sauce, season with salt and pepper, and serve with the duck.

ANATRA ALL'ARANCIA

Orange Roast Duck *(Makes 4 servings)*

WE ITALIANS RARELY USE FRUIT, COOKED or uncooked, as a condiment or sauce. Duck is an exception, and orange is undoubtedly a fruit that voluptuously embraces this remarkable bird beautifully.

DUCK

One 4- to 5-pound fresh duck
Salt to taste, optional
Freshly ground pepper to taste
1 medium-size carrot, peeled and
    cut into 6 pieces
1 small onion, quartered
1 rib celery, trimmed and cut into 8 pieces
1/2 teaspoon dried rosemary
1/2 teaspoon dried thyme

SAUCE

2 seedless oranges
1/4 cup sugar
1 teaspoon cornstarch
1 cup chicken broth, preferably homemade
    (page 61), or a good canned one
2 tablespoons balsamic vinegar
1/4 cup Marsala wine

1. Remove the neck, gizzard, heart, and liver, if any, from the duck. Chop the neck into 3 to 5 pieces; cut the gizzard in half. Place both and the heart in a baking pan fitted with a rack and large enough to contain the duck. Reserve the liver. Set aside.

2. Bring a large pot of water to a boil. Add the duck, bring back to a boil, and cook 5 to 7 minutes. Drain and dry the duck completely. This can be done the day before. Keep loosely covered in the refrigerator.

3. Preheat the oven to 450°F.

4. Sprinkle the duck with salt, if used, and pepper. Insert the carrot, onion, and celery into the cavity of the duck. Combine the herbs and rub all over the duck. Truss the duck and set it on the rack in the prepared pan. Reduce the heat to 375°F and roast until the duck is brown and the skin looks crisp, about 1 1/2 hours. In the middle of cooking, pierce the skin in several places. Baste once or twice. Add the liver to the bottom of the pan during the last 5 minutes. Remove the duck from the oven. Let it rest 15 minutes.

5. With a vegetable peeler, peel the outer skin of the oranges, avoiding the bitter white pith. Cut the peel into long, thin julienne strips, and blanch for 2 to 3 minutes. Drain and reserve. Remove all the white pith from the oranges and carefully remove the sections. Do this over a bowl to collect all the juices.

continues

6. In a medium-size saucepan, combine the sugar, cornstarch, and $3/4$ cup of the broth. Cook over medium-high heat, stirring, until slightly thickened, about 5 minutes. Add the julienned orange strips and cook until slightly softened, 5 to 8 minutes longer. Set aside.

7. Cut the duck into serving pieces. Discard the vegetables inside the duck, or cut the carrot into rounds and the celery and onion into slices. Discard the neck. Chop the gizzards, heart, and liver and add to the pan with the sauce. Keep the duck warm, uncovered, in a warm oven. Pour off all the fat from the roasting pan. Add the remaining broth, the vinegar, and Marsala to the pan. Stir with a wooden spoon, scraping all the brown particles clinging to the bottom and sides of the pan. Add this to the pan with the sauce. Reheat the sauce and add the orange sections with any accumulated juices from the bottom of the bowl. Simmer 5 minutes and serve with the duck.

NOTE: SOMETIMES, AFTER THE DUCK IS CUT UP, I PUT THE PIECES, SKIN SIDE UP, FOR 5 MINUTES, UNDER A PREHEATED BROILER TO MAKE IT CRISPY.

PICCIONI ALLA CONTADINA

Farmer's Squabs (Makes 6 servings)

AS A CHILD I REMEMBER FEEDING pigeons, which where reared in a distant corner of my grandmother's house where there was a large terrace. Nobody lived in that part of the house where we children also went to play. Pigeons need space to roost and fly, and in Pescara we only had a civilized balcony overlooking a main street.

Fortunately, we could buy them at the local market, and I remember how delicate and flavorful their taste was. Here I buy my pigeon, or better,

1/4 cup dried porcini mushrooms, soaked in 1 cup of lukewarm water for 20 minutes
Extra virgin olive oil
1 clove garlic, peeled and smashed
3 fresh squabs, split in half
Salt to taste, optional
Freshly ground pepper to taste

1 medium-size onion, finely chopped
1 sprig fresh rosemary, or 1/2 teaspoon dried
1/2 cup dry wine
1 tablespoon tomato paste
2 cups peeled tomatoes, cut into pieces
3 cups sliced mushrooms
The livers from the squabs, if any
1 tablespoon minced fresh parsley

1. Gently, so as not to disturb the sediment resting at the bottom, lift the porcini mushrooms from the water and strain the soaking liquid through a paper towel or coffee filter. Set aside.

squabs, which are young pigeons, 20 to 30 days old, from D'Artagnan. They come cleaned and ready to cook.

This is a family recipe in which the squabs are cooked in a sauce and served with a potato puree (page 383). A polenta would also do nicely since the dish is a kind of a stew.

2. In a large heavy skillet, or using two, heat 3 tablespoons of the oil and add the garlic and squabs. Brown on all sides, sprinkle with salt, if used, and pepper. Add the onion and rosemary. Cook 5 to 8 minutes, stirring, and add the wine; let evaporate.

3. Combine the water reserved from the porcini with the tomato paste and add to the skillet. Simmer 5 minutes and add the peeled tomatoes. Cover and cook at a simmer.

4. In another skillet, heat 2 more tablespoons of the oil and add the fresh mushrooms. Chop the dried porcini coarsely and add. Cook until the water exuded by the mushrooms has evaporated, 8 to 10 minutes, then add them to the squabs. Cover and continue cooking until the squabs are done, about 30 minutes longer. Add the livers during the last 5 minutes. Sprinkle with parsley and serve half a squab per person.

PICCIONI AL FORNO VILLA SANTA MARIA

Roasted Pigeons Villa Santa Maria **(Makes 6 servings)**

CHEF ANTONIO STANZIANI OF VILLA SANTA Maria gave me permission to use this recipe from his book *La Cucina dei Grandi Cuochi di Villa Santa Maria* (Mario Solfanelli, Editore). "This is," he says, "a traditional preparation from our village, since all farmers at one time, and even today, would raise pigeons."

It is a simple and delicious recipe. Make sure your pigeons or squabs are young and do not come from Venice, where they die a natural death . . . !

3 young pigeons or squabs, ready to cook
Salt to taste, optional
Freshly ground pepper to taste
3 cloves garlic, peeled and smashed

3 sprigs fresh rosemary
6 sage leaves
3 strips lemon peel
¼ cup extra virgin olive oil

1. Preheat the oven to 375°F.

2. Sprinkle the pigeons with salt, if used, and pepper. Insert into the cavity of each bird 1 clove of garlic, 1 sprig of rosemary, 2 leaves of sage, and 1 strip of lemon. Pour the olive oil over the birds and bake 30 to 40 minutes. Let the pigeon rest 10 minutes, then cut into serving pieces and serve.

Variation: If pigeons are unavailable, use Cornish hens.

CONIGLIO IN PORCHETTA

Roasted Rabbit "Porchetta" Style **(Makes 8 servings)**

I AM SO GLAD TO SEE THAT RABBIT IS becoming quite popular in this country. For the Italians and the French it is like eating chicken, and often rabbits are cooked similarly. This one, being an Abruzzese recipe, is prepared in the style of our famous *porchetta*, with the aromatic perfume of wild fennel.

2 young fresh rabbits, approximately 3 pounds each; or 1 rabbit, about 5 pounds, innards included
1/2 cup wine vinegar
20 sprigs fresh wild fennel (see Note)
4 cloves garlic, peeled
2 1/2 cups water

1/4 cup extra virgin olive oil
1/4 pound prosciutto, chopped
1/4 pound pancetta, chopped
1/4 cup dry Marsala wine
Salt to taste, optional
Freshly ground pepper to taste

1. Remove all the innards from the rabbits, wash them, and set aside. Wash the rabbits well and keep them under running water for about 20 minutes. Place them in a nonreactive bowl with the innards, add the vinegar and enough water to cover. Let stand about 1 hour, then drain and pat dry.

2. Preheat the oven to 375°F.

3. In a pot, place the fennel sprigs, 2 cloves garlic, and water. Bring to a boil and simmer 15 minutes. Drain, but reserve the fennel and water. Discard the garlic.

4. In a medium-size skillet, heat 1 tablespoon of the oil and add the chopped prosciutto and pancetta. Cook a few minutes. Cut the innards in pieces, if large, and add to the skillet. Cook over high heat, stirring, about 10 minutes. Add the wine and let evaporate.

5. Squeeze the fennel dry and add to the skillet. Cook, stirring, 5 to 8 minutes. Place this mixture in the bowl of a food processor. Peel the remaining garlic cloves and add. Chop coarsely.

6. Sprinkle the rabbits inside and out with salt, if used, and pepper. Stuff them with an equal amount of the chopped mixture and sew the openings. Place the rabbits in an oiled baking pan and pour the remaining oil over them. Add 1/4 cup of the reserved water from the fennel and set in the oven. Roast 25 minutes and turn both rabbits.

7. Continue roasting until the rabbits are done, about 1 hour. Baste often and add a little more of the fennel water to keep the meat moist. Continue cooking until the meat is done, about 20 to 30 minutes longer.

8. Cut the rabbits into serving pieces and keep warm. Deglaze the baking pan by adding a little more of the fennel water, or plain water, to the pan. Scrape to remove the brown particles clinging to the bottom and sides of the pan. Pour this sauce over the rabbits and serve.

NOTE: IF YOU CANNOT FIND FRESH WILD FENNEL, USE THE GREEN PARTS FROM A FRESH FENNEL, OR 2 FENNEL BULBS.

CONIGLIO FARCITO

Stuffed Rabbit (Makes 6 servings or more)

MY AUNT ELA, A MASTER AT MAKING rabbit, did not bone it. She felt that the bones were essential for flavor, and I agree. But since this rabbit is stuffed, I think that it is a good idea to partly bone it, as I do.

One 4 to 5 pound rabbit, split at the belly, from neck to tail, its carcass removed
1/4 cup vinegar
Extra virgin olive oil
Salt to taste, optional
Freshly ground pepper to taste
1/4 pound coppa (see Note) or soppressata
1 clove garlic, peeled
3 fresh sage leaves, or 1/4 teaspoon dried

1 small sprig fresh rosemary, or 1/2 teaspoon dried
3/4 pound ground veal
2 tablespoons unsalted butter
2 cups chicken broth, approximately, preferably homemade (page 61), or a good canned one
1/2 cup dry white wine

1. Place the rabbit in a nonreactive bowl. Add the vinegar, pour in enough cold water to cover, and let it stand for 30 minutes or longer.

2. Preheat the oven to 375°F. Lightly oil a baking dish large enough for the rabbit to fit snugly.

3. Pat the rabbit dry. Place it, skin side down, on a large work surface. Sprinkle with salt, if used, and pepper, and cover the interior cavity with the *coppa*, or *soppressata*. Set aside.

continues

4. Chop together the garlic and herbs. Place in a mixing bowl, add the ground veal, and mix well. Fill the rabbit with this mixture. Close the rabbit up and secure with string. Place the rabbit in the prepared pan and dot with butter. Pour $^1/_2$ cup of the broth into the bottom of the pan. Place in the oven and roast until the rabbit is done, about $1^1/_2$ hours. If necessary, keep adding more broth while cooking and sprinkle often with wine. The rabbit should cook *in umido*, with a little humidity. If it tends to color too much too quickly, reduce the heat to 350°F, or cover loosely with aluminum foil. The finished rabbit's color should be a dark brown.

NOTE: *COPPA* IS AN ITALIAN SALAMI SOLD IN ITALIAN SPECIALTY SHOPS AND SOME SUPER-
MARKETS.

CONIGLIO ALLA PECORARA

Shepherd's Rabbit **(Makes 6 servings)**

THIS RABBIT IS BAKED IN A DELICIOUS tomato sauce, and with the accompaniment of potatoes. It is called *alla pecorara*, for its addition of grated cheese, which makes the sauce even more succulent.

One 4- to 5-pound rabbit,
   cut into serving pieces
$^1/_4$ cup of vinegar
1 pound potatoes, cut into wedges
3 tablespoons extra virgin olive oil
$^1/_2$ teaspoon dried rosemary

1 medium-size onion, sliced
Salt to taste, optional
Freshly ground pepper to taste
One 16-ounce can strained or peeled tomatoes
3 tablespoons freshly grated parmesan or
   grana padano cheese

1. Place the rabbit in a nonreactive bowl. Add the vinegar and enough cold water to cover. Let stand 1 hour or longer.

2. Preheat the oven to 375°F.

3. In a medium-size bowl, combine the potatoes, oil, rosemary, and onion.

4. Drain the rabbit and place it in a large roasting pan. Surround with the potato mixture, season with salt, if used, and pepper. Add the tomatoes. (If using the peeled kind, chop them somewhat.) Bake 1 hour, add the grated cheese, and continue baking until the rabbit and potatoes are done, about 15 minutes longer. Serve hot.

CHAPTER 11

CARNE

Meat

I have always loved meat. In these days of "food terrorists," as our inimitable Julia Child calls some nutritionists, I still have my good American beef steak whenever I feel like it. There is nothing better.

Of course I enjoy other meats as well. When I speak of my carnivorous penchant, I am not limiting myself to red meat. I love the delicacy of veal, although I find American veal a little underflavored. Another favorite of mine is pork, whose flavor is a little better. But still, even in Italy, pork today does not have the intensity of flavor that I remember enjoying when I was growing up. Since Abruzzo is the "pastoral" land, lamb is a great specialty and is, of course, quite prevalent in our gastronomy. I find American lamb delicious and suitable for all my recipes including those made with kid.

About Beef

I didn't grow up with good beef. When I was a child in Italy, one could have good tender steaks only in Florence, and perhaps Milan or Turin. Beef elsewhere was always tough. That is why we Italians have such wonderful pot roasts.

Some of them are earthy and comforting, others are elegant, sophisticated for the choice of ingredients, and often quite expensive to prepare. The famous *Carne al Barolo,* from Piedmont, is potted with an entire bottle of expensive Barolo wine, but what a succulent dish!

These days, you can eat good beef anywhere in Italy. In fact, the Italians are so proud of this new beef that my relatives and friends always try to entice me with a nice *bistecca.* But no matter how good this *bistecca* might be, I politely refuse. Nothing compares to a good American steak. In Italy, I can eat many other delicious things.

So this section of the book is inspired by the quality of good American beef, but it is cooked with Italian and Abruzzese flavors. When I cook steak, I simply add a good pinch of my Seven Herbs (see head note, pages 297–98) after lightly coating the steak with a little olive oil.

Buy red meat one or two days before you intend to use it. Red meat tenderizes if kept in the refrigerator for a couple of days.

Stick to Your Steak

Sometime ago, at a food convention, I was part of a panel discussing cooking schools. A question went to Jacques Pepin, the noted food expert writer and instructor at the French Culinary Institute of New York. He was asked what he liked to eat after a long day of travel and teaching away from home. He was sitting next to me. Jacques looked around as if to find inspiration, and then with that sardonic French accent, so familiar to those who watch him on television, he said, "Oh, I don't know, perhaps a soup." Turning to me, he continued, "What about you, Anna Teresa?"

Without hesitation, I answered, "Me? A good American steak."

He immediately tapped his forehead and chuckled, "You're right. Why didn't I think of it!"

Salsa Agrodolce di Peperoni e Pomodori Zia Ela

Aunt Ela's Pepper and Tomato Sweet and Sour Sauce (Makes 4 to 5 cups)

THIS SAUCE, WHICH YOU CAN PREPARE IN advance, keeps well in glass jars for a few months and you will have enough for several meals. However, since I do not have the cool cellar my aunt had, I store it in the refrigerator.

For the tomatoes in this recipe, buy plum tomatoes which are not fully ripe, or at least the hardest you can find.

3 pounds mixed green, red, and yellow
   bell peppers
1 pound plum tomatoes, seeded and diced
2 tender ribs celery, washed, trimmed,
   and diced

2 large red onions, coarsely chopped
2 medium-size carrots, peeled and diced
2 cups white wine vinegar
3 tablespoons extra virgin olive oil
1/4 cup sugar

Wash, core, and cut the bell peppers into thin strips. Dice the strips and place in an enameled pot. Add the tomatoes, celery, onions, carrots, vinegar, oil, and sugar. Bring to a boil, reduce the heat to low, and simmer until the peppers are very soft, 15 to 20 minutes. Cool and store in glass jars.

NOTE: THIS SAUCE IS SERVED COLD AND GOES WELL WITH BOILED AND GRILLED MEAT AND FISH.

LOMBATINE PEPATE E FIAMMATE

Flamed Beef Steaks with Pepper **(Makes 4 servings)**

PAPÀ USED TO MAKE THIS DISH ON THE terrace in Pescara. Our neighbors were amused, although they were a little startled by the flames.

Now, I make it only over charcoal when I am on vacation in East Hampton. I use a charcoal grill and serve them *al fresco*, in the garden!

Not only is the flaming of the steaks an amusing spectacle, but the grilled flavor is quite delicious and well worth the effort.

My father used an Abruzzese liqueur called *Centerbe*, which means 100 herbs, for flavoring, but it is not sold in the States. I have resorted to grappa and a pinch of my Seven Herbs.

4 shell steaks, about 8 ounces; or 2 porter-house steaks, 10 to 12 ounces each

2 to 3 tablespoons extra virgin olive oil

1 tablespoon or more black peppercorns, crushed, or cracked with a mallet

$\frac{1}{2}$ teaspoon Seven Herbs mixture (see head note, pages 297–98)

Salt to taste, optional

$\frac{1}{4}$ cup grappa

1. Rub the steaks with the oil. Combine the peppercorns with the herbs and pat this mixture on both sides of the steaks. If your taste finds delight in it, use more pepper. Let it rest in a cool place for 1 hour.

2. Prepare a charcoal fire or gas grill well in advance. Have your barbecue ready and grill the steaks on both sides to your likeness. We Italians prefer our steaks medium to well-done, and this takes at least 5 to 7 minutes or more per side, depending on the size of the steak. Sprinkle the steaks with salt, if used.

3. Transfer the steaks to a large platter, pour on the grappa, ignite, and serve with flare.

NOTE: INSTEAD OF GRAPPA YOU CAN USE GIN, BUT THEN LEAVE OUT THE SEVEN HERBS, AS GIN HAS A PRONOUNCED HERBIVOROUS FLAVOR ANYWAY.

LA MIA HAMBURGER

My Hamburger **(Makes 2 servings)**

TO TELL THE TRUTH, THE FIRST TIME I HAD a classic hamburger with cheese, ketchup, and maybe even relish was during my British campaign, as I call the three years I spent in England. This hamburger was called a Wimpy, and I liked it. Returning home to Pescara, I told my father how I enjoyed the Wimpy. Our chopped meat was always transformed into meatballs or a meatloaf! Papà immediately started to reproduce the Wimpy. I must confess we both liked ketchup (which my father referred to as "that good American thing") and used it often with steaks.

Anyway, this is the hamburger I make today for my husband. The American version is quite different and he claims it is the best he has ever eaten. See what you think!

I use ground chuck for it because it has more flavor. And my special secret—but do not tell anyone—is the addition of *cornichon*. I use an iron skillet to cook my hamburgers, but they are just as good grilled.

³/₄ to ¹/₂ pound ground chuck meat
1 teaspoon Worcestershire sauce
1 or 2 cornichons, finely chopped

Freshly ground pepper to taste
Salt to taste, optional

1. Combine all the ingredients but the salt. Shape into 2 hamburgers.

2. Place a cast-iron skillet on medium-high heat with nothing in it. When very hot, add the hamburgers. Cook 4 to 5 minutes per side for rare, 6 to 7 minutes per side for medium, and 9 to 10 minutes per side for well done. Turn them a few times until you achieve the desired doneness. Sprinkle with salt. And . . . by all means, serve it with ketchup.

L'Arrosto

The Roast *(Makes 8 servings or more)*

WITHIN THE FAMILY THIS DISH WAS SIMPLY called "the roast" because it was made rarely, and only when we could get a good piece of fillet of beef, which was hard to come by and expensive.

But when we had one, it was treated with tender loving care, not only by the one who was cooking it, but by all of those giving advice and instructions as well.

This is the family recipe. It has a delicious herby flavor and, to obtain it, one must use fresh herbs.

2 cloves garlic, peeled
6 juniper berries
3 sprigs fresh parsley
5 blades chives
7 to 8 fresh basil leaves
2 to 4 fresh mint leaves
1 tablespoon fresh rosemary leaves
1/4 teaspoon ground allspice
1/4 cup unsalted butter
1 fillet of beef, about 6 pounds, trimmed of all fat
2 tablespoons extra virgin olive oil
1 medium-size onion, thickly sliced
2 medium-size carrots, peeled and cut into small pieces
1 1/2 cups beef or veal broth, preferably homemade (see Variation 2, page 61), or a good canned broth
4 to 5 strips prosciutto fat; or same amount bacon
1/2 cup dry red wine

1. In a food processor, place the garlic, juniper berries, parsley, chives, basil, mint, rosemary, and allspice. Process until very finely chopped. Mix 1 teaspoon of this mixture with 2 tablespoons of the butter. Cover this and refrigerate. Reserve the remaining herb mixture.

2. Tie the beef to give it a round shape. Pat the remaining herb mixture all over the meat. Cover loosely with aluminum foil and let it marinate in the refrigerator for 2 to 3 hours or overnight.

3. When ready to cook, let the beef come to room temperature.

4. Preheat the oven to 400°F.

5. In the bottom of a roasting pan, place the oil, onion, and carrots. Mix well and add 1/4 cup of the broth. Set the roasting rack in place and add the meat on top. Dot with the remaining butter. Arrange the prosciutto strips or bacon lengthwise on top of the meat. Roast 30 minutes, then add the wine to the bottom of the pan. Cook until it starts to brown, about 1 hour. (The center will be rare. Cook a little longer if desired.) Baste occasionally with the juices at the bottom of the pan. (My father always recommended that this meat be cooked *al sangue*—bloody, or rare.) Remove to a platter and cover loosely with foil to keep warm.

6. Remove the vegetables from the bottom of the pan, place them in a food processor, and puree. Pour the puree into a saucepan. Add a little of the broth to the roasting pan and scrape the brown particles clinging to the bottom and sides of the pan. Add to the saucepan. Add some, or all, of the remaining broth to the saucepan according to the consistency you prefer your sauce. Bring to a boil. Reduce the heat to medium and simmer for a few minutes to warm through. Add the reserved butter-herb mixture, stir, and remove the sauce from the heat. Cover to keep warm.

7. Slice the beef and arrange on a serving platter. Pour some of the sauce on the beef and serve the remaining sauce on the side.

NOTE: MY MOTHER ALWAYS SERVED A CREAMY POTATO PUREE (PAGE 383) AND A GREEN VEGETABLE WITH THIS DISH.

BISTECCONA SUCCULENTA

Succulent "Big" Steak   *(Makes 6 to 8 servings)*

WE CALLED THIS DISH SUCCULENT BECAUSE of its sauce, redolent with an unusual combination of spices.

This ancient recipe goes back to the days of the Saracens and when L'Aquila, the capital of Abruzzo, was a flourishing commercial center. Many new spices were introduced to Italy at that time.

In those ancient days, spices were a necessity, especially pepper, which, together with salt, helped to conserve food. The famous Via Salaria goes from the Adriatic coast to Rome, and was the famous route by which the

1 large onion, peeled and quartered
2 medium-size carrots, peeled and cut into pieces
3 ribs celery, trimmed and cut into pieces
1 clove garlic, peeled
One ¼-inch slice fresh ginger, peeled
2 whole cloves
¼ teaspoon ground allspice
¼ teaspoon freshly ground pepper
3 tablespoons extra virgin olive oil
3 pounds beef chuck, in 1 thick slice
½ cup Marsala wine
1 teaspoon tomato paste

1. Preheat the oven to 375°F. In a food processor, combine the onion, carrots, celery, garlic, ginger, cloves, allspice, and pepper. Process until quite finely chopped.

2. In a baking pan large enough to hold the beef, pour in the vegetable mixture and 1 tablespoon of the oil. Toss and spread the mixture on the bottom of the pan. Place the meat on top and pour in the Marsala wine.

continues

Romans brought salt from the sea. The prices for these commodities were astronomical. In the fifth century A.D. during the Barbarian invasions, Alaric, the king of the Visigoths, asked for a thousand kilos of pepper in exchange for abandoning the siege of Rome. In the Middle Ages, a pound of ginger, a new spice, commanded the price of a sheep, and a pound of cloves, that of a cow.

This dish, therefore, must have cost a fortune in ancient times. But today, it is a rather inexpensive dish yet still rich in succulent flavor.

3. Combine the tomato paste with $^1/_4$ cup water and pour this over the beef and vegetables. Cover with aluminum foil and bake for 2 hours, or until the beef is tender. Baste the meat with its own juices once or twice. If there appears to be too much liquid at the bottom of the pan once the cooking is finished, remove the meat to a platter and cover with aluminum foil to keep warm. Raise the temperature of the oven to 400°F and return the baking pan to the oven. Cook for a few minutes or as long as necessary to reduce the amount of liquid. Be careful not to scorch the sauce. Slice the beef and serve with the sauce.

NOTE: A TOUCH OF SOY SAUCE OR WORCESTERSHIRE SAUCE, COMBINED WITH THE MARSALA, ADDS AN EXTRA ZIP.

STINCO BRASATO

Braised Beef Shank   (*Makes 6 to 8 servings*)

I KNOW, I KNOW, THE ITALIAN NAME sounds funny. Many a journalist has called me in alarm, when reviewing an Italian cookbook, fearing that it was a terrible misspelling. I reassure them that it is a perfectly polite Italian word and it means shank. We Italians love shank meat so much that when we want to describe a very good person, we call him a *Stinco di Santo*, a saint's shank.

The *stinco*, though, should not be confused with *ossobuco*. Although the *ossobuco* refers to the shank of the veal, it is cut into pieces. *Stinco* is the whole

MARINADE

1 beef shank, about 5 to 6 pounds, or 2 smaller shanks weighing the same amount
1 bottle Montepulciano d'Abruzzo wine
3 medium-size carrots, peeled and cut into pieces
3 medium-size red onions, quartered
1 rib celery, trimmed and cut into pieces
10 whole cloves

5 juniper berries
5 bay laurel leaves
1 cinnamon stick
10 crushed black peppercorns, cracked

COOKING

2 tablespoons extra virgin olive oil
Meat
Salt to taste, optional
Freshly ground pepper to taste

THE DAY BEFORE:

1. Prepare the marinade: Place the shank in a large, nonreactive bowl. Add the wine, carrots, onions, celery, cloves, juniper berries, bay leaves, cinnamon, and peppercorns. Marinate, turning occasionally, for 12 hours in the refrigerator.

shank, and the meat is cooked on the bone. *Stinco Brassato* is a succulent dish with many different preparations. This one, in particular, has a subtle hint of cinnamon and the harmonious taste of the clove. Again, a typical Abruzzese combination.

This recipe can also be made with veal and pork shank. Remember that the meat must marinate 12 hours, so plan accordingly.

THE NEXT DAY:

2. Remove the meat to a platter and pat dry with paper towels. Set aside. Reserve the marinade.

3. In an oval pot large enough to hold the shank, heat the oil. Add the shank and cook, turning often, until brown on all sides, 10 to 20 minutes. Add salt, if used, and the pepper. Remove the meat to a platter, pour off the fat from the pot, and set the pot aside. Reserve the pot.

4. Remove the bay leaves and cinnamon from the marinade and set aside. Strain the marinade and reserve the liquid. Place the solids from the marinade into a food processor and puree.

5. Return the pot to the heat and add the pureed mixture. Cook over medium-high heat until warmed through, about 5 minutes. Return the shank to the pot and add the bay leaves and cinnamon. Add the liquid marinade and season with salt, if used, and pepper. Bring to a boil, reduce the heat to low, and cook until the meat is falling off the bone, about 3 to 4 hours or longer. To serve, discard the bay leaves and cinnamon, stand the shank on end, and, holding the bone with a towel, slice or chunk the meat.

NOTE: MY MOTHER REUSED THE BONE FOR A BROTH. YOU CAN FREEZE IT UNTIL YOU'RE READY TO USE IT AGAIN.

Variation: Lamb shank is delicious this way.

INVOLTINI DI MANZO RIPIENI

Stuffed Beef Rolls *(Makes 6 servings or more)*

THE STUFFING FOR THESE *INVOLTINI* IS A pleasing delicate combination of prosciutto, mozzarella cheese, and asparagus. The dried tomatoes add a savory touch to the sauce. String beans, broccoli stalks, or other greens can be substituted for the asparagus. My mother also used the stems of the artichokes, and I assure you, the dish acquired a special delicious flavor.

12 large braciole, *about 4 ounces each,*
  (5 × 6 inches, approximately) cut
  from a piece of top round of beef,
  well pounded
Freshly ground black pepper
1/2 teaspoon dried rosemary, crumbled
1/2 teaspoon dried thyme, crumbled
12 slices mozzarella cheese, 1/4-inch thick
24 asparagus, trimmed and blanched

12 thin slices prosciutto
3 tablespoons extra virgin olive oil
1/4 cup dry red wine
Water
1 cup oil-cured sun-dried tomatoes,
  cut into thin strips
1 cup broth or bouillon, if needed
1/4 cup minced fresh parsley

1. Sprinkle each *braciola* with pepper, rosemary, and thyme, to your taste. Cover each with a slice of mozzarella. Trim the stems of the asparagus so that they do not protrude from the meat when rolled and place on the mozzarella. Cover with the prosciutto, folding it to fit the slices of meat. Roll up the meat and secure with string.

2. In a large skillet, heat the oil. Add the rolled beef and cook over medium-high heat, turning often, until the meat is browned on all sides, 5 to 8 minutes. Add the wine and let evaporate. Add enough water to come halfway to the tops of the meat rolls. Cover, bring to a boil, reduce the heat, and cook until the meat is tender, about 1 1/2 to 2 hours. Turn the meat often. Add the dried tomatoes about 10 minutes before the meat is done. If you do not have enough liquid add some of the broth as needed to prevent scorching. Add the parsley just before serving, and serve hot.

NOTE: YOU CAN USE VEAL CUTLETS FOR THIS DISH INSTEAD OF BEEF, BUT COOK THEM 45 MINUTES TO 1 HOUR.

Variation: These *involtini* can be stuffed with a mixture of ground veal, pork, and a "finger" of mozzarella inserted in the middle. Done this way, they are called *uccelli scappati*, runaway birds. I sometimes cook them in a tomato sauce.

CODA DI MANZO BRASATA

Braised Oxtail **(Makes 6 servings)**

THIS IS A DELICIOUS STEW WHICH THE whole family will love. But pass plenty of napkins in case anyone wants to nibble on the bones.

My mother always made it the day before because, as with other dishes, she felt it was better the next day. And she was absolutely right. Besides, you can remove the fat on the surface much more easily at that point, since it will have congealed during the night.

3 pounds oxtail

2 tablespoons extra virgin olive oil

2 medium-size onions, coarsely chopped

2 medium-size carrots, peeled and cut into ¹/₂-inch rounds

1 tablespoon all-purpose flour

¹/₂ cup dry wine, white or red

2 ribs celery, trimmed and cut into slices

2 bay leaves

2 to 3 sprigs fresh parsley

8 peppercorns, crushed

3 whole cloves

4 cups hot water

1 top-quality Knorr beef bouillon cube

1. Trim the oxtail of all possible fat. In a large pot, heat 1 tablespoon of the oil. Add the oxtail and cook over medium-high heat, turning often, until brown on all sides, about 10 to 15 minutes. (Do not overcrowd the pot or the oxtail will not properly brown. Brown in two batches if necessary.)

2. Remove the meat to a bowl and discard all but 1 tablespoon of the fat from the pot. Add the remaining oil to the pot and add the onions. Cook over medium-high heat, stirring often, until soft and translucent, about 5 to 8 minutes. Stir in the carrots.

3. Sprinkle the flour over the onions and carrots, stir well, and return the meat to the pot. Add the wine and let evaporate. Add the celery, bay leaves, parsley, peppercorns, cloves, water, and bouillon cube.

4. Cover the pot, reduce the heat to medium-low, and cook until the meat is tender, about 3 to 4 hours. Stir every once in a while. Remove the bay leaves before serving.

NOTE 1: THIS IS NOT A SOUP AS IT IS CONCEIVED OF IN AMERICA, BUT A STEW. HOWEVER, MAKE SURE WHILE COOKING THAT THE SAUCE DOES NOT DRY OUT TOO MUCH. IF THIS HAPPENS ADD SOME HOT WATER.

NOTE 2: TO SKIM THE FAT OFF THE SURFACE, PLACE SOME PAPER TOWELS LOOSELY ON THE TOP AND PEEL OFF. YOU WILL SEE HOW MUCH FAT REMAINS ATTACHED TO THE PAPER. JULIA CHILD TAUGHT ME THIS TRICK.

BOLLITO MISTO

Boiled Meats **(Makes 8 or more servings)**

THIS IS A QUINTESSENTIAL, CLASSIC Italian dish which, for some strange reason, has never become popular in the United States. Comparable dishes can be found in almost every nation of the world. France has *pot au feu,* Austria *tafelspitz,* Ireland has its beef and cabbage. In the Middle East shines the Iranian *kalipacheh,* which literally means "head-to-foot," and that says it all. This type of food can contain almost every part of an animal.

It is only in New England that a similar dish appears. That is the famous and delicious Boiled Dinner. But even this very American rendition remains localized to that region.

Jasper White, the *mezzo Italiano* (half Italian) Bostonian chef, who considers himself a traditionalist, calls this type of food "hearty, earthy, and satisfying." And he is so right. In his restaurant the Boiled Dinner is delicious.

We Italians consider *il bollito misto* a great classic dish. In the best restaurants it is brought to the table on a special steam cart made of copper, with highly ornate brass handles and cupola lids. I am so fond of this dish that, although I make it often at home, when I go back to Italy I never fail to visit the elegant restaurant at the hotel Hassler–Villa Medici in Rome, where it is served with great flourish.

1 fresh beef tongue; or 2 calves' tongues
3 pounds beef rump or chuck roast
1 pound beef brisket
3 pounds veal shoulder, preferably with bone
2 pounds veal breast
1 calf's head
2 calf's feet
3 pounds turkey legs and thighs
1 large onion, cut with a cross at the bottom
2 whole cloves
2 to 3 sprigs fresh parsley

2 bay leaves
2 ribs celery, with leaves if possible
2 large carrots, peeled
10 peppercorns
1 large, ripe tomato; or 4 to 5 cherry tomatoes
1 jigger (2 ounces) vinegar
Salt to taste, optional
1 recipe Salsa Verde *(page 93)*
1 recipe Salsa per Bollito Misto di Mamma *(page 94)*

1. To remove the skin from the tongue, plunge the tongue or tongues into boiling water and cook 15 minutes. Cool and pull off and discard the skin. Set aside.

2. In a large stockpot, combine the tongue, chuck, brisket, and shoulder of veal. Add water to come 2 inches above the meats. Bring to a boil, reduce the heat to medium-low, and cook 1 hour. Add the breast of veal, the calf's head and feet, and the turkey. Stud the onion with the 2 cloves and then add to the pot. Add the parsley, bay leaves, celery, carrots, peppercorns, tomatoes, vinegar, and salt. Add more water to come 2 inches above the solids. Bring to a boil, reduce the heat to medium-low, cover the pot, and cook at a simmer for 2 to 3 hours. At a certain moment you may want to lift out the calf's head in order to remove the brains, which will otherwise overcook. Return the head to the pot.

3. Cool the meat in its broth for 15 minutes.

4. Strain the broth. Remove the vegetables and puree them in a food mill. (This will make a delicious creamy vegetable soup.)

5. Cut the larger pieces of meat into chunks, cut the tongue into thin slices. Serve with one or both of the sauces.

Their *bollito misto* is one of the best. Furthermore, the panorama from their terraced facade above the Spanish Steps is magnificent.

This dish can be accompanied by a number of sauces. The *salsa verde,* green sauce (page 93), is the classic one. My mother's favorite was *salsa di peperoni e pomodori,* pepper and tomato sauce (page 94). In northern Italy, a sauce with *cren,* or horseradish, is popular also. Still another favorite is an accompaniment of *sottaceti,* a colorful mixture of savory pickled vegetables, which can be found in Italian specialty stores.

The secret of *il bollito misto* is not just slow cooking, but the selection of the meats. One should have a mixture of veal, beef, and poultry. The best veal cuts are brisket, flank, breast, calf's head and feet, and, indispensably, one or two calves' tongues. For the beef, use shoulder, leg, round, rump, brisket, chuck, and of course, tongue. For poultry, I like to use turkey thighs and legs, which are available without having to buy the entire bird. The amounts of these meats depend on how many people you are going to serve. Keep in mind, though, that it doesn't pay to make a small quantity. First of all, the flavor will suffer, and second, leftovers do not pose a problem, because the meat can be reheated in its broth several times. And finally, the superb broth, of course, can be used in soups or risotto.

Since nowadays we have to care about our intake of fat, be sure to cool the broth overnight. I always make *bollito misto* the day before. This way I can remove all the fat which congeals on the top and reheat the meat in its own defatted broth.

You will not have a problem finding most of the recommended meats, but you may have to special order the head, feet, and tongue from a reliable butcher. Make sure to tell your butcher to trim all meats of as much fat as possible.

LA TRIPPA

(Makes 6 to 8 servings)

THIS DISH WAS SIMPLY CALLED THE TRIPE. We knew what it meant.

4 1/2 pounds tripe
2 leeks, halved lengthwise and well rinsed
2 ribs celery, washed and trimmed
2 medium-size carrots, peeled
2 strips lemon peel
2 tablespoons extra virgin olive oil
3 slices prosciutto with fat included, chopped

1 small diavoletto *(dried Italian hot red pepper), optional*
Salt to taste, optional
Freshly ground pepper to taste
1/2 cup dry white wine
One 16-ounce can tomato puree
Freshly grated parmesan or grana padano cheese to taste

1. Wash the tripe in several changes of water. Place in a pot and cover with water. Add the green parts of the leeks, 1 rib celery, 1 carrot, and the lemon peel. Bring to a boil over high heat, reduce the heat to medium-low, and simmer for 1 hour to soften the tripe. Cool in its own broth until it can be handled. Remove the tripe

continues

to a cutting board. Discard the broth and vegetables, and cut the tripe into thin strips, about $^{1}/_{4}$-inch thick and 3 to 4 inches long.

2. Cut the remaining leek, celery, and carrot into pieces and finely chop all together.

3. In a large skillet, heat the oil and add the prosciutto, cook a few seconds until it releases its flavor, then add the tripe, the *diavoletto*, the chopped vegetables, and season with salt, if used, and pepper. Cook over medium-high heat, stirring often, to develop the flavors, about 10 minutes. Add the wine and let evaporate. Add the tomato puree. Rinse the can with half a can of water, stirring to loosen any bits of tomato and add. Cover the pot, reduce the heat to low, and cook over very low heat until the tripe is tender, about 2 hours. Serve sprinkled with the grated cheese.

NOTE: THIS TRIPE IS BETTER THE DAY AFTER. REHEAT AND SIMMER 15 MINUTES.

Variation: *I turcinelli.* Mother's *turcinelli*, rolls, were famous. The recipe is so simple you do not need one. After boiling the tripe as in the above recipe, she used to cut the tripe into rectangular pieces 5 inches long and 3 inches wide. She sprinkled a generous mixture of chopped parsley and garlic on them. After rolling and tying the *turcinelli,* she would cook them in broth, any kind she had around, even one made with bouillon cubes. A small amount of diced carrot was added toward the end to make the dish more attractive when it was served.

LA TRIPPA
Tripe

It wasn't an everyday meal, but Papà would buy it fairly often whenever our butcher would tell him that he had some nice tripe. Although my mother was a master at preparing this, my father wouldn't leave her alone, making several excursions to the kitchen to tell her to add this or that. I was usually always around too, because tripe has always been one of my passions.

Quite often, on Sunday nights, after a movie, we would go to a *birreria*, a beer hall, where they serve beer and prepared food, to eat tripe. Some in Pescara were reknown for their tripe, but none compared to my mother's.

In this country there are only two kinds of tripe available, honeycomb and flat, because the government allows only certain parts of the intestine to be sold. Whichever you buy, make sure it is well cleaned. I always boil my tripe for 1 hour before using it.

ABOUT VEAL

Varro, a prolific Latin writer, called Italy the land of veal. And to this day, the preferred meat of Italy is, undoubtedly, veal. Even in Abruzzo, where lamb and pig reign supreme, veal is nevertheless greatly appreciated and deliciously cooked in many, many ways.

The meat of our veal is particularly flavorful because the cows, like the lamb, graze on the aromatic grass covering the slopes of our mountains.

However, not much of the veal sold in the markets nowadays, either in Abruzzo or the rest of Italy, is "nature veal," or *vitellino da latte*, milk-fed, which means that the animal has drunk only milk before coming to the butcher shop. This meat is very expensive and is usually reserved for cuts like *scaloppine*, cutlets, medallions, etc., and requires only brief cooking.

The conventional American veal, which is what we eat in this country, is the meat from 400-pound calves. It is still nice and flavorful, but not as tender as the Italian kind.

Veal, a delicate meat and easily combined with other elements, lends itself to be prepared with a myriad of condiments—wines, broth, vinegar, and most vegetables. It is an ideal meat to stuff, particularly with pork products, which provide the most interesting flavor, enhancing the subtlety of the veal and pleasantly contrasting sweet and strong elements. Some cuts take very swift cooking, others can stand long, gentle simmering. And, happily, veal is a nourishing meat, easily digestible, with very little fat, therefore a bonus for our modern diet.

SCALOPPINE AL MARSALA

Veal Marsala   (Makes 6 servings)

THIS IS PERHAPS ONE OF THE MOST COMmon ways of cooking veal scaloppine. It is simple and delicious, and is always appreciated.

I prefer to use a dry Marsala with this recipe rather than the traditional sweet one.

1 cup all-purpose flour
1 teaspoon sage, fresh or dried, finely chopped
Salt to taste, optional
Freshly ground pepper to taste

3 pounds veal scaloppine, pounded thin
2 tablespoons unsalted butter
2 tablespoons extra virgin olive oil
¼ cup Marsala wine
1 tablespoon minced fresh parsley

1. In a large bowl, combine the flour with the sage, salt, if used, and pepper. Dredge the scaloppine in this, but shake off the excess flour.

2. In a skillet large enough to hold the scaloppine in one flat layer, heat the butter and oil over high heat. (Do not overcrowd the skillet or the scaloppini will not brown properly. Brown in two batches if necessary, adding more butter and oil as necessary.) Add the scaloppine and sauté over medium-high heat, turning often, until lightly browned, 2 to 3 minutes on each side. Pour off the fat and add the wine. Scrape the bottom of the skillet underneath the scaloppine until the wine evaporates and the juices are slightly thickened. Sprinkle with parsley and serve.

continues

Variation 1: *Scaloppine al Limone*

For a more tangy flavor, substitute the Marsala with the juice of half, or more, lemon. Proceed as above.

Variation 2: *Medaglioni di Vitello al Marsala,* **Medallion of Veal Marsala**

Although similar to the scaloppine, these medallions have a more succulent sauce. After browning, the meat is removed to a plate and kept warm. Marsala is added to the pan, cooked over high heat for a few seconds, then 1 cup of broth and $^1/_2$ cup heavy cream are combined in the pan and simmered until the mixture starts to thicken. The sauce is then either poured on the medallion or served on the side. I like to serve them on a bed of spinach cooked in butter, or with a creamy potato puree (page 383).

NODINI DI VITELLO DELIZIA

Veal Chops Delizia *(Makes 4 servings)*

AS THE NAME OF THE RECIPE SAYS, THESE chops are a *delizia*, a delight.

Generally, I do not like undercooked meat, unless it is a good American steak, but be sure not to overcook these chops. The secret to a well-prepared chop is in not overcrowding the pan.

4 veal loin chops, about 12 to 14 ounces each, $1^1/_2$ inches thick
$^1/_4$ pound lean prosciutto, finely chopped
4 fresh sage leaves
Freshly ground pepper to taste
1 cup all-purpose flour, approximately, for dredging

2 tablespoons unsalted butter
1 tablespoon extra virgin olive oil
$^1/_4$ cup Marsala wine
About 1 cup chicken broth, preferably homemade (page 61), or good quality canned

1. Remove the ribbon of fat surrounding the chops and cut the larger side horizontally as to form a pocket. Fill each chop pocket with an equal amount of the chopped prosciutto and 1 leaf of sage. Sprinkle the chops with pepper and dredge lightly in the flour. Be careful that the stuffing does not fall out.

2. In a skillet large enough for the chops to fit in one flat layer, heat the butter and oil. Add the chops and cook over medium-high heat until brown, 4 to 5 minutes per side. Add the Marsala and scrape the bottom of the pan with a wooden spoon to dislodge the brown particles. Let the wine evaporate. Cook 5 to 8 more minutes, adding a little broth as needed to prevent scorching (see Note 1). Serve hot.

NOTE 1: THIS IS WHEN MY FROZEN BROTH CUBES (SEE BOX, PAGE 62) COME IN HANDY. A FEW CUBES WILL KEEP THE CHOPS FROM STICKING. THIS ELIMINATES THE NEED FOR MORE BUTTER OR OIL. I ALWAYS USE THEM WHEN BROWNING OR SAUTÉING. I ADD ONE OR TWO CUBES IF THE FOOD STARTS TO STICK, INSTEAD OF MORE BUTTER OR OIL. THEY ARE, OF COURSE, GREAT TO DEGLAZE A PAN.

NOTE 2: SWEET, TENDER PEAS ARE THE BEST ACCOMPANIMENT FOR THIS DISH.

Variation: *Costoletta di Vitello alla Me,* **Veal Chops My Style**

This is a quick recipe for when there is not much time to cook. The chops are lightly smeared with grainy mustard and browned in a little oil and butter.

COSTOLETTA DI VITELLO ALL'ORTOLANA

Veal Chop a la "Backyard" **(Makes 6 servings)**

ORTOLANA, AS I EXPLAINED PREVIOUSLY, means that a recipe contains ingredients from the backyard garden. In this case, tomatoes and arugula are used.

Choose rib chops that are not too thick. If they are too thick, ask your butcher to cut them in half as they should be no more then $^1/_2$-inch thick. Also ask your butcher to "French" them. This means to scrape the meat off the "handle" bone of the chop up to where the solid part is attached. When my brother was a child, he used to call this type of chops *la costoletta col manico*, the chop with the handle. He loved to brandish one and bite into it like a savage. At first, my mother would be furious, but then we would all laugh at his antics.

6 rib chops, cut in half lengthwise
About 2 cups plain bread crumbs
1 sprig fresh parsley, minced
3 sage leaves, minced, or $^1/_2$ teaspoon dried, crumbled
Freshly ground pepper to taste
3 large eggs
2 tablespoons milk

4 tablespoons extra virgin olive oil
1 to 2 tablespoons balsamic vinegar
1 bunch arugula, trimmed, well washed, and coarsely chopped
3 firm ripe tomatoes, diced
1 cup canola oil
Salt to taste, optional

1. If your chops are too thick, ask the butcher to split them in half and to scrape the "handle" of the chop, as suggested above. Place each chop between two pieces of waxed paper. With a meat pounder, flatten the meat to $^1/_4$-inch thickness. Be careful not to tear the meat.

2. In a large bowl, combine 1 cup or more of the bread crumbs with the parsley, sage, and pepper.

3. Beat the eggs with the milk, dip 1 chop at a time into the eggs and dredge the chops in the bread-crumb mixture. Pat the chops to make the crumbs adhere. Chill for 1 hour.

continues

4. Just before cooking the chops, combine 2 tablespoons of the olive oil and the balsamic vinegar in a large bowl. Add the arugula and tomatoes, but do not toss.

5. Pour the canola oil in a large skillet and add 2 tablespoons of the olive oil. Heat to the smoking point and fry the chops until nicely golden, 3 to 5 minutes on each side. Drain on paper towels. Sprinkle with some salt, if used.

6. Toss the arugula and tomato salad. Set 2 chops on individual plates, top with some of the salad, and serve.

Variation: For *Cotoletta alla Milanese,* proceed as per *Costoletta,* but omit the arugula and tomatoes.

VIVA LA COTELETTA
Hail the Cutlet

We loved cutlets with a passion. They seemed ever-present in our home. It was our school meal, our quick supper, an elegant second course for dinner, and always in a *panino,* sandwich, when we went skiing or boating. They are good hot and excellent cold. For some reason, they seem less popular in the United States these days. One rarely sees a simple cutlet in an Italian restaurant.

In Italy, the *cotoletta* is still widely appreciated, from Milano, where it originated, to Roma and Palermo, and in between.

Perhaps the "food terrorists" (to use Julia Child's favorite term for these nutritionist guardians of our health) have defeated the *cotoletta.* Of course, the real one is often dipped in egg and fried in butter, but once in a while, why not indulge in this delightful dish?

These cutlets can be prepared in advance and cooked at the last minute.

By the way, the real *cotoletta alla Milanese* is on the bone, but my mother made it the more commonly served way, with no bone.

ARROSTO DI VITELLO ALLE ERBE

Roast Veal with Herbs **(Makes 6 servings)**

Oil for the pan
2 slices prosciutto
1 clove garlic, peeled and smashed
1 tablespoon fresh rosemary leaves,
  or ¹/₂ tablespoon dried
1 teaspoon fresh thyme leaves,
  or ¹/₄ teaspoon dried

2 sprigs fresh parsley
4 pounds shoulder of veal,
  boned and tied
2 tablespoons extra virgin olive oil
Freshly ground pepper to taste
¹/₂ cup dry white wine
Salt to taste, optional

1. Preheat the oven to 375°F. Lightly oil a baking pan into which the veal fits snugly.

2. In a food processor, place the prosciutto, garlic, and herbs. Process until very finely chopped.

3. Pierce holes into the meat and lard it by inserting some of the chopped mixture into the holes. Smear the meat with the oil and place it in the prepared pan. Sprinkle with pepper. Roast until the veal starts to color, about 1 hour. Add half the wine and baste with the accumulated pan juices. Sprinkle with salt, if used. Continue cooking 30 to 45 minutes longer. Test for doneness by piercing the veal meat with a skewer; if juices are clear, the meat is done. Otherwise cook a little longer. Let rest 10 minutes before slicing.

4. Spoon off the fat from the pan in which the meat cooked. Add the remaining wine to the pan and scrape the brown particles clinging to the bottom and sides of the pan. If you want more sauce you can also add a little broth. Reheat and serve it with the meat.

VITELLO CON LA ROGNONATA

Veal with Kidney Stuffing **(Makes 6 to 8 servings)**

It is a pity that in this country, organ meats—apart from liver—are not popular at all. Apart from the available liver, it is almost impossible today even to find kidney, which is highly appreciated in French and other cuisines. All the regions of Italy have their own special ways of cooking these succulent morsels. In Abruzzo, the *coratella d'agnello*, a stew made with the organ meats of the lamb, is considered a delicacy, and it is absolutely delicious.

The following recipe was, and is, a favorite Sunday roast in my home. If the visibility of the kidney in it worries you, chop it coarsely and combine it with the rest of the filling. I am sure that if you do not elucidate about the ingredients, everybody will love the dish.

3 to 4 pounds veal loin

FILLING

1 large egg
2 tablespoons extra virgin olive oil
1/2 cup bread crumbs
1/4 cup milk, approximately
1 medium onion, chopped
1 carrot, chopped
1 to 3 sprigs fresh parsley, minced
1 rib celery, chopped
1 to 2 fresh sage leaves, or
  1/2 teaspoon dried
4 slices prosciutto, chopped
1/2 pound ground veal
Salt to taste, optional

Freshly ground black pepper
2 tablespoons butter
1 veal kidney, about 1 1/2 pounds, cut
  in half

ROASTING

2 tablespoons extra virgin olive oil
1 onion, quartered
1 carrot, cut into 4 pieces
1 rib celery, cut into 4 pieces
Salt to taste
Freshly ground pepper to taste
2 tablespoons unsalted butter
1/2 cup water
1/2 cup dry wine

1. Preheat the oven to 400°F.

2. Cut the veal in half lengthwise without cutting through to the bottom. Spread the veal meat in a rectangle by opening up the two sides of the veal as you would a book. Set aside.

3. In a mixing bowl, beat the egg and add the ingredients for the filling, except the kidney.

4. Spread half the filling on the inside of the roast. Arrange the 2 pieces of kidney in a line down the center lengthwise. Cover with the remaining filling to cover the kidney. Fold over the meat to enclose the filling. Secure with string. Cover the two ends of the roast with aluminum foil to secure the filling in.

5. In a roasting pan toss together the oil, onion, carrot, and celery. Set the meat on top of the vegetables, sprinkle with salt, if used, and pepper, and dot with the butter. Pour the water into the bottom of the pan and roast 20 minutes to condense the juices. Reduce the heat to 350°F. Turn the roast and baste often with the wine and the accumulated pan juices. Continue roasting until the juices of the roast run clear when pierced with a skewer, about 50 minutes longer. Remove the aluminum foil from the ends about 10 minutes before the roast is done.

6. Remove the roast from the pan and cover with foil to keep warm. With a slotted spoon, transfer the vegetables to a food processor and puree.

7. Untie the meat and slice it. Skim off the fat from the pan juices and pour the juices from the meat into a small pan. Add the pureed vegetables and rewarm. Pour some of the sauce on the meat; serve the remaining sauce separately.

BRACIOLONA RIPIENA DI CARCIOFI

Big Braciola Stuffed with Artichokes (Makes 6 to 8 servings)

THIS IS A GREAT-TASTING RECIPE. I CALL it *braciolona* because it is a large *braciola*, a slice of rolled stuffed meat. For this recipe you need a large slice of veal, which your butcher can prepare for you. Otherwise buy a loin of veal and, with a sharp knife, open it up like a book lengthwise, then open the two sides of the loin the same way and pound the meat flat with a meat pounder. Thus prepared, the meat can be stuffed and rolled as you please.

I am using artichokes for this *braciolona*, but other vegetables are also good.

4 baby artichokes
Juice of ¹/₂ lemon
5 tablespoons extra virgin olive oil
1 clove garlic, peeled and smashed
2 sprigs fresh parsley
3 pounds veal roast, preferably loin, opened, and pounded like a large braciola (see the description in head note)

Salt to taste, optional
Freshly ground pepper to taste
3 tablespoons extra virgin olive oil
3 large eggs, well beaten
¹/₄ cup dry wine
¹/₄ cup or more chicken broth, preferably homemade (page 61), or good quality canned broth

1. Trim away the tough leaves of the artichokes, cut off the tops, and slice them very thinly. Place in a bowl, add cold water to cover, and the juice of the lemon. (This is called acidulated water, and will prevent the artichokes from discoloring before being cooked.)

2. In a medium-size skillet, heat 2 tablespoons of the oil. Add the garlic and 1 sprig of parsley. Drain the artichokes but reserve some of the acidulated water. Add the artichokes to the skillet and cook over medium-high heat, stirring often, 2 to 3 minutes. Add ¹/₄ cup of the reserved water. Cover, reduce the heat to low, and steam, stirring occassionaly, until the artichokes are tender, about 10 minutes. Add a little more water if necessary to prevent scorching. Remove the sprig of parsley and the garlic, mince both together with the remaining sprig of parsley, and add to the artichokes. Set aside.

3. Make sure your meat is well pounded. Sprinkle the veal with salt, if used, and pepper, and set aside.

4. In a medium-size skillet, heat 1 tablespoon of the oil and pour in the eggs. Cook over medium heat until the bottom is set, 2 to 3 minutes. Turn and cook the *frittata* on the other side until set, about 3 minutes.

5. Lay the meat flat on a work surface, cover with the *frittata,* and spread the artichokes all over. Roll and tie with string. Wrap both ends of the roll with aluminum foil to secure the filling.

6. In a heavy-bottomed oval pan large enough to hold the roast, heat the remaining 2 tablespoons of oil. Remove the aluminum foil from the meat and cook over medium-high heat until brown on all sides, 10 to 15 minutes. Add the wine and let evaporate. Add the broth, reduce the heat to low, and cook, covered to concentrate the flavor, about 30 minutes. Remove the lid and continue cooking while the sauce reduces. Turn the meat often. When done, let the roll rest 15 minutes, covered with aluminum foil, before slicing it.

NOTE: THE *BRACIOLONA* CAN BE SERVED COLD. IT IS AN IDEAL DISH FOR A BUFFET, FOR WHICH IT CAN BE PREPARED ONE DAY IN ADVANCE. WHEN CUT, IT LOOKS VERY PRETTY.

VITELLO AROMATICO

Aromatic Veal **(Makes 6 servings)**

THIS DISH IS A TRULY EXCEPTIONAL ONE, and easy to cook, but calls for an unusual combination of spices and herbs.

How did this recipe come about? One explanation is that over the centuries, Abruzzo, like many parts of Italy, having been dominated by various invaders, absorbed some of the customs and usages introduced by these people. This is especially noticeable in cooking. *Vitello Aromatico* has a mixture of spices and herbs denoting Saracen, Spanish, and French influences.

It was during the Middle Ages that the use of spices, a sign of affluence, became prominent and continued to be so throughout the Renaissance. One reason for their popularity stemmed from the fact that the aroma

1/2 teaspoon freshly ground pepper
1/2 teaspoon cinnamon
1/2 teaspoon powdered cloves; or 2 whole cloves, ground
1/4 teaspoon nutmeg
Salt to taste, optional
1 1/2 teaspoons thyme
1 1/2 teaspoons marjoram
1 1/2 teaspoons rosemary
1 1/2 teaspoons tarragon
3 tablespoons extra virgin olive oil
2 tablespoons unsalted butter
3 pounds veal roast, shoulder or loin, tied with string

2 medium-size carrots, peeled and cut into pieces
1 rib celery, cut in two
1 bay leaf
1/2 cup dry Marsala wine
2 cups or more chicken or veal broth, preferably homemade (page 61)
24 pearl onions, with a cross cut at the bottom
1 teaspoon sugar
Sprigs of curly parsley for garnish

1. In a small bowl, combine all the spices, salt, if used, and herbs, but not the bay leaf, which is used later. Rub the meat all over with this mixture.

2. In a heavy-bottomed oval pan in which the meat can fit snugly, heat 2 tablespoons of the oil and 1 tablespoon of the butter. Add the veal, carrots, celery, and

continues

of meat had to be camouflaged with a lot of spices to offset the development of some unpleasant odors, due to the lack of refrigeration. Well, no matter the reason, some of these Renaissance dishes are still part of the cooking in the "grand manner" (important, fancy) of today's cuisine. This *Vitello Aromatico* is a good example. But the sapient mixing of the condiments is what turns this veal into an elegant, sophisticated dish whose assertive and yet elusive flavor will please the most educated palate.

Keep in mind that veal often exudes liquid. So add the broth a little at a time. The meat has to cook *in umido*, with humidity, meaning with a little liquid at all times, but not in a bath.

the bay leaf. Cook over medium-high heat until brown on all sides, 10 to 15 minutes. Add half of the Marsala, let evaporate. Add $^1/_4$ cup of the broth, cover the pan, and reduce to a simmer. Reserve $^1/_2$ cup of the broth and set aside. Add $^1/_2$ cup of the remaining broth, cover, and reduce the heat to low. Simmer until very tender, about $1^1/_2$ to 2 hours, adding more broth as necessary to keep the veal *in umido* (see head note, at left).

3. Remove the meat; reserve the pot. Cover the meat with aluminum foil and keep warm. Discard the bay leaf. Place all the sauce and vegetables in a food processor and puree. Set aside.

4. Add the remaining oil and butter to the pot. Heat and add the onions and cook over medium-high heat, stirring often, until they start to color, about 5 minutes. Sprinkle with the sugar, stir, and add the remaining Marsala. Cook over medium heat, stirring often, until the onions are tender, about 20 minutes. Remove the onions to a plate. Keep warm. Add $^1/_4$ cup of the remaining broth and, with a wooden spoon, scrape the brown particles clinging to the bottom and sides of the pot. Add more broth. You should have $1^1/_4$ cups of liquid in the pot. If not, add a little water. Bring to a boil and reduce to 1 cup. Add the pureed vegetables, stir, and warm up.

5. Slice the meat and place it on a serving plate. Surround the meat with the onions. Pour some of the sauce on the meat; serve the remaining sauce on the side. Garnish the plate with the parsley.

NOTE: PORK CAN BE MADE THIS WAY TOO.

CARNE ALLA GENOVESE

Carne Genovese Style (Makes 6 to 8 servings)

MY AUNT ELA WAS FAMOUS FOR HER *Carne alla Genovese*, which is a pot roast, and it means "meat in the style of Genoa." So what does this dish have to do with the cooking of Abruzzo? It seems that during the sixteenth century the region was a center for commerce in wool, sheep, and saffron. Its capital, L'Aquila, at the very center of Italy, hosted merchants from all over the country and from abroad. Some of these "foreigners" remained and settled in small colonies. In fact many streets in the city are named after the regions or nationalities of these people. So there is a *via dei Veneziani, via dei Francesi, via dei Lombardi,* and *via dei Genovesi.* It is from the Genovese colony that the locals learned to cook meat according to their custom, hence *Carne alla Genovese.*

The sauce of this dish is also excellent to dress pasta, especially penne, rigatoni, and fusilli.

1 slice prosciutto
1 teaspoon rosemary
1 clove garlic, peeled
3 pounds shoulder of veal
2 large onions
2 whole cloves
2 tablespoons unsalted butter

2 tablespoons extra virgin olive oil
1 carrot, peeled and cut in two
1 or 2 sprigs fresh parsley
Salt to taste, optional
Freshly ground pepper to taste
1/2 cup dry white wine

1. Chop together the prosciutto, rosemary, and garlic. Lard the meat with this mixture (see Step 3, page 323). Tie the meat with string to keep in shape.

2. Peel the onions and cut a cross at the bottom. Stick the cloves into the onions.

3. In a heavy-bottomed pot in which the meat can fit snugly, heat the butter and oil. Add the meat, onions, carrot, and parsley. Cook over medium-high heat until the meat is browned on all sides, 10 to 15 minutes. Season with salt, if used, and pepper, and add the wine. Let evaporate.

4. Add enough water to come halfway up the meat. Bring to a boil over high heat, cover, reduce the heat to low, and cook until the meat is tender, about $1^{1}/_{2}$ hours. The liquid should reduce by half. If the evaporation is too fast, add a little more water as needed to keep the veal quite moist.

5. When the meat is done, transfer the vegetables to a food processor or a food mill, using a slotted spoon, and puree.

6. Remove the meat to a cutting board and cover with foil to keep warm. Degrease the liquid in the pot and add the pureed vegetables. Slice the meat, warm the sauce, and serve.

NOTE: YOU CAN SERVE THE MEAT WITH POLENTA, PLAIN RICE, OR YOUR FAVORITE VEGETABLE.

VITELLO SAPORITO ALL'ADRIANA

Flavorful Veal Adriana   (*Makes 8 servings or more*)

ADRIANA IS THE YOUNGEST OF MY THREE beloved cousins. Although I am older than she, we are like sisters. She was like my "baby" when I was a teenager. I taught her how to read when she was barely five, but even before that, I made her swim with the "grown-ups," and climb mountains at four o'clock in the morning. She used to follow me like a puppy, at times unwillingly. She is now the happy mother of six off-spring and married to a pediatrician, fortunately. In the summer, her children come to visit from Italy and it is a joy. Their father says that each one has the personality of an only child, and this is so true. But because of their individualism, it is such fun to have them around, one or two at a time! It seems that all of them are interested in food, and often give me recipes. What can you expect? It was one of them, Carlo, not yet five, whom I caught slivering truffles on bread and butter for his afternoon snack. Good taste must run in the family!

This simple recipe is in Adriana's *repertorio*, and now mine. We call it *saporito*, flavorful, because the taste and perfume of the porcini mushrooms are the enhancers that make this delectable dish so *saporito*. The addition of milk in the sauce of the veal is an ancient Abruzzese tradition.

4 pounds veal, loin or shoulder, boned
¼ pound thin prosciutto slices
2 tablespoons unsalted butter
1 tablespoon extra virgin olive oil
1 medium-size onion, thinly sliced
¼ cup dry Marsala wine
½ cup dried porcini mushrooms, soaked
   in 1 cup lukewarm water for 20 minutes
1 tablespoon all-purpose flour
2 cups milk

1. Wrap the veal entirely with the prosciutto slices. Tie with string.

2. Place the butter and oil in a heavy pot in which the veal can fit snugly. Heat and add the meat and the onion. Cook over medium-high heat, turning often, until brown on all sides, 10 to 15 minutes. Add the Marsala and let evaporate.

3. Gently lift the mushrooms from the water without disturbing the sediment at the bottom. Strain the soaking water through a paper towel or coffee filter. Set aside. Chop the mushrooms coarsely and add to the meat. Filter the water from the mushrooms through a paper towel and combine it with the flour and milk, then add to the meat. Cover the pot, reduce the heat to low, and simmer until the meat is tender and the sauce has condensed, about 1½ to 2 hours. If the sauce tends to thicken too much, add a little water. When the meat is done, remove it to a platter, cover it with aluminum foil, and let it rest 15 minutes. Slice the meat, reheat the sauce if necessary, and serve.

NOTE: SERVE WITH POLENTA OR RICE.

Variation: Instead of dried porcini, use the same amount of dried tomatoes.

PETTO DI VITELLO BRASATO

Braised Breast of Veal (Makes 4 to 6 servings)

THIS IS A SIMPLE AND INEXPENSIVE MEAL. The meat is gently simmered in a pot. Pearl onions are added in the last half hour or so.

When we were children, my brother and I loved to chew the white cartilage bones that are part of the breast. In Milan, these are considered a delicacy and are an important part of a tangy, lemony, garlicky antipasto called *insalata di nervetti*.

Keeping in mind that there are a lot of bones in a piece of breast, the quantity in pounds suggested for this recipe, which will serve 4 to 6 people, is appropriate.

8 to 9 pounds breast of veal, with bones in
1 tablespoon extra virgin olive oil
Salt to taste, optional
Freshly ground pepper to taste
1 tablespoon mixture of Seven Herbs (see head note, pages 297–98)

¹/₂ pound pearl onions, peeled and with a cross cut at the bottom of each onion
¹/₂ cup wine, red or white

1. Trim all the visible fat from the breast of veal.

2. Lightly oil the bottom of a heavy pot in which the breast can fit snugly. If necessary, cut the breast into 2 to 3 pieces and add to the pot. Pour in enough water to just cover the meat. Add the seasoning and the herbs. Cover and cook over medium-low heat until the water has evaporated and the meat has started to brown, about 2 hours. At this point turn the meat once or twice. It should be fork tender; if not, add a little water and continue cooking. Remove the meat to a platter.

3. Skim off the excess fat from the pan juices and add the onions to the pan. Sauté until lightly browned, 3 to 5 minutes. Return the meat to the pan and add the wine, cover, and simmer until the onions are cooked, 10 to 15 minutes. You may need to add some hot water, but keep the onions a little al dente. Let the meat rest for 5 minutes before slicing. Serve with the onions and its own sauce.

NOTE: OTHER VEGETABLES LIKE CARROTS, POTATOES, AND BROCCOLI CAN BE ADDED. ADD THE POTATOES HALF AN HOUR BEFORE FINISHING THE MEAT.

FEGATO DI VITELLO CON LE CIPOLLE E CAPPERI

Calf's Liver with Onions and Capers *(Makes 2 servings)*

IN MY HOME THIS DISH ALSO INCLUDED the lungs and the heart. It was a succulent stew and we all loved it.

3 tablespoons all-purpose flour

¼ teaspoon Seven Herbs (see head note, pages 297–98)

2 slices calves' liver, about 1 ¼ pounds total

2 tablespoons unsalted butter

2 tablespoons extra virgin olive oil

1 large red onion, sliced

1 tablespoon capers in brine, drained

1 small bunch rosemary

2 tablespoons Marsala wine

1 tablespoon minced fresh parsley

1. Combine the flour with the Seven Herb mixture. Dredge the liver in it and shake off the excess flour. Set aside.

2. In a large skillet, heat 1 tablespoon of the butter and 1 tablespoon of the oil. Add the onion and cook, stirring often, over low heat until the onion is quite soft, 8 to 10 minutes. Add the capers and cook just a few seconds to blend briefly. With a slotted spoon, remove the onion mixture to a bowl and keep warm.

3. Add the remaining butter and oil to the skillet, if needed. If you have enough fat in the skillet, add only the remaining butter or the remaining oil. Add the rosemary and liver and cook over medium-high heat until lightly browned, about 2 minutes per side. Remove the liver to a serving plate, pour off the fat, and add the Marsala to the skillet and let evaporate. Return the onion to the skillet to warm up and then spoon over the liver, sprinkle with the minced parsley, and serve.

ABOUT LAMB

Abruzzo is indeed a pastoral land where sheep—the white herds and their colorful shepherds—roam. In September they descend from the mountains and move south to their winter pastures in Apulia. I remember how beautiful it was to see the herd winding along the beach, which we, the locals, had finally reconquered from the tourists. It meant that the shepherds had started the ancient rite of the *trasumaza*, the herding which is repeated every year. They travel on the ancestral *tratturo*, a trail which runs along the coast of the Adriatic. In the spring, they will return the same way to their mountain habitats. There is a wonderful poem written by Gabriele D'Annunzio which describes this bucolic journey. It starts:

September, let's go—it is time to migrate— it is now that my shepherds leave the mountains and go towards the sea . . .

Such animal husbandry has a long history in Abruzzo and, not surprisingly, traditional cuisine has always centered on lamb and kid. Their meat is renowned for the lean, delicate, not fatty taste. This is due to the aromatic herbs on which the herds graze.

Even mutton is appreciated in Abruzzo. Some of the recipes for it go back to time immemorial. Unfortunately, one can only enjoy these specialties locally, often cooked by the shepherds themselves.

There are other ancient recipes for the cooking of goat. *Capra alla montanara* (page 344), a typical recipe from the mountains, is an exquisite prepara-

tion done mostly in September when this meat is most flavorful.

The *castrato*, meat of a castrated male sheep, is another great specialty that is seldom cooked in the home. Fortunately, it is sometimes served in local restaurants of the chain Buon Ricordo, The Good Remembrance, an association of restaurateurs dedicated to re-creating dishes from the past.

In the United States, as a practical matter, it is impossible to reproduce these ancient dishes exactly. Certain types of meats mentioned above are not available here. But a number of recipes can be adapted. I have tried them using American lamb, which I find excellent. It doesn't taste exactly the same as the genuine dish, but why not try it anyway? The dishes are still delicious in their own "American" way.

COSTOLETTE DI AGNELLO IN PORCHETTA

Porchetta-style Lamb Chops (Makes 6 servings)

PORCHETTA IS THE METHOD USED TO COOK a young pig on a spit in a wood-burning oven. This recipe puts together the two most beloved flavors of Abruzzo, lamb and pork. The pork in this case is caul fat, which is a lacy membrane covering part of the intestine, sold in butcher shops, usually frozen. I suggest you order yours in advance.

2 cups loosely packed basil leaves
1 sprig fresh parsley
2 cloves garlic
2 tablespoons extra virgin olive oil
12 lamb rib chops, no more then 1 inch thick, trimmed of all fat

6 pieces of caul fat large enough to wrap 2 chops together
1 sprig fresh rosemary, or 1 teaspoon dried
1/2 cup dry white wine

1. In a food processor, place the basil, parsley, and garlic. Add the oil and process until finely chopped.

continues

It is a very aromatic recipe with the sweet flavor of basil and the pervasive aroma of rosemary.

2. Preheat the oven to 375°F.

3. Choose 2 chops of similar size. Spread some of the basil mixture on one side of a chop, cover with the second chop, like a sandwich, and set aside. Repeat until you have sandwiched all the chops. Wrap each sandwich with a piece of caul and set them in a baking pan large enough to hold them in one layer. Break the sprig of rosemary into pieces and add to the pan among the packages. Place the pan in the oven and roast until the chops start to brown, about 1½ hours. Remove the pan from the oven, pour off all the fat, and add the wine. Return the pan to the oven and cook until the chops are done, about 10 to 15 minutes longer. Serve hot.

NOTE: ITALIANS DO NOT LIKE PINK LAMB. ADJUST COOKING TIME ACCORDINGLY IF YOU LIKE IT LESS DONE.

AGNELLO ALLO STAZZO

Roast Stuffed Lamb Shepherd's Style (Makes 8 servings)

LO STAZZO IS AN ENCLOSURE WHERE SHEEP are kept in the warm season during the night. Shepherds sleep under tents while their beautiful Abruzzesi sheep-dogs keep watch. This is a dish that the shepherds cook in improvised stone ovens. I remember, during my mountain-climbing days, marveling at these primitive constructions when-ever we encountered a *stazzo*. If we were lucky and the shepherds were cooking, pieces of meat were gener-ously offered, and they tasted absolutely delicious. As a matter of fact, when my friends rave about this dish, I cannot help telling them, "You should have tasted the one cooked by the shepherds!"

¼ cup extra virgin olive oil
1 small diavoletto *(dried Italian hot red pepper)*
¾ pound lamb liver or chicken livers, diced
Salt to taste, optional
1 large egg, lightly beaten
2 to 3 tablespoons grated pecorino cheese (Abruzzese, romano, or sardo)

One 4- to 5-pound leg of lamb, boned but not butterflied
Freshly ground black pepper to taste
1 sprig fresh rosemary, or ½ teaspoon dried
2 to 3 cloves garlic, peeled
½ cup dry red wine

1. Preheat the oven to 375°F.

2. In a medium skillet, heat 2 tablespoons of the oil over medium heat and add the *diavoletto* and liver. Cook over medium-high heat, stirring, until the liver starts to color, 2 to 3 minutes. Add the salt, if used. Remove to a mixing bowl, discard the *diavoletto*, and stir in the egg and cheese. Cook until the eggs are scrambled. Fill the cavity of the lamb from which the bone has been removed with this mixture. Secure the meat with kitchen string.

Ask the butcher for a leg of lamb with the bone removed, but without splitting or butterflying the flesh.

3. Place the remaining oil in a baking pan large enough to hold the lamb snugly. Add the lamb and roll it in the oil so that it is nicely coated. Sprinkle with pepper and add the rosemary. Scatter the garlic around. If necessary, cover the two ends of the roast with a bit of aluminum foil to keep the stuffing in place. Roast until the lamb starts to brown, about 45 minutes. Pour the wine over the lamb.

4. Wet a brown paper bag and cover the lamb with it. This will keep the roast moist. Continue baking 1 to 1 1/2 hours, depending on how well done you like your meat. Baste every once in a while with the cooking juices. Let rest 15 minutes before slicing.

NOTE: AS I SAID PREVIOUSLY, WE ITALIANS DO NOT LIKE LAMB PINK. FOR US THE MEAT IS DONE IF THE JUICES RUN CLEAR WHEN PIERCED WITH A SKEWER. HOWEVER, WHEN USING A MEAT THERMOMETER, INSERT IT INTO THE MEAT, AWAY FROM THE BONE, REMOVE IT, AND TAKE A READING. DO NOT LEAVE THE THERMOMETER IN THE MEAT. THESE ARE THE INTERNAL TEMPERATURES FOR ROASTING LAMB:

130°....................................RARE
150°....................................MEDIUM
170° TO 180°......................WELL-DONE

ABBACCHIO AL FORNO

Roasted Abbacchio **(Makes 8 servings or more)**

ABBACCHIO IS MILK-FED BABY LAMB. THE name is dialect and it is used mostly in Rome where the *abbacchio* is a specialty. But in adjacent regions, such as Abruzzo, the same name is used because of its proximity to the region of Rome, the Latium. In fact, the recipes are quite similar. The meat is so tender with its unique flavor that most of the time it is simply roasted with very little embellishment. Kid, or baby goat, can be roasted the same way.

This recipe has a pinch of pecorino cheese which, together with the ubiquitous *diavoletto*, makes it quite Abruzzese.

Since this type of lamb is very bony, I recommend you buy an entire half of the lamb. It is so delicious you will not have much left.

1 cup plain bread crumbs
3 tablespoons grated pecorino romano cheese
3 cloves garlic, minced
2 tablespoons minced fresh parsley
¼ cup extra virgin olive oil

Half a baby lamb, about 10 pounds (available from specialty butcher shops)
¾ cup dry wine, red or white
2 bay leaves
Salt to taste, optional
Freshly ground pepper to taste

1. In a small bowl, combine the bread crumbs, cheese, garlic, and parsley.

2. Lightly oil a baking pan with 1 to 2 tablespoons of the oil and place the lamb in it. Preheat the oven to 400°F.

3. With your hands, rub the oil all over the lamb. Pat the bread-crumb mixture over and underneath the lamb to adhere. Place in the oven, pour the wine all around but not on top. Add the bay leaves. Season with salt and pepper. Bake 30 minutes to seal in the juices. Reduce the heat to 350°F and continue baking until very tender, about 1½ hours. Baste often. Cut the meat into serving pieces and serve with the pan juices.

NOTE: I LIKE TO PUT SOME POTATOES AROUND OR UNDERNEATH THE LAMB BEFORE BAKING. DRESS THE POTATOES WITH A LITTLE OIL AND ROSEMARY.

ABBACCHIO ALLA CACCIATORA

Baby Lamb Cacciatore (*Makes 6 servings*)

THIS VERY TYPICAL ABRUZZESE RECIPE IS succulent and delicious. It is not easy to find *abbacchio* here, but a good Italian butcher can get it for you. I use good American baby lamb for this recipe, also with excellent results. Kid can be made this way, as well.

6 pounds abbacchio, *or baby lamb, cut into serving pieces*

¹/₄ cup wine vinegar

1 diavoletto *(dried Italian red hot pepper)*

8 cloves garlic, peeled

4 anchovy fillets, drained

2 sprigs fresh parsley

2 sprigs of fronds of a fennel bulb; or use dill

1 sprig fresh rosemary

¹/₄ cup extra virgin olive oil

1 rib celery, trimmed and cut into thin slices

Juice of 1 lemon

Salt to taste, optional

1. Place the pieces of meat in a bowl, cover with water, and add 2 tablespoons of the vinegar. Let stand for 15 minutes.

2. Break the *diavoletto* in half and remove the seeds. In a food processor, make a pesto with half of this pepper, 4 cloves of the garlic, 2 anchovy fillets, 1 sprig of parsley, 1 sprig of the fennel fronds, and half of the rosemary. Process until finely chopped. Transfer to a small bowl and add to it 1 tablespoon of the vinegar. Set aside.

3. Drain the meat and pat dry. In a large skillet, heat the remaining oil, and without chopping, add the remaining *diavoletto*, garlic, herbs, and celery. Sauté briefly and add the meat. Cook over medium-high heat, stirring often, until the celery is softened and the meat is brown, about 10 minutes.

4. Add the remaining 1 tablespoon of vinegar, the juice of the lemon, and salt, if used. Cook, stirring, until the juices are slightly reduced. Add the pesto and stir, then add ¹/₂ cup of water. Stir, cover the skillet, and cook over medium heat until the meat is tender, about 25 to 30 minutes. If the juices tend to evaporate, add a little more water so that a little sauce remains. Serve hot.

> **NOTE:** IF YOU WISH, REMOVE THE UNCHOPPED HERBS AND GARLIC. SINCE THIS IS SUCH A RUSTIC DISH, I DO NOT BOTHER. I SEE THAT WHOEVER GETS THEM, EATS THE SPRIGS AND GARLIC WITH GREAT GUSTO!

AGNELLO ALLE ERBE VITA-COLONNA

Lamb with Herbs Vita-Colonna **(Makes 8 servings or more)**

THIS RECIPE HAS ALWAYS INCLUDED OUR family name. It has an intensely herbivorous flavor. When I cannot find fresh mint, I use the bottled mint sauce and it works well with this preparation. I do not recommend using dried mint.

3 slices prosciutto, fat included
2 cloves garlic, peeled
2 teaspoons fresh rosemary leaves,
  or 1 teaspoon dried
2 teaspoons fresh oregano,
  or 1 teaspoon dried
2 to 3 sprigs fresh parsley
1/4 cup fresh mint leaves
6 tablespoons wine vinegar
  or balsamic vinegar

2 tablespoons water
1 teaspoon sugar
One 5- to 6-pound leg of lamb,
  trimmed of fat
2 to 3 tablespoons extra virgin olive oil
Freshly ground pepper to taste
Salt to taste, optional
3/4 cup fresh plain bread crumbs
1/2 cup finely minced fresh parsley

1. Preheat the oven to 400°F.

2. In a food processor, chop the prosciutto, garlic, rosemary, oregano, and parsley. Process until finely chopped. Remove from the bowl and set aside.

3. In the same food processor, combine the mint leaves, vinegar, water, and sugar. Process until the mint is finely chopped. Remove from the bowl and set aside.

4. Pierce several holes in the leg of the lamb and lard the meat with the chopped prosciutto mixture (see Step 3, page 323).

5. Pour the oil into a baking pan. Roll the leg of lamb in it so that the meat is evenly coated with the oil. Grind a good amount of pepper over and pour 3/4 cup water into the bottom of the pan. Roast 20 minutes to seal in the juices. Reduce the heat to 350°F. Season with salt, if used, and roast until the meat is almost done, about 2 hours longer. Baste once in a while with the pan juices.

6. Combine the bread crumbs and the minced parsley with the mint and vinegar mixture. Spread this mixture on a large platter or cookie sheet. Using rubber gloves or a kitchen towel grab the lamb by the bone and roll the leg in the bread-crumb mixture. Make sure the lamb is evenly coated, if not, pat some of the mixture on the bare spots. Return the lamb to the oven and continue roasting 10 to 15 minutes

longer, or until the lamb is cooked as desired and the crust is lightly browned, 10 to 15 minutes longer. Baste once or twice. Cool 15 minutes before carving.

NOTE: WHEN USING THE MINT SAUCE, ELIMINATE THE VINEGAR FROM THE RECIPE. IF YOU LIKE, AFTER POURING OFF MOST OF THE FAT, DEGLAZE THE PAN WITH A LITTLE WINE OR BROTH TO MAKE A NICE SAUCE AND SERVE IT WITH THE MEAT.

AGNELLO ALLA BRACE

Barbecued Lamb **(Makes 8 to 10 servings)**

THE ABRUZZESI COOK LAMB IN MANY ways, from simply grilled, like this recipe, to elaborate casseroles, stews, *ragù* (page 100), and lamb sauces which can be used to dress *l'sagne* (page 155), the local broad noodles, similar to *pappardelle*.

One 5-pound leg of lamb, cut into 3/4-inch steaks
2 cloves garlic, sliced
2 sprigs fresh mint, chopped, or 1 teaspoon dried

2 sprigs fresh rosemary, chopped, or 1 teaspoon dried
Juice of 1 lemon
3 tablespoons extra virgin olive oil
Salt to taste, optional
Freshly ground pepper to taste

1. Place the lamb steaks in a nonreactive pan.

2. In a small bowl, combine the garlic, mint, rosemary, lemon juice, oil, salt, and pepper. Mix well and pour over the lamb. Let stand 1 hour at room temperature, or 2 to 3 hours longer if refrigerated. Turn the meat a few times.

3. Remove the meat from the marinade and grill, preferably over charcoal, about 8 minutes per side, basting often with the marinade.

NOTE: FOR A DIFFERENT FLAVOR, USE 1/4 CUP BALSAMIC VINEGAR INSTEAD OF LEMON JUICE.

AGNELLO AGRODOLCE

Sweet and Sour Lamb (Makes 6 servings)

THE SHEEP OF ABRUZZO SPEND THE WIN-
ter on the southern plains of Apulia.
Lamb is popular there too. This is why
I decided to include this recipe which
comes from the Guerra family who
live in that region. They own the
exclusive hotel Il Melograno, an oasis
of peace and subdued elegance, near
the region's capital city of Bari. The
white, gracious buildings of the complex (one of which dates back to the
seventeenth century) are nestled in a
bucolic landscape of thousand-year-
old olive trees. It is one of my most
favorite places to spend a holiday, and
this recipe is delightful, simple, and
tasty.

3 tablespoons extra virgin olive oil
3 bay leaves
6 cloves garlic, peeled and smashed
3 pounds lamb meat from the leg,
  cut into large cubes
Salt to taste, optional
Freshly ground pepper to taste
3/4 cup dry white wine
Juice of 1 lemon
2 teaspoons sugar
2 sprigs fresh parsley

1. In a large skillet, heat the oil and add the bay leaves and 5 of the cloves of garlic. Cook over medium-high heat until the garlic starts to sizzle, 2 to 3 minutes.
Add the lamb and cook until browned, 5 to 8 minutes. You may need to do this in
batches. Return all the meat to the skillet if you have separated it, season with salt,
if used, and pepper, and add the wine. Reduce the heat to low, cover the skillet,
and cook, stirring every once in while, until the lamb is tender, about 1 1/2 hours. If
you should have too much liquid, remove the lid and reduce. Add the lemon juice
and sugar. Stir well.

2. Chop together the remaining clove garlic and parsley and add to the skillet, stir,
and serve at once.

FRICASSEA DI CAPRETTO ALL'OSCURA

Kid Stew "in the Dark" *(Makes 6 servings)*

I ADAPTED THIS DELICIOUS RECIPE FROM one from the School of Villa Santa Maria. It reflects the efforts of their teachers to blend with past traditions while adding touches of modern sophistication.

It is called "in the dark" because at the end, between the mushrooms and the truffles, the dish appears rather dark.

2 legs of kid, 4 to 5 pounds each, approximately, cubed, with bone left in
1/4 cup wine vinegar
Salt to taste, optional
1 cup all-purpose flour, approximately, plus 1 tablespoon
2 tablespoons extra virgin olive oil
2 ounces fresh lard, chopped, or same amount prosciutto fat

1 small onion, finely chopped
1 pound fresh mushrooms, trimmed and coarsely chopped
1 cup sparkling wine, preferably Prosecco
1/2 cup chicken or beef broth, preferably homemade (page 61), or good quality canned broth or bouillon
1 small black truffle

1. Place the kid meat in a bowl with the vinegar. Cover with water and let stand for 20 minutes. Drain and pat dry with paper towels. Combine the salt, if used, and the 1 cup of flour and dredge the pieces of kid in this mixture. Shake off the excess flour. Reserve the flour.

2. In a large skillet, heat the oil, add the lard or prosciutto fat, and cook 5 minutes, then add the kid. Cook over medium-high heat, turning often, until slightly colored, about 10 minutes. Add the onion and let the meat brown, then add the mushrooms. Cook over medium-high heat until the water put out by the mushrooms has been absorbed.

3. Add the wine and let evaporate. Sprinkle the whole with 1 tablespoon of the reserved flour, stir, and add the broth. Reduce the heat to low and cook, stirring often, until the meat is tender, about 1 1/2 hours total.

4. Brush off any possible residue of sand from the truffle, slice it very finely, and add to the meat. Cook 5 minutes and serve.

NOTE: TRUFFLES ARE EXPENSIVE, BUT ONCE IN A WHILE ONE CAN INDULGE IN THIS DELICACY. HOWEVER, A LESS EXPENSIVE SOLUTION IS TO USE A GOOD TEASPOON OR TWO OF TRUFFLE PASTE.

CREPATELLA DI AGNELLO
ALLA TERAMANA

Lamb Stew in the Style of Teramo (Makes 6 servings)

Crepatella is a dialect variation of *capra* (goat). This dish, a specialty of Teramo, a city famous for its gastronomy, is traditionally made with goat.

I use lamb, which, in the United States, is more readily available than goat. But if you can find goat, this will be a treat. For this dish, the most appropriate part of the goat to use is *il muscolo,* the shin.

6 lamb shins; or 3 pounds lamb meat cut from the leg, cubed
$\frac{1}{2}$ cup water
$\frac{1}{2}$ cup white wine
4 bay leaves
2 sprigs fresh rosemary
1 small diavoletto *(dried Italian hot red pepper)*
2 medium-size onions, cut in half and each half cut into 3 pieces
2 tablespoons extra virgin olive oil
1 teaspoons tomato paste
One 8-ounce can tomato puree
1 tablespoon minced fresh parsley

1. If using the shins, remove the bones and reserve. Cube the meat and remove all visible fat.

2. Place the meat, water, wine, bay leaves, and 1 sprig of rosemary in a large pan. Add the bones of the shins, if you are using them. Bring to a boil over high heat. Reduce the heat to low and simmer 30 minutes. Add the pepper, onions, olive oil, tomato paste, and the tomato puree. Cook at a simmer, covered, until the meat is tender, about 1 hour. If the liquid tends to evaporate too much, add some more water. Serve sprinkled with parsley.

NOTE: IF YOU SHOULD WANT TO DO THIS DISH WITH GOAT, FIRST BOIL THE MEAT IN WATER FOR 1 HOUR. DISCARD THE WATER AND PROCEED AS ABOVE.

Agnello o Capretto Cacio e 'Ovo

Lamb or Kid with Cheese and Egg Sauce (Makes 10 to 12 servings)

THERE IS NO HOUSEHOLD IN ABRUZZO that does not make this delicious dish at Easter. In my home, we always wondered why we didn't have it more often.

During the Easter season, it is served first in the middle of Lent, when, as the Catholic calendar allows, there is a break in the strict rule of almost no meat for forty days, and then again on Easter Sunday. In my household, on Easter we almost always served kid (baby goat) instead of the lamb, which was made, as the tradition commands, *cacio e 'ovo* (cheese and egg).

This is an ancient dish with Greek origins. It was probably imported by Abruzzesi shepherds who, in winter, traveled south with their herds toward the friendly colonies of Magna Grecia (today the regions of Apulia, Calabria, Campania, and Sicily).

The reason the kid or lamb is cooked with this egg sauce is because the lamb and the egg are the traditional symbols of Easter. During Holy Week, shops are decorated with these symbols. Processions pass through the streets, where the balconies are adorned with splendid hangings of silk and velvet, colorful lanterns, and flowers. The churches display great representations of the death of Christ with antique statuary and depicting scenes

continues

*1 baby lamb, about 10 pounds; or a
    12- to 14-pound kid, cut into small
    pieces without removing the bone*
¹/₄ cup extra virgin olive oil
1 medium-size onion, sliced
1 sprig fresh rosemary, or 1 teaspoon dried
Salt to taste, optional
Freshly ground pepper to taste

1 cup dry red wine
*1 cup chicken or beef broth, preferably
    homemade (page 61), or a good quality
    canned broth*
6 large eggs
²/₃ cup freshly grated parmesan cheese
Juice of ¹/₂ lemon
¹/₄ cup minced fresh parsley

1. Quickly rinse the meat, pat dry, and set aside.

2. In a large skillet heat the oil. Add the onion and sauté over medium-high heat, stirring often, until softened, about 5 minutes. Add the meat and brown, turning the pieces often, about 10 minutes. (Do in two batches if necessary. Do not overcrowd the pan.) Add the rosemary, salt, if used, and pepper. Add the wine and let evaporate. Add ¹/₄ cup of the broth, cover the skillet, reduce heat to low, and cook slowly, adding more broth as needed to prevent scorching. Do not let the liquid dry up completely. This step will take 1 to 2 hours, depending on how tender the meat is. Taste the meat to make sure it doesn't overcook.

3. In a bowl, beat the eggs, add the cheese, a pinch of pepper, the lemon juice, and parsley. Pour the mixture over the meat. Stir and cook a few minutes until the eggs coagulate. Serve at once.

NOTE: THE BEST ACCOMPANIMENT FOR THESE SPECIALTIES IS A SEASONAL *SPEZZATINO* (A QUICK SAUTÉ) OF BABY ARTICHOKES AND TENDER PEAS (PAGE 370).

dating back to the sacred theater of the Middle Ages.

The city of Chieti, near Pescara, is famous for its Easter celebration. Great lyric artists come to sing during its historic procession. People come from all over Italy to see the spectacle, and it is often shown on national television.

Children are always given an Easter egg made of chocolate but hollow inside, which contains a surprise toy or tinsel. Some of these eggs are majestic and beautifully decorated, with flowers or cupids made of sugar.

When I was a child, my grandmother, and later my mother, always made a cake in the shape of a lamb for me and my brother. The Easter dinner would include this cake, and always a bowl of hard-boiled eggs. Everyone had to eat at least one for tradition.

The next day, more hard-boiled eggs are put into a picnic basket with a *fiadone* (page 40), or some other *pizza rustica,* for the traditional picnic. On that day, almost the entire population of Italy is on the road. It is our 4th of July!

If you want to make a really authentic *cacio e 'ovo,* be sure to order your kid, or baby lamb, on time. If you order the kid, buy an entire one. The average weight of one kid is no more then 14 pounds, and that includes many bones.

CAPRA ALLA MONTANARA

Goat in the Style of the Mountaineers **(Makes 6 to 8 servings)**

One 3- to 4-pound leg of goat, bone removed
$^{1}/_{2}$ cup vinegar; or juice of 1 lemon
3 tablespoons extra virgin olive oil
1 small diavoletto *(dried Italian hot red pepper)*
Salt and pepper to taste
1 large onion, coarsely chopped

1 cup dry wine, white or red
1 tablespoon butter
$^{1}/_{2}$ pound pearl onions, peeled and with a cross cut at the bottom of each onion
1 tablespoon sugar
2 tablespoons balsamic vinegar
1 tablespoon minced fresh parsley

1. Place the meat in a large pot, cover with water, and add $^{1}/_{4}$ cup of the vinegar or the lemon juice. Bring to a boil. Immediately drain the meat, return it to the pot, and add cold water to cover. Let it cool, then cube the meat and dry it with paper towels.

2. In a large skillet in which the meat can fit snugly, heat the oil and the *diavoletto.* Add the meat and brown, about 10 minutes. Season with salt and pepper, then add the onion and cook until soft, about 5 minutes. Add the remaining $^{1}/_{4}$ cup vinegar, cook 5 minutes, and add the wine. Reduce the heat, cover the skillet, and cook over low heat for about 2 hours. If the liquid tends to evaporate, add a little water.

3. In a small skillet, heat the butter, add the pearl onions, sauté for 5 to 8 minutes, then add $^1/_4$ cup water. Cover the skillet and cook over medium heat until the onions are soft, about 10 minutes. Add the sugar and balsamic vinegar. Cook 5 minutes, stirring. If the mixture is too dry, add a little water.

4. When the meat is done, add the pearl onions, stir, and serve with a sprinkling of minced parsley.

AGNELLO A CUTTURO

Lamb in a Pot (Makes 6 to 8 servings)

DURING THE SUMMER, THE SHEPHERDS live *all'addiaccio*, in the open air, and cook lamb in a copper cauldron hanging from a rustic trestle made with three wooden poles stuck in the ground.

As Nice Cortelli Lucrezi writes in her charming book *Le Ricette Della Nonna* (*Grandmother's Recipes*; Japadre Editore), "the shepherds cut the meat . . . and put it in the *cutturo* (the cauldron), and cook it . . . slowly so that the *brodetto* (soupy meat, as she calls it) does not dry too much."

The shepherds toast slices of crusty bread which they put at the bottom of their dishes before topping it with the meat and its broth.

Once, I actually felt very ambitious and cooked my kid in the fireplace of our living room, and in a real *cutturo*—a present from my brother who didn't want me to forget the traditions of my pastoral land!

However, cooking this dish on a modern stove, using a pot with two handles and a tight-fitting lid, will do.

5 pounds boneless lean lamb,
cut from the leg, cubed
2 teaspoons kosher salt
$^1/_4$ cup ($^1/_2$ stick) unsalted butter
1 tablespoon extra virgin olive oil

1 large onion
1 teaspoon thyme
2 bay leaves
$^3/_4$ cup water

1. Set the meat in a bowl and sprinkle with the salt. Set aside at room temperature for 1 hour, or 2 to 3 hours refrigerated.

2. Cut the butter into small pieces and spread it over the bottom of a large, heavy-bottomed pan. Drizzle the oil over.

3. Quickly rinse the meat and add to the pan without draining it too much.

4. Cut a cross at the root end of the onion (this prevents the onion from falling apart and collapsing). Bury the onion in the middle of the meat and add the thyme, bay leaves, and water. Cover and cook over very low heat until the meat is tender, about 1 hour, shaking the pan every once in a while without removing the lid. Check the meat, give it a stir, and continue cooking until the meat is very tender, about 30 to 40 minutes longer. Serve hot with its little broth.

IL COATTO

(Makes 6 servings)

It is difficult to translate the name of this dish—which is an ancient dish of pastoral origins whose name comes from the Latin *coactus*. Literally translated, it means imprisoned or enclosed.

In fact, the meat in this recipe is cooked, or "imprisoned," in its sauce but does not float in it. Coffee beans are added to the sauce as a reminder of our dealings with the Saracens.

Il Coatto is a specialty of the mountain regions and around the village of Arsita.

3 pounds lean, boned lamb, cubed
2 cups water
3 cloves garlic, peeled and smashed
1 onion, quartered
1 sprig fresh rosemary, or 1 teaspoon dried
4 fresh sage leaves, or ½ teaspoon dried
¼ teaspoon marjoram
5 to 6 fresh basil leaves, or 1 teaspoon dried

¼ cup extra virgin olive oil
1 small diavoletto *(dried Italian hot red pepper)*
One 16-ounce can peeled tomatoes
4 to 5 toasted coffee beans
5 to 6 juniper berries, crushed
Salt to taste, optional
¾ cup dry white wine
1 tablespoon minced fresh parsley

Place the meat in a pan with a tightly fitting lid. Add the water and boil 15 minutes over high heat, uncovered. Drain the meat and add the garlic, onion, rosemary, sage, marjoram, basil, olive oil, *diavoletto*, tomatoes, coffee beans, juniper berries, and salt. Cover the pan and continue cooking over low heat about 1 hour. Stir once or twice. Add the wine, cover, and cook 1 hour longer, or until the meat is tender and the sauce has reduced. Sprinkle with parsley and serve.

NOTE: I DO NOT REMOVE THE COFFEE BEANS AND THE GARLIC. I ALWAYS SAY THAT WHOEVER GETS THEM IS THE LUCKY ONE. MY FRIENDS LOVE THIS.

MAZZARELLE

Lamb Parts in Lettuce Rolls *(Makes 4 to 6 servings)*

THIS IS A CELEBRATED SPECIALTY FROM Teramo. Similar preparations are done all over Abruzzo, the South of Italy, and even on the island of Sardinia. The name changes but the ingredients are the same. It is an ancient dish which goes back to pre-Roman days.

I didn't know if I should include this recipe in this book because the ingredients are difficult to obtain here. But I have adapted it and perhaps, with a friendly butcher, one can manage.

I would have liked to have included more recipes of this kind, like the *coratella*, a stew made with the innards of a lamb, the *marritte*, made with the intestines, and similarly, lamb tripe. But apart from the difficulty of finding the ingredients, I am afraid the dishes might not appeal to the American palate. So I will give you only this one, a little sanitized, but oh, so delicious!

2 pounds lamb innards, heart, lung, liver, spleen, and sweetbreads
1 large onion, finely chopped
4 cloves garlic, peeled and minced
3 sprigs minced fresh parsley
Salt to taste, optional
Freshly ground pepper to taste

1 bunch romaine lettuce
1 tablespoon extra virgin olive oil
2 ounces fresh lard, chopped; or same amount prosciutto fat
1/2 cup dry white wine
One 8-ounce can tomato puree
1 teaspoon tomato paste

1. Chop the innards very coarsely, place in a bowl, and add the onion, garlic, and parsley, and season with salt and pepper. Set aside.

2. Remove about 12 of the largest leaves from the lettuce and blanch them. Spread the leaves on kitchen towels. Distribute the mixture of the innards among the leaves and roll, tucking the sides to enclose the filling. Tie with kitchen string. Set aside.

3. In a large pan in which the *mazzarelle* can fit in one layer, heat the oil and lard or prosciutto fat. Add the *mazzarelle* and cook over medium heat, turning them gently, until evenly browned, about 10 minutes. Add the wine and let evaporate, then add the tomato puree.

4. Dissolve the tomato paste in 1/2 cup water and add to the pan. Cover, bring to a boil, and cook over medium-low heat about 30 minutes. Serve hot.

NOTE: THE ORIGINAL *MAZZARELLE* ARE TIED WITH THE TENDER GUTS OF THE LAMB.

ABOUT PORK

Nobody prevented me, when I was a child, from witnessing the slaughter of chickens, rabbits, and pigeons. It was part of the daily routine. It meant preparing dinner. Our maid, Annina, of whom I speak often, considered it a good diversion for a child, a way to keep me occupied while I learned. She would invite me to go with her to the stable to commit the deed. It was a natural act and I felt very grown-up when she would let me pluck a chicken with the understanding that I could keep the most colorful feathers for my games.

I remember when our farmer, at the beginning of the summer, would bring the *maialino*, piglet, to the house. I am, of course, talking of my grandmother's house in Guardiagrele, which had stables. There, the little pig would be raised under the ever-wise supervision of the aforementioned maid, and the advice of the entire household, which included my uncle Tommaso, the doctor, and of course, my uncle Agostino, the vet.

I was kept away on the day of the pig's demise which occurred sometime during the month of November. Frankly I didn't mind it, because I had gotten fond of the little beast since I would often feed it. Upon my return from school, I would find the carcass already washed and hanging from the ceiling of the cellar. I remember being astonished by its luminous whiteness. I am a little ashamed to confess that after the first pang of guilt, I felt no remorse. I was already thinking of the *maialatura*. This is an ancient ritual during which the meat of the pig is cut. Then begins the laborious process of making turgid sausages and salami, and of curing the chewy prosciutti and the delicate pancetta. Since nothing is wasted in a pig, on the night of this event, friends and relatives are invited for a *cenetta*, a repast. During this feast, delicious dishes concocted in the kitchen with tripe, snout, ears, head, and all the innards come in succession. It is really a great banquet during which all my remorse was washed away. I was even allowed to drink half a glass of wine. Well, let's face it, I was a food person even then.

But my favorite part of this event came before the dinner. It was the making of the *sanguinaccio*, a sweet blood pudding, which even today is made all over Italy and sold in ice-cream cones in the most elegant coffee shops. This must be made quickly before the blood coagulates.

My uncle Filippo would sit in front of the fireplace, which had a huge, resplendent copper cauldron hanging on its chain over the fire. On the side, a little table displayed all the utensils necessary for the preparations and the ingredients, like sugar, chocolate, tons of cocoa, and some spices, were exhibited, too. The young maids and I where the handlers of these things which were passed to him, on request, much the way a surgeon asks for instruments in an operating room. Soon a subtle perfume of chocolate and cinnamon would permeate the kitchen and infiltrate itself in the most remote nooks of the house. It drew even my mother, who would keep away from the kitchen if others were laboring for her, to see how the *sanguinaccio* was doing. When the guests arrived for dinner, their contentment in smelling this delicious pudding spread over their faces.

We Abruzzesi have a great affinity for pork. As with lamb, our pigs were special because, apart from feeding on corn and the aromatic herbs of the meadows, they also ate scraps from the kitchen. Nowadays, and this is most unfortunate, the scrap business is ending; pigs now are fed with commercial feed because kitchen scraps are no longer kept. Very few people raise a pig in the house. I know, I will never eat pork the way I had it at my grandmother's home.

Of course pork nowadays is called "the other white meat." It is very lean and good for you, but the flavor of the past is lost forever.

Fortunately, pork meat lends itself to many condiments and can be made quite flavorful with herbs and spices. Because of the danger of trichinosis, pork must be cooked properly, but not to death. Cook it with attention in order not to dry it out. Check it often and, most of all, use your own best judgment.

PROSCIUTTO FRESCO AL FINOCCHIO

Fresh Ham with Fennel **(Makes 8 servings or more)**

IT ISN'T EASY TO SECURE A FRESH BACKSIDE leg of pork, which is the part from which the wonderful Italian *prosciutto* is made. However, a good butcher will get it for you. If all else fails, you can use the rib side of a roast. If you do, ask the butcher to dislodge the meat from the bones but before cooking it, reasseamble the ribs using the bones as a rack (see recipe below).

You can also cook the meat with the bone intact, but it will be difficult to slice.

4 to 5 pounds fresh ham (backside leg of pork)

3 sprigs fresh wild fennel, or dill, or the same amount from the fronds (green feathery part) of a fresh fennel

1 sprig fresh rosemary, or 1 teaspoon dried

1 clove garlic, peeled

3 tablespoons extra virgin olive oil

1 1/2 cups dry wine, approximately, white or red

Freshly ground pepper to taste

Salt to taste, optional

1 rib celery, sliced into 2-inch pieces

1 carrot, peeled and sliced into 2-inch pieces

1 medium-size onion, sliced

1. Trim the ham of excess fat. Reserve 1 tablespoon of the fat.

2. Chop together 2 sprigs fresh fennel, the rosemary, garlic, and the reserved fat. Lard the meat with this mixture (see Step 3, page 323) and tie the roast to keep its shape. Pour a little oil in your hand and "massage" the meat with it.

3. Preheat the oven to 400°F.

4. Lightly oil a baking pan large enough to hold the ham snugly. Combine 1/4 cup of the wine and 1/4 cup water, pour into the pan, and add the meat. Roast 45 minutes, turning once. Baste often with its own juices.

5. Reduce the heat to 375°F. Sprinkle the meat with pepper and salt, if used. Cook 1 1/2 hours, basting often and adding more of the remaining wine little by little. Scatter the vegetables all around and continue cooking until the the meat is done, when juices run clear when pierced with a skewer, about 45 minutes.

6. Remove the roast from the pan and keep warm. Remove the vegetables with a slotted spoon and place in a food mill or a food processor. Puree. Spoon off the excess fat from the pan and combine the pan juices with the vegetable puree. Warm up the sauce.

7. Slice the meat, pour some sauce over, and serve the remaining sauce in a sauce boat. Decorate the meat with sprigs of fennel.

ARROSTO DI MAIALE AL LATTE ADRIANA

Pork Roast with Milk Adriana **(Makes 6 to 8 servings)**

I AM AFRAID MY OTHER TWO COUSINS, Gianna and Franca, who are Adriana's sisters, will get a little peeved with me. You see, I am using Adriana's name more then theirs in this book. They two are excellent cooks, but it seems to me that Adriana is the one who has carried the torch of the family recipes. Her sisters, when they married, moved away from Abruzzo and expanded their repertoires according to the use and customs of the places where they are now living. Adriana, remaining in Abruzzo, had her mother nearby, and being very close to my mother, continued cooking our traditional dishes.

She likes to put her own imprint on a recipe and this one is very Adriana. She also likes to cook with milk. Is it because she has had 6 children, whom she personally nursed. . . ? Jokes aside, this is a delicious recipe, a little unusual, but with a delicate taste.

3 tablespoons unsalted butter
3 tablespoons extra virgin olive oil
3 pounds pork loin, boned and tied
Freshly ground pepper to taste

1 leek, trimmed, washed well, halved,
    and cut into strips
1 quart fat-free milk
1 tablespoon flour
Juice of 1/2 lemon

1. Preheat the oven to 350°F.

2. In a heavy pot large enough to hold the meat snugly, heat 2 tablespoons of the butter and 2 tablespoons of the oil. Add the meat and cook over medium-high heat, turning often, until brown on all sides, 10 to 15 minutes. Sprinkle with the pepper. Remove the meat to a platter. Discard the fat and wipe the pot clean, then return the pot to the heat and add the remaining butter and oil. Sauté the leek and cook over medium-high heat, stirring, until it starts to color, 4 to 6 minutes.

3. Return the meat to the pot. Combine the milk and flour and add. Cover the pot, place in the oven, and bake, turning once in awhile, until the juices from the meat run clear when pierced with a skewer, about 2 hours. Add the lemon juice, stir, and let the meat rest 15 minutes before slicing. Serve with its own sauce.

NOTE: THIS MEAT CAN ALSO BE COOKED ON THE STOVE OVER VERY LOW HEAT. STIR AND TURN OFTEN.

BRASATO DI MAIALE IN SALSA SAPORITA

Braised Pork in Flavorful Sauce *(Makes 6 servings)*

THE MEAT IN THIS RECIPE IS COOKED VERY simply using the braising method. The sauce, prepared separately, is a savory combination of chicken livers and prosciutto, flavored with cloves and herbs.

PORK

3 tablespoons extra virgin olive oil

1 sprig fresh rosemary, or $^1\!/_2$ teaspoon dried

3 pounds boneless shoulder of pork, tied securely with kitchen string

Salt to taste, optional

Freshly ground pepper to taste

$3^1\!/_4$ cups chicken or beef broth, preferably homemade (page 61), or good quality canned broth, or use bouillon

SAUCE

2 chicken livers

4 ounces prosciutto

2 cloves garlic

2 fresh sage leaves, or $^1\!/_4$ teaspoon dried

$^1\!/_2$ teaspoon dried rosemary

4 ounces sweet Italian sausage, skinned and crumbled

Freshly ground pepper to taste

2 or 3 tablespoons broth, preferably homemade (page 61), or good quality canned

2 tablespoons white wine vinegar

$^1\!/_4$ cup dry wine, white or red

1. In a heavy pot large enough in which the meat can fit snugly, heat the oil. Add the rosemary and cook over high heat, letting the flavor explode, for 1 to 2 minutes. Add the meat and reduce the heat to medium-high. Cook, turning often, until brown on all sides, 10 to 15 minutes. Season with salt, if used, and pepper. Add $^1\!/_4$ cup of the broth, cover, reduce the heat, and cook about 2 hours. Continue adding the broth, a little at a time, and turning the meat often. The pork meat should cook *in umido,* with moisture.

2. For the sauce, chop all together the livers, prosciutto, garlic, sage, and rosemary. Place in a bowl, add the sausage meat, and stir to combine. Transfer to a medium-size saucepan. Add the broth, vinegar, and wine. Cook over low heat, covered, until slightly reduced, about 30 minutes. Stir often, and if the sauce tends to dry out, add a little more broth as needed.

3. Slice the meat and pour the sauce over, or serve the sauce separately.

PORCHETTA CASALINGA

Home-style Porchetta **(Makes 8 servings)**

PORCHETTA IS A GREAT SPECIALTY OF Abruzzo and the bordering regions of central Italy. But Villa Santa Maria, a town famous for its professional cooking school, whose beginnings go back to the Middle Ages, stages a festival every summer, dedicated to the *porchetta*. Many Abruzzesi chefs, graduates of the school, return to Villa Santa Maria from all over the world to attend the festival and cook the *porchetta*. The event takes place on the main street and the best *porchettaro* (the one who cooks the *porchetta*) wins a prize. Their recipes are secret and never revealed.

In any case, since real *porchetta* is made with a full-grown young pig (not a suckling pig), it would be a little difficult to make it in a conventional oven. The authentic *porchetta* is cooked on a pole in a wood-burning oven and eaten at room temperature. My recipe, *alla casalinga*, home-style, is a little more manageable, and because I have eaten *porchetta* since my childhood I think I was able to guess the ingredients correctly.

Porchetta is a must at any big Abruzzese banquet. Incidentally, Abruzzo is renowned for its gargantuan feasts, especially the one called *panarda*. What is a *panarda*? The origin

PORK

6 to 7 cloves garlic, peeled and minced
1 1/2 teaspoons fresh rosemary, chopped
1 teaspoon freshly ground pepper
Kosher salt to taste
6 pounds boned fresh pork, preferably
    from the butt

SKIN

1/2 cup wine vinegar
1/2 teaspoon fresh rosemary, chopped
1 teaspoon freshly ground pepper
Kosher salt to taste
1 or 2 sheets fresh pork skin,
    or enough to wrap the pork in

THE DAY BEFORE:

1. Combine the garlic, rosemary, pepper, and salt in a small bowl. Rub the meat with this mixture. Set the meat on a dish, cover, and refrigerate overnight.

2. Combine the vinegar, rosemary, pepper, and salt in a large nonreactive pan. Add the skin to the pan, pour this mixture over the skin, cover, and refrigerate overnight.

THE NEXT DAY:

3. Preheat the oven to 450°F.

4. Remove the skin from the marinade. Discard the marinade. Wrap the meat in the skin and tie securely with kitchen string. Set the meat on the rack of a roasting pan and roast until the skin starts to color, about 20 minutes. Turn the roast and reduce the heat to 375°F. Continue cooking until the skin is quite brown and crackling, about 2 1/2 to 3 hours. Turn once in a while. To make sure the meat is cooked, pierce it deeply in the thickest part with a skewer. If the juices run clear, the meat is done. Cool 15 minutes before removing the skin. Cut the skin into strips (this is easily done with scissors or poultry shears). Slice the meat and serve the *porchetta* surrounded by the strips of skin.

NOTE: IDEALLY THIS *PORCHETTA* SHOULD BE COOKED ON A SPIT. THE SKIN SHOULD BE VERY CRISP. IF THIS DOESN'T HAPPEN IN YOUR OVEN, AFTER CUTTING THE SKIN, PLACE THE CUT STRIPS ON A BAKING SHEET AND PUT IT BACK INTO THE OVEN FOR A FEW MINUTES AT A TEMPERATURE OF 500°F.

of the name is unknown. Perhaps it comes from *pane,* bread, but I doubt it. It is a grand banquet, given for many occasions: a wedding, a homecoming, the return of an emigrant, a very special birthday, a promotion, a political event, a business convention and, in the old days, even for a funeral. Someone called it the phoenix of the Abruzzese banquet, because when it seems about to end, it starts all over again. A minimum of thirty courses to a maximum of sixty are served. It starts with a prologue of many antipasti. And, in a real theatrical manner, three "acts" follow, each "act" with eleven entrées (main courses) each.

There is a well-known story about a *panarda,* as told by Eduardo Scarfoglio, a famous writer of the past century. Enjoying a *panarda* in his native city of L'Aquila, after the thirtieth course he felt he could eat no more. When his host realized what was happening, he approached him with a hurt face, brandishing a rifle. Scarfoglio immediately regained his appetite!

My husband, Harold, was given a *panarda* by my friend and schoolmate, Mirella Capobianchi. We had just been married and this was the first time we were spending a summer in Pescara. The feast was held in her beautiful farmhouse on a verdant hill overlooking the Adriatic. After many courses, the *pièce de résistance* arrived— the *porchetta.* My husband is Jewish and I had a moment of panic when this imposing *porchetta* appeared, carried by four colorful peasants wearing local costumes. The pig, too, was all decked out, sporting a necklace of vibrant multicolored peppers and an apple in its mouth. Remembering the Scarfoglio episode, I didn't say anything, but my husband's amused expression reassured me. He ate it with gusto, and he liked it a lot.

A *panarda* nowadays is seldom done, mostly for lack of capable stomachs. But *porchetta* is always present in Abruzzo.

This recipe is not difficult at all, but you must start your preparations the day before. The skin of the pig must be ordered in advance. Your butcher should be able to get it for you, but if all else fails, you can wrap the pork with pancetta, or even bacon.

MAIALE IN SALSA DEL DOTTORE SERAFINI

Dr. Serafini's Pork in Sauce (Makes 6 servings)

GOING TO DINNER AT NINO AND ANNA Serafini's house in Lanciano is always a special treat. The husband and wife team are excellent gastronomes. Their dinners are extremely well executed. This dish is Nino's invention, but Anna cooked it for me and I found it utterly delicious and novel.

The best pork cut of meat for this dish is the *capicollo,* which is found near the neck. Since it is not sold here, I use the butt or the upper shoulder with good results.

3 tablespoons extra virgin olive oil
1 large onion, thinly sliced
One 4-pound pork butt or shoulder
2 bay leaves
1/4 teaspoon cinnamon
1/2 cup wine vinegar, preferably white
1/2 cup dry wine
1/4 cup Italian sottaceti *(see Note);*
  or 1 sour Jewish pickle, chopped
1 3/4 cups or more chicken broth,
  preferably homemade (page 61),
  or good quality canned broth
1 tablespoon unsalted butter
1 tablespoon all-purpose flour
3/4 cup plain yogurt

1. In a heavy pan large enough to hold the meat snugly, heat the oil and onion. Cook over medium heat until the onion is softened, about 5 minutes. Add the meat and cook until brown on all sides, 10 to 15 minutes. Add the bay leaves, cinnamon, and vinegar. Let evaporate and add the wine. Cover, reduce the heat to low, and cook 30 minutes, turning the meat once or twice. Add the pickles and continue cooking until the meat is done, about 2 hours longer. Reserve 1 cup of the broth and add 3/4 cup of it to the meat. Cook 1 hour longer. Turn often, and if the meat tends to dry, add a little of the broth as needed.

2. Remove the meat to a platter and cover with aluminum foil to keep warm. Discard the bay leaves. Degrease the sauce at the bottom of the pan. Add the butter and the flour, stir well, then add, little by little, the reserved 1 cup of broth. Bring to a boil, reduce the heat to low, and simmer until slightly thickened, about 5 minutes. Turn the sauce into a food processor and puree.

3. Rewarm the sauce, add the yogurt, stir, and if too thick, add more broth. Simmer a few seconds to warm but do not boil again.

4. Slice the meat and serve with the sauce on the side.

NOTE: *SOTTACETI* ARE PICKLED VEGETABLES SOLD IN ITALIAN SPECIALTY STORES AND SOME SUPERMARKETS. THEY ARE ALSO CALLED *GIARDINIERA.*

ARROSTICINI COL MANICO

Roasted Pork Ribs *(Makes 4 servings)*

My brother Mimmo called these extremely tasty ribs *col manico,* with the handle. Indeed they have a handle.

2 racks pork spareribs, about 4 pounds
1 teaspoon kosher salt
Freshly ground pepper to taste
1 cup wine vinegar
3/4 cup water

1 teaspoon tomato paste
1 cup chicken broth, preferably homemade (page 61), or good quality canned broth, or bouillon

1. Sprinkle the meat with the salt and the pepper. Cover and refrigerate 6 hours or overnight.

2. Preheat the oven to 400°F.

3. Place the ribs in a large baking pan, pour the vinegar over the meat, and pour the water in the bottom of the pan. Bake about 1 hour. Rotate the ribs once in a while and baste with the juices at the bottom.

4. Combine the tomato paste with $^{1}/_{2}$ cup of the broth. Brush the ribs with this mixture and bake until the ribs are tender and quite brown, about 1 hour longer. Remove the ribs to a platter and cover with foil to keep warm. Pour off the fat from the pan and add the remaining broth into the pan where the ribs cooked. With a wooden spoon, scrape to remove the brown particles clinging to the bottom of the pan. Pour the sauce into a sauce boat and keep warm. Cut the ribs into serving portions and serve with the sauce. Pass plenty of paper napkins.

NOTE: THESE RIBS CAN ALSO BE SERVED WITH AUNT ELA'S SAUCE (PAGE 307).

PICCATA DI MAIALE AI CAPPERI

Pork Piccata with Capers (Makes 6 servings)

AS A VARIATION OF VEAL *PICCATA*, THIS recipe is just as easy to prepare and quite delicious. In my home it was usually served with a delicate potato puree (page 383) which made a perfect foil for the piquancy of the capers.

12 pork cutlets, about 1 1/2 pounds, cut from the loin and pounded
All-purpose flour for dredging
2 tablespoons extra virgin olive oil
1 tablespoon butter

Salt to taste, optional
Freshly ground pepper to taste
Juice of 1/2 lemon
1/2 cup of wine
2 tablespoons capers in brine, drained

1. Dredge the cutlets in flour. Shake off the excess flour.

2. In a large skillet in which the cutlets can fit in one layer (or cook them in batches), heat the oil and butter and quickly sauté the cutlets on both sides until brown. Sprinkle with salt, if used, and pepper. Add the lemon juice, cook a few minutes, and remove the cutlets to a plate. Add the wine to deglaze the pan and return the cutlets to the skillet. Let the sauce reduce a little and add the capers. Serve immediately.

NOTE: TURKEY CUTLETS WORK VERY WELL WITH THIS RECIPE. PORK CHOPS CAN ALSO BE COOKED THIS WAY. FOR 6 CHOPS, I ADD 1 TEASPOON GRAINY MUSTARD WITH THE CAPERS.

Variation: *Costoletta di Maiale all'Arancia*, Pork Chops with Orange
We Italians do not particularly like fruit with meat. But pork in certain cases, and perhaps duck, are exceptions. These chops are cooked like the above *piccata*. Instead of the lemon, use the juice of 1 orange, and instead of the capers, add the pulp of an orange, coarsely chopped.

Cotechino con le Lenticchie

Cotechino with Lentils (Makes 8 servings or more)

THERE WAS NO NEW YEAR'S IN MY FAMILY without this dish at our festive table. *Cotechino* with lentils is traditionally eaten all over Italy at this time. It also has a folkloristic significance. The meat with which the *cotechino* is made represents abundance, and the lentils, fortune in business and money. The dish must be garnished with parsley since, as the ancient Romans believed, it wards off the evil eye. And since we in Abruzzo are a little superstitious, we oblige. Isn't this the land where *malocchio*, the evil eye, is feared and revered?

Speaking of *malocchio*, when we were children, the moment we announced a bellyache or a toothache, Annina, our maid who was also a bit of a witch, would arrive with her paraphernalia to remove the *malocchio*. She, of course, was positive that someone had given us the evil eye. Fascinated, we sat in front of her magic implements: a basinet, a pitcher of oil, olive of course, and a bowl of salt. She would start with an unintelligible mumbo jumbo and, making cross signs on the aching parts of our bodies and the foreheads, she would proceed to remove the *malocchio*. She knew when it had worked because, when she sprinkled a few drops of oil in the water, the drops would spread in a certain way. I do not remember what she

COTECHINO
Two 1-pound cotechini
1 medium-size onion, quartered
1 rib celery, trimmed and cut into 2 pieces
1 medium-size carrot, peeled and cut into 4 pieces
1 bay leaf
10 peppercorns
1/2 teaspoon thyme

LENTILS
1 1/2 pounds lentils, picked over and washed
1 large onion, with a cross cut at its root end
1 rib celery, trimmed and cut into 2 pieces
2 sprigs fresh parsley
1 clove garlic
1 bay leaf
2 medium-size carrots, peeled and each cut into 4 pieces
Salt to taste, optional
Freshly ground pepper to taste
3 tablespoons extra virgin olive oil
1 bunch curly parsley for garnish

1. Prepare the *cotechini*: Pierce the *cotechini* in several places. Set them in a pot and add all the remaining ingredients. Add water to come 2 inches above the solids. Bring to a boil, reduce the heat, and simmer, over low heat, 1 hour. Remove from the heat but keep warm.

2. Prepare the lentils: Place the lentils in a pot. Add all the remaining ingredients but the oil and parsley. Add enough water to come 2 inches above the solids. Bring to a boil and add 2 tablespoons of the oil.

3. Cover the pot, reduce the heat, and simmer until the lentils are soft but not mushy, about 45 minutes. Taste often because some lentils will cook faster than others. At this point the water should be all absorbed; if not, remove the lid and reduce the water. If, by any chance, the lentils are still hard, add some water from the *cotechini* and continue cooking until they are done. Remove the bay leaf and garlic and discard. Remove the onion, celery, and carrots and discard or keep for another use.

continues

did with the salt. My grandmother, a religious woman, didn't approve at all, and my mother and father laughed at it, but we children always felt better afterward.

The parsley, however, always garnished our dish of *cotechino e lenticchie*. You do the same, one never knows; besides, it is also pretty.

For those who do not know, *cotechino* is a special Italian sausage, similar to a salami, but sold fresh in Italian specialty stores or Italian butchers.

4. Slice the *cotechini* and arrange around the rim of a serving plate. Spoon the lentils in the middle and garnish the dish with the parsley.

NOTE: I USUALLY CHOP THE VEGETABLES AND MIX THEM WITH THE LENTILS. THE CARROTS ADD COLOR TO THE DISH.

CHAPTER 12

CACCIAGIONE

Game

$\mathcal{P}$reparing game at home is something we seldom think of these days. One reason is that many people are tender-hearted and do not like the idea of shooting or trapping animals. In the old days, hunting was not just sport. Professional hunters would bag large numbers of birds, wild fowl, hare, venison, etc., and then sell them in the marketplace. Unfortunately, as a result of such indiscriminate hunting, some types of game which used to be plentiful are now scarce. Today laws regulate the time during which certain game can be hunted and limit what a hunter can bag. Now, to increase supply, a large variety of game, especially birds, are being raised on farms like chickens. Their meat is tender and perhaps more pleasing to a modern palate. The meat is often lean, an added bonus in these days of cholesterol and fat abomination.

In Europe, during the nineteenth century, serving varied and large portions of game was the hallmark of the wealthy classes. Meat was scarce and hunting was a necessity. Quite often, the only people who could hunt were the noblemen because they owned almost all the land for vast distances around their castles. Unfortunately, if not invited, you could not hunt in their territory. For the nobles, it was a prestigious sport and even ladies participated.

Today, game is not as popular and no longer symbolizes wealth and plenty. It simply seems exotic, perhaps because not everybody knows how to cook it. Actually, it is not difficult. It can be cooked like other meats, but there are important preliminary preparations. Game bought at a butcher shop is usually ready to cook, but it is always a good idea to wash the meat with water and vinegar. Some of these meats should be kept under running water for a while to eliminate excessive gamy taste, and then placed in a good marinade which will tenderize and increase the flavor of the meat.

LEPRE IN SALMÍ

Hare in Salmí **(Makes 6 servings)**

WE ATE *LEPRE* SEVERAL TIMES DURING THE year. Perhaps a friend who hunted would bring the hare. And we would receive it with grateful enthusiasm.

But the best hare I have eaten was one my brother Mimmo and I hunted . . . unwillingly. Driving back from a trip to Roccaraso, the enchanting holiday resort on the Maiella Mountain, where we had spent a weekend skiing, we hit a hare crossing the road. Rather upset, we stopped the car and searched for the wounded animal. Well, we found it, dead. After a few *mamma mia* and *che peccato*, what a pity, we decided that it would be more of a pity if we left it there to rot. So we took it home, and father's comment was, "*Mors tua, vita mea*," which in Latin means your

MARINADE

One 3- to 4-pound hare, cut into serving pieces
2 medium-size carrots, peeled and sliced into rounds
1 medium-size onion, sliced
2 ribs celery, trimmed and diced
2 cloves garlic, peeled and minced
1 sprig fresh thyme, or ¹/₂ teaspoon dried
1 sprig fresh marjoram, or ¹/₂ teaspoon dried
1 sprig fresh sage, or ¹/₂ teaspoon dried
2 bay leaves
3 to 5 juniper berries; or 1 jigger of gin
4 to 5 peppercorns
5 cups good dry red wine, like Barolo, Barbera, or Chianti

COOKING INGREDIENTS

2 tablespoons unsalted butter
2 tablespoons extra virgin olive oil
1 tablespoon all-purpose flour
Salt to taste, optional
Freshly ground pepper to taste

ANCHOVY SAUCE

3 to 4 anchovy fillets, drained
1 clove garlic, peeled
3 tablespoons balsamic vinegar
3 tablespoons red wine

TO SERVE

³/₄ cup chicken broth, preferably homemade (page 61), or good quality canned broth
1 tablespoon minced fresh parsley

death [is] my life. He then proceeded to plan the making of a splendid meal!

My father marinated the hare—which incidentally weighed more than 5 pounds—for two days, and then he cooked it in *salmí*. This is a method used for the preparation of game. The best *salmí* is done with hare.

Generally, the best time to buy hare is from September to February. The unbeatable food supplier, D'Artagnan, imports them fresh from Scotland. You can also buy fresh hare from a reliable butcher shop in New York, such as Ottomanelli on Bleecker Street, or Balducci's. They come ready to cook, but I recommend a good, long marinade.

TWO DAYS BEFORE:

1. Place the hare in a nonreactive bowl and add all the ingredients listed for the marinade. Refrigerate for 1 to 2 days. Let it come to room temperature outside the refrigerator for at least 3 hours before cooking. Ideally, this would not be refrigerated but kept in a cool place.

TO COOK THE HARE:

2. Remove the hare from the marinade and pat dry. Strain the marinade and reserve the liquid and solids separately.

3. In a large covered casserole, heat the butter and oil. Add the meat and brown over medium-high heat on all sides. Add the vegetables and the herbs from the marinade. Cook, stirring, until well flavored, about 5 minutes. Sprinkle with the flour, stir, and add $1/_2$ cup of the liquid marinade. Let evaporate. Season with salt, if used, and pepper, then add the remaining liquid marinade. Cover the casserole, reduce the heat to medium-low, and cook until the hare is tender, about 2 hours. Stir occasionally.

4. Prepare the sauce by chopping together the anchovies and garlic. Combine this mixture with the balsamic vinegar and wine. Set aside.

5. Remove the hare to a serving platter and cover loosely with foil to keep warm. Discard the sprigs of herbs and degrease the casserole, if necessary. Add the anchovy mixture. If you do not have much sauce, add some of the broth to the casserole. Bring to a boil, reduce slightly, and spoon this sauce over the hare, or serve it on the side. Sprinkle the hare with the minced parsley just before serving.

NOTE: IT IS CUSTOMARY IN ITALY TO SERVE THIS DISH WITH POLENTA.

Lepre alla Cacciatora

Hare Hunter Style *(Makes 6 servings)*

THIS IS AN ANCIENT RECIPE FROM SAN Giovanni, a quaint village set on a hill overlooking the picturesque Lake Sinizzo. This recipe works well with rabbit also.

One 3- to 4-pound hare, cut into
   small pieces
3/4 cup wine vinegar
3 to 4 cloves garlic, peeled and sliced
1 large sprig fresh rosemary,
   or 1 1/4 teaspoons dried

1 small diavoletto *(dried Italian*
   hot red pepper), optional
Salt to taste, optional
Freshly ground pepper to taste
1/4 cup extra virgin olive oil
1 tablespoon minced fresh parsley

1. Place the hare under running water for half an hour. Transfer to a large bowl, add 1/4 cup of the vinegar, and cover with cold water. Let stand 20 minutes.

2. Place half the hare in a heavy-bottomed pan in which the pieces can be set in two layers. Add the remaining vinegar, spread the garlic over, break the rosemary sprig into pieces and add it together with the *diavoletto*, if used. Add the salt, if used, the pepper, and the remaining pieces of hare. Cover with water, add the oil, and place the pan on high heat. Bring to a boil, reduce the heat to medium-low, and cook at a simmer without stirring, about 2 hours, or longer if the hare is a tough one. Shake the pan a few times. At the end you should have a delicious little sauce at the bottom of the pan. Sprinkle with parsley and serve.

QUAGLIE IN PADELLA

Quails in a Skillet (Makes 6 servings)

QUAILS ARE LEAN CREATURES AND CARE must be taken so as not to dry them in the process of cooking. Quick searing in a skillet, or broiling, are the ideal cooking methods to preserve the juices inside. Quail are easy to cook and require little time, as this recipe demonstrates.

I recommend buying fresh quail, not frozen, for best full flavor.

12 quails, about 5- to 6-ounces each, ready to use
6 thin slices pancetta, each slice halved; or bacon slices, cut in half
12 leaves fresh sage, or 1 teaspoon dried
Juniper berries for the quail plus 1 teaspoon slightly crushed juniper berries

¼ cup extra virgin olive oil
Salt to taste, optional
Freshly ground pepper to taste
¼ cup gin
½ cup dry white wine

1. Wash the quail and pat dry. Insert into the cavity of each quail ½ slice of pancetta, 1 sage leaf, or a pinch of the dried, and 2 to 3 juniper berries. Tie the legs together with kitchen string.

2. In a large skillet, or using a smaller one to cook them in batches, heat the oil. Quick-sear the quails and cook over medium-high heat, turning often, until brown on all sides, 7 to 10 minutes. (Do not overcook.) Season with salt, if used, and pepper. Add the gin and let evaporate. Remove the quails and keep warm.

3. Add the crushed juniper berries to the skillet. Pour in the wine. Cook over medium-high heat a few minutes, scraping to remove the brown particles clinging to the bottom and sides of the skillet. Strain the sauce over the birds and serve.

Variation 1: There is a method of cooking birds in Abruzzo called *alla Vignaiola*. The word comes from *vigna,* the grape arbor. Simply wrap the birds in grape leaves and a slice of pancetta and cook as above. Grape leaves are available at Greek specialty stores.

Variation 2: It is nice to serve the bird on large bread croutons, either fried or baked like *bruschetta.*

FAGIANO TARTUFATO

Truffled Pheasant *(Makes 4 servings)*

WHEN MY FATHER COULD GET HOLD OF A truffle, the first thing he would think of was a pheasant. But in those days pheasant had to be hunted, and therefore were not easy to come by. Sometimes he would settle for a *maiale* or *vitello tartufato*, truffled pork or veal, both equally good. Of course, both dishes should be preceded by a nice bowl of homemade tagliatelle topped by a slivering of truffles.

When truffles are available in our markets, indulge in this dish. I do not recommend using canned truffles. In my opinion, the true aroma of the truffle is not there. It is better to invest in a tube of truffle paste or a bottle of truffle oil, which usually has an intense perfume. The truffle paste, by the way, works well in a sauce, especially one based on butter or cream.

It is always better to treat the pheasant with some sort of marinade and let the bird sit in it overnight. This will tenderize the meat which, by nature, can be a little dry.

2 young pheasants, about 2½ pounds each
4 tablespoons prosciutto fat (see Note)
1 medium-size black truffle
Extra virgin olive oil
Salt to taste, optional
Freshly ground pepper to taste
63 slices pancetta
¾ cup water
½ cup or more chicken broth, preferably homemade (page 61), or a good quality canned one
1 tablespoon minced fresh parsley

THE DAY BEFORE:

1. Remove the neck and giblets (including the liver) from the pheasants. Rinse under cold water, pat them dry, and refrigerate.

2. Chop the prosciutto fat into a creamy consistency and rub into the cavity of the birds.

3. Brush off, but do not wash, any residue of earth from the truffle, and slice it very thinly, preferably with a truffle slicer. Place the slices in the cavities of the birds and truss. Set the birds in a large china or glass bowl, cover with plastic wrap, and place at the bottom of the refrigerator for 1 to 2 days.

THE FOLLOWING DAY:

4. Preheat the oven to 400°F. Rub the birds with some olive oil and sprinkle with salt, if used, and pepper. Cover the breasts with the slices of pancetta and place them on a rack in a roasting pan. Add the reserved neck and giblets, pour the water into the bottom of the roasting pan, and reduce the heat to 350°F. Roast until browned and tender, 1 hour or more, depending on the age of the birds. Baste often with their own juices. If the legs of the pheasants tend to color too much, reduce the heat to 325°F. Add the liver during the last 10 minutes. To test for doneness, pierce the pheasant in a meaty part of the leg; if the juices run clear, not pink, the pheasant is done.

5. Remove the birds to a plate and keep warm. Discard the neck but chop the giblets and liver.

6. Pour the broth into the roasting pan in which the pheasant cooked. With a wooden spoon scrape the brown particles clinging to the bottom and sides of the pan. If you have too much liquid, boil on top of the stove to reduce the sauce a little. Cut the pheasants into serving pieces. Coarsely chop the truffle slices from the cavities and distribute on top of the pheasants. Do the same with the chopped giblets and livers. Pour the sauce over and serve sprinkled with the minced parsley.

NOTE 1: A LITTLE CREAM IN THE SAUCE WOULDN'T BE BAD!

NOTE 2: WHEN YOU BUY PROSCIUTTO, TRIM SOME OF THE FAT OFF, PUT IT IN A PLASTIC CONTAINER AND REFRIGERATE OR FREEZE. IT IS EXCELLENT TO LARD ANY MEAT (SEE STEP 3, PAGE 323).

NOTE 3: NICE PHEASANT CAN BE ORDERED BY MAIL FROM D'ARTAGNAN. THEIR PHONE NUMBER IS 1-800-DARTAGNAN. MANY GREEN MARKETS ALSO SELL THEM.

CERVO IN PADELLA

Venison in a Skillet **(Makes 6 servings)**

HERE IS A SIMPLE AND QUICK WAY OF cooking this delectable meat.

3 to 4 pounds venison, cut into cutlets and pounded
Juice of 1 lemon
7 to 8 juniper berries, crushed
Freshly ground pepper to taste
2 cloves garlic, sliced
1 cup all-purpose flour, approximately, for dredging
2 tablespoons extra virgin olive oil

2 tablespoons unsalted butter
Salt to taste, optional
1 bunch broccoli, trimmed, cut into flowerets, and blanched
1/4 cup Marsala wine
1 cup chicken broth, preferably homemade (page 61), or good quality canned broth
1 tablespoon minced fresh parsley

1. Place the venison in a large bowl, add the lemon juice, and sprinkle with the juniper berries and a good grinding of pepper. Scatter the garlic over and let it stand in a cool place for 1 hour or overnight.

continues

2. Remove the cutlets from the marinade and pat dry. Reserve the marinade. Dredge the cutlets with flour, shaking off the excess.

3. In a skillet large enough to contain all the cutlets in one layer, or using a smaller one and cooking in batches, add the oil and butter. Add the cutlets and cook over medium-high heat, turning often, until lightly browned on both sides. Season with salt, if used. Add the reserved marinade, cook a few minutes, then add the broccoli, and cook 2 to 3 minutes longer to warm through. Add the Marsala and let evaporate. Remove the meat and broccoli to a platter.

4. Add the broth to the skillet. Increase the heat to high and bring to a boil. Cook, scraping the brown particles clinging to the bottom and sides of the skillet with a wooden spoon, until the sauce is slightly reduced. Return the cutlets and broccoli to the pan and warm through. Serve sprinkled with the fresh parsley.

Variation: *Cerbiatto del Duca*, Venison of the Duke
The reason this recipe was called "of the Duke" in my family is that the venison came from a wooded area that had belonged to the local duke. The dish, a succulent one, goes back to the time of chivalry, when hunting was a noble sport.

Instead of cutlets, as used in the previous recipe, the meat is cut into cubes. No lemon in the marinade but a good bottle of dry red wine, like Montepulciano d'Abruzzo or Chianti. To the juniper berries, I add 3 bay leaves. The meat marinates for 2 days. After draining the cubes from the marinade, they are browned in oil and butter as in the above recipe. The marinade is then added little by little during the cooking, which takes about 2 hours, or until the meat is tender. For an elegant touch, 1/4 cup heavy cream can be added during the last 5 minutes.

VERDURE

Vegetables

*B*ecause of the geographical position of Abruzzo, vegetables are cultivated abundantly on the neatly tended farms gracing both the coastline and the interior. We love vegetables in our region, and their preparations are imaginative and varied. In fact, all over Italy, vegetables are an important part of the meal and are always cooked with care.

Italians are masters at preparing delectable casseroles with vegetables, layering them with cheeses, cured meats, or sauces. We love stuffed vegetables like peppers, zucchini, eggplant, and onions. The stuffing can be a light mixture of bread crumbs and herbs, or rice, meat, fish, or even pasta. These vegetable dishes can be served as main courses at a simple family dinner, accompanied by soup or salad.

STUFFING FOR VEGETABLES

(Makes enough filling for 6 to 8 vegetables)

My PARENTS LOVED *VERDURE* (VEGETABLES). We would have them with every meal. My mother used to make wonderful, colorful trays of assorted stuffed vegetables like peppers, eggplant, zucchini, tomatoes, onions, and potatoes.

Stuffed vegetables were often served at dinner, preceded by a bowl of *pastina in brodo* (small pasta, cooked in a homemade broth), followed by a salad, and then the usual basket of assorted fruits.

The stuffing was typically made with bread crumbs. I use my own bread crumbs, which I make by lightly toasting leftover bread and crushing it in the food processor (see Tips, page XIV).

To fill vegetables like eggplant, zucchini, or onions, cut these vegetables in half, scoop out some of the inside, dice, and sauté the dices with the onion.

5 to 6 tablespoons extra virgin olive oil
1 large onion, chopped
1½ cups bread crumbs
6 tablespoons freshly grated parmesan cheese
Salt to taste, optional
Freshly ground pepper to taste
One 8-ounce mozzarella, shredded
1 teaspoon anchovy paste, optional
2 to 3 basil leaves, chopped, or ¼ teaspoon dried
2 sprigs fresh parsley, minced

1. Preheat the oven to 375°F. Heat 2 tablespoons of the oil in a medium-size skillet. Add the onion and sauté over medium-high heat, stirring often, until soft and translucent, about 5 minutes. If you have the scooped out dices from some of the vegetables, add at this point. Cook until soft. Add the bread crumbs and cook until the juices are absorbed, 2 to 3 minutes. Turn the mixture into a mixing bowl. Add 3 tablespoons of the oil. Stir well and add the parmesan, salt, pepper, mozzarella, anchovy paste, basil, and parsley. Toss well.

2. Fill the vegetables of your choice with the bread-crumb mixture, but do not pack solid. Place the vegetables in an oiled pan, drizzle over a little of the remaining oil, and bake until the vegetable shells are soft and the tops are lightly browned, 45 minutes to 1 hour.

BIETOLE AL BURRO

Buttered Swiss Chard *(Makes 6 servings)*

HERE IS A SIMPLE AND DELICATE WAY OF cooking Swiss chard. I reserve the white core of this vegetable to put in a salad.

2 tablespoons unsalted butter
1 tablespoon extra virgin olive oil
1 bunch Swiss chard, about 2 pounds, trimmed and cut up
Salt to taste, optional

Freshly ground pepper to taste
1 cup broth, preferably homemade (page 61), or bouillon
Freshly grated parmesan or grana padano cheese

In a large skillet, heat the butter and oil. Add the chard and cook over medium-high heat, stirring often, until slightly softened, 2 to 3 minutes, add the salt, pepper, and broth. Cover the pan and cook until tender, about 8 minutes. Serve sprinkled with the grated cheese.

NOTE: I COOK BRUSSELS SPROUTS THIS WAY, TOO.

BROCCOLI STRASCINATI

Sauté of Italian Broccoli *(Make 6 servings)*

BROCCOLI DI RAPE IS THE REAL NAME OF the Italian broccoli. This quintessential Italian vegetable is becoming quite popular. The only problem is that Americans, and especially food writers, seem reluctant to spell out its name properly. I think that the word *rape*, which means beets, scares them. Well, I do not mind when people call it *rapini,* but it is not acceptable to call it *rabbe or rabe.* That is not Italian!

Broccoli di rape has a pleasant, bitter flavor which blends splendidly with fruity olive oil and garlic. I like it just

2 bunches broccoli di rape, about 2 pounds
1/4 cup extra virgin olive oil
2 cloves garlic, peeled and smashed

1 small diavoletto (dried Italian hot red pepper), optional
Salt to taste, optional

1. Trim the broccoli, but do not remove the stems (you may want to peel them, but it is not necessary). Cut each spear into 3 or 4 pieces, wash the greens well, and keep them in water until ready to use.

2. In a large skillet over medium-high, place the oil, garlic, and *diavoletto,* if used, and heat.

3. Lift the broccoli with your hands, shake off excess water, and place in the skillet. Stir and cover with a lid. Reduce the heat to medium-low and steam the broccoli

continues

boiled and dressed with a little oil and lemon, or a splash of balsamic vinegar.

The following recipe is the classic one, and it also makes a great condiment for pasta, especially *orechiette*.

in its own water until wilted, about 5 minutes. Remove the lid. If you still have too much liquid, boil to reduce it; otherwise, raise the heat slightly and stir-fry the broccoli until they are tender, about 5 to 6 minutes.

SPEZZATINO DI CARCIOFI E PISELLI

Artichokes and Peas Stew **(Makes 6 servings)**

THIS HAS BEEN A FAVORITE VEGETABLE dish of mine ever since I was a child. Sometimes I make it as a simple lunch just for myself. If I make too much, I scramble a couple of eggs into the leftovers for a meal the next day. What a feast!

For the best results, choose baby or medium-size artichokes and make sure their leaves are closed into a solid ball. To see if they are fresh, squeeze the artichokes with your hands. They should squeak. Avoid those monstrous American types with spiked leaves. They might look impressive but they are tough and there will be a lot of waste. They will also contain a large choke which must be removed.

In Italy, we were always aware of growing seasons. When my mother would find a choke in an artichoke, she would sigh with regret and announce that the season for this delightful vegetable had ended.

8 small (baby) artichokes; or use one 10-ounce package frozen artichokes, thawed
Juice of ¹/₂ lemon
¹/₄ cup extra virgin olive oil
1 sprig fresh Italian parsley

2 cloves garlic, peeled and smashed
One 10-ounce package frozen peas, thawed
Salt to taste, optional
Freshly ground pepper to taste
4 to 5 sprigs fresh Italian parsley, minced

1. Snap back the top of the artichoke leaves one at a time and break off the tough part, leaving the tender part of the bottom of the leaf attached to the stem. Do this all around the artichoke until you reach the pale green leaves. Cut off about 1 inch from of the top of the trimmed artichoke. If there are stems, peel them. Cut the artichokes into wedges and place in a bowl of water. Add the lemon juice to prevent discoloring. (This step is unnecessary if using frozen artichokes.)

2. In a nonreactive, medium-size skillet, heat the oil over medium heat and add the sprig of parsley and the garlic. Cook over medium-high heat, stirring often, until the garlic starts to sizzle, 1 to 2 minutes. Add the fresh artichokes and ¹/₂ cup water. Cover and cook until almost tender, about 15 minutes. (If using frozen artichokes, do not add water and cook only 5 to 6 minutes.)

3. Add the peas, season with salt, if used, and pepper. Cook until the peas are heated through. Sprinkle with the minced parsley and serve.

NOTE: I DO NOT KNOW IF I HAVE SAID THIS BEFORE, BUT IN THIS COUNTRY FRESH PEAS ARRIVE AT THE MARKETS WHEN THEY ARE TOO OLD AND TASTE WOOLLY. FROZEN PEAS ARE BETTER AND, TOGETHER WITH ARTICHOKES, ARE THE ONLY FROZEN VEGETABLES I BUY.

CARCIOFI AL MARSALA

Artichokes in Marsala Wine **(Makes 6 servings)**

CONTRARY TO THE BELIEF THAT IT IS DIFFI-
cult to combine wine with artichokes,
the light sweetness of the Marsala
nicely subdues the natural bitterness of
the artichokes.

This recipe was an invention of my
father. When it came to wine, he knew
well what to do with it.

Choose medium-size artichokes,
with some stem attached, if possible. I
always go to the bin of baby artichokes
and choose the biggest ones.

6 medium-size artichokes
Juice of ¹/₂ lemon
1¹/₂ tablespoons unsalted butter
2 tablespoons extra virgin olive oil
1 medium-size onion, chopped
1 sprig fresh parsley

¹/₂ cup bread crumbs
*³/₄ cup chicken broth, preferably home-
    made (page 61), or good quality
    canned broth*
¹/₄ cup Marsala, preferably dry

1. Trim the artichokes of the tough leaves (see previous recipe), and cut off about
1 inch from the tops. Cut off and peel the stems but leave the artichokes whole.
Plunge the artichokes and stems into a bowl of water with the lemon juice.

2. In a small skillet, heat 1 tablespoon of butter and the oil. Sauté the onion over
medium-high heat, stirring, until soft and translucent, about 5 minutes.

3. Chop together the stems of the artichokes and the parsley and add to the onion.
Cook until the stems are tender, about 5 minutes. Stir in the bread crumbs.

4. Drain the artichokes and insert some of the crumb mixture among the leaves and
into the center. Set the artichokes on their bottoms in a pan large enough to hold
them snugly. Add the broth and the Marsala, dot with the remaining butter, and
cover the pan.

5. Cook over medium heat until the artichokes are done, 30 to 40 minutes. Test by
pulling a leaf off one of the artichokes. If done, the leaf should come out easily.

CARDI CON CAPPERI E OLIVI

Cardoons with Capers and Olives *(Makes 6 to 8 servings)*

THIS IS A SAVORY SIDE DISH PARTICULARLY good with grilled or roasted meat or fish.

1 bunch cardoons, about 2 pounds
Juice of ½ lemon
1 tablespoon all-purpose flour
1 tablespoon capers in brine, drained

3 anchovy fillets, drained
½ cup pitted, cured olives
2 to 3 sprigs fresh parsley
3 tablespoons extra virgin olive oil

1. Clean the cardoons (see Cardoon Soup, page 74). Cut them into 4- to 5-inch pieces, place in a bowl of cold water, and add the lemon juice. Let stand 20 to 30 minutes.

2. Bring water to a boil, add the flour and cardoons, and boil until tender, 5 to 10 minutes.

3. In a food processor, combine the capers, anchovies, olives, parsley, and oil. Process until pureed.

4. Drain the cardoons and quickly rinse them under cold running water. Dry with a paper towel and place on a serving plate, pour the sauce over, and serve.

CIOFFA 'MBRIACA

Drunken Cauliflower *(Makes 6 servings)*

IN ABRUZZO WE LIKE TO COOK VEGETABLES in a covered pan where they slowly absorb the flavor of the condiment in which they are dressed. In this case, wine gives flavor and makes the cauliflower "drunk." Cooked this way the cauliflower remain nice and white.

1 or 2 medium-size heads of cauliflower, about 3 pounds
5 tablespoons extra virgin olive oil
1/2 cup white wine
2 bay leaves
3 cloves garlic, peeled and sliced

1 small diavoletto *(dried Italian hot red pepper)*
Salt to taste, optional
1 cup water
1 tablespoon minced fresh parsley

1. Separate the cauliflower into flowerets and cut the stems into bite-size pieces, or reserve them for use in a salad.

2. Place the cauliflower in a large, heavy pan. Add the oil, wine, bay leaves, garlic, *diavoletto*, salt, and water. Cover and bring to a boil. Reduce the heat to medium and simmer until the cauliflower is tender and all the water has evaporated, about 20 minutes. Stir occasionally.

3. Sprinkle with parsley and serve.

VERDURE IN AGRODOLCE

Greens in Sweet and Sour Sauce *(Makes 6 servings)*

THE SWEET-SOUR TASTE OF THIS RECIPE is a perfect foil for pork dishes.

About 3 pounds mixed greens, such as cabbage (red or savoy), endive, or spinach
1 tablespoon extra virgin olive oil
1 tablespoon prosciutto or bacon fat

2 cloves garlic, peeled
¼ cup wine vinegar
1½ teaspoons sugar
Freshly ground pepper to taste
Salt to taste, optional

1. Shred all the greens and set aside.

2. Heat the oil in a heavy-bottomed pan. Chop the prosciutto or bacon fat together with the garlic and add to the pan. Cook over medium-high heat, stirring often, until the flavors are released, about 1 minute. Add the greens, vinegar, sugar, pepper, and salt. Cover, reduce the heat to low, and stew the greens until tender, about 30 to 35 minutes. Check the liquid in the pan from time to time. If necessary, add a little water to prevent scorching.

Variation: Broccoli, cauliflower, and Brussels sprouts can be prepared this way.

FAGIOLINI AL BURRO E LIMONE

String Beans with Butter and Lemon *(Makes 6 servings)*

THIS IS A FAVORITE WAY TO EAT STRING beans in my house—simply blanched and dressed with a little butter and lemon. Nowadays, I often switch to olive oil instead of butter. Both are good.

1½ pounds string beans, ready to cook
Salt to taste, optional

2 tablespoons unsalted butter
Juice of ½ lemon

Plunge the string beans into boiling, salted water. Cook until tender but not mushy, about 8 to 10 minutes. Drain, dress with the butter and lemon, and serve.

NOTE: PRACTICALLY EVERY VEGETABLE AND GREEN CAN BE COOKED THIS WAY.

FUNGHI TRIFOLATI

Sautéed Mushrooms *(Makes 6 servings)*

WHEN I WAS A CHILD, MY PARENTS SELdom bought mushrooms. They were always picked in the woods and brought to us by a farmer or a friend. I have already told elsewhere the story of our washerwoman in Pescara, who always came with a basket of mushrooms she had picked in her nearby *pineta*, pine wood. Who had ever heard of cultivated mushrooms at that time? Even if we had known of them, we probably would not have bought any. What flavor would they have?

True, there was always a certain fear that some of the freshly picked mushrooms could be poisonous. But we ate them anyway, hoping for the best.

Today, a great variety of mushrooms are found in American stores, and they are perfectly safe to eat. I love to make this recipe with a mixture of cremini, shiitake, portobello, porcini, or whatever is available. This kind of dish can be quite expensive. But I have a little trick. First of all, invest in a bag of dried porcini mushrooms. A handful of those, cooked together with the everyday, inexpensive kind of white mushrooms, is enough to give that special bosky flavor, lost in cultivated mushrooms, to your dish.

¹/₄ cup extra virgin olive oil
2 cloves garlic, peeled and chopped
2 pounds mixed fresh or wild mushrooms, cleaned, stems trimmed and sliced, caps sliced or cut into wedges

¹/₄ cup dried porcini mushrooms, soaked in ³/₄ cup lukewarm water for 15 minutes
Freshly ground pepper to taste
4 sprigs minced fresh parsley
Salt to taste, optional

1. In a large skillet, heat the oil and garlic. Add the fresh mushrooms and cook over medium-high heat, stirring often, until they start to give off liquid.

2. Gently, so as not to disturb the sediment resting at the bottom, lift the porcini mushrooms from the bowl of water with a slotted spoon and strain the soaking liquid through a paper towel or coffee filter. Reserve the soaking water. Chop the porcini and add to the skillet. Add half the parsley and continue cooking until the water put out by the mushrooms has been absorbed.

3. Add the reserved soaking water to the skillet, a little at a time. Cook until all the liquid has been absorbed, about 15 minutes. Season with salt, if used, and pepper, sprinkle with the remaining parsley, and serve.

Variation: This is also a way of cooking zucchini.

TRIFOLATI

Trifolati is a term used for food prepared in the manner in which you would prepare truffles.

Of course nowadays, one has to be a Croesus to be able to afford a *Trifolata di Tartufi* (Sautéed Fresh Truffles). I feel lucky when I have *one* to shred onto some food!

L'INDIVIA DI EMANUELA

Emanuela's Endive *(Makes 4 to 6 servings)*

MY NIECE EMANUELA, OR EMI, AS WE call her familiarly, is not interested in cooking—well, not at this point in her life. She is only twenty-three. However, when she heard that I was writing a new cookbook, she gave me a recipe she likes to make. Vegetables are her favorite food and here it is.

2 or 3 bunches Belgian endive, trimmed and washed
3 tablespoons extra virgin olive oil
2 cloves garlic, peeled and smashed
1 sweet sun-dried pepper, available in Italian specialty food stores

¼ cup cured black olives, pitted and coarsely chopped
1 tablespoon capers in brine, drained
1 tablespoon pinoli nuts
1 tablespoon raisins
1 anchovy fillet, drained and chopped, optional

1. Cut the leaves of the endive into 2 or 3 pieces and plunge into boiling water. Cook until slightly softened, about 5 minutes. Drain.

2. In a large skillet, heat the oil and add the garlic. Using scissors, cut the pepper into round strips and add to the skillet. Cook over medium-high heat, stirring, until the pepper has softened, 3 to 5 minutes. Add the endive, stir, and cook 5 minutes longer. Add the olives, capers, pinoli nuts, raisins, and anchovy. Cook until the flavors come together, 4 to 5 minutes.

NOTE: SERVE THIS DISH WITH ROASTED MEATS, ESPECIALLY PORK.

FAGIOLI FRESCHI

Fresh Beans **(Makes 6 servings)**

I AM SO GLAD TO SEE, MORE AND MORE IN our produce stores, and some super-markets—fresh beans sold in their bright red pods. They cook quickly and can be prepared by just boiling and dressing with oil and lemon, or oil and balsamic vinegar.

The following is a family recipe which was served hot as an accompaniment to meat or fish.

No need to tell you that cooked this way, the beans can be combined with pasta for a delicious *pasta e fagioli* dish.

1 ½ pounds fresh beans, shelled
Extra virgin olive oil
2 cloves garlic, peeled and smashed
2 fresh sage leaves, or ½ teaspoon dried

1 ripe, firm tomato
Salt to taste, optional
Freshly ground pepper to taste

1. In a medium-size pan, place the beans, 2 tablespoons of the oil, the garlic cloves, sage, and tomato. Add enough water to come 1 inch above the beans. Cover the pan, bring to a boil, reduce the heat, and simmer until the beans are tender, about 20 to 45 minutes.

2. Drain the beans, remove the garlic and tomato, mash the garlic, peel and chop the tomato, and stir both back into the beans. Add the salt, if used, a good grinding of pepper, and 3 tablespoons of olive oil, mix, and serve.

FAVE ALL'ABRUZZESE

Fava Beans Abruzzo Style **(Makes 4 to 6 servings)**

FRESH FAVA BEANS (*FAVE* IS THE PLURAL in Italian) have become quite available in this country. In my home, the first fava beans of the season were eaten as fruit, often accompanied by shards of pecorino cheese.

Easy to cook, fava beans accompany meat or fish beautifully. At a dinner party they always generate a pleasant surprise and are a welcome change to the usual run of the mill vegetables.

4 to 5 pounds fava beans, unshelled
2 tablespoons extra virgin olive oil
1 large onion, thinly sliced
1 clove garlic, minced

1 tablespoon minced fresh parsley
Salt to taste, optional
Freshly ground pepper to taste

1. Shell the fava beans from their pods. Bring a pot of water to a boil, add the shelled fava beans, and cook about 10 minutes. Drain, cool, and pull off their outer skins.

2. In a medium-size skillet, heat the oil. Add the onion and cook over medium-high heat, stirring often, until soft and translucent, about 5 minutes. Add the garlic and parsley. Stir in the fava beans and season with the salt, if used, and a little pepper. Cook until the fava beans are tender, about 5 to 8 minutes.

FAVE E PATATE

Fava Beans and Potatoes (Makes 6 servings)

THIS RECIPE CALLS FOR DRIED FAVA beans, but one can very well use the fresh kind.

1 pound dried fava beans, soaked overnight
1 sprig fresh thyme; or 2 bay leaves
2 to 3 medium-size potatoes, peeled and cubed
3 tablespoons extra virgin olive oil

1 medium-size onion, thinly sliced
3 ripe tomatoes, cubed
Salt to taste, optional
Freshly ground pepper to taste
1 tablespoon minced fresh parsley

1. Drain the fava beans, rinse, and place in a large pot. Pour in enough cold water to come 2 inches above the beans. Add the thyme or bay leaves and bring to a boil. Reduce the heat to medium-low and cook until the beans are tender, about 45 minutes to 1 hour. Add the potatoes during the last 15 to 20 minutes.

2. In a large skillet, heat the oil. Add the onion and sauté over medium-high heat, stirring often, until soft and translucent, about 5 minutes. Add the tomatoes and cook 5 minutes longer. Drain the fava beans and the potatoes. Add them to the skillet and cook, stirring often, until the potatoes are tender but not mushy, about 10 minutes. If necessary, add a little hot water or broth to prevent scorching. Season with the salt, if used, and pepper. Serve sprinkled with the parsley.

FINOCCHI AL TEGAME

Baked Fennel (Makes 6 servings)

FENNEL IS BECOMING POPULAR IN THIS country, and it's a good thing, too. Cooked, as in this recipe, fennel also makes a flavorful accompaniment to meat or fish. Do not discard the green "beard" or fronds of the fennel. They can be used in broths, soups, or as an

Unsalted butter as needed
3 fennel bulbs, trimmed, tough leaves removed, cut into quarters, and washed well.

Salt to taste, optional
2 tablespoons grated parmesan cheese

1. Preheat the oven to 375°F. Butter an oven-to-table baking dish large enough to hold the fennel in one flat layer.

herb for a marinade, and as garnish. It has a pleasant anise flavor.

2. Blanch the fennel in boiling, salted water for about 10 minutes. Drain, reserving the cooking liquid.

3. Place the fennel in the prepared dish. Add 1 cup of the reserved cooking liquid, dot with butter, and sprinkle with the cheese.

4. Bake until the fennel is tender when pierced with a fork, about 10 to 15 minutes.

MELANZANE ALLA MEDITERRANEA

Mediterranean Eggplant (Makes 6 servings)

LONG BEFORE THE WORD *MEDITERRANEAN* became fashionable, we were cooking things in Abruzzo in this style—and calling it just so.

It means simple preparations in which the food is cooked with the fragrance of olive oil, tomatoes, herbs, and . . . love.

6 medium-size eggplants
$\frac{1}{4}$ cup, approximately, extra virgin olive oil
2 cloves garlic, very finely minced
1 teaspoon grainy mustard

Juice of 1 lemon
$1\frac{1}{2}$ teaspoons capers in brine, drained
1 tablespoon minced fresh parsley

1. With a fork, pierce the eggplants in 2 or 3 places. Roast the eggplants over the flame of a gas burner, turning them often until the skin is charred. Or, without piercing the skin, bake in a 375°F oven until the vegetables "collapse." Peel and cube the eggplants, removing some of the seeds, if any.

2. In a small bowl, combine the oil, garlic, mustard, lemon juice, capers, and parsley. Mix well and pour over the eggplant and toss.

NOTE: | SOMETIMES PUREE THE EGGPLANT AND SERVE IT AS A DIP WITH A BASKET OF WARM PITA BREAD WEDGES.

MELANZANE A FUNGHETTO
Eggplant Sauté

Melanzane a funghetto means eggplant cooked in the style of mushrooms. This is a common method of cooking vegetables in Italy. It is a sauté done in oil and garlic. Another term used for these kinds of dishes is *trifolati*.

Some people believe in salting the eggplants before cooking them. This helps, of course, to remove the natural bitterness of the vegetables. I sometime do it too, especially if I cannot find small eggplants and have to use large ones, but personally I do not mind a little bitterness in my eggplant.

Eggplants are oil guzzlers. I remember my mother using quite a bit of it and always adding a little more while cooking them. But I have a trick. Every time I need a little more oil or butter, I use my magic cubes of broth. (See the box on page 62.)

For cooking these eggplants just follow the recipe for *Funghi Trifolati* on page 375, and for an eggplant *ragù*, which can be used also as a pasta sauce, toward the end add 1 teaspoon tomato paste and 5 to 6 fresh tomatoes, cubed.

PATATE DELLA DUCHESSA

Duchess Potatoes   (*Makes 6 to 8 servings*)

As its name implies, this is a classic and elegant dish.

1 pound baking potatoes
Salt to taste, optional
Freshly ground white pepper
3 tablespoons unsalted butter, plus more
   for the pan

¹/₂ cup freshly grated parmesan or
   grana padano cheese
¹/₂ teaspoon nutmeg
2 large egg yolks
1 tablespoon milk

1. Boil the potatoes, peel, and puree. Add the salt, if used, pepper, 3 tablespoons of the butter, the grated cheese, nutmeg, and 1 of the egg yolks. Mix well.

2. Preheat the oven to 375°F. Butter a standard-size cookie sheet.

3. Place the potato puree in a pastry bag. Pipe out 6 or 8 round *pizzette* (patties), of equal size onto the prepared cookie sheet.

4. Combine the remaining egg yolk with the milk. Mix well and brush the *pizzette* with this mixture. Bake until golden brown, about 15 minutes.

PATATE ALL'ABRUZZESE

Abruzzo-style Potatoes (*Makes 6 to 8 servings*)

SIMPLE AND RUSTIC, THIS POTATO DISH IS a great accompaniment for a variety of dishes. It also makes a good lunch entrée.

My friend Dr. Arnaldo Cerasoli, a fellow Abruzzese, gave me this "forgotten" recipe. I say forgotten because it reminded me of home, where a similar dish was also made.

8 medium-size baking potatoes
2 tablespoons extra virgin olive oil
4 cloves garlic, finely chopped
1 sprig fresh parsley, minced
Salt to taste, optional
Freshly ground pepper to taste

1. Boil the potatoes until tender, peel, and mash.

2. Heat 1 tablespoon of the oil in a cast-iron skillet. Add the garlic and cook over medium heat, stirring, until it starts to sizzle, about 1 minute. Pour this into the mashed potatoes and add the parsley, salt, if used, and pepper.

3. Add the remaining oil to the skillet, heat over medium heat, and add the potato mixture. Flatten with a fork and cook over very low heat until a golden crust forms on the bottom, 8 to 10 minutes. Turn out the potato pancake onto a plate, slide it back into the skillet again, top side down, and cook on the other side until brown and crisp, about 5 minutes.

NOTE: WITH PATIENCE, THIS RECIPE CAN BE MADE INTO INDIVIDUAL SMALL PANCAKES.

PATATE FRITTE AL FORNO

Fried Potatoes in the Oven (**Makes 6 servings**)

THIS IS ANOTHER HEALTHY SOLUTION TO "real" fried potatoes. These are baked but taste nice and are crisp like the real thing.

3 large baking potatoes, washed and peeled
3 tablespoons extra virgin olive oil

Salt to taste, optional
Freshly ground white pepper to taste

1. Preheat the oven to 400°F.

2. Slice the potatoes as you would for french fries. Place in a mixing bowl, add the oil and season with salt, if used, and pepper. Toss and spread the mixture onto a nonstick cookie sheet large enough to hold them in one flat layer. Bake 30 minutes. Toss them around and continue baking until golden, about 10 minutes longer. Switch the oven off and leave the potatoes in 5 to 10 minutes longer to crisp. Serve hot.

PATATE AL ROSMARINO

Rosemary Potatoes (**Makes 6 servings**)

THIS IS ONE OF THE MOST COMMON WAYS of cooking potatoes in Abruzzo, where the rosemary grows wild on the slopes of our hills. This is a great accompaniment to meat or fish. Fresh rosemary should be used to achieve the special aromatic flavor typical of this dish.

1 1/2 pounds baking potatoes, peeled and
cut into 1/4-inch slices
2 cloves garlic, peeled and quartered
1 sprig fresh rosemary, chopped, or
1/2 teaspoon dried

4 tablespoons extra virgin olive oil
1/4 teaspoon freshly ground pepper
Salt to taste, optional

1. Preheat the oven to 375°F.

2. In a large mixing bowl, place the potatoes with the garlic, rosemary, oil, salt, if used, and pepper. Toss well and pour into a baking dish large enough to hold the potatoes in one flat layer. Bake until potatoes are done, 45 minutes to 1 hour.

NOTE: ONE OR TWO TOMATOES, SLICED AND MIXED WITH THE POTATOES IS A NICE ADDITION.

Variation: Instead of rosemary use bay leaves.

PURÈ DI PATATE

Potato Puree **(Makes 6 servings)**

Sɪʟᴋʏ ᴛᴇxᴛᴜʀᴇᴅ ᴀɴᴅ ᴅᴇʟɪᴄɪᴏᴜs ᴛᴀsᴛɪɴɢ, this puree makes an elegant accompaniment for meat and poultry.

The *purè di patate* is also a classic *contorno* (side dish) served all over Italy.

5 medium-size all-purpose potatoes, about 2 pounds
5 tablespoons unsalted butter, at room temperature

$^1/_2$ cup milk, or more
Pinch of salt
3 to 4 tablespoons freshly grated parmesan cheese

1. Boil the potatoes until soft, peel, and strain them through a food mill or ricer. Add the butter and mix well. Add the milk and continue mixing until smooth and creamy.

2. Pour the mixture into a pan and cook over low heat, stirring constantly until the puree is light and starts to bubble, about 10 minutes. Add a little more milk, if necessary. Remove from the heat and stir in the parmesan cheese. Serve hot.

NOTE: Lᴇꜰᴛᴏᴠᴇʀ ᴘᴜʀᴇᴇ ᴍᴀᴋᴇs ᴅᴇʟɪᴄɪᴏᴜs ᴘᴀɴᴄᴀᴋᴇs; ᴏʀ, ʟᴀʏᴇʀ ᴛʜᴇ ᴘᴜʀᴇᴇ ᴡɪᴛʜ ᴍᴏᴢᴢᴀʀᴇʟʟᴀ ᴄʜᴇᴇsᴇ ᴀɴᴅ ʙᴀᴋᴇ.

PEPERONI ARROSTITI

Roasted Peppers **(Makes 6 servings)**

Iᴛ ᴡᴀs ᴀ sᴜᴍᴍᴇʀ ʀɪᴛᴜᴀʟ. Pᴇᴘᴘᴇʀs ᴡᴇʀᴇ roasted for our daily meal everyday. The smoky perfume permeated the house. The peppers were usually served as a *contorno*, an accompaniment, to the main course. The leftovers went into a delicious *frittata*, or were pureed to dress some spaghetti.

6 peppers, a mixture of green, yellow, and red
1 clove garlic, minced

2 to 3 tablespoons extra virgin olive oil
1 tablespoon minced fresh parsley

1. Roast the peppers by placing them directly over the flame of a gas burner until the skin is charred. Turn the peppers often. Or place on a cookie sheet and roast in the oven at 375°F. Drop them into a paper bag and seal the top. This will facilitate peeling. Let the peppers cool, then peel, core, and seed the peppers. Cut into strips.

continues

2. In a serving bowl, combine the garlic, oil, and parsley. Add the peppers and serve.

NOTE: THOUGH TEMPTING BECAUSE IT IS SO EASY, DO NOT SUCCUMB TO THE TEMPTATION OF PEELING THE PEPPERS UNDER RUNNING WATER. YOU WILL WASH OUT THE FLAVOR ALONG WITH THE SKIN AND SEEDS.

PEPERONI FRITTI

Fried Peppers **(Makes 6 servings)**

THIS *CONTORNO*, SIDE DISH, GOES WITH everything: fish, meat, and poultry. Choose peppers of several colors for an impressive presentation.

A bit of advice: Buy your peppers in advance and keep them in a basket for a few days. They make a lovely still life in your kitchen or living room. When they start to wrinkle, they are better and more mature.

If you buy them at a green market, choose the peppers which are in the midst of changing colors and let them become fully red or yellow. Green peppers are actually immature peppers.

3 tablespoons extra virgin olive oil
2 cloves garlic, peeled and smashed
1 sprig fresh rosemary, or ½ teaspoon dried

5 to 6 large peppers, washed, cored, and cut into strips
1 sprig fresh rosemary, or ½ teaspoon dried

In a large skillet, heat the oil. Add the garlic and rosemary, if using the fresh kind. Cook over medium-high heat, stirring, until the garlic starts to sizzle, about 1 minute. Add the peppers and the dried rosemary, if used. Cook, stirring often, until the peppers are soft and lightly browned, about 15 minutes. Serve hot.

PISELLI STUFATI

Stewed Peas **(Makes 6 servings)**

THIS IS THE MOST COMMON WAY OF cooking peas in Italy. The Abruzzesi use the cheek of the pork or pancetta. The Romans use pancetta or prosciutto.

Italian fresh peas are tender and cook in a minute, so the word "stewed" is a little misleading, but this is what the recipe is called in Italian. I find that in the United States, one can buy fresh peas only at the beginning of the season. Afterward, or later in the season, it is better to use frozen peas for this preparation. I actually find frozen peas to be quite satisfactory.

1 tablespoon extra virgin olive oil
3 ounces pork cheek, or pancetta, or
  prosciutto, diced (see Note)
1 large onion, chopped
2 cups frozen peas, thawed
1 tablespoon minced fresh parsley

In a medium-size skillet, heat the oil. Add the pork cheek, pancetta, or prosciutto, and cook over medium-high heat, stirring often, until the fat is rendered. Add the onion, reduce the heat to medium, cover, and let the mixture stew for about 10 to 15 minutes. Stir often. If you feel you have too much fat in the skillet, remove some and discard. Add the peas, cook 5 minutes, add the parsley, and serve.

NOTE: IF USING PROSCIUTTO, BUY IT IN ONE SLICE, SO YOU WILL BE ABLE TO DICE IT.

Variation: Fava beans are also excellent cooked this way.

ZUCCHINE ALLA CAMPAGNOLA

Country-style Zucchini **(Makes 6 servings)**

ITALIANS LIKE SIMPLE FOOD FOR THE everyday table. These zucchini are easy to prepare and a good side dish for meat or fish. As an extra bonus, it can be used as a sauce for pasta.

3 tablespoons extra virgin olive oil
1 large onion, sliced or chopped
6 small zucchini, about 2 pounds,
*   cut into small cubes*
4 to 5 ripe plum tomatoes, coarsely chopped;
*   or one 8-ounce can peeled tomatoes*

2 to 3 fresh basil leaves, or ¹/₄ teaspoon
*   dried*
Salt to taste, optional
Freshly ground pepper to taste
¹/₂ tablespoon unsalted butter
1 tablespoon minced fresh parsley

1. In a large skillet, heat the oil and add the onion. Cook over medium-high heat, stirring often, until the onion is soft and translucent, about 5 minutes. Add the zucchini and cook 5 minutes longer. Add the tomatoes and basil. Stir, cover, and continue cooking over medium heat until the zucchini are tender, about 8 to 10 minutes. If the mixture is too watery, remove the lid, increase the heat to high, and boil until the liquid has evaporated.

2. Add the salt, if used, and pepper. Remove from the heat, add the butter, stir, and sprinkle with the minced parsley.

Variation: Eggplant and string beans can also be cooked this way.

ZUCCHINE IN SALSA NOBILE

Zucchini in a "Noble" Sauce *(Makes 6 servings)*

THIS IS AN ANCIENT ABRUZZESE RECIPE from the time of my great-great-grandmother.

The preparation is quite modern in appearance, since the zucchini are elegantly cut into thin julienne strips.

3 to 4 medium-size zucchini, about 1 pound
2 tablespoons extra virgin olive oil
1 clove garlic, peeled and chopped
4 to 5 oregano leaves, chopped, or ¼ teaspoon dried

Salt to taste, optional
Freshly ground pepper to taste
1 tablespoon wine vinegar
2 anchovy fillets, drained; or 1 teaspoon anchovy paste
2 to 3 sprigs minced fresh parsley

1. Cut the zucchini in half, julienne them, and place in a large saucepan. Add the oil, garlic, oregano, salt, pepper, and vinegar. Cover and cook over medium-low heat until the zucchini are tender done, about 10 minutes.

2. Spoon some of the liquid from the zucchini into a bowl. With a fork, crush the anchovy into a thick paste and add to the bowl. (Or stir in the anchovy paste.) Add this to the zucchini, mix, and serve sprinkled with the parsley.

Variation: A preparation for zucchini, similar to the above, entails cooking the zucchini with ½ cup white wine, 3 tablespoons olive oil, salt, pepper, 1 bay leaf, and a little thyme. Proceed as indicated. You'll find this dish to be simple and delicious.

CHAPTER 14

INSALATE

Salad

During my cooking classes, when it comes to salad, I always direct this question

to students who have traveled to Italy: How many times were you asked during a

meal at a restaurant in Italy, "Which kind of dressing would you like on your

salad?" The answer is invariably, "Never!" Simple salads served with meals are

always dressed with oil and vinegar, often mixed by your waiter, right at your

table. When the dressing is different, the salad acquires a name, like *alla Siciliana,*

which contains oranges, *alla Genovese,* which includes potatoes and string beans,

and so forth.

Salad is almost never served at the beginning of a meal, at least not in the home or in serious Italian restaurants. In Italy, we believe that salad should cleanse the palate. Therefore, it either accompanies the main dish or follows as a separate course after the main one.

Some composite salads, like the *Insalata Russa* (page 14), a melange of cooked vegetables dressed with mayonnaise, or a rice salad, are served at times as an antipasto. But most often, these are main courses for a lunch or a light supper.

You have read in the pasta chapter how I feel about pasta salads, so I shall not repeat myself. (I don't like them!)

Dressing For My Every Day Salad (Makes about 1 cup of dressing)

As ITS NAME IMPLIES, THIS DRESSING enhances my daily salad. It is a simple combination which I usually prepare in a small jar. It lasts a week or so.

1 clove garlic, peeled and smashed
1 sprig fresh dill; or a small sprig from the "beard" or fronds of a fennel
1 teaspoon grainy mustard

3/4 cup extra virgin olive oil
1/4 cup balsamic vinegar
Salt to taste, optional
Freshly ground pepper to taste

1. Place the garlic and dill in a screw-top glass jar large enough to contain all the remaining ingredients.

2. Add the mustard, oil, vinegar, salt, if used, and pepper. Close the jar and shake well to thoroughly blend the ingredients before serving.

NOTE: THIS DRESSING GOES WITH EVERY KIND OF LETTUCE.

INSALATA AL GORGONZOLA

Gorgonzola Cheese Dressing *(Makes ³/₄ cup dressing)*

I DO NOT PARTICULARLY LIKE CHEESE IN MY salad, but the puckery taste of gorgonzola combines well with a mayonnaise dressing.

2 ounces mild gorgonzola cheese
¹/₃ cup reduced-fat mayonnaise

3 tablespoons coarsely chopped walnuts
1 tablespoon minced fresh parsley

Crumble the cheese and combine it with the mayonnaise. Mix until smooth. Stir in the walnuts and parsley. Refrigerate if not used at once.

NOTE: THIS IS NOT ONLY A GOOD DRESSING FOR EVERY KIND OF GREEN, BUT ALSO FOR COOKED VEGETABLES.

INSALATA DI ARANCE

Orange Salad *(Makes 6 servings)*

THIS DISH IS ONE OF THE FIFTEEN COURSES that are traditionally served at the San Joseph (or San Giuseppe) feast table on March 19th in Castelbottaccio. This is a village of Norman origin in the region of Molise—originally part of Abruzzo.

The feast is usually accompanied by copious amounts of red wine. This is a little unorthodox for the "cognoscenti" who believe that the sour taste of the citrus fruits does not go with wine, but it has a long history. Tradition!

In Campobasso, where the salad accompanies pork dishes, an abundant pinch of sugar is added to the salad instead of the salt.

4 navel oranges
¹/₄ cup extra virgin olive oil

Pinch of salt, optional
1 small clove garlic, peeled and minced

1. Peel the oranges and use a serrated knife to cut the flesh into ¹/₄-inch round slices. Place in a serving dish or platter.

2. In a small bowl, combine the oil, salt, if used, and garlic. Mix well, pour the mixture over the slices, and serve.

Variation: With only one orange you can make a lovely dressing for a salad of radicchio, Belgian endive, and arugula.

INSALATA DI FAGIOLI

Bean Salad (*Makes 6 servings*)

SALADS MADE WITH BEANS, CHICK PEAS, and lentils are quite popular in Italy. They are served cold or lukewarm and are an ideal accompaniment to many dishes, but especially fish.

This salad, because of the beets, appears to be nicely streaked with red when tossed.

1 cup dried white beans
2 bay leaves
1 small red onion, finely chopped
¼ cup extra virgin olive oil
3 tablespoons wine vinegar

Salt to taste, optional
Freshly ground pepper to taste
2 large red beets, boiled, peeled, and cubed
6 small red potatoes, boiled in their skins
*   and cut in half or quartered*

1. Place the beans in a pan of cold water. Bring to a boil, reduce the heat to medium, and simmer 10 minutes. Drain, rinse with cold water, and return the beans to the pan. Cover with water, add the bay leaves, bring to a boil, reduce the heat to medium-low, and simmer until done, but not mushy, about 45 minutes. Drain and set aside.

2. In a serving bowl, combine the onion, oil, vinegar, salt, if used, and pepper. Mix well and add the beans. Toss and add the beets and the potatoes. Toss again and serve.

NOTE: INSTEAD OF BEANS YOU CAN USE CHICK PEAS OR LENTILS. WITH LENTILS, YOU DO NOT NEED TO DO THE PRELIMINARY 10-MINUTE BOILING. ALSO, THE LENTILS WILL COOK IN MUCH LESS TIME, ABOUT 20 TO 30 MINUTES.

INSALATA DI FAGIOLINI MIMOSA

String Bean Salad Mimosa *(Makes 8 servings)*

THIS IS ONE OF MY FAVORITE SALADS. IT IS ideal for a buffet table. It is pretty and easy to serve and eat.

¼ cup extra virgin olive oil
1 clove garlic, peeled and minced
1 teaspoon grainy mustard
Juice of 1 lemon
Salt to taste, optional

Freshly ground pepper to taste
2 pounds string beans, trimmed and
*   blanched*
2 hard-boiled large eggs

1. In a serving bowl, combine the oil, garlic, mustard, lemon juice, salt, if used, and pepper. Mix well. Add the string beans and toss. Place in a serving bowl.

2. Peel the eggs and separate the whites from the yolks. Coarsely chop both, separately. Sprinkle the yolks on top and in the center of the beans, and distribute the whites decoratively all around the yolks. Serve.

DUETTO DI INSALATA CON FINOCCHIO

Salad "Duet" with Fennel *(Makes 6 to 8 servings)*

THIS IS A COLORFUL SALAD WITH A DIFFER-ent dressing and the refreshing crunchiness of fennel. The presentation is quite appealing if one uses the radicchio di Treviso, whose reddish leaves are long, similar to the Belgian endive ones, and not wound up in a ball like the regular radicchio.

1 head radicchio leaves, preferably the
*   Treviso kind*
2 heads Belgian endive, separated into leaves
2 heads fennel, trimmed, tough outer
*   leaves removed, and cut into thin*

rounds (reserve some of the
*   green "beards" or fronds)*
½ cup reduced-fat mayonnaise
1 teaspoon grainy mustard
1 teaspoon ketchup

1. On a round platter, alternate, all around, the radicchio and endive leaves to form a decorative border. Pile the fennel in the center of the platter.

2. In a small bowl, combine the mayonnaise, mustard, and ketchup. Mix the ingredients well and drizzle the dressing all over the salad. Decorate with some of the reserved fennel "beard."

INSALATA DI LATTUGA, CARCIOFI SOTT'OLIO E BARBABIETOLE

Lettuce, Marinated Artichoke, and Red Beet Salad **(Makes 6 to 8 servings)**

I LOVE RED BEETS AND I OFTEN ADD THEM to my regular salad. They also go well mixed with oranges and dressed with olive oil and a splash of balsamic vinegar.

10 to 12 romaine lettuce leaves, or any other green lettuce, torn into bite-size pieces
1 small jar (about 5 ounces) marinated artichokes, drained

2 red beets, boiled and peeled
3 to 4 tablespoons Dressing for My Everyday Salad (page 389)
Freshly ground pepper to taste

1. Place the greens in a large salad bowl. If necessary, cut the artichokes into wedges and place in the center.

2. Cut the red beets into wedges and arrange all around the artichokes. Add the dressing and a little pepper. Toss just before serving.

NOTE: I OFTEN SUBSTITUTE THE ARTICHOKES WITH MARINATED MUSHROOMS AND ALSO HEARTS OF PALM.

INSALATA DI MELANZANE

Eggplant Salad **(Makes 6 servings)**

THIS IS AN UNUSUAL SALAD WITH A STRONG garlicky flavor. Select medium-size eggplants, preferably "male" ones (female eggplants have too many seeds). How do you recognize the gender? The end of the male eggplant is pointed!

3 medium-size eggplants
¼ cup extra virgin olive oil
2 tablespoons balsamic vinegar; or
*   juice of ½ lemon*
1 teaspoon chopped fresh oregano, or
*   ¼ teaspoon dried*

1 to 2 cloves garlic, peeled and slivered
Salt to taste, optional
Freshly ground pepper to taste
2 sprigs fresh parsley

1. Cut the eggplants lengthwise into 4 wedges each. Blanch the wedges 5 minutes. Drain and cool.

2. In a salad serving bowl, combine the oil, vinegar, oregano, garlic, salt, if used, and pepper. Set aside.

3. Cut each wedge of the eggplants into ½-inch triangles. Add to the salad mixing bowl and toss. Set aside for a couple of hours. Just before serving, mince the parsley, sprinkle it over the salad, and serve.

MISTICANZA

"Mixture" Salad **(Makes 6 to 8 servings)**

THIS IS THE ULTIMATE ABRUZZESE SALAD. It is called "mixture" because it is made with a combination of greens and vegetables.

I have been eating this salad since I was a child, and this is why I do not understand all the current fuss about *mesclun*, the mixture of leaves sold in supermarkets and vegetable stores. Mesclun costs *un'occhio della testa* (an eye of the head) and most of the time looks tired and limp. Mix the greens yourself—believe me, it will be much fresher than one you buy.

DRESSING

1 clove garlic, peeled and very finely minced

2 to 4 fresh mint leaves, or basil leaves, minced

3 tablespoons extra virgin olive oil

1½ tablespoons wine vinegar; or 2 tablespoons balsamic vinegar

Salt to taste, optional

Freshly ground pepper to taste

SALAD

8 radicchio leaves

5 to 6 endive leaves

4 to 5 romaine leaves

4 to 5 chicory leaves

10 to 12 arugula leaves

1 small fennel bulb, trimmed, tough leaves removed, and thinly sliced into rounds

1 medium-size carrot, peeled and thinly sliced

2 ripe, firm tomatoes, sliced or cubed, optional

1. At the bottom of a large salad bowl, combine the garlic, mint, oil, vinegar, salt, if used, and pepper. Mix well.

2. Add the leaves, tearing them into bite-size pieces. Add the fennel, carrot, and tomatoes. Toss just before serving.

NOTE: YOU CAN ADD ANY OTHER GREENS YOU LIKE.

INSALATA ROSSA

Red Salad (Makes 6 servings)

IN THE WINTERTIME, WHEN LETTUCE WAS A little scarce, Mother used to make this salad which we enjoyed a lot.

It is best prepared in advance and refrigerated, or left overnight in a cool place.

3 tablespoons extra virgin olive oil
3 tablespoons balsamic vinegar
1 clove garlic, peeled and minced
1 small onion, chopped
2 thin slices peeled fresh ginger, chopped
2 tablespoons raisins
1 small head red cabbage, shredded

In a large salad bowl, combine the oil, vinegar, garlic, onion, ginger, and raisins. Add the cabbage and toss well.

INSALATA CON VERDURE

Salad with Vegetables **(Makes 6 to 8 servings)**

THIS IS ONE OF THE MANY SALADS MY mother made with blanched or boiled vegetables. In Italy, vegetables are often served as a salad, especially broccoli, cauliflower, string beans, and zucchini. These are blanched and simply dressed with oil and lemon. Especially in summertime, they are a refreshing accompaniment to simply grilled meat or fish.

1/4 cup extra virgin olive oil
3 tablespoons wine vinegar
Salt to taste, optional
Freshly ground pepper to taste
1 clove garlic, peeled
1 cup loosely packed fresh basil
2 sprigs fresh parsley
2 medium-size potatoes, boiled, peeled, and cut into small cubes
1/2 pound string beans, blanched and cut into bite-size pieces

1 cup pitted, cured black olives, preferably from California
2 tablespoons capers in brine, drained
1 small head Boston lettuce, or another kind of lettuce, trimmed and washed
3 hard-boiled large eggs, peeled and cut into wedges
1 tablespoon minced fresh parsley

1. In a food processor place the oil, vinegar, salt, if used, pepper, garlic, basil, and parsley. Process until very finely chopped. Set aside.

2. In a mixing bowl combine the potatoes, string beans, olives, and 1 tablespoon of the capers. Add the dressing and toss well.

3. Line the bottom and sides of a salad bowl with the lettuce leaves. Spoon the dressed vegetable mixture in the middle. Sprinkle with the remaining capers and parsley, and decorate with the eggs.

NOTE: THE VEGETABLES MENTIONED IN THE HEAD NOTE CAN ALSO BE ADDED TO THIS SALAD.

PART IV

LA CASA
DI LANCIANO

The House in Lanciano

n every year. After we sold the house in

ght an apartment in Pescara, my Aunt Cla

l, turn of the century villa in the not too

n my brother was married and I was living

each winter with them and even had their

own quarters in the villa. My father and Uncle Raf, lovers of good food

Lanciano is where I now return every year. After we sold the house in Guardiagrele and my parents bought an apartment in Pescara, my aunt Ela and uncle Raf bought a beautiful turn-of-the-century villa in the not-too-distant town of Lanciano.

Later when my brother was married and I was living abroad, my parents spent part of each winter with them and even had their own quarters in the villa. My father and Uncle Raf, lovers of good food and drink, were often caught sneaking down to the cellar, brandishing goblets and a corkscrew. They were only going to taste "this new wine" to see if it was appropriate for the table. They made a funny couple, my father tall, dark, handsome and a little rakish, and Uncle Raf smallish, blond, and dignified. Not withstanding their political disagreements, would you believe my father was the conservative one while Uncle Raf was quite liberal? They could not be without each other for long.

Actually, I had been going to Lanciano since I was a child of seven, before and after my aunt and uncle were married and before they bought the villa. Uncle Raf's many younger brothers and sisters practically adopted my brother and me. They took us everywhere.

It was in the house in Lanciano that my aunt and uncle raised their three children, Gianna, Franca, and Adriana. The house was eventually left to their daughter Adriana, who was the only one of the three girls to remain in Lanciano.

Adriana married a pediatrician, Federico, and they have six children. It is a lovely family and all the children have turned out well. My cousin Adriana always says her children have only one problem, which she calls the complex of the only child, meaning each one wants special attention. But, in fact, they are quite independent, bright, industrious, and have their father's sense of humor. Francesca, the eldest, married to an architect and the mother of two delightful little girls, is a restorer of ancient books. Luigi is a lawyer and a banker, David a teacher, Raffaele an accountant, and the two youngest are still at university.

Lanciano is an ancient and prosperous town which, since the Middle Ages, has been known for its big commercial fairs. Each September, the Fiera di Lanciano calls back all the wayward citizens living in other parts of Italy and reunites them with the families who have remained.

During this month-long fair there are many activities, including horse races, picnics in the park, and elegant balls at the local club. One year during the festival, I was elected Miss Abruzzo and invited to compete for the Miss Italian Competition. But, at the last moment, my mother forbid me to go because she didn't think it was dignified. The one who was upset about mother's adamant refusal was my father, who was already planning to be my chaperone. As a true Italian, a little macho, of course, Papà relished the idea of all those beautiful girls parading around. So he was disappointed and I lost my shot at becoming another Sophia Loren. She competed that year but didn't win. So you see, I might have had a real chance. Sophia though, was elected Miss Cinema, and from there the rest of her life is history.

Lanciano is also famous for its beautiful romanesque churches, an ancient Roman bridge of the Diocletian era, and a Hebrew district, where the Jews involved in local commerce lived. On one side, the city is enclosed by the remains of a twelfth-century castle with imposing towers. I love to walk by these ancient walls at sunset, the flaming sky turning into shades of blue, smoothing the contour of our beautiful mountains. At night the valley below becomes an upside-down sky with the little lights of the farmhouses and villages lighting up and twinkling in the night.

In my university days, I would come back from Rome just before Christmas. Often my mother and father were already in Lanciano. My young cousins were anxiously waiting to start setting up the *presèpio*, or crèche, whose artistic pieces had been accumulated during the years. The crèche was placed in a corner of the main foyer for everybody to see. Presents were hidden away and placed near the crèche the night before

Epiphany, January 6th, after the children had gone to bed. This is when La Befana, the benevolent witch and dispenser of gifts, arrives. In these last years, St. Nicholas has won over La Befana, and now it is from him that the children receive their presents. It is a pity, because while St. Nicholas is not a frightful figure, La Befana, always represented astride a broom amidst thunderous clouds, was.

In fact, it was with a certain apprehension, a mix of fear and expectation, that we children would descend the staircase in the morning to see what was left for us. The sight of large baskets would immediately reassure us. The Befana had not been so nasty.

In Lanciano, on the 23rd of December, a unique rite takes place called La Squilla, which is the sound coming from a bell placed on the civic tower. This bell rings for one hour, from 6 to 7 in the evening, to call families together. It is the time to set aside quarrels, resentments, and ancient wounds.

I remember with anticipation, although I was not raised with this tradition, how we and our cousins would all rush home to kiss and embrace our dear ones and wish each other a "Buon Natale," a Merry Christmas.

The tradition of La Squilla was started in the sixteenth century by a local archbishop to commemorate the loving journey of the shepherds to Bethlehem to honor the Baby Jesus. The saintly man would leave his palace barefoot and walk several kilometers to a little church in the valley. All through the journey he would incessantly ring a bell summoning the faithful to follow him. This pilgrimage is still reenacted today. For the people of Lanciano it is such a strong tradition that when, living away and not able to visit on that date, they telephone each other from wherever they are.

If my remembrance of Pescara invariably turns me back to summer, the beach, and first romances, Lanciano is forever intertwined with the festivals of September and Christmas holidays. It is here that as a young person and an adult the continuation of family traditions took place. My brother, Mimmo, who lived in the nearby city of Chieti, used to arrive unannounced for lunch or dinner just because he was driving by. When he went there with his family, it was more of a planned affair. If my aunt Ela was not prepared for surprise guests, she would send him downstairs, where Adriana lived. She felt that her daughter, with her six children, was used to surprise guests and would not be bothered by one more person. My cousin Adriana misses Mimmo very much; they were particularly close. In fact, everybody said that there was more family resemblance between the two of them than with me, his twin.

The house in Lanciano in many ways has replaced the one in Guardiagrele. It is here that when our families still get together, events and traditions are replayed as they were in the past. Now when Harold and I return to Italy, it is from here that we move around Italy visiting my other cousins, who live in the South, and friends in other cities.

We have brought our own friends from America to Lanciano and my hospitable cousins have impressed them with their generosity and pleasure in entertaining them. My family, true to our motto *Abruzzo forte e gentile,* Abruzzo strong and gentle, uphold the tradition.

CHAPTER 15

DOLCI

Desserts

ABOUT DESSERTS

I should know something about sweets. My maternal great-grandfather, Giacinto Palmerio, started a factory in 1889 making *confetti,* almond-coated candies that soon became a celebrated specialty of Abruzzo, as did his *torroni* (nougat), particularly his *torroni croccanti.*

Today, three cities in Abruzzo are famous for such confections. Sulmona, with its Fabbrica di Confetti Pelino, continues a tradition dating back to the fifteenth century. L'Aquila is known for its tender chocolate *torroni* invented by the sisters Nurzia, who transformed a family operation into an international company.

And in my hometown of Guardiagrele, at the Pasticceria Lullo, a cousin of mine still makes great-grandfather Giacinto's *torroni croccanti*.

When I was growing up, the family factory was run by my uncle Filippo, who years before had reluctantly abandoned his university studies to take over the business. You see, Nonna Sabina, my grandmother, after having seventeen children, was left a widow and pregnant with yet another child. She tried to run the operation by herself, but Uncle Filippo, one of the eldest children, soon realized she was overwhelmed. He took control of this large family and ran the business with both great ability and a touch of tyranny. As time went on, everybody was afraid of Zio Filippo—his employees, his wife, his daughters, nieces, and nephews—but not me. I adored him! When he came home each evening, I would watch from the window and run downstairs to meet him. We would sit in the entrance, me on his lap, and play a game. I had to guess which hand held the "goodie." It was great fun, but of course, I was not allowed to have it until after dinner!

Visitors to Guardiagrele today, after admiring its natural beauties and the ancient romanesque cathedral, cannot go away without stopping at the Pasticceria Lullo. They go to eat the *torroni*, of course, but also to try one of the most singular pastries ever invented. No one knows for sure which family member invented it, but

it remains a very special dessert indeed. The pastry's profane name is *Sise de le Monache*, dialect for nuns' breasts, but in more polite terms they are called *Tre Monti*, for the three peaks of the Maiella Mountain. Each pastry has a sponge cake base stuffed with custard, and a top shaped like three pointed breasts. They are delicious, almost ethereal. The well-known writer and movie director Mario Soldati wrote of these pastries in glowing terms. He mentions them in his book *Viaggio in Italia*, a journey of discovery, recording his personal search for the hidden wine and food treasures of Italy.

The last descendent of the Palmerio family, my charming cousin Francesco, still runs the shop where these pastries are sold. He did not abandon his university studies, though. He is a patissier with a doctorate in Italian literature, and in fact, is the director of the town's library.

Last October, while visiting the Del Verde Pasta Factory in Fara San Martino with a group of my students from Seattle, our hosts uncovered a table laden with *Sise de le Monache*. In response to my astonished, questioning look, they revealed that they had done their research, discovered that I was born in Guardiagrele, and that the owner of the Pasticceria Lullo was my cousin. I confess I was profoundly touched.

You will not find the recipe for these pastries here. It remains a family secret and you will have to go to

Guardiagrele to taste them! I confess I tried to make them once . . . and failed miserably. My darling cousin Francesco consoled me saying that I did not have the right oven. Perhaps! Or maybe my ancestors were indeed keeping an eye on this century-old family secret.

Fortunately, Abruzzo is a region rich in desserts of all kinds. We have specialties for every occasion—religious festivities, birthdays, marriages, and even funerals. In this book I focus on family recipes for desserts which were a feature in my house, and those from the places most familiar to me and my family. One could write an entire book on the sweets of Abruzzo—perhaps one day I will.

Thanks to the shop, my childhood never lacked pastries and cookies. However all the traditional desserts were still prepared in the home. For Christmas we made *cavicionetti* (page 415) to give to friends and offer to well-wishers. At *Carnivale* (our Mardi Gras), we made decorative *cicerchiata* (page 417), a kind of honey cake. We prepared fritters called *zeppole di San Giuseppe* (page 442) in honor of the saint and my father, whose name was Giuseppe. At Easter we had several *pizze*, some savory, some served as dessert, like the *fiadone* (page 40) and *bocconotti* (page 412), as well as special almond pastry cakes in the shape of a horse or a lamb for the boys, and a doll for the girls.

You'll notice, we Abruzzesi are quite partial to nuts and honey.

Hazelnuts and almonds grow wild in the mountains around us. Honey has been a staple since the time of the Romans when sugar was rare and costly; to this day, it remains an ingredient in many of our favorite recipes.

Finally, any discussion of sweets from Abruzzo must include liqueurs, which always accompanied dessert. In the past, many liqueurs were homemade. My father was a master at it. I inherited his recipe book, but unfortunately, in this country, it is illegal to buy pure alcohol, the base for liqueurs. I remember the delicate *rosoli* reserved for the ladies, the dark *nocino*, made with walnuts, or the *cerasuolo*, with the fragrant perfume of cherries. But the art of making liqueur actually dates to the Middle Ages. Monks were passionate herbalists who concocted many elixirs with herbs furnished by *madre terra* (mother earth) for the purpose of curing all ills, including love maladies and the black death.

One such is the fierce *centerbe*, a potent digestive containing one hundred herbs from the Maiella. It is referred to as "green fire" for its color and its 70-proof strength. The Toro family, makers of this strong liqueur since 1817, insist that, apart from the herbs indeed gathered by the monks, the liqueur is the absolute creation of a Dr. Beniamino Toro, a pharmacist.

Then there is *corfinio*, a name derived from the mythical capital of a state called Italia founded by the fierce people of Abruzzo. They rebelled against Rome and defeated the formidable Roman Legions in the year 328 B.C.

To commemorate this event, Michetti, a celebrated painter of the turn of the century, designed the typical bottle for the *corfinio* in the shape of a Roman amphora. He decorated it with Italic warriors to whom the liqueur is supposed to give strength and courage.

Nowadays most liqueurs are commercially produced and the most renowned one is the golden Aurum, from Pescara. It is flavored with the sweet oranges growing along the Adriatic. Yet, when I go to visit relatives or friends in some remote parts of Abruzzo, the *rosolio* is still served, often with the lacy *pizzelle* (page 430), the sweet symbol of Abruzzo.

CREMA DI MAMMA

Mother's Custard (**Makes 2 cups**)

I CALL IT *CREMA DI MAMMA*, MY COUSINS call it *crema di zia*, aunt's custard, and friends will say *la crema della signora Raffaella . . . .* The fact is, this custard is so good and so foolproof that everybody who has tasted it has asked for the recipe. It is a basic custard that works well as a filling for cakes and can be combined with many flavors and other ingredients.

4 large egg yolks	*2 cups milk*
3/4 cup sugar	*2 strips lemon peel*
3 tablespoons all-purpose flour	*1 teaspoon vanilla extract*

1. In the pot, combine the yolks, sugar, and flour. Mix with a wire whisk until smooth. Slowly add the milk, stirring, until the mixture liquifies. Add the lemon peel.

2. Place the pot over medium-low heat and cook the custard, stirring constantly, until it starts to condense and a few bubbles appear at the top of the custard. Simmer gently for about 1 minute but do not boil.

continues

The best pot in which to make this *crema* is a copper zabaglione pot. You can also use an enameled pot.

3. Remove from the heat, stir in the vanilla, transfer to a bowl, and cool.

NOTE: MY MOTHER ALWAYS USED A VANILLA BEAN WHICH SHE ADDED WITH THE LEMON PEEL. WHEN FINISHED SHE WOULD REMOVE THE BEAN, RINSE IT, LET IT DRY, AND STORE IN A JAR FULL OF SUGAR. IT WAS REUSED MANY TIMES.

Variation: For chocolate custard, place 2 tablespoons of cocoa in a bowl. Add a few tablespoons of the hot custard and mix until smooth. Add the remaining custard and a pinch of ground cinnamon. Mix until smooth.

PAN DI SPAGNA LUCIANA AMORE

Sponge Cake Luciana Amore **(Makes 8 servings or more)**

THIS IS AN EASY WAY TO MAKE SPONGE cake. Contrary to tradition, a pinch of baking powder is added to the flour. The mixture is then stirred into the egg yolks before folding into the whites. It never fails, I say, making the usual sign against the evil eye, and I thank my cousin Luciana for devising this easy method.

Unsalted butter for pan
2 tablespoons all-purpose flour mixed with a pinch of sugar
4 large eggs, separated

¼ teaspoon lemon or vanilla extract
¾ cup sugar
¾ cup all-purpose flour
1 teaspoon baking powder

1. Preheat the oven to 350°F. Lightly butter a 9-inch cake or springform pan. Dust with the flour-sugar mixture, making sure that the bottom and sides of the pan are well coated. Shake out excess flour mixture.

2. Beat the egg yolks, add the flavoring and sugar, and continue beating until the mixture is fluffy and lemon-colored. Mix the flour and the baking powder together and stir into the yolk mixture. The dough will be stiff.

3. Beat the egg whites until stiff. Stir one third of the whites into the dough mixture and mix to lighten it. Add the rest of the egg whites, a little at a time, and gently, but swiftly, fold into the mixture. Pour into the prepared pan.

4. Bake 45 minutes without opening the oven. If a toothpick inserted in the middle of the cake comes out clean, the cake is done; otherwise cook a little longer. Cool on a wire rack and unmold.

PASTA FROLLA SEMPLICE

Simple Pie Dough **(Makes 1 double crust 9-inch pie crust)**

THIS IS A BASIC DOUGH, ESPECIALLY suited for fruit pies.

2 cups all-purpose flour
¼ cup sugar
½ cup (1 stick) unsalted butter,
    cut into ½-inch cubes

3 tablespoons solid vegetable shortening,
    chilled
1 large egg
½ cup, or more, ice water

1. In a food processor fitted with a steel blade place the flour and sugar. Process a few seconds. Add the butter and shortening. Process until the mixture resembles coarse meal. Add the egg, process just to blend, and start adding the water a little at a time. Stop as soon as a ball starts to form on the blades.

2. Remove the dough from the processor and with floured hands form into a ball. Cut the ball in half, shape each half into a smaller ball, flour them lightly, and wrap in plastic wrap. Chill for 1 hour or more.

SALSA DI RICOTTA PER FRUTTA

Ricotta Sauce for Fruit **(Makes 2 cups sauce)**

INSTEAD OF WHIPPED CREAM, TRY THIS sauce on berries, any kind, or top sliced fruit such as peaches, nectarines, apricots, and bananas with a spoonful of it.

You can add melted chocolate or a fruit puree like raspberry to the ricotta and serve it as an accompaniment to cakes. You can make the sauce as fluid as you like by adding more liquid, such as orange juice, or you can use ¼ cup liqueur, such as Curacao, Grand Marnier, or Amaretto, for example.

1 pound whole milk ricotta, drained
¼ cup sugar or honey
1 teaspoon vanilla extract

Rind of 1 orange, minced
Juice of 1 large orange

Place all the ingredients in a food processor fitted with a plastic blade. Process until smooth. Chill before using. Serve the sauce over berries or fresh fruit.

SCORZETTE D'ARANCE CANDITE

Candied Orange Peel (**Makes 2 cups**)

I USE THESE ORANGE PEELS TO DECORATE cakes or as a flavoring for cakes, *semifreddi*, ice cream, and fruit desserts.

I cut the oranges in wedges, remove the peel, and scrape off the bitter white pith. I store the peels in a plastic bag in the refrigerator until I have the right amount. The finished orange peels keep for a long time in the refrigerator.

1 cup sugar
1 teaspoon cream of tartar

$^1/_2$ cup water
2 cups orange peel

1. In a nonreactive pan, combine the sugar, cream of tartar, and water. Bring to a boil, reduce the heat to low, and simmer 15 minutes.

2. Cook the orange peels in boiling water, about 10 minutes. Drain and add to the sugar mixture. Simmer 30 minutes. Cool completely. Place the peels and syrup in a covered jar. It lasts refrigerated for several months.

NOTE: WHEN YOU WANT TO USE SOME OF THE PEELS, REMOVE THEM WITH A FORK. NEVER STICK YOUR FINGERS INTO THE JAR—THIS CAUSES THE REMAINING PEELS TO GET MUSHY. THE PEELS CAN BE CUT INTO THIN JULIENNE STRIPS BEFORE COOKING, IF DESIRED.

BANANE E FRAGOLE ALLE NOCI

Bananas and Strawberry with Pecans (**Makes 6 to 8 servings**)

THIS IS A VERY SATISFYING LITTLE DESSERT I invented one day when a bunch of almost green bananas suddenly ripened and had to be used immediately. This is what I did.

1 pint strawberries
3 tablespoons honey
*1 tablespoon chopped Candied Orange
   Peel (above), optional*

2 tablespoons Aurum or other orange liqueur
5 ripe bananas
$^1/_2$ cup pecans or walnuts, coarsely chopped
Mint leaves for garnish

1. Wash, dry, and hull the strawberries. Slice lengthwise.

2. In a mixing bowl, combine the honey, orange peel, and liqueur. Add the strawberries and set in a cool place for 30 minutes. Toss every once in a while.

3. Peel the bananas and cut in half lengthwise. Cut the halves into thin slices, add to the strawberries, toss, add the nuts, and toss again. Serve in individual bowls, garnished with the mint leaves.

BARRETTE DI CIOCCOLATA E NOCI

Chocolate Pecan Bars (Makes 24 bars)

In addition to my favorite younger aunts, Cettina and Ela, I had other fabulous older aunts as well. They were distributors of cookies, narrators of exciting fables, and lived in houses full of mysterious rooms with enchanting corners and secluded gardens.

One of these older aunts was Zia Nina, a cousin of my mother. She lived in a town named *Torre dei Passeri* (tower of the sparrows). We used to visit her once or twice during the year and stay for a week or so. She was a widow who had been married to a charming man, considered by the family to be a scoundrel. But she adored him! It was rumored that Uncle Camillo, her husband, had squandered her fortune with his extravagant living, which she had willingly shared. Aunt Nina lived in genteel poverty, with a faithful, unpaid maid, in an old house, with elegant rooms surrounded by beautiful objects. I have an inlaid table in my living room that comes from her house. I love it, not only for its beauty but also for the memories it brings. She was a grand lady and we children were enchanted by her stories. This recipe for pecan bars comes from my friend, Marietta Poerio, but they are similar to those made by Zia Nina's maid. The first time I ate them at Marietta's, I knew I had found again the delicious "bars" of Zia Nina.

CRUST

3/4 cup (1 1/2 sticks) unsalted butter, cut into pieces, plus more for the pan

1 1/2 cups all-purpose flour

2/3 cup sugar

1/2 teaspoon salt, optional

1 large egg, lightly beaten

FILLING

1/2 cup (1 stick) unsalted butter, at room temperature

1 cup brown sugar

2 large eggs

1/4 cup all-purpose flour

1 1/2 teaspoons vanilla extract

3 cups chopped pecans

2 cups semisweet chocolate chips

1. Preheat the oven to 350°F. Lightly butter a 13 × 9-inch baking pan. Set aside.

2. Prepare the crust: Combine the flour, sugar, butter, and salt in a food processor. Process until the mixture reassembles coarse meal. Add the egg and process until a dough forms on the blades.

3. With floured hands, press the dough evenly into the bottom of the prepared pan. Bake until lightly golden, 20 to 25 minutes.

4. Prepare the filling: Cream the butter and sugar in a mixing bowl and beat until light and fluffy. Add the eggs, one at a time, beating well after each addition. Beat in the flour, add the vanilla, and stir in the pecans and the chocolate chips. Spread this mixture over the crust and bake until the top is golden brown, 30 to 35 minutes. Cool on a rack and then cut into 24 bars.

Biscotti alle Mandorle

Almond or Hazelnut Cookies (**Makes about 2 dozen cookies**)

My grandmother, Nonnina, as she was affectionately called, used to make these *biscotti* all the time. She would have them ready for friends, who in Italy often arrived without notice, the gardener, who came once a week, the washerwoman, and other acolytes who gravitated to her big house. The beverages varied according to whom the cookies were served—tea or hot chocolate for the ladies, some special wine such as *Marsala* or *vino cotto* for the others. My father always managed to be the one serving "the others" so that he could dip his cookies into the *vino cotto*, which he loved.

These *biscotti* can be made with hazelnuts. Incidentally, The name *biscotti* means "twice cooked," from the Latin *bis,* which means "two." Nowadays, though, it stands for all sorts of cookies.

3 cups all-purpose flour, plus more for kneading
2 teaspoons baking powder
4 large eggs
1 cup sugar
³/₄ cup (1¹/₂ sticks) unsalted butter, melted
3 tablespoons olive oil
1 teaspoon almond extract
1 teaspoon vanilla extract
1 cup almonds or hazelnuts, lightly toasted, skinned, and coarsely chopped

1. Preheat the oven to 350°F. Butter a standard-size sheet pan.

2. Sift the flour and the baking powder together. Set aside. In a large mixing bowl, combine the eggs and sugar. Beat 5 minutes and add ¹/₂ cup of the melted butter. Add the olive oil, almond extract, vanilla, and nuts. Gradually add the flour mixture and beat until well combined.

3. Line a standard-size cookie sheet with parchment or waxed paper. Brush lightly with some of the remaining butter.

4. Turn the dough onto a floured pastry board or other work surface and knead for 5 to 8 minutes, adding more flour as needed to prevent sticking. Shape the dough into two 14 × 2-inch logs. Place on the prepared pan and bake until golden, about 25 minutes. Cool on a rack. Reduce the oven temperature to 275°F.

5. Cut the loaves diagonally into ¹/₂-inch-thick slices. Place the slices back onto the cookie sheet and bake for 10 minutes, turn once, and bake 10 minutes longer. Cool completely before storing in airtight containers.

BISCOTTI AL MASCARPONE

Cookies with Mascarpone (**Makes about 2 dozen cookies**)

THESE DELICATE COOKIES ARE EASY TO make and delicious. They also lend themselves to a few variations. You can add nuts such as pecans, almonds, hazelnuts, and other dried fruits.

1 1/2 cups sugar
1/2 cup (1 stick) unsalted butter, at room temperature
1 large egg
1/2 cup mascarpone cheese

1 teaspoon vanilla extract
2 1/4 cups all-purpose flour
1/2 teaspoon baking powder
1/2 cup semisweet chocolate chips
1/2 cup raisins

1. Preheat the oven to 300°F.

2. In a food processor, combine the sugar and butter. Process briefly to blend. Add the egg, mascarpone, and vanilla. Mix just to combine; do not over process. Add the flour and baking powder. Process a few seconds to mix and turn into a bowl. Stir in the chocolate chips and raisins.

3. Use tablespoons to drop rounded bits of dough, about 2 inches apart, onto non-stick cookie sheets.

4. Bake until edges are golden, about 25 minutes. Do not brown. The cookies will spread and touch each other. Cool before separating. Store in airtight containers.

BOCCONOTTI ABRUZZESI

Abruzzesi "Mouthfuls" **(Makes 10 to 12 bocconotti)**

THESE ARE STUFFED PASTRIES MADE IN special molds available in stores selling Italian kitchen ware. Individual brioche molds can also be used.

In Abruzzo we have pastries to celebrate almost every occasion, and these *bocconotti* are traditional Easter fare.

DOUGH

1 ½ cups all-purpose flour, plus more as needed
½ cup sugar
½ cup (1 stick) unsalted butter, cubed and chilled
2 large eggs, at room temperature
2 large egg yolks

FILLING

1 cup toasted almonds
6 tablespoons sugar
6 tablespoons cocoa
Grated rind of 1 lemon
¼ teaspoon cinnamon
Sweet wine like Malvasia, Marsala, or sherry
Unsalted butter for the molds
Confectioner's sugar for dusting
Cinnamon for dusting

1. Prepare the dough: Combine the flour and the sugar in a food processor. Process briefly, add the butter, and process again until the mixture resembles coarse meal. Add the eggs and the egg yolks. Process until a ball forms on the blades. Wrap in plastic wrap and chill for 30 minutes, or until ready to use.

2. Prepare the filling: Combine the toasted almonds and sugar in a food processor. Process until finely chopped. Add the cocoa, lemon rind, cinnamon, and enough wine to make the mixture creamy but not wet.

3. Butter 12 *bocconotti*, or individual brioche molds.

4. Roll out the dough ⅛ inch thick. Cut the dough into rounds large enough to fit the molds. Set the remaining dough and all the scraps aside. Line the molds with the cut dough and let overhang slightly. Fill the *bocconotti* shells with the almond mixture to just below the rim.

5. Preheat the oven to 375°F.

6. Gather the remaining dough and scraps into a ball, roll out thinly, and cut to fit the tops of the filled *bocconotti*. Seal all around by pressing with your fingers so that the overhanging dough is cut away.

7. Place the *bocconotti* on a cookie sheet and bake until the tops are golden, 20 to 25 minutes. Cool, unmold, and dust with sugar and cinnamon.

NOTE: THE *BOCCONOTTI* CAN BE STORED IN AN AIRTIGHT CONTAINER FOR 1 WEEK TO 10 DAYS.

BUDINO DI RICOTTA E CIOCCOLATA

Chocolate and Ricotta Pudding (Makes 6 to 8 servings)

I STILL REMEMBER THE DIN OF THE SHEEP'S bells in the courtyard of my grandmother's house announcing the shepherds and their wares. We would run down to caress the woolly animals while the grown-ups bargained for fresh cheeses and ricotta. Back in the kitchen, my three younger cousins, Gianna, Franca, Adriana, and I would make a dessert of our own invention. Our maid Annina mischievously let us be a bit naughty and use the homemade orange liqueur.

This simple, quick dessert can be elegantly embellished with kiwis or berries.

1 tablespoon cocoa
3 tablespoons orange liqueur
1 teaspoon vanilla extract

4 cups ricotta, drained
¹/₄ cup honey
4 ounces bittersweet chocolate, grated

1. In a small bowl, combine the cocoa, liqueur, and vanilla. Mix into a smooth paste. Turn the mixture into a food processor, add ¹/₄ cup of the ricotta, and process until smooth and creamy. Add the honey, chocolate, and the remaining ricotta and process thoroughly.

2. Spoon into individual glasses and serve.

NOTE: ORANGE GOES WELL WITH CHOCOLATE. IF NOT USING THE ORANGE LIQUEUR, ADD THE GRATED PEEL OF A SMALL ORANGE OR CANDIED ORANGE PEEL (PAGE 408).

Variation: Sometimes I omit the cocoa to keep the pudding white and I melt the chocolate. I place the prepared ricotta in individual goblets. Slowly I pour some of the hot chocolate in and gently I swirl it around two to three times with a small knife. The black-and-white effect in the glass is very appealing.

BUDINO DI RICOTTA

Ricotta Pudding **(Makes 8 servings)**

THIS IS CALLED A PUDDING, PERHAPS FOR its soft texture, but is actually more like a cake. My aunt Cettina used to make it for my birthday.

I prepare it in a medium-size soufflé dish and often serve the pudding hot, with raspberry sauce on the side. Or I let it cool in the dish and then unmold it. When cool, the pudding falls, and can be served sliced as a cake. Either way, the flavor is delicious.

Some people recoil at the mention of candied fruit as it is often stale. When you buy it, be sure the fruit is moist and not too dry. Or you can use my *Scorzette d'Arance*, Candied Orange Peel (page 408).

Butter for pan
Very fine bread crumbs for dusting the pan
$^1/_4$ cup raisins
$^1/_4$ cup mixed dried fruits, diced
$^1/_4$ cup rum
4 large eggs, at room temperature
$1^1/_2$ pounds whole milk ricotta, drained
$^1/_4$ cup all-purpose flour
5 tablespoons sugar
$^3/_4$ teaspoon cinnamon
Rind of 1 lemon, finely chopped
1 teaspoon vanilla extract
Confectioner's sugar

1. Preheat the oven to 350°F. Lightly butter a 6-cup-capacity soufflé dish and sprinkle the bottom and sides with bread crumbs. Set aside.

2. Combine the raisins and candied fruit in a small bowl. Pour the rum into the bowl and let stand 10 minutes. Stir once or twice.

3. In a large bowl, combine 1 whole egg with the yolks of the remaining 3 eggs. (Set the whites aside.) Beat the egg and yolks until frothy. Slowly add the ricotta and mix well.

4. Combine the flour, sugar, and $^1/_4$ teaspoon of the cinnamon and add to the ricotta mixture. Add the lemon rind and vanilla. Mix well and add the candied fruit with the rum. Mix again.

5. Beat the egg whites, preferably in a copper bowl, until stiff and fold into the ricotta mixture. Pour into the prepared soufflé dish and bake until a cake tester inserted into the middle of the cake comes out clean and the top is nicely colored, about 1 hour.

6. If not serving immediately, let cool in the oven before unmolding. Serve with a dusting of confectioner's sugar and the remaining cinnamon.

Cavicionetti all'Abruzzese

Abruzzese-style Christmas Fritters (**Makes about 60 to 70 pastries**)

CAVICIONETTI ARE HALF-MOON SHAPED pastries. In Abruzzo they are made all through the Christmas season, both to have around the house for visiting well-wishers and to send to friends and relatives. Although we would receive several trays as presents, I always thought that my grandmother's *cavicionetti* were the best. And this is her recipe. *Cavicionetti* are sometimes called *caggionetti*.

FILLING

2 cups Marsala wine, sweet or dry
1 1/2 cups almonds, blanched, toasted,
   and finely chopped
1/2 cup walnuts, finely chopped
1/2 teaspoon ground cinnamon
2 cups boiled chick peas, pureed
4 ounces semisweet chocolate, coarsely
   chopped
3/4 cup sugar
2 tablespoons candied fruit, finely chopped
Grated rind of 1 lemon

DOUGH

3/4 cup white wine
3/4 cup water
1/2 cup oil
3 1/2 cups all-purpose flour
1 teaspoon baking powder
Oil for deep-frying
Confectioner's sugar
1/4 teaspoon cinnamon

1. Prepare the filling: Heat the Marsala in a nonreactive pan. In a mixing bowl, combine the nuts, cinnamon, and chick pea puree. Add enough hot Marsala to obtain a thick but not stiff cream. Add the chocolate and stir until the chocolate melts. Add the sugar, candied fruit, and lemon rind. Refrigerate at least 20 minutes or longer. The filling can be prepared the day before.

2. Prepare the dough: Combine the wine, water, and oil in a food processor. Process a few seconds and start adding the flour and baking powder. Stop as soon as a ball forms on the blades. Turn the dough onto a floured work surface and knead 15 minutes, adding more flour if necessary. The dough should be a little stiff but pliable. Cover with a bowl and let rest 15 minutes.

3. Roll out the dough as thinly as possible. (This can be done with a pasta machine, stopping before the last notch.) Cut the dough into 4-inch circles. Reuse the scraps by rerolling them into the remaining dough. Place 1 tablespoon of the filling on each circle. Run a wet finger around the edge of the circle, fold the dough over to form a half moon, and press edges firmly to seal. Keep the finished pastry on a tray lined with kitchen towels.

continues

4. Heat the oil to the smoking point and fry pastries, without crowding the pan, until golden brown. Drain on paper towels. Mix the confectioner's sugar and cinnamon together and dust them with the mixture. *Cavicionetti* can be served hot or cold.

NOTE: THESE PASTRIES CAN ALSO BE BAKED AT 375°F FOR 35 MINUTES.

A PUREE OF CHESTNUTS, ALTHOUGH LESS TRADITIONAL, IS A GOOD SUBSTITUTION FOR CHICK PEAS.

CIAMBELLONA

(Makes 18 slices or more)

IT IS DIFFICULT TO TRANSLATE THE NAME of this recipe. A *ciambella* is a round cake with a hole in the middle. A big one is called a *ciambellona*. Small ones, like doughnuts, are called *ciambelline*.

This cake is like a brioche and wonderful for breakfast. Mother made it often. I must confess that before the war I never ate bread for breakfast. It was either the *ciambellona*, or *susamelli* and *cornetti* (pastries similar to croissants), or the ever-present *biscotti*. The war changed all this, and we were lucky when we had bread.

Slices of *ciambellona* with jam and preserves were also offered at teatime, when the ladies (those were the days!) came to visit.

Like brioche, this is better when eaten freshly baked and still warm. The slices can be toasted and make wonderful French toast as well.

5 cups all-purpose flour
1 cup whole wheat flour
2 cups milk, scalded
3/4 cup sugar
1 envelope dry yeast
1/2 cup (1 stick) unsalted butter,
*   at room temperature*
4 large eggs

1/2 cup honey
1 teaspoon vanilla extract
1 teaspoon cinnamon
1 cup pitted, chopped dates, or raisins
2 tablespoons chopped Candied Orange
*   Peel (page 408)*
Unsalted butter for pan

1. Combine the flours together in a large bowl and set aside.

2. Place 1/2 cup of the milk in a mixing bowl. Add 2 tablespoons of the sugar, the yeast, and 1 tablespoon of the combined flours. Stir and let stand until the mixture foams, about 10 minutes.

3. Stir the butter into the remaining milk and let melt.

4. Lightly beat the eggs and add to the milk and butter mixture. Add the remaining sugar, honey, vanilla, and cinnamon. Mix well. Add the yeast mixture, stir, and start adding the flour, 1 cup at a time, while beating with a wooden spoon. Stir in the dates and the orange peel. The dough will be soft and sticky. Cover the bowl with buttered plastic wrap and kitchen towels. Set in a warm place and let rise until doubled in bulk, about 1 1/2 hours.

5. Butter a 12-inch tube or Bundt cake pan (12-cup capacity) and spoon the dough into it. Cover the pan with buttered plastic wrap and kitchen towels. Set in a warm place and let rise again for 1 hour.

6. Preheat the oven to 350°F. Remove the coverings from the pan and place in the lowest third of the oven. Bake the cake until a toothpick or cake taster inserted into the middle of the dough comes out clean, 50 minutes to 1 hour. Cool 5 to 10 minutes in the pan, then unmold. Serve warm, or toast the slices.

LA CICERCHIATA

(Makes about 16 servings)

THE NAME OF THIS CAKE COMES FROM *cece* (chick pea) because it is formed with hundreds of little balls of dough the size of chick peas. It takes a little patience to shape them but is worth the trouble. It is traditionally made for *Carnevale*, the Italian Mardi Gras.

La Cicerchiata is an ancient dessert that actually comes from the Jews living in Italy at the time of the Romans. Therefore, I was not surprised when served a similar confection called *teiglach* at Rosh Hashanah dinners.

In other parts of Italy this type of cake has different names and shapes. In Naples it is called *strufoli*, meaning wads of cotton, and it is conically shaped. In Sicily, since the dough is pinched off in little pieces, it is called *pizzicati* (pinched).

Children love this dessert because it looks so festive with its decoration of candied fruits and almonds.

"CHICK PEAS"
4 large eggs, at room temperature
3 tablespoons sugar
½ cup extra virgin olive oil
1 tablespoon liqueur, preferably an orange liqueur
3 cups or more all-purpose flour
Oil for deep-frying, preferably canola

ASSEMBLY
1½ cups honey
3 to 4 tablespoons blanched almonds
2 tablespoons diced candied fruit
¼ cup Candied Orange Peel (page 408), diced
6 red candied cherries, or a mixture of red and green, halved

1. To make the "chick peas": Place the eggs and sugar in a food processor. Process a few minutes to blend, then add half the olive oil and the liqueur. Process to mix well. Start adding the flour a little at a time until a ball forms on the blades. Remove the dough to a floured work surface and knead until smooth and pliable, adding more flour as needed to prevent sticking.

2. Break off pieces of dough and roll with your hands into long, thin, round strips. Cut the strips into small pieces the size of chick peas. (If you have the patience, roll the little pieces into balls.) Keep the balls on a platter, which will make it easier to slide them into the hot oil.

3. In a frying pan, combine the frying oil and the remaining olive oil. Heat to the smoking point and start frying the little pieces, in batches, until golden. Remove with a slotted spoon and drain on paper towels.

continues

4. In a large skillet, heat the honey over medium-high heat until it starts to darken, 3 to 4 minutes. Add the fried little balls and stir gently with a slotted spoon until well coated. Add the almonds and the candied fruit, but not the orange peel and cherries, which are used at the last minute.

5. Wet a large platter and turn the mixture into it. When cool enough to handle, wet your hands and shape the mass into a ring (like a large doughnut). Scatter the orange peel on top of the ring and decorate with the cherries.

NOTE: MY MOTHER, WITH MY HELP, USED TO SHAPE EACH LITTLE PIECE OF DOUGH TO MAKE IT REALLY LOOK LIKE A CHICK PEA. THE NEAPOLITANS, ON THE OTHER HAND, MAKE THE BALLS THE SIZE OF HAZELNUTS. BUT THE REAL *CICERCHIATA* IS THE WAY MY MOTHER DID IT!

CRESPELLE FRANGIPANI

Frangipani Crepes *(Makes 24 to 30 crepes)*

THE FRENCH INVASION DURING THE EIGHteenth century left many influences, from street names to customs, and of course, gastronomically as well. The penchant for crepes found in the territory around Teramo, the culinary center of the region, is proof enough.

There are many simple and unusual recipes that can be made with crepes. This is one of the most intriguing and never fails to please.

The origins of the name *frangipani*, is also interesting and intertwined with French culture. It came from Muzio Frangipani, an Italian nobleman living in Paris during the sixteenth century.

CREPES
3/4 cup milk
3/4 cup water
3 large egg yolks
1 tablespoon sugar
3 tablespoons orange liqueur, triple sec, or rum
1 1/2 cups sifted all-purpose flour
5 tablespoons melted unsalted butter
1 tablespoon solid unsalted butter

FILLING
2 cups Crema di Mamma *(page 405)*
1/4 teaspoon almond extract
1/2 cup toasted almonds, finely chopped
1 to 3 tablespoons amaretto liqueur

FINISH
Butter for pan
Crepes
Filling
2 ounces semisweet chocolate, grated

1. Prepare the crepes: Combine the milk, water, yolks, sugar, liqueur, flour, and melted butter in a food processor or blender. Process until the mixture is well blended. Cover and refrigerate 2 to 3 hours, or overnight.

He invented a perfume with the scent of bitter almonds. This inspired pastry chefs to create a cream to which ground almonds and a touch of the bitter essence of the nut were added. My mother always used a few drops of bitter almond essence with the almonds. In the United States, I have never been able to buy this essence, which is considered toxic if used without knowledge. Therefore I buy the regular almond extract sold in supermarkets.

The recipe for these crepes is a little involved. But if one plans accordingly, steps can be done in advance, simplifying the task.

2. When ready to make the crepes, melt a little of the solid butter in a crepe skillet and wipe with a paper towel. Using a measuring cup, pour $1/4$ cup of the batter into the skillet. Tilt the skillet and allow the batter to cover its entire bottom. As soon as the edges of the crepe start to color, turn it over. Cook very briefly and turn the crepe onto a platter. Continue making crepes until all the batter is used. You may need a little more butter in the process.

3. Prepare the filling: In a large bowl, combine the *Crema di Mamma*, almond extract, almonds, and amaretto. Mix well.

4. To assemble the dish, butter an oven-to-table baking pan large enough to contain all the crepes in one flat layer.

5. Spread 2 to 3 tablespoons of the filling on each crepe and fold the crepes into quarters.

6. Place the filled crepes in the prepared pan; they can slightly overlap. Sprinkle with the grated chocolate.

7. Preheat the oven to 350°F. Bake the crepes until hot in the center and the chocolate has completely melted, about 20 minutes. Serve warm.

NOTE: FOR A DIFFERENT FLAVOR, USE OTHER NUTS IN THE FILLING SUCH AS HAZELNUTS, PRALINE, OR EVEN PULVERIZED AMARETTI COOKIES.

CROSTATA DI CREMA ALLE MANDORLE

Custard Pie with Almonds (*Makes 8 servings or more*)

LEFTOVERS ARE A GREAT INSPIRATION. MY mother used to make a lot of things with leftover egg whites. This pie is a good example.

DOUGH

2²/₃ cups all-purpose flour

¹/₂ cup sugar

³/₄ cup (1¹/₂ sticks) unsalted butter

2 large egg yolks

2 tablespoons or more sweet wine, such as Marsala, Malvasia, or sherry

¹/₂ teaspoon baking powder

FILLING

1¹/₂ cups toasted almonds

³/₄ cup sugar

¹/₄ teaspoon cinnamon

1 teaspoon lemon extract

Butter for pan

1 tablespoon orange marmalade

1 tablespoon sweet wine like Marsala, Malvasia, or sherry

1¹/₂ cups Crema di Mamma (*page 405*)

6 large egg whites

Confectioner's sugar for dusting

1. Prepare the dough: Combine the flour and sugar in a large bowl. Add the butter and quickly work with your fingers until the mixture resembles coarse meal. Add the yolks, wine, and baking powder. (Add more wine if the mixture is too crumbly.) Turn onto a floured work surface and form into a ball. Do not handle too much. Wrap in plastic wrap and chill 20 minutes.

2. Prepare the filling: Combine the almonds and sugar in a food processor. Process until finely chopped and transfer to a mixing bowl. Add the cinnamon and the lemon extract.

3. Preheat the oven to 375°F. Lightly butter a 10-inch pie pan.

4. On a dampened counter, place 1 sheet of waxed paper. Place the dough on top and flatten with a floured rolling pin. Cover the dough with a second sheet of waxed paper and roll out the dough to a thickness of ¹/₂-inch. (The crust should not be too thin.) Lift the waxed paper from the top of the dough and turn the dough into the prepared pan. Peel the remaining paper off and trim the edges with scissors.

5. Combine the orange marmalade with the wine and brush the bottom of the dough. Add the custard and smooth the top.

6. Lightly beat the egg whites and combine with the almond mixture. Pour this over the custard and smooth the top of the pie. Bake until the top is set and slightly brown, about 40 minutes.

7. Cool completely. Just before serving dust with confectioner's sugar.

CROSTATA DI MELE AL CROCCANTE

Apple Tart with Almond Brittle (Makes 6 to 8 servings)

CROSTATE ARE SIMPLE TARTS MADE WITH a crumbly dough and filled mostly with fresh fruits in summer, or jams in winter. In the summer, I use peaches or apricots instead of apples, and in the winter I use pears.

These are easy to make and the fruit can be flavored with many ingredients, such as nuts, chocolate, liqueurs, etc. This one is enhanced by a 4-ounce bar of *croccante*, an Italian almond brittle that one can find around Christmas time in Italian specialty shops. You can use pralines or American almond brittle candy as well. Because I live in Manhattan, if desperate, I can run to the street corner and follow the aroma of the peanut man, toasting away his nuts and sugar, and buy a packet!

Butter for the pan
1 recipe Simple Pie Dough (page 407)
4 to 5 crisp medium-size apples
4 ounces croccante, *chopped*

2 tablespoons sugar
3 to 4 tablespoons peach or apricot jam
1 tablespoon grappa or kirsch

1. Butter a 10-inch pie pan.

2. On a floured marble or wooden surface, roll out the dough to about $1/8$-inch thickness. Slide a long, metal spatula underneath the pastry to detach it from the surface. Drape the dough around a rolling pin and cover the bottom and sides of the prepared pan. Press with your fingers to make the dough adhere. Alternatively, with floured hands, pat down the dough, without stretching, directly into the prepared pan. Cut away excess dough. Chill 10 to 20 minutes.

3. Peel, core, and very thinly slice the apples. Keep the slices in a bowl of acidulated water (water with the juice of $1/2$ lemon) while working. Drain the apples and pat dry with paper towels.

4. Preheat the oven to 400°F. Pierce the bottom of the dough in several places with a fork. (This will prevent the dough from buckling.) Scatter the *croccante* over the bottom of the dough, then arrange the apple slices in a concentric pattern around the edges and bottom of the pan. Sprinkle the sugar over the apples and dot with butter. Bake until the crust is golden, 45 to 50 minutes.

5. Combine the jam with the grappa, and with a pastry brush, paint or drizzle the top of the tart. Serve warm or cold.

CROSTATA DI PESCHE DEL FATTORE

Peach Pie of the Farmer **(Makes 6 to 8 servings)**

IN ABRUZZO, WE HAVE A LOT OF PEACHES. In early spring the flowering trees are wonderful to behold. I remember descending the Gran Sasso Mountain after our last ski expedition of the season and finding peach trees blooming in the valley, their white flowers looking as if fresh snow had fallen on them.

Every summer while living in Pescara, we were invited to a friend's farm to pick peaches. Afterward the farmers prepared a fabulous picnic and peach pie was its delightful conclusion.

Apricots, pears, and cherries (and when you can find them, sour cherries) can be used as a substitute for peaches. Do not blanch the cherries, though!

DOUGH

2 $^1/_2$ cups all-purpose flour
$^1/_2$ cup sugar
1 cup finely chopped almonds
Rind of 1 lemon, minced
$^3/_4$ cup (1 $^1/_2$ sticks) unsalted butter, cut into cubes and chilled
3 large eggs
Ice water, if necessary

FILLING

5 medium-size peaches
Juice of $^1/_2$ a lemon
$^1/_4$ cup confectioner's sugar
$^3/_4$ cup ricotta
$^1/_4$ teaspoon almond extract
$^1/_4$ teaspoon vanilla extract
Butter for pan
1 cup blanched almonds, coarsely chopped
$^2/_3$ cup peach jam
2 tablespoons peach liqueur, or another of your choice

1. Prepare the dough: Combine the flour, sugar, almonds, and lemon rind in a food processor. Process briefly to mix and add the butter. Process until the mixture resembles coarse meal. Add the eggs and process until a ball forms on the blades. If this does not happen, add small amounts of the ice water. Wrap in plastic wrap and chill 30 minutes.

2. Prepare the filling: Bring a large pot of water to a boil. Remove from the heat, add the peaches and set aside until the skins comes off easily, about 5 minutes. Cool the peaches and remove the peels. Set aside one whole half of a peach to place in the center of the pie and slice the remaining peaches. Place the sliced peaches in a bowl and sprinkle the slices with the lemon juice and 1 tablespoon of the sugar. Toss and set aside.

3. In a food processor fitted with a plastic blade, combine the ricotta, remaining sugar, almond extract, and vanilla. Process until smooth.

4. Lightly butter a 10-inch pie pan. Preheat the oven to 425°F.

5. On a floured work surface, preferably marble, roll out the dough into a circle large enough to cover the bottom and sides of the prepared pan. Line the prepared pan with the circle of dough and pierce the bottom all over with a fork. Top the dough

with foil and fill with aluminum pie weights or dried beans. Bake 15 minutes, remove the foil and pie weights, and bake 5 minutes longer. Remove from the oven.

6. Scatter $^1/_2$ cup of the almonds on the bottom on the pie crust, add the ricotta mixture, smooth the top, and sprinkle with the remaining almonds. Place the half peach in the center of the pie and arrange the slices all around.

7. In a small pan, combine the peach jam with the liqueur. Warm over low heat to melt. Strain the mixture and drizzle over the peaches. Serve at room temperature.

GRANITA DI CAFFÈ CON PANNA

Coffee Granita with Whipped Cream (Makes 6 servings)

THERE WAS, AND STILL IS, A CAFFÈ IN Pescara called Il Lido. It is on the Lungomare, the avenue stretching along the sea, overlooking the beautiful beach. In summer, it was the place to meet before and after dinner. Our parents sat with their friends. We, the young people, used to "hang out" there too. We didn't know we were doing that, the word had not yet been coined. But this was the place where we spent hours with our friends deciding what to do.

Meanwhile we would have a *granita*. Especially after dinner, there is nothing more soothing and refreshing than sitting in the open air, and savoring a *granita di caffè*. When I prepare one, I think of those happy, carefree days and my *granita* tastes even better.

It is an easy dessert to make at home and a wonderful finish for any dinner.

$^1/_2$ cup sugar
1 cup water

2 cups brewed strong espresso coffee
1 cup heavy cream

1. Combine the sugar and water, bring to a boil, reduce the heat to low, and simmer 15 minutes. Add the coffee, stir, and pour the mixture into a shallow pan.

2. Place in the freezer. As soon as ice crystals start to form around the edges, stir the mixture. Freeze again and repeat the stirring every 30 to 40 minutes until the *granita* is formed.

3. When ready to serve, whip the heavy cream. Spoon the *granita* into tall glasses and top with the whipped cream.

NOTE 1: YOU CAN GARNISH THE GLASSES WITH 1 OR 2 COFFEE BEANS. I SOMETIMES ADD A SPLASH OF SAMBUCA LIQUEUR TO THE COFFEE.

NOTE 2: BREWED DECAFFEINATED COFFEE CAN ALSO BE USED, BUT NOT THE POWDERED KIND.

NOTE 3: BY THE WAY, IF YOU FORGET TO STIR THE GRANITA EVERY 30 TO 40 MINUTES, AND YOU FIND IT SOLID AS A ROCK, DO NOT PANIC. DO AS I DO AND BREAK INTO PIECES, PLACE IN THE FOOD PROCESSOR, AND PROCESS UNTIL SMOOTH.

MACEDONIA DI FRUTTA

Fresh Fruit Salad (Makes 6 servings)

Undoubtedly fruit is the favorite dessert of the Italians. Sweet desserts like cakes, pastries, and ice cream, are not eaten at every meal. These are reserved for Sunday dinners, special occasions, or afternoon outings sitting at a *caffè* with a friend. Fruit is the finish of every meal in Italy, festive or not.

I still remember the discussions at home, when guests were coming, about what to serve first, *il dolce o la frutta,* the sweet or the fruit. The sweet-toothed family members, quoting the Roman dictum *Dulcis in fundo,* which means sweet at the end, opted for this. The ladies, instead, insisted on fruit for the last course. "More refined," they said, "it cleans the palate." And in the end, the almost Solomonic decision was left up to the guests.

At home a variety of fresh fruit was always served in an elegant fruit bowl, and one took care peeling and cutting the chosen piece. Occasionally, the fruit was embellished either by poaching or baking, or dressing it with a special sauce. *Macedonia* was a favorite. Like the country of Macedonia, which at the time of Alexander the Great was made up of several states, so is this dessert made up of several fruits. Its assembly also changed according to the season. In winter, for instance, nuts and dried fruit were included.

2 1/2 cups fresh fruit, diced, small berries left whole
1 tablespoon honey
2 tablespoons confectioner's sugar
1/4 cup rum, Cognac, grappa, or preferred liqueur
Mint leaves for garnish

In a bowl, combine the fruit, honey, and sugar. Mix well and stir in the rum. Cover with plastic wrap and chill. Serve in individual bowls, garnished with mint leaves.

NOTE: I OFTEN ADD CHOPPED NUTS TO MY FRESH FRUIT SALAD. FOR A MORE SOPHISTICATED DESSERT, LAYER THE FRUIT WITH LADY FINGERS AND A MOUSSE MADE OF 1/2 POUND MASCARPONE OR CREAM CHEESE AND 1/2 CUP PUREED, STRAINED STRAWBERRIES OR RASPBERRIES.

MATTONELLA DI GELATO ALLA FRANCESCA SPERA

Ice Cream "Brick" Francesca Spera *(Makes 12 servings or more)*

FRANCESCA, AN ABSOLUTE SPOILED BRAT and the oldest of my cousin Adriana's six kids, surprised everyone when she got married and became quite domesticated. We go to visit her and her darling husband, Leonardo, and their two adorable girls whenever we are in Italy. They live in the papal city of Viterbo, famous for its beautiful architecture, and Francesca always prepares for me a new dish, like this dessert.

¹/₄ cup unsweetened cocoa
1 cup sugar
3 large eggs, separated

2 tablespoons liqueur, preferably hazelnut
1 cup heavy cream
Whipped cream for serving, optional

1. In a large bowl, combine the cocoa and half the sugar. Gradually stir in enough boiling water to make a dense cream.

2. Beat the egg yolks with the remaining sugar until thick and lemon-colored. Fold in the liqueur and the cocoa mixture.

3. Whip the cream until it forms stiff peaks. Beat the egg whites until stiff and combine the two. Fold into the cocoa mixture.

4. Line a 9 × 12-inch rectangular pan with plastic wrap. Let the ends overlap to facilitate unmolding after freezing. Pour in the mixture, smooth the top, and cover with more plastic wrap. Freeze overnight.

5. Remove from the freezer 30 minutes before serving. Peel the plastic wrap off the top and invert the pan onto a large platter. Peel off the remaining plastic wrap, cut into large squares and serve with whipped cream on the side, if desired.

PARROZZO DI PESCARA

Rough Christmas Bread (Makes 8 or more servings)

Parrozzo is a contraction of *pane rozzo*, rough bread. A rustic sweetened bread was traditionally made by the shepherds of Abruzzo at Christmas time. A clever pastry maker at the well-known patisserie D'Amico in Pescara refined it, creating the now famous *parrozzo*. It has become an emblem of the city just like *panettone* is for Milan.

Obtaining the recipe for *parrozzo* was quite impossible. The D'Amico people considered it their secret. However, a worker from the D'Amico patisserie opened his own shop near our house. My clever father patronized the place and befriended the owner who was making a cake similar to *parrozzo*. For obvious reasons, he called it *pan bru* (dark bread).

My father would buy it often, and while praising it, he would ask the owner, "But you do not put semolina in it, do you?" And the man would answer, "Oh yes, Dottore, just one cup." And at another time he asked, "I tasted more almonds than usual, did you put in more?" "No Dottore," was the answer, "one and a half cups as I do all the time, and you know, I do not put any butter in the cake, only a bit when I melt the chocolate for the cover." And so the conversations went, until Papà had the entire recipe. To this day, in the family, we still call it *Parrozzo di Papà*.

CAKE

Butter for pan
2 tablespoons all-purpose flour for dusting the pan
6 large eggs, separated
1³/₄ cups sugar
1¹/₂ cups almonds, blanched, lightly toasted, and finely ground
1 cup semolina
1 lemon

GARNISH

4 ounces semisweet chocolate
1 tablespoon unsalted butter
1 teaspoon instant espresso powder, optional
About 1 cup chocolate sprinkles

1. Make the cake: Preheat the oven to 375°F. Lightly butter and flour a 9-inch, dome-shaped Pyrex mixing bowl.

2. In a separate bowl, beat the egg yolks and sugar until fluffy and lemon-colored. Add the almonds and stir in the semolina. The mixture will be stiff. Grate the peel of the lemon into the mixture and squeeze in the juice of the lemon. Mix well.

3. Beat the egg whites until stiff and fold into the egg-yolk mixture. Pour into the prepared bowl and bake until a cake tester inserted in the middle comes out clean, about 1 hour. Cool and unmold.

4. Prepare the garnish: Combine the chocolate and butter in the top of a double boiler set over simmering water. Stir until melted. Add the espresso and mix well. Pour all over the cake and spread with the help of a spatula. Scatter the chocolate sprinkles generously over the entire cake. Cool completely.

NOTE: THE SPRINKLES ARE NECESSARY TO GIVE THE CAKE THE LOOK OF A ROUGH BREAD. THIS CAKE IS BETTER THE NEXT DAY. IT WILL KEEP FOR A WEEK OR SO, WELL-WRAPPED IN ALUMINUM FOIL OR STORED IN AN AIRTIGHT CONTAINER.

PERE AL LIQUORE

Pears with Liqueur **(Makes 6 servings)**

ITALIAN MEALS END WITH FRUIT, BUT sometimes the fruit gets a special treatment as in this case, with the addition of liqueur.

2 tablespoons unsalted butter, plus more
  for pan
6 firm but ripe pears

2 tablespoons sugar
$^{1}/_{4}$ cup amaretto, triple sec, Strega, or
  other liqueur

1. Preheat the oven to 350°F. Lightly butter an 11-inch ovenproof pie dish from which you can serve. Set aside.

2. Peel the pears, cut them in half, and remove the cores. Drop into a bowl of acidulated water (water with the juice of $^{1}/_{2}$ lemon).

3. Place the pears, cut side down, in the prepared dish. Sprinkle with the sugar and dot with the butter. Bake until the pears are soft when pierced with a fork, 35 to 40 minutes.

4. Remove from the oven and douse the pears with the liqueur of your choice. Cool before serving.

Variation: Puree a cup of strawberries or raspberries, to serve as a sauce for the pears. Flavor the sauce with some of the liqueur used for the pears.

PESCHE AL LAMBRUSCO

Peaches with Lambrusco **(Serves 6)**

THERE WAS NO PICNIC WITHOUT THIS dessert, one of my father's favorites. As soon as we would arrive on the chosen spot, my father would search for a stream into which to place his bottles of Lambrusco di Sorbara, the best of its kind. The peaches were already sliced, and when ready to eat, they were spooned into goblets (glass, not plastic, which probably didn't even exist at that time!). The sparkling Lambrusco was gently poured over the fruit resulting in a brilliant pink foam. Of course during the picnic a few bottles had already been consumed by the grown-ups, while we children drank *gazzosa,* a soft drink similar to Fresca. Papà poured the Lambrusco on our peaches too, but keeping the bottle very high so that when the wine splashed on the fruit, it immediately became foamy. We felt very grown-up with our sips of Lambrusco.

6 large ripe peaches
Sugar to taste, optional

Lambrusco wine, preferably from
Sorbara, well chilled

You may or may not peel the peaches. In either case, slice them and place in individual goblets. Sprinkle with sugar, if desired. Fill the goblets with Lambrusco and serve cold.

PIZZA DI CREMA E RICOTTA ALL'ABRUZZESE

Custard and Ricotta Cream Abruzzo Style (**Makes 8 to 10 servings**)

OFTEN IN ABRUZZO, A CAKE OR A PIE IS called "pizza." In fact a *zuppa inglese* is also called *pizza dolce* (sweet pizza).

This recipe is a little different from the usual Italian ricotta cake or pie found in New York. It is a family recipe, and as is customary in Abruzzo, it contains custard.

Butter for pan
1 batch Simple Pie Dough (page 407)
1 batch Crema di Mamma (page 405), chilled
2 cups whole milk ricotta, well drained
¼ cup unsweetened cocoa
¼ cup sugar

1 tablespoon minced Candied Orange Peel (page 408)
1 cup candied citron, optional
½ teaspoon cinnamon
1 teaspoon vanilla extract
Confectioner's sugar

1. Butter a 10-inch pie pan.

2. Reserve one-fourth of the dough in the refrigerator. Roll out the remaining dough into a circle large enough to cover the prepared pan. Line the pan with the circle and keep chilled until ready to add the filling.

3. Place the custard in a mixing bowl and set aside.

4. Preheat the oven to 375°F.

5. Place the ricotta in a food processor and process briefly. Add the cocoa, sugar, orange peel, candied citron, cinnamon, and vanilla. Process until well mixed. Add this mixture to the custard, mix well, and pour into the prepared pie shell.

6. Thinly roll out the reserved dough, cut into strips, and form a lattice top on the pie. Bake until set, about 1 hour. If the top tends to brown too much, cover loosely with aluminum foil. Cool before serving, sprinkled with confectioner's sugar.

Le Pizzelle

Pizzelle Wafers (Makes about 60 pizzelle)

LE PIZZELLE ARE COOKIES MADE WITH A special kind of waffle iron. They look like pretty lace doilies, and their taste is addictive. It is customary in Abruzzo to offer *pizzelle* when visiting a soon-to-be bride. They are almost always present at festive occasions, especially when there are children.

A *pizzelle* machine is necessary for this recipe. They are sold in kitchen supply stores. But I wish I had the *ferro* (iron) with which my grandmother used to make her *pizzelle*. Each home had their *ferro* stamped with the initials of the head of the family.

On rainy days, grandmother used to convey her knowledge of preparing *pizzelle* to the children gathered around the fireplace. We had to master the heat of the iron, the amount of batter to use, and how long to keep it over the fire. A few cookies got burned, but what fun it was. Nowadays, the electric *pizzelle* machine renders the task quite easy. I find that the nonstick *pizzelle* makers do not work as well as the regular ones.

The *pizzelle*, when they come out of the machine, are soft and pliable, but after a few seconds they become crispy. While still soft, they can be shaped into *cannoli*, or cones. When fitted into a cup, they make little baskets that can be filled with custard, ice cream, or fruit.

6 large eggs
1 1/2 cups sugar
1 teaspoon vanilla extract
1 cup (2 sticks) unsalted butter, melted
  and cooled

About 3 1/2 cups all-purpose flour
4 teaspoons baking powder
1 cup very finely chopped nuts, optional
Unsalted butter for the machine

1. Place the eggs in a food processor and process briefly to mix. With the blades in motion, gradually add the sugar. Add the vanilla, butter, 3 cups of the flour, the baking powder, and nuts. Process until well blended. The batter should be dense and not liquid. Add more flour as needed.

2. If you have never used the *pizzelle* machine, follow the manufacturer's instructions. Butter the inside of the machine very lightly and wipe off any excess with a paper towel.

3. When the machine is ready, drop 1 heaping teaspoon of the batter into the center of each griddle. Press the lid down and cook 30 seconds. Remove the *pizzella* and lay flat on a board. Continue until all the batter is used. Serve in a basket.

ROTOLO BIANCO E NERO DI MIMMO

Mimmo's Black-and-White Roll (**Makes 10 to 12 slices**)

As a teenager, my brother, Mimmo, loved this dessert. Being my twin, his preference for this cake created a family problem when deciding which cake would be made for our mutual birthday. I definitely preferred one with ricotta, like a *cassata*. Fortunately in Italy, saints are also a cause for festivity, so when my brother's name day came up, I made this cake for him.

I do not know where I got the recipe, probably from my aunts' fancy magazines. Over the years, I have adapted it many times, and I can really say that it is my recipe.

It is an elegant cake, and, as often happens, better the next day. So make it one day in advance.

The crunchiness of the *croccante* or *torrone* (Italian nougats) adds a special texture to the filling. Almond brittle can be a good substitute. The nougats are available in Italian specialty stores, especially around Christmas. They keep for a long time.

CAKE

Butter for pan
8 ounces semisweet chocolate
8 large eggs, separated
1 cup sugar
1/2 teaspoon almond extract
2 tablespoons toasted almonds, finely ground
2 tablespoons unsweetened cocoa

FILLING

1 1/2 cups heavy cream
3 tablespoons confectioner's sugar
1 teaspoon vanilla extract
1 tablespoon Candied Orange Peel
  (page 408), very finely chopped
2 ounces croccante or torrone, chopped
2 tablespoons unsweetened cocoa

1. Make the cake: Lightly butter a 17 × 12-inch jelly-roll pan and line with parchment paper. Let the paper extend a little on all sides. Set aside. Preheat oven to 350°F.

2. Place the chocolate, broken into pieces, in the top of a double boiler set over simmering water. Stir until the chocolate has completely melted. Set aside to cool.

3. In a large bowl, beat the egg yolks until fluffy and lemon-colored. Gradually add the sugar and continue beating. Add the almond extract, ground almonds, and cocoa. Fold in the cooled chocolate.

4. In a separate bowl, preferably copper, beat the egg whites until stiff. Fold the whites into the chocolate mixture. Pour into the prepared pan and smooth the top. Bake until the top has puffed and the center has set, 10 to 15 minutes. Remove from the oven and cover the pan with a slightly damp kitchen towel. This will keep the cake moist and easy to roll.

5. Prepare the filling: Whip the cream until it starts to hold soft peaks. Add the sugar, a little at a time, and continue beating. Add the vanilla, candied orange peel, and *croccante* or *torrone*. The filling should be stiff but spreadable.

6. Without removing the towel, turn the cake upside down. Peel off the parchment paper and evenly spread the filling over the surface of the cake. Roll the cake from the long side nearest to you onto a cake platter or board. Chill at least 1 hour, or overnight, loosely covered with aluminum foil. Just before serving, trim away the end pieces to even the cake. Dust with cocoa and serve.

QUADRATI BIANCHI E NERI

White and Black Squares **(Makes 12 large or 24 small squares)**

RICOTTA IS A FAVORITE INGREDIENT OF mine and I use it often, either for savory dishes or for desserts. This recipe is something I concocted when confronted with an unused container of ricotta.

RICOTTA MIXTURE
Butter for pan
One 15-ounce container whole milk ricotta
1/2 cup sugar
1 tablespoon cornstarch
1 large egg, lightly beaten
2 tablespoons orange liqueur
1/4 cup heavy cream

BATTER
1 1/4 cups sugar
3/4 cup (1 1/2 sticks) unsalted butter, melted
4 ounces semisweet chocolate, melted and cooled
4 large eggs, lightly beaten
1 teaspoon vanilla extract
1 1/4 cups all-purpose flour

1. Preheat the oven to 375°F. Lightly butter a 13 × 9-inch baking pan.

2. In a large bowl, combine the ricotta, sugar, cornstarch, egg, liqueur, and heavy cream. Mix until smooth.

3. Prepare the batter: Combine the sugar, butter, chocolate, eggs, vanilla, and flour in a separate bowl. Blend until smooth.

4. Spread two-thirds of the chocolate batter into the prepared pan. Pour the ricotta mixture on top and spread with a spatula. Add the remaining chocolate batter in spoonfuls, leaving some of the ricotta exposed. Draw a small knife through the batter, swirling it lengthwise and crosswise to form a marbled pattern.

5. Bake until a cake tester inserted in the center comes out clean, 40 to 45 minutes. Cool completely before cutting into squares.

SAMOCA AFFOGATO

Drowned Samoca (Makes 6 servings)

As kids, the Caffè Lido in Pescara was a favorite hangout where we used to meet *la ganga*, the gang, as we called ourselves, not knowing the pejorative meaning of the word. At that time, we thought it was chic, grown-up, and American.

Because it was summertime, we naturally ordered ice cream. The *affogato*, ice cream drowned in some liqueur, was all the fashion. Mind you, we were teenagers, but *viva l'Italia*, there was no law that prevented kids from drinking a little alcohol. True, in one serving of the concoction there was very little of it. Even our parents, who were probably sitting a few tables away, didn't object!

I serve this dessert at impromptu dinners. It is a cinch to prepare and, especially in summer, very pleasing.

1 pint ice cream, vanilla or coffee
⅓ cup Sambuca Romana or anisette liqueur
¼ cup coffee liqueur

18 coffee beans, or chocolate curls, for decoration
Pirouette cookies, optional

1. Place the ice cream in individual glasses or bowls.

2. In a cup, combine the liqueurs and pour equal amounts over each glass. Decorate with coffee beans or chocolate curls. If serving pirouettes, insert 2 into each serving.

NOTE: Any ice cream can make a great *affogato*. Just choose the flavor you like and "drown" it with an appropriate liqueur.

SEMIFREDDO AL CAFFÈ

Coffee Semifreddo (Makes 6 to 8 servings)

WHAT IS A SEMIFREDDO? IT LITERALLY means a semicold dessert, which is chilled but not necessarily frozen. They are also called *dolci al cucchiaio*, spoon desserts. The famous *tirami sù*, for instance, is a *semifreddo*.

Italy has a passion for these sorts of desserts and they were always a favorite in my house.

They can be prepared in advance and are easy to make.

6 large egg yolks
1 cup sugar
$^1/_4$ cup cornstarch
1 cup freshly brewed espresso, chilled
1 cup milk
1 ounce semisweet chocolate, grated

1 teaspoon vanilla extract
3 tablespoons Sambuca Romana or
   anisette liqueur
1 cup heavy cream
Coffee beans, optional, for garnish

1. In a *zabaglione* or enamel pot, beat together the egg yolks and sugar. Slowly add the cornstarch, espresso, and milk. Whisk until the mixture is smooth. Cook over low heat, stirring constantly, until the mixture thickens. Do not boil. Remove from the heat. Whisk in the chocolate, the vanilla, and liqueur. Cool.

2. Whip the cream until stiff. Reserve $^1/_2$ cup of the cream for garnish. Fold the remaining cream into the coffee mixture. Spoon into individual goblets. At this point the *semifreddo* can be chilled. Garnish with a dollop of the reserved whipped cream and a few coffee beans before serving.

TARALLUCCI

(Makes about 30 tarallucci)

LI TARALLUCH, AS THEY ARE CALLED IN Abruzzo, are the quintessential conclusion to a family reunion, and also to celebrate the signing of a contract, or the end of a job well done. In fact, they are such a tradition for many occasions that often, in recounting a squabble among friends or family, people will conclude their tale by saying "and then it all ended with *tarallucci e vino*," meaning that all was well at the end.

Tarallucci are crunchy rings of dough with the texture of breadsticks. They are an invitation to drink and are usually dunked in wine. Some may contain sugar, therefore are sweet, but the real ones are savory. I included them in the dessert chapter because they are always served at the end of a meal or as a snack.

I did not have a recipe for *tarallucci*. My mother seldom made them and my father would rely on the local bakery. My grandmother, on the other hand, made them "with her eyes closed," as the saying goes, with no recipe and at the spur of the moment.

But one day my friend and colleague Nick Malgeri arrived at my house with a basket of *tarallucci* and the recipe, because he knew I would want it. They looked and tasted just like grandmother's and the evening ended happily with *tarallucci e vino*.

1 cup warm water
1 envelope dry yeast
¼ cup extra virgin olive oil
3 cups all-purpose flour
2 teaspoons salt
1 tablespoon fennel seeds
1 teaspoon coarsely ground pepper

1. Place the water in a bowl and whisk in the yeast. Stir in the oil after the yeast has dissolved.

2. Place the flour and salt in a food processor and process to mix. Add the yeast mixture and process until a dough forms on the blades. Add the fennel and pepper and process again to combine.

3. Turn the dough into an oiled bowl and cover with plastic wrap and several kitchen towels. Place away from any drafts and let rise until doubled in bulk, about 1 hour.

4. Punch the dough down and turn onto a floured work surface. Shape into a long roll and cut into 30 pieces. Roll each piece into a 6- to 8-inch stick, then overlap the ends and pinch to form rings. Place the rings on a floured cloth.

5. Bring water to a boil in a large pot. Preheat the oven to 375°F.

6. Place the *tarallucci* in the boiling water, a few at a time, and poach until they rise to the surface. Arrange on oiled racks placed on cookie sheets. Bake until the *tarallucci* are golden and crisp, about 30 minutes. Cool and store in airtight containers.

NOTE: IF THE *TARALLUCCI* GET SOFT THEY CAN BE CRISPED AGAIN IN THE OVEN.

TORTA DI AMARETTI

Amaretti Cake **(Makes 10 to 12 slices)**

This is probably my favorite cake. When I make it in my cooking school I always apologize for its look—quite plain and a little flat. I have tried embellishing it with a glaze, but it was like gilding a lily, and in my opinion, not necessary. However, I sometimes use small amaretti, *amarettini*, or my homemade Candied Orange Peel (page 408) as a garnish. But, believe me, this cake, with its fudgy consistency, is so good that a simple dusting of confectioner's sugar is all that is needed.

Butter and flour for pan
10 amaretti cookies
4 ounces semisweet chocolate
1 cup (2 sticks) unsalted butter, at room temperature
1 cup sugar
5 large eggs, separated

1/2 cup all-purpose flour, plus more for pan
1 tablespoon Aurum or other orange-flavored liqueur
Orange marmalade, optional
5 to 6 small amaretti cookies (amarettini), optional
Confectioner's sugar

1. Preheat the oven to 350°F. Lightly butter and flour a 10-inch cake pan.

2. In a food processor, pulverize the amaretti and chocolate. Remove and set aside.

3. In the same processor, cream the butter and sugar. Add the egg yolks, one at a time, and process for 5 minutes.

4. Gradually add the flour and the amaretti-chocolate mixture. Process until well mixed. Add the liqueur and process again to blend. Transfer to a large bowl.

5. Beat the egg whites until stiff and fold into the amaretti mixture. Pour into the prepared pan and bake until a toothpick inserted in the middle of the cake comes out clean, about 45 minutes. Cool and unmold.

6. If using *amarettini* to garnish the cake, spread a little orange marmalade on the bottom of each cookie to make it stick to the cake. Sprinkle with confectioner's sugar just before serving.

NOTE: THIS CAKE IS BETTER THE NEXT DAY.

TORTA DI MANDORLE

Almond Cake *(Makes 8 servings)*

THIS ALMOND CAKE WAS MADE ONLY when my mother had an accumulation of egg whites, never just for its own sake. She also made delicious cookies that she called *spumette,* foams, or *sospiri,* sighs. We loved all of them.

Walnuts, hazelnuts, or a mixture of these nuts can be used instead of the almonds.

I sometimes use cornmeal instead of flour because I have a friend who is allergic to wheat. The cake comes out crunchy and is delicious.

Butter for pan
All-purpose flour for pan
1 cup almonds, blanched and peeled
1¹/₃ cups sugar
8 large egg whites

¹/₄ teaspoon cream of tartar
Grated peel of 1 orange or lemon
6 tablespoons all-purpose flour or cornmeal
1 teaspoon baking powder
Confectioner's sugar

1. Preheat the oven to 350°F. Lightly butter and flour a 9-inch springform pan.

2. In a food processor, combine the almonds and 1 tablespoon of the sugar. Process until the almonds are finely chopped. Set aside.

3. In a large bowl, combine the egg whites with the cream of tartar. Beating constantly with an electric mixer, gradually add the remaining sugar. Beat until the mixture holds stiff peaks. Fold in the orange or lemon peel and the almond mixture.

4. Sift the flour and baking powder into the bowl and carefully fold until the mixture is thoroughly blended. Pour into the prepared pan and smooth the top.

5. Bake until a toothpick inserted in the middle of the cake comes out clean, about 1 hour. Cool and unmold.

6. Sprinkle with the confectioner's sugar just before serving and cut with a serrated knife to prevent crumbling.

Variation: To make *spumette* or *sospiri* cookies, fold 1¹/₂ cups nuts, chopped very coarsely, into the egg-white mixture. If the mixture seems too thin, add a little more flour. Spoon the batter into mounds on buttered and floured cookie sheets. Bake in a preheated 350°F oven until slightly colored, 15 to 20 minutes. Turn the oven off and leave the cookies until the oven is cold. Store in airtight containers. (Pine nuts and few chocolate chips are delicious in these cookies, too.)

Torta alle Mele, Noce di Cocco e Noci

Apple Cake with Coconut and Walnuts (*Makes 8 servings*)

When I was a child it was a treat to have a piece of coconut which was sold by street vendors from Africa. But one Christmas we received a present of four whole coconuts. This cake came out of that "donation." And now, since shredded coconut is so available, I make it often.

Butter for pan
Flour for pan
2 to 3 green apples (preferably Granny Smith), diced and unpeeled
¼ cup raisins
1 cup walnuts, coarsely chopped with 1 tablespoon sugar
½ cup shredded coconut
1½ cups all-purpose flour

1 teaspoon baking powder
1 teaspoon cinnamon
1 teaspoon nutmeg
2 large eggs
¾ cup sugar
¾ cup (1½ sticks) unsalted butter, melted
2 tablespoons Nocino or Amaretto liqueur
Confectioner's sugar

1. Lightly butter and flour a 9-inch cake pan. Preheat the oven to 350°F.

2. In a small bowl, combine the apples, raisins, walnuts, and coconut. Mix well and set aside.

3. In a bowl, combine the flour, baking powder, cinnamon, and nutmeg.

4. In a separate bowl, beat the eggs and sugar until light and lemon-colored. Beating constantly, add the butter and liqueur. Stir in the flour mixture and the apple mixture. Turn into the prepared pan and bake until a tester inserted in the middle of the cake comes out clean, about 45 minutes. Cool and unmold.

5. Dust with confectioner's sugar just before serving.

TORTA DI MELE ALLA LUIGI

Apple Cake Luigi (*Makes 8 to 10 servings*)

MY YOUNG NEPHEWS AND NIECES ARE ALL lovers of good cooking. One of them, Luigi, is a busy banker, who, along with his girlfriend, Simona, enjoys experimenting in the kitchen.

This is a simple, uncomplicated cake which can be made in a short time.

2 pounds apples
Juice of ½ lemon
2 tablespoons unsalted butter, plus more for the pan
½ cup all-purpose flour, plus more for the pan
¾ cup sugar
½ teaspoon cinnamon
1 large egg, beaten
2 tablespoons rum
1 teaspoon baking powder
Milk as needed
Confectioner's sugar

1. Peel, core, and cut the apples into small pieces. Place in a large bowl, sprinkle with the lemon juice, toss, and set aside.

2. Preheat the oven to 375°F. Lightly butter and flour a 10-inch cake or quiche pan. Set aside.

3. In a food processor, combine the butter, flour, sugar, cinnamon, egg, rum, and baking powder. Process to combine. Add enough milk to make a rather soft dough. (It should be a little wet.) Turn the dough into the bowl of apples and mix well. Pour the mixture into the prepared pan and bake until a toothpick inserted in the middle comes out clean, 45 minutes to 1 hour. Cool, unmold, and serve sprinkled with confectioner's sugar.

NOTE: I HAVE MADE THIS CAKE WITH PEARS AND APRICOTS, WITH EXCELLENT RESULTS.

TORTA NATALIZIA ALLA ANTONIETTA

Christmas Log Cake Antonietta (**Makes 12 slices or more**)

ANTONIETTA SORRENTINO IS A SECOND cousin who lives in Pescara. My mother and father were very close to her parents with whom they spent pleasant afternoons. The ladies embroidered (I did it too, for a period of time) and the men talked politics. With Antonietta's two brothers and mine, we made a lovely group. Antonietta and I were inseparable. One of the things that bound us together was reading. She already had her degree in literature and often steered me toward the classics. We promised ourselves that one day, we would reread in Latin Ovid and Horace, whom we had studied in school! But then she got married and I left Pescara. Our reunions are always affectionate and full of memories. No doubt she kept her promise about our Roman poets; she teaches them in school. Me . . . I am waiting for when I have more time. Perhaps when I finish this book. Antonietta, like most Abruzzesi, uses *mosto cotto* in this recipe which is the cooked must of the wine. You will never find it here. I have used a sweet Marsala or a Malvasia. They both work well.

DOUGH
1 recipe Simple Pie Dough (page 407)
1 tablespoon cocoa
Butter for pan
All-purpose flour for pan

FILLING
2 cups shelled walnut, almonds, and
* hazelnuts combined*
5 to 6 dried figs
1/4 cup honey
1/2 cup pinoli nuts
3/4 cup raisins
1/4 cup candied fruit
Rind of 1 orange, minced
3 tablespoons cocoa
1/2 teaspoon cinnamon
Sweet Marsala or Malvasia wine
* as needed*

1. Prepare the dough according to the recipe but add the cocoa to the ingredients. Wrap in plastic wrap and chill for 1 hour.

2. Prepare the filling: Coarsely chop together the 2 cups of nuts and the dried figs.

3. In a mixing bowl, combine the chopped nut mixture with 3 tablespoons of the honey. Add the pinoli, raisins, candied fruit, orange rind, cocoa, and cinnamon. Mix well. Add the wine a little at a time to combine. Do not make the mixture too wet. Cover with plastic wrap and chill for 1 hour.

4. Preheat the oven to 350°F. Lightly butter and flour a standard-size cookie sheet.

5. On a floured pastry board or other work surface, thinly roll out the dough into a rectangle. Spread the filling over the dough leaving the edges clean all around. Roll as you would for a strudel. Tuck in the ends. Place the roll on the prepared pan, seam side down, and bake until golden, about 20 minutes.

6. In a small bowl, combine the remaining honey and 1 tablespoon of the wine. Stir to blend and brush over the top of the cake. Bake 5 to 10 minutes longer. Cool before slicing.

TORTA DI NOCCIOLE E CIOCCOLATA

Hazelnut and Chocolate Cake **(Makes 6 to 8 servings)**

THIS IS ONE OF THE MOST DELICIOUS CAKES you can eat. At home, we were all chocolate lovers and this cake was a favorite. It is a rich cake, but, once in a while, let's indulge.

5 ounces (9 tablespoons) unsalted butter
1 cup shelled hazelnuts, toasted
1 cup sugar
6 ounces semisweet chocolate, broken
  into pieces

5 large eggs, separated
2 tablespoons Amaretto or Fra Angelico
  liqueur
Confectioner's sugar
1 cup heavy cream, whipped, optional

1. Preheat the oven to 350°F. Lightly butter a 9-inch cake pan. Line the bottom with waxed paper, butter the paper again with $1/2$ tablespoon of the butter, and set aside. Keep the remaining butter at room temperature.

2. In a food processor, combine the nuts and 1 tablespoon of the sugar. Process until finely chopped.

3. Combine the remaining butter, sugar, and the chocolate in the top of a double boiler. Cook over simmering water, stirring, until the mixture is smooth. Let cool.

4. Beat the egg yolks, one at a time, into the chocolate mixture. Fold in the nuts and the liqueur. Beat the egg whites until soft peaks form and fold into the chocolate mixture. Pour into the prepared pan. Bake until a cake tester inserted in the middle of the cake comes out clean, about 45 minutes. Cool on a rack and unmold. Remove the waxed paper. When completely cool, dust with confectioner's sugar and serve with a bowl of whipped cream, if desired.

ZABAGLIONE (OR ZABAIONE) CLASSICO

(Makes 6 dessert servings, more as a sauce)

WOULD YOU BELIEVE THAT I ATE *zabaglione* almost every day while I was growing up in Italy? And I loved it. Parents thought that it was good for children, and perhaps they were right. After all, cholesterol had not been invented yet.

Zabaglione is served warm or cold, in small glasses, bowls, or goblets, and eaten with a spoon like a pudding. Nowadays, though, it is mostly used as a sauce.

6 large egg yolks
$^{1}/_{2}$ cup sugar

$^{1}/_{4}$ cup Marsala wine, preferably sweet

1. Place all the ingredients in a *zabaglione*, or enameled pot.

2. Place the pot over boiling water and beat constantly with a wire whisk until the mixture thickens and starts to form ribbons. Do not boil. Serve in individual goblets as a spoon dessert with cookies, or as a sauce for fruit or cakes.

NOTE: *ZABAGLIONE* CAN ALSO BE MADE WITH OTHER SWEET WINES, LIKE *MALVASIA*, OR A LIQUEUR LIKE *AMARETTO*, *STREGA*, OR *GRAND MARNIER*.

ZEPPOLE DI SAN GIUSEPPE

Saint Joseph's Fritters *(Makes about 50 fritters)*

THE FEAST OF SAINT JOSEPH IS A NATIONAL holiday in Italy. After Mass, everybody goes to their favorite *caffè* to have an *aperitivo* and of course *zeppole*.

It is also customary to pay visits to all the friends and relatives called Giuseppe or Giuseppina. Saints' name days are more important in Italy than birthdays, and celebrated accordingly.

In my household the *zeppole* were made in great quantities because my father's name was Giuseppe. We always had a big party for family and friends.

1 cup water
$^{1}/_{4}$ cup ($^{1}/_{2}$ stick) unsalted butter
Rind of 1 lemon, or small orange
Pinch of salt
1 cup all-purpose flour

5 large eggs
1 cup sugar
Oil for frying
$^{1}/_{2}$ teaspoon cinnamon

1. In a heavy pan, combine the water, butter, lemon, and salt.

2. Bring to a boil, remove the pan from the heat, and add all the flour at once. Mix vigorously until smooth. Return the pan to the heat and cook over medium heat, stirring constantly, until the batter starts to come away from the sides of the pan. Remove to a mixing bowl and continue beating for a few minutes to cool.

These fritters are traditional all over Italy, but particularly in the South. In Sicily they are also called *sfingi.*

3. Add the eggs, one at a time, and 2 tablespoons of the sugar. Mix well and turn the mixture into a pastry bag fitted with a star tube. Pipe onto individual pieces of parchment paper or aluminum foil in the shape of a doughnut.

4. Heat the oil and drop in the *zeppole,* a few at a time, peeling the paper off. Fry on both sides until golden, about 5 to 8 minutes. Drain on paper towels. Cool.

5. In a large bowl, combine the remaining sugar and the cinnamon. Mix well and use to dredge the zeppole while hot. Set on a serving plate.

NOTE: THE MIDDLE OF THE *ZEPPOLE* CAN BE FILLED WITH A VARIETY OF FILLINGS LIKE RICOTTA, NUTELLA, OR A TEASPOON OF PRESERVES, ESPECIALLY SOUR CHERRY PRESERVES.

Index